WINNING
— ON THE —
NORTH SIDE
THE 1929 CHICAGO CUBS

EDITED BY GREGORY H. WOLF

ASSOCIATE EDITORS:
RUSS LAKE, LEN LEVIN AND BILL NOWLIN

SOCIETY FOR AMERICAN BASEBALL RESEARCH, INC.

PHOENIX, AZ

Winning on the North Side: The 1929 Chicago Cubs
Edited by Gregory H. Wolf
Associate Editors: Russ Lake, Len Levin and Bill Nowlin

ISBN 978-1-933599-89-2
(Ebook ISBN 978-1-933599-88-5)

Cover and book design: Gilly Rosenthol

Cover photo: Hack Wilson and Rogers Hornsby
(National Baseball Hall of Fame)

The Society for American Baseball Research, Inc.
4455 E. Camelback Road, Ste. D-140
Phoenix, AZ 85018
Phone: (800) 969-7227 or (612) 343-6455
Web: www.sabr.org
Facebook: Society for American Baseball Research
Twitter: @SABR

TABLE OF CONTENTS

INTRODUCTION
WINNING ON THE NORTH SIDE:
THE 1929 CHICAGO CUBS

By Gregory H. Wolf

A TRIP TO VENERABLE WRIGLEY FIELD, the century-old baseball institution on the North Side of Chicago, is an exciting event for most spectators and a rite of passage for many baseball fans and tourists from all over the country. Spectators are transported back to a simpler time, and reconnect to the early days of baseball. Whether the Cubs win or lose, Wrigley Field and the hundreds of bars and restaurants throughout Wrigleyville are packed in the summer. Most of those who venture to the intersection of Clark and Addison streets probably know that it's been a long time since the Cubs have won a World Series or even been in one.

If you conduct a Google search with the phrase "lovable losers," the Chicago Cubs pop up. That's probably not too comforting to Cubs fans who hope to follow the footsteps of long-suffering fans in Boston and on the South Side of Chicago, who waited in excess of 80 years before their beloved Red Sox and White Sox won the World Series in the first decade of the new millennium. The Cubs' World Series championship drought is now in its second century. They last captured the title in 1908, in the Deadball Era, the days of Tinker-to-Evers-to-Chance, and during Theodore Roosevelt's presidency. The last time the Cubs made it to the World Series, World War II had just ended and scores of big-league players were returning from military service to the diamond. Since Chicago's loss to the Detroit Tigers in that fall classic, three generations of Cubs fans can talk about fate, frustration, loss, and hope. Cubs teams have lost at least 90 games in a season a whopping 23 times since 1945, yet the club, despite its record, maintains its hold on the hearts of ardent and even casual fans. Fandom, of course, transcends logic and reveals an emotional, even psychological bond between fan and team. Maybe Cubs fans have come to expect the worst while hoping for the best. Intermittently a team appears to be in position to

break the dreaded "Curse of the Billy Goat" from 1945, when tavern owner Billy Sianis was forced to leave Wrigley Field during the World Series because of the stench of his pet goat he had brought to the game. On the few occasions that victory and a World Series berth seemed so close, the baseball gods frowned on the Cubs' faithful. Their collective hearts and psyches bear the scars of the Cubs' tragedies — their monumental late-season collapse in 1969, their soul-crushing defeat in the 1984 NLCS, and the bizarre "Bartman" catch in the 2003 NLCS with the Cubs just outs from their first World Series appearance in 59 years.

There was a time, however, when the Cubs were the model franchise in the National League and expected to compete for, if not win, the pennant every year. From 1926 to 1939 the Cubs enjoyed a franchise-record 14 consecutive winning seasons. [That record, by the way, can't be broken until at least 2029]. This book is about arguably the best team from that successful era, the 1929 Cubs, the first of four pennant winners (1929, 1932, 1935, and 1938) in a 10-year span.

Millionaire chewing-gum magnate and passionate baseball fan William Wrigley spared no expense in transforming the Cubs into one of baseball's most exciting teams and establishing a winning culture once he assumed majority ownership in the club by 1921. He created a utopian spring-training facility on his own personal paradise, Catalina Island, off the California coast. With his trusted and innovative right-hand man, team president Bill Veeck, Sr., Wrigley systematically combed Organized Baseball for the best possible talent and put together a well-rounded team. In 1926 the duo hired Joe McCarthy, a 39-year-old minor-league manager with no big-league playing experience. That same season they acquired two castoffs, Hack Wilson and Riggs Stephenson, both of whom subsequently paid big dividends. Wilson, a center fielder who had failed to crack the starting lineup with New York Giants, unexpectedly transformed into the NL's biggest drawing card, leading the league in home runs four of the next five seasons. Stephenson, who was languishing in the minor leagues because of his supposed fielding problems despite a .337 batting average in parts of five seasons with the Cleveland Indians, may be one of the most overlooked players in big-league history. He batted at a .346 clip the next five seasons (1926-1930) while playing left field. Prior to the 1928 season, the Cubs pulled off a stunning trade by obtaining one of the most dynamic players in the game, fleet-footed Kiki Cuyler, from the Pittsburgh Pirates. Cuyler, one of the heroes of the Pirates' 1925 championship but in the club's doghouse in 1927, led the major leagues in stolen bases his first three years with the Cubs (1928-1930), while batting. 335. Incidentally, the Cubs had also acquired first baseman Charlie Grimm, of the most popular players and managers in club history, from the Pirates after the 1924 season.

The Cubs appeared headed for the pennant in 1927, only to lose 21 of their last 33 games and squander a 3½-game lead, fall out of first place, and finish in fourth place. The next season, they turned it on in September, winning 24 of their last 34 games, but could not overcome the St. Louis Cardinals, their biggest rivals of the period, and finished in third place, four games behind the Redbirds. After that near-miss, Wrigley and Veeck made arguably the boldest move in Cubs history by acquiring the NL's best hitter, Rogers Hornsby, from the Boston Braves for the staggering price of $200,000 and five players.

Favored to win the pennant in 1929, the Cubs did not disappoint. They battled the Pirates and Giants in the first half of the season before taking sole position of first place on July 24 and cruising to the pennant with a record of 98-54, 10½ games in front of the Pirates. In a high-scoring era, the Cubs were an offensive juggernaut, leading the majors with 982 runs scored. Their 3-4-5-6 hitters (Cuyler, Hornsby, Wilson, and Stephenson) formed one of the most potent quartets in baseball history, collectively scoring 493 runs and knocking in 520. In his last full season in the big leagues, Hornsby won the NL MVP award by batting .380, driving in 149 runs, walloping 39 home runs, and scoring a major-league high 156 runs in 156 games. As awe-inspiring as the Cubs offense was, their pitching was almost as good, finishing second in team ERA (4.16) and leading the league in shutouts (14). Right-handers Guy Bush, Pat Malone, and Charlie Root formed the National League's best trio, winning 59 games, and were regularly used in relief, too. A resilient club, the Cubs benefited from the good season of shortstop Woody English (131 runs scored) and from role players. Norm McMillan took over third base when Clyde Beck went down with an injury early in the season; Chick Tolson played first base for about a month late in the season when Grimm was injured; and Cliff Heathcote batted .313 while filling in for Cuyler in right field. The team's weak link was at catcher. While their inspirational leader, catcher Gabby Hartnett, missed almost the entire season because of arm pain, the Cubs used five backstops before acquiring Zack Taylor in early July.

The 1929 Chicago Cubs National League Pennant Winners.
L-R: Zack Taylor (C), Hank Grampp (P), Johnny Moore (OF), Norm McMillan (3B), Ken Penner (P), Hal Carlson (P), Grover Land (Coach), Charlie Root (P), Jimmy Burke (Coach), Cliff Heathcote (OF), Woody English (SS), Joe McCarthy (Mgr.), Mike Cvengros (P), Clyde Beck (3B), Footsie Blair (UT), Art Nehf (P), Pat Malone (P), Guy Bush (P), Johnny Schulte (C), Kiki Cuyler (RF), Sheriff Blake (P), Mike Gonzalez (C), Hack Wilson (CF), Gabby Hartnett (C), Riggs Stephenson (LF), Rogers Hornsby (2B). (Library of Congress)

The atmosphere in and around Wrigley Field was festive all summer long. The fan base was energized by weekly Ladies Days, when women received free admission to games, as well as by radio broadcasts of games. The Cubs set a major-league record for attendance with 1,485,166, marking the fourth of seven consecutive seasons that they led the NL in attendance.

The Cubs' season came to an ignominious conclusion when they faced Connie Mack's Philadelphia Athletics. The A's, winners of 104 games and favored to capture their first championship since 1913, had a star-studded cast to match the Cubs, with future Hall of Famers Mickey Cochrane, Jimmie Foxx, Al Simmons, and the best pitcher in baseball, Lefty Grove. Long before the "lovable loser" moniker was attached to the Cubs, Chicago's defeat in the World Series helped craft the narrative of fateful losses. Trailing two games to one, the Cubs had a commanding 8-0 lead in the bottom of the seventh inning in Game Four and seemed to be on the verge of tying the Series. Then the A's exploded for a series-record 10 runs in the seventh en route to a 10-8 victory. In Game Five, hard-throwing Pat Malone, who had led the NL with 22 victories, had a two-hit shutout through eight innings before surrendering four hits in the final frame, including Bing Miller's walk-off, Series-clinching double.

Fifteen days after the Cubs' loss in the World Series, the stock market crashed in New York. "Black Tuesday" ushered in the Great Depression, which would affect the country and baseball throughout the 1930s. The Cubs continued winning throughout the decade, but the cast of characters was in flux. By the time Chicago won its next pennant, in 1932, Wrigley was dead, McCarthy and his replacement Hornsby had both been fired, Wilson had been traded, and the slugging Cubs had transformed into a scrappy, line-drive-hitting team led by player-manager "Jolly Cholly" Grimm.

This book commemorates the 1929 Chicago Cubs, one of the most memorable and exciting in baseball history. I invite you to read the life and baseball stories of all 31 roster players, the three coaches, and the manager of that team, and relive an important part of baseball history. Also included are biographies of William Wrigley and Bill Veeck, Sr., as well as Margaret Donahue, the first female executive in baseball history, sportswriters Ed Burns and Irving Vaughan, who covered the Cubs for the *Chicago Tribune*, and radio announcer Bob Elson. A summary of the regular season and World Series, as well as essays on the 1929 Athletics, Wrigley Field, Catalina Island, and fate of the Cubs after 1929 round out this volume.

Members of the Society for American Baseball Research (SABR) researched and wrote all of the biographies and essays in this book. Their interest in baseball history and commitment to preserving its heritage have made the volume possible.

Gregory H. Wolf, editor
Arlington Heights, Illinois
March 15, 2015

ACKNOWLEDGEMENTS

This book is the result of tireless work of many members of the Society for American Baseball Research (SABR). I express my gratitude to Mark Armour, chairman of SABR's BioProject, and Bill Nowlin, in charge of team projects, for their encouragement and support when I initially suggested a book about the 1929 Chicago Cubs.

I am indebted to the associate editors and extend to them my sincerest appreciation. Bill Nowlin, the eagle-eyed second reader; fact-checker Russ Lake; and copy editor Len Levin read every word of the text and made numerous corrections to both language and statistics. Their attention to detail has been invaluable.

I thank all of the authors for their contributions, meticulous research, cooperation through the revising and editing process, and finally their patience.

This book would not have been possible without the generous support of the staff and Board of Directors of SABR, SABR Publications Director Cecilia Tan, and designer Gilly Rosenthol (Rosenthol Design). Special thanks to Matthew Grace of Retro Images Archive and John Horne of the National Baseball Hall of Fame for supplying the overwhelming majority of photos.

WILLIAM WRIGLEY, JR.

By David Fletcher and George Castle

Tuesday, October 8, 1929, should have been the peak day of 68-year-old William Wrigley, Jr.'s life.

His Chicago Cubs had throttled the rest of the National League, winning the pennant by 10½ games after leading by as many as 14½ in mid-September. The thunder in the lineup, led by prize acquisition Rogers Hornsby's .380 average and Hack Wilson's 159 RBIs, powered the Cubs to 982 runs, 224 more than their regular-season opponents scored. And on this day, the march to Wrigley's coveted World Series title would begin at Clark and Addison against the Philadelphia Athletics and 35-year-old right-hander Howard Ehmke, who had pitched in just 11 games in 1929.

What could possibly go wrong? Supersalesman Wrigley, who had built his gum and baseball empire out of its humble origins of soap-peddling, couldn't see how his dream ballclub could fail. Neither could the 50,740 who crammed into the newly double-decked Wrigley Field to culminate four seasons of ever-rising Cubs mania in wide-open Chicago. Even Al Capone, the city's top businessman, so to speak(easy), was caught up in the baseball enthusiasm, posing for a photo with Cubs catcher Gabby Hartnett.

To cap off the euphoria, *Time* magazine was going to press with its October 15 issue featuring Wrigley as its cover boy. Henry Luce was not honoring Wrigley for his confectionery feats. "…Graduated from green shirts" was the caption below Wrigley's name, and referred the reader to the "Sport" section:

"This year, playing to 1,500,000 patrons in Chicago alone, the team must have been returning a profit on its investment at which General Motors or Standard Oil would probably turn enviously green. When his team made certain of winning the pennant, Mr. Wrigley told all the players to have a big evening at his expense; adding that he would not honor any expense account for less than $50."[1]

The outgoing Wrigley, who spared no expense to make his Cubs champion and build them to New York Yankees level and beyond, was sports' most successful mogul of the end of the Roaring Twenties, building upon the fabulous success of the gum empire to which he turned over day-to-day management to son Philip in 1925.

"During the first six months of this year the Wrigley Co. (chewing gum) had net earnings of $5,211,990, more than $300,000 more than the net income of the first six months of 1928 when the total annual net earnings were $11,068,618 or $6.15 a share. His business, still increasing, has tripled since 1920. He spends an average of $4,000,000 dollars a year on advertising," *Time* wrote.

"Red-cheeked, dewlapped and genial, given to exercise, to backslapping, to the indulgence of strange whims that usually turn out to be investments, and fond of uttering pungent aphorisms on salesmanship, of gravely handing new acquaintances packages of his gum, a supply of which he carries around with him at all times, William Wrigley Jr. is at 68 well-equipped to enjoy his amazing prosperity."[2]

Even from the context of history, Wrigley seemingly had the tiger by the tail with a lineup that would have stocked the All-Star team had the midsummer classic existed in 1929.

"These ('29) Cubs were a rip-snorting team which played its baseball for all it was worth. Small wonder then that Chicago went completely overboard for it, setting up a seasonal attendance record of 1,485,166. In this highly productive season it was more of a novelty for a game to be played weekday or Sunday, without an overflow crowd on the field than with one," observed writer Warren Brown.[3]

Wrigley and his dynamic team president, William L. Veeck, were so popular they were tabbed to do a straw-hat advertisement at the beginning of the summer in '29, when men typically switched to their skimmers. The baseball world and more was his oyster in 1929.

Deep down, though, Wrigley must have understood that baseball is the cruelest sport. Failure is the constant companion at all levels of the game when a .330 percentage, which would earn a performer a seat on the bench or a boot off the team in football and basketball, wins a batting title. From the dawn of the modern World Series in 1903, favorites have been unceremoniously toppled by the most unexpected turns of events. On this day, the balloon-popping was not the stock market — its day would come soon enough by the end of the month — but the Cubs and Wrigley's dreams. It started in the form of Ehmke.

The 35-year-old journeyman right-hander, 7-2 in the regular season, shut out Hornsby, Wilson, Woody English, Riggs Stephenson, Kiki Cuyler, and Charlie Grimm for eight innings, during which he fanned an astounding 12 hitters. Ehmke took a 3-0 lead in the ninth, weakening a bit on Stephenson's one-out RBI single. But after another single followed by a force out, he reached back for his last reserves and struck out pinch-hitter Chick Tolson, stranding two runners to end the game and finishing with his baker's dozen whiff total. The Athletics won, 3-1.

Ehmke's shocking mastery of the Cubs set a bad tone for the World Series. The A's pounded the Cubs in Game Two the next day, 9-3, before 49,987 at Wrigley Field. The Cubs had lost the first two games, both at their home park. Shifting to Philadelphia's Shibe Park on October 11, the Cubs jumped back into the Series with a sixth-inning rally toward their 3-1 victory. However, the next day produced the most crushing postseason loss in Cubs history up until October 14, 2003 (the infamous "Bartman Game.")

Leading 8-0 going into the bottom of the seventh behind ace Charlie Root, the Cubs staged a collapse for the ages. They gave up ten runs in the inning as Hack Wilson misplayed two fly balls to center field in the late-afternoon Philadelphia sun. The 10-8 loss completely stunned the Cubs family. When Game Five was played, two days later (because Philadelphia did not allow Sunday baseball), the Cubs were a beaten ballclub as the A's clinched the fall classic with a 3-2 come-from-behind walk-off win

behind Rube Walberg's 5⅓-inning, two-hit shutout stint in relief of Ehmke.

"There (would) be some changes made. All winter long that 1929 World Series was given a kicking around," a sportswriter penned years later. "That William Wrigley, Jr. was bitterly disappointed is putting it mildly. Whether there were words between him and Manager (Joe) McCarthy, or between President Bill Veeck and McCarthy, no one can say for sure.

"However, it can now be revealed here that on the way to the training camp at Catalina [Island] in the spring of 1930, McCarthy confided to one sports writer that win, lose, or draw, he would not be with the Cubs for longer than the current season — if that long. The sports writer was asked not to print it — and hasn't, until now," revealed Warren Brown in the seminal 1946 book *Chicago Cubs* (dedicated "To PK Wrigley and the World Championship That Has Yet to Come").[4]

Everything self-made man William Wrigley, Jr. had poured into the Cubs had been dashed. There's always next year, but that's never a given. And it wasn't. On September 4, 1930, the Cubs had a 79-54 record with a 4½-game lead. Hack Wilson had slugged his way to an eventual 56-homer, record 191-RBI season. No matter. The Cubs lost ten of their next 15 to fall three games back of the archrival St. Louis Cardinals. The pratfall brought back that crushing feeling of the World Series. That was enough for Wrigley, who suddenly made the ground even shakier underneath McCarthy's feet. As the season slipped away, Wrigley wouldn't even give McCarthy the dreaded vote of confidence.

"I will not say that McCarthy will not be manager next year," Wrigley told the *Chicago Tribune's* Irving Vaughan. "Neither will I say he will not be offered a new contract. … We have no way of knowing what McCarthy might demand in salary. He might ask $100,000 in salary. Or maybe McCarthy might not want the job any longer."[5]

Meanwhile, the *Chicago Herald and Examiner's* Warren Brown, discovered from a source close to Yankees owner Jacob Ruppert that Ruppert and Wrigley had agreed to shift McCarthy to the Yankees, who were dissatisfied with second-year manager Bob Shawkey. Brown had the scoop: Wrigley would name Rogers Hornsby, for whom he paid $200,000 to the Boston Braves late in 1928, as McCarthy's replacement. Wrigley craved the championship McCarthy had not given him. Hornsby already had won the World Series with the Cardinals in 1926 in the second of his four seasons as a player-manager.

"Rajah" — irascible and demanding to the players who had worked under him, and an inveterate horseplayer — had charmed Wrigley in a manner McCarthy never could. The astute team-builder/character judge Veeck was not fooled, but the decision to hire Hornsby was made at the only pay grade above him in the Cubs organization.

"We planned to offer Hornsby a contract a few days after the season closes," Wrigley said as the season dribbled to its conclusion in 1930 and his plan to elevate Hornsby leaked out. "We didn't want to embarrass McCarthy."

"I have always wanted a world's championship team and I am not sure that Joe McCarthy is the man to give me that kind of team."[6]

The Cubs would continue to win on an every-three-years schedule through the Depression-ravaged 1930s, beyond Wrigley's own passing on January 26, 1932, of heart disease in Phoenix. But the McCarthy-for-Hornsby switch tarnished all the good that he had done to bring the Cubs to the peak of franchise history, even beyond their 1908 World Series title. Granted ownership power under Wrigley's son, Philip K. Wrigley, Veeck fired Hornsby in 1932 as his gambling debts mounted and the Cubs clubhouse soured under Rajah's stifling yoke in the pennant race. Charlie Grimm proved to be an able replacement to rally the Cubs to the '32 flag and win 100 games and the pennant in 1935 — but he was still no Joe McCarthy. Marse Joe won seven World Series titles with the Yankees, taking two different teams, one helmed by Babe Ruth and Lou Gehrig, another led by Joe DiMaggio (whom the Cubs passed over signing as a minor leaguer) to the top. Only Casey Stengel equaled McCarthy's championship record.

Amazingly, the suspicion of Hornsby was not passed down to the next generation in the Veeck family. The younger Bill Veeck hired Rajah to juice the headlines for his sagging St. Louis Browns in 1952.

Veeck Junior recalled: "When I hired Rogers Hornsby, my mother (Grace Veeck) wrote me a note 'What you think — smarter than your daddy was?'... When I fired him before the season was two months old she wired: 'What DID I tell you?'... Before I had signed him, I had consulted [sportswriter] Gordon Cobbledick in Cleveland. 'Don't get involved with that guy,' Cobby warned me, 'You've got troubles enough already.'"[7]

In the end, the bungling away of McCarthy cannot tarnish the William Wrigley, Jr. record. He and Veeck built the Cubs' standing in Chicago to a level that the subsequent 45 years of eccentric, misinformed ownership by Philip K. Wrigley could never wipe away.

A millionaire self-made man and chewing gum magnate, Wrigley purchased a minority stake in the Cubs in 1916 and became the largest shareholder two years later. His deep pockets helped transform the Cubs into one of the game's model franchises. (National Baseball Hall of Fame)

The demarcation line of father-and-son Wrigley couldn't have been more stark.

In spite of the ill-advised cashiering of McCarthy, William Wrigley, Jr. presided over a Cubs Golden Age that outlasted him by three pennants in six years, and even enjoyed some residual positive effects as late as the 1945 World Series. Philip Wrigley surely triggered the team's Dark Ages, placing them in so deep a rut with mismanagement that it sometimes seems two successor ownerships have not yet dug out of the hole.

Where William Wrigley, Jr. was an outgoing, nearly outspoken seeker of the limelight, a pure salesman, his son was an introvert who coolly mentioned that there was no need for a guest bedroom in his Phoenix home. The elder Wrigley loved sitting in his front-row seat, being recognized and photographed. Philip Wrigley was renowned for not attending Cubs games, at least in his public persona. In reality he slipped in in near-disguise to the bleachers and grandstand. The old man loved being recorded monitoring out-of-town Cubs scores via a ticker in his office. He even had a cable laid at the bottom of the San Pedro Strait to get scores on his beloved Catalina Island. Philip Wrigley was portrayed as watching games on TV, almost out of sight and out of mind, at his Lake Geneva, Wisconsin, estate.

The empire-building Wrigley Jr. developed baseball's most capable baseball executive in William L. Veeck. Ever the tinkerer with mechanical objects and manager of his father's gum business, Philip Wrigley was a prolific meddler in baseball management for which he had no aptitude. His inward-turning nature prevented him from networking throughout the game to find the most capable man to run the Cubs on his behalf. He instead continually recycled mediocrities throughout the baseball organization.

And where William Wrigley, Jr. spared no expense to make the Cubs into baseball's powerhouse, his offspring more often than not put on the financial brakes. Philip Wrigley even went as far as forbidding new signings of amateur players by his scouts in 1962 due to perceived wasted bonuses on failed prospects.

The Cubs were a family heirloom to be properly maintained, but not lovingly or knowledgeably nurtured, by Philip Wrigley.

The contrasts were simply the difference of generations. William Wrigley, Jr. was a business innovator and promoter. Unlike the Veeck family, something was lost in the next generation, with Philip growing up in wealth and being charged with running a far-flung confectionery empire rather than building it brick-by-brick, product-by-product.

Two interesting stories, but the second could not have happened without the first. The sorrow was that the successor timeline did not match the original.

The Cubs William had built were an extension of his own Horatio Alger story. A native of Philadelphia who had dropped out of school at 13, he was the son of a soap manufacturer. He also loved baseball, sneaking off work and school to watch games. Moving to Chicago in 1891 at 29, Wrigley arrived with just $32 in his pocket. He sold Wrigley's Scouring Soap.

Adhering to Marketing 101, Wrigley offered premiums to customers to stoke sales. His first premium was baking powder, which proved more popular than the soap. Wrigley switched to selling baking powder. The successor premium was two packages of chewing gum with each can of baking powder.

He finally found his niche. Under his own name, Wrigley introduced his first two gum brands, Lotta and Vassar, in 1892. The legacy Juicy Fruit and Spearmint brands made their debuts in 1893. The gum empire was off and running as the William Wrigley Jr. Co. soon took its place among the stalwarts of American industry.

William's self-made affluence enabled him to buy into his favorite game. When cafeteria king Charley Weeghman folded his Federal League Whales — playing at their two-year-old Weeghman ballpark at Clark and Addison — into the Cubs in 1916, he took on additional partners. Meatpacking king J. Ogden Armour came aboard and persuaded Wrigley to join him, each investing $50,000 while joining the Cubs' board. Wrigley fast became first among equals on the board. As Weeghman's business interests slumped, Wrigley persuaded him to sell his shares to him late in 1918. With Weeghman's departure, the North Side ballyard was renamed Cubs Park. By 1921 Wrigley had become majority owner, buying out Armour and other partners.

Wrigley's backing of Veeck to shift from sportswriter with the *Chicago American* to team treasurer and soon afterward president proved a stroke of genius. Even as the Cubs flirted with mediocrity through the first half of the 1920s, Veeck proved he could manage a baseball team as well as write about it under the alias Bill Bailey. One by one, starting with Gabby Hartnett in 1922, he acquired the future stars who would bring Wrigley to the edge of his championship promised land at the end of the decade.

Wrigley ran the Cubs, his ballpark, and other properties with the same philosophy as architect and urban designer Daniel Burnham with Chicago as a whole: "Make no small plans." He gave Veeck the approval to permit wall-to-wall exposure via the booming medium of radio, and Cubs games took to the airwaves regularly in 1925. Soon after, he boosted the capacity of Cubs Park, renamed Wrigley Field, with a two-year project to double-deck the stadium in 1927-1928. Wrigley took ballpark upkeep seriously. Wearing a pair of white gloves, he'd run his hands along grandstand railings to search for smudges or dust.

Wrigley Field was not the only lasting piece of real estate with Wrigley's hands, gloved or not, all over them.

As he gained control of the Cubs, he plowed back $3 million of his gum fortune into the purchase of Santa Catalina Island, in the Pacific 22 miles southwest of Los Angeles. Wrigley turned the island into a Jazz Age playpen for his family, his Cubs, and tourists. With the exception of four seasons during World War II, the Cubs conducted spring training on a field at Avalon Canyon from 1921 to 1951. Careers in and out of baseball were launched in the balmy climate. Covering spring training in 1937, a sportscaster from WHO-Radio in Des Moines was invited to go back to Los Angeles to take a screen test at Warner Brothers. Producers liked what they saw in the genial

Ronald Reagan, native of Dixon, Illinois, and the rest was history.

At the same time as he became baron of Catalina, Wrigley commissioned the construction of the double-towered Wrigley Building, the white-colored, clock-bedecked, after-dark-floodlit gateway to North Michigan Avenue. Starting the 1920 construction boom north of the Chicago River, the 30-story main south tower was opened in April 1921. The 20-story north tower opened nearly three years later. Setting up as headquarters of the William Wrigley Jr. Co. and later radio stations WBBM and WIND along with its famous restaurant, the Wrigley Building was Chicago's first air-conditioned office building. From this landmark edifice inspired by a tower in the Seville (Spain) Cathedral, three generations of Wrigleys would go on to conduct the Cubs' business as platoons of players trooped in to discuss financial and philosophical matters.

With the physical trappings of success all around his office and 2,000 miles distant, William Wrigley, Jr. decided to forgo some paid attendance to run with another Veeck-inspired innovation: Ladies Day, in which all women would be admitted free. The promotion proved wildly successful with as many as 30,000 women cramming into the ballpark for a 1930 game. The Cubs' popularity — and that of Wrigley himself — soared.

He would purchase a pennant if need be. Wrigley tried. With the Cubs climbing upward through the first division from 1926 to 1928, he and Veeck traded five players with $200,000 in cash to the Boston Braves on November 7, 1928, for the only man alive to hit .424 in a season. Rogers Hornsby may have moved from the St. Louis Cardinals to the New York Giants to the Braves in three years with his demanding, prickly personality, but he knew how to handle a bat better than anyone else in baseball.

Hornsby paid dividends immediately. Scoring a career-high 156 runs batting in front of Hack Wilson, he also slugged 39 homers and drove in 149 runs to set up an NL "Murderer's Row" in the Cubs lineup. But all went for naught in the cruel outcome of the 1929 World Series, in which a hot pitcher and bad breaks crushed the mightiest of Cubs lineups.

William Wrigley, Jr. spent the last two seasons of his life a frustrated man. He never realized his championship dream. But he probably could never have conceived that his team would enter the long, strange journey on which in the 21st century it was still traveling. He didn't scout his son well enough as successor owner.

Philip Wrigley stubbornly held on to the Cubs and Wrigley Field as family heirlooms and monuments to his father. William Wrigley, Jr. had bequeathed the Cubs directly to his son, who reportedly promised his father on his deathbed that he would never sell.

"The club and the park stand as memorials to my father," the younger Wrigley said in 1933. "I will never dispose of my holdings in the club as long as the chewing-gum business remains profitable enough to retain it." Decades later, he reconfirmed his position to the *Chicago Sun-Times'* Irv Kupcinet: "I inherited the Cubs from my father and I feel an obligation to carry on in respect to him. But I'll leave the team to my son Bill and he can do whatever he pleases."[8]

Wrigley fulfilled these vows, resisting tempting offers from the likes of McDonald's impresario Ray Kroc, a Cubs fan since childhood. Sure enough, it was Bill Wrigley who finally sold to Tribune Co. in 1981, an inside deal of blueblood corporate partners meant to pay off a $40 million inheritance-tax bill after the 1977 deaths of Philip and Helen Wrigley.

In between his eccentric schemes, the younger Wrigley tried to emulate his father's moves, with mixed success:

- Imitating the cash acquisition of the NL's most prominent player in Hornsby in 1928, Philip Wrigley sent $185,000 and three players to the Cardinals at the start of the 1938 season to acquire lame-armed Dizzy Dean. In spite of widespread knowledge throughout spring training in '38 that Dean had lost his fastball as the after-effects of a sore arm caused by a broken toe suffered in the 1937 All-Star Game, Wrigley went ahead and acquired the colorful pitcher. Pitching only with guts and guile, Dean never became more than a part-time starter for the Cubs and was through four years later.

- Mimicking his father's hiring of sportswriter Veeck as team president, Philip Wrigley tapped James Gallagher, like Veeck a baseball writer for the *Chicago American*, as general manager in 1940. Gallagher was no Veeck, though. He got off on the wrong foot by trading second baseman Billy Herman to the Brooklyn Dodgers. Gallagher presided over a franchise decline through World War II as he and manager Jimmie Wilson were sarcastically dubbed the "James Boys."

- The in-over-his-head GM's best deal was snaring ace Hank Borowy on waivers from the Yankees in mid-1945. Borowy's 11-2 record was the difference in a pennant race against the St. Louis Cardinals, lacking a Navy-bound Stan Musial for the only season missed in "The Man's" career. The Cubs resumed their downhill course in 1946. Gallagher was shifted to business manager in 1949 amid a front-office shakeup, eventually leaving the Cubs seven years later.

- A strategy that did pay off down the line was exposing the Cubs at low cost to the new medium of TV in 1949, as William Wrigley, Jr. and William L. Veeck had done with the rise of radio in the 1920s. Three of the four Chicago TV stations on the air in '49 — WGN, WBKB, and WENR — broadcast the Cubs simultaneously with their own announcers and equipment. To accommodate their needs, Philip Wrigley paid $100,000 for construction of new camera positions and broadcast booths. The cost to each station was merely $5,000 toward construction; none were charged rights fees.

Eventually, when WGN obtained the exclusive TV deal in 1952, the Tribune Co.-owned outlet paid under-market rate for rights. The station made an assured profit while whetting generations of future fans' appetites for buying Cubs tickets. Kids would run home from school to catch the end of the daytime telecasts, then eventually found their way to Wrigley Field as they grew older and acquired more disposable income.

But the passion that William Wrigley, Jr. had for baseball and Wrigley Field never was shared by his tinkering son, self-professed as an auto mechanic at heart, and more comfortable with machines than with his fellow man. The Cubs basically lost their future when the elder

Wrigley and William L. Veeck died in consecutive years, 1932-1933. They were never replaced as a one-two punch that spared no expense in putting winning as the first, second and last priority of the Chicago National League Ballclub.

NOTES

1   *Time,* October 15, 1929.

2   Ibid.

3   Warren Brown, *Chicago Cubs* (New York, G.P. Putman, 1946), 108.

4   Warren Brown, 118.

5   Roberts Ehrgott, *Mr. Wrigley's Ballclub: Chicago & The Cubs During the Jazz Age* (Lincoln: University of Nebraska Press, 2013), 251.

6   *The Sporting News,* September 25, 1930.

7   Bill Veeck with Ed Linn, *Veeck As In Wreck* (New York, Putnam, 1962), 23.

8   Roberts Ehrgott, 251.

TOM ANGLEY

By Jack Morris

TOM ANGLEY WAS A BALLPLAYER BORN 50 years too soon. Born in an era nearly 70 years before the designated hitter, he was a short but powerfully built player who hit for average and power. However, defensively, he was a catcher more because of his physical size than prowess behind the plate. *The Sporting News* once called Angley "the stout hitting catcher with the effeminate throwing arm."[1] Pop flies around the plate were also a problem for Angley. So despite a career minor-league batting average well over .330 and two league batting titles, his major-league career was limited to five games with the 1929 Chicago Cubs.

A graduate of Georgia Institute of Technology, Angley as of 2014 still held the Georgia Tech record for career batting average (.436) and career slugging percentage (.763).[2] In his first three years in Organized Baseball (1927-1929), he led the South Atlantic League in batting, hit .323 in the Southern Association, and then topped the American Association in batting. His offensive numbers were so good that in 1929 Cubs manager Joe McCarthy kept Angley on the club as a fourth-string catcher and pinch-hitter. But when fate thrust him into the starting catcher's role after injuries to three Cubs catchers, McCarthy quickly found a replacement, ending Angley's major-league career at five games. No other major-league team took a chance on the poor fielding Angley.

Thomas Samuel Angley was born on October 2, 1904, in Baltimore, the first of two children born to Thomas and Lelia Viola Burrows Angley. His father was a career Army man so the family was always moving. Five years before Angley's birth, his father was stationed in the Philippines during the Philippine-American War. In 1910 the family was living in South Portland, Maine, when the senior Angley was stationed at Fort Williams, and in 1920 they were at Fort Howard in Baltimore. From Baltimore the family moved to Fort McPherson in East Point, Georgia, just outside Atlanta.[3]

It was in Atlanta while attending the University School for Boys that Angley blossomed as an athlete. He participated in four sports at the prep school, playing football, basketball, and baseball for four years, and running track and field for two years. In football Angley set what was purported to be the "world's record" for the most dropkicks in a game against Georgia Military Academy, when he booted 13 through the goalposts in an 86-0 win. He was the captain of the basketball and baseball teams in his senior year.[4]

After high school, straying not too far from home, Angley chose Georgia Tech to attend. By his sophomore year, he was a starter on the varsity baseball team. As a right fielder, he batted .422 in 21 games with seven home runs. In 1926 he switched to catcher, leading Georgia Tech to the Southern Conference championship with a 21-4-1 record. Angley batted .500 in 26 games with nine home runs. On April 10, against Auburn, he banged out three doubles to set the Georgia Tech record for the most doubles in a game. During the season, nationally syndicated sportswriter Roy Grove called Angley "the greatest hitter ever to appear in southern college baseball."[5]

Angley wasn't the only talented player on that 1926 Yellow Jackets team. Bobby Reeves, also a junior, went straight to the Washington Senators after the season and played in the majors for six years. Junior center fielder Doug Wycoff, who hit .430, went on to play in the National Football League for the New York Giants. And first baseman John Brewer played five seasons in the minors after college.[6]

Angley also played football at Georgia Tech and in his senior year he made the starting varsity as a guard. After the football season, when January 1927 rolled around, it was announced that the Atlanta Crackers of the Class A Southern Association had signed Angley. He was to report after graduation to Macon of the Class B South Atlantic League. While the 1927 Georgia Tech baseball team wasn't quite as good as it had been in 1926, the team went 15-6. Angley, the captain, had another fine season, batting .388 in 28 games with two home runs.[7]

After graduating, Angley left for Macon. In his first game with the Peaches, he crushed a grand slam. He easily picked up where he left off in college and was hitting well over .300 as the season progressed.

On July 13 Angley was involved in probably the most disturbing event of his career. Playing against Asheville at Macon, with the game scoreless in the bottom of the third, Angley singled. He took a big lead on Asheville pitcher Tom Ferrell while Raymond "Pete" Mann, Macon's third baseman, squared to sacrifice Angley to second. The first two pitches were wide and outside. Anticipating another wide offering, Mann stepped far out toward the plate. Instead of throwing outside, Ferrell fired a pitch that bore in toward Mann. Before Mann could get out of the way, the ball struck him in the chest. He collapsed and died. An autopsy revealed that his rib had shattered and pierced his heart. Mann is the only minor-league player to die after a pitched ball struck him in the chest.[8]

After the tragedy, Angley continued his torrid hitting, batting .357 as of August 1. On September 15 it was announced that he had been purchased by the Atlanta Crackers for 1928. By season's end, Angley led the league in hitting with a .386 mark. He pounded out 19 doubles, 6 triples, and 2 home runs.[9]

When Angley reported to Atlanta, he weighed in at 212 pounds. At 5-feet-8, he was decidedly heavy. But in ten days he managed to shed 17-plus pounds. He came into camp as the second-string catcher and his fielding didn't help his chances. Dick Hawkins of the *Atlanta Constitution* wrote of him during spring training, "Tom Angley's failing on foul balls may buy him a ticket back to Macon for a bit more seasoning."[10] But Angley's bat not only kept him on the team, it pushed him into the starting lineup.

Angley finished with a .323 batting average, and on October 4, the Chicago Cubs drafted him from the Crackers. And to top off a great year for Angley, he married the former Harriet O'Neal of Atlanta.[11]

Angley appeared in five games with the Cubs in 1929, his only season in the majors. (Retro Images Archive. George Brace Collection)

As the 1929 Cubs' spring training went along, it appeared that Angley was ticketed for Atlanta for another season. The Cubs had future Hall of Famer Gabby Hartnett as their first-string catcher. Behind him was steady veteran Mike Gonzalez. Rookie Earl Grace had batted .336 in Little Rock of the Southern Association the year before and was more polished behind the plate. But toward the end of spring training, Hartnett came up with a lame throwing arm. With his return uncertain, Angley, based on his hitting, made the squad. For the first five games of the season, he sat the bench waiting for his chance. Then against the St. Louis Cardinals in Chicago on April 23, first Gonzalez and then Grace hurt fingers while catching in the top of the fifth inning. Angley was forced into the game. He acquitted himself well with both the bat and glove. He drove in two runs on sacrifice flies in a 9-6 loss to the Cards.[12]

With no backups, Angley started the next day in Pittsburgh. He went 3-for-5 with two RBIs and a walk.

The first hit of his career came off future Hall of Famer Burleigh Grimes. But despite Angley's batting, Joe McCarthy frantically sought a starting catcher. He acquired veteran Johnny Schulte from Double-A Columbus. Schulte started the next three games but on April 28 he was spiked and forced out of a game at Cincinnati. With both Grace and Gonzalez still laid up, Angley again stepped in. He scored a run and drove in another. He started the next two games. The second of them, on April 30, was his last major-league game. Despite driving in six runs and batting .250 in five games, Angley was back on the bench. Grace recovered enough to take over the catching duties on May 1. Two weeks later Gonzalez was back into the lineup as was Schulte.[13]

With four catchers, plus Hartnett available for pinch-hitting duties, Angley was sold to Reading of the International League. But under the Organized Baseball rules, because Angley had been drafted from Atlanta, he was to have been offered back to the Crackers. Since he wasn't, Commissioner Kenesaw Mountain Landis declared him a free agent. By June 8 he had signed with Kansas City of the American Association. Two months later, Angley was second in the league in hitting with a .369 mark. By season's end he was the leading hitter in the American Association (.389). His offense helped propel Kansas City to not only the American Association title but also a Little World Series victory over the Rochester Red Wings of the International League.[14]

In 1930 Angley started the season with Kansas City but the Blues tired of his poor fielding. In his fourth season in Organized Baseball as a catcher, he still had trouble on pop flies. Typical of Angley's play was this sequence as related by the *Milwaukee Sentinel* about a game on May 30 against the Brewers: "Tom Angley must have had another one of his 'nervous' spells, judging by the way he chased a couple of popups around the plate. He muffed [Ed] Grimes' foul in the third and then failed to touch [Buck] Stanton's popup in front of the plate in the sixth. Buck's ball bounced foul and on his next chance tripled against the scoreboards."[15]

On July 15 Kansas City had had enough. Angley was sold to Indianapolis of the American Association. The Indians

were in need of catching help after losing Joe Sprinz to Cleveland. Angley ended the season with a batting average of .334 with six home runs. That winter he went to Cuba to play in a short-season winter league. He played for Marianao where he was the teammate of future Hall of Famer and Negro League great Oscar Charleston. Angley batted .267 in the three-week-long season.[16]

In 1931 Angley had his best year in professional baseball. Playing for Indianapolis, he finished tied for second in the league in batting to Art Shires with a .375 mark. He belted out 18 home runs and had a slugging percentage of .595. Midway through the season *The Sporting News* wrote that if "Angley continues his terrific hitting, it is difficult to see how he … can be kept out of the majors in 1932." The paper even saw improvement in his defense: "(H)is work behind the bat also has been excellent."[17]

But no major-league team came calling for Angley. He returned to Indianapolis's spring-training site in Sarasota, Florida, for a second time in 1932. Angley had enjoyed his time the previous winter and now was a Sarasota resident in the offseason. (He was part of a large contingent of baseball players who wintered in the area.) Angley played in January with a group of them called the Sarasota All-Stars in a mini-barnstorming tour through Florida.[18]

During the 1932 season, Angley was almost a part of another tragic event. Indianapolis was facing Kansas City when Angley smashed a line drive off rookie pitcher Frank Gabler's skull. The ball hit so hard that it ricocheted back to home plate. Gabler spent three months in the hospital with a fractured skull but eventually returned to baseball and pitched for several seasons in the major leagues.

But despite Angley's offensive fireworks, Indianapolis soon wearied of his defensive play. On June 22 he was released to Terre Haute of the Class B Illinois-Indiana-Iowa (Three-I) League. The Indians said that Angley "failed to come up to expectations this season." But by July 9, he was back playing with Indianapolis. For the season, he batted .311 for the Indians in 95 games and pounded out nine home runs.[19]

Sometime before wintering in Sarasota, Angley and his wife, Harriet, had divorced. While in Sarasota, Angley met Eloise Lorraine Archibald, the daughter of a prominent businessman, and on January 14, 1933, they were married in Sarasota. Shortly after the wedding, Angley was back in spring training with Indianapolis. This time, the Indians held onto Angley for the entire season. He batted .303 in 92 games.[20]

After the season was over, Angley took a job as an assistant football coach for Sarasota High School in the fall and then was the head basketball coach for the Ringling College of Art team in the winter. He would continue in those capacities for the following year as well.[21]

In March 1934 Angley crossed paths with Joe Sprinz again when they were traded for each other. With the deal, Angley ended up with Columbus, the fourth team he had played for in the American Association. In May, with Columbus having to pare down its roster to meet the 20-player limit, the Red Birds sent Angley to Elmira of the Class A New York-Pennsylvania League. He tore up NYPL pitching, batting .367 in 29 games. On June 25 Columbus recalled Angley. His chief job for the rest of the season with Columbus was pinch-hitting. By season's end, he had batted .338 in 57 games. Columbus went on to win the American Association title and then beat Toronto of the International League for the Little World Series crown.[22]

In January 1935 Columbus sold Angley to Houston of the Texas League. As usual, he continued hitting well. *The Sporting News* wrote in May that Angley "can wear out that nugget but his throwing and fielding have left much to be desired."[23] On June 13 Houston left Angley home as it departed for a 16-day road trip, saying that "his catching has not reached expectations."[24] In reality, Angley and Houston owner Fred Ankenman were in a salary dispute. Ankenman, unhappy with having to pay Angley the $400 a month that his contract with Columbus called for, tried to cut his salary. When Angley balked at that move, Ankenman threatened to suspend him and then tried to ship him to Jacksonville of the Class C West Dixie League, where the salary limit was $100 per month.

On June 17 Houston announced that Angley had been optioned to Jacksonville. Instead of reporting, though, Angley retired from Organized Baseball and took a position with Sun Oil in Brenham, Texas. His main job with Sun was player-manager for the company baseball team, the Brenham Sun Oilers. It was the start of a long semipro playing career for Angley.[25]

Angley stayed with Brenham for a couple of seasons then moved on to play for teams in Waco and Conroe, Texas. In 1939 he hooked up with a Houston team called the Grand Prize Brewers. For the next few years, the Brewers were the class of the state of Texas in semipro baseball. In 1940 the Brewers played in the National Baseball Congress Semi-Pro World Series in Wichita, Kansas, finishing in third place. Angley set a record by launching three home runs in consecutive at-bats against Lancaster, South Carolina, during a game in the tournament.[26]

In 1941 Angley took a job at the Boeing Aircraft plant in Wichita and played for its company team, the Wichita Stearman Trainers, who also played in the prestigious NBC tournament. The following year the team became the Boeing Bombers and with fellow former major leaguers Woody Jensen and Fred Brickell joining Angley on the roster, the Bombers won the NBC tournament. Angley continued to play with the team through the 1946 season. He also took over as the official scorer of the NBC tournament. He eventually left Boeing and became a sporting-goods salesman. On the side, he refereed sports. He continued to live in Wichita with his wife and three daughters.[27]

During the summer of 1952, Angley was admitted to St. Francis Hospital in Wichita with kidney problems. *The Sporting News* reported in August that he was critically ill. Reports said Angley's weight had fallen from 220 pounds to 115. On September 3 the Boeing Bombers played the Fort Myer Colonials in a benefit game for Angley. On October 26, 1952, Angley died in the hospital at the age of 48 of pneumonia brought on by complications from kidney failure. He was survived by his wife and three daughters and was buried in Wichita Park Cemetery and Mausoleum in Wichita.[28]

In 1970 Angley was inducted into the Georgia Tech Hall of Fame and in 1991 he went into the Kansas Baseball Hall of Fame.[29]

The author would like to thank Karl Green, the chairman of the SABR Collegiate Baseball Research Committee, and Marilyn Somers, director of the Georgia Tech Living History Program, for their time and effort. It was greatly appreciated.

NOTES

1   *The Sporting News*, March 21, 1935.

2   *2013 Georgia Tech Media Guide*, ramblinwreck.com/sports/m-basebl/13mediaguide.html.

3   *Washington Evening Star*, December 18, 1899.

4   *Brooklyn Daily Eagle*, January 15, 1929; *The Technique* (Georgia Tech school newspaper), December 2, 1926; *Macon Telegraph*, March 4, 1923.

5   *2013 Georgia Tech Media Guide*; *Hagerstown Morning Herald*, April 24, 1926.

6   *1926 Georgia Tech Yearbook*.

7   *Thomasville (Georgia) Times Enterprise*, October 26, 1926; *The Technique*, November 25, 1926; *Salamanca (New York) Republican-Press*, January 25, 1927; *2013 Georgia Tech Media Guide*.

8   *Greensboro (North Carolina) Daily News*, July 14, 1927; *The Sporting News*, July 21, 1927; Robert Gorman, *Death at the Ballpark* (Jefferson, North Carolina: McFarland, 2009), 29.

9   *The Sporting News*, August 11 and November 10, 1927; *Greensboro Daily News*, September 16, 1927.

10 *Atlanta Constitution*, March 16 and 27, 1928.

11 *Baton Rouge State-Times*, February 23, 1928; *Danville (Virginia) Bee*, October 5, 1928; Unidentified newspaper article dated October 4, 1928, in Angley's Baseball Hall of Fame player file.

12 *Syracuse Herald*, February 9, 1929; Alan Levy, *Joe McCarthy: Architect of the Yankee Dynasty* (Jefferson, North Carolina: McFarland, 2005), 127; *Rockford (Illinois) Morning Star*, April 16, 1929; *Davenport (Iowa) Democrat and Leader*, April 24, 1929.

13 *Rockford Register-Gazette*, April 25, 1929; *Appleton (Wisconsin) Post-Crescent*, April 29, 1929.

14 *Logansport (Indiana) Pharos-Tribune*, May 21,1929; *Brooklyn Daily Eagle*, September 16, 1929; *Lebanon (Pennsylvania) Daily News*, June 3, 1929; *Joplin (Missouri) Globe*, June 9, 1929; *Centralia (Washington) Daily Chronicle*, July 30, 1929; *Sheboygan (Wisconsin) Press*, December 10, 1929.

15 *Milwaukee Sentinel*, June 1, 1930.

16 *Omaha World-Herald*, July 16, 1930; Jorge S. Figueredo, *Cuban Baseball: A Statistical History 1878-1961* (Jefferson, North Carolina: McFarland, 2003), 194.

17 *The Sporting News*, August 6, 1931; *Seattle Daily Times*, November 21, 1931.

18 *Sarasota Herald-Tribune*, October 27, 1952; *Tampa Morning Tribune*, January 18, 1932.

19 *The Sporting News*, August 27, 1936; *Canton Repository*, June 22, 1932.

20 Letter from Nancy Angley Armstrong to Lee Allen in Angley's Baseball Hall of Fame player file.

21 *Sarasota Herald-Tribune*, October 19, 1933, and March 6, 1934.

22 *The Sporting News*, March 1 and October 18, 1934; *Canton (Ohio) Repository*, May 11, 1934; *Dallas Morning News*, June 26, 1934; *Toledo News-Bee*, July 4, 1934.

23 *The Sporting News*, May 16, 1935.

24 *San Antonio Light*, June 13, 1935

25 *Canton Repository*, January 22, 1935; *The Sporting News*, May 16, 1935;*San Antonio Light*, June 13, 1935; *Galveston Daily News*, June 8, 1939; *Dallas Morning News*, June 18 and September 2, 1935; *Sarasota Herald-Tribune*, June 29, 1935.

26 *The Sporting News*, April 1, 1937; *Pampa (Texas) Daily News*, July 23, 1937; *Baton Rouge Morning Advocate*, June 15, June 16, and August 10, 1939; *Greensboro Daily News*, August 26 and September 2, 1940; *Omaha World-Herald*, August 26, 1940.

27 *Sarasota Herald-Tribune*, January 20, 1946; *Wichita Morning Eagle*, October 27, 1952; Bob Rives, *Baseball In Wichita* (Mount Pleasant, South Carolina: Arcadia Publishing, 2009), 67.

28 *Wichita Morning Eagle*, October 27, 1952; *The Sporting News*, August 20 and November 5, 1952; *Arizona Republic (Phoenix)*, September 4, 1952; Tom Angley's Kansas Certificate of Death.

29 *Wichita Eagle*, February 1, 1991.

CLYDE BECK

By Norm King

CLYDE BECK WAS YOUR PROTOTYPICAL good-field, no-hit utility infielder. He was by no means a star in an era when players like Babe Ruth and Jimmie Foxx made headlines with their prodigious blasts. But he was the kind of player every team needs, someone who provided the bench depth and versatility that helped the 1929 Cubs make it to the World Series.

The new century had barely dawned when Clyde Eugene Beck was born on January 6, 1900, in the Los Angeles suburb of Bassett, California.[1] He was the third son and youngest of four children of Charles Beck of California and Melvira (McGarvin) Beck of Missouri.

Beck acquired his baseball skills playing semipro ball around California. He finally got his chance in the professional ranks with the Los Angeles Angels of the Pacific Coast League in 1922. As a rookie, Beck got into only 46 games, but batted a respectable .279 with eight doubles and one triple among his 38 hits.

There was some uncertainty over what team he would play for in 1923. The Angels had tried to sell Beck to the Wichita Izzies of the Class A Western League prior to the season and appeared to have difficulty consummating the deal. In fact, *The Sporting News* reported in its February 8, 1923, edition that the proposed trade had fallen through and that Beck would play for the Angels that season. The sale to Wichita was completed in late March.[2]

Minor leaguers sometimes played many more games in those days than their major-league counterparts. The Western League season was a grueling 169 games long and Beck played in 168 of them.[3] He averaged close to one hit per game (167) and batted .284. In the field he compiled a .941 fielding percentage at shortstop while committing 49 errors. He was recalled by the Angels at the end of the season and played six games for them, getting four singles in 20 at-bats for a .200 average.

Beck's performance with the Izzies was impressive enough for the Angels to bring him back in 1924. He played in

148 Pacific Coast League games that year, batted .268, and showed some sock with six home runs. More significantly, he set a league record for second basemen that still stood in 2014 when he had 12 assists in a game on October 5 against the Seattle Indians.

The 1925 season was a strange one for Beck. He played in a whopping 188 games, all at second base. He hit 17 home runs, an astounding total for someone who never hit more than six homers in any other professional season. It's impossible to determine what accounted for Beck's power surge, especially when he never came close to hitting that many home runs in a season before or after. The Angels did move into a new ballpark late in the season but that didn't explain it. They played most of their home games that year at old Washington Park where the dimensions were 325 feet down the lines and 411 feet to straightaway center field. On September 29 they moved into brand-new Wrigley Field. That ballpark's dimensions were even bigger: It was 340 feet down the left-field line, 339 feet down the right-field line, and 412 to straightaway center.

The large number of games played doesn't account for the difference, either, as Beck played in only 40 games more than the previous season yet hit almost three times as many home runs. Whatever batting stroke or stroke of luck that worked for him that year never worked for him again.

Of course no one could have predicted his future paucity of power, but Beck's 1925 numbers prompted the Cubs to buy his contract. In return, the Angels received cash and four players.[4]

Beck wasn't used very much when the 1926 season started. His first major-league appearance came as a pinch-runner in a May 19 game against the Boston Braves. He was optioned to Milwaukee of the Double-A American Association on May 22 and had an immediate impact with the Brewers. He did so well, in fact, that he became a pawn in a feud between the Milwaukee and Chicago owners.

The Brewers had a player named Fred "Fritz" Schulte whom Brewers owner Otto Borchert wanted to sell for $100,000.[5] Cubs president Bill Veeck wanted Schulte for his team, but Borchert sold him to the St. Louis Browns. At the time, the Brewers were in a tight race for the American Association pennant — they finished in third place with a 93-71 record, 12½ games behind the league champion Louisville Colonels — and Beck was an integral part of the Brewers' success:

"Beck was fielding like a big leaguer, covering a world of ground and playing the keystone sack so brilliantly that he has made fans forget all about (former Brewer) Oscar Melillo," wrote George F. Downer in the *Milwaukee Sentinel.* "Coming here reputed to be a weak hitter, Beck had developed into a dependable clubber, having hit safely in the in the last sixteen consecutive games."[6]

"As a backlash of the failure of Wrigley's money to sway Borchert," said *The Sporting News*, "the big-league club took a retributive poke at the Brewers by recalling second baseman Clyde Beck. …"[7]

Of course Beck was just caught in the middle of all this, and considering that he played in only 30 games for the Cubs that season and hit only .198, he probably was not integral to the Cubs' 1926 pennant hopes. (They finished fourth with an 82-72 record, seven games out of first.)

The Cubs gave Beck a chance to strut his stuff in 1927 and he had a solid if not spectacular season, getting into 117 games, mostly at second base. He batted .258 with 101 hits, 2 home runs, 44 RBIs, and 44 runs scored. In the field, he committed 19 errors, a respectable total (Brooklyn's Jay Partridge led National League second basemen with 52 errors).

An offseason move assured Beck of regular playing time in 1928. The Cubs acquired future Hall of Famer Kiki Cuyler from the Pirates for second baseman Sparky Adams and outfielder Pete Scott. Beck played in 131 games that year, splitting his time primarily between third base (87 games) and shortstop (47 games). He hit .257 with

three home runs, one of which was a grand slam that drove in all the Chicago runs in a 4-3 victory on July 17 over the Philadelphia Phillies, the team's eighth and last victory during a midseason winning streak.

Beck was married by the time the 1928 season began, and his wife, Gertrude, wasn't one to let him off the hook if he played poorly, as a September 20 newspaper article amply illustrated:

"Clyde Beck of the Chicago Cubs has a wife whose heart and soul are on winning ballgames and there is no smile at home for the Chicago infielder when he fails to do his part.

"Recently, Mrs. Beck sat in the grandstand in the Cubs' park. In a nearby seat was a rooter who had no idea of the lady's identity. Beck came up in a pinch and struck out.

"'Damn that Beck!' exploded the irate fan. 'I could shoot him for that.'"

"Then noticing the lady looking at him, and thinking she disapproved of his profanity, he started to offer an apology.

"'Not at all, not at all,' said Mrs. Beck. 'I echo your sentiments. You see, I happen to be Clyde's wife, and believe me, I could shoot him myself!'"

"But all ball players' wives are like that."[8]

Beck probably slept wearing a bulletproof vest during the 1929 season. Even before the season began, the media speculated that the Cubs would swing a trade for Les Bell of the Braves to get some better hitting from the third-base position.[9] That trade fell through, but journeyman Norm McMillan replaced an injured Beck at third base early in the year and held on to the hot corner for the remainder of the season. Beck played in only 54 games at third base and shortstop, hitting a meager .211. He didn't play in the World Series, in which the Cubs fell to the Philadelphia Athletics in five games.

The Cubs acquired Bell off the waiver wire on October 29, 1929, the same day as the US stock-market crash that signaled the beginning of the Great Depression. Hopefully this turn of events didn't cause Beck any great depression, for even though Bell's presence on the Cubs should have severely limited his playing time in 1930, injuries to team-mates forced manager Joe McCarthy to use Beck in his infield. Bell suffered an arm injury that prompted McCarthy to move regular shortstop Woody English to third and install Beck at short.[10] For the season, Beck got into 83 games (57 at shortstop), but his weak hitting (.213 batting average) ensured that he would not be a regular player. Oddly enough, he hit six home runs that year, more than he hit in any other major-league season and exactly half of his career total of 12.

Beck's 1931 season did not get off to a good start. In fact, it didn't get off to any start as he sat on the bench for the Cubs' first 37 games before being released on June 3. He was picked up by the Cincinnati Reds, ostensibly the "player to be named later" in a preseason trade for utility outfielder Cliff Heathcote.[11] In what turned out to be his last season in the majors, Beck hit just .154 in 53 games as a part-time infielder, primarily at third base. The Reds sent Beck down to the St. Paul Saints of the American Association at the end of the 1931 season, ending his major-league career.

Beck played two seasons for St. Paul before returning to his old California stamping grounds with the PCL's Mission Reds of San Francisco. At 34, he proved there was still some life in the ol' glove yet when he led PCL shortstops in fielding in 1934 with a .970 fielding percent-age in an exhausting 188 games. And to prove that 1934 was no fluke, he repeated the feat again in 1935, topping PCL shortstops with a .957 fielding percentage.

After playing one more year with the Mission Reds in 1936, Beck was traded to the Oakland Oaks for pitcher Tom "Dutch" Conlan. Apparently the Oaks adopted an "if you can't beat 'em, join 'em" approach in acquiring him.

"Although he is no DiMaggio at the plate, Beck, nevertheless, has been a thorn in the side of Oakland hurlers," wrote Emmons Byrne in *The Sporting News*. "The front office thought something should be done about it and henceforth, if he is going to hit in the clutch, it will be for the Oaks."[12]

Well, it seems that the front office changed its mind because the Oaks released Beck on May 20, 1937. He was

immediately picked up by the Seattle Indians. Between the two teams Beck played in 20 games and hit a paltry .171. This was his final season as a professional base-ball player.

After his playing days ended, Beck moved back to Los Angeles with his wife and two children, Evelyn (born 1927) and Charles (1931), and made his living as a motor winder.[13] Even though he never went back to baseball, he participated in activities commemorating events that took place during his career. He played in an old-timer's game held on October 7, 1950, to honor the 25th anniversary of the first game played at Wrigley Field in Los Angeles. He attended dinners put on by the Pasadena Sports Ambassadors to honor former ballplayers who played in the World Series. (The fact that Beck didn't actually play in the 1929 Series with the Cubs didn't seem to matter.)

Beck may also have been surprised by the results of an opinion poll of Cubs fans commissioned by the Chicago

Beck was the Cubs' Opening Day third baseman in 1929 before he suffered an injury in the 22nd game of the year. (Retro Images Archive. George Brace Collection)

club that was published in 1950. One of the questions was, "Who do you think is the greatest Cub player of our time?" Stan Hack, who retired in 1947, led the results with 14.2 percent of the vote and Gabby Hartnett was second respondents with 13.9 percent. Other Hall of Fame players such as Hack Wilson and Grover Cleveland Alexander were on the list. Beck also made the list, with 0.9 percent of the vote, which is strange considering that even Joe Tinker didn't make the list.[14]

Clyde Beck lived in the Los Angeles area until he died of an acute myocardial infarction on July 15, 1988, in Temple City, California. He was 88 years old.

SOURCES

Ancestry.com

Ballparksofbaseball.com

Baseball-Reference.com

Borchertfield.com

Milb.com

The Sporting News

Clyde Beck player file, National Baseball Hall of Fame

NOTES

1   Different sources cite different places and dates of birth. The 1910 US Census indicates Beck was born in 1899, and an undated newspaper article lists his date of birth as January 6, 1902, in bordering El Monte, California. Beck himself listed January 6, 1900, as his birthdate.

2   "Clyde Beck Sold to Wichita Ball Club," *Dubuque* (Iowa) *Herald*, March 26, 1923.

3   In a review of Western League statistics on baseball-reference.com for the 1923 season, no player appeared in more than 169 games.

4   Associated Press, "Angels Do Well in Beck Deal," *The Deseret News*, Salt Lake City, Utah, December 11, 1925.

5   "If the Ice Plants Will Only Hold Out," *The Sporting News*, July 22, 1926 .

6   George F. Downer, "Following Through With Downer," *Milwaukee Sentinel*, July 16, 1926.

7   *The Sporting News*, July 22, 1926.

8   Clipping, publication unknown, from Beck's file at the National Baseball Hall of Fame.

9   Associated Press, "Cubs and Braves Plan to Swing Trade," *St. Petersburg* (Florida) *Evening Independent*, January 31, 1929.

10 William Weekes, "Reserve Player Sent Into Lineup of Cubs as Hornsby Breaks Ankle Leads Chicago to Double Victory," *St. Petersburg Evening Independent*, May 31, 1930.

11 Associated Press, "Cubs Release Beck to Cincinnati Club," *Milwaukee Sentinel*, June 4, 1931.

12 Emmons Byrne, "Well Thinned Oaks Wait on New Buds," *The Sporting News*, January 28, 1937.

13 The birth years are based on Evelyn's being listed as 13 years old and Charles as 9 at the time of the 1940 US Census.

14 "Barber Shop Poll 86.6 Per Cent for Farm Aid," *The Sporting News*, January 25, 1950.

CLARENCE "FOOTSIE" BLAIR

By Norm King

IMAGINE YOU'RE ONE OF TWO WIDGET-winders working in the same factory and that you have to compete for the Number One job with one of the greatest widget-winders in history. That is exactly the situation that Clarence "Footsie" Blair found himself in when he played second base for the Chicago Cubs. That is, he played when the other guy, future Hall of Famer Rogers Hornsby, didn't.

Clarence Vick Blair was born in Enterprise, Oklahoma, approximately 130 miles east of Oklahoma City, on July 13, 1900. He was the oldest of three children born to Charles H. Blair, originally from Arkansas, and Cora E. Blair, from Tennessee. Charles Blair held a number of jobs over the years. He is known to have worked as a night watchman at a mill and as a fireman in an oilfield.

Blair grew up in Texarkana Ward 4, Bowie, Texas. He didn't receive much education, leaving school after completing the seventh grade.[1] Blair began his professional career close to home in 1924 with the Texarkana Twins of the Class D East Texas League, where he batted an undistinguished .245 in 88 games as an infielder, including 36 games at second base.

There are no records of where Blair played in 1925, but by 1926 he had moved up to the Class A Southern Association with the Little Rock Travelers, a team that included future New York Yankees catcher Bill Dickey, himself a future Hall of Famer. Blair appeared in only 41 games that year, all at shortstop. Offensively, he hit a respectable .284, but his defense had highs and lows; of the three shortstops on the team that year, he had the most errors, 23, and the lowest fielding percentage, .896.

Blair's mediocre season resulted in his demotion to the Columbia (South Carolina) Comers of the Class B South Atlantic League for 1927. It seems that returning to a lower level and going back to a more natural position at second base agreed with him. He got a lot more playing time, appearing in 128 games, and his batting average shot up to .301. He committed the same number of errors as

the previous season, 23, but in more than three times as many chances (759 compared with 221 in 1926). Blair finished the season with an excellent .970 fielding percentage and a return engagement to Little Rock for 1928.

This time he was ready. His batting average dipped slightly, to .294, but he hit a career- high nine home runs, only one fewer than he hit in his three major-league seasons combined. He dazzled with the glove as well, committing only 13 errors in 121 games at second base for an excellent .983 fielding percentage. These numbers were good enough for a ticket to "The Show" with the Chicago Cubs in 1929.

In baseball, as in life, timing is everything. Unfortunately for Blair, he arrived in Chicago at the same time as the aforementioned Hornsby, considered by many the greatest right-handed hitter of all time. With the Boston Braves in 1928, the 32-year-old Hornsby had led the National League in batting average (.387), on-base percentage (.498), and slugging average (.632). A 28-year-old rookie like Blair couldn't expect much playing time backing up an all-time great, and he didn't get much, a mere 77 plate appearances and a smattering of starts at first base and third (seven at each), along with two appearances at second base. He did bat .319 and hit one home run, but he spent a lot of time riding the pines. He had one plate appearance in Game One of the 1929 World Series against the Philadelphia Athletics, but the only positive aspect about it was that he wasn't one of Howard Ehmke's record-setting 13 strikeout victims.

One could have forgiven Blair for having a feeling of déjà vu when the movie *42nd Street* came out in 1933. That's the famous movie where the leading lady of a Broadway show broke her leg just before opening night and plucky Ruby Keeler went out in her place as a nobody and came back a star.

In Blair's case, the star second baseman, Hornsby, broke his ankle sliding into third base in the first game of a doubleheader on May 30, 1930, against the St. Louis Cardinals. Blair replaced Hornsby in the first game, and

A versatile infielder, Blair debuted with the Cubs in 1929 batting .319 in 72 at-bats. He replaced the injured Rogers Hornsby as the Cubs second baseman in 1930. (National Baseball Hall of Fame)

was the Cubs' leadoff hitter in the second game. He wowed the audience, going 3-for-5 with a home run and six RBIs.

The similarity to *42nd Street* ends there, unfortunately for Blair, because he went out in Hornsby's place as a nobody and came back as, well, still a nobody. Granted, he took full advantage of his playing time. In 134 games, he batted .273 with six homers and 59 runs batted in. But his 1930 season didn't have a Hollywood ending because he simply didn't get on base enough to be the offensive catalyst a good leadoff hitter should be. His batting average was mediocre for the top spot in the order, and his .306 on-base average was the lowest among the starting eight in the Cubs' lineup. True, he crossed the plate 97 times, but three teammates had substantially higher run totals, including Kiki Cuyler (155), Woody English (152), and Hack Wilson (146). Even accounting for these players having played more games than he did, Blair's total was

low, especially for a player hitting at the top of the order for a good offensive team.

Research indicates that 1930 is also the year that Blair got his nickname of Footsie. In his book on baseball nicknames, J.K. Skipper says that the sobriquet stems from a quote in a 1930 article in the *Chicago Tribune*, which reads, "Blair is a speedy fellow despite enormous contact with the ground, which accounts for his nickname."[2]

Blair probably knew his playing time would be limited when spring training for 1931 rolled around. Not only had Hornsby's ankle healed, he was now the Cubs player-manager, having replaced Joe McCarthy with four games left in the 1930 season. The Cubs also had a blue-chip prospect in 21-year-old Billy Herman, who gave a hint of his own Hall of Fame career to come by hitting .327 in 25 games. For the 30-year-old Blair, his .258 batting average in 86 games simply didn't cut it.

To Hornsby's credit, he did sit himself down when he was mired in a 1-for-26 slump in early June 1931 and had Blair play in his place. At the time, Hornsby's average had fallen to .297. By the third game of Hornsby's self-benching, Blair's average for the season was at .191, so Hornsby figured the team was better off having himself in the lineup. The rest no doubt did the Rajah some good because he ended up leading the team in home runs (16) and RBIs (90), and tying for the team's highest batting average (.331). Blair's last major-league appearance came in the final game of the 1931 season, when he pinch-hit in the fifth inning for starting pitcher Guy Bush. He struck out.

The Cubs sold Blair to the Los Angeles Angels of the Pacific Coast League in March 1932. It seems the Texarkana resident didn't much like the California sunshine. He played 46 games for the Angels and then quit the team abruptly in June after fans got on him for his play.

"Fans had been riding Blair since he committed four errors in one game, then threw the ball into the grandstand at his caustic critics," wrote the *San Jose News*.[3]

Not surprisingly, the Angels suspended Blair for the remainder of the season, then sold him to the Cincinnati Reds. As training camp for 1933 approached, Blair, who had to pay his own way to spring training, as did all other players, couldn't get any money out of his bank because of the Great Depression. He wired the Reds about his predicament, and they arranged for a train ticket on credit for him to get from Texarkana to Tampa, Florida, by rail. Blair didn't make the Reds during spring training and was sent to the International League's Jersey City Skeeters. He never reported to the Skeeters, perhaps because they were a financial disaster. The club was in such dire financial straits that each of the other International League clubs had to supply it with players.[4]

The Skeeters scooted up to Syracuse to become the Chiefs before the 1934 season started, and Blair did play for them that year. He had an undistinguished season, batting .266 with two home runs, although he tied the Rochester Red Wings' Tom Winsett for the league lead in triples with 13.

That number was unlucky for Blair because the Boston Red Sox, the Chiefs' parent team, demoted him to the Class A Southern Association's Knoxville Smokies for the 1935 season. He began a three-year stint with the Smokies (1935-37) that began the winding down of his professional career. His batting averages declined with each season, from .293 in 1935 to .285 in 1936, then to .263 in 1937. In 1938 Blair went down to the Jackson (Mississippi) Senators of the Class B Southeastern League. He had a good year, batting .318 in 127 games with a .418 slugging average.

The following year in Jackson, Blair added the manager's title to his business card and still managed to get into 108 games, batting .275 with three home runs — his highest total in three years — and a .379 slugging average.

The following two years Blair played some for the Senators, 12 games in 1940 and 50 games in 1941, but he devoted himself primarily to managing, and the results showed. The Senators won the Southeastern League championship in 1940 and lost in the league final the following season. The 1941 season was his last in baseball.

After his diamond career ended, Blair returned to Texarkana, where he ran a service station. He and his wife, Lois, had three children, six grandchildren, and one great-grandchild. He died in Texarkana just 12 days shy of his 82nd birthday, on July 1, 1982.

Clarence Blair's baseball career may not have been distinguished, and he may not have spent much time in the big leagues. But he was probably the only player in major-league history who could honestly boast that the great Rogers Hornsby the manager benched Rogers Hornsby the player in favor of him. A great story for the grandkids.

SOURCES

BaseballReference.com

Texarkana (Texas) *Gazette*, July 3, 1982

Tuscaloosa(Alabama) *News*, September 25, 1940, and September 17, 1941

NOTES

1   1940 US Census.

2   J.K. Skipper, *Baseball Nicknames: A Dictionary of Origins and Meanings* (Jefferson, North Carolina: McFarland and Company Inc., 2011), 23.

3   "Suspend Blair, Angels Outfielder," *San Jose News*, June 22, 1932, 4.

4   "Brief Bits of Gossip," *The Sporting News*, December 28, 1933, 3.

SHERIFF BLAKE

By Gregory H. Wolf

SHERIFF BLAKE WAS NOT REALLY A sheriff, but rather a hard-throwing right-handed pitcher whose best days came during a six-year period for the Chicago Cubs, from 1925 to 1930, when he averaged 12 wins and 216 innings per season as a dependable starter and occasional reliever. After winning a career-high 17 games and tying for the league lead in the National League with four shutouts in 1928, Blake helped guide the Cubs to the pennant in 1929.

John Frederick Blake was born on September 17, 1899, in Ansted, West Virginia, to Jesse Alfred and Lula Mae (Holder) Blake. He grew up in the rugged Appalachian terrain of central West Virginia, where coal mining was a way of life for most families. His parents were hard-working, industrious people of Scotch-English descent. His father worked in the coal mines for more than 40 years, rising to the post of foreman. His mother raised eight children born over the course of two decades. Fred, as his parents called him, was the third born and the first of two sons. With access to education limited and money scarce, it seemed like a foregone conclusion that young Fred would join his father in the mines by the time he was 14. His father trained him to operate mining machinery as a way to escape backbreaking and dangerous manual work.

Baseball offered miners and small towns in Appalachia a temporary respite from the harsh realities of their surroundings. Blake's father was an accomplished amateur pitcher and taught his son the art of pitching. By the time Fred was 16, he was pitching with adults on local coal-field teams. In light of American's imminent entry into the World War, the Blakes sent Fred to the Greenbrier Military School in Lewisburg in 1916, hoping that a military career would provide their son an escape from the perils of mining. Fred played football and baseball at the boarding school, but despised the rigid discipline and quit after about two years.

Blake's big break occurred when he enrolled at West Virginia Wesleyan College in Buckhannon, where he made a name for himself as "one of the most phenomenal young pitchers" in the northwest part of the state, reportedly striking out 63 batters in four games in 1919.[1] Blake caught the attention of Earle "Greasy" Neale, who had coached the college's football team and was also a fleet-footed outfielder for the Cincinnati Reds at the time. On Neale's recommendation, Reds scout Gene McCann signed the hard-throwing right-hander.

For reasons Blake never understood, the Reds placed him on waivers some time after their World Series triumph over the Chicago White Sox in 1919. The Pirates, who had attempted to sign Blake the previous year, claimed him. Blake suffered a severely sprained ankle at the Pirates' spring training in Hot Springs, Arkansas, and was subsequently released. He returned to West Virginia, and began pitching for the semipro Charleston Senators, a former team in the Class D Ohio State League. Recalled by the Pirates in midseason, 20-year-old Blake made his big-league debut on June 29 during the second game of a doubleheader against the Chicago Cubs at Cubs Park. He tossed the final inning of relief in a 14-3 drubbing, yielding two hits and two runs. He pitched five more times in relief and finished with a lofty 8.10 ERA over 13⅓ innings.

The Pirates assigned Blake to the Rochester (New York) Colts, and then Tribe, of the Double-A International League for the 1921 and 1922 seasons, where he was managed by George Stallings, best known as the skipper of the "miracle" Boston Braves championship team of 1914. "He was the greatest man there ever was," Blake told oral historian Eugene Murdock.[2] According to Blake, Stallings was a demanding manager who taught him to keep the ball low and encouraged him to rely on his fastball and curveball. Though Rochester finished in second place behind the Lefty Grove-led Baltimore Orioles both years, Blake developed into one of the league's premier pitchers. In his first year in the IL, he established career bests in wins (21) and innings (300); the following year he won 17 and posted a 2.76 ERA. Like the young Grove, Blake suffered from poor control and finished second to the future Hall of Famer in walks in 1921; however, while Grove developed impeccable control, Blake battled bouts of wildness throughout his 21-year professional baseball career.

Blake credited Stallings for giving him the nickname Sheriff. "[It] was back during Prohibition," he explained. "Stallings knew I was from West Virginia [and also knew] that there was a lot of moonshining going on in West Virginia. He went to call me one day and could not think of my name, so he said 'Hey you moonshining sheriff, come here.'"[3] The name remained with Blake for the rest of his life. He learned to embrace it, but admitted that he had to explain for the remainder of his baseball days that he was not really an elected official in charge of enforcing the law.

After his fourth consecutive spring training with the Pirates, Blake was sent to the Seattle Indians of the Double-A Pacific Coast League for the 1923 season. Described by *The Sporting News* as a "terrible bust," Blake limped to a 13-20 record and his ERA ballooned to 4.71.[4] During the National Association meeting in December, the Pirates traded him to the Chicago Cubs. Blake had been the subject of rave reports from Cubs scout Jack Doyle, who considered his record to be an anomaly and predicted success for him. According to *The Sporting News*, Blake was "dissatisfied and indifferent" about playing so far from home and his pitching consequently suffered.[5]

Standing an even 6 feet tall and weighing about 180 pounds, Blake was quiet and easy-going, especially compared to his more rambunctious teammates Pat Malone and fellow West Virginian and good friend Hack Wilson. With his gray eyes, black hair, and bushy eyebrows, Blake spoke with an unmistakable Appalachian drawl that newspapers in Chicago often mentioned. Recognized by his slow, unpretentious gait, Blake was known to conserve his energy before he pitched. While a member of the Cubs, he married Marguerite H. "Madge" Cross, who, like other well-known wives of Cubs players, was a constant presence at home games at Wrigley Field. Despite the trappings and lifestyle the big city had to offer, Blake was a country boy at heart, and spent his offseason at home in West Virginia where he occasionally pitched in

Blake posted a 14-13 record and logged 218 1/3 innings for the Cubs in 1929. The previous year he tied for the NL lead with four shutouts and won a career-high 17 games. (National Baseball Hall of Fame)

late-season coal-field league games, hunted, fished, and golfed.

Touted as a "stuff" pitcher for most of his career, Blake began his first season with the Cubs in the bullpen. Against the St. Louis Cardinals at Cubs Park on April 24, he pitched a scoreless frame of relief in the ninth inning, and picked up his first big-league win when the Cubs scored two in the bottom of the ninth to win the game, 5-4. On July 5 he tossed a complete game to defeat the Cardinals in St. Louis, 6-2, in his first major-league start, then hit his stride by winning five of six decisions through late August. But he struggled down the stretch, losing his last four decisions. With 11 starts among his 29 appearances, Blake finished the season with a 6-6 record and a high, 4.57 ERA in 106⅓ innings.

While the last-place Cubs took a large step backward in 1925, finishing with a losing record for the first time in four years, Blake became a regular in the starting rotation, joining his boyhood hero, 38-year-old Grover Cleveland "Pete" Alexander. Like the Cubs, who burned through three different managers during the season, Blake was maddeningly inconsistent. He led the team with 31 starts, and had 10 wins but also 18 losses (tying for the second-most in the league). He tossed complete games in all of his victories (including a ten-inning, ten strikeout performance) and carved out a nifty 2.47 ERA; yet in his other 36 appearances his ERA was well over 6.00. The root of Blake's Jekyll and Hyde act was a lack of control. He finished second in the league with a career-high 114 walks. During the course of his six-year run in the starting rotation (1925-1930), Blake's 591 free passes were the most among NL hurlers, but he led the league just once in the dubious category (1926).

Switch-hitter Blake's seven RBIs in 1925 were his most in a given season; he batted .211 in 558 career at-bats. In his only postseason at-bat, he singled to shortstop during Game Two of the 1929 World Series.

A turning point in Cubs history occurred in 1926 when they hired Joe McCarthy to pilot the club. McCarthy endeared himself to his players by his unwavering support for them, even when they struggled. Blake discovered that trait two months into the season. The lanky West Virginian's ERA was north of 7.00 as a swingman and reliever, but with the Cubs just three games off the pace in a tight pennant race, McCarthy gave his beleaguered pitcher another chance on the mound. Blake responded by hurling a four-hitter to defeat the Phillies at the Baker Bowl. Two starts later, Blake authored the best game in his big-league career as he held the eventual champion St. Louis Cardinals to one hit and matched his career high with ten strikeouts en route to a 5-0 victory at Sportsman's Park during the second game of a double-header. Though a poor September (13-14) doomed the Cubs' pennant aspirations, Blake's 6-3 record and sparkling 2.64 ERA in the pressure-packed games of August and September proved to McCarthy that he was an invaluable member of the staff despite his overall pedestrian record of 11-12.

Blake had a reputation as a quick worker on the mound and regularly completed games in well under two hours. He claimed he learned to speed up his rhythm from home-plate umpires, like legendary Bill Klem. "Klem always told young pitchers to work fast," he recalled. "In one of the first games I pitched when he was umpiring, he brought the ball out to me and said to me, 'Young fellow, now let's have a real fast game. These fans want to get home for supper. All good pitchers pitch fast games.'"[6] And despite all of his walks, undoubtedly many on full counts, the level-headed Blake rarely argued with umpires or became emotionally unhinged because of a bad call like teammates Charlie Root or Pat Malone, and was never ejected from a professional baseball game in his 21-year career. Blake's only pitching vice might have been his liberal use of the rosin bag, which drew the attention of *The Sporting News* in 1926 when the bag was introduced to the big leagues.[7]

For most of the 1927 season, the Cubs played streaky baseball. After Chicago's fourth consecutive loss and sixth in seven games to fall to 22-19, Blake tossed a five-hit shutout against the Boston Braves on June 5 to commence the North Siders' 12-game winning streak and rekindle the club's pennant aspirations. The Cubs moved into first place on July 7 (owing to nine straight wins), but were unable to pull away from the second-place Pittsburgh Pirates. After losing 10 of 13 games to fall back into second place, the Cubs and Blake got hot at the same time. In his first three starts in August, the West Virginian tossed three consecutive complete-game victories, allowing just one earned run in 28 innings. Included was a season-long ten-inning effort against the Cincinnati Reds on August 13 and a five-hit shutout of the Brooklyn Robins in the first game of a doubleheader on August 19 to maintain the Cubs' five-game lead over the Pirates. But the Cubs lost 16 out of their next 20 games to fall out of contention, and ultimately finished in fourth place. For the season, Blake won 13 and lost 14 and posted a 3.29 ERA (tenth-best in the NL) in 224⅓ innings.

Blake reported to the Cubs spring-training facility on Catalina Island in 1928 still reeling from the team's late-season collapse the previous September. Up by two games on August 30, the North Siders lost 18 of their last 30 contests to finish in fourth place again. Blake started the 1928 season red hot, wining five consecutive decisions with a sub-1.00 ERA. "[He's] the backbone on the Cubs pitching staff to date," exclaimed *The Sporting News*.[8] Led by the pitching quintet of Bush, Malone, Root, Blake, and Art Nehf (who combined to start 129 games and log in excess of 1,100 innings) and the home-run slugging of Wilson, the Cubs climbed to within two games of the league-leading Cardinals on September 13, when Blake limited them to four hits in a complete-game victory. Though the Cubs were collectively disappointed by their third consecutive "near-miss" and third-place finish, Blake enjoyed his first winning season, setting career highs in victories (17), innings (240⅔), ERA (2.47), and complete games (16); his four shutouts tied for the league lead with four other hurlers.

During the closing weeks of the season, Blake suffered a career-altering injury to the fingers on his right hand when a line drive damaged several of them. "I didn't pitch at all for about a week or so and then when I started again I held the ball a little differently," said Blake. "I even threw underhand for a while. I couldn't grip the curveball very well."[9] Unfortunately for Blake, the height of his personal success also marked his steady, but swift decline. Without his "fast breaking curve" Blake was out of the big leagues three years later.[10]

Chicago acquired the extremely talented yet equally divisive second baseman Rogers Hornsby in the offseason making them the favorites to win the pennant in 1929. While the Cubs battled the Cardinals and Pirates for first place through July, the fingers on Blake's right hand continued to bother him. Described as a "mystery" by *The Sporting News*, Blake lost eight of his first ten decisions despite a sub-3.00 ERA.[11] His control worsened (he walked at least five batters in 12 of 29 starts) as the season progressed, and his ERA steadily rose to 4.29 by season's end. Aided by the high-scoring Cubs offense, Blake won 12 of 15 decisions to finish with a winning record for the second and last time in his career (14-13) and logged 218⅓ innings. The Cubs cruised to their first pennant since 1918.

McCarthy opted for a three-man rotation (Root, Malone, and Bush) against the overwhelming favorite Philadelphia Athletics in the World Series. The Cubs lost the first two games in Chicago; Blake pitched 1⅓ innings of scoreless relief in Game Two before being lifted for a pinch-hitter during the Cubs' fifth-inning rally. Bush's win in Game

Three at Shibe Park breathed new life in the North Siders, who were seemingly on the verge of tying the series, two games apiece. Leading the A's, 8-0 in the seventh inning of Game Four, the Cubs collapsed, surrendering ten runs in the bottom of the frame in an eventual 10-8 loss. Blake was the third of four pitchers in that fateful inning. With the Cubs still in the lead, 8-7, Blake relieved Art Nehf with one out and Mickey Cochrane on second base. "I lost that game," said Blake, "pitching to only two batters. [Al] Simmons bounced one over the third baseman's head and [Jimmie] Foxx grounded another one through the infield."[12] Blake was lifted for Pat Malone, and subsequently was charged with the defeat when Jimmy Dykes cranked a double scoring Foxx, representing the lead run, and Bing Miller to complete the comeback. Miller's dramatic walk-off, Series-clinching double with two outs in the ninth inning of Game Five ended the Cubs' nightmare.

For the first and only time in his career, Blake was named Opening Day starter in 1930, and went six innings to defeat the Cardinals. He tossed a complete game in his next outing to start the season at 2-0. It went downhill after that. He lost seven of his next eight decisions with an ERA hovering over 6.30. Blake was still capable of strong outings, such as an 11-inning complete-game victory over the Brooklyn Robins in August; however, he surrendered hits and walks at an alarming rate (1.67 per nine innings), exceeding even the league average in the Year of the Hitter. The Cubs appeared poised to take their second consecutive pennant but squandered a five-game lead during the last month of the season as pressure and mounting dissent led to McCarthy's resignation with four games remaining. Relegated to the bullpen, Blake made just two starts in the last five weeks of the season, finishing with a 10-14 record and 4.82 ERA in 186⅔ innings.

Just 31 years old, Blake reported to spring training early and was still considered an important cog in the Cubs staff. But Blake chafed under the authoritarian rule of manager Hornsby, struggled in the field, and was ultimately placed on waivers. With an 0-4 record, Blake was claimed by the Philadelphia Phillies on July 20. He took his acquisition in stride, but had little to offer the league's worst pitching staff. He won four of nine decisions, but posted a dismal 5.58 ERA, and was released at the end of the season.

Blake spent the next nine years as a baseball nomad, wandering the upper minor leagues hoping to catch on with a big-league club in need of a cagey veteran. He also pitched annually in coal-field leagues in West Virginia once the professional season was over. Two years pitching in the St. Louis Cardinals farm system earned him an invitation to the Cincinnati Reds spring training in 1934. Among the last cut, Blake spent the next three years in the Double-A International League with the Toronto Maple Leafs and Baltimore Orioles, where he averaged about 13 wins and 225 innings per season.

The pitching-starved St. Louis Browns, managed by his one-time tormentor Rogers Hornsby, invited Blake to spring training in 1937. He made the team as a reliever, but was released on July 15 owning an astronomical 7.61 ERA. Two days later the St. Louis Cardinals unexpectedly signed the veteran as insurance in light of Dizzy Dean's injury in the All-Star Game. He tossed a 10⅓-inning complete game but lost in his first appearance as a Redbird. Though he pitched well in his 14 outings (3.71 ERA), he lost all three of his decisions and was released at season's end.

Blake hung on for three more seasons (1938-1940), winning 30 games and logging in excess of 500 innings for the Class A1 Birmingham Barons and Oklahoma City Indians, before retiring. "I was one of those fellows who never got a sore arm," said Blake.[13] Except for the injury to his fingers, Blake never suffered from shoulder or elbow woes. He logged 3,967 innings in his professional career; 1,620 of them were in the big leagues, where he won 87 games and lost 102.

Blake tried his hand at managing, but lasted less than a full season with the Huntington (West Virginia) Aces of the Class D Mountain State League in 1941. He returned to his home in Beckley, West Virginia, and worked for a coal-mining company for more than 20 years. He continued to pitch well into his late 40s for various mining teams and was a local celebrity of sorts.

Sheriff Blake died on October 31, 1982, in Beckley after a long illness. He was 83 years old and never lost his childhood enthusiasm for baseball. He was buried at the Sunset Memorial Park.

SOURCES

Ehrgott, Roberts, *Mr. Wrigley's Ball Club. Chicago & the Cubs During the Jazz Age* (Lincoln, Nebraska, and London: University of Nebraska Press, 2013).

Golenbock, Peter, *Wrigleyville: A Magical History Tour of the Chicago Cubs* (New York: St. Martin's Griffin, 1999).

Murdock, Eugene, *Baseball Players and Their Times: Oral Histories of the Game, 1920-1940* (Westport, Connecticut: Meckler, 1982).

Stout, Glen, *The Cubs: The Complete Story of Chicago Cubs Baseball* (Boston: Houghton Mifflin Harcourt, 2007).

Stewart, Johnny, "Sheriff Blake Recalls 20-Years Baseball Career." *Raleigh Register* (Beckley, West Virginia), April 30, 1957.

Charleston (West Virginia) *Gazette*

Chicago Daily Tribune

New York Times

Raleigh Register (Beckley, West Virginia)

The Sporting News

Ancestry.com

BaseballLibrary.com

Baseball-Reference.com

Retrosheet.org

SABR.org

Sheriff Blake player file, Baseball Hall of Fame, Cooperstown, New York.

NOTES

1   "Glen White, W. Va," *Raleigh Register* (Beckley, West Virginia), April 24, 1919, 9.

2   Eugene Murdock, *Baseball Players and Their Times: Oral Histories of the Game, 1920-1940* (Westport, Connecticut: Meckler, 1982), 193.

3   Murdock, 194.

4   *The Sporting News*, July 26, 1923, 3.

5   *The Sporting News*, December 20, 1923, 1.

6   Murdock, 199.

7   *The Sporting News*, July 8, 1926, 7.

8   *The Sporting News*, July 5, 1928.

9   Murdock, 189.

10   *The Sporting News*, July 1, 1926, 1.

11   *The Sporting News*, July 25, 1929, 1.

12   Murdock, 190.

13   Murdock, 188.

GUY BUSH

By Gregory H. Wolf

AN OFTEN OVERLOOKED PITCHER ON successful Chicago Cubs teams of his era, Guy Bush was among the National League's winningest pitchers from 1928 to 1934 and finished with 176 victories in his 17-year career. Success was far from foretold when the 21-year-old Mississippi Mudcat made an unlikely debut for the North Siders in September 1923. After his Class D league folded, Bush was afraid to leave the friendly confines of the rural South for those of Wrigley Field (at the time known as Cubs Park); consequently, he assumed an alias and hid out in another low-level league for six weeks before being persuaded to come to the Windy City.

Guy Terrell Bush was born on August 23, 1901, in Aberdeen, a small town and once a busy port on the Tombigbee River in northeastern Mississippi.[1] His parents, George W. and Willie (Gray) Bush, married in 1899 and raised six children (Gahal, Guy, Getrude, Granville, Gay, and Gazell) on their cotton farm in Monroe County and later Lee County, about 150 miles southeast of Memphis. Growing up in hard economic times, Guy had little time to pursue sports and worked year-round on his family's farm. Sensing an opportunity for Guy to pursue a career as a soldier, George and Willie sent him to the nearby Tupelo Military Institute to start high school in 1916. Working on campus to pay for his tuition, room, and board, Guy became interested in baseball. Tall and lanky, he impressed his coaches with his ability to throw and pitched for four years in high school (and in some accounts for an additional year as a postgraduate). Bush often told the story that when he left the school, headmaster George W. Chapman gave him $250 and told him, "Pay it back out of your baseball earnings."[2] Playing semipro and independent ball in leagues throughout the northern part of the state, Bush had a stroke of luck while pitching for a team that played in Shelby and Merigold, two small towns in Bolivar County, Mississippi, in 1923, when George Wheatley, president and scout of the Greenville (Mississippi)

Swamp Angels, saw him pitch and signed him to a professional contract.

Crediting manager Harold Irelan for helping him harness his fastball, Bush overpowered competition in the Class D Cotton States League.[3] After tossing shutouts against Vicksburg to win both games of a doubleheader, the 21-year-old Bush was signed by Chicago Cubs scout Jack Doyle for a reported $1,200. When the league folded in late July 1923, the Cubs wired Bush to report to Chicago immediately. "I was afraid of all the sinful things I had heard existed in Chicago," said Bush, whose idea of Chicago was based on Al Capone and gangsters.[4] Deciding not to report to the Cubs, but not informing Bill Veeck, Sr., Bush joined the Milan (Tennessee) Twins in the Class D Kentucky-Illinois-Tennessee League under an assumed name and without a contract. In early September Bush finally reported to the Cubs after a harrowing overnight train ride to the big city. The green "recruit pitcher" made his major-league debut on September 17 by pitching a scoreless ninth inning, striking out two and surrendering one hit, in a loss to the New York Giants at Cubs Park.[5]

On Catalina Island, California, in 1924, Bush, participating in his first Cubs spring training, impressed manager Bill Killefer with a "mighty neat curve ball and plenty of speed."[6] He made the Cubs' Opening Day roster, but the 6-foot right-hander was optioned to the Wichita Falls (Texas) Spudders of the Class A Texas League in May after just two appearances. With a 9-3 record in 99 innings as a starter and reliever, Joe, as sportswriters began calling him for "no particular reason,"[7] was recalled two months later to replace the ailing Grover Cleveland Alexander. Years later, Bush said that Alexander, more than any other player, had helped him make the transformation from a "thrower" into a big-league pitcher.[8] After a strong eight-inning outing in his first major-league start, surrendering three runs (two earned) and getting the loss, 3-2, against the Phillies on July 16, Bush pitched a complete game and struck out seven to defeat the Boston Braves 7-4 on July 20 and earn his first victory. With his 16 appearances evenly divided between starts and relief appearances, he won two of seven decisions and notched a 4.02 ERA in 80⅔ innings. For the last-place Cubs in 1925, the inexperienced Bush tied for the NL lead in saves (4) and tied for second in the league in appearances (42) while proving that he was equally valuable as a starter, reliever, and all-around fireman, logging 182 innings, but winning just six times in 19 decisions.

With the hiring of a new manager, Joe McCarthy, the Cubs and Bush were in transition in 1926. While Marse Joe ushered the team into an era of hitting, Bush was developing into a trustworthy and effective starter. After flopping just before midseason during a stint as a starter (with an ERA approaching 6.00), he was given another opportunity to prove himself in August with the Cubs just 6½ games out of first place, Bush arguably had the best month of his career. He won all five of his starts and another game in relief, and pitched consecutive shutouts over the Giants and the Brooklyn Robins in Chicago as part of a stretch of 25 consecutive scoreless innings. For the month Bush surrendered just one earned run in 51⅔ innings for a microscopic 0.17 ERA. Extending his winning streak to eight games in September, Bush finished with 13 wins (the first of ten consecutive years of at least ten wins), and had a 2.86 ERA in 157⅓ innings, while the Cubs became stagnant down the stretch to finish in fourth place.

Named a starter to begin the 1927 campaign, Bush hurled an 18-inning complete game on May 14 to defeat the Braves 7-2 in Boston. Always a quick worker on the mound, he faced 71 batters in that game, which lasted just 3 hours and 42 minutes. In his next start (one week later), Bush pitched another complete game to defeat the Robins and it appeared as though he had become one of the game's elite pitchers. But he was stricken by a case of mumps and missed four weeks in June. In his first start in six weeks, he shut out Brooklyn on five hits, winning 1-0 on July 10 to give the Cubs a surprising one-game lead in the pennant race. Often a victim of poor run support, Bush won just three more times (losing seven) while the Cubs faltered from late August into September by losing 11 of 13 games to fall out of contention and end again with a fourth-place finish. During the first game of a doubleheader on September 17 Bush pitched a 13-inning complete game to defeat the Braves 3-2 in Chicago for his tenth and final victory of the season. He logged 193⅓ innings and posted a team-best 3.03 ERA.

From 1928 to 1934, Bush, Pat Malone, and Charlie Root formed one of the best pitching trios in baseball. Although Malone and Root attracted most of the press and adulation of the fans, Bush was more consistent, winning 15 or more games in each of those seven seasons, and led the trio in wins with 121 to Malone's 115 and Root's 100; his .621 winning percentage was easily the best. While Root and Malone burst on the scene by winning 18 games in 1926 and 1928 respectively after outstanding minor-league seasons, Bush had limited experience pitching before sticking with the Cubs in 1925 and came across as having struggled and labored for his success. Irving Vaughan of the *Chicago Daily Tribune* called Bush "one of the National League's outstanding 'finds'" whose success resulted when he learned to "master a curve ball [and] also control."[9]

After a successful 1928 campaign, in which he won 15 times and logged 200-plus innings for the first of seven times in his career, Bush braced for even more personal and team success in 1929. After the Cubs' offseason acquisition of Rogers Hornsby, many experts picked them to take the pennant. Bush tossed a three-hit shutout to defeat the reigning NL champion Cardinals 4-0 on April 21 in his season debut. Starting regularly (30 starts) and used in relief consistently (20 times), Bush was the hottest pitcher in baseball for most of the season. He pitched a ten-inning complete game to defeat the Robins, 6-5, in the first game of a doubleheader on July 20 and put the Cubs in a first-place tie with the Pittsburgh Pirates. Bush tossed a three-hit, 1-0 shutout over the Braves on August 1 and a complete-game victory against the Phillies on August 9 to improve his record to 16-1. His personal-best 11-game winning streak was broken by the Braves on an unearned run in a relief outing on the 12th, but three days later Bush hurled his tenth complete game in 11 starts to defeat the Robins. At that point he was running on fumes. McCarthy had a tendency to overuse hot pitchers even as the Cubs ran away with the pennant. With 11 appearances in the month of August (six starts), Bush's complete-game win over the Reds on August 25 was his 18th and final victory of the season. After a disastrous September (0-3 and a 6.03 ERA), Bush's position in the starting rotation was in jeopardy for the World Series, the Cubs' first since 1918. By season's end Bush had appeared in a major-league-high 50 games (including 30 starts), pitched a career-high 270⅔ innings, won 18 games, and tied for the NL lead in saves (8).

After the Cubs lost World Series Games One and Two in Chicago with Root followed by Malone on the mound, McCarthy "decided to gamble" (in the words of the *Chicago Daily Tribune*) by choosing Bush to start Game Three against Connie Mack's vaunted Philadelphia Athletics, the overwhelming Series favorites.[10] Bush, who had pitched two innings of relief in Game One, was surprised to be named the starter, but not by the outcome of the game: He held the A's to nine singles while going the distance in a 3-1 victory in Philadelphia's Shibe Park. F.C. Lane wrote in *Baseball Magazine* that Bush was underappreciated during his career "and generally not rated as a great pitcher." Bush approached the art of pitching cerebrally and "dissect[ed] every game with painstaking care," Lane wrote.[11] After Bush's victory, the A's crushed Root and three Chicago relievers during the seventh inning for 10 runs in Game Four to come back from an eight-run deficit and then edged out Malone with a walk-off win in Game Five to win their first Series since 1913.

Bush's success in 1929 brought him added notoriety in Chicago. Local sportswriters began calling him the Mississippi Mudcat instead of Joe and portrayed him as a good-natured country boy with a "deep Southern drawl" (phonetic spelling of his words added local color) who learned about life, money, and baseball in the big city.[12] In 1927 Bush married Frances Richardson, a college graduate from Virginia and a department head in a North Side Chicago bank. By all accounts, Bush was an approachable, friendly, fun-loving teammate. He and Pat Malone were good friends. Bush regularly attended hockey and football games, and golfed and hunted during the offseason. But his most time-consuming pursuits involved money. He opened and personally ran gasoline stations and sponsored baseball and basketball teams. He had a fondness for fast, luxurious cars and was known as the best-dressed

Cubs player with "more than a score of suits and hundreds of neckties."[13]

Weighing just about 165 pounds for most of his career, Bush was often described as "frail."[14] Catcher Gabby Hartnett thought Bush was a nervous type whose slight stature came from worrying too much. Bush himself admitted, "I would get more hop on my fastball if I had a little more beef behind my throws," but never packed on the pounds like the portly Root and the husky Malone.[15] Bush is "stronger physically than he looks," wrote Chicago sportswriter Ed Burns, and was "fidgety" on the mound.[16] Prone to bouts of wildness, Bush survived on his fastball, which he threw with a "hop-toad" lunge.[17] He had a high windmill windup, threw overhand to three-quarters overhand, had a high leg kick and a long stride toward the plate, and sprang forward to finish in a squat position. "I found that I can get more on the ball,"

The "Mississippi Mudcat," Bush went 18-7 for the Cubs in 1929 and led major-league pitchers with 50 appearances. From 1928 to 1934 the dependable Bush averaged 17 wins and 227 innings for the North Siders. (Retro Images Archive. George Brace Collection)

said Bush, "if I come forward with everything I got. I naturally throw myself off balance."[18] He'd stretch forward as far as he possibly could (much like Tom Seaver 40 years later) which he thought shortened the distance from the mound to home plate and made his fastball even faster. "In a tight hard pitched game," he recalled, "I'll generally skin my right knee."[19]

Bush had a disastrous start in 1930. Pounded in his first five appearances (two starts) and saddled with an 11.02 ERA in 16⅓ innings, Bush slipped while fielding a ball, twisted his elbow, and missed three weeks in May. After several relief appearances, he rejoined the starting rotation but his fastball lacked velocity. Pummeled by opponents (they batted .316 against him), Bush surrendered a staggering 174 runs and a new (post-1900) National League-record 155 earned runs in just 225 innings, and led the major leagues in wild pitches (12). Amazingly, he won 15 games (thanks to the Cubs' offense) and lost just ten times. In the "Year of the Hitter," Bush's 6.20 ERA was not the worst in the league; that honor went to the Phillies' Les Sweetland, who posted a 7.71 ERA in 167 innings. Betrayed by their pitching and inconsistent offense in September, the Cubs were overtaken by the St. Louis Cardinals in the last two weeks of the season and finished in second place.

Tall, dark, and handsome, with slicked-back hair and sideburns, Bush had a reputation of a quirky player who "pride[d] himself as a slugger," even though he batted just .161 (143-for-888) during his major-league career with no home runs and 52 runs batted in.[20] Sportswriters often joked that when the National League introduced new baseballs with thicker stitches to improve pitchers' grip and a thicker hide to slightly deaden the ball in 1931 in reaction to the record-setting hitting barrage the previous season, Bush bemoaned that his hitting would suffer. He was also an accomplished fielder, despite his delivery, and tied for the NL lead in fielding percentage (1.000) for three consecutive seasons (1935-1937).

Cubs batters continued to bash the ball in 1931, but the pitching staff was mired in another collective funk, ranking sixth in earned-run average and runs surrendered. Bothered by an early-season arm injury through most of

July, Bush pitched inconsistently and rumors circulated that he was washed up. However, he unexpectedly turned his season around beginning on July 31 when he pitched a complete game to defeat the league-leading Cardinals 10-3 in St. Louis. Recording eight complete games in his last 12 starts, Bush was the "mainstay of the team" and finished with a 16-8 record.[21] Within a span of five weeks, Bush threw his only two career one-hitters and both were unusual. At the conclusion of his dominating 1-0 victory over the Cardinals on August 9, teammates rushed to congratulate Bush for his first no-hitter. Minutes later, the mood turned somber when word emerged from the press box that George Watkins' first-inning grounder, which shortstop Woody English had fielded poorly then dropped, was scored a hit and not an error. The episode sparked national debate. Outraged by the general lack of information given to players and fans during games, such as the number of hits and errors, *The Sporting News* led efforts to require that scoreboards show hits and errors.[22] On September 13 at Wrigley Field in the second game of a doubleheader, Bush surrendered just a legitimate single, but two errors led to an unearned run in an 8-1 drubbing of the Braves.

Bush had the reputation of being one of the most athletic and physically fit players on the Cubs. Reporting on his legendary workouts at spring training in Catalina Island, the Associated Press wrote that "no one can outwork him."[23] Asked about his offseason preparation, Bush responded, "I smoke several cigars a day, eat sparingly, and just study baseball,"[24] (which might also explain his rail-thin physique).

In 1932 the Cubs became the last major-league team to put numbers on players' uniforms. With four complete-game victories in his first six starts, Bush, donning number 14 (and later switching to 24), was off to a fast start for second-year manager Rogers Hornsby. The 30-year-old Bush pitched a 13-inning masterpiece, defeating the Braves, 5-3, in Boston on June 12 to give the first-place Cubs a 1½-game lead, but the team was on the verge of unraveling. In the midst of player injuries and inconsistencies, shortstop Billy Jurges was shot twice by a local chorus girl in early July. The team sputtered to a 26-29 record in June and July. Hornsby was fired on August 2. The manager was a chronic gambler and had racked up an estimated $40,000 of debt. He borrowed money from players, including Bush, to pay his bookies. In early August the *Chicago Daily Tribune* reported that Commissioner Kenesaw Landis had launched an investigation into gambling on the Cubs. "I don't give a damn what anybody says, the gambling stories printed in Chicago are lousy," said Bush, who was one of the targets of the investigation.[25] Eventually five players, including Bush, were exonerated during a hearing conducted in St. Louis in August.

The Cubs rallied around first baseman Charlie Grimm, who succeeded Hornsby. A player-manager, Jolly Cholly was easygoing and helped relax the team, whose players had been on edge all season from Hornsby's autocratic ways. As Bush won eight of ten decisions in the last six weeks of the season, the Cubs went 37-18 for Grimm to overtake the Pirates and cruise to the pennant. For the first time since 1926, the Cubs pitching staff paced the NL in team ERA (3.44), led by 23-year-old Lon Warneke's 2.37. Bush's 19 wins ranked third in the league (behind Warneke's 22 and Brooklyn's Watty Clark's 20). He posted a 3.21 ERA in 238⅔ innings.

Facing the overwhelming favorite New York Yankees in the opening game of the World Series at Yankee Stadium, Bush surrendered just three hits in 5⅓ innings but was unexpectedly wild, issuing five walks and giving up eight runs in a 12-6 shellacking. *The Sporting News* reported that Bush was still smarting from a finger injury suffered in his last start of season, and that the "top of his right finger looked like the sawed-off end of a raw ham."[26] With the Cubs down three games to none, Bush had a chance to redeem himself in Game Four, but lasted only one-third of an inning, facing five Yankee hitters and surrendering two singles and a walk and hitting a batter. The Yankees, cruising to another lopsided win and their first World Series championship since 1928, helped manager Joe McCarthy exact revenge on the team that had fired him just before the 1930 season ended. The Series is better known today for Babe Ruth's "called shot" in Game Three off Charlie Root.

Bush was among the highest paid pitchers in the National League from 1930 through 1933. He injured his arm during spring training in 1933, but remained confident in the Cubs' ability. Bush was confident that the Cubs would win the pennant again.[27] But for the first ten weeks of the season, he struggled (failing to make it beyond the fifth inning in five of ten starts), and the Cubs treaded water in fourth place, barely above .500. Tensions and frustrations were high even at the beginning of the season when, during an especially poor start against St. Louis, Bush challenged Dizzy Dean to a fight during the game. While Dean heckled Bush, Grimm clashed with Cardinals manager Gabby Street. Bush was a streaky pitcher and at 31 had just perfected a new pitch to replace his slowing fastball. "I got my new screwball down," Bush said. "Last year I couldn't throw it as often as I wanted because it made my finger sore."[28] A complete-game victory over the Pirates at Wrigley Field on June 16 commenced one of his best and longest streaks. Used almost exclusively as a starter for the first time in his career, Bush responded by winning 15 of his final 21 starts, including 16 complete games. For just the second time in his career, he tossed shutouts in consecutive starts when he blanked the Phillies on three hits in a 5-0 victory in Philadelphia on August 24, and then on short rest tossed a 2-0 two-hitter against the Dodgers in Brooklyn. Aiming for his 20th victory in his last start of the season, against his rival Dizzy Dean in St. Louis, Bush hurled a five-hitter and struck out a season-high seven batters in a 12-2 thumping of the Redbirds. "I get more satisfaction out of beating that guy once than I do winning from anyone else twice," Bush said of facing Dean.[29] Bush set career highs in wins (20), starts (32), complete games (20), and shutouts (4), while posting a career-low 2.75 ERA in 259 innings. Despite his preseason predictions, the Cubs finished a disappointing third.

Bush won his first seven decisions (including six complete games) to start the 1934 season, finished with 18 victories, and recorded a winning percentage of .600 or better for the seventh year in a row, despite missing almost five weeks because of a rib injury in June and an ear infection in July. But the season was practically a repeat of 1933 for the Cubs: They plodded along (still struggling with the death of team president Bill Veeck, Sr. in the offseason) and the offense never got on track in 1934. Appearing in relief in both games of an August 16 doubleheader against the Braves two days after being clobbered by them in a start, Bush clashed with Grimm because he felt he was being overworked. He had an increasingly acrimonious relationship with his skipper, and Bush's days in Chicago were numbered. In "the sensation of the week" during baseball's postseason winter meetings in Louisville, 32-year-old Bush, outfielder Babe Herman, and pitcher Jim Weaver were traded to the Pittsburgh Pirates for workhorse pitcher Larry French and future Hall of Famer Fred Lindstrom.[30]

Despite his claim that he was excited to be going to Pittsburgh, Bush regretted leaving Chicago (he continued to live there during the offseason) and had difficulty adapting to his new team and surroundings in 1935. Plagued by inconsistencies, he twice lost his position in the starting rotation, but still managed 25 starts in 41 appearances. Proclaimed a "bust" by The Sporting News,[31] Bush finished with a disappointing 11-11 record and a 4.32 ERA in 204⅓ innings.

Like his teammate Charlie Root, Bush's legacy is inextricably tied to Babe Ruth. In a fateful game on May 25, 1935, against the Boston Braves, Bush relieved Red Lucas and surrendered the final two home runs of Ruth's career. (Ruth had already hit a home run off Lucas.) The second of the two surrendered by Bush, Ruth's 714th, was the first home run ever to clear the right-field grandstand at Pittsburgh's Forbes Field. "I got a signal for another fastball and I came through with one," Bush recalled in 1974 when Hank Aaron broke Ruth's home-run record. "[Ruth] got ahead of the ball and hit it over the triple deck, clear out of the ballpark. I'm telling you, it was the longest cockeyed ball I ever saw in my life."[32] The 1992 film The Babe underscored the rivalry between Bush and Ruth which began in the 1932 World Series when Bush led the Cubs' merciless harassment of Ruth.

Bush's fall from an 18-game winner in 1934 to ineffective mop-up artist in 1936 was a startling and unexpected surprise.[33] Bush, who at the time ranked second in the National League in career wins behind Jesse "Pop" Haines

of the Cardinals, was released in July and signed with the Boston Bees (so named since 1936 after their horrendous 38-115 record the previous season). Manager Bill McKechnie, well known for his handling of cast-off pitchers, coaxed a 4-5 record and 11 starts out of Bush in the second half of the 1936 season. On arguably the major leagues' best pitching staff in 1937 (the Bees led baseball with a 3.22 ERA), Bush rebounded with an above-league-average 3.54 ERA in 180⅔ innings. He had 11 complete games in his first 16 starts. But Bush was often the victim of poor run support, struggled the last two months of the season, and finished with an 8-15 record while starting 20 times in 32 appearances.

Like many players of his era, Bush wrung every possible inning from his arm before retiring. He was sold to the Cardinals before the 1938 season, but was released by St. Louis in early May. He signed with the Los Angeles Angels, the Cubs' affiliate in the Double-A Pacific Coast League, for an estimated $5,000 bonus, and helped lead them to the league title in 1938 as a spot starter and reliever.

Retiring in Chicago with his wife, Bush opened a tavern, suffered the loss of his gas stations due to fuel rationing during World War II, and worked for the Pullman sleeping-car company. With baseball rosters thinning because of the war, Bush staged an unlikely comeback at the age of 42. After working out with the Cubs, he signed a contract with the Chattanooga Lookouts of the Class A-1 Southern Association in July 1944. Bush's 5-3 record and 3.13 ERA in ten games (nine starts), caught the attention of his former Braves manager and current Cincinnati Reds skipper Bill McKechnie, who invited him to spring training in 1945. Bush made four appearances in relief and, with players beginning to return from military service, was released in late May. Retiring for the second time, Bush finished his 17-year major-league career with a 176-136 record and a 3.86 ERA in 2,722 innings.

A farmer and Southerner by heart, Bush spent a few years after his playing days in Chicago before retiring permanently to Shannon, Mississippi, near where he grew up. Raising vegetables and soybeans on his 50-acre farm, Bush never tired talking about baseball and moving from the small town to the big city to find fame on the mound. On July 2, 1985, he died of cardiac arrest at the age of 83. Funeral services were held at the First Baptist Church in Shannon and he was buried in the Shannon cemetery.

SOURCES

Ancestry.com

BaseballLibrary.com

Baseball-Reference.com

Chicago Daily Tribune

New York Times

Retrosheet.com

The Sporting News

NOTES

1   There is some debate about Bush's birthdate. Throughout his playing career he listed it as 1903 or 1904 to appear younger. His Social Security Death Index says 1900; his gravestone says 1901, as do most of his obituaries. Guy Bush player file at the National Baseball Hall of Fame, Cooperstown, New York

2   Edward Burns, "Page Mr. Alger! Home Town Boy Makes in Good in Big City," undated *Chicago Daily Tribune* article in Guy Bush player file, National Baseball Hall of Fame.

3   "Irelan's Pupil," *Decatur* (Illinois) *Review,* April 3, 1924, 14.

4   Edward Burns, "Page Mr. Alger," Guy Bush player file, National Baseball Hall of Fame.

5   "Kelly Gets the Hammer, Giants Win," *Wisconsin State Journal,* Madison, Wisconsin, September 18, 1923, 16.

6   Irving Vaughn, "Cubs Come Back With Twin Win in Coast Games," *Chicago Daily Tribune,* March 17, 1924, 25.

7   For example, see Irving Vaughn, "Cubs Splash Whitewash on Giants," *Chicago Daily Tribune,* August 8, 1926, 23.

8   Irving Vaughn, "Tireless Energy and Desire to Learn Lift Bush to Top," *Chicago Daily Tribune,* September 14, 1932, 19.

9   Irving Vaughn, "Guy Bush's 20-Year-old Brother Signs With Cubs," *Chicago Daily Tribune,* February 1, 1928, 29.

10   Irving Vaughn, "Guy Bush Picked to Face Athletics Today," *Chicago Daily Tribune,* October 11, 1929, 23.

11   F.C. Lane, "The Only Winning Pitcher," *Baseball Magazine,* November 1930, 555.

12   "The Series Cast in Person," undated, unidentified publication in Guy Bush player file, National Baseball Hall of Fame.

13   Ibid

14   F.C. Lane, "The Only Winning Pitcher."

15   Ibid.

16   *Chicago Daily Tribune,* July 9, 1930, 30.

17   F.C. Lane, "The Only Winning Pitcher."

18   Ibid.

19   Ibid.

20   Edward Burns, "Wilson Clouts 53d Homer; Cubs Win 6-3," *Chicago Daily Tribune,* September 23, 1930, 17.

21   *The Sporting News,* August 13, 1931, 1.

22   *The Sporting News,* August 20, 1931, 4.

23   Paul Michelson, "Bud Tinning Is Cause of Cubs Winning Streak," Associated Press article in *Biloxi* (Mississippi) *Daily Herald,* July 16, 1933, 3.

24   "Salads and Cigars," Associated Press article. 1932, Guy Bush player file, National Baseball Hall of Fame.

25   *The Sporting News,* August 18, 1932, 1.

26   *The Sporting News,* October 13, 1932, 3.

27   Paul Michelson, "Guy Bush certain Cubs will retain loop championship," Associated Press article in *Biloxi* (Mississippi) *Daily Herald,* April 11, 1933, 5.

28   Ibid.

29   "Bush, Dizzy Have Feud," United Press article in *Milwaukee Journal,* April 25, 1934, 19.

30   *The Sporting News,* November 29, 1934, 2.

31   *The Sporting News,* July 25, 1935, 1.

32   Robert Shaw, "Babe's 714th a monumental blast," Associated Press article in *Cleveland Plain Dealer,* May 25, 1974, 6-C.

33   *The Sporting News,* July 23, 1936, 1.

HAL CARLSON

By Ernie Fuhr

OCCASIONALLY, A PLAYER IS TAKEN out of the lineup due to personal misfortune. But in 1930 a scheduled pitcher didn't take the mound (or ever pitch again) because he died an agonizing death on that very morning. Hal Carlson was a right-handed journeyman who pitched for three teams in the National League. He was a fairly talented pitcher, but his success hadn't come easily. His 14-year career was disrupted by World War I, the spitball ban, chronic health problems, and, finally, an early grave.

Harold Gust Carlson was born on May 17, 1892, in Rockford, Illinois, close to the border with Wisconsin. He was the oldest of four children[1] of working-class Swedish immigrants who instilled in him the values of hard work and self-reliance, qualities that later served Carlson well. While growing up, he attended Wight School, a neighborhood school in the heart of Rockford's Swedish-American community.[2] On the sandlots of Rockford's east side, young Hal honed his skills, pitching for the semipro Rockford Maroons.

The Maroons, an independent team of Swedish-American men, worked regular jobs during the week, and on weekends they traveled to play other teams in the region, often in Wisconsin, Indiana, or Iowa. Hal started pitching for the Maroons in 1911.[3] He enjoyed the camaraderie of playing baseball and remained friends with many of his teammates for the rest of his life. He experimented with the spitball, soon discovering many ways that he could magically affect the weight, motion, and trajectory of the baseball. The spitball pitch would become Carlson's specialty.

Baseball scouts soon noticed Carlson's talents and in 1912 he joined the Rockford Wolverines of the Class C Wisconsin-Illinois League. Although Carlson showed potential and was popular with hometown crowds, he struggled somewhat. In April 1913 the *Rockford Register Gazette* reported that he had been cut from the team: "Harold Carlson, a Rockford boy who did some pitching for the team last season, was dropped today. It was hard

to find room for him, against the greater experience of others on the staff."[4] This temporary setback did not discourage Carlson, nor did the Rockford club lose interest in him. The next season, he was picked up again. According to the *Rockford Morning Star*, "Harold Carlson, the local pitcher who has shown considerable promise when wearing the Rockford uniform, was yesterday added to the pitching staff at the insistence of manager Orville Wolfe, who thinks he can develop him into an effective hurler."[5]

Carlson had a good year in 1914, posting a winning percentage of nearly .550, and was considered "to possess the best spitter of any pitcher in the W-I Circuit."[6] On August 24, 1914, he was sold to the Milwaukee Brewers of the Double-A American Association for $750.[7] Carlson's time in Milwaukee was short; he soon came down with a bad case of the flu and was unable to report to the team.[8] It is uncertain whether Carlson recovered enough to actually pitch, as there is no formal record of his performance. Apparently, Milwaukee was unimpressed. In January 1915 the Brewers sold Carlson to the Central League's Grand Rapids Black Sox.[9] In the early months of the season he was 4-5 with an earned-run average of 2.96. In June Carlson obtained his release from Grand Rapids and joined the hometown Rockford Wakes of the Class B Three-I (Illinois-Indiana-Iowa) League. After a subpar 1915 season with the Wakes (4-11, 3.07 ERA), Carlson's best performance in the minors came in 1916, when he posted a record of 23-13 and an ERA of 2.79. In a game against Moline, Carlson pitched 18 innings, with a no-hitter going into the ninth.[10] Although Rockford eventually lost, 1-0, the game illustrated Carlson's endurance and solidified his growing reputation.

Clarence "Pants" Rowland, who had scouted in the Three-I League and often seen Carlson pitch,[11] was now managing the Chicago White Sox and in 1916 he invited Carlson to team tryouts in the spring of 1917.[12] Had things worked out differently, Carlson might have spent his rookie year playing with the world champion White Sox of 1917. For reasons unclear, the White Sox canceled their invitation to him.[13]

Carlson got another opportunity on September 21, 1916, when the Pittsburgh Pirates signed him for $1,200.[14] In his rookie year of 1917, as a spot starter and reliever, he went 7-11, with a respectable ERA of 2.90. In May 1918 Carlson joined the Army to serve in the World War.[15] He was able to play a little more baseball before being shipped to Europe, pitching for the 86th Division team at Camp Grant, in Rockford.[16] When he got overseas he served as a machine gunner in the Battle of the Argonne Forest.[17] Like many of his comrades, he was exposed to poison gas, and there was speculation that this contributed to the health problems that plagued Carlson and eventually took his life 20 years later.[18] Carlson was discharged as a sergeant and returned home in May 1919, in time to rejoin the Pirates.

While Carlson was overseas, a major controversy brewed regarding spitball pitching. Club owners felt that the time had come to ban the practice for ethical reasons as well as safety concerns. The ban was instituted for the 1920 season, except for two pitchers on each team whose stock in trade was the spitball. They were given one season to adjust. After the 1920 season club owners were allowed to submit the names of spitball pitchers who would be allowed to continue using the pitch until they retired. This list of 17 spitball pitchers did not include Carlson because Pirates owner Barney Dreyfuss did not submit any names. This was probably more than just a clerical oversight; Dreyfuss was a staunch opponent of the spitball who served on the commission that banned it. He may have tried to get Carlson's name on the list, but, according to at least one sportswriter, was rebuffed by the other owners.[19]

Carlson was forced to reinvent his repertoire and again master some fundamentals: throwing curves and fastballs, and altering speeds. His pitching faltered and his statistics declined. In 1919 he was 8-10 with an ERA of 2.23. In 1920 he was 14-13, but his ERA had risen more than a full run, to 3.36. On July 7, 1921, in an exhibition game against the New York Yankees, Carlson struck out Babe Ruth twice.[20] But he was soon sidelined with a sore arm,

and ended the season with a dismal 4-8, 4.27 record. There was no noticeable improvement in 1922 (9-12, 5.70). In 1923 Carlson made only four appearances before the Pirates demoted him to the Wichita Falls Spudders of the Class A Texas League, where he spent the rest of the season. In Texas Carlson was rejuvenated, ending the season 20-10. It was enough of an improvement for the Philadelphia Phillies to take a chance on Carlson, acquiring him for 1924.

On October 24, 1924, Carlson married Eva Nelson, a local schoolteacher, whom he had met while she was attending Northwestern University in Evanston, Illinois. Carlson's granddaughter, Kristine Pratt, recalled that her grandmother said a friend asked her to go to a party where a "famous baseball player" was going to be. "My grandmother refused initially, as she couldn't care less about baseball players of any kind, famous or otherwise," Pratt said. "I wonder if that's what interested him in her initially; the fact that she wasn't in awe of him or one of his groupies?"[21] The Carlsons' first child, daughter Betty, was born two years later.

With a new team came new opportunity. When Carlson joined the Phillies in 1924, they were struggling. In 1924 and 1925, Philadelphia finished next to last in the National League, then dead last in 1926 and 1927. Against this backdrop, a mediocre hurler like Hal Carlson could distinguish himself, if he performed well. His first two years in Philadelphia were unspectacular, but in 1925 he led the National League with four shutouts. The 1926 season was his best year yet, when he posted a record of 17-12 and the best ERA (3.23) since his rookie days. Carlson also earned a few votes for 1926 National League MVP, placing 11th in the vote tally. Withal, on June 7, 1927, Carlson was traded to the Cubs for pitcher Tony Kaufmann and shortstop Jimmy Cooney.

Carlson's hometown of Rockford is 75 miles northwest of Chicago, so when he was traded to the Cubs, it felt like a "homecoming" in many respects. Carlson continued to be very popular with the people of Rockford. Whether he was winning or losing, he was widely admired and always captured local headlines. On August 25, 1926, when he was still pitching for the Phillies, more than 500

A trusty swingman for the Cubs in 1929, Carlson won 11 games. The following season the 14-year big-league veteran died tragically at the age of 38 from a stomach hemorrhage. (Retro Images Archive. George Brace Collection)

fans from the Rockford area journeyed to Wrigley Field to honor their hometown hero. They presented Carlson with a grandfather clock.[22] (After many decades keeping time in the Carlson family's home, the clock, along with other baseball artifacts, was presented to Rockford's Erlander Home Museum.)

Carlson made his debut with the Cubs on June 8, 1927, the day after he had been traded, at Wrigley Field against Dazzy Vance and the Brooklyn Robins. Carlson pitched a complete game and allowed only two runs as the Cubs edged the Robins, 3-2. In his first four weeks in Chicago, Carlson won six games, helping put the Cubs in first place by July 7. He won 12 games and lost 8 for the Cubs with an ERA of 3.17. (His combined record was 16-13 with an ERA of 3.70.)

Carlson suffered a setback in the Cubs' 1928 spring training camp on Catalina Island; he was stricken with a bad case of the flu. This and serious bouts of pleurisy rendered him ineffective for most of the season. He was dropped

from the pitching rotation and started only four games, ending the year 3-2 with an ERA of 5.91. Carlson's chronic health problems were a permanent condition, related to his being gassed in World War I. A doctor in California told him that he probably only had months to live.[23] Carlson didn't share this grim news, nor did he let it deter him from playing.[24] He returned to Chicago hopeful for one more comeback, both for himself and for the Cubs' postseason hopes.

In spite of his age (36) and ill health, Carlson did his best to stay in shape. One day before he had to pitch, he asked the Cubs trainer, Andy Lotshaw, for a deep tissue massage on his sore elbow. Lotshaw advised Carlson to lie face down. Then, while the ailing pitcher wasn't looking, he rubbed Hal's arm with Coca-Cola from the bottle he'd been drinking. Carlson pitched successfully that afternoon, and from that day on, Lotshaw continued to give him this "special therapy" without telling him what it was.[25]

The 1929 World Series, against the Philadelphia Athletics, was the pinnacle of Carlson's 14-year career. By then he had recuperated and was pitching better than ever, with a record of 11-5 and an ERA of 5.16. In the World Series he pitched twice in relief, giving up seven hits and three runs in four innings. The three runs he gave up came in Game Two, when he was one of three pitchers who hurled in relief of Pat Malone as the Cubs list, 9-3. One of the five hits he gave up in three innings was a two-run homer by Al Simmons. In Game Four, in which the Cubs took an 8-0 lead but gave up 10 runs in the seventh inning, Carlson pitched a scoreless eighth inning.

Carlson began the 1930 season feeling healthy and upbeat. He and his wife were expecting their second child that summer, and his Cubs salary allowed them to build a home in Rockford. Carlson also enjoyed the camaraderie of his teammates, even though he was older than most of them. Despite being called "The Silent Swede" with his reserved personality, he had a fun-loving, mischievous side. "He could be a practical joker," said his granddaughter Kristine Pratt.[26]

Carlson relished his role as the dugout bench jockey. *Chicago Tribune* sportswriter Edward Burns wrote, "A job such as Hal's, of course, involves a great deal of research. If, for instance, any one of the opposing pitchers ever was in jail for horse stealing, Hal should know about it. To be a good jockey as Carlson is, his timing must be perfect."[27]

On May 27, 1930, an unseasonably cold day, the Cubs home game against the Cincinnati Reds was rained out. The Cubs were 19-19 and Carlson led the pitching staff with a 4-2 record. After an early dinner, Carlson returned to his apartment at Hotel Carlos, just up the street from Wrigley Field. He knew that he would be starting in the next day's game and, feeling a little under the weather, he turned in early that night.[28]

In the middle of the night, the 38-year-old Carlson awoke with an awful pain in his stomach. Though it was about 2:15 A.M., the pain was bad enough that he called Ed Froelich, the Cubs' clubhouse attendant, who also stayed in the hotel. "I feel pretty bad. You better call a doctor," Carlson said. Froelich rushed to Carlson's room. Carlson told him that it was probably just an attack of his stomach ulcers. He thought that if the pain abated, he might be okay. Concerned, Froelich sat with him for a while. By 3 A.M., blood started to come up into Carlson's mouth. Now in a state of panic, Froelich called three other Cubs players who were in the building: Kiki Cuyler, Riggs Stephenson, and Cliff Heathcote. By the time they arrived, Carlson was fading fast. Immediately they summoned the team physician, Dr. John Davis, who was nearby. By the time Dr. Davis arrived, Hal was losing consciousness. An ambulance was called, but by the time it arrived, it was too late. At 3:30 A.M., as his teammates watched helplessly, Carlson breathed his last. The cause of death was officially listed as a stomach hemorrhage.[29]

There is some debate as to the exact cause of Carlson's stomach hemorrhage and whether his death could have been prevented. One theory is that Carlson was injured when he was struck in the abdomen by a batted ball at spring training that year.[30] This may have damaged the fragile artery within the stomach, proving fatal if undetected. Another possibility is that the poison gas in World War I did long-term organ damage, and eventually caught up to Carlson. It is uncertain which of these things is more directly responsible for Carlson's death, as medical

knowledge was much more limited in 1930, and Carlson closely guarded his medical privacy.[31]

Eva Carlson was not with Hal at the hotel because she was eight months pregnant and was resting at their home in Rockford. This was not uncommon, as late-term pregnancies and childbirth could become risky in those days. Kristine Pratt said she believed her grandfather was unconscious by the time Froelich and the players arrived, and that he had actually died alone. "He felt the pain and he knew something was wrong and started calling the other players on the team, crying out in agony and begging them to do something, as he was dying," she said. "Unfortunately, he was known for being a practical joker. So he died alone in his room. Of course it's a game we can all play isn't it? If he hadn't played practical jokes, if someone had come, if my grandmother had been there, would it have turned out differently? Medical care isn't what it is now. Could anyone have helped him? Regardless, the end result is the same."[32]

The Cubs, stunned and wearing black armbands for their fallen pitcher, played their scheduled game against the Reds that afternoon, winning 6-5. Kiki Cuyler, who had been at Carlson's deathbed hours before, hit a two-run homer in the first inning. The next game was postponed, as a delegation of Cubs players accompanied Carlson's body back to Rockford.

Carlson was buried that weekend. Crowds lined the streets as the funeral procession passed, and 5,000 mourners gathered at Rockford's Arlington Cemetery.[33] Carlson's pallbearers were local friends with whom he had played ball in his early days with the Rockford Maroons. Honorary pallbearers were Cubs personnel, including fellow pitchers Charlie Root and Pat Malone.[34] The rest of the Cubs soldiered on. On the afternoon that Carlson was buried, they won a doubleheader from the St. Louis Cardinals.

On July 7, 1930, five weeks after Carlson died, Eva gave birth to their second daughter, Kathleen. As a single mother and with only her meager schoolteacher's income, Mrs. Carlson successfully raised both girls, no small accomplishment during the Great Depression. She never remarried and lived another 59 years. She kept a portrait of Carlson hanging over her bed and would say goodnight to him every night for the rest of her life.[35]

Carlson was remembered by his friends and colleagues for his hard work, patriotism, and perseverance, on and off the field. Perhaps the most fitting eulogy was given by Cubs president Bill Veeck, Sr. who said: "Hal Carlson was a splendid example of moral courage and was loved by everyone who knew him. While he was fighting for his country in the World War, his stock in trade as a pitcher, the spitball, was taken from him through an oversight. But instead of quitting like most humans, he came back to greater success than ever. In all my life I have never known a finer type than Carlson. He was strong in every way, morally and physically."[36]

SOURCES

Asprooth, Fritz, *Hal Carlson: A Rockford Legend.* (booklet), Library of Congress

No. TXu 000330544, 1988.

Boone, Robert, and Gerald Grunska, *Hack: The Meteoric Life of one of Baseball's First Superstars* (Highland Park, Illinois: Highland Press, 1978).

Ehrgott, Roberts, *Mr. Wrigley's Ball Club: Chicago and the Cubs During the Jazz Age* (Lincoln: University of Nebraska Press, 2013).

Rockford Daily Republic

Rockford Morning Star

Rockford Register Gazette

Rockford Register Star

Baseball-Reference.com

Retrosheet.com

Genealogybank.com

Ancestry.com

Kristine Pratt, email correspondence with author, October 2013

NOTES

1   Carlson was born in 1892, although the author came across several stories and biographies that stated, inaccurately, that he was born in 1894. In one instance, Carlson himself spoke this mistruth to a reporter: "The Cub Takes A Week Off and Goes to Work," *Rockford Daily Republic,* June 22, 1927, 6.

2   Fritz Asprooth, *Hal Carlson: A Rockford Legend.* (booklet) Library of Congress No. TXu 000330544. 1988, 6.

3   Ibid.

4   "Team Chosen By Marshall," *Rockford Register Gazette,* April 29, 1913, 7.

5   "Series of Dances Planned in Aid of Baseball Club," *Rockford Morning Star,* January 30, 1914, 7.

6   "Sell Carlson to Milwaukee Club," *Rockford Register Gazette,* August 24, 1914, 5.

7   Ibid.

8   "Drizzle Prevents Clash of Indians With Rockfords," *Rockford Morning Star,* August 29, 1914, 9.

9   "Breakfast Table Chat," *Rockford Morning Star,* January 1, 1915, 10.

10 Asprooth, 8.

11 "Carlson to Get Trial With Sox," *Rockford Register Gazette,* May 5, 1916, 9.

12 Ibid.

13 "Carlson Star for Pirates," *Rockford Register Gazette,* May 5, 1917, 5.

14 "League Meets Oct. 10," *Rockford Daily Republic,* October 6, 1916, 10.

15 "May Brings Rockford Baseball Fans Memories of Hal Carlson," *Rockford Morning Star,* May 11, 1952, 20.

16 Asprooth, 12.

17 Dick Ramey, "Hal Carlson, Rockford's Only Major League Player, Dies Suddenly in Chicago," *Rockford Register Gazette,* May 28, 1930, 2.

18 Robert Boone and Gerald Grunska, *Hack: The Meteoric Life of One of Baseball's First Superstars* (Highland Park, Illinois: Highland Press, 1978), 93.

19 Burt Whitman, "Aid Pitching By Letting Down Bars to Spit Ball Delivery," *Boston Herald,* December 28, 1924, 3.

20 "Harold Carlson Fans Babe Ruth Twice Thursday," (Associated Press article) *Rockford Register Gazette,* July 8, 1921, 14.

21 Kristine Pratt, correspondence with author, October 27, 2013.

22 Dooney Trank, "Carlson Loses but Gets Gift from Fans Here," *Rockford Register Gazette,* August 26, 1926, 11.

23 Robert Ehrgott, *Mr. Wrigley's Ball Club: Chicago and the Cubs During the Jazz Age* (Lincoln: University of Nebraska Press, 2013), 127.

24 Ehrgott, 104.

25 Ehrgott, 108.

26 Kristine Pratt, correspondence with author, October 17, 2013.

27 Edward Burns, "Who Are These Cubs?" *Omaha World Herald,* September 30, 1929, 10.

28 Ehrgott, 232.

29 Ibid.

30 Bill Wolverton, "Who was Hal Carlson?" *Rockford Register Star,* April 3, 1996, 4B.

31 Ehrgott, 104.

32 Kristine Pratt, correspondence with author, October 17, 2013.

33 "Friends Pay Last Respects to Hal Carlson," *Rockford Daily Republic,* June 1, 1930, 1.

34 Ibid.

35 Ibid.

36 Bob O'Neal, "Local Pitcher Loses Battle To Ill Health," *Rockford Daily Republic*, May 29, 1930, 1.

KIKI CUYLER

By Gregory H. Wolf

THOUGH CONTEMPORARY NEWSPAPER reports typically referred to Hall of Fame outfielder Hazen Cuyler by his given name, the right-hander is more easily recognized by one of the most unique, yet most often mispronounced nicknames in baseball history: Kiki. "It came from shortening my name," Cuyler explained about acquiring the moniker (which rhymes with "eye-eye") as a minor leaguer in 1923. "Every time I went after a fly ball, the shortstop would holler 'Cuy' and the second baseman would echo 'Cuy' and pretty soon the fans were shouting 'Cuy Cuy.' The papers shortened it 'Kiki.'"[1] According to another story, the sobriquet had less glamorous origins: It arose as a way to mock Cuyler, who struggled to overcome his stuttering.

Cuyler had been dead for almost two decades and his accomplishments had largely faded with memory when the Veterans Committee elected him to the Baseball Hall of Fame in 1968. But during his heyday in the mid-1920s through mid-1930s with the pennant-winning Pittsburgh Pirates and Chicago Cubs, Cuyler was considered one of the most popular and most exciting players in baseball. Blessed with uncanny speed, quick reflexes, and a powerful arm, Cuyler was a solid line-drive hitter with surprising power. In an 18-year career (1921-1938) that was also marred by injuries and an enduring controversy with a manager, he batted .321, collected 2,299 hits, led the major leagues in stolen bases four times, and had a legacy-defining, Series-winning hit in Game Seven of the 1925 World Series for the Pirates.

Hazen Shirley Cuyler was born on August 30, 1898, in Sturgeon Point, a small village in northeast Michigan on the coast of Lake Huron. Cuyler's Canadian-born parents, George Alonzo and Anna Rosalind (Shirley) Cuyler, married in 1891 and were naturalized as US citizens in 1895, about three years after their first child, Edna, was born. While Anna found piecemeal work as a dressmaker, George, a former semipro baseball player, served in a local coast guard, the Life Saving Service of Sturgeon Point. He suffered an injury in the line of duty in 1906, prompting the family to relocate five miles to the south, to

Harrisville, where he became a respected public servant. "Cuy," as Cuyler was known to his friends and family, was an active youth who enjoyed fishing and hunting, and an all-around athlete. By the age of 14 he was playing baseball in local sandlot and semipro leagues. At Harrisville High School he played baseball, basketball, and football, and ran track. He graduated in 1917 as the valedictorian of his class of five students. After finishing high school he enlisted in the US Army and served in Company A of the 48th Infantry Regiment, but was not sent to France during World War I. He briefly attended the US Military Academy at West Point before returning to Michigan and marrying his high-school sweetheart, Berta M. Kelly, in 1919.

Cuyler and his young bride (soon to be joined by their first child, Harold) moved to Flint, Michigan, where Cuyler worked in a Buick factory and carved out a reputation as a hard-throwing right-handed pitcher in competitive industrial leagues in Flint and Detroit, about 70 miles south. According to Ronald T. Waldo in his informative biography of the player, George H. Maines, president of the Class B Michigan-Ontario League, signed Cuyler to a contract for the Bay City (Michigan) Wolves in 1920.[2] When Cuyler was spiked while sliding into second base, Wolves manager Calvin Wenger moved him permanently to the outfield. During the season Cuyler batted .258 in 69 games.

With a vastly improved batting average in his second season (.317), Cuyler attracted the attention of big-league clubs. Ty Cobb, in his first year as player-manager of the Detroit Tigers, wanted to sign the local star; however, the Tigers' owner, Frank Navin, refused. Undeterred by reports that Cuyler had difficulty hitting a curveball, the Pittsburgh Pirates, acting on the recommendation of scout Frank Haller, purchased the speedy outfielder for an estimated $2,500.

A gifted yet green prospect, Cuyler needed to prove he could hit big-league pitchers. After the Michigan-Ontario League playoffs, the Pirates called up Cuyler in September

1921. He made his major-league debut on September 29, starting in right field in the second game of a doubleheader against the St. Louis Cardinals, going 0-for-3 in the 5½-inning contest. He had to wait nearly a year to get into another major-league game, and then appeared in only one, as a ninth-inning pinch-runner.

Cuyler was optioned to the minors for more seasoning after participating in spring training in 1922 and 1923. He batted .309 for the Charleston (South Carolina) Pals, champions of the Class B Sally League, in 1922, followed by his breakout season with the Nashville Volunteers of the Class A Southern Association. Named the league's most valuable player, Cuyler, whom fans and sportswriters had begun calling "Kiki," led the circuit in runs scored (114) and stolen bases (63) while batting .340. Cuyler attributed his hitting success to a decision to stand deep in the batter's box. In his third consecutive late-season call-up with the Pirates, Cuyler rapped five hits in his last 11 chances to finish with a .250 average in 40 at-bats.

A perennial first-division team, the Pirates got off to a slow start in 1924 in their quest to unseat the three-time NL pennant-winning New York Giants. Cuyler had played primarily center field in the minors, but that position belonged to veteran Max Carey, long acknowledged as the best basestealer and one of the fastest players in the NL. Relegated to the bench as the season started, Cuyler went 3-for-4 with a double and triple in his first start of the year, on May 6, en route to collecting 11 hits in 17 at-bats in the first four games he started, and he worked himself into batting third in the regular lineup.

By early June Cuyler had replaced the slumping veteran Clyde Barnhart in right field. In early July he was moved to left field in place of the struggling Carson Bigbee. He collected six hits, including three doubles and a triple, in the Pirates' 16-4 drubbing of the Philadelphia Phillies on August 9 during the first game of a doubleheader. "Cuyler has had much to do with the success of the Pirates," wrote Pittsburgh beat reporter Ralph. S. Davis. "[He's] won a place in the heart of Pittsburgh fans."[3] In the Pirates' doubleheader sweep of the St. Louis Cardinals on September 6, Cuyler homered in each contest and drove in a total of six runs, raising his batting average to .380,

to keep the Pirates just one game behind the league-leading Giants and a half-game behind the Brooklyn Robins in a tight three-team pennant race.

The Sporting News described Cuyler's rise to stardom as "meteoric" and compared his aggressive hitting to that of Rogers Hornsby. But Cuyler, suffering from a sore right shoulder, slumped in September, batting .211 in 17 games beginning September 7. His season came to a premature end on September 25 after a crushing three-game series sweep by the Giants at the Polo Grounds. Almost universally praised as "one of the season's sensations,"[4] Cuyler easily led the Pirates in batting (.354, fourth best in the NL) and home runs (9) while scoring 94 runs and rapping 16 triples in just 117 games.

Despite the success in his rookie campaign, Cuyler began his sophomore season under pressure to prove that he was not a "flash" and that his late-season slump was merely an aberration. Though the Pirates started the season poorly again, occupying last place as late as May 9, Cuyler re-emerged as the offensive catalyst for the club. On June 4 he hit for the cycle for the only time in his major-league career and drove in three runs in the Pirates' 16-3 throttling of the Philadelphia Phillies in Forbes Field. He experienced a career day on June 20, belting two home runs for the first of three times that season (and five times in his career), driving in a personal-best six runs, and tying a career high with five runs scored in Pittsburgh's 21-5 victory over the Brooklyn Robins in the Smoky City. Continuing his relentless hitting, Cuyler guided the Pirates to a 55-32 record from July through September as they captured the pennant by 8½ games over the Giants. Described by The Sporting News as "closing the season in a blaze of glory,"[5] Cuyler tied an NL record by collecting ten consecutive hits over three games September 18-21, and then went 4-for-4 on September 22, giving him 14 hits in 16 at-bats. Syndicated sportswriter Norman E. Brown compared Cuyler to the Pirates' 35-year-old center-fielder, Max Carey (en route to leading the NL in stolen bases for the tenth and final time in 13 seasons). Carey tutored the youngster in the finer points of baserunning, including sliding technique and avoiding pickoff attempts. After swiping 32 bases in 1924, the "Flint Flash" was successful on 41 of 54 attempts in 1925, and then led the major leagues in stolen bases in four of the next five seasons. In one of the most prolific seasons in Pirates history, Cuyler set a post-1900 NL record with 144 runs scored, led the majors with 26 triples among his 220 hits, clouted a career-best 18 home runs, and finished fourth in batting average (.357). His 369 total bases still rank as the most in Pirates history (as of 2014). Cuyler finished second in the NL MVP race to the Cardinals' Rogers Hornsby.

Cuyler's clutch hitting helped propel the Pirates to victory over the reigning champion Washington Senators in the 1925 World Series. After Pittsburgh lost Game One to Walter Johnson at home, Cuyler belted a game-winning two-run homer off starter Stan Coveleski in the eighth inning of Game Two to give the Pirates a 3-2 victory. Losses in Games Three and Four left them down three games to one, but the Pirates battled back to force a Game Seven, which the Associated Press at the time described as "perhaps the most thrilling seen in World Series history."[6] In a "rain-soaked, furious dramatic struggle" at Forbes Field, Cuyler came to bat with the bases loaded against Walter Johnson in the bottom of the eighth inning with the game tied, 7-7.[7] He hit what appeared to be a home run down the right-field foul line; however, the ball dropped in the outfield, buried itself in a tarpaulin, and was ruled a ground-rule two-run double. It gave the Pirates a 9-7 lead, and the championship.

With the offseason acquisition of hitting phenom Paul Waner, a center fielder, from the San Francisco Seals of the Pacific Coast League, the Pirates were expected to duplicate their success of the previous season; however, the 1926 season devolved into one of the most disappointing and acrimonious in Pirates history. In light of his World Series heroics, Cuyler held out for more money, and his ensuing wrangle with Pirates owner Barney Dreyfuss played out in the papers before Cuyler signed a contract. After a slow start, he batted .449 (53-for-118), scored 25 runs, and knocked in the same number over a 28-game span to raise his average to a league-leading .381 on June 11.

On July 26 the Pirates took sole possession of first place and seemed destined to claim another pennant. The

turning point in the season came to be known as the ABC affair. The controversy started when Pirates vice president Fred Clarke, who was sitting on the bench and acting in the role of assistant coach, made disparaging remarks about Max Carey, who was struggling uncharacteristically with a .214 batting average, and demanded that McKechnie replace him during a doubleheader shutout loss on August 7 to the seventh-place Braves at Boston. Veterans Babe Adams, Carson Bigbee, and Carey held a team meeting to decide whether Clarke should be allowed to remain on the bench. On August 13 Pirates brass quashed the insurrection by releasing all three players; however, the damage had been done. Pittsburgh limped to a 23-24 record and a third-place finish after the players were released. The tensions in the team clubhouse seemed to affect Cuyler, too. In his final 51 games after the initial brouhaha, he seemed at times indifferent, batted just .288, and drove in only 21 runs. Cuyler led the

Outfielder Kiki Cuyler batted .360, drove in 102 runs, and led the league with 43 stolen bases for the Cubs in 1929. A member of the World Champion Pittsburgh Pirates in 1925, the Future Hall of Famer batted .321 in his 18-year career. (Retro Images Archive. George Brace Collection)

league in games played (157), runs (113), and stolen bases (35); however, critics pointed to his lower batting average (.321) and drop in home runs (18 to 8) and RBIs (102 to 92) as evidence of a poor season.

Donie Bush replaced McKechnie as manager of the Pirates in 1927 and vowed to run a more disciplined ship. Rekindling his aggressive approach, Cuyler was batting .329 for the first-place Pirates on May 28 when he tore ligaments in his ankle sliding into third. During the weeks after he returned to the lineup on July 9, tensions between the player and his manager flared, resulting in one of the most enduring mysteries in Pirates history. Not only upset that he was moved from center field to right field, Cuyler objected to batting fifth and especially second, instead of his customary third position.

The situation came to a head when Cuyler failed to slide during a force play at second base in a game against the New York Giants on August 6, earning him a $50 fine. The controversy became a national story when Cuyler was subsequently benched and started only one game for the remainder of the season even though the Pirates were battling for the pennant. *The Sporting News* reported that Dreyfuss instituted the benching because he still fumed over the player's holdout after the 1925 season; others countered that the player was moody and egotistical, and wanted more publicity.[8] The fans, however, were unanimous in their desire to see Cuyler on the field. Even without Cuyler, the Pirates captured the pennant and faced the New York Yankees in the fall classic. "The 'Cuyler Case,'" wrote Ralph S. Davis, "almost overshadowed interest in the World Series."[9] While theories for his benching and rumors of his trade swirled, Cuyler did not play in the Series, and the Pirates were swept in four games by the Bronx Bombers. Other than a few superficial remarks, neither Dreyfuss, Bush, nor Cuyler ever publicly discussed the behind-the-scenes machinations of the controversy.

While Cuyler's departure from Pittsburgh was a foregone conclusion, it was a surprise on November 28, 1927, when the Chicago Cubs acquired the player in exchange for infielder Sparky Adams and outfielder Pete Scott. *The Sporting News* quickly dubbed Riggs Stephenson, Hack Wilson, and Cuyler as the "best fly chasing trio in baseball,"

and predicted that Cuyler's arrival "will tip the scales in favor of the Cubs" in the pennant race.[10] With an exceptional spring training, Cuyler eased worries that he was a self-absorbed player or, worse, a troublemaker. Cubs manager Joe McCarthy boasted, "I've got the best hitting outfield in the National League," fueling expectations that Cuyler would duplicate his success from 1925 and 1926.[11] In a preseason exhibition game in Kansas City, Cuyler seriously injured his right hand when he ran into a wall attempting to catch a fly ball. The injury, which made it difficult to hold a bat, plagued the outfielder the entire season, and contributed to his poor start. Furthermore, he was an aggressive, first-pitch hitter and had difficulty adjusting to McCarthy's approach of taking pitches when ahead in the count. Batting third and playing right field, Cuyler was hitting just .206 on June 11, and his season appeared to be a washout. However, he surged in his last 49 games, batting .338 and scoring 39 runs. Cuyler led the major leagues with 37 stolen bases and the team with 92 runs, offsetting a disappointing .285 batting average.

With the Cubs' offseason acquisition of Rogers Hornsby from the Boston Braves, many experts picked them to take the pennant in 1929. Chicago boasted one of the most imposing lineups in NL history with Cuyler, Hornsby, Wilson, and Stephenson batting third through sixth. The quartet, affectionately called Murderers' Row, collectively batted .362, belted 110 home runs, drove in 520 runs, and scored 493.[12] Other than a leg injury that limited him to pinch-hitting duties for three weeks in July, Cuyler enjoyed relatively good health all season and excelled in an environment where the national spotlight focused on Hornsby and Wilson. "There was never a more valuable team player," said McCarthy.[13] A hallmark of consistency, Cuyler surged over the last 55 games of the season (he batted .396, scored 51 runs, and knocked in 48) as the Cubs built an insurmountable lead over the Pittsburgh Pirates to capture their first pennant since 1918. No player in the NL could match Cuyler's unique combination of speed and power. He batted a career-best .360, led the majors with 43 stolen bases, mashed 15 home runs, and drove in 102 runs.

In their highly anticipated matchup with the Philadelphia Athletics, the Cubs lost Games One and Two at Wrigley Field. Cuyler, who struck out five times and managed just one hit, was roundly castigated as a "goat."[14] With the score tied, 1-1, in the sixth inning of Game Three, Cuyler "whistled a single through the box and out to centre [center field]," driving in Woody English and Hornsby to give the Cubs the lead and eventual victory.[15] In Game Four Cuyler connected for three singles and drove in two runs. In Game Five he collected his first extra-base hit of the Series (a double). But the Cubs lost both games in monumental fashion. The A's overcame an eight-run deficit by scoring a series-record ten runs (tied in 1968) in the seventh inning of Game Four, and then staged another dramatic comeback in Game Five when they scored three runs in the bottom of the ninth inning to capture the title.

In an era when many ballplayers were considered uncouth for their excessiveness off the field, Cuyler was an exception. Often described as one of the "gentlemen of baseball," he neither drank nor smoke, and rarely argued with umpires or opposing players.[16] Standing 5-feet-10½ and weighing a trim 175 pounds, Cuyler was good-looking, with wavy, dark hair and dark, penetrating eyes. Sportswriter J.T. Meek called him the "game's fashion plate" and an "exponent of diamond neatness."[17] Cuyler kept his svelte figure by playing sports year-round. He resided in the offseason with his wife and two children (daughter Kelly June was born in 1928) in Harrisville, and played in nascent professional basketball leagues. He led his various teams on barnstorming tours to Pittsburgh and Chicago (among other cities) to capitalize on his notoriety and publicize the emerging sport. His interests included hunting and fishing, but also the arts. He was an accomplished dancer who frequently won waltz tournaments at the Cubs' spring training site in Catalina Island. Blessed with a fine voice, Cuyler enjoyed singing, and not just in the clubhouse showers. He spent four weeks in 1930 on a vaudeville stage in Chicago with teammates Wilson, Gabby Hartnett, and Cliff Heathcote.[18]

The Cubs' title aspirations were dashed when they lost the reigning National League MVP, Rogers Hornsby to a broken ankle in late May 1930, but Cuyler assumed a greater role in the Cubs' offensive juggernaut, which set a franchise record by scoring 998 runs in the "Year of the Hitter." Over a 13-game stretch beginning on June 23, Cuyler batted .483 (28-for-58), scored 17 times, and drove in an eye-popping 27 runs to help the Cubs transform a 2½-game deficit into a 1½-game lead in the pennant race. "So accustomed are the fans to watching this fellow burn up the bases," wrote *The Sporting News*, "that it goes almost unnoticed with his constant hitting, running, fielding, and throwing."[19] Behind the hitting of Cuyler, Woody English (152 runs scored, 214 hits, .335 average), and the record-setting slugging of Hack Wilson (56 home runs, 191 runs batted in, .356 average), the Cubs increased their lead to 5½ games by August 30 and seemed poised for another NL pennant. "Cuyler's brilliant work and the 'never say die spirit' of the team are reasons why the Cubs hold first place," reported the *Chicago Daily Tribune*. But on August 31 they began an epic collapse by losing 14 of 21 games leading to finger-pointing and McCarthy's ouster with just four games remaining. Hornsby, who had been jockeying behind the scenes for the managerial position, took the reins of the team for the final four games. In a dramatic and disappointing season, Cuyler played in all 156 of the team's games (the third time he led or co-led the league in games played), scored 155 runs (tied for 24th-most in big-league history as of 2014), set career highs in hits (228), doubles (50), and RBIs (134), and led the major leagues in stolen bases with 37.

A five-tool player, Cuyler drew comparisons to Ty Cobb, Tris Speaker, and Shoeless Joe Jackson. Veteran Cubs scout Jack Doyle considered Cuyler the "most graceful player of all time, a fellow who could do more things with a glove than Cobb, who could throw better than Cobb, who could pick up groundballs on his outfield patrol like grounders."[20] Cuyler played all three outfield positions equally well; his strong arm made him an ideal right fielder and his speed was invaluable as a center fielder. Six times he ranked among the top five in assists for outfielders. "There is no center fielder who runs farther for long fly hits," opined syndicated sportswriter John B. Foster.[21]

Ironically Cuyler's athleticism, seemingly effortless play, and gentlemanly persona also drew criticism. "Cuyler had only one flaw that kept him from being rated with the immortals of the game," suggested *The Sporting News* in his obituary, echoing sentiments heard throughout the player's career. "He lacked the ruthlessness that might have carried him to greater heights and made his record even more brilliant."[22] Considered sensitive to criticism, Cuyler responded best to players' managers, like McKechnie and McCarthy, instead of authoritarian types (Bush and Hornsby).

Cuyler proved to be one of the few bright spots in the Cubs' mediocre and inconsistent season in 1931, during which players bristled at Hornsby's autocratic managerial methods. Batting leadoff through most of June, Cuyler was moved back to the third spot to provide the team with more offense in light of Wilson's precipitous drop in power (13 home runs). He batted .330, tied for third in the league with 202 hits, and ranked fourth by scoring 110 runs.

Cuyler's reputation as one of the fastest players in baseball ended after he suffered serious injuries in 1932 and 1933. While rounding third base on April 24, 1932, Cuyler cracked a bone in his left foot and missed six weeks. Robbed of his ability to take an extra base, Cuyler struggled after his return on June 8. In a weak year in the NL, the Cubs occupied first place for much of May and June, but the season was careening out of control. Players were increasingly resentful of the tyrannical Hornsby, who was also under investigation by Commissioner Kenesaw Mountain Landis because of his gambling debts. On July 6 starting shortstop Billy Jurges was shot twice by showgirl Violet Popovich Valli (Jurges survived). In an odd twist, Valli blamed her actions on Cuyler, who had apparently tried to persuade Jurges to end the sordid affair. The Cubs began a miraculous transformation when affable first baseman Charlie Grimm replaced Hornsby as manager on August 4. The Cubs responded by winning 23 of their first 27 games under "Jolly Cholly" and cruised to an unlikely pennant. Cuyler surged under his former Pittsburgh teammate (.373 average with 28 RBIs in the last 28 games) to finish with a .291 average and 77 RBIs in 110 games.

In the World Series the Cubs lost four straight games to the overwhelmingly favorite New York Yankees, led by Joe McCarthy. There were few Cubs highlights in a Series best remembered for Babe Ruth's supposed "called shot" in Game Three. In that dramatic contest, Cuyler went 3-for-4 with a double and solo home run to deep right field, but was otherwise quiet (5-for-18).

In 16 World Series games, Cuyler batted .281 (18-for-64), scored nine runs, and knocked in 12.

Cuyler splintered the fibula bone in his right leg during a spring-training game in 1933 and was limited to just 70 games (batting .317) for the third-place Cubs. While the rumor mill churned out reports of Cuyler's trade to the Cincinnati Reds in the offseason, he reported to spring training in 1934 with his status as a starter in doubt. Cuyler's productive spring enabled Grimm to juggle his outfield, moving offseason acquisition and reigning NL Triple Crown winner Chuck Klein to left field, inserting Cuyler in center, and keeping strong-armed Babe Herman in right field. While the Cubs contended for the title most of the season before finishing in third place, the 35-year-old Cuyler made a remarkable comeback. He ranked third in hitting (.338) and led the league with 42 doubles, and his 15 stolen bases trailed only St. Louis's Pepper Martin's 23. In the second year of the midsummer classic, Cuyler was named to his first and only All-Star team. Starting in right field, he went 0-for-2.

The Cubs caused a "minor sensation" when they released Cuyler (batting .268) on July 3, 1935.[23] The Cincinnati Reds outbid at least five other teams to sign the aging star. On July 11 Cuyler debuted for the Reds as their center fielder. While the Cubs won 21 consecutive games in September to capture an unlikely pennant, Cuyler played on a losing team for the first time in his big-league career, and batted just .251 for the Reds.

The oldest regularly starting position player in the NL, Cuyler made yet another comeback in 1936. After batting primarily in the leadoff position through May, he went back to his customary third spot and hit at a .345 clip from June 4 on. He celebrated his 38th birthday by going 5-for-9 with two triples in the Reds' doubleheader sweep of the Philadelphia Phillies at Crosley Field on August

30. He led the fifth-place Reds in hits (185), extra-base hits (47), runs (96), and RBIs (74), and batted .326.

During the Reds' youth movement in spring training 1937, Cuyler suffered a broken cheekbone when he collided with Cincinnati second baseman Alex Kampouris during an exhibition game against the Detroit Tigers on April 1. Though he was ready to play by Opening Day, Cuyler revealed that the injury bothered his timing all season long. He batted just .271 with no homers and 32 RBIs for the NL cellar-dwellers. On September 21 he announced that he was retiring at the end of the season, and was granted his release on October 4.

A student of the game, Cuyler had long made it known that he wanted to transition into managing. After considering several minor-league managerial positions, he surprisingly signed with the Brooklyn Dodgers as a player on February 2 with the hope of moving into a coaching position that season. The NL's oldest player, Cuyler started 58 games in the outfield and tutored a trio of 20-something flychasers — Buddy Hassett, Ernie Koy, and Goody Rosen. Cuyler was released as a player on September 16 and re-signed as a coach for the remainder of the season.[24]

A respected teacher, Cuyler spent his final 11 years in the dugout of minor- and major-league teams, but never achieved his dream of piloting a big-league club. Less than three months after retiring as an active big leaguer, Cuyler accepted a position as player-manager of Chattanooga in the Class A1 Southern Association. In his rookie season, he led the Lookouts to the pennant. He resigned after 2½ seasons with the club to accept a coaching position with the Chicago Cubs, serving under manager Jimmie Wilson through the 1943 season. Cuyler piloted the unaffiliated Atlanta Crackers of the Southern Association for five seasons (1944-1948), guiding them to first-place finishes in his first three years and to the league title in 1946. He spent his final year in baseball (1949) as a member of Joe McCarthy's coaching staff for the Boston Red Sox.

Cuyler suffered a heart attack on February 2, 1950, while ice fishing near his home in Harrisville. Two days later, while he was in a local hospital, a blood clot formed in his leg. The likely cause was varicose veins, which plagued Cuyler his later years.[25] When the situation worsened, he was sent by ambulance to a hospital in Ann Arbor but died in transit on February 11 at the age of 51. His funeral service was held on February 14 at St. Anne's Catholic Church in Harrisville, and he was buried in St. Anne's Cemetery.

SOURCES

Ancestry.com

BaseballLibrary.com

Baseball-Reference.com

Chicago Daily Tribune

New York Times

Pittsburgh Press

Pittsburgh Post-Gazette

Retrosheet.com

SABR.org

The Sporting News

Hazen "Kiki" Cuyler player file from the Baseball Hall of Fame, Cooperstown, New York.

NOTES

1   *The Sporting News*, February 10, 1968, 18.

2   Ronald T. Waldo, Hazen "Kiki" Cuyler. *A Baseball Biography* (Jefferson, North Carolina: McFarland, 2012) 14.

3   *The Sporting News*, July 24, 1924, 1.

4   *The Sporting News*, August 7, 1924, 1.

5   *The Sporting News*, October 1, 1925, 1.

6   Associated Press, "Pittsburgh Defeats Washington, 9-7, to Win World's Baseball Championship," *Berkeley* (California) *Daily Gazette*, October 15, 1925, 1.

7   Associated Press, "Pirates Win Seventh Game and World's Championship," *Scranton* (Pennsylvania) *Republic*, October 16, 1925, 1.

8   *The Sporting News*, August 18, 1927,1.

9   *The Sporting News*, October 20, 1927, 1.

10 *The Sporting News*, February 9, 1928, and March 1, 1928, 3.

11 John B. Foster, "Kiki To Play in Right Field, Latest Plan Of Cubs," *Pittsburgh Post-Gazette*, March 8, 1928, 15.

12 The term Murderers' Row is most readily associated with the 1927 New York Yankees, and Babe Ruth, Lou Gehrig, Bob Meusel, and Tony Lazzeri, who batted three through eighth.

13 Werner Laufer, "Lady Luck At Last Shines On Kiki Cuyler" (NEA), *Freeport* (Illinois) *Journal-Standard*, September 7, 1929, 10.

14 "Cubs Goats Become Heroes," *Chicago Tribune*, October 12, 1929, 23.

15 John Drebinger, "Cubs Triumph, 3-1, In 3d Series Game Before 30,000
    Fans, *New York Times*, October 12, 1929, 1.

16 *The Sporting News*, August 4, 1932, 4.

17 *The Sporting News*, March 31, 1932, 5.

18 Associated Press, "Hack Wilson Puts on Vaudeville Act," *Sarasota*
    (Florida) *Herald-Tribune*, October 9, 1930, 1.

19 *The Sporting News*, July 24, 1930, 3.

20 *The Sporting News*, February 22, 1950, 20.

21 *The Sporting News*, March 24, 1932, 3.

22 *The Sporting News*, February 22, 1950, 20.

23 *The Sporting News*, July 11, 1935, 1.

24 Waldo, 212.

25 *The Sporting News*, February 22, 1950, 20.

MIKE CVENGROS

By Chip Greene

CONSIDERING HOW DREADFUL HIS first full professional season was, it's a wonder Mike Cvengros made it to the major leagues at all. Yet make it he eventually did, and he went on to win 25 major-league games over parts of six seasons, plus 177 in the minors. Over the course of his career, two themes constantly recur: the lefthander's diminutive size, which led journalists to frequently refer to him as "little" Mike Cvengros, and what must have been the relative complexity of pronouncing his unique last name. A "tongue-twister," the scribes liked to call it. (Contemporary efforts to discover the correct pronunciation have proved fruitless.) No doubt sluggers like Babe Ruth knew just how to say the pitcher's name.

Pana, Illinois, Cvengros's hometown, lies in the heart of coal country. The fifth of the nine children of Michael J. Cvengros, a laborer, and Helen (Buray) Cvengros, Michael John, the future major leaguer, was born on December 1, 1900. According to Cvengros's Hall of Fame file, his parents were natives of Austria, as were their parents. In 1923, after Cvengros joined the Chicago White Sox, manager Kid Gleason told the *New York World* that Cvengros "is Czecho-Slovak."[1] In 1927, when Cvengros pitched for the pennant-winning Pittsburgh Pirates, newspapers described him as the son of Polish parents.[2] Triangulating from these separate sources, it's a safe guess to say that Cvengros's parents' homeland was the Austro-Hungarian Empire, which before World War I encompassed parts of Poland and Czechoslovakia.

Young Michael labored for a time in the coal mines; a newspaper described him as a "powerful youngster who got that way in the coal mines of Central Illinois."[3] He learned to play baseball with teams in and around Pana before he found his way at the age of 19 to Little Rock of the Southern League. How he ended up there is unclear, but Cvengros's professional baseball career had begun.

There appears some contradiction over his first season. Online sources indicate that Cvengros first took the mound professionally in 1921, for Chickasha, Oklahoma,

in the Class D Western Association, and that he joined Little Rock in 1922. However, a January 16, 1927, article in the *Pittsburgh Sunday Post* said that Cvengros had been "given two trials with Little Rock by Manager Kid Elberfeld. In his first trial [in 1920] he relieved J. Hank Robinson after the fifth inning in a game against New Orleans at Little Rock on August 27," and "allowed just 3 hits in 4 innings" during a 6-1 Little Rock victory. Two days later, the article said, Cvengros pitched in relief against Memphis and was lifted after walking five batters in less than an inning. Cvengros "never appeared again that season," the article said, but he "was reserved for Little Rock for 1921." Those two games appear to be the true beginning of Cvengros's professional career.

After spring training with Little Rock in 1921 during which he received "no chances to pitch,"[4] Cvengros was sent to Chickasha. It's difficult to imagine what that experience must have been like for the 20-year-old. To contemplate the statistical story of that season is to envision a constant barrage of baserunners and runs scored by the opposition, as in 152 innings over 47 games he compiled a mind-boggling WHIP (walks plus hits per inning pitched) of 3.104 and lost 22 games (although he also won 17). Perhaps the team was short on pitchers, or maybe Cvengros's batting skills (he played 17 games in the outfield and produced averages of .275 batting and .358 slugging) gained him a reprieve; nevertheless, he remained with the Chicks the entire season and apparently learned some lessons. For by the following season, his performance resulted in a dramatic change of fortunes. After a nightmarish 1921 season, Cvengros found himself atop a big-league mound in 1922.

Returning to Little Rock in 1922, the 21-year-old Cvengros caught the eye of major-league scouts while posting 17 wins, a 2.88 ERA, and a 1.372 WHIP. He also batted .295, and even played a game in left field. New York Giants scout Dick Kinsella saw Cvengros and recommended him to Giants manager John McGraw. In September the Giants signed Cvengros, and on September 30 at the Polo Grounds in New York, he made his major-league

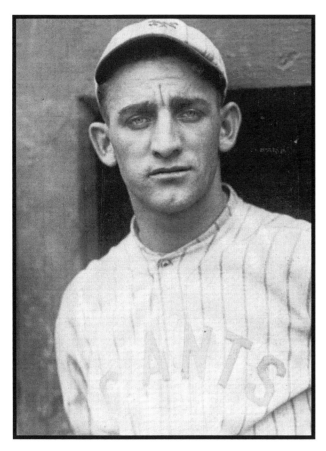

Cvengros made 28 of his 32 appearances as a reliever for the Cubs in 1929, his last of six seasons in the big leagues. (National Baseball Hall of Fame)

debut, starting against the Boston Braves. Though he lost, 5-1, Cvengros pitched a complete game and allowed just six hits, although his four walks assuredly didn't help his cause. (The *New York World* commented the next season that Cvengros's pitching "made folks sit up and take notice."[5]) Just two years removed from the coal mines, Cvengros was a major leaguer. Staying there, though, often proved problematic.

Tracking down what kind of player Cvengros was and gauging his ability is frustrating; there's not much available reference material. What is readily apparent, though, is that at 5-feet-8 and just 159 pounds he was "somewhat undersized"[6] for a major leaguer. Over his career Cvengros often struggled with control, as attested by his 1.582 WHIP; he also walked more batters (285 in 551 innings) than he struck out (201). Cvengros was an effective hitter, particularly in the minors, where he sometimes played the outfield and frequently pinch-hit. In 1,309 minor-

league at-bats, the left-handed swinger batted .265 and smashed six home runs.

Of his contemporaries, Cvengros probably bore the closest resemblance as a pitcher to another man of similar stature. In June 1923, the *New York World* suggested that Cvengros "gives promise of being something of the same sort of pitcher as Dickie Kerr," of the White Sox, also a left-hander, who was just 5-feet-7 and weighed 155 pounds. That Kerr would be offered as an example was probably not a mere coincidence. In 1923 Cvengros and Kerr had become teammates.

Fresh from his major-league debut, Cvengros returned home to Pana after the 1922 season and joined the local ballclub. He was sensational. On October 16 he pitched a no-hitter against Nokomis, giving up just one walk. On the 22nd he handed the Decatur All-Stars and their 51-year-old pitcher, Joe "Iron Man" McGinnity a 7-1 defeat. At the end of January 1923 Cvengros joined 19 other pitchers at the Giants' spring-training camp at Marlin Springs, Texas. "McGraw apparently thinks very well of Cvengros," said a sportswriter, "and seems to think the Pole has quite an opportunity before him."[7] But on Opening Day, April 17, Cvengros was returned to Little Rock, which released him the same day.

Cvengros wasn't without a team for long. During his previous stay with Little Rock, White Sox manager Kid Gleason had seen him work and been impressed with the southpaw's skills. So when Little Rock waived Cvengros, Gleason "was quick to grab him."[8] Cvengros joined Chicago for the 1923 American League season and posted a 12-13 record for the seventh-place team. Cvengros spent three seasons with the White Sox, and if his work that first season was respectable, it was a performance he was never able to replicate. After that, in fact, he was just not very good. (In 88 career appearances for the White Sox, Cvengros finished 18-34 with a 4.74 ERA.) Cvengros did, however, produce a few highlights for the White Sox, particularly in 1923. In his debut appearance, on April 22 at St. Louis, in relief of starter Ted Blankenship, he was the winner when the White Sox came from behind to beat the Browns, 4-3; in 4⅓ innings, he allowed just two hits. On June 8 at Yankee Stadium, he pitched a complete-game victory, twice striking out Babe Ruth. In late July he pitched complete-game victories against the Philadelphia Athletics and Boston Red Sox, allowing just one run in each contest.

In 1924 things fell apart. Perhaps it was the loss of his benefactor, Gleason, who had been fired after the 1923 season and replaced by Frank Chance (who was himself replaced by Johnny Evers after Chance became ill prior to Opening Day; he died on September 15). From his first appearance, the season was a disaster for Cvengros; he won just three games while losing 12 and posted a 5.88 ERA. On April 26, at Detroit's Navin Field, Cvengros again made his season debut by relieving starter Ted Blankenship. In four innings the Tigers rocked Cvengros for nine hits and 11 runs (six earned). In the fifth inning, after giving up five runs, Cvengros "walked out of the box and went to his hotel."[9] Asked to explain his sudden disappearance, Cvengros tersely replied, "I took myself out."[10] Evers later fined the pitcher $200. Cvengros never recovered.

Neither did he ever solve The Bambino. Like many other pitchers of his era, Cvengros struggled mightily against Ruth. With the exception of the two strikeouts in 1923, Ruth usually got the best of their confrontations. During his career Cvengros allowed 24 regular-season home runs, five of them by Ruth. None was more dramatic than the first. In 1944, in a syndicated newspaper series called "My Biggest Baseball Day," Ruth recalled that blast.

"One day we were playin' in Chicago against the White Sox," Ruth told sportswriter John P. Carmichael, "and Mark Roth, our secretary, was worryin' about holdin' the train because we were in extra innings. He was fidgetin' around behind the dugout lookin' at his watch, and I saw him when I went up to hit in the 15th. 'All right, quit worrying,' I told him.' I'll get this over with right now. Mike Cvengros was pitchin' and I hit one outta the park [on the first pitch]. We made the train easy. It was fun."[11] In a Herculean effort, Cvengros lost the complete-game 15-inning affair, 3-1.[12]

Cvengros's final season with the White Sox was 1925. Working that year for manager Eddie Collins, he pitched in just 22 games, 11 as a starter, and finished 3-9. On

September 1 he was released by Chicago, and the next day signed with the New Orleans Pelicans of the Southern Association. He took the mound that same day for New Orleans, and over the remainder of the season went 4-0. Returning to the Pelicans in 1926, Cvengros posted an impressive 18-5 mark and batted .352, as he was often called on to pinch-hit. After the season the Pirates drafted him, and, just one season removed from the big stage, Cvengros returned to the major leagues.

There were few highlights for Cvengros during the 1927 season. Having won the World Series just two years before, Pittsburgh fielded a veteran team. With solid starters Lee Meadows, Vic Aldridge, and Ray Kremer returning, there seemed few opportunities for Cvengros, and he was rarely used, making just four starts among 23 appearances and pitching just 53⅔ innings as the Pirates marched to the pennant. Cvengros hadn't had much of a season, but he was in the World Series, against the Yankees.

The seldom-used Cvengros didn't appear to have much chance of working in the World Series. Bush said he "probably would use no left-handed pitchers against the Yankees unless emergency relief so demanded."[13] As Emil Yde and Cvengros were the only "port-side hurlers and neither is in Class A,"[14] Cvengros undoubtedly prepared to spend the Series on the bench.

But Cvengros did indeed take the mound against the Yankees. In Game Two, at Forbes Field, with New York leading 4-1, he relieved starter Aldridge with one out in the top of the eighth and the bases loaded. He hit the first batter he faced, Earle Combs, forcing home a run, then gave up a single to Mark Koenig, allowing another run to score. Ruth and Lou Gehrig grounded out. Cvengros was pinch-hit for in the bottom of the inning.

The next day, at Yankee Stadium, he again met his nemesis. With one out in the bottom of the seventh, three runs in and runners on second and third with the Yankees now leading, 5-1, Cvengros relieved starter Meadows. The first batter Cvengros faced was Ruth and The Babe crushed a three-run homer, putting the game out of reach. Cvengros then struck out Gehrig and Bob Meusel. He allowed a single and coaxed three groundouts in the eighth before being lifted for a pinch-hitter in the ninth. Cvengros worked 2⅓ innings in his two Series appearances and allowed three hits, including the Ruth home run, in the only postseason action of his career.

The 1928 season once again found Cvengros in the minor leagues. The Pirates' offseason acquisition of left-hander Fred Fussell from Wichita Falls of the Texas League made Cvengros expendable, and he and catcher Ike Danning were sent to Wichita Falls to complete the Fussell deal. Again Cvengros was outstanding against minor-league hitters, going 21-8 (his career mark in 408 minor-league appearances was 177-130, with a 3.29 ERA),and again drawing the attention of major-league scouts. On October 3 the Cubs drafted him, and Cvengros returned to the major leagues.

Things were looking up in Chicago. In 1928, their third season under manager Joe McCarthy, the Cubs had produced 91 wins and finished third. Management felt all the pieces were in place to improve, save for a big-time bat. Then came the blockbuster: the acquisition of second baseman Rogers Hornsby from the Boston Braves in exchange for five players and $200,000. One of the five players was left-handed pitcher Percy Jones, who had tossed ten wins that season for the Cubs. Seeking to replace Jones's productivity, the Cubs added Cvengros to their roster for 1929.

In an experience similar to that with the 1927 Pirates, Cvengros was again used sparingly. He nonetheless made his presence felt. Starting on April 23, Cvengros had five consecutive scoreless relief appearances, working 12⅔ innings and allowing just seven hits. On May 21 Cvengros made his first start and was hammered, surrendering nine hits and six runs in 4⅔ innings. For the season he pitched in 32 games, four as a starter, and produced five wins, all in relief. He did not pitch in the World Series. In December the Cubs sent him to Indianapolis of the American Association in exchange for pitcher Arthur "Bud" Teachout. It was the final major-league deal in which Cvengros was involved. After 25 wins in 144 games, he never again appeared on a major-league roster.

Cvengros pitched eight more seasons in the minor leagues. After going 15-9 for Indianapolis in 1930 and opening the

1931 season with the club, he was traded during that season to league rival Columbus. After a 10-10 season Cvengros was traded to Houston of the Texas League, where in six seasons he compiled a record of 79-62 (including 21-11, 2.38 in 1933). After a 4-16 season in 1937, the 36-year-old Cvengros retired.

In 1932 Cvengros had married Dolores Mary Hurve Vandalia, Illinois. By 1937, Cvengros's final season, the two were living, apparently childless, on Clay Avenue in Houston. Cvengros had a job as a laborer for the Gulf Brewing Company.

In February 1938 Cvengros was announced as the manager of Abbeville of the Class D Evangeline League,[15] but by May he had "resigned due to ill health."[16] That appears to be Cvengros's final connection with Organized Baseball.

A final reference to Cvengros appears in the 1940 US Census, which recorded Mike and Dolores living, with no children, in Ramsey Township, Fayette County, Illinois. He was a tavern keeper and she a tavern helper.

Cvengros died August 3, 1970, aged 69, at St. Joseph Hospital in Hot Springs, Arkansas. Three months earlier he had been diagnosed with stomach cancer with metastasis. He was buried in the Calvary Cemetery, in Hot Springs.

SOURCES

My sincerest appreciation to SABR member Bill Mortell for his diligent genealogical research.

Mike Cvengros player file at the National Baseball Hall of Fame in Cooperstown, NY.

Biloxi (Mississippi) *Daily Herald*

Bridgeport (Connecticut) *Telegram*

Decatur (Iowa) *Daily Review*

Eau Claire (Wisconsin) *Leader*

Kingston (New York) *Daily Freeman*

Newark (Ohio) *Advocate*

New York World

Oakland (California) *Tribune*

Ogden (Utah) *Standard Examiner*

Pittsburgh Sunday Post

San Antonio Light

Sheboygan (Wisconsin) *Press*

Twin Falls (Idaho) *Daily Times*

Uniontown (Pennsylvania) *Morning Herald*

Winnipeg (Manitoba) *Free Press*

Baseball-Reference.com

Retrosheet.org

NOTES

1   *New York World*, June 9, 1923.

2   *Pittsburgh Sunday Post*, January 16, 1927.

3   Undated clipping in Cvengros's file at the Baseball Hall of Fame, Cooperstown, New York.

4   *Pittsburgh Sunday Post*, January 16, 1927.

5   *New York World*, June 9, 1923.

6   Undated clipping in Cvengros's Hall of Fame file.

7   *Bridgeport* (Connecticut) *Telegram*, February 16, 1923.

8   *New York World*, June 9, 1923.

9   Undated clipping in Cvengros's Hall of Fame file.

10 *Pittsburgh Sunday Post*, January 16, 1927.

11 *Winnipeg Free Press*, November 13, 1944.

12 The game took place on May 22, 1923, at Comiskey Park.

13 *Twin Falls* (Idaho) *Daily Times*, October 4, 1927.

14 Ibid.

15 *Biloxi Daily* (Mississippi) *Herald*, February 23, 1938.

16 *San Antonio Light*, May 17, 1938.

WOODY ENGLISH

By Dan Fields

AS THE LEADOFF OR NUMBER-TWO batter for some of the highest-scoring teams in baseball history, Woody English scored 400 runs from 1929 through 1931 while playing shortstop or third base for the Chicago Cubs. As noted by Bill James, "English in 1930 had 214 hits and 100 walks, which enabled him to score 152 runs, and set up Hack Wilson's 191-RBI season. He is one of [the] few players to have had 200 hits and 100 walks in the same season."[1] That year, English had 755 plate appearances — a single-season major-league record until 1938, a National League record until 1962, and still (as of 2014) a Cubs record. In 1933 he played in the first All-Star Game.

Not a large man, English had large hands. Their size was an asset to an infielder but a source of embarrassment as a child (he would hide them in class by sitting on them). English was also known for getting along with the notoriously prickly Rogers Hornsby, with whom he roomed during the second baseman's stint with the Cubs. Said Bill James, "If you can get along with Rogers Hornsby you can probably get along with anybody, and that was English. He was a likeable, upbeat person who always had something good to say about everybody."[2]

But he also had an impish side: English "was like 'Peck's bad boy' in the grade-school books of the day. He looked innocent but wasn't. English's favorite prank was to crawl across the floor of a hotel lobby and sneak up on an unsuspecting businessman reading the newspaper. English would light the bottom of the paper and slip away as the newspaper caught fire."[3]

Elwood George English was born on March 2, 1906, on a farm in Fredonia, Licking County, in central Ohio. He was the oldest of four children born to Wilbur English and Gladys (Carpenter) English. He attended primary school in Centerburg and played second base for the school team. In 1916 his uncle Paul Carpenter pitched in five games with the Pittsburgh Pirates. When English was only 12 years old, his father died at the age of 34. English moved with his mother to Newark, Ohio. He attended high school there and again played second base on the school team. In his senior year, the team didn't lose a game.

After high school English worked part-time at local plants operated by the Pure Oil Company and the Firestone Tire and Rubber Company. He played on the Pure Oil baseball team on Sundays and on another industrial company team during the week. In 1924 he tried out for semipro teams in Hamilton and Zanesville and played for the Zanesville Greys at shortstop. He captured the attention of Al Schweitzer, who had played outfield for the St. Louis Browns from 1908 to 1911. Schweitzer recommended English to the Toledo Mud Hens of the Double-A American Association. At the season's close, English went to Toledo and signed a contract for the 1925 season for $300 a month. "It seemed like a million dollars to me," he said later.[4]

English batted only .220 in 131 games with Toledo in 1925. "I was probably pretty good with the glove and I always had excellent speed," he said, "so I guess that is why they stayed with me while I was having trouble at the plate. Jimmy Burke was the manager that year. In 1926 Casey Stengel took over and he was a real help to me in my hitting. Casey and I would go to the ballpark early and he would pitch to me and give me little tips here and there until my average began to pick up. I hit .301 that year and Casey was almost as happy about it as I was."[5] English had a .948 fielding percentage in 162 games at shortstop in 1926 and led the American Association in total chances at the position.

Late in the 1926 season, while the Mud Hens were on the road to play the Milwaukee Brewers, English learned from the local paper that he had been sold to the Chicago Cubs for $50,000. Cubs skipper Joe McCarthy had managed the Louisville Colonels in the American Association in 1925 and was impressed by English's overall performance, despite a weak year at the plate. After his batting improved, McCarthy went after him.

English made his major-league debut on April 26, 1927; he was 21 years old. On June 7 the Cubs traded their starting shortstop, 32-year-old Jimmy Cooney, to the Philadelphia Phillies. The day of the trade, McCarthy told English, "You're my shortstop now."[6] English batted .290 in 87 games during his rookie year, and his 23 sacrifice hits were second-most on the team. In 1928 he became the Cubs' leadoff batter; that year, he had a .299 batting average in 116 games. In a July 21 doubleheader against the New York Giants, he hit two doubles in each game.

When Rogers Hornsby joined the Cubs in 1929, he told team president William Veeck that "he wanted a room-mate who didn't talk in his sleep, didn't snore, didn't get up early and didn't come in late, didn't whistle while shaving, and didn't keep gin in his room."[7] Mild-mannered English filled the bill, and a team's second baseman and shortstop would often room together so that they could talk over opposing hitters.

Said English, "Hornsby liked me. He taught me quite a bit about hitting. I didn't weigh but 150 pounds. I choked the bat. He said, 'Woody, you stand closer to the plate. Stand about even with it, and if anything, one foot a little bit in front of the other. Then you'll get that curve ball before it snaps off too fast.' He said, 'Push the ball past the pitcher. You can run good. Make the pitcher cover first base, and you'll beat him over there nine times out of ten.'"[8] Of Hornsby, English also said, "You know, I liked the guy, because, see, he was so good to me, I couldn't help but like him, but a lot of players didn't like Rogers."[9]

In 1929 English batted .276 in 144 games and was in the NL's top ten in plate appearances (699), at-bats (608), runs scored (131), and sacrifice hits (21). From June 21 to July 26, he had a 34-game on-base streak. He also had a fine year defensively, finishing second among major-league shortstops in double plays turned (107) and third in fielding percentage (.955).

English said, "In 1929 we had a very powerful lineup. We had Hornsby, Gabby Hartnett, Hack Wilson, Riggs Stephenson, Kiki Cuyler. Kidding, we'd say, 'Let's get our eight runs early and then take it easy. That's what we used to say."[10] But the Cubs faltered in the World Series, losing to the Philadelphia Athletics in five games. English had

four errors in the first three games, including miscues against consecutive batters in the ninth inning of Game One, and he batted 4-for-21 (.190) during the Series.

English's best year offensively was 1930. Playing in all 156 games, he set a major-league record with 755 plate appearances and led the NL with 320 times on base (still, as of 2014, a Cubs record). He finished third in the league in runs scored (152) and walks (100), tied for third in triples (17), fifth in at-bats (638), and in the top ten in on-base percentage (.430), hits (214), and total bases (326). He batted .335 and had 14 home runs. In December he eloped with Helen Golan, and the pair was wed by a justice of the peace in Crown Point, Indiana, just across the state line. English and Golan had been introduced by friends after a game in July 1930.

English had another outstanding year at the plate in 1931. Again playing in all 156 games, he batted .319 and finished first in the NL in plate appearances (727), second in

The starting shortstop on the pennant-winners, English scored 131 runs and batted .276 in 1929. The following season he set career-highs with 152 runs and a .335 batting average. (Retro Images Archive. George Brace Collection)

at-bats (634) and times on base (277), third in runs scored (117), tied for third in hits (202), fourth in sacrifice hits (18), fifth in walks (68), and in the top ten in total bases (262), doubles (38), and stolen bases (12). He led the league's shortstops in putouts (322) and was third in the majors in fielding percentage at short (.965). That year English was fourth in voting for the National League MVP Award and runner-up to Philadelphia's Chuck Klein in *The Sporting News's* sportswriters' poll of the league's MVP.

In February 1932 Emily Evans Haag of Newark, Ohio, filed a breach-of-promise suit against English. Writes Roberts Ehrgott in *Mr. Wrigley's Ball Club*, "Her attorney told the newspapers that his client had been engaged to English for three years. English had already tried at least once to settle things with Haag. A few weeks after he eloped with Helen Golan in December 1930, he had made his ex-fiancée a settlement offer of $1,500, which she declined."[11]

English did not play in April because of a broken finger. When he returned, he had lost his old job at shortstop to slick-fielding Billy Jurges; English moved to third base. In early August, after Rogers Hornsby was let go as manager and team captain Charlie Grimm was named the new manager, Grimm picked English as his replacement as captain. In 1932 English batted .272 in 127 games, and he finished in the top ten in the NL in walks (55) and sacrifice hits (12).

After the Cubs won the pennant, English presided over the clubhouse meeting at which the players decided not to pay a World Series share to Hornsby, the departed player-manager, and to pay a half-share to infielder Mark Koenig, who was acquired in August from the Mission Reds of the Pacific Coast League and played a key role in the pennant run. Hornsby filed a protest with Commissioner Kenesaw Mountain Landis, claiming that he was entitled to some World Series money. In a public statement, Landis turned down Hornsby's plea, saying that the current players could distribute the shares as they saw fit.

As for Koenig, Babe Ruth and others on the New York Yankees accused the Cubs of shortchanging their former teammate by giving him only a half-share, and Landis summoned English to his home to discuss the allotment. Landis attended Cubs games regularly, in a box seat near the dugout, and English chatted with him when taking the lineup to home plate. Because Koenig had played in only 33 games with the Cubs, Landis told English that he didn't think Koenig was entitled to a full share. English replied, "Judge, I never voted against Koenig to get a full share. Only two of the players voted against a full share for him and the vote had to be unanimous."[12] (English later revealed that the two holdouts were Billy Herman and Billy Jurges.)

In the 1932 World Series, which the Cubs lost to the Yankees in four games, English went 3-for-17 (.176). As third baseman, he had a clear view of Babe Ruth's supposed called-shot home run off pitcher Charlie Root in the fifth inning of Game Three: "He's got two strikes on him. The guys are yelling at him from our dugout. He's looking right in our dugout, and he holds up two fingers. He said, 'That's only two strikes.' But the press box was way back on top of Wrigley Field, and to the people in the press, it looked like he pointed to center field. But he was looking right into our dugout and holding two fingers up. That *is* the true story."[13] Added English, "Ruth would never do a thing like that, point. Charlie Root would have murdered him."[14]

English led NL third basemen in fielding percentage (.973) in 1933. He played in 105 games and batted .261; he was in the top ten in the league in walks (53). Long after his baseball career, English said that his biggest thrill was playing in the first All-Star Game, at Comiskey Park on July 6, 1933. He flied out in his only at-bat and played two innings at shortstop.

In 1934 English batted .278 in 109 games, and Stan Hack took over as the starting third baseman for the Cubs. The following year English played in only 34 games owing to an ankle injury and an injured thumb, with a .202 batting average. He did not play in the 1935 World Series, which the Cubs lost to the Detroit Tigers in six games. In 1936 English played in 64 games and batted .247; he was not aware that he was marked for the trading block.

"I had no idea about it beforehand," said English. "Burleigh Grimes had been with the Cubs and he went over to manage the Brooklyn Dodgers in 1937. At the end of the 1936 season he told me that I would be playing for the Dodgers the next season I said 'never.' But he was right. I was down at Hot Springs during the winter when I got a letter from Bob Lewis, the traveling secretary, which said, 'You are now the property of the Brooklyn baseball club.' I felt pretty bad about it because I had spent my whole career with the Cubs. You hate to leave a place where you had been for 10 enjoyable years."[15]

As of 2014 English was 12th in Cubs history in sacrifice hits (120), 17th in walks (498), 18th in runs scored (747), and 20th in times on base (1,774). He ranked in the top 25 in games (1,098), plate appearances (4,941), at-bats (4,296), hits (1,248), doubles (218), and on-base percentage (.368).

In 1937 English played in 129 games with the Dodgers, mostly at shortstop, and batted .238. That year he won a suit of clothes for batting a ball against a sign for Abe Stark's store. The sign was located directly under the Ebbets Field scoreboard in right field, less than 350 feet from home plate. Said English. "The right fielder usually played right in front of the sign so it was almost impossible to hit it."[16] But he lucked out when Paul Waner slipped in the mud one day and the ball got past him. English went to the store and was greeted by "about 99 photographers," he said. "Stark got a lot of publicity out of it and I got my new suit."[17] In December 1937 English and his wife, Helen, divorced.

English played in 34 games in 1938, with a batting average of .250. He appeared as a pinch-hitter during his final major-league game, on July 1, 1938; he was 32 years old. Over his 12-year career, he hit .286 in 1,261 games. In 2001, Bill James ranked English as the 59th best shortstop in baseball history.

After hanging up his spikes, English worked for a manufacturing plant in Chicago. During World War II, he worked at an airplane factory where O'Hare Airport was later built. In 1952 he got a call from an old friend asking if he would manage the Grand Rapids Chicks in the All-American Girls Professional Baseball League. English

had a pretty good job, so he sought to discourage his friend by asking for a generous salary. The friend replied, "Can you come tomorrow?"[18] English managed the team from mid-1952 to 1954, when the league disbanded. He led the team to a championship in 1953.

English returned to Newark, Ohio, in the early 1960s and worked for State Farm Insurance as a night supervisor; he retired in 1971. A section of Ohio's Route 16 was renamed Woody English Parkway in his honor in 1996. There is also a gym at a YMCA in Newark that is named for him. English died in Newark on September 26, 1997; he was 91 years old. The epitaph on his tombstone in Fredonia Cemetery says simply "A Great Baseball Player."[19]

SOURCES

Ancestry.com

Baseball-Reference.com

Retrosheet.org

Woodyenglish.com

Satterfield, Jerry, "Woody English's major league baseball career remembered," *Newark* [Ohio] *Advocate*, July 14, 2013.

Wilson, Terry, "Woody English: Played for Cubs in World Series," *Chicago Tribune*, September 28, 1997.

NOTES

1   Bill James, *The New Bill James Historical Baseball Abstract* (New York: Free Press, 2003), 628.

2   Ibid.

3   Roger Snell, *Root for the Cubs: Charlie Root and the 1929 Chicago Cubs* (Nicholasville, Kentucky: Wind Publications, 2009), 134.

4   Eugene Murdock, *Baseball Players and Their Times: Oral Histories of the Game, 1920-1940* (Westport, Connecticut: Mecklermedia, 1991), 293.

5   Ibid.

6   Murdock, 294.

7   Peter Golenbock, *Wrigleyville: A Magical History Tour of the Chicago Cubs* (New York: St. Martin's Press, 1999), 210.

8   Golenbock, 211.

9   Golenbock, 226.

10 Golenbock, 212.

11 Roberts Ehrgott, *Mr. Wrigley's Ball Club: Chicago and the Cubs During the Jazz Age* (Lincoln, Nebraska: University of Nebraska Press, 2013), 292.

12   Murdock, 292.

13   Golenbock, 234.

14   Ibid.

15   Murdock, 298.

16   Murdock, 299.

17   Ibid.

18   Murdock, 301.

19   thedeadballera.com/GravePhotos/GravePhotos_E/English.Woody.
      Grave.html

MIKE GONZÁLEZ

By Joseph Gerard

MIGUEL GONZÁLEZ ENJOYED A long and prolific career as a major-league catcher and coach, and along with Adolfo Luque is considered to be one of the two true patriarchs of baseball in Cuba, where he was a player, manager, and owner in the Cuban League from 1910 through 1960. He was a coach on the 1934 world champion St. Louis Cardinals, and although it was only on an interim basis, in 1938 he became the first Latin American to manage in the major leagues. He was the third-base coach who, depending on your point of view, either waved home or tried in vain to stop Enos Slaughter when the latter made his celebrated "mad dash" from first base on a double by Harry Walker to score the deciding run in Game Seven of the 1946 World Series. Despite these accomplishments and the recognition that came with them, González is probably best remembered for coining one of the most famous phrases in the lexicon of baseball while on a scouting expedition for John McGraw and the New York Giants.

Miguel Angel González Cordero was born on September 24, 1890, in the town of Regla, across the bay from Havana. Not much is known about his early life, other than that he and his family lived humbly in modest surroundings. Baseball had become enormously popular on the island by the time Miguel was a boy, as Cubans began to disavow any ties to Spanish colonialism, including its sports, while looking to the US for inspiration. Like many young Cuban boys at the time, Miguel and his friends learned the game on the fields and lots of the city, using whatever makeshift equipment they could find.

Miguel quickly grew to a height of 6-feet-1 but was extremely gaunt for his size. It was said that he resembled a long loaf of thin Cuban bread, and his physique, along with his childhood occupation delivering bread to his neighbors in Regla, earned him the nickname Pan de Flauta, after a loaf of bread so narrow as to resemble a pan flute. González had played baseball during his school years at the Institute of Havana, and he was working as a bank clerk when he was recruited by Fé, the baseball club that had originated decades earlier in the Havana neighborhood of Jesús del Monte. He made his first appearance for Fé as a shortstop in the professional Cuban League in 1910, appearing in six games and amassing 21 at-bats.

González was catching in Cuba during the following winter when he was noticed by Georges Henriquez, a physician who had purchased the Long Branch, New Jersey, club in the fledging Class D New York-New Jersey League, along with his brothers Carlos and Richard. The three brothers had emigrated from Colombia to the United States with their parents, settling in Manhattan, but evidence suggests they spent time in Cuba as well and were familiar with the brand of baseball played on the island.

They decided to stock the Long Branch club with Cuban players. In addition to González, the brothers lured Cuban stars like Adolfo Luque (at that time Gonzalez's batterymate), Angel Aragón, Manuel Cueto, Luis Padrón, Tomás Romañach, and Juan Violá; the team was aptly named the Cubans. Richard Henriquez, who had played baseball at Columbia while attending medical school, joined the team himself. Long Branch quickly outclassed its opposition, winning the 1912 pennant by approximately 20 games. While Luque was undoubtedly the star attraction, González hit for an average of .333 and was behind the plate for every game.

After the summer of 1912 the Henriquez brothers sold González's contract to the Boston Braves, and he made his major-league debut on September 28, appearing in one game and walking once in three plate appearances. He was on the roster of the Braves to begin 1913, but manager George Stallings sent him down to Buffalo, which passed González along to Class B Wilkes-Barre. González refused the assignment and the Long Branch club purchased his optional release from Boston. The Braves recalled González briefly in the fall of 1913, but Long Branch subsequently purchased his outright release.

When González returned to Cuba he was traded from Fé to Habana for the 1913-14 season, which began his affiliation with the Rojos or, as they came to be known later, the Leones, a connection that lasted until the demise of the Cuban League.

At the same time, a letter from William H. Peal, secretary of the Eastern League, to Louis Heilbroner of the Baseball Statistical and Information Bureau described González as a very good hitter who is "catching great ball" in Cuba against American squads, at least one of which, the Birmingham Barons of the Southern Association, had made an offer for his services.[1] Heilbroner forwarded the letter to Garry Herrmann, president of the Cincinnati Reds, who signed González for the 1914 season.

In the fall of 1914, González, 24 years old, was named manager of Habana by new owner Abel Linares, who apparently had already taken note of the reserved, studious, and loyal nature of his protégé. González rewarded Linares with a championship in the 1914-15 season, the first of 13 Cuban League titles he would win as manager of Habana.

Meanwhile, González had appeared in 95 games for Cincinnati in 1914, catching in 83 of them and batting .233. Tommy Clarke was established as the regular backstop in Cincinnati, but in early April of 1915 the Reds traded González to the Cardinals for catcher Ivey Wingo. The Cardinals were looking to free up playing time for young catching prospect Frank "Pancho" Snyder. González played the next four seasons with the Cardinals, beginning as a backup for Snyder, who was one of the best catchers in the National League in 1915 at the age of 21, while occasionally filling in at first base.

Despite his size, González had a reputation as a stellar defensive catcher who possessed a strong, whip-like throwing arm, very quick feet, and soft hands for blocking pitches. Snyder himself was considered to be an excellent defensive catcher, one of the best of his era, yet manager Miller Huggins began to use González as his starting catcher as early as 1916, penciling him in as the starter in 84 games compared with 69 for Snyder. J.J. Ward of *Baseball Magazine* observed, "There are a few better catch-

ers in big league ball than Miguel A. González, but they are very, very few indeed."[2]

González batted .262 in 1917. His best season with the bat came in 1918, when he hit .252 with 39 walks and 20 extra-base hits. He stole 14 bases. Despite his success, González was placed on waivers by the Cardinals in May 1919, and was selected by the New York Giants. Manager John McGraw had spent much time in Cuba and had seen González play there in winter ball. On one occasion after Gonzalez's arrival, McGraw gave his team a pep talk convincing them of victory in the 1919 season, and looked to González, the newcomer, for validation. "We won't win, Cincinnati has the best team," replied González, who turned out to be quite prescient on the matter, even if his characteristic candor did not sit well with McGraw.[3]

McGraw kept González on his roster for four seasons, but Mike's playing time diminished as the Giants used first Lew McCarty as well as Frank Snyder, whom they had brought on board in 1919, as their starters. González spent considerable time as a bullpen catcher, and McGraw often sought his input on the relative merits of the pitching staff. But by 1922, at age 31, Gonzalez was considered through as a hitter, and the Giants sold his contract to the St. Paul Saints of the American Association.

González had two good seasons with the Saints, batting .298 and .303, and his contract was purchased in the spring of 1924 by the Cincinnati Reds. The Reds subsequently sold him to Brooklyn and González spent spring training with the Robins in Clearwater. The day before the season began, Brooklyn traded González to the Cardinals for infielder Milt Stock.

González had a good season with the Cardinals in 1924, playing in 120 games and batting .296, but in May 1925 he was traded to the Chicago Cubs along with infielder Howard Freigau for catcher Bob O'Farrell, who at the time was considered to be one of the finest defensive catchers in the league. González arrived in Chicago only to find young sensation Gabby Hartnett firmly entrenched as the starting catcher for the Cubs; he served primarily as Hartnett's backup for the better part of the next two seasons.

When Joe McCarthy took over as manager of the Cubs in 1926, he created some controversy by increasing Gonzalez's playing time at Hartnett's expense. "There aren't many players who can't outhit González, and maybe he doesn't spiel our language so well, but somehow he makes those pitchers understand him and they'll learn about pitching to hitters from him," McCarthy said.[4] Of course, Hartnett eventually blossomed into a star, and González did not appear in more than 60 games in any of the next three seasons for the Cubs, although he was a member of the pennant-winning squad of 1929 and appeared twice in the 1929 World Series, won by the Philadelphia Athletics in five games, striking out as a pinch-hitter in Game Two in his lone at-bat.

Undeniably, González's career in the big leagues represented only half of his baseball life — the rest was spent in Havana. The Cuban League arranged its schedule around that of American baseball, allowing González and many other Cuban players to have dual careers. In the winter they played against fellow Cubans, the finest players from the Negro Leagues, and American major leaguers. The competition was fierce, and the level of play superb. Many major-league teams and mixed barnstorming squads visited the island each winter to play the local teams, only to be startled by the quality of play of Cuban stars like Jose "The Black Diamond" Mendez, Cristobal Torriente, Alejandro Oms, and Dolf Luque. Many of their legendary feats have lived on, such as Mendez's streak of 25 scoreless innings for Almendares against Cincinnati in a series at Almendares Park in 1908.

Professional baseball in Cuba existed as far back as 1878, but the Cuban League never represented a cross-section of the population on the island — it was centered in Havana, and for all intents and purposes, it really existed as a mechanism for perpetuating one of the greatest and most intense rivalries in the history of the sport, the battle between the Habana Leones, or the Reds, and the Almendares Alacranes, the Blues. Attempts to add clubs from the provinces over the years generally met with failure; one of the steadier teams, Cienfuegos, rarely bothered to schedule games in its own city, traveling to Havana for "home" games in search of a bigger gate.

Cuban-born, 38-year-old Miguel Gonzalez made 47 starts behind the plate for the Cubs in 1929. He enjoyed a 17-year career in the big leagues and also coached in the St. Louis Cardinals organization for 13 years. (Retro Images Archive. George Brace Collection)

The first glory years of the Cuban League are generally considered to have taken place between World War I and the onset of the Great Depression, and it was during this period that the two great patriarchs of the sport in Cuba, González and Luque, became the faces of the two "eternal rivals." While the league shuttled third and fourth teams in and out over a period of years, the one constant was the competition between the Reds and the Blues, between González and Luque, which literally divided the city in two.

By the time this period ended, in 1929, González had managed Habana to six championships, in the seasons of 1918-19 (notable for the participation of the Cuban Stars, a team of Cubans who played in the American Negro Leagues), 1920-21, 1921-22 (an abbreviated season of nine scheduled games, of which only five were completed), 1926-27, 1927-28, and 1928-29, while still serving as a full-time player.

His only notable absence from the league during this period was in the 1923-24 season, won by the Santa Clara Leopardas, considered by many to be the best team ever assembled in Cuba, with an outfield of Oscar Charleston, Pablo "Champion" Mesa, and Alejandro Ohms. González left Habana to form a league of his own in Matanzas, which would feature all Cuban players, and he was replaced at the helm of Habana by his rival, Luque.

There were many reasons for his defection. González was becoming increasingly disaffected with the control promoter Abel Linares exerted over the league. Linares owned all three teams — Habana, Almendares, and Santa Clara — that participated in the 1923-24 season. Also, more American players were traveling to Cuba for the winter campaign, and Gonzalez's gesture of creating an all-Cuban insurgent league was seen as a protest against this development. Finally, and most significantly, González may have been trying to avert the gaze of Major League Baseball. Commissioner Kenesaw Mountain Landis, aware that the veneer of invincibility enjoyed by the major leagues was being peeled back by losses to Latin teams, had banned barnstorming in the offseason, which could easily have been construed to include the Cuban League.

When the Roaring Twenties gave way to the Depression, the golden age of the Cuban League ended, and by this time González's major-league career seemed over as well. The Cubs released him after the 1929 season, saying he had lost his arm strength. González denied it. "I am sorry to leave the Cubs for I have many friends in Chicago, but I have changed teams so many times that one more will make no difference," he said. "I am through as a Cub, but not as a ballplayer. My arm is all right, although I will have to admit that it is not what it used to be. Someone has said that the Cubs let me go because it went back on me, but that is very funny, because I never noticed it."[5]

Unable to find a major-league job, he played for the Minneapolis Millers of the American Association, at age 39. He hit .263 in 92 games and led the league's backstops with a .993 fielding percentage.

González's performance caught the attention of Branch Rickey, the general manager of the Cardinals, who signed him for the 1931 season. González played for the Cardinals

in 1931 and 1932, but had only 33 plate appearances over the two seasons, serving mostly as a bullpen coach. He did make a significant contribution to the Cardinals' world championship team in 1931. During the deciding Game Seven against the Athletics, Gonzalez walked from the bullpen to the dugout under the guise of getting a drink of water. What he had in mind was getting a good look in the eyes of starting pitcher Burleigh Grimes, who appeared to be struggling to hold a 4-0 lead late in the game. González hastened back to the bullpen and instructed left-hander Bill Hallahan to start warming up. "Burleigh, she tired," González said.[6] As it turned out, Grimes was indeed tired, and needed Hallahan to enter in the ninth inning with two outs, two runs in, and Philadelphia runners on first and second. Hallahan retired Max Bishop on a fly ball and the Cardinals held on for a 4-2 victory.

After the 1932 season González's major-league playing career came to an end. He was 41 years old. He finished with a lifetime batting average of .253, but his value was mainly on defense, where he compiled a fielding percentage of .980 and threw out 47 percent of baserunners attempting to steal. He finished within the top three in the National League in caught-stealing percentage five times. In assists as a catcher, he ranks immediately behind Hall of Famers Johnny Bench, Ernie Lombardi, and Mickey Cochrane, and just ahead of Yogi Berra.

For 1933 Rickey sent González to the Double-A Columbus Red Birds as a player-coach. González was credited with assisting in the development of the Red Birds' top pitching prospects, including Paul Dean and Bill Lee. He also managed, at 42, to accumulate 111 at-bats as a backup catcher, with a batting average of .324.

When Cardinals player-manager Frankie Frisch needed a coach for the 1934 team, he did not hesitate to select González, calling him "a great guy, loyal and true."[7] The Gas House Gang won 95 games and the National League pennant, then defeated the Detroit Tigers in seven games in the World Series.

González coached for Frisch and the Cardinals into the 1938 season as the Cardinals' fortunes faded under the Fordham Flash; they dropped from 96 wins in 1935 to 71 in 1938. Frisch was fired with 16 games remaining in 1938, and González was named interim manager, the first Latin American to manage in the big leagues. This was a bittersweet moment for González, for his promotion came at the expense of his mentor and close friend. "I hate to see him go. He's a real pal and a good man. I didn't want him to leave," he said.[8]

In the offseason, Rickey and owner Sam Breadon sought out González for his advice on a new manager for the Cardinals, and followed his recommendation that they hire Ray Blades, his tutor at Columbus. González returned to his role as coach under Blades until June 1940, when he briefly took over the reins as manager again after Blades was fired and before Billy Southworth succeeded him. González's final record as a major-league manager was 9-13.

In Cuba, 1930 was a precursor of an extremely difficult decade for the Cuban League. A contract dispute between the teams and the owners of La Tropical Stadium in Havana reduced the schedule to a mere five games. Over the next three years, the political stability in the country deteriorated as labor strikes and other, more violent measures were taken against the ruthless, heavy-handed government of President Gerardo Machado, who was finally forced out of office in 1933. The playoffs to settle a tie in the 1932-33 season were canceled, and then the entire 1933-34 season was wiped out. The 1934-35 campaign was notoriously weak, with all three professional teams going down to defeat at the hands of the amateur Rum Havana Club.

An improvement in the Cuban economy in the mid- to late 1930s, as well as the exploits of some of the great Cuban players of the era, among them as Martin Dihigo, Raymond "Jabao" Brown, and Lazaro Salazar, led to a revival of interest in the Cuban League. González, who had taken a two-year hiatus, returned for the 1938-39 campaign, but despite a pitching staff that included Dihigo, Tomás de la Cruz, Negro League great Ted "Double Duty" Radcliffe, and Luis Tiant the elder, Habana could finish no higher than second place, five games behind Santa Clara.

The revitalization of the league was also due to a rebirth of the rivalry between Habana and Almendares that began in the following season. Beginning with the 1939-40 campaign, the championship was won by either Habana or Almendares for five consecutive seasons, before Cienfuegos dethroned them in the 1945-46 season, the last to be played at La Tropical Stadium.

González had owned a tobacco and cigar business in Cuba, and was always a level-headed businessman and a good steward of his finances. When the widow of Abel Linares was ready to sell both the Almendares and Habana franchises, González put together a group of investors, and bought the Habana team for $25,000 in 1946. By 1947 he owned the team outright, and a decade later it was appraised at $500,000. But his rise to ownership directly resulted in the end of his career in American baseball.

González had continued coaching under Southworth in 1941, and the Cardinals improved to finish second behind the Brooklyn Dodgers. Beginning in 1942, the Cardinals entered the most hallowed era in their history, winning 106, 105, and 105 games in their next three seasons. In 1942 they edged out Leo Durocher's Brooklyn team to win the pennant by two games, and went on to defeat the New York Yankees in five games in the World Series. They won the pennant again in 1943 but lost to the Yankees in the World Series. The Cardinals won the Series in 1944, defeating their city rivals, the St. Louis Browns, in six games.

After leading the Cardinals to a second-place finish in 1945, Southworth signed a lucrative contract to manage the Boston Braves, and the Cardinals hired Eddie Dyer as manager. In a testament to how well González was regarded within the organization, and by owner Sam Breadon himself, he was retained and made the third-base coach, at which position he would be involved in one of the most famous plays in World Series history.

With both the Series and Game Seven knotted at 3-3, Enos Slaughter was on first base with two outs in the bottom of the eighth inning. On a 2-and-1 pitch to Harry Walker, Slaughter broke for second. Walker lined a double to left-center field, where Leon Culberson, who had just replaced the injured Dom DiMaggio, raced to his right to field it and throw to the cutoff man, shortstop Johnny Pesky. Slaughter had kept on going around third and beat the startled Pesky's throw to the plate to score the go-ahead run. The Cardinals held on and won their third World Series in five years.

The winning play was surrounded by some confusion that has caused continuing dispute. Walker's hit was called a single by some members of the media, which magnified Slaughter's achievement. Also, DiMaggio, standing on the dugout steps, had yelled to Culberson to move to his right prior to the pitch, but the crowd noise drowned him out, and Culberson did not notice. Pesky, stunned to see Slaughter heading for home, was said to have hesitated upon catching Culberson's throw, allowing Slaughter to score. The available film of the play shows that Pesky wheeled and threw home without much more than a momentary hesitation. Unfortunately for the Red Sox, his throw was well up the third-base line, allowing Slaughter to score.

Another dispute is whether González put up the stop sign or waved Slaughter home. The video is inconclusive on this matter. The video shows González coming into vision as Slaughter approached third base with his head down, and the only clearly discernible movement the coach made was to backpedal rapidly, almost as if to get out of Slaughter's way. Slaughter himself was ambivalent on the subject, siding with each point of view on different occasions. Perhaps his most telling comment on the play took place during a television interview in 2000, when he said, "I never saw Mike González, the third-base coach. Whether he tried to stop me or not, I don't know. I never looked up."[9]

For his part, González was persistent in his account of the play, insisting that with two outs and the bottom of the order coming up, he did not hesitate to wave Slaughter around third. If so, he may have been influenced by a play in the fourth inning of Game One, when Slaughter tripled to left-center field with two outs, but was left stranded, with the Cardinals losing the game in extra innings. On this occasion, Pesky fumbled the relay from DiMaggio, but González held Slaughter at third base when he clearly could have scored. González was criticized by some observers of that play for being out of position to make the proper call.

Game Seven marked the end of Miguel González's career in the major leagues. In many ways his departure was symbolic of the conflict that had arisen between the owners of Organized Baseball in the United States and the independent interests of league owners outside of their purview.

The Mexican League, which had come into existence in the 1930s, had always depended for its success on the participation of many of the greatest Latin American players, including Cubans, as well as the finest African-American players from the Negro Leagues. The president and kingpin was Jorge Pasqual, a multimillionaire who was eager to expand the influence and importance of his league in Mexico's postwar economic boom. The return from World War II of many gifted baseball players was flooding the available talent pool, and Pasqual wanted his share of the overflow. He offered exorbitant bonuses and salaries to American major leaguers in an effort to get them to jump their contracts and join his league. When his plan began to bear fruit, Commissioner Happy Chandler and the team owners were quick to take action to defend their interests.

Chandler proclaimed that any player who jumped to Mexico, as well as those who played against them in winter leagues, would be blacklisted from Organized Baseball. This was a direct blow to the Cuban League, which had for years drawn on talent from the Mexican League, including famous jumpers like Sal Maglie, Max Lanier, and Lou Klein. The two leagues had formed a summer/winter combination that was attractive to many African-American and Latin players. Many of the top Cuban players, like Dihigo, Luque, and Salazar, had played and managed in Mexico — the baseball connection between the two countries was close. Regardless, Major League Baseball was now in effect restricting Cuban players from playing in their own country.

González and Luque, as well as at least 18 other Cubans, were formally banned from Organized Baseball. On October 17, 1946, González, with eyes on purchasing the

Habana franchise, resigned as a coach of the Cardinals. Owner Sam Breadon expressed disappointment, saying, "We'd like to see him come back at any time, and hope he will."[10]

As the controversy swirled throughout Cuba, "the eternal rivals" engaged in a pennant race in February 1947 that enthralled the entire nation. The 1946-47 Cuban League season was moved to the new Gran Stadium. The ballpark accommodated 35,000 fans and was centrally located in Havana, which was enjoying an outbreak of postwar tourism that had bolstered the economy. González's Leones had built a large early lead in the standings, but a tremendous late run by Luque's Alacranes that saw them win 12 of 13 games at one point, left the outcome hanging in the balance on the last day of the season. Finally, Max Lanier defeated Habana to reward Almendares with the pennant.

With the threat of further sanctions very much in mind, the executives of the Cuban League decided to seek peace. An agreement between Organized Baseball and the Cuban League in the summer of 1947 ended Cuban autonomy over its own professional baseball. The jumpers would be banned, and from then on the major leagues would have control over the flow of players between the United States and Cuba. The Cuban League would in essence become a training ground, a minor league, for developing major league players.

González continued to manage the Leones under the agreement, winning three consecutive championships, in 1950-51, 1951-52, and 1952-53. In the winter of 1953, he made the surprising announcement that he would retire as manager of Habana at the end of the season, but would remain as owner. He retired with many Cuban League managerial records that would never be eclipsed, including most games (1,525), most seasons (34), most wins (917), and most pennants (14). He was elected to the Cuban Baseball Hall of Fame in 1955. Habana never won another Cuban League title.

There are many stories about González, some certainly apocryphal and others existing in various forms. Many center on his inability to speak English well; in the perhaps unwitting racism that was commonplace at the time, most sportswriters painstakingly spelled out every word González spoke phonetically, as a rather cruel way of pointing out his problems with the language.

However, González did have a few characteristic mannerisms as well as phrases that he used throughout his baseball career, almost as calling cards. Like many Spanish speakers first learning to speak English, he had trouble with pronouns, often referring to males as "she." His stock phrase for a person of superior intelligence or intuitive wisdom was a "smart dummy," while a person who lacked those qualities was a "humpy-dumpy."[11]

Gonzalez's problems with the language did lead to some challenges for his teammates. One of the most famous tales involved a play in a game against the Giants at the Polo Grounds on September 13, 1936. The Cardinals were batting in the third inning of the first game of a doubleheader before a crowd of 64,417, a record National League one-game attendance at the time. With pitcher Henry "Cotton" Pippen on second base and Terry Moore on first, Art Garibaldi hit a line drive into right-center field. Pippen took off but quickly stopped between second and third, unable to understand the instructions of his third-base coach, González. Moore had by then rounded second only to find Pippen directly in his path. The Giants tagged both Pippen and Moore out while Garibaldi, despite having ostensibly doubled, was back on first base. After the inning, an angry González stormed into the dugout. "They no understand, Frank," he told manager Frisch. "I tell Pippen go and she stop. I tell Moore stop and she go ahead. What do you do with dummies like them? I do my best, Frank, I cannot do some more."[12]

Of course, González's issues with the language resulted in his coining one of the most famous phrases in baseball. After the 1921 season, Giants manager John McGraw told González to scout a young prospect in Cuba over the winter. González, never one for verbosity, replied with a four-word telegram. It read simply, "Good field, no hit," a phrase that has lived on in the scouting community ever since.

Despite these humorous anecdotes, Gonzalez was never considered to be anything less than an astute baseball man and evaluator of talent. He was renowned among his teammates for his ability to unravel the most complicated signs of the opposing team. In particular, he was excellent at cracking the code that opposing infielders used to signal the forthcoming pitch, and discreetly informed the batter from the third-base coaching box. He had a remarkable memory that allowed him to recall the strengths and weaknesses of every player, both at bat and in the field, and he could recite batting averages at the drop of a hat.

While at first the Cuban League showed signs of surviving the revolution of 1959 that brought Fidel Castro to power, by 1961 professional baseball had been banned in Cuba. It was later reported that some of González's property was confiscated, but due to his stature and fame, he was allowed to reside in his principal residence, a marble home in the exclusive Vedado neighborhood of Havana, and maintain his car and chauffeur. Because of travel restrictions instituted by the Castro government, he became isolated from his friends and colleagues in American baseball, who quickly lost track of his whereabouts.

One of González's last reported public appearances was at the final game of the World Amateur Baseball Championship in Havana in January 1972. A Havana newspaper reporter covering the event wrote for *The Sporting News*, "Now 81 years old, Miguel Angel still has a strong voice, recalls his lifetime baseball records, and his keen eyes observe everything on the diamond."[13]

González's was last heard from when Preston Gomez returned from a visit to Cuba with pictures taken at González's 85th birthday party. He is seen smiling from behind a large birthday cake, holding a bottle of beer in each hand. He is missing his toes, suggesting that he suffered from diabetes.

González was married twice. After his first wife, Esther, died of cancer, he took his mother, Juana Cordero, into his home in the Havana suburb of Cerro. He later remarried and had a son, Miguel Jr., with his second wife, who was still alive when he died on February 19, 1977, from a heart attack at the age of 86. He is buried in the Christopher Columbus Cemetery in Havana.

SOURCES

Billheimer, John, *Baseball and the Blame Game: Scapegoating in the Major Leagues.* (Jefferson, North Carolina: McFarland & Co, 2007).

Bjarkman, Peter C., *A History of Cuban Baseball 1864-2006* (Jefferson, North Carolina: McFarland & Co, 2007).

Figueredo, Jorge S., *Cuban Baseball: A Statistical History 1878-1961* (Jefferson, North Carolina: McFarland & Co, 2011).

Gonzalez Echevarria, Roberto, *The Pride of Havana: A History of Cuban Baseball* (New York: Oxford University Press, 2001).

McNeill, William F., *Black Baseball Out of Season: Pay for Play Outside of the Negro Leagues* (Jefferson, North Carolina: McFarland & Co, 2007).

Perez, Louis A. Jr., *On Becoming Cuban: Identity, Nationality and Culture* (Chapel Hill, North Carolina: University of North Carolina Press, 1999).

Riley, James A., *The Biographical Encyclopedia of the Negro Baseball Leagues* (New York: Carroll & Graf Publishers, 1994).

Ruck, Rob, *Raceball: How the Major Leagues Colonized the Black and Latin Game* (Boston: Beacon Press, 2011).

Stockton, J. Roy, *The Gashouse Gang* (New York: Bantam Books, 1948).

Broeg, Bob. "Ex-Cardinal Gonzalez Added Accent to Coaching," *St. Louis Post-Dispatch*, August 19, 1971.

——— "Mike Gonzalez — Smart Dummy Coach," *St. Louis Post-Dispatch*, January 29, 1972.

——— "Mike, She's Gone — Grins Linger," *St. Louis Post-Dispatch*, April 30, 1977.

Hamilton, Jim, "Gonzales (sic) Made Views Known," *Oneonta* (New York) *Daily Star*, August 25, 1985.

Holmes, Thomas, "Aged Gonzales (sic) Returns to St. Louis to Teach Cardinal Kid Pitchers," *Brooklyn Eagle*, January 25, 1931.

McKenna, Brian, "The Henriquez Long Branch Cubans," Baseballhistoryblog.com, accessed June 25, 2013.

Stockton, J. Roy, "Mike Gonzales (sic), He Coach Third Base and Keep Cardinals from Fumbling Around This Year," *St. Louis Post-Dispatch*, March 17, 1934.

Ward, John J., "Gonzales (sic), the Cuban Backstop," *Baseball Magazine*, February 1917.

——— "Cuba's Best Catcher With the Cubs," *Baseball Magazine*, July 1927.

"Gonzalez, Miguel Angel (Mike)," no author, title or date given. From González's file at the Baseball Hall of Fame.

Karst, Eugene F., "Cardinal Newcomers for 1931," undated press release from St. Louis Cardinals.

Peal, William H., Letter to Louis Heilbroner, February 5, 1914.

Baseball-reference.com

NOTES

1   William H. Peal, letter to Louis Heilbroner. February 5, 1914.

2   John J. Ward, "Gonzales (sic), The Cuban Backstop." *Baseball Magazine*, February 1917.

3   Jim Hamilton, "Gonzales (sic) Made Views Known." *Oneonta* (New York) *Daily Star*, August 25, 1985.

4   Thomas Holmes, "Aged Gonzales (sic) Returns to St. Louis to Teach Cardinal Kid Pitchers," *Brooklyn Eagle*, January 25, 1931.

5   Joe Massaguer, personal interview with Miguel González. Quoted in *The Sporting News*, January 23, 1930.

6   Bob Broeg, "Mike, She's Gone — Grins Linger," *St. Louis Post-Dispatch*, April 30, 1977.

7   J.G. Taylor Spink, "Mike Gonzalez — Cuban Caballero of the Cardinals," *The Sporting News*, October 20, 1938.

8   Miguel Angel (Mike) "González," No author, title or date given. From González's file at the Baseball Hall of Fame.

9   John Billheimer, *Baseball and the Blame Game: Scapegoating in the Major Leagues*, 14.

10 United Press, "Card Coach Job Given Up by González," October 17, 1946.

11 Miguel Angel (Mike) "González," from González's file at the Baseball Hall of Fame.

12 J.G. Taylor Spink, "Mike González — Cuban Caballero of the Cardinals," *The Sporting News*, October 20, 1938.

13 J.G. Taylor Spink, "Mike González Attends Title Contest in Havana." *The Sporting News*, January 22, 1972.

EARL GRACE

By Greg Erion

As the 1929 season began, the Chicago Cubs were in trouble. They were without the services of their starting catcher, 28-year-old Gabby Hartnett, whose arm had gone dead. While Hartnett would eventually regain his throwing abilities, he played in only 25 games that year, just one as a catcher.[1] Initially, 38-year-old Mike Gonzalez and Earl Grace, whose professional experience had consisted of just 159 games in the minor leagues, took his place. The Cubs, a close third behind the New York Giants and the pennant-winning St. Louis Cardinals in 1928, needed someone other than an old veteran or an inexperienced rookie to handle their talented pitching staff. Mike Gonzalez eventually shared the catching duties with Zack Taylor. Although Grace would go on to be one of the better defensive catchers of his era, he had not yet reached his potential and was gone from the Cubs in midseason.

Robert Earl Grace was born in Barlow, Kentucky, on February 24, 1907, to Robert Edward and Nannie Grace. Earl, as he came to be known, was the second of five children.[2] In 1916 the family moved to Phoenix, Arizona, where the elder Grace became a real-estate broker, eventually forming his own realty company, and subsequently became a leader in civic affairs, including involvement on the Phoenix baseball scene.[3]

Earl played ball at Union High School, and his talent caught the eye of a scout, Grover Land, a former Cleveland Indians catcher. Grace signed a contract to play for the Lincoln Links of the Class A Western League. He later recalled, "My contract called for $200 a month for five months, but I only lasted a month. By the time I got my first paycheck I was so homesick I quit the club and went fishing. Oh boy, was I homesick. I thought my heart had withered away. That's the way you get at the age of 17."[4] Somewhat chastened by this experience, he gave it another try the following spring.

"By the time the next spring rolled around I had grown up and decided to give baseball another try. I reported to Little Rock and was transferred to Muskogee, where I played first base, the outfield and caught." Appearing in 69 games for the Muskogee Athletics of the Class C Western Association in 1926, Grace hit .298, playing alongside future Hall of Famer Bill Dickey. Still not good enough to stay in professional baseball, he was released again. Grace played semipro ball in the Phoenix area the following year hoping to catch on in Organized Baseball. His perseverance paid off as he signed with the Little Rock Travelers of the Class A Southern Association. Again teamed up with Dickey, he caught the bulk of the games for the Travelers and batted .336[5]

With the Cubs opening the 1929 season minus the services of their veteran catcher Hartnett, they purchased Grace's contract from Little Rock in hopes that he could fill in. It was a tremendous burden to place on the shoulders of a 22-year-old. At that point, Grace just had parts of two seasons in the minor leagues, essentially only one as a catcher. The Cubs were expected to be contenders, having finished third just four games behind the pennant-winning Cardinals the year before. Over the winter, to improve their chances, the Cubs had obtained Rogers Hornsby via a trade with the Boston Braves for five players and an estimated $200,000. The pressure was on to win.

With the high expectations, there was a great deal of stress on Grace to help handle a veteran pitching staff headed by Guy Bush, Pat Malone, and Charlie Root. He made his debut on April 23 against the St. Louis Cardinals, entering the game in the late innings. Just over a week later, he got his first start, going hitless in four at-bats against Cincinnati. On May 4 Grace caught both ends of a doubleheader against the Philadelphia Phillies at the Baker Bowl in Philadelphia. Hitless in the first game, he came to bat in the second inning against pitcher Claude Willoughby and collected his first major-league hit, a three-run home run that started the Cubs on their way to a 9-7 victory to complete a sweep.

Although Grace played passably well, alternating behind the plate with Mike Gonzalez, the Cubs could not pull away from the pack. By late June Grace had given way to another veteran catcher, Johnny Schulte, who had been signed as a free agent in late April. In early July, the Cubs claimed another veteran receiver, Zack Taylor, on waivers from the Braves. Taylor proved adequate to the job and the Cubs went on to win the pennant. With the acquisition of Taylor, Grace went to the Reading Keystones of the Double-A International League, where he finished the season. Under different rules than are now in place, Grace did not receive a players' share of World Series proceeds, because he had been sent out in July.[6]

Grace spent all of 1930 with Reading, where he hit .324 in 137 games. It was there he recalled having his biggest day in baseball. In a doubleheader against Newark he got six hits in seven at-bats including two home runs. [7]

Grace's play earned a trip back to the Cubs in 1931. He made the team only to be traded to the Pittsburgh Pirates on May 29 for catcher Rollie Hemsley in the first of what would be Grace's three major-league transactions each involving a fellow receiver. Thanks to a couple of late-night escapades, Hemsley had worn out his welcome in Pittsburgh. He had caught the eye of the Cubs manager, Rogers Hornsby, which made Grace expendable.[8] It proved a beneficial trade for Grace. Hartnett was back at full strength and all Grace could have hoped for with the Cubs was to serve as a backup. Joining Pittsburgh, he alternated with Eddie Phillips, again facing mostly right-handed pitching. He finished the season with a credible batting average of .280 for Pittsburgh (combined .270, including his stay with Chicago).

Grace made his last error of the 1931 season on August 29, in a game against St. Louis, an error that would obtain greater significance the following season. In 1932 Grace emerged as the first-string catcher for Pittsburgh, playing in 115 games, hitting .274 with 17 doubles and 8 home runs. Overall it was the best offensive season of his career. But it wasn't for his hitting that Grace gained attention in 1932. He broke several fielding records for catchers. On July 24, playing against his old teammates at Wrigley Field, Grace handled four chances and set a major-league record for the most consecutive chances without an error, 282. His streak continued until September 8, when he made a poor throw to second, allowing the Brooklyn

Dodgers' Tony Cuccinello to score. In all, Grace had handled 444 chances without an error over the course of 121 games, another record.[9] The season ended a few weeks later with Grace setting yet another record, a .998 fielding average.[10] His record fielding percentage stood until 1946, when the Philadelphia Athletics' Buddy Rosar had a perfect 1.000 average in 117 games.[11] These fielding records were set in competition with Ray Hayworth of the Detroit Tigers. Hayworth had run up streaks of errorless games and chances accepted before dropping a called third strike against the Athletics on August 29, just ten days before Grace's streak ended, allowing Grace to surpass his effort.[12]

If 1932 proved something of a breakthrough for Grace, 1933 was less so. Barely a month into the season, the *Boston Globe* reported that Grace's left foot had become infected.[13] A few weeks later, after Grace had missed several games, the *Globe* reported that the infection was not healing and

Grace made his big-league debut as a catcher for the Cubs in 1929. He later played for the Pittsburgh Pirates and Philadelphia Phillies in his eight-year career. (Retro Images Archive. George Brace Collection)

that Grace would probably have to undergo an operation, missing two to three weeks of play. The estimate was accurate; Grace went out of the lineup on June 22 and returned on July 12. He played the rest of the season without incident and only a late-season slump prevented him from finishing over .300. He settled for a .289 mark, his highest major-league average.

Over the next few years, Grace platooned with Tom Padden. He happened to be playing in a game of historic proportions in late May of 1935. The Pirates were facing the Braves in a series at Forbes Field. The Braves had drawn a lot of attention for signing the aging Babe Ruth as a player and team vice president. Ruth's main value to the team was as a drawing card. In the first game of the series, on May 23 with Grace behind the plate, Ruth was hitless. The next day, with Padden catching, he singled in four at-bats. On May 25, with Grace again catching, Ruth went 4-for-4 with three home runs, the last of them judged to be the longest homer hit in Pittsburgh up to that time. They proved to be Ruth's last major-league home runs. A week later he retired. Years later, Grace was asked about that day. "I don't recall much about it," he said. "But I remember I was 0-for-4 and my name was misspelled in the box score."[14] (Interestingly enough, a review of various newspaper accounts of the game found Grace's name being spelled correctly.[15])

On November 21, 1935, Grace was traded again, this time to the Philadelphia Phillies along with 21-year-old pitcher Claude Passeau for catcher Al Todd. Over the next two seasons, Grace hit .249 and .211 with the second-division club, appearing almost exclusively against right-handed pitchers. On October 3, 1937, he pinch-hit for pitcher Pete Sivess against Boston at Braves Field, drawing a walk. That turned out to be his last major-league game. For his career, Grace played in 627 games, batted .263, and set several fielding records, which stood for several years.

After the season ended, Grace was traded once again, to the St. Louis Cardinals for catcher Cap Clark. Grace was assigned to the Cardinals Columbus farm team in American Association.[16] He was not happy with the transaction and considered retiring from the game.[17] He eventually decided to report to Columbus, playing there

until he was traded in mid-June to the Minneapolis Millers. Grace hit a combined .233 with the two high-level minor-league teams in 117 games. In 1939 his playing time fell off while he played for both the Millers and the Nashville Volunteers of the Class A1 Southern Association. In 1940 Grace batted once for the Millers before being released. That ended his professional career.

Grace returned to Phoenix, where his father and brother Bill had established themselves in the real-estate business. He had little time to consider his post-baseball career before World War II beckoned. Grace went into the Army Air Corps and eventually was assigned as athletic director at Luke Field in Phoenix.[18]

Several years earlier, when asked about being single, Grace had noted, "I have been spoiled by three sweet sisters, but I am willing to be spoiled by someone else's sister." Just as long as she could cook and darn socks, he added.[19] Grace's affection for his sisters went beyond talk. While playing ball, he provided financial support for two of them, both of whom eventually became teachers.[20]

An opportunity to be spoiled by someone other than his sisters presented itself when certain out-of-town visitors came to Phoenix. As related by Grace's daughter Vickie, businessman Herbert Johnson of Evanston, Illinois, came to town, accompanied by his daughter, Shirley Mae, who was introduced to Earl. Whether Miss Johnson could cook or darn socks may or may not have been a factor, but she did marry Grace on December 25, 1941, just weeks after the United States entered World War II. The new Mrs. Grace had attended DePauw University in Greencastle, Indiana.[21]

From Luke Field, Grace was transferred several times, among other places to Camp Grant, Illinois, and Daytona Beach, Florida.[22] At Daytona Beach his and Shirley's first daughter, Vickie, was born. Several years later they had another daughter, Cheryl.

By then Grace was out of the service and back in Phoenix. While still playing he had begun to purchase land in the Phoenix area, eventually coming to own cotton and citrus farms in the Peoria, Phoenix, and Yuma areas as well as land near what is now the Phoenix Sky Harbor

International Airport. He kept close ties to the baseball community, and played golf and hunted doves with his neighbor and friend Dizzy Dean.

Grace's name occasionally popped into the news whenever someone made a run at his fielding records. Although Rosar bested Grace's record for the highest fielding percentage for a major-league catcher, Grace still held the National League record. After 18 years, it was broken by the New York Giants' Wes Westrum, who surpassed Grace in 1950 with a .999 percentage.[23]

Grace was often on hand for various events connected with baseball, among them welcoming the Giants to spring training at Phoenix in 1948 and gathering at sports award banquets with players and ex-players.[24] He frequently ran into Grover Land, who had recommended him for his first contract. Grace kept in touch with other ballplayers as well through such organizations as the Arizona Organized Baseball Oldtimers Association, formed in 1953 with Grace as its secretary-treasurer.

Grace's daughter Vickie, recalled her father as a quiet and private person. He seldom spoke of his baseball career; it had ended several years before she and her sister were born. But when he occasionally scouted for the Yankees, she went with him to games as he sized up the local talent. Vickie went to spring-training games, at one time getting the autograph of Wes Westrum with mixed feelings — she knew from her dad's scrapbook Westrum's significance as it related to her father. Golf was a major activity for her parents. Her mother was an accomplished golfer; they were both members of the Arizona Country Club, where they played golf, and frequently went on golfing trips together.[25]

In 1966 Jerry Eaton of the *Arizona Republic* interviewed Grace at one of his citrus fields. Grace was less than nostalgic about his career in baseball. Sitting in his Thunderbird alongside Easton, he watched workers weed his field as he spoke of his baseball career and life since retiring from the game. "The first two or three years in the big leagues were fun, but after that it turned into a doggone hard job. We did all our traveling by train then and a fellow would have a hard time keeping track of where he was. I'd wake up in a sweat in a hotel room at night sometimes not knowing for a moment what city I was in or where the door was. We were always on the go and it was tough to stay oriented or adjusted." Of his time with the Pirates, Grace said, "I played on some pretty good Pittsburgh teams, but we never quite seemed to have the pitching."[26]

By this time Grace had experienced several heart attacks, which limited his mobility. The old ballplayer lamented his slower pace of life, "I've had a couple of heart attacks and I can't get around like I once did. It wears me out not roaming around the fields anymore. I sure am jealous of those young fellows in the fields. Look at them move around. That kind of activity tuckers me out these days — makes me furious that it does."[27]

That slower pace of life continued until December 22, 1980, when Grace died of congestive heart failure at 73. He was buried at Greenwood Memorial Lawn Cemetery in Phoenix.[28] He was survived by his wife, Shirley, and daughters, Vickie and Cheryl. Numerous letters of condolences were received, which reflected a convivial spirit. Former US Senator and Arizona Governor Paul Fannin said in a letter, "He told great stories in a humble way." Another friend spoke of his laugh and sense of humor.[29]

Grace played in heady company. He was a teammate of several Hall of Fame players. While not much of a hitter, Grace had a reputation for defense and was known as one who had particular savvy in handling pitchers. Unlike many players, he did not let baseball define his life. It was an adventure along the way, not a destination, as he proved in his subsequent career as a successful businessman, and perhaps more important as a family man and friend.

NOTES

1   Peter Golenbock, *Wrigleyville, A Magical History Tour of the Chicago Cubs*, (New York: St. Martin's Press, 1996), 206.

2   Ancestry.com

3   *The Sporting News*, January 126, 1952, 23.

4   Unidentified newspaper dated March 21, 1936, in Grace's file at the Hall of Fame.

5   All baseball statistics from retrosheet.org/boxesetc/T/Ptaylz101.htm and baseball-reference.com/players/g/graceea01.shtml.

6   Grace's Hall of Fame player file.

7   Grace's Hall of Fame player file.

8   "Pirates Trade Hemsley to Cubs for Earl Grace," *Chicago Daily Tribune*, May 30, 1931, 11.

9   "It's Bad Day for Pirates; Beaten 12-2; Grace Errs," *Chicago Daily Tribune*, September 9, 1932, 23.

10 "Grace, Pirates Set 2 Fielding Marks," *New York Times*, December 28, 1932, 21.

11 "Rosar Sets Fielding Mark," *The Sporting News*, December 19, 1946, 12.

12 Unidentified newspaper dated September 1, 1932, in Grace's Hall of Fame player file.

13 "Earl Grace Out of Game With Infected Foot," *Boston Globe*, May 13, 1933, 7.

14 "Obituaries," *The Sporting News*, January 10, 1981, 45.

15 An informal review of news accounts of the game in the *Boston Globe*, *Chicago Daily Tribune*, *New York Times* and *Washington Post* in their May 26, 1935, showed Grace's name spelled correctly in the box score.

16 "Slow Trading Mars Meeting At Chicago," *The Sporting News*, December 16, 1937, 3. Both Baseball.Reference and Retrosheet at the time of this research incorrectly showed Grace being traded to the St. Louis Browns. Other articles from the *New York Times* and the Washington *Post* note Grace going to the Cardinals. Clark had been in the Cardinals' minor-league organization before being traded for Grace.

17 "Leiber Holds Out Again," *New York Times*, January 23, 1938, 76.

18 "Bride of Army Athletic Director," *Chicago Daily Tribune*, January 4, 1942, N5.

19 Unidentified newspaper dated March 21, 1936, in Grace's file at the Hall of Fame.

20 Telephone interview with Vickie Lund, Grace's daughter, on June 13, 2013

21 Telephone interview with Vickie Lund on June 6, 2013.

22 "In The Service," *The Sporting News*, August 3, 1944, 12, and July 26, 1945, 11.

23 "Six N.L. Defense Marks Broken and Three Tied," *The Sporting News*, December 27 1950, 16.

24 "Del Webb Host at Gala Party for Giants," *The Sporting News*, March 17 1948, 20;"Casey Salutes Giants, Lippy Hails Giants," *The Sporting News*, January 30, 1952, 24.

25 Telephone interview with Vickie Lund, June 6, 2013.

26 Jerry Eaton,"Arizona Agriculture: From Athletics to Agriculture — The Tale of Catcher Earl Grace," *Arizona Republic*, April 10, 1966, 18-B.

27 Ibid.

28 Telephone interview with Vickie Lund, June 6, 2013.

29 Telephone interview with Vickie Lund, June 13, 2013.

HANK GRAMPP

By Peter Morris

ENRY GRAMPP, JR. WAS BORN IN New York City on September 28, 1903, the only child of Henry and Frieda Grampp. There is some confusion about Henry's middle name, which was long listed as "Erchardt" in baseball encyclopedias. But since his paternal grandfather's given name was Eckhard and his father provided his name as Henry Joseph Eckhard Grampp when he filled out his World War I registration card, it is likely that that was also Henry Jr.'s name.

Henry Sr. was employed as chief attendant at the New York Museum of Art and by 1920 his son was working as a bank messenger. But the younger Henry was also dreaming of a career in baseball, and in 1923 pitched in six games for Hartford of the Eastern League (Class A) followed by seven games for Newark of the International League. By 1926 his work for Petersburg of the Virginia League (Class B) had caught the eye of a Chicago Cubs scout, and he was drafted by the Cubs at the end of that season.[1]

When Grampp arrived at the Cubs' spring-training home on Catalina Island the next spring, his mind must have been full of dreams of making the team and going on to major-league stardom. As it turned out, he made the team all right, but his role was not one he could have envisioned. Day after day, he was asked to pitch batting practice to Cub hitters, but when the real game began, his work ended.

Almost a month into the season, Chicago arrived in Grampp's hometown for a series against the New York Giants. Before one of the games, the local boy who'd made good was presented with a watch by the boys who belonged to a German-American club headed by Senator Robert Wagner of New York.[2] But even back in this most inviting of atmospheres, Chicago manager Joe McCarthy never called upon Grampp to face live action.

Grampp finally made his major-league debut in the second game of a doubleheader in St. Louis on June 21, 1927. The game was already a lost cause when Grampp was called from the bullpen, and he surrendered three more runs in two innings of work. Then it was another two months before his next appearance, on August 30 in New York. This time he pitched a shutout inning, but it was not enough to earn him any more work that year.

But while game action was in extremely short supply, Grampp had no trouble staying busy. Until this point, it had been customary for batting practice to be thrown by a member of the staff who was between starts. But Grampp changed this; as sportswriter Edward Burns observed, "All other major league clubs rotate the job of pitching in batting practice among pitchers several days away from any possible turn to pitch. Not so the Cubs — that's Hank's job 154 days of the season."[3]

Naturally the job of full-time batting practice pitcher attracted some sarcastic commentary. Sportswriter James S. Collins quipped that the umpire's cry of "Play Ball" was "Grampp's cue to call it a day and see himself to the showers. Next to managing the Phillies, Mr. Grampp's seems the most unattractive job baseball has offered since an unsung hero filled a line on the Giants' pay roll as keeper of the late 'Bugs' Raymond."[4]

But Grampp took the assignment seriously and so did his teammates, who never made his role "the subject of some flippant comment." As Burns explained, "Batting stars in the thick of a pennant fight won't stand for careless pitching. To get beaned in batting practice is an accident not looked upon as a legitimate way to get injured. So to be a successful batting practice pitcher an athlete must have control and at the same time keep his offerings difficult to hit. Hank has control and he doesn't lob 'em over. That's the reason he has been called the world's champion batting practice pitcher."[5]

It was also a demanding job: "Hank's work is on a definite schedule, and while the club is at home begins earlier than on the road, for the home team has first call on batting practice. The practice is ended on schedule, but the home club starts as early as the manager orders. In a game the pitcher rests while his club is at bat, but the practice pitcher stays in for a certain number of 'rounds,' in which the batters practice in the same order as in the game, each hitting the ball three times in each round."[5]

And, perhaps most importantly, Grampp never showed any sign of resenting his role. "Grampp never complains that his light is being hidden under a bushel," Burns noted. "His smile is perpetual. He is content. Other ball players nervously wonder what each day holds for them. Hank knows what he's going to do."[6]

Because of his value to the club, Grampp was invited back to spring training in 1928 and again made the team — but never once pitched in a major-league game that season. Asked why he didn't give Grampp an occasional chance in a mop-up role, McCarthy replied, "Grampp has done his full quota of work long before there ever is occasion for a relief pitcher. Taking those rounds of pitching practice is just as hard work as pitching in a game."[7]

Grampp returned to Catalina in 1929 amid vague speculation that he might finally see regular work during regular-season games.[8] But Grampp understood his role and so did most observers. An Associated Press story even claimed that "official batting [practice] pitcher" was his title.[9]

By this time, Grampp had developed a "talent for impersonation" of other teams' pitchers that made him all the more valuable.[10] "If the Cubs are to face Carl Mays, for instance," sportswriter James S. Collins explained, "Mr. Grampp goes out there and throws up a few underhand balls to the Cub sluggers. If [Grover Cleveland] Alexander is expected to be the opposing pitcher, we are told, he gives an imitation of Alexander's style."[11]

Thus the 1929 season again saw Grampp as usual take the mound for batting practice each and every day, but just as consistently depart the scene before the start of the game itself. There was one difference that year: The Cubs were headed for the World Series.

That prospect was very exciting for Grampp and all the Cubs, but it did raise a concern. Grampp threw batting practice only when the opposing starter was to be a right-hander. Eric Nadel and Craig R. Wright in *The Man Who Stole First Base* claimed that Grampp was ambidextrous, but numerous contemporary sources make clear that he threw only right-handed.[12] There were relatively few southpaws in the National League, so he worked nearly every day during the regular season, but the Philadelphia Athletics featured two left-handed starters, Rube Walberg and Lefty Grove, meaning that Grampp might not see much work.

A column by Edward Burns maintained that Grampp was beginning to worry and lose weight over this prospect. It seems safe to assume that the claim was at least partially — if not entirely — tongue in cheek. After three years of keeping a "perpetual smile" while performing a role that others might have resented, Grampp must have been thrilled about being involved in the fall classic.[13]

Before it started, however, Grampp did finally get a chance to start a major-league game. On October 4, 1929, McCarthy told the team's beat writers they could select the Cub starter for the last day of the season three days later. Grampp was their unanimous choice, but after pitching one solid inning, he was rocked for six runs in the second inning and had to be removed.[14]

Grampp's concerns about not being needed during the World Series — if indeed they were real — proved unfounded. Athletics manager Connie Mack, wary of Chicago's right-handed hitters, surprised everyone by starting right-hander Howard Ehmke in the opener and used his two left-handers only in relief during the Series. Unfortunately for Grampp and the Cubs, Mack's strategy proved effective, and Philadelphia won in five games. Grampp did at least have the distinction of being on his team's active roster for the World Series, though naturally he did not pitch.[15]

Grampp went to spring training in Catalina again in 1930, but it would prove a very different spring than the three previous ones for him. On April 9 he married a 19-year-old local woman named Elaine Hammond. Before the end of the year, the marriage had disintegrated. Grampp was

Right-handed pitcher Grampp made his last of three big-league appearances for the Cubs in 1929. (Retro Images Archive. George Brace Collection)

trying to obtain a divorce, while Hammond was seeking an annulment, claiming that they had been married hurriedly by a deputy sheriff because Grampp told her the team was about to leave. Meanwhile, the deputy sheriff was maintaining that he thought the whole thing was a joke.[16]

Three days after his disastrous marriage, the Cubs released Grampp to Reading of the International League.[17] He somehow compiled an 8-3 record for this club, but his 6.10 earned-run average shows that he did not pitch well. He began the 1931 season with Reading, but was released after only two games and picked up by Buffalo, which in turn cut him loose in July.[18] After a final stint with Norfolk, he decided to return to New York City and retire from baseball.

Grampp worked for several years as a special patrolman for the National Bank and was married again, to a woman named Lena — this time successfully.[19] But Grampp didn't entirely turn his back on baseball. In 1934 he was back in a familiar role as batting-practice pitcher for the Yankees.[20] And in 1950 he was hired as a full-time scout by the Cubs, with responsibility for New York, New Jersey, New England, and Pennsylvania.[21]

In 1968 Henry's wife Lena, died at the age of 57. Henry Grampp survived for another 18 years, dying in New York City on March 24, 1986, at the age of 82.

NOTES

1   *New York Times*, October 2, 1926.

2   *Sheboygan* (Wisconsin) *Press*, May 9, 1927.

3   Edward Burns, "Henry Grampp's In Town, So All Cubs Feel Fine," *Chicago Tribune*, January 31, 1929.

4   James S. Collins, "Almost the Naked Truth," *Washington Post*, March 21, 1929.

5   Edward Burns, "Home Folks Won't See His Series' Stuff, Grampp Wails," *Chicago Tribune*, August 7, 1929.

6   Burns, "Henry Grampp's In Town."

7   Burns, "Home Folks."

8   *Lincoln* (Nebraska) *Evening State Journal and Daily News*, February 14, 1929.

9   *Galveston Daily News*, March 21, 1929.

10 Burns, "Henry Grampp's In Town."

11 Collins, "Almost the Naked Truth."

12 Eric Nadel and Craig R. Wright, *The Man Who Stole First Base* (Dallas: Taylor Publishing, 1989), 14.

13 Burns, "Home Folks."

14 *Oakland Tribune*, October 5, 1929.

15 *Chicago Tribune*, September 11, 1929.

16 *Los Angeles Times*, April 5 and 9, 1930; *Olean* (New York) *Herald*, December 16, 1930.

17 *Port Arthur* (Texas) *News*, April 12, 1930.

18 *Syracuse Herald*, May 4 and July 19, 1931.

19 *New York Times*, April 10, 1936, and December 27, 1941.

20 *Chicago Tribune*, June 27, 1934.

21 *Chicago Tribune*, February 19 and 24, 1950; *Canandaigua* (New York) *Daily Messenger*, June 7, 1950.

CHARLIE GRIMM

By Dan Fields

CHARLIE GRIMM WAS A MAN OF MANY talents. Called "perhaps the best ever" defensive first baseman by Bill James,[1] he led the National League in fielding percentage at the position seven times and finished in second place three times between 1920 and 1933 with the Pittsburgh Pirates and Chicago Cubs. He was a .290 hitter over his 20-year career, with nearly 2,300 hits and more than 1,000 RBIs. He managed the Cubs to three pennants, and as of 2014 no one except Cap Anson had won more games as the team's skipper. Grimm's career winning percentage of .547 was as of 2014 the 17th highest among managers with at least 1,000 wins.

Grimm was one of baseball's premier entertainers, and not just for his acrobatic play. He would serenade fans before games with his singing and banjo playing. "In the on-deck circle he might brandish two bats in imitation of a butcher sharpening his knives. He and [Cubs catcher Gabby] Hartnett liked to play 'burnout' in front of the fans, advancing up the line and firing the ball toward each other at closer and closer quarters. To the roars of the crowd, he might mimic an umpire's walk behind his back — an act that at least once earned him an ejection as a manager."[2]

"I had fun playing baseball," wrote Grimm in his 1968 autobiography. "I tried to make it fun for my players after I became manager. I was 'Jolly Cholly' and I always thought a pat on the back, an encouraging word, or a wisecrack paid off a lot more than a brilliantly executed work of strategy."[3]

Charles John Grimm was born on August 28, 1898, in St. Louis. Of his childhood, Grimm said, "We were a happy family. Pop played the bass fiddle, Mom the harmonica. My older brother, Bill, could do a job on almost any instrument. My other brother, Albert, played the old honky-tonk style of piano. My sister, Margaret — we called her Mutz — was the only one of us who ever took a music lesson. She played piano. I was a banjo man from the start."[4]

Grimm dropped out of school after the sixth grade. That "wasn't unusual in those days," he said. "That's how far my father had gone too."[5] Grimm's German-born father wanted him to join the family painting business, but young Charlie had other ideas. "On the weekends I worked as a peanut vendor in old Robison (Field), the Cardinals' park on Natural Bridge Road," he said. "That's where I really got started, shagging flies for the ballplayers before the games. I came to know the great stars — Ed Konetchy, Hal Chase, Bobby Wallace, Roger Bresnahan, Slim Sallee, Bill Doak, and all the others. Chase took a liking to me and tried to teach me the footwork of a first baseman, but I never did learn to shift properly. It was easier for me to catch a wide throw, in the air or in the dirt, with my bare left hand than backhanding it with the glove."[6]

The 17-year-old Grimm signed with the Philadelphia Athletics on July 28, 1916. He appeared in his first major-league game on July 30, starting in left field; one teammate taking the field that day was second baseman and future Hall of Famer Nap Lajoie, who retired less than a month later. On September 1 Grimm had a memorable encounter: "Connie Mack sent me up to hit against Walter Johnson in Washington, but I wasn't at the plate long. I didn't even swing on one of the three strikes, and I still have the bat I carried to the plate that day. It's just like new. All I can tell you about Johnson is that I saw him raise his arm."[7] Grimm batted .091 with two hits in 22 at-bats during 12 games with the 1916 Athletics, whose record of 36-117 (.235) was one of the worst ever.

Grimm was sold by the Athletics to the Durham Bulls of the Class D North Carolina State League. He played in 29 games with the Bulls in 1917. He returned to his hometown in 1918 and appeared in 50 games with the Cardinals; he had a .220 batting average. Among his teammates were 22-year-old shortstop Rogers Hornsby and 44-year-old infielder Bobby Wallace. Grimm also played in 56 games that year with the Little Rock Travelers of the Class A Southern Association.

In 1919 Grimm appeared in 131 games with Little Rock, batting .285 and compiling a .993 fielding average at first base. He was acquired by the Pittsburgh Pirates and played in 14 September games, with a .318 batting average. On September 11 against the Philadelphia Phillies, Grimm went 4-for-4 (all singles), scored two runs, drove in two runs, and stole a base.

During spring training in 1920, "George Whitted, a third baseman-outfielder, asked me if I could sing bass," Grimm said. "I accepted his invitation for an audition and easily made the Pirates' quartet, which included Cotton Tierney and some other substitutes until Rabbit Maranville came along a year later."[8] According to Grimm, "Before each game we'd gather behind the batting cage at home plate and serenade the fans. We weren't inflicting our harmony on them, they demanded it. Deep in my memory of those days are the fans who arrived from the coal mines with lamps still attached to their caps. Then, after the ballgame, we'd get together almost every evening to knock off a few tunes after dinner."[9]

Grimm played five full seasons with Pittsburgh. In 1920 he led National League first basemen in fielding percentage (.995) while batting .227. In 1921 he raised his batting average to .274 and had a 20-game hitting streak. He tied for third in the NL in triples, with 17, and led the Pirates in RBIs, with 71. His fielding percentage of .994 at first base was second highest in the NL. In 1922 he batted .292 and drove in 76 runs despite hitting no home runs. His rate of 39.5 at-bats per strikeout was fifth best in the NL. For the second year in a row, his fielding percentage of .994 was second best among NL first basemen.

Grimm had his best year offensively in 1923, with a .345 batting average and 99 RBIs. After a five-game hitting streak to end the 1922 season, Grimm had a base hit in the first 25 games of 1923. He led the NL in fielding percentage as a first baseman (.995).

In 1924 Grimm had a standout year defensively. He led the majors in putouts (1,596) and led all first basemen in double plays turned (139) and fielding percentage (.995) while batting .288. Pittsburgh was only 1½ games behind the first-place New York Giants on September 21, then lost three straight to the Giants at the Polo Grounds

before finishing in third place. Pirates owner Barney Dreyfuss believed the fun-loving ways of Grimm and second baseman Maranville (a heavy drinker) were a distraction to the team, and on October 27 he traded the pair, along with pitcher Wilbur Cooper, to the Chicago Cubs for pitcher Vic Aldridge, infielder George Grantham, and first-base prospect Al Niehaus.

At spring training in 1925 on Catalina Island in California, it didn't take long for Grimm for find kindred spirits: "Even before I had unloaded my stuff in the locker I had become a member of the Cubs' string band. Hack Miller, the muscular outfielder, played a guitar that was held together with bicycle tape. Barney Friberg, the third baseman, played the mandolin. Cliff Heathcote's instrument was the ukulele. I quickly brought my left-handed banjo out of hiding. We had a group."[10]

That year he batted .306 and had a four-hit game in five consecutive months (April through August). He led the

"Jolly Cholly" Grimm played for the Cubs for 12 seasons, anchoring first base on the 1929 and 1932 pennant winners. He also guided the club to the 1935 pennant as manager. (Retro Images Archive. George Brace Collection)

Cubs in RBIs (76) and on-base percentage (.354) and tied for 13th in the NL MVP voting (the only member of the last-place Cubs to receive votes). He was also named team captain by Rabbit Maranville, who served as a player-manager for less than two months. (Grimm remained the captain, or "Der Kaptink," until 1932.)

In 1926 Grimm batted .277 and had 82 RBIs. In 1927, he had a .311 batting average. And in 1928, he led the league in fielding percentage as a first baseman (.993) and turned 147 double plays in 147 games. He batted .294, with a five-hit game on June 18 and four-hit games on July 26 (14 innings) and August 4.

In 1929, when the Cubs won the pennant, Grimm had a .298 batting average and drove in 91 runs even though he missed 35 games in August and September with a broken hand. In Game Four of the World Series against the Philadelphia Athletics, Grimm hit a two-run homer off 46-year-old Jack Quinn. During the Series, which the Cubs lost to the Athletics in five games, Grimm batted .389 and drove in four runs.

In his autobiography, Grimm wrote, "The best team I ever played on was [Joe] McCarthy's twenty-niners. It was strictly power all the way. No tricky baseball. Kiki Cuyler was the only one who could take an extra base, but who needs finesse with sluggers such as [Hack] Wilson, Hornsby, [Riggs] Stephenson, and Cuyler? And to think that Hartnett was on the bench [with an arm injury] most of the season!"[11]

In 1930 Grimm led NL first basemen in fielding percentage for a fifth time (.995) while batting .289. He had one of his better years offensively in 1931, with a batting average of .331 and an on-base percentage of .393. On June 21 against the Brooklyn Robins, he went 5-for-5. He again topped in the league in fielding percentage as a first baseman (.993). Grimm was eighth in the NL MVP voting.

On August 2, 1932, with the Cubs trailing the Pirates by five games, Hornsby was let go as manager, and Grimm accepted the position. The next morning he called the team together: "[H]e told the men that he had served under good managers who had taught him what he had to do to help the club. His success, and theirs, he said, would come down to one thing: 'Hustle. We're facing a fight and we have a fine chance to win this pennant. I'm depending on every fellow on the club to give his best. And I know he will.' He also announced that English would replace him as captain."[12] August 16 was Charlie Grimm Day at Wrigley Field, and the player-manager was presented with five-foot-high baskets of roses, bouquets, and a platinum watch.

The Cubs, who had chafed under the dictatorial style of Hornsby, responded well to the affable Grimm. The team went 37-18 (.673) under his leadership in 1932, with 14 consecutive wins from August 20 to September 3, and took the pennant by four games over the Pirates. Grimm batted .307 for the season and had 80 RBIs. He tied for fifth in the NL in doubles (42). He led NL first basemen in double plays turned, with 127. The Cubs were swept in the World Series by the New York Yankees; Grimm batted .333. His former manager on the Cubs, Joe McCarthy, won the first of seven World Series titles with the Yankees.

In 1933 Grimm's first full season as a manager, he played in 107 games and batted .247. He also led the majors in fielding percentage as a first baseman (.996). The Cubs had an 86-68 record and finished third. The following year, Grimm batted .296 in 75 games as the Cubs went 86-65 and again finished in third place.

Grimm won his second pennant as a manager in 1935. (He played in only the first two games of the season.) The Cubs had 100 wins — the most by the team since 1910 — and 54 losses. Chicago won 21 straight games from September 4 to 27, allowing more than three runs in a game only once during the streak. The Cubs had the lowest ERA in the majors (3.26) and led the NL in batting average (.288) and runs scored (847). Standouts included NL MVP Gabby Hartnett (.344, 91 RBIs), Billy Herman (.341, 227 hits, 57 doubles), Augie Galan (203 hits, 133 runs), and pitchers Bill Lee (20-6), Lon Warneke (20-13), and Larry French (17-10).

In his autobiography, Grimm wrote, "The best team I managed was the 1935 group. It had balance with slick pitching, fielding, batting, and some speed. A team has to be great to win twenty-one in a row. It also has to be a trifle lucky. And I don't believe any club ever won a pennant unless five or six of its key players had a top season."[13] But the team's luck faltered in the World Series, as the Cubs lost to the Detroit Tigers in six games.

In 1936 Grimm's last season as a player-manager, he played in 39 games, batted .250, and played his final major-league game on September 23; he was 38 years old. Over his career, he played in 2,166 games, got 2,299 hits, hit 79 home runs, and drove in 1,077 runs. His fielding percentage at first base was .993. When he retired as a player, only Jake Beckley and Cap Anson had played more games at the position. As of 2014, Grimm was among the top ten first basemen in games, putouts, and double plays turned.

Grimm guided the Cubs to an 87-67 record in 1936 (tied for second place) and a 93-61 record in 1937 (second place). On July 20, 1938, with the Cubs at 45-36 and trailing the first-place Pirates by 5½ games, Grimm was replaced by Gabby Hartnett. He moved to the broadcast booth, and the Cubs won the pennant that year. Grimm rejoined the Cubs as a coach in 1941, then left after he and Bill Veeck, Jr. (son of the former president of the Cubs) bought the Milwaukee Brewers of the American Association. Grimm went on to manage the team, which had a working agreement with the Cubs.

According to Grimm, "One of Veeck's first projects was organizing a little musical group that played concerts before each game. Bill's instrument was a big whistle with holes in it and a plunger to control the air. Rudie [Schaffer] played a home-made bass fiddle, consisting of a five-gallon paint can and a broomstick with a cord on it, which produced a thumping noise. George Blaeholder, a veteran pitcher who has been credited with introducing the now popular slider, played the accordion, and I chimed in with my banjo."[14] Grimm managed the Brewers through 1943, winning a pennant and the Little World Series that year.

The Cubs got off to a miserable start in 1944 and wanted Grimm back at the helm. He called on an old friend to replace him as manager in Milwaukee: Casey Stengel, who at the time had an undistinguished record of 581-742 piloting the Brooklyn Dodgers and Boston Braves. With the Cubs having lost ten straight after an Opening Day win, Grimm took over as manager on May 5. The Cubs lost the next three games. Then on May 11, before Chicago starter Ed Hanyzewski took the mound against Philadelphia, Grimm gave him a four-leaf clover, which the pitcher wore under his cap; the Cubs won 5-3. The team went 74-69 under Grimm in 1944, winning 11 consecutive games from July 25 through August 5. He wrote in his autobiography, "I like to think that the sharp turnabout of these 1944 Cubs might have been due, at least in part, to my philosophy that a manager should keep his players relaxed and save the whip for a lion tamer."[15]

Grimm won his third pennant as a manager in 1945, with a record of 98-56. The Cubs topped the NL in batting average (.277), ERA (2.98), and fielding percentage (.980). First baseman Phil Cavarretta led the league in batting (.355) and on-base percentage (.449), drove in 97 runs, and won the NL MVP Award. Pitcher Hank Borowy, purchased from the Yankees on July 27, went 11-2 with the Cubs and had the lowest ERA (2.13) in the senior circuit; he won the *Sporting News* NL Pitcher of the Year Award.

Grimm relied heavily on his new ace during the World Series against the Tigers, a strategy that proved costly. Borowy threw a shutout in Game One and pitched into the sixth inning in Game Five (giving up five runs). The next day he threw four scoreless innings in relief as the Cubs won, 8-7 in 12 innings. Two days after that, Grimm sent Borowy to the mound again to start Game Seven. The hurler did not retire a batter, giving up singles to the first three batters (all of whom would score). Leading 5-0 before the Cubs came to bat, the Tigers won, 9-3.

The Cubs slumped under Grimm over the next three seasons, going 82-71 in 1946 (third place), 69-85 in 1947 (sixth place), and 64-90 in 1948 (eighth and last place). In mid-June of 1949, with the Cubs at 19-31, Grimm was fired and replaced by Frankie Frisch. He became vice president in charge of player operations. He resigned in early 1950 to manage the Dallas Eagles of the Double-A Texas League. In 1951 Grimm returned to Milwaukee to manage the Brewers in the Triple-A American Association. He led the team, a Boston Braves affiliate, to another pennant and Little World Series title. Grimm won *The Sporting News* Minor League Manager of the Year Award.

On May 30, 1952, Grimm was named manager of the Boston Braves, replacing Tommy Holmes. The Braves, who had a 13-22 record when Grimm took over, went 51-67 the rest of the season. He remained the manager when the team moved to Milwaukee the next year. Under his leadership, the Milwaukee Braves were 92-62 in 1953 (second place), 89-65 in 1954 (third place), and 85-69 in 1955 (second place). With a 24-22 record in 1956 Grimm was fired and replaced by Fred Haney. Grimm later wrote of his disappointment at being let go before being able to bring a pennant to Milwaukee. (The Braves won the 1957 pennant and the World Series over the New York Yankees.)

Grimm returned to the Cubs, serving as vice president from 1957 through 1959 and managing the first 17 games of the 1960 season, with a 6-11 record. In an unusual swap, Grimm replaced Lou Boudreau in the WGN radio broadcast booth, and Boudreau became manager of the Cubs. In Grimm's three stints as manager in Chicago, he had a record of 946-782. His career record during 19 seasons as manager was 1,287-1,067. He is one of the few men in the major leagues to both play in 2,000 games and manage 2,000 games.

Grimm served on the Cubs' coaching staff from 1961 to 1963, then rejoined the front office, where he remained until 1981. He was inducted into the Wisconsin Athletic Hall of Fame in 1978. Just north of Madison, Wisconsin, is the town of Windsor, where one can drive on Charlie Grimm Road.

Grimm died of cancer on November 15, 1983, in Scottsdale, Arizona; he was 85 years old. Adhering to his wishes, Grimm's wife, Marion, scattered his ashes over Wrigley Field. In 2009 he was one of ten finalists for the Veterans Committee managers/umpires ballot for the Baseball Hall of Fame.

SOURCES

Ehrgott, Roberts, *Mr. Wrigley's Ball Club: Chicago and the Cubs During the Jazz Age* (Lincoln, Nebraska: University of Nebraska Press, 2013).

Finoli, David, and Bill Ranier, *The Pittsburgh Pirates Encyclopedia* (New York: Sports Publishing, 2003).

Grimm, Charlie, with Ed Prell, *Jolly Cholly's Story: Baseball, I Love You!* (Chicago: Henry Regnery Company, 1968).

James, Bill, *The New Bill James Historical Baseball Abstract* (New York: Free Press, 2003).

Porter, David L., ed., *Biographical Dictionary of American Sports: Baseball* (volume 2) (Westport, Connecticut: Greenwood Press, 2000).

Skipper, John C., *The Cubs Win the Pennant! Charlie Grimm, the Billy Goat Curse, and the 1945 World Series Run* (Jefferson, North Carolina: McFarland and Company, 2004).

Snyder, John, *Cubs Journal: Year by Year and Day by Day With the Chicago Cubs Since 1876* (Cincinnati: Emmis Books, 2005).

Spatz, Lyle, ed., *The SABR Baseball List & Record Book* (New York: Scribner, 2007).

Stout, Glenn, *The Cubs: The Complete Story of Chicago Cubs Baseball* (New York: Houghton Mifflin, 2007).

Sugar, Bert Randolph, ed., *The Baseball Maniac's Almanac*, third edition (New York: Sports Publishing, 2012).

"Charlie Grimm Is Dead at 85; Baseball Player and Manager," *New York Times*, November 17, 1983.

"Ex-Braves skipper Charlie Grimm dies," *Milwaukee Sentinel*, November 16, 1983.

Baseball-Reference.com

Retrosheet.org

NOTES

1 Bill James, *The New Bill James Historical Baseball Abstract*, 471.

2 Roberts Ehrgott, *Mr. Wrigley's Ball Club: Chicago and the Cubs during the Jazz Age*, 83.

3 Charlie Grimm with Ed Prell, *Jolly Cholly's Story: Baseball, I Love You!*, 4.

4 Grimm, 8.

5 Grimm, 9.

6 Grimm, 9-10.

7 Grimm, 11.

8 Grimm, 15.

9 Grimm, 17.

10 Grimm, 25.

11 Grimm, 236.

12 Ehrgott, 305.

13 Grimm, 236.

14 Grimm, 149-150.

15 Grimm, 160.

GABBY HARTNETT

By William H. Johnson

ECOUNTED AND SAVORED OVER generations, four iconic moments share a single connective thread. In each tableau, Chicago Cubs catcher Gabby Hartnett was not only present at the moment, but was an active participant in the various scenes. Even without those brushes with what came to approach mythological status, Gabby Hartnett was a Hall of Fame player. He carved out a career as one of the finest catchers ever to play the game, and into the 21st century was still widely acknowledged as the best catcher in the National League during his playing career in the 1920s and 1930s. In his life span of 72 years, almost to the minute, he wasted few moments, on the diamond or off. In any litany of baseball memories from the 1930s, perhaps no event stands out more than Babe Ruth's "called shot" home run off Cubs pitcher Charlie Root in the 1932 World Series, unless it was the feat of New York Giants pitcher Carl Hubbell and his consecutive strikeouts of five future Hall of Fame hitters (Ruth, Gehrig, Foxx, Simmons, and Cronin) in the 1934 All-Star Game. For Cardinals fans and baseball historians, the 1937 All-Star Game will remain forever cast in notoriety because of the injury to Dizzy Dean's big toe from Earl Averill's shot back through the box, an injury that caused Dean to change his delivery and led to an all-too-premature career-ending injury. Finally, though certainly not least, was the famous 1938 "Homer in the Gloamin'," a shot whose momentum propelled the Cubs past the Pittsburgh Pirates and into the World Series. Gabby Hartnett was a critical part of each of those dramas.

Charles Leo Hartnett was born on December 20, 1900, in Woonsocket, Rhode Island, the eldest of 14 children born to Fred and Ellen "Nell" (Tucker) Hartnett. Fred, a laborer, moved his family to Millville, Massachusetts, just over the state line from Woonsocket, when he took a job at Banigan's Millville Rubber Shop. Fred played semipro baseball in his younger years and managed the Millville town team for a period, and was considered to have a tremendous throwing arm. It was a genetic legacy he passed to his son, Leo.

The boy, known as Leo but called Dowdy by the locals, after his father, grew up listening to his father talk baseball. As soon as Leo was able, he began playing baseball, and gravitated to the role of catcher, just as his father had. At 14 Leo finished the eighth grade at Longfellow Grammar School and took a job as a laborer at the Rubber Shop.[1] He also joined the town's baseball team, along with another future professional, Tim McNamara, who went to Fordham University and pitched for the Boston Braves and New York Giants from 1922 through 1926. Though Leo later left the Rubber Shop to attend the prestigious Dean Academy in nearby Franklin, Massachusetts, it was on the baseball diamond that he got his education.

The young catcher had a terrific throwing arm, so good that in 1920 the American Steel and Wire Company in Worcester offered him a job in its shipping department just so he could play on the company baseball team. Hartnett thrived, perhaps even discovering that work was occasionally getting in the way of baseball, instead of the reverse. There is a story, impossible to prove but widely recounted and intriguing, that the New York Giants' John McGraw heard of Hartnett and sent scout Jesse Burkett to have a look at the prospect. Evidently Burkett felt the catcher's hands were too small for major-league baseball, so the Giants passed. What is a matter of record is that Hartnett signed his first professional baseball contract with the Worcester Boosters of the Class A Eastern League on March 12, 1921.

Appearing in 100 games for Worcester, Hartnett played well enough that Cubs scout Jack Doyle offered him $2,500 to sign with Chicago. Leo accepted and the Cubs sent him to spring training with the team on Catalina Island, off the Southern California coast. Hartnett did not immediately impress manager Bill Killefer, who already had Bob O'Farrell on the roster as his primary backstop, and it took Doyle's intervention to persuade Killefer to give Hartnett a legitimate trial at catcher. The manager had the youngster catch Grover Cleveland Alexander for a full game, and afterward the pitcher told his manager that Hartnett was "all right."² That verdict was enough to keep Leo on the Chicago roster.

Backing up starting catcher O'Farrell in 1922, the 21-year-old Hartnett barely spoke to anyone, especially not to newspaper reporters. In view of his awkward shyness, teammates and the press dubbed him Gabby, an ironic moniker at the time, but one that he actually grew into as he aged, developing a reputation as something of a chatterbox crouched behind home plate. "… Bill Killefer still wasn't sure where (Hartnett) would best fit in, since the Cubs had one of the best catchers in the league in Bob O'Farrell. Killefer considered playing Hartnett in the outfield, or at first base, but the outfield was finally ruled out because of Hartnett's lack of speed. … He was tabbed as O'Farrell's understudy and a backup at first base."³

After making his major-league debut on April 12, 1922, Hartnett appeared in only 34 games and collected a mere 14 hits for the season. Behind the plate, though, he made only two errors, a mark that highlighted his value as a defensive backup and kept him on the roster for the next season. In 1923 Gabby's batting average climbed over 70 points, and when O'Farrell was injured in 1924, Hartnett was poised to fill the void. Making the most of the opportunity, he hit .299 and homered 16 times in 111 games, and finished tied for 15th in voting for the National League's Most Valuable Player.

From then on Hartnett played his position better than any of his predecessors and most of his successors. Large for the time, the 6-foot-1, 195-pound Gabby became the first player to hit five or more homers in the first six games of a season, and then went on to break the single-season record for home runs by a catcher in 1925 with 24. "… (Harnett) discovered how to exploit the newly inviting left-field fence and smashed a one-season team record 22 home runs (and moreover, the major league's venerable single-season mark for catchers) by midseason, then slumped badly in the second half after Veeck removed most of the left-field bleachers. …"⁴ In spite of the slump, he finished second in the league in home runs, trailing only Rogers Hornsby's 39. In 1924 and 1925, only 136 bases were swiped off Hartnett, compared with a league average of 178 against other starting catchers.⁵ During his 1926 season he demonstrated the necessary maturity behind the plate by throwing out 60 percent of the runners attempting steals against him while finishing third among National League catchers in assists and tied for third in putouts.

Hartnett's 1927 season saw his offensive production increase to the point that he finished tenth in the league's Most Valuable Player balloting. The Cubs carried two catchers for most of the year, 26-year-old Gabby and Cuban-born Mike Gonzalez, a decade older. Hartnett carried the brunt of the catching load for the fourth-place team, appearing in 127 games while improving his batting average to .294, and leading the circuit in putouts, assists, errors, and runners caught stealing.

He continued his growth the following year, 1928, with a .302 batting average, 26 doubles, 9 triples, and 14 homers in only 388 at-bats, but the Cubs managed only a one-place improvement, to third. He also earned yet another nickname. "As he grew older and added weight, the big catcher developed a ruddy complexion, resulting in the nickname 'Old Tomato Face,'" a biographer wrote. "According to one sportswriter, 'There were three distinguishing characteristics associated with the likeable Irish-American — a red face, a big cigar, and a laugh in which he simply wound up and let go, laughing all over. His frame shook like a dilapidated jalopy.'"⁶

As spring training began in 1929, on Catalina Island just off the coast of Los Angeles, Hartnett and his new bride, Martha Henrietta (Marshall) Hartnett, planned to use the trip as both preseason conditioning and a honeymoon on the isolated resort.⁷ The couple, married on January 28, had a son, Charles Leo Jr. (known as Bud), born in December 1931, and a daughter, Sheila, born in June 1935.

Mitigating the matrimonial bliss, though, was unexplained deadness in Hartnett's right arm, which ultimately limited his season to one game in the field and 25 pinch-hit appearances. Unable to throw well and unresponsive to treatment, Hartnett rested for the year. While he did come to bat three times as a pinch-hitter during the 1929 World Series against the Philadelphia Athletics, he did not record a hit in his first postseason contests. Whatever the cause of the malady, Hartnett recovered to the point that he was able to post a .339 batting average in 1930, with career highs in hits (172), runs scored (84), home runs (37), RBIs (122), slugging (.630) and OPS (1.034), while committing only eight errors in 136 games behind the plate. Also, on the defensive side, Hartnett led the league catchers in putouts (646), assists (68), and runners caught stealing (36).

In 1932 the Cubs won the pennant by four games over the Pittsburgh Pirates, and faced the Yankees in the World Series. The Cubs pitchers sported the lowest earned-run average in the league that year (3.44), in part due to Hartnett's experience calling the games. During the top of the fifth inning in Game Three of the Series, Hartnett was behind the plate when Babe Ruth raised his arm and gestured toward the pitcher and the outfield. According to Hartnett biographer William McNeil, Gabby later said, "I don't want to take anything from the Babe, because he's the reason we made good money, but he didn't call the shot. He held up the index finger of his left hand … and said, 'It only takes one to hit.'"[8] Regardless of whether Ruth did or did not "call his shot," the story has become an apocryphal slice of baseball lore, one that refuses to fade with time.

Hartnett, however, was too busy with the 1933 season to fret over Chicago's sweep by the Yankees in 1932 despite his .313 batting average in the Series. At the top of his game, he was selected as a National League reserve in the inaugural All-Star Game. The next year, batting .336 with 13 home runs by the time of the game, he was named the starting catcher in a battery with Giants ace Carl Hubbell. It was in the top of the first inning, after a leadoff single by Charlie Gehringer and a walk to Heinie Manush, that Hubbell started his historic streak. He struck out Ruth, Lou Gehrig, and Jimmie Foxx to end the inning, and then picked up where he left off in the second, whiffing Al Simmons and Joe Cronin before Bill Dickey broke up the string with a base hit. Hartnett went 0-for-2 at the plate, but never played a more memorable All Star Game.

The following season, 1935, was one of Hartnett's best. His body was 34 years old, but he played as if he were ten years younger, and his mind was as sharp as ever. He batted .344, made only nine errors in 110 games and led the Cubs to the World Series against the Detroit Tigers. Hartnett played well that postseason, batting .292, but the Cubs fell in six games. After the season he was named the National League's Most Valuable Player, over pitcher Dizzy Dean of the St. Louis Cardinals and Arky Vaughn of the Pittsburgh Pirates, a small comfort for again falling short of a championship.

In 1937 Harnett was again selected for the All Star Game, his fifth consecutive appearance, and found himself behind the plate paired with Cardinals rival Dizzy Dean. In the bottom of the third inning, with two outs and the game scoreless, Dean gave up a single to Joe DiMaggio and a home run to Lou Gehrig. Earl Averill then smote a sharp drive directly back to the mound, a hit so hard that it clipped the pitcher's left foot before finding second baseman Billy Herman's glove for the eventual throw and the putout at first base. Dean left the game, his career

A Chicago institution, Hartnett was injured for most of the 1929 season and played in only one game behind the plate. The six-time All-Star and recipient of the 1935 NL MVP award, Hartnett starred on the club's three pennant-winning teams in the 1930s, the final of which he led as player-manager. (Retro Images Archive. George Brace Collection)

changed forever. Averill's low line shot had broken the big toe on Dean's left foot, and when the pitcher tried to come back before it had fully healed, he altered his delivery to avoid the pain. That caused Dean to permanently damage his arm and finally retire from the game prematurely (but not before pitching for three seasons for the Hartnett-managed Cubs).

Hartnett finished a close second behind the Cardinals' Joe Medwick in MVP voting in 1937, but he saved his greatest moment for 1938, and another Chicago pennant chase. On July 20, 1938, the Cubs languished in third place in the standings, 5½ games behind league leader Pittsburgh, despite having won seven straight games after a six-game losing skid during the preceding two weeks. Chicago owner Philip Wrigley fired established manager Charlie Grimm and replaced him with novice Hartnett. The move worked. By late September the Cubs were 1½ games out of first and had a three-game series in Chicago remaining with the Pirates. After the Cubs won the first game to pull within a half-game of the lead, the teams met again at Wrigley Field on September 28.

With the score tied at 5-5 after eight innings, and as the early-autumn darkness threatened the unlighted stadium, the umpires agreed that the ninth inning would be the last of the day. They also decided that, in the event of a makeup the following day, the entire game would be replayed, and not just picked up where it was stopped. Hartnett came to bat against the Pirates' standout relief pitcher, Mace Brown, with two out in the bottom of the ninth. Brown used the reduced visibility to his advantage and got two quick fastball strikes on the catcher. With darkness setting in and visibility decreasing, Brown inexplicably threw Hartnett a high curve. Gabby knocked the pitch over the fence in left-center field, and into immortality. "Most fans were unable to follow the flight of the ball in the darkness, but when it settled into the left field seats for a walk-off home run, Wrigley Field erupted with a deafening roar that could be heard for blocks. Thousands of … spectators came spilling out of the stands screaming and racing toward the diamond."[9]

Hartnett said, "I swung with everything I had, and then I got that feeling, the kind of feeling you get when the blood rushes out of your head and you get dizzy. A lot of people have told me they didn't know the ball was in the bleachers. Well, I did. Maybe I was the only one in the park who did. I knew the moment I hit it. … I don't think I saw third base … and I don't think I walked a step to the plate — I was carried in."[10] The "Homer in the Gloamin'," as it is remembered, remains one of the signature walk-off home runs of all time. The Cubs won again the next day to complete a series sweep of the Pirates. The 10-1 victory capped a ten-game Chicago winning streak that placed the Cubs on the path to win the NL pennant by two games. The ending was not entirely happy, however, as the Cubs were swept in the World Series by the Yankees.

Hartnett, now under media scrutiny as the Cubs' manager, began to show the strain. He was accused by some players of favoring pitcher Dizzy Dean; there were other petty squabbles; and Gabby found himself catching more often than he'd have liked simply because his was the best bat on the team among the catchers. On August 28, 1939, Hartnett's durability was formally acknowledged when he caught his 1,728th game, breaking Ray Schalk's major-league record for games caught by a catcher. (The record has since been broken by several catchers.)

After the 1940 season, following nearly two decades with the club and despite a three-season record of 203-176 (.536), Hartnett was abruptly fired as manager on November 13. Less than a month later, on December 10, he signed as a player-coach with the New York Giants, and, at the age of 40, hit .300 in 64 games in 1941. On September 24 of that season, Hartnett went 1-for-4 against the Philadelphia Phillies in what proved to be his final big-league game.

Not quite done with baseball, Hartnett managed five seasons in the minors from 1942 through 1946. In 1942 he managed Indianapolis of the American Association to a 76-78 record, and from 1943 through 1945 led Jersey City of the International League. In 1946, his final year managing, he piloted Buffalo of the International League.

After retiring from baseball, Hartnett opened Gabby Hartnett's Recreation Center in Lincolnwood, a Chicago suburb. The enterprise ultimately grew to 20 bowling lanes, a barbershop, a soda fountain, a cocktail lounge, and a sporting-goods store. On January 26, 1955, with a career major-league batting average of .297, 1,912 hits, and one of the most famous home runs in the history of the game, he was elected to the Baseball Hall of Fame with an illustrious class that also included Joe DiMaggio, Ted Lyons, and Dazzy Vance.[11]

Hartnett lived his entire post-baseball life in Illinois. He was a coach and scout for the Kansas City Athletics for two years in the mid-1960s, but spent much of his time playing golf, hunting, and enjoying his golden years. His health deteriorated. In 1969 he was taken to the hospital after spitting blood on the golf course. The next year his spleen was removed, but it was an unwinnable fight. At 5:20 A.M. on his 72nd birthday, December 20, 1972, in Park Ridge, Illinois, Gabby Hartnett died of complications from cirrhosis of the liver. He is buried in All Saints Cemetery in Des Plaines, Illinois.

Hartnett's obituaries conveyed a portrait of a genuinely good man: "(It) was his winning personality that set him apart on the field — a friendly wave to the men in the press box, a hundred handshakes with friends he had made in every city in the circuit, and autographs for everyone, young and old, who asked him to sign."[12]

Nearly three decades after his death, as Major League Baseball built its All Century Team in 1999, Hartnett's achievements were sufficiently notable that he was a finalist, but he finished behind Johnny Bench and Yogi Berra in the voting. His greatest epitaph, though, was penned in his obituary: "'Old Tomato Face' they called him. His last game long since played, but his love of baseball undiminished to the end. … As man and player … Rhode Island can be proud to call him a native son."[13]

NOTES

1   William McNeil, *Gabby Hartnett: The Life and Times of the Cubs' Greatest Catcher* (Jefferson, North Carolina: McFarland, 2004), 31.

2   Roberts Ehrgott, *Mr. Wrigley's Ballclub* (Lincoln: University of Nebraska Press, 2013), 77.

3   McNeil., 50.

4   Ehrgott, 37.

5   McNeil, 64.

6   McNeil, 112.

7   McNeil, 152.

8   McNeil, 174.

9   McNeil, 256

10 Eddie Gold and Art Ahrens, *The Golden Era Cubs: 1876-1940* (Chicago: Bonus Books, 1985), 149.

11 William Mead, *Low and Outside: Baseball in the Depression, 1930-1939* (Alexandria, Virginia: Redefinition Books, 1990).

12 Irv Haag, "Baseball's All-Time Greatest Catchers," *Baseball Digest,* April 1973.

13 "Gabby Hartnett, Noble Son of R.I.," *Pawtucket Times,* December 26, 1972.

CLIFF HEATHCOTE

By William H. Johnson

Cliff Heathcote spent 14 of the 40 years of his life in the major leagues, and is largely remembered as half of one of the more memorable trades in baseball history; He was swapped for Max Flack between games of a 1922 doubleheader between the Cubs and the St. Louis Cardinals. That sliver of memory is an inadequate legacy for the talented defender, who was an important supporting piece in Chicago's 1929 pennant chase, batting .313 in 82 games and committing only two errors in the outfield.

Clifton Earl Heathcote was born in Pennsylvania on January 24, 1898, to woolen mill owner Spurgeon Heathcote and his wife, Annie (Kraft) Heathcote. Raised in the Glen Rock area, near York, Cliff attended the York Collegiate Institute, where proved better at basketball than at baseball. He entered Pennsylvania State University in 1917, but did not play baseball there, even though the school had a team. He accumulated two years of college credits while there,[1] but when the opportunity to give baseball a try presented itself, Cliff couldn't resist.

Heathcote signed with the St. Louis Cardinals in 1918, after impressing at a tryout camp, and was assigned to the Houston Buffaloes in the Class B Texas League. After 20 games, and only a month before the league suspended operations because of World War I, the young outfielder was called up to the big club, and made his major-league debut on June 4, 1918. The Cardinals were then at the very beginning of building an organization that would produce the great Gas House Gang teams of the 1930s, although predictions of their subsequent rise would have been ridiculed when the team signed Heathcote. That 1918 season had been shortened because of the government's work-or-fight order requiring men to join the armed forces or take defense jobs, and the Cardinals finished the campaign securely in last place. The following year Branch Rickey replaced Jack Hendricks as manager, and the team climbed to seventh place. The new manager began scouring the region for prospects, finding future stars like Jim Bottomley and supporting-cast members like outfielders Ray Blades and Heinie Mueller. Led on the field by Rogers Hornsby and piloted by the shrewd Rickey, the Cardinals tied for fifth place in 1920 and ascended to third place in 1921. It was a quiet nascence for what would prove to be a coming dynasty.

Just over a week after his promotion, Heathcote enjoyed what would prove to be the finest offensive day of his career on June 13, 1918, in front of 3,500 spectators at Philadelphia's Baker Bowl. During a 19-inning tilt that ended in an 8-8 tie, he led off and ended up hitting for the cycle, a home run, triple, double, and a single in nine at-bats. The opportunity for Heathcote's feat should never have arisen, but for the fact that the Phillies blew a six-run lead and let the Cardinals tie the game, 8-8, in the seventh. Despite Hornsby's four errors that afternoon, the two teams played 12 scoreless innings before the game was finally called at 9 P.M. The 20-year-old Heathcote batted a respectable .259 in 88 games with the Cardinals that season, although that was slightly offset by the 16 errors he committed playing in left field and center field.

It was his fielding, in fact, that earned Heathcote the sobriquet Rubberhead, after he lost a fly ball in the sun and it bounced off his head.[2] Despite that bit of notoriety, though, Heathcote became a regular in the St. Louis outfield for the next two seasons, batting .282 and stealing a total of 48 bases to accompany his demonstrably improved fielding. In 1921 his average slid below .250, and remained there during the first part of the 1922 season, and the dropoff led to one of the more notable trades in baseball history.

It happened at a Decoration Day (now called Memorial Day) doubleheader on May 30, 1922. The Cardinals sought to continue their climb. Rickey decided he needed a top-of-the-order hitter more than he did a young outfielder, and traded Heathcote for Cubs outfielder Max Flack.

Flack was almost a decade older than Heathcote, but was a competent baserunner and had stolen 37 bases in two different seasons. The entire Cardinals squad had stolen only 94 bases in 1921, and Flack represented an instant improvement. After the trade, in the second game of the doubleheader, Flack indeed led off for the Cardinals, but Heathcote went 2-for-4 at the plate in his new uniform, and helped the Cubs to a 3-1 win for a sweep. Later that season, on August 25, Heathcote proved the wisdom of the Chicago management when he set a modern National League record by reaching base seven times in a nine-inning game, in a wild 26-23 Cubs victory over the Phillies. Heathcote went 5-for-5 at the plate, walked twice, and scored five runs in contributing to a final tally that remains the highest score for a major-league game in the modern era. In 76 games with his new team, Heathcote hit .280 and scored 37 runs, and went a long way toward establishing a slot on the team for the next season.

He started in the Cubs' outfield in 1923 and 1924, recording a .309 batting average during the latter season, and by 1925 the slim player also came to be regarded as something of a females' fan favorite in Chicago. Heathcote's offseason job, overseeing a dairy route in Pennsylvania, was somewhat less than glamorous.[3] Before the 1925 season began, Cliff married a York native, Olga Beard. Sadly, both she and their baby son died during childbirth that year. He never remarried.

In 1926 Heathcote posted career highs of 10 home runs, 98 runs scored, 141 hits, and 33 doubles. He stole 18 bases. All this he accomplished while competing to hold a spot in an outfield that also included Riggs Stephenson and Hack Wilson. The Cubs, managed by Joe McCarthy, finished in fourth place in the National League. The next two seasons Heathcote platooned with Earl Webb in right field,[4] as center field and left field were semi-permanently occupied by Wilson and Stephenson. Heathcote fit in well with the team regardless of where he played,[5] and he teamed with Kiki Cuyler and Charlie Grimm to perform as a musical trio on occasions. Not only would Heathcote serenade teammates accompanied by his ukulele,[6] often unbidden, during train rides, but the combo occasionally performed at various Chicago clubs, generally whenever they were offered the opportunity.[7]

In 1929 Heathcote had his sole opportunity to play in the World Series. Despite batting .313 during the season,

Heathcote started 44 games in right field in place of the injured Kiki Cuyler in 1929 and batted a career-best .313 in 224 at-bats. (National Baseball Hall of Fame)

the outfielder was on the bench for Game One of the Series, the first ever played at Wrigley Field, against the Philadelphia Athletics and 35-year-old pitcher Howard Ehmke with more than 50,000 spectators. The Athletics' pitcher was a side-arm specialist and with more than 50,000 spectators in one of the more notable games in World Series history, he struck out a World Series-record (later broken) 13 Cubs batters. With one out in the bottom of the seventh, Heathcote pinch-hit for catcher Zack Taylor with Cuyler on third and Stephenson on second and the Cubs trailing 1-0. He flied out to short left field for the second out and Chicago failed to score. Philadelphia held on for a 3-1 win and Heathcote's World Series batting career was over.

In 1930 Heathcote's batting average dipped to .260, and he became even less relevant to the team. Before the 1932 season the Cubs put the outfielder on waivers and Cincinnati claimed him. As a reserve outfielder on the worst team in the league (43 games out of first place and 22 out of the first division), he batted .258 in 90 games.

After only three at-bats in eight games in 1932, the Reds released Heathcote. On June 25 the Phillies picked him up to serve as a backup to first baseman Don Hurst, but he played in only seven games at first, and in only 30 games overall. On September 24 in the first game of a doubleheader, Heathcote pinch-hitter in his final professional baseball game. The following April the Phillies released him. With no other suitors, he retired from baseball and returned to the dairy business in Pennsylvania.

On January 19, 1939, less than seven years after leaving baseball, Heathcote died of a pulmonary embolism in his hometown of York.[8] He is buried in the Mount Carmel Cemetery in nearby Littlestown, Pennsylvania.

Heathcote's major-league career spanned 15 seasons and 1,415 games, in which he amassed 1,222 hits and batted .275. He scored 643 runs and drove in 448. On balance, Heathcote was a gifted ballplayer but never a star, and was half of one of the oddest trades in baseball. He was a cog in the 1929 Cubs' juggernaut, and while only rarely did he personally determine the outcome of a game, he left his faint but indelible mark on one of the great seasons in Chicago baseball.

NOTES

1 Roberts Ehrgott, *Mr. Wrigley's Ball Club: Chicago and the Cubs During the Jazz Age* (Lincoln: University of Nebraska Press, 2013), 111.

2 Ehrgott, 103.

3 Ehrgott, 104.

4 Ehrgott, 98.

5 "Carlson, Heathcote Win First Tribune Awards," *Chicago Daily Tribune*, August 10, 1927, 21.

6 Irving Vaughan, "Cubs Spin Yarns, Eat, and Sing as Train Goes West," *Chicago Daily Tribune*, February 26, 1927, 21.

7 Ehrgott, 189.

8 Heathcote's file at the National Baseball Hall of Fame, Cooperstown, New York.

TRADER HORNE

By Dan Fields

THE MAJOR-LEAGUE CAREER OF BERLYN "Trader" Horne was brief. From April to July 1929, he threw 23 innings during 11 games with the Chicago Cubs, with a record of 1-1 and an earned-run average of 5.09. He was gone from the team before it won the pennant that year. But Horne (whose nickname came from an ivory trader and African adventurer known as Trader Horn) played in the minor leagues for 11 years before reaching the Cubs and for ten years after, winning 229 games and pitching more than 3,700 innings. He was also a serviceable hitter, with a batting average of about .250 in the minors; he could even claim a .400 average in the majors, with two hits in five at-bats. In the more than 40 years after his baseball career ended, Horne "never lost his love and enthusiasm for the sport."[1]

Berlyn Dale Horne was born on April 12, 1899, in Bachman, Ohio, about 15 miles northwest of Dayton. His parents, Joseph and Pearl Horne, also had two daughters, Mary (born in 1900) and Pearlyn (born in 1901). Horne wrote of his early years playing ball in a personal diary:

"Bachman was the beginning of baseball for me. They needed a pitcher so with the help of my Uncle Alex Hammel and his son, Howard "Dutch" Hammel, I was taught to pitch and how to throw the spitball. We had a good team of good ole farmer boys. We played all the good teams from Dayton and surrounding towns including Texters Lady Tourists who played three men on the team.

"We beat them easily and they wanted me to join their team, but my folks put thumbs down on that deal. They insisted I join them and guaranteed me $5 a game. Much more than I made with the Bachman team, which was $2 a game, but my folks resisted as I was too young, 14 years old. I continued to pitch for teams in Dayton as we moved there. I pitched for a church team, Tri M's, and we won all games but one over all the amateur teams and I averaged 18 strikeouts a game and had two no-hit games."[2]

Even as an adult, Horne was considered small for a ballplayer, standing 5-feet-9 and weighing 155 pounds. He threw right-handed and batted from both sides of the plate. Horne began in the minor leagues in 1917 with the Jacksonville Roses in the Class C Southern Atlantic League; he pitched in 25 games and had a record of 11-11. He didn't appear in the minors in 1918 but played on a team representing Plant 3 of the Dayton-Wright Airplane Company, which produced planes and aircraft engines for the US military in the World War.

After the war, Horne joined the Battle Creek Custers of the Class B Michigan-Ontario League. In 1919 he had a record of 19-9 and an ERA of 2.61. The next year his record fell to 8-15 despite an ERA of 3.07. He also played in the outfield for Battle Creek and displayed fine form at the plate. In 1920 he batted .276, with nine doubles, ten triples, and two home runs in only 228 at-bats.

In 1921, with the Port Huron Saints (also in the Michigan-Ontario League), Horne had a record of 16-13 and an ERA of 3.28. He also played the outfield and continued to hit well; he batted .270, with nine doubles, three triples, and a home run in 174 at-bats. With the Port Huron-Sarnia Saints the next year, Horne pitched in only 16 games (with a record of 6-7 and an ERA of 4.41) and played the outfield in 72 games. He batted .287, with 14 doubles, 11 triples, and 2 home runs in 296 at-bats. "I got to hitting pretty good, so they put me in the outfield regularly in 1922," said Horne. "And one day I went back for a line drive over my head that hit the wall. I stopped real fast to get the rebound off the fence and tore the ligaments in my left ankle."[3] The injury prevented a deal that would have sent him to the Pittsburgh Pirates.

In 1923, playing for the Saginaw Aces of the Michigan-Ontario League, Horne appeared in 27 games as a pitcher (with a 7-8 record and 3.87 ERA) and 29 games as a nonpitcher, with a batting average of .260 in 123 at-bats. By 1924 he was primarily being used as a pitcher. Horne began the year in Saginaw, with a record of 11-4 and an ERA of 2.80. Then he was acquired by the Rochester

(New York) Tribe of the Double-A International League. The team's owner and manager was George Stallings, who had managed the Miracle Boston Braves of 1914 to a World Series title. During the remainder of 1924, Horne won only three games while losing 11, with a 4.58 ERA.

But Horne was a productive starter for Rochester in 1925 (13-12, ERA of 3.86); 1926 (15-16, ERA of 4.26); and 1927 (18-10, ERA of 4.79). In 1926 he pitched in an exhibition game against the Cleveland Indians. After the game, Horne and future Hall of Famer Tris Speaker, the center fielder and manager of the Indians, crossed paths in the showers. "Young fellow, shut off that shower for a minute," said Speaker. "I want to talk to you. You pitched some pretty good ball out there today. I think you can get somewhere in this game. You should aim at the big leagues."

"I got two doubles off of you this afternoon," continued Speaker. "How'd I get them? I could tell you were going to give me the change of pace. You didn't hide the ball. The pitch was an open book."[4] Speaker then spent the next several minutes showing Horne how to hide the ball before making the pitch.

Horne had perhaps his finest year in the minors in 1928. Playing for the Jersey City Skeeters, who finished last in the International League, he had an ERA of 3.01 and a

In his only season in the majors, Horne made 11 appearances and won one game for the Cubs in 1929. He notched 229 wins in his 21-year career in the minors. (Library of Congress)

record of 16-17. Horne was a workhorse, pitching 266 innings in 44 games.

One of Horne's favorite memories from the minors was pitching to Babe Ruth for the first time, in a 1928 exhibition game. (Ruth had hit a record-setting 60 home runs for the Yankees in 1927.) Horne got Ruth to pop up in their initial encounter and was feeling pretty pleased with himself. "But in a later at-bat, Ruth hit a line drive up the middle so hard that Horne thought it would take his hat (and head) all the way to the center field fence, where paint chips went flying."[5]

While in Jersey City, Horne sometimes ate at a restaurant that Ruth frequented. "I used to go up Hudson Boulevard to Dick's Inn, a great eating place with great steaks," said Horne. "The Babe used to come over there and he used to call me 'boy' whenever he saw me."[6] Once, Ruth called him over to share a drink. "It was during Prohibition. But Dick always had a bottle for the Babe and a private room," according to Horne. "A friend of mine, another ballplayer, and I were in there one night eating and we looked in there and Babe said, 'Hey, little boy, come here. You gotta have a little nip with me or you don't eat tonight.' I said, 'I'll be right there, Babe.'"[7]

Thanks to Horne's success in 1928, he was sold to the Chicago Cubs and invited to 1929 spring training on Catalina Island, about 25 miles off the coast of Los Angeles. On February 14 Horne and other players boarded a train in Chicago that was bound for Los Angeles. During the journey he snapped photos of the landscape and sparked a flap with the news photographers on board. In a *Chicago Tribune* story filed from Flagstaff, Arizona, Edward Burns wrote, "Horne has been taking pictures of everything from the abode houses to mountain peaks so this morning the cameramen demanded he show his union credentials before snapping another picture.

"Horne, a quiet chap, explained that neither he nor his folks ever had been west of Danville, Ill., and that he was merely loading the family album. But the ornery photographers remained adamant and he sadly packed away his machine."[8] The Cubs players and manager Joe McCarthy rallied to Horne's defense, and the incident strengthened his bond with the rest of the team.

On April 11 Horne learned that he was one of nine pitchers to make the team. He made his major-league debut on April 24 against Pittsburgh; he was 30 years old. Horne relieved Charlie Root in the seventh inning and retired the first eight batters he faced. Through the 12th inning, Horne had faced 21 batters, striking out three and allowing two singles, a walk, and no runs. In the 13th inning, however, he walked two and then gave up a game-winning single.

On April 28, pitching against the Cincinnati Reds, Horne gave up three hits, three walks, and five runs (only one earned) in two-thirds of an inning. On May 21 he got his only major-league win, allowing no runs in 1⅓ innings of relief work against Pittsburgh. He also hit a single and scored his only major-league run. Horne pitched one inning each against the St. Louis Cardinals on May 25 and against the New York Giants on June 2, and allowed no hits or runs.

On June 5 Horne made his only major-league start. He pitched five innings against the Brooklyn Robins and allowed three runs, only one earned. He struck out three batters but walked seven. He hit a single and had a sacrifice hit. He left the game trailing 3-1 lead, but the Cubs won the game with four runs in the ninth inning. Horne allowed no runs against the Philadelphia Phillies on June 15 (one inning) and June 16 (two innings). At this point, he had an ERA of 1.47, with only two earned runs in 18⅓ innings (eight games). But he was rocked by St. Louis on June 17, allowing five earned runs, including a three-run home run to Chick Hafey, in a third of an inning, and by Pittsburgh on June 21, allowing four earned runs in two innings.

On July 11, in the second game of a doubleheader against the New York Giants, Horne worked 2⅓ innings and gave up one hit (a home run by Mel Ott) and two walks. He also threw a wild pitch. It turned out to be Horne's last game in the majors.

Horne was still with the Cubs in mid-August, when columnist Ernest J. Lanigan described how welcoming the team had been to the newcomer. "[Horne] informs me that [Rogers] Hornsby has been great to him, that Charlie Root has been great to him, that Joe McCarthy

has been wonderful to him and that he has gone out of his way to give him a pat on the back or to praise him for some little thing in which he was showing improvement."[9]

According to Lanigan, "Horne is always a favorite with the managers he works for, the reason being that he is a worker and not a moaner. He was tickled pink when he was purchased from Jersey City last fall. He had been kicking round the minor leagues for quite a few seasons and scouts were passing him up because of his size."[10]

In the column, Lanigan quoted from a letter Horne sent to him: "I certainly have been in luck getting with the Cubs and now I will have to stay with them. I never saw such a ball club in my life, though there may be others like it. For the good of the pastime, I hope there are. This club has spirit, teamwork, everybody pulling for the other fellow and everybody making it pleasant for rookies like myself. I had to wait a long time to get in fast company and when I did get in I got with one of the most remarkable baseball organizations."[11]

Less than a week after the column was published, first baseman Charlie Grimm slipped while running to catch a foul popup and broke a bone in his hand. The Cubs wanted Chick Tolson, playing for the Los Angeles Angels in the Pacific Coast League, to replace the injured Grimm, but Los Angeles wouldn't send Tolson unless they could have Horne. So the deal was made, although Joe McCarthy said that he "really didn't want the lad to get away."[12]

Horne played in Los Angeles for the remainder of 1929, with a record of 5-4 and an ERA of 6.06. After the season the Cubs divided the loser's share of the World Series money. Each player on the final roster was entitled to about $4,000, and the Cubs voted for Horne to get $2,000. He used the money to buy a new 1930 Chrysler. (He was said to have driven the car until it was a rusted heap, not wanting to part with what he called his "World Series car."[13]) In 1930 Horne had a 13-7 record and 4.47 ERA with Los Angeles.

In 1931 and 1932 Horne played for teams in five leagues: the Indianapolis Indians in the American Association (Double-A), the Jersey City Skeeters in the International

League (Double-A), the Knoxville Smokies in the Southern Association (Class A), the Omaha Packers in the Western League (Class A), and the Scranton Miners in the New York-Pennsylvania League (Class B). His longest stint was in Indianapolis, where he pitched in 30 games in 1931 and had a record of 9-9 and an ERA of 4.50.

In mid-1931, while Horne's wife, Hazel, was seven months pregnant, she had surgery to remove a brain tumor. Neurological damage from the surgery left her with some paralysis on one side of her face. The couple's son, Murray, was born on August 2, 1931.

From 1933 through 1937, Horne played for six teams in the Double-A Pacific Coast League: the Hollywood Stars, the Mission Reds, the Oakland Oaks, the Sacramento Senators, the San Diego Padres, and the Seattle Indians. During those five years, he had a record of 37-38 and an ERA of 4.09 in 170 appearances.

Horne's teammates in San Diego in 1936 included Vince DiMaggio, Bobby Doerr, and Ted Williams. According to teammate George Myatt, "We had a quartet on the club — Vince DiMaggio, Red Campbell, Berlyn Horne, and another player — and they sang 'Those Wedding Bells are Breaking Up that Old Gang of Mine.'"[14] Williams was fresh out of high school, where he was a star pitcher. "Frank [Shellenback], our manager, made an outfielder of Ted," said Horne. "He always had a bat in his hand and carried a bat on the train on our trips in the Coast League."[15]

Horne added that Williams "liked to eat and wanted to go eat with the older players so he could get our desserts, three or four extra desserts after our evening meals."[16]

In 1938, at the age of 39, Horne finished his professional career. He played for the Vancouver Maple Leafs and the Yakima Pippins in the Class B Western International League, with an overall record of 12-8 and an ERA of 3.91. Over the course of his 21-year minor-league career, Horne pitched 3,726⅓ innings in 676 games, with a record of 229-211 and an ERA of about 3.50 (statistics for earned runs in 1931 and 1932 are incomplete).

Horne and his family settled in California, where he worked as a carpenter. Horne's daughter-in-law Joan Scott said, "As a person, I found him to be delightful. He loved his son and his wife. He was never a large wage earner but was hardworking and steady in his company, Virtue Brothers furniture manufacturing in Torrance, California. The family were Republicans and Christian Scientists. Their home was modest, but warm and welcoming."[17]

After his wife died of colon cancer in 1957, Horne moved to Arcanum, Ohio, and later cared for his ailing mother, who died in 1977. As a child, writer Roger Snell walked past Horne's house on his way to and from school. "He lived five doors down the street," Snell recalled. "He often would be on his front-porch swing, listening to the Reds on [the] radio. I'd chat with him a little, and in the course of discussion I learned he played professional ball."[18] Snell later described the baseball career of this "quiet and kindly gentleman"[19] in his 2009 book on Charlie Root and the 1929 Cubs.

In 1981, while Horne was living in Franklin, Ohio, a bank awarded him two tickets to the World Series as part of a contest, but an arthritic hip made traveling difficult. Horne showed up at the bank in his Cubs warm-up jacket and chose a 19-inch color television so that he could watch the Series at home.

On February 3, 1983, Horne died in Franklin from complications of atherosclerosis; he was 83 years old. Nephew Andrew Kopp scattered his uncle's ashes from a plane over Bachman, Ohio. In a postcard to his family, Kopp wrote: "I took Berly on his last flight. … He wanted me to tell you that he is resting peacefully."[20] As noted by Roger Snell, the postcard was postmarked February 14, 1983 — exactly 54 years from the day Horne boarded a westbound train from Chicago toward spring training with the Cubs on Catalina Island.

On file at the Baseball Hall of Fame is a survey that Horne filled out when he retired from professional baseball. When asked if he would do it all again, he responded, "Absolutely!"[21]

SOURCES

Snell, Roger, *Root for the Cubs: Charlie Root and the 1929 Chicago Cubs* (Nicholasville, Kentucky: Wind Publications, 2009).

Ancestry.com

Baseball-Reference.com

Retrosheet.org

NOTES

1 Terry Baver, *Franklin* (Ohio) *Chronicle*, February 9, 1983, cited in Roger Snell, *Root for the Cubs: Charlie Root and the 1929 Chicago Cubs* (Nicholasville, Kentucky: Wind Publications, 2009), 231.

2 Snell, 119-120.

3 Snell, 121.

4 Al Nickerson, *Boston Sunday Advertiser*, 1929 (date unknown), cited in Snell, 122.

5 Snell, 122.

6 Terry Baver, *Franklin* (Ohio) *Chronicle*, August 5, 1980, cited in Snell, 122.

7 Ibid.

8 Edward Burns, *Chicago Tribune*, February 17, 1929.

9 Ernest J. Lanigan, "Fanning with Lanigan," August 15, 1929, cited in Snell, 158.

10 Snell, 159.

11 Ibid.

12 Snell, 160.

13 Snell, 230.

14 William G. Swank and James D. Smith III, "This Was Paradise: Voices of the Pacific Coast League Padres, 1936-1958," *Journal of San Diego History*, Winter 1995.

15 Snell, 230.

16 Ibid.

17 Joan Scott, personal communication with the author, August 2013.

18 Mike Curtin, "Cubs Star 'Nobody Knows' Given His Due Decades Later," *Columbus* (Ohio) *Dispatch*, April 14, 2009.

19 Snell, 2.

20 Snell, 231.

21 Snell, 2.

ROGERS HORNSBY

BY C. PAUL ROGERS, III

ANY CONVERSATION ABOUT THE greatest hitter in baseball history must include Rogers Hornsby in the opening gambit.[1] His .358 lifetime batting average in 23 big-league seasons is second all-time to Ty Cobb's .367 and well ahead of such all-time greats as Tris Speaker (.345), Ted Williams (.344), Babe Ruth (.342), Lou Gehrig (.340), and Stan Musial (.331). Further, there is really no debate that Hornsby is the greatest right-handed hitter of all time; he is significantly ahead of such notables as Harry Heilmann (.342) and Al Simmons (.334).

Along the way, Hornsby won seven National League batting titles and batted over .400 three times, including an unbelievable .424 in 1924, the best single season batting average in modern baseball history. Perhaps his most remarkable season was 1922, when he captured the Triple Crown. He not only led the league in seven major offensive categories, but he dominated the league in a way few others have. For example, his .401 batting average was almost 50 percentage points higher than that of Ray Grimes, who finished second; his 42 home runs were 16 more than anyone else; his 152 RBIs led the league by 20; his 250 hits led the league by 35; his 450 total bases were 136 more than Irish Meusel, who finished second; and his .722 slugging percentage led the league by 150 points.

Hornsby was so good that even umpires accorded him special reverence. One story, perhaps apocryphal but oft-repeated, described the time a pitcher complained after the legendary umpire Bill Klem called a close pitch a ball rather than strike three. Hornsby hit the next pitch out of sight for a home run and Klem allegedly told the pitcher, "See, Mr. Hornsby will tell you when it's close enough to be a strike."[2]

It is no wonder that Hornsby earned the sobriquet "the Rajah." After Rudolph Valentino starred in the silent film classic *The Sheik* in 1921, America became enthralled with all things "Arabian." As a result, Babe Ruth became known as the "Sultan of Swat," and Hornsby the "Rajah of Swat," soon shortened to "the Rajah."[3]

Hornsby, however, was almost as well known for his bluntness and complete lack of diplomacy as his prowess with a bat. He rarely argued with umpires but said whatever crossed his mind to anyone else, including the owners he worked for. Longtime Cardinals owner Sam Breadon remarked that listening to Hornsby was like have the contents of a rock crusher emptied over his head.[4]

Once when he was playing second base for the New York Giants in 1927, he was eating dinner with Eddie "Doc" Farrell, the team's young shortstop. A sportswriter stopped by the table and asked Hornsby if he thought the Giants could win the pennant.

"Not with Farrell playing shortstop," was his answer.[5]

No wonder Hornsby mostly ate alone.

Hornsby's managerial career was far less successful than his playing career, however, especially at the major-league level. He managed for all or part of 15 big-league seasons with six franchises, achieving by far his greatest success as player-manager of the 1926 world champion St. Louis Cardinals.[6] However, his overbearing, often irascible personality created poor relations with both players and owners, and led to his being fired at every post, sometimes in midseason. Like many great ballplayers who try to manage, he couldn't teach what had come so naturally to him, and he was easily frustrated by mediocrity.[7] As one writer put it, "Hornsby knew more about baseball and less about diplomacy than anyone I ever knew."[8]

Hornsby was born on April 27, 1896, on a farm two miles outside of the small town of Winters in Runnels County, Texas. He was the fifth child of Ed and Mary Rogers Hornsby and was named after his mother's family name. His father died when young Rogers was 2½ years old. Left with five children, the oldest of whom was only 14, Mary Hornsby moved the family back to her parents' farm about nine miles from Austin, Texas. There Rogers began playing baseball as a youngster in overalls and insisted on getting to play with the big kids.[9]

In the winter of 1902 and 1903, Mary moved her five children to the small city of Fort Worth, which had lured large meat-processing and packing houses to its stockyards, creating many jobs. The three older boys went to work as packers, while Rogers attended elementary school and played baseball with the neighborhood children. By the time he was 9, he was the leader of a semi-organized local team that had blue flannel uniforms sewn by his mother. The team sometimes traveled to games in other neighborhoods by trolley.[10] Young Rogers so loved his uniform that he wore it as much as possible, even around his own yard.[11]

By the age of 10, he was working in the summer as a messenger boy at the Swift & Company plant and serving as a batboy for one of the adult teams. He also sometimes played as a substitute infielder because he was adept in the field. At 15 he was playing with grown men for the North Side Athletics in the Fort Worth City League, as well as hiring out to other teams in the area. For example, in 1911 he played a dozen games for a team in Granbury, an hour southwest of Fort Worth, for $2 a game plus rail fare and room and board. He was already quite cocky. When the manager praised Hornsby's play at second base after a win over Weatherford, Hornsby replied, "Yeah, and there are eight other positions I can play just as good."[12]

The following year, Hornsby answered a local newspaper ad and joined the Boston Bloomer Girls, a traveling girls' baseball team that was touring Texas. Even though he learned that he was expected to wear a wig and bloomers and pretend to be a girl, the prospect of playing ball and making some money led him to sign on and play a number of games in North Texas.[13]

Hornsby had entered Fort Worth's new North Side High School in 1909 and played both baseball and football, playing in the same backfield with future football Hall of Famer Bo McMillin.[14] He dropped out, however, after two years to go to work as an office boy for the superintendent of the Swift & Company packing plant to help support his mother and sister. Although he played baseball whenever and wherever he could, he didn't overwhelm anyone with his talent. At 17 he was almost 6 feet tall but skinny as a rail. The result was that he was an adept fielder but, hard as it might be to believe, a weak hitter.[15]

In the spring of 1914 the 17-year-old Hornsby talked his older brother Everett, who was a 30-year-old journeyman minor leaguer, into arranging a tryout with the Dallas Steers of the Class B Texas League. The Steers were impressed enough to sign Rogers to a contract, but he was released on April 29, two weeks after the season started, without ever getting off the bench.

Undaunted, Hornsby caught a bus to Hugo, Oklahoma, to try out for the Hugo Scouts of the Class D Texas-Oklahoma League. He made the team as its shortstop and signed for $75 a month.[16] The franchise folded, however, on June 11 after just 51 games,[17] but Hornsby's contract was sold to the Denison Champions in the same league for $125. All in all, however, it was not an auspicious beginning. Hornsby committed 45 errors in 113 games and, at 5-feet-11 and 135 pounds, hit only .232. His teammate Herb Hunter remembered a frustrated Hornsby pleading, "Won't somebody teach me how to hit?"[18]

For 1915 Hornsby reported back to Denison, which had changed its name to the Railroaders and was now affiliated with the Western Association, still a Class D league. The St. Louis Cardinals trained that spring in Hot Wells, Texas, outside San Antonio, and, with a split squad, played their way north to St. Louis at the end of the spring. Their second team stopped for a three-game series against the Railroaders in Denison. Hornsby caught the eye of the Cardinals' one and only scout, Bob Connery, who liked the way he fielded tough hops. Connery was so impressed he even bought Hornsby new spikes and a glove out of his own pocket.[19]

Hornsby played the season with Denison and improved his batting average to .277 in 119 games, as the Railroaders won the pennant by 4½ games over the Oklahoma City Senators. His erratic play at shortstop continued, however, as he made 58 errors in the field, or one almost every two games.

Near the end of the season, Hornsby received the startling news that the Cardinals had purchased his contract from Denison for $600. He was ordered to join the team in

Cincinnati for the remaining month of the National League season. Hornsby's meteoric rise was no doubt helped by the fact that the Federal League was in its second and last season and had depleted the American and National League rosters.[20]

Hornsby had never been north of Tulsa, Oklahoma, when he reported to the Cardinals on September 3, 1915, after a two-day, 1,200-mile train ride in a day coach. Cardinals' manager Miller Huggins did not see fit to put Hornsby into a game until September 10, by which time the Cardinals had returned home to St. Louis. With the club trailing the Reds 7-0 in the sixth, Rogers entered the game at shortstop in place of Artie Butler. Hornsby's 23-year big-league career began inauspiciously as he went hitless in two at-bats against Reds rookie pitcher Charles "King" Lear and had no chances in the field.[21]

After riding the bench for two more games, Hornsby finally got his first start on September 13, against Brooklyn and the veteran right-hander Jack Coombs, who held him hitless in four at-bats. The following day the 19-year-

"The Rajah" batted .380, belted 39 home runs, drove in 149, and led the league with a career-best 156 runs scored to win the NL MVP Award in 1929. (National Baseball Hall of Fame)

old got his first major-league hit, a single, off Brooklyn's future Hall of Famer Rube Marquard. Huggins then played Hornsby at shortstop in all 15 remaining games, batting him eighth in the order. Following Huggins' instructions, Rogers choked up about six inches on the bat, seldom striking out but seldom hitting the ball hard. His first extra-base hit, a double, was off none other than Grover Cleveland Alexander, who was pitching the Phillies to their first pennant.[22]

All told, the rookie managed 14 hits, all but two of which were singles, in 57 official at-bats for a .246 batting average. He continued to be erratic in the field, committing eight errors in his 18 appearances. Hornsby tailed off in the six-game annual postseason city series against the St. Louis Browns, with only two hits in 20 at-bats and four more errors in the field.

Hornsby was not shy even as a 19-year-old getting his first taste of the big leagues, and after the season approached manager Huggins for his assessment. Huggins said, "Kid, you're a little light, but you've got the makings. I think I'll farm you out for a year."

As hard as it is to believe, Hornsby completely mistook what Huggins meant and spent the winter on his uncle's farm near Lockhart, Texas, doing farm labor, eating fried chicken and steak, and drinking as much milk as he could hold.[23]

By the time he reported to the Cardinals' 1916 spring-training base in Hot Wells, Texas, Hornsby had gained about 30 pounds of muscle. He displayed so much exuberance and hustle that his teammates starting calling him "Pep."[24] At bat, he stopped choking up, stood back in the box, and immediately began lacing line drives all over the field. Huggins, who didn't think much of Hornsby's future at shortstop, now thought he had a future at third base.[25]

When the season opened on April 12, however, the still 19-year-old Hornsby was at shortstop against the Pittsburgh Pirates and their 42-year-old shortstop legend Honus Wagner. Batting seventh, Hornsby drove in both runs with two singles in a 2-1 Cardinals win. Although St. Louis was destined for seventh place, Hornsby was a genuine spark, crossing the .300 barrier in late June and moving to fifth and then fourth place in the batting order.[26] Very quickly several National League teams attempted to trade for or purchase Rogers from the cash-strapped Cardinals, but ownership resisted. By September 14 he was all the way up to .326, which tied him for the league lead with Cincinnati's Hal Chase.[27]

Playing more third base than shortstop, Hornsby finished the season at .313, fourth best in the league, but only .003 away from second place. He led the team in most offensive categories and was among the league leaders in many. It was truly a meteoric rise for a young man who had batted .277 the previous year in Class D.

By the time Hornsby reported to the Cardinals' 1917 spring training in Hot Wells after a winter working for Swift & Company as a checker on the loading docks in Fort Worth, the club had new ownership and had installed Branch Rickey as president.[28] For the next 20 years the careers of the two would be intertwined, although not always happily so. Under Rickey's leadership the Cardinals won 22 more games than in 1916 and moved up to third place. Hornsby played shortstop exclusively for manager Huggins and raised his batting average to .327, second in the league behind Cincinnati's Edd Roush's .341. Rogers hit a powerful .327 as he led the league with 253 total bases and a .484 slugging percentage.

Huggins left the Cardinals after the season to manage the New York Yankees, and Rickey replaced him with Jack Hendricks, late of the Indianapolis Indians of the American Association. It was not a happy match for Hornsby, who late in the war-shortened season publicly called his manager "a boob," and his teammates "stool pigeons." Earlier when he failed to slide on a play at home plate and was tagged out, he told his teammates, "I'm too good a ballplayer to be sliding for a tail-end team."[29]

The Cardinals were in fact a last-place team, finishing 33 games out of first place. Hornsby's discontent showed on the field as he struggled out of the gate before a mid-season hot streak got his batting average to a respectable level. He finished at .281 but committed 46 errors in 115 games, almost all of which were at shortstop.

Before heading to his war-essential job at a shipyard in Wilmington, Delaware, Hornsby loudly announced that he would never again play for Hendricks. Soon after his arrival in Wilmington he was joined by his fiancée Sarah Martin, whom he had met during his time in Denison. They were married in a civil ceremony on September 23.[30] When the war ended in November, they returned to Fort Worth, where Hornsby set about using his baseball connections to try to arrange automobile dealerships in Texas.

The Cardinals board of directors did not bring Hendricks back for 1919 but instead persuaded Branch Rickey to manage as well as serve as team president. The team could only improve to seventh place, thanks in large measure to the woeful Phillies (47 victories), but Hornsby fared much better under Rickey's leadership. He batted .318, second only to Edd Roush's .321, and was among the league leaders in most categories.

Hornsby's play in the field continued to be indifferent. According to teammate Bill Doak, Hornsby wouldn't think of working on his fielding and cared only about his batting average. Doak even suggested that manager Rickey switch Hornsby from third base to second because Milt Stock could play third and "Hornsby couldn't be any worse at second base than he is at third."[31] Even so, Hornsby managed to reduce his error total to 34 for the year, playing 72 games at third base, 37 at shortstop, 25 at second base, and five games at first.

In the offseason John McGraw made a concerted effort to acquire Hornsby for his New York Giants, offering the Cardinals $70,000 plus four players, but Rickey was not interested. Giants owner Charles Stoneham eventually offered $300,000 straight cash with St. Louis to keep Hornsby through 1920, but Rickey still wouldn't bite for his cash-strapped club.[32]

Hornsby settled into second base as the 1920 spring training began in Brownsville, Texas, and stayed there, playing all 149 games at the position during the regular season. He led second basemen in errors with 34, but no one cared because offensively he moved from star to superstar, leading the league with a .370 average for the Cardinals, who tied for fifth place with the Chicago Cubs.

Only 24 years old, he also led the league in hits (218), doubles (44), and slugging percentage (.559), and tied for the lead in runs batted in (94) with New York's George "High Pockets" Kelly.

It was the beginning of an incredible run of batting prowess. For the next five seasons, 1921 through 1925, Hornsby batted .397, .401, .384, .424, and .403, arguably the most dominant stretch in baseball history. His overall average for that five-year stretch was an astounding .402.[33] Coupled with 1920, he strung together six straight National League batting championships. He won the Triple Crown in 1922 and 1925 and led the league in every major category multiple times. Hornsby was the top player in the National League for the decade, a true superstar well before that phrase was coined.

Off the field, however, life was not so rosy. His wife, Sarah, gave birth in November 1920 to a boy whom they named Rogers Hornsby, Jr., but by the fall of 1922 their marriage was falling apart, due in no small part to Hornsby's dalliance with a married woman named Jeannette Pennington Hine.[34] By June 1923 Hornsby was defending an alienation-of-affections lawsuit by Jeannette's husband and an action for divorce by Sarah. He settled both, agreeing to pay Sarah $25,000 in exchange for her public exoneration of Rogers for the Hine affair.[35]

Then late in the season Hornsby became embroiled in a dispute with Cardinals management, who accused him of feigning injury, fined him $500, and suspended him for five games. For his part, Hornsby was bothered by his knee, which he had badly injured in May, and a severe skin rash that forced him to be swathed in bandages and ointment.[36] He was limited to 107 games for the season and "slumped" to .384.

Hornsby's troubles with Branch Rickey, which included the normally mild-mannered Rickey twice charging and swinging at Hornsby after a game,[37] and the Cardinals allowed John McGraw to renew his efforts to trade for Hornsby. The talks fell apart when the Cardinals insisted on Frankie Frisch in return. During the winter meetings in Chicago, the Brooklyn Robins offered Cardinals owner Sam Breadon $275,000 for Hornsby but, although shocked by the offer, Breadon said no.[38] In February

Hornsby and Rickey eventually talked through their troubles and made up. Then, on the eve of leaving for spring training for the 1924 season, he married Jeannette Pennington in a private ceremony in a courtroom in St. Louis.[39]

With the tumultuous 1923 behind him, Hornsby attained new heights in 1924, attaining a modern-day record .424 batting average, with 227 hits in 536 at-bats. He was held hitless in only 24 of the 143 games he appeared in and never more than two games in a row. During July and August, the peak of the hot, humid St. Louis summer, he batted .486. Although he missed eight games with a sore back beginning with the very end of August, he hit an incredible .509 for the month. During an August 21-23 four-game series against the Giants in Sportsman's Park, he smashed out 11 hits in 16 at-bats. [40]

Hornsby was the consummate gap hitter and an RBI machine, leading or tying for the league lead four times. He also hit with power, leading the league with 42 home runs in 1922 and 39 in 1925. Although he stole only 135 bases in his career, he was regarded as one of the speediest men in baseball and often legged out infield hits. Pro football hero Bo McMillin, Hornsby's old high-school teammate, once dropped in to Sportsman's Park to visit, and ended up donning baseball shoes and challenging Hornsby to a footrace, which Rogers won by a good margin.[41]

In the field Hornsby had become a more than adequate second baseman with a perceived weakness for going back for pop flies. That reputation may in part be due to the fact that with a runner on first he liked to cheat toward second in anticipation of a double-play groundball, which allowed some popups to fall in that he might have otherwise reached.[42] On the other hand, teammate Dick Bartell remembered that Hornsby would often tell his shortstop to take all the pop flies around second base because the sun was in his eyes, even on cloudy days.[43] His real defensive strength was turning the double play, at which he was the acknowledged master of his era.[44]

Hornsby's personal habits and lifestyle were almost as exceptional as his prowess at baseball. He didn't drink alcohol or use tobacco products but was a big red-meat eater, always with quantities of whole milk. He also had a particular fondness for ice cream, which he consumed every evening. He thought it important to get his rest, which in his case meant 12 hours of sleep a night.

He famously didn't read anything but the sports pages or go to the movies, reputedly to save strain on his eyes. On the road, he became known as the champion lobby sitter in baseball history, not reading, but sitting for hours watching the people go by. His interests and topics of conversation were pretty much limited to baseball and horse racing. During spring training in 1925, Branch Rickey talked Hornsby into playing nine holes of golf for the first time. He shot a 39 and never played again. He tended to be aloof from his teammates, usually rooming by himself on the road, and often showering, dressing, and exiting the clubhouse after a game without saying a word to anyone.[45]

Hornsby parlayed his almost incomprehensible 1924 season into a three-year contract totaling $100,000, behind only Babe Ruth and commensurate with the deals player-managers Ty Cobb and Tris Speaker had. When the Cardinals won only 13 of their first 38 games in 1925, Sam Breadon fired Branch Rickey as the field manager, while retaining him as the general manager, and persuaded the 29-year-old Hornsby to take over the club as player-manager. Just three days later, second wife Jeannette gave the Rajah a second son when William Pennington Hornsby was born in St. Louis.[46]

Under Hornsby the Cardinals went 64-51 and rose to fourth place with an overall 77-76 record.[47] Managing certainly didn't affect Hornsby's playing as he batted .403 for the year to win his sixth consecutive batting title. He also garnered his second Triple Crown, smacking 39 home runs and driving in 143 runs to go with his second straight .400-plus year and third overall.[48]

Hornsby suffered from a variety of physical ailments during the 1926 season and his batting average fell to .317. Nonetheless, the year was the pinnacle of Hornsby's long baseball career, as under his managerial guidance the Cardinals won their first National League pennant by two games over the Cincinnati Reds and then the world

championship in a thrilling seven-game World Series over the powerful New York Yankees.

The club was bolstered by Hornsby's midseason acquisitions of outfielder Billy Southworth and the 39-year-old Grover Cleveland Alexander, who both played key roles in clinching the pennant.[49] While the Cardinals were preparing for the Series opener in New York, Hornsby received word that his 62-year-old mother had died. She had gotten word that the Cardinals had won the pennant and let it be known that she didn't want anything to interfere with her son playing in the World Series. Rogers heeded her wishes and the funeral was delayed until after the Series was over.[50]

The Series itself was a seesaw affair with Alexander striking out ten Yankees in a complete-game win in Game Two to even the games at one apiece.[51]

After St. Louis won Game Three, Babe Ruth hit a record three home runs to lead the Yankees to a 10-5 win, tying the Series at two games each. When the Yankees rallied to win Game Five in extra innings in St. Louis, the Cardinals headed for Yankee Stadium down three games to two and having to win two consecutive games for the title. With Alexander back on the mound, the Cardinals won Game Six, 10-2, as Ol' Pete scattered eight hits, struck out six, and threw only 29 balls in his 104 pitches.

Alexander was known to have a serious drinking problem. After the game Hornsby approached him and urged him not to celebrate too much because he might be needed in Game Seven. Alexander reportedly assured Hornsby that he could "throw four or five of the damnedest balls they ever saw" and maybe could go a couple of innings.[52]

Game Seven turned into a classic. The Cardinals led 3-2 in the bottom of the seventh, but after the Yankees loaded the bases with two outs, Hornsby signaled for Alexander to come in from the bullpen. No one knows for certain what kind of shape Alex was in, but he told Hornsby he felt fine when he reached the mound.[53] He took only three warm-up pitches before facing Tony Lazzeri, who hit a long foul on a 1-and-2 pitch that was almost a grand slam. But Lazzeri then struck out to end the threat. Alexander retired the Yankees in order in the eighth but in the ninth walked Babe Ruth with two outs. Ruth inexplicably tried to steal second base, but Cardinals catcher Bob O'Farrell threw to Hornsby at second base to nail Ruth by a wide margin and win the Series for St. Louis.[54]

For the rest of his life Hornsby would say that making a simple tag at second base to end the 1926 World Series was the biggest thrill of his baseball career.[55] Perhaps that is not a surprising answer, for it was the only time in his long career that he was part of a world championship team.

Hornsby received very high praise for his managerial abilities after the World Series from his players[56] and sportswriters alike.[57] Not surprisingly after the success of 1926, Hornsby sought to rework his contract, which had a year to go, demanding a new three-year deal at $50,000 a year. Breadon countered with one year at $50,000, providing Hornsby stayed away from the race tracks. Unbeknownst to Rogers, Breadon had so tired of Hornsby's act that he had arranged to trade him to the Giants if talks fell through. McGraw had coveted Hornsby for years and was now willing to trade Frankie Frisch, with whom he'd had a bitter falling-out. When Hornsby blew up at Breadon's counteroffer, the deal was done, to the shock and consternation of everyone in St. Louis.

Breadon later confessed that he so much wanted to get rid of Hornsby that he had been afraid he might accept the one-year offer.[58] For his part, Hornsby termed the trade "the biggest disappointment I had in my life."[59] It came less than two months after his biggest thrill in baseball, winning the World Series.

Hornsby rebounded on the field with the Giants in 1927, batting .361, second in the league, slugging 26 home runs, third-most in the league, and driving in 125 runs, also third-most. He also frequently took over the managerial reigns due to John McGraw's annual bouts with sinusitis. His club finished third in a tight pennant race, only two games from the pennant, but the Rajah managed to wear out his welcome in New York after only one year. Not surprisingly, his overbearing personality managed to get him cross-ways with McGraw and Giants star Freddy Lindstrom.[60] Then his criticism of Giants owner Horace Stoneham and a highly-publicized lawsuit by a bookie claiming that Hornsby owed him over $70,000 for unpaid

horse-race bets led the Giants to dump him to the Boston Braves in January 1928 for outfielder Jimmy Welsh and catcher Shanty Hogan, both front-line ballplayers but hardly stars.[61]

Hornsby's time in Boston was also short, although he batted .387 to claim his seventh National League batting title. With the Braves off to an 11-20 start, manager Jack Slattery resigned on May 23, to be replaced by the Rajah. But the team continued its inept performance even after the acquisition of George Sisler, and finished with only 50 wins against 103 losses, ahead of only the dismal Phillies.

The Braves' dreary record did not temper Hornsby's attitude. Late in the season, the Pirates and Paul Waner, who had been chasing the Rajah in the batting race all summer, came to Boston to play the Braves. Waner had a rough series and afterwards ran into Hornsby in the runway under the stands. Waner said, "Well, Rog. It looks like you're gonna beat me."

Hornsby scowled at him and said, "You didn't doubt for a minute that I would, did you?"[62]

On the other hand, Hornsby had a good relationship with George Sisler, both on and off the field, and lived in the same upscale residential hotel. Displaying his fondness for children, the Rajah often took George's 7-year-old son Dick (later a major leaguer with the Cardinals, Phillies, and Reds) down to the local drugstore for an ice cream or a soft drink.[63]

The Braves were deep in debt and after the season, Hornsby, armed with a new three-year $120,000 contract and working both sides of the aisle, urged the owner, Judge Emil Fuchs, to swing a deal with the up-and-coming Chicago Cubs. On November 7 Fuchs did just that, sending Hornsby to the Cubs for five players and a record $200,000.[64] The reigning star of the National League thus joined his fourth different team in four years.

Hornsby told reporters that he highly respected Cubs manager Joe McCarthy and knew they would get along, and they did. Playing on a powerhouse team with the likes of Hack Wilson, Kiki Cuyler, and Riggs Stephenson no doubt helped. The Cubs swept to the National League pennant by 10½ games as the Rajah, now 33 years old, lived up to his name, hitting .380 for the season. Despite persistent pain in his heel, Hornsby played in all 156 games and led the league in runs scored with 156.[65]

The Cubs fell flat in the World Series against the Philadelphia Athletics, losing in five games, and so did Hornsby. The pain in his heel probably had an impact, as he batted only .238 and struck out an uncharacteristic eight times.

After the season, Hornsby was awarded his second Most Valuable Player Award by the Baseball Writers of America. He also had surgery to remove bone spurs from his heel, which helped ease the pain temporarily. He fell victim to the stock-market crash, but the bulk of his losses on his RCA stock were on paper only.[66]

Hornsby was highly praised in 1929 for his leadership and for being a consummate baseball man who "lives, breathes, and dreams baseball." It was about this time that the Rajah uttered his most famous quote when asked what he did in the offseason. He answered, "I stare out the window and wait for spring."[67]

Unfortunately, the spring of 1930 brought more pain from his heel which made it difficult for Hornsby to hit with any power, run, slide, or cover any ground on defense. After working his way into the lineup, he broke his ankle sliding in late May.[68] When he returned to the team late in the season, the Rajah was mostly relegated to pinch-hitting duties.[69] Ironically, in the National League's most prolific offensive season, Hornsby, its premier hitter, appeared in only 42 games and finished with a .308 average.

Cubs owner William Wrigley had become disenchanted with Joe McCarthy and announced with four games left in the season that Hornsby would take over as player-manager for 1931.[70] Although there were rumors that Hornsby had undermined McCarthy and actively sought his job, the Rajah denied it, saying the two had parted as friends. Others, like teammates Gabby Hartnett and Charlie Grimm, were not convinced.[71] Cubs president William Veeck, Sr. was so upset at Hornsby's hiring that he resigned, only to come back when Wrigley promised he would never interfere again.[72]

Veeck put up with what has been characterized as Hornsby's "reign of terror" for about a season and a half before firing him on August 2, 1932.[73] In the interim Hornsby had gotten cross-ways with just about everyone on the team, including stars like Gabby Hartnett, Hack Wilson, Kiki Cuyler, and Billy Herman.[74] Hornsby was so disliked that when a firecracker in the stands went off during a lull in a game, Woody English, who actually liked the Rajah, remembered thinking that somebody must have just shot Hornsby.[75]

Hornsby also became entangled with the IRS for under-stating his income and had borrowed money from a number of his teammates to cover his losses at the race track.[76] The team had slipped to third in 1931, although Hornsby had his last good year as a player, batting .331 in 100 games. They were in second place in 1932 when Veeck lowered the boom, five games out of the lead.[77] Under the genial Charlie Grimm, the team swept to the pennant by four games over the Pittsburgh Pirates. Afterward, the Cubs spoke loudly about their feelings for the Rajah when they voted him a zero share of the World Series money.[78]

Although Hornsby's heel limited him to only 58 at-bats in 1932, he wasn't out of work for long. His old nemesis Sam Breadon of the Cardinals had a hole at third, thought the Rajah could still hit, and so signed him for the 1933 season. Foot and leg ailments plagued the 37-year-old, but he did hit .325 for the Cardinals in 46 games, many as a pinch-hitter. By midseason, however, St. Louis was mired in fifth place and asked waivers on Hornsby, who was unable to play regularly.

Once again Hornsby found a taker, this time in the American League. Phil Ball, owner of the last-place St. Louis Browns, quickly signed him to a three-year contract as player-manager. For the first time Hornsby actually lasted beyond his initial contract, running the Browns until midway through the 1937 season before the axe finally fell. The team was dismal, finishing in eighth, sixth, seventh, seventh, and eighth place. They paled in comparison to the Cardinals' Gas House Gang and, in the height of the Depression, drew as few as 81,000 fans for an entire season.[79]

Bill Werber remembered a one-sided conversation with the Rajah late in the 1933 season when the Boston Red Sox and the Browns happened to be on the same train west to open a series in St. Louis. Midway through the long trip, Hornsby made his way into the Red Sox Pullman car and took center stage. Werber was in first full major-league season and so was all ears as Hornsby expounded on hitting and eye care. Hornsby said he had never seen a movie because they were bad for one's eyes. He also thought reading weakened them, as well, whether through newspapers, magazines, or books. He also stressed the importance of plenty of sleep and the avoidance of whiskey. After Hornsby had exhausted his fund of advice, he rose and abruptly departed.[80]

Hornsby's playing days were for all intents and purposes over, although he remained on the active roster, occasionally filling in at second base or pinch-hitting. For example, at 41 years of age in 1937, he hit .321 in 56 at-bats. Off the field, he continued be plagued by gambling debts and bad investments, which caused his farm to be foreclosed on, and a crumbling second marriage.[81] Indeed, his inveterate playing of the horses finally caused the Browns to give him the heave-ho.[82]

This time there was no big-league club waiting in the wings, so Hornsby managed to land a job as player-coach with the Baltimore Orioles of the International League for 1938.[83] In early June, flamboyant Chattanooga Lookouts owner Joe Engel, looking for box-office appeal, signed Hornsby to manage for the rest of the season. He even hit a pinch-hit home run and went 2-for-3 in limited playing duty.[84] He returned to Baltimore, this time as manager, in 1939 but guided the team only to sixth place.

Hornsby then found himself out of a job until the following June, when he signed on to manage the Oklahoma City Indians in the Class A1 Texas League. Under his tutelage the team rose from the cellar to fourth place, making the league playoffs. That earned him a return engagement for 1941, but with the team languishing below .500, he resigned in late June and returned to his home in St. Louis.[85]

Hornsby's hometown Fort Worth Cats, also in the Texas League, came calling for 1942, and gave him authority over the business operations of the team in addition to naming him manager. He was in Fort Worth in January when he received word of his election to the Baseball Hall of Fame in his first year of eligibility. He said it was a "mighty nice honor," and went about selling season tickets for the Cats, without "a single turndown."[86]

The Cats, buoyed by a late-season nine-game winning streak, finished third in 1942 with an 84-68 record before losing to Beaumont in seven games in the league playoffs. Although Hornsby was rehired for 1943, the Texas League shut down operations due to World War II, leaving him with a reduced salary with the Cats and renewed money problems.[87] Mexican baseball mogul Jorge Pasquel came to the rescue, hiring the Rajah as manager of the Vera Cruz Blues in Pasquel's six-team circuit for 1944.[88]

He lasted nine days in Mexico, quitting when Pasquel expressed disappointment that the Blues had won a Saturday game that meant a smaller crowd on Sunday. When Hornsby got back to St. Louis, he said, "I finally decided I'd rather be a lamppost in America than a general down there."[89]

There were suspicions that Commissioner Kenesaw M. Landis had blacklisted Hornsby from the major leagues because of his inveterate playing of the horses and generally disagreeable personality.[90] Landis died in November 1944, however, and Hornsby was not quick to get back to the majors even afterward. He had a brief stint as a spring-training hitting instructor for the Chicago White Sox in 1946 and then with the Cleveland Indians the following spring.

Hornsby and Lefty O'Doul were widely considered to be the best batting instructors of their time, especially when it came to the mechanics of hitting.[91] But the Rajah's effectiveness as a teacher of hitting was probably affected by his prowess as a hitter. A struggling Eddie Robinson, the Indians first baseman, sought Hornsby out during spring training to ask him if he should be a guess hitter, looking for a certain pitch in a given situation. Hornsby told him, "No, just hit what you see." As a result, Robinson decided not to be a guess hitter and continued to struggle. Then, when Robinson was with the Washington Senators in 1949, his manager, Joe Kuhel, told him that "guessing" was really just looking for a certain pitch until you have two strikes. That advice turned Robinson's career around; he would eventually make four All-Star teams.[92]

Hornsby was so good a hitter that he could just react to the pitch and hit .400. But even most good major-league hitters could not.

Hornsby spent much of the late 1940s as director of a youth baseball program in Chicago sponsored by the *Chicago Daily News*, and operating the Rogers Hornsby Baseball School in Hot Springs, Arkansas. He separated from his second wife, Jeanette, in 1945, effectively ending their marriage.[93] In December 1949 he got word that his estranged 29-year-old son from his first marriage, Rogers Hornsby, Jr., had been killed in a training mission in a modified B-29. His first wife refused to allow Hornsby to attend the funeral.[94] Thus ended a rough decade for the Rajah.

The 1950s started off better for Hornsby when the New York Yankees hired him to manage their Beaumont farm team in the Texas League. After a slow start the Roughnecks, led by league Player of the Year Gil McDougald, played .709 baseball after June 7, winning the regular-season pennant by 2½ games over the Fort Worth Cats. The Yankees, liking what they saw, sent him to manage Ponce in the Puerto Rican Winter League, where his team finished third.[95]

Hornsby was again in demand and was recruited to manage the independent Seattle Rainiers of the Pacific Coast League for 1951. He was again successful, guiding the Rainiers to their first PCL championship in ten years, even though the team was picked to finish in the second division.[96] Led by Jim Rivera, a player Hornsby had drafted after seeing him in the Puerto Rican League, they won the pennant by six games and then the league playoffs against the Los Angeles Angels and Hollywood Stars.[97] Hornsby didn't allow alcohol in the clubhouse, but after the Rainiers won the pennant, the players asked if they could have champagne or something in the clubhouse to celebrate. "Not till I'm out of here," he said.[98]

His son Bill was attempting to make it as a ballplayer and hooked on with Oklahoma City in the Texas League

that year. After hitting only .206 after 69 games, Bill was released. When the Rajah learned of it, he said he was "glad Billy learned early that he wasn't a real player. … Imagine how I would have felt, seeing the Hornsby name down in the batting averages with the pitchers."[99]

On a misty night in Seattle during the season, Hornsby and Lefty O'Doul put on a pregame batting exhibition. O'Doul, one of the all-time great left-handed hitters, who was 54 years old, hit line drive after line drive deep to left field. The Rajah, who was 55, then nailed line drive after line drive deep to his opposite field, right. The two old rivals could still smash the ball.[100]

After his successes in Beaumont and Seattle, Hornsby's long road back to the majors was soon at an end. He quickly received similar three-year offers from both the St. Louis Browns and the Cardinals to manage for 1952. The Browns, owned by Bill Veeck, son of former Cubs president William Veeck, were coming off a 102-loss, last-place finish. The Rajah chose that job because he thought the upside was much greater than with the perennial contending Cardinals. Thus, at the age of 55, the Rajah was back in the majors, hired by the franchise that had 14 years earlier fired him from his last big-league job, and hired by the son of the man who fired him from the Cubs in 1932.[101]

Hornsby lasted only 51 games before Veeck gave him the boot. During spring training, he quickly got cross-ways with the legendary Satchel Paige, who liked to keep his own training rules.[102] The club got off to a strong start but soon faded to seventh place, as Hornsby became more and more irascible.[103] The acerbic Hornsby had general contempt for pitchers and continued his long-standing practice of making pitching changes from the dugout.[104] According to Ned Garver, he was completely aloof and wouldn't speak to a player except to ridicule him. Once in a hotel elevator, Hornsby derided Garver for walking the opposing pitcher in the game that day. The problem was that it had been Cliff Fannin, not Garver, who had done the deed.[105]

When Veeck got rid of the Rajah on June 8, the players were thrilled and presented their owner with a three-foot trophy that they had inscribed, "To Bill Veeck: For the greatest play since the Emancipation Proclamation." Pitcher Gene Bearden said, "They ought to declare a national holiday in St. Louis."[106] Outfielder Bob Nieman was quoted as saying that "the news was like lifting a hundred-pound sack of sand from each player's back." For his part, Hornsby claimed that the trophy was a publicity stunt dreamed up by one of Veeck's underlings, and that many of the Browns had let him know they had nothing to do with it.[107] In his autobiography, however, Veeck asserted that he was completely surprised by the trophy.[108]

As amazing as it seems in hindsight given the debacle with the Browns, Hornsby was hired to take over the Cincinnati Reds about six weeks later. The club was languishing in seventh place when general manager Gabe Paul selected the Rajah to replace Luke Sewell because he "wanted a hard-nosed baseball man."[109] He certainly got one.

The Reds went 27-24 under Hornsby to finish in sixth place. He was signed through the 1953 season and began spring training in a more relaxed mode, telling his players, "Baseball is fun, not work." He couldn't curtail his bluntness, however, and soon rubbed everyone the wrong way. One day after watching weak-hitting infielder Rocky Bridges take batting practice, he turned away from the batting cage and said, "I can piss farther than he can hit."[110]

Bubba Church, like most pitchers, was less than fond of Hornsby, in part because he wouldn't come to the mound to change pitchers. Church also objected to the Rajah's inveterate second-guessing. Once Church threw a 3-and-2 curveball that the batter hit for a home run. When he got back to the dugout, Hornsby said loudly, "Why did you throw him a curveball in that situation?"

Church replied, "Because I wanted him to hit a home run."[111]

Hornsby couldn't avoid controversy with the Reds, making an anti-Semitic remark to Gabe Paul, who, although Hornsby didn't know it, was Jewish, and getting into a well-publicized spat with sportswriter Earl Lawson over his failure to remove a battered pitcher from a game.[112] Thus, just before the conclusion of a lackluster 68-86 year

and a sixth-place finish, the Reds announced that Hornsby would not return for 1954.

Although the Rajah would never again have a manager's job, he continued to find baseball-related work for the rest of his life. His long-estranged second wife, Jeanette, died in 1956, and about six months later he married Marjorie Bernice Frederick Porter, a 49-year-old widow.[113] He continued to work with Chicago's Youth Foundation; participated in his baseball camp in Hot Springs, Arkansas; and then Hannibal, Missouri;[114] served as a spring training hitting instructor for the Cubs and did some scouting for the team. In 1961 the expansion New York Mets hired Hornsby as a scout and then manager Casey Stengel brought him on board as a coach with the original 1962 Mets team that finished 40-120.

In the fall of 1962 Hornsby entered a Chicago hospital for cataract surgery and suffered a stroke. He was unable to leave the hospital during the holidays and on January 5, 1963, the Rajah suffered a fatal heart attack. He was 66 years old.

Like all men with superior athletic ability of one kind or another, Hornsby was far from perfect. He mostly made a mess of his personal life and his blunt, opinionated, outspoken, speak-your-mind-at-any-time approach to life kept him in turmoil and cost him any number of jobs. He was, not surprisingly given his Texas upbringing at the time, bigoted and anti-Semitic, although he had a number of Jewish friends.[115] Although he always claimed that he was hurting no one but himself, his betting on the horses got him cross-ways with Commissioner Landis, who may have blackballed Hornsby for a number of years.[116]

On the other hand, Hornsby had a real fondness for children, working with thousands over many years. He was a more successful minor-league than major-league manager, suggesting that he had more patience at that level. But as a player he was so good that any all-time team without him at second base is highly suspect. The Rajah was indeed royalty with a bat in his hands.

SOURCES

Allen, Lee, and Tom Meany, *Kings of the Diamond: The Immortals of Baseball's Hall of Fame* (New York: Putnam's, 1965).

Alexander, Charles C., *Rogers Hornsby — A Biography* (New York: Henry Holt & Co., 1995).

Alexander, Charles C., *John McGraw* (New York: Viking, 1988).

Bartell, Dick "Rowdy Richard," with Norman L. Macht, *Rowdy Richard* (Berkeley, California: North Atlantic Books, 1987).

Boone, Robert S., and Gerald Grunska, *Hack — The Meteoric Life of One of Baseball's First Superstars: Hack Wilson* (Highland Park, Illinois: Highland Press, 1978).

Broeg, Bob, *Bob Broeg's Redbirds — A Century of Cardinal Baseball* (Kansas City: Walsworth Publishing Co., 1992 revised ed.).

Broeg, Bob, *The Pilot Light and the Gas House Gang* (St. Louis: The Bethany Press, 1980).

Broeg, Bob, and Jerry Vickery, *The St. Louis Cardinals Encyclopedia* (Chicago: Contemporary Books, 1998).

Broeg, Bob, *Super Stars of Baseball* (St. Louis: The Sporting News, 1971).

Brown, Warren, *The Chicago Cubs* (Carbondale and Edwardsville, Illinois: Southern Illinois Univ. Press, reprint ed., 2001).

Cataneo, David, *Hornsby Hit One Over My Head — a Fan's Oral History of Baseball* (San Diego: Harcourt, Brace & Co., 1997).

Curran, William, *Big Sticks — The Batting Revolution of the Twenties* (New York: William Morrow & Co., 1990).

D'Amore, Jonathan, *Rogers Hornsby — A Biography* (Westport, Connecticut: Greenwood Press, 2004).

Debs, Victor, Jr., *Baseball Tidbits* (Indianapolis: Masters Press, 1997).

Dickson, Paul, *Bill Veeck — Baseball's Greatest Maverick* (New York: Walker Publishing Co., Inc, 2012).

Dobbins, Dick, *The Grand Minor League — An Oral History of the Old Pacific Coast League* (Emeryville, California: Woodford Press, 2009).

Doutrich, Paul E., *The Cardinals and the Yankees, 1926* (Jefferson, North Carolina: McFarland & Co., Inc., 2011).

Durso, Joseph, *The Days of Mr. McGraw* (Englewood Cliffs, New Jersey: Prentice-Hall, Inc., 1969)

Ehrgott, Roberts, *Mr. Wrigley's Ball Club — Chicago and the Cubs During the Jazz Age* (Lincoln, Nebraska: University of Nebraska Press, 2013).

Fuchs, Robert S., and Wayne Soini, *Judge Fuchs and the Boston Braves* (Jefferson, North Carolina: McFarland & Co., Inc., 1998).

Garver, Ned, with Bill Bozman and Ronnie Joyner, *Touching All the Bases* (Pepperpot Productions USA, Inc., 2003).

Golenbock, Peter, *The Spirit of St. Louis — A History of the St. Louis Cardinals and Browns* (New York: Avon Books, Inc., 2000).

Golenbock, Peter, *Wrigleyville — A Magical History of the Chicago Cubs* (New York: St. Martin's Press, 1996).

Gorman, Bob, *Hornsby's Heroes of 1926* (Baldwin, New York: Amereon House, 1997).

Graham, Frank, *The New York Giants — An Informal History of a Great Baseball Club* (Carbondale and Edwardsville, Illinois: Southern Illinois Univ. Press, reprint ed., 2002).

Graham, Frank, *Baseball Extra — An Album of Profiles* (New York: A.S. Barnes & Co., 1954).

Grayson, Harry, *They Played the Game* (New York: A.S. Barnes & Co., 1944).

Grimm, Charley, with Ed Prell, *Baseball, I Love You!* (Chicago: Henry Regnery Co., 1968).

Guinn, Jeff, with Bobby Bragan, *When Panthers Roared — The Fort Worth Cats and Minor League Baseball* (Fort Worth: TCU Press, 1999).

Hornsby, Rogers, and Bill Surface, *My War with Baseball* (New York: Coward-McCann, Inc., 1962).

Hornsby, Rogers, edited by J. Roy Stockton, *My Kind of Baseball* (Philadelphia: David McKay Co., Inc., 1953).

Huhn, Rick, *The Sizzler — George Sisler, Baseball's Forgotten Great* (Columbia, Missouri: University of Missouri Press, 2004).

Johnson, Lloyd, and Miles Wolff, eds., *The Encyclopedia of Minor League Baseball* (Durham, North Carolina: Baseball America, Inc., 2d ed., 1997).

Kavanagh, Jack, *Ol' Pete — the Grover Cleveland Alexander Story* (South Bend, Indiana: Diamond Communications, Inc., 1996).

Lawson, Earl, *Cincinnati Seasons — My 34 Years with the Reds* (South Bend, Indiana: Diamond Communications, Inc., 1987).

Leutzinger, Richard, *Lefty O'Doul — The Legend That Baseball Nearly Forgot* (Carmel, California: Carmel Bay Publishing Co., 1997).

Levy, Alan H., *Joe McCarthy — Architect of the Yankee Dynasty* (Jefferson, North Carolina: McFarland & Co., Inc., 2005).

Lieb, Frederick G., *The Baltimore Orioles — the History of a Colorful Team in Baltimore and St. Louis* (Carbondale and Edwardsville, Illinois: Southern Illinois Univ. Press, reprint ed., 2005).

Lieb, Frederick G., *The St. Louis Cardinals — the Story of a Great Baseball Club* (Carbondale and Edwardsville, Ilinois: Southern Illinois Univ. Press, reprint ed., 2001).

Lieb, Fred, *Baseball As I Have Known It*, (New York: Coward, McCann & Geoghagen, Inc., 1977).

Lowenfish, Lee, *Branch Rickey — Baseball's Ferocious Gentleman* (Lincoln, Nebraska: University of Nebraska Press, 2007).

McGraw, John J., *My Thirty Years in Baseball* (Lincoln, Nebraska: Bison Book Edition, 1995).

McGraw, Mrs. John, edited by Arthur Mann, *The Real McGraw* (New York: David McKay Co., Inc, 1953).

McKelvey, G. Richard, *Mexican Raiders in the Major Leagues — The Pasquel Brothers vs. Organized Baseball, 1946* (Jefferson, North Carolina: McFarland & Co., Inc., 2006).

McNeil, William F., *Gabby Hartnett — The Life and Times of the Cubs' Greatest Catcher* (Jefferson, North Carolina: McFarland & Co., Inc., 2004).

Meany, Tom, *Baseball's Greatest Hitters* (New York: A.S. Barnes & Co., 1950).

Offit, Sidney, ed., *The Best of Baseball — the Game's Immortal Men and Moments* (New York: G.P. Putnam & Sons, 1956).

Parker, Clifton Blue, *Fouled Away — The Baseball Tragedy of Hack Wilson* (Jefferson, North Carolina: McFarland & Co., Inc., 2000).

Petree, Patrick K., *Old Times to the Goodtimes — Oklahoma City Baseball* (Self-published, 1980).

Pietrusza, David, *Judge and Jury: The Life and Times of Judge Kenesaw Mountain Landis* (South Bend, Indiana: Diamond Communications, Inc., 1998).

Rains, Rob, *The St. Louis Cardinals* (New York: St. Martin's Press, 1992).

Raley, Dan, *Pitchers of Beer — The Story of the Seattle Rainiers* (Lincoln, Nebraska: University of Nebraska Press, 2011).

Ritter, Lawrence S., *The Glory of Their Times* (New York: Macmillan & Co., Inc., 1966).

Shoemaker, Robert H., *The Best in Baseball* (New York: Thomas Y. Crowell Co., 1959).

Skipper, John C., *Billy Southworth — A Biography of the Hall of Fame Manager and Ballplayer* (Jefferson, North Carolina: McFarland & Co., Inc., 2013).

Skipper, John C., *Wicked Curve — The Life and Troubled Times of Grover Cleveland Alexander* (Jefferson, North Carolina: McFarland & Co., Inc., 2006).

Skipper, John C., *A Biographical Dictionary of Major League Baseball Managers* (Jefferson, North Carolina: McFarland & Co., Inc., 2003).

Snell, Roger, *Root for the Cubs — Charlie Root and the 1929 Chicago Cubs* (Nicholasville, Kentucky: Wind Publications, 2009).

Tye, Larry, *Satchel — The Life and Times of an American Legend* (New York: Random House, 2009).

Waldo, Ronald T., *Hazen "Kiki" Cuyler — a Baseball Biography* (Jefferson, North Carolina: McFarland & Co., Inc., 2012).

Warburton, Paul, *Signature Seasons — Fifteen Baseball Legends at Their Most Memorable, 1908-1949* (Jefferson, North Carolina: McFarland & Co., Inc., 2010).

Werber, Bill, and C. Paul Rogers, III, *Memories of a Ballplayer — Bill Werber and Baseball in the 1930s* (Cleveland: Society for American Baseball Research, 2001).

Wilbert, Warren N., *A Cunning Kind of Play: The Cubs-Giants Rivalry, 1876-1932* (Jefferson, North Carolina: McFarland & Co., Inc., 2002).

Williams, Peter, *When the Giants Were Giants* (Chapel Hill, North Carolina: Algonquin Books of Chapel Hill, 1994).

Williams, Ted, with John Underwood, *My Turn at Bat* (New York: Fireside Books, 1988).

Veeck, Bill, with Ed Linn, *Veeck — As in Wreck* (New York: G.P. Putnam's Sons, 1962).

Breit, Harvey, "'Mister Baseball' Starts His Second Career," *New York Times Magazine*, May 11, 1952.

Hornsby, Rogers, as told to Bill Surface, "You've Got to Cheat to Win in Baseball," *True* magazine, August 1961.

Hornsby, Rogers, as told to J. Roy Stockton, "How to Get Fired," *Look*, July 14, 1953.

Hornsby, Rogers, as told to Tim Cohane, "Rogers Hornsby: 'It's Still Baseball Cobb,'" *Look*, June 17, 1952.

Lieb, Frederick G., "Hornsby Badges — Blazing Bat, Sharp Tongue," *The Sporting News*, January 19, 1963.

Sher, Jack, "Rogers Hornsby — The Mighty Rajah," *Sport*, July 1949.

Stull, Dorothy, "Subject: Rogers Hornsby," *Sports Illustrated*, Sept. 10, 1956.

Surface, Bill, "The Last Days of Rogers Hornsby," *Saturday Evening Post*, June 15, 1963.

Teel, William S., "The Strange Stock Deal and the Rajah," *Baseball Magazine*, September, 1953.

Toporcer, George "Specs," "Rogers Hornsby — The Greatest Hitter of All-Time," *Baseball Bluebook*, May 1953.

NOTES

1   George "Specs" Toporcer, "Rogers Hornsby — The Greatest Hitter of All-Time," *Baseball Bluebook*, May, 1953.

2   Bob Broeg, *Super Stars of Baseball*, 128.

3   Jonathan D'Amore, *Rogers Hornsby, A Biography*, 37.

4   Dick "Rowdy Richard" Bartell with Norman L. Macht, *Rowdy Richard*, 223.

5   Broeg, *Super Stars of Baseball*, 127.

6   Bob Gorman, *Hornsby's Heroes of 1926*; Paul E. Doutrich, *The Cardinals and the Yankees, 1926*.

7   John C. Skipper, *A Biographical Dictionary of Major League Baseball Managers*, 153-54; Bartell, 222, 326.

8   Harry Grayson, *They Played the Game*, 135.

9   Charles A. Alexander, *Rogers Hornsby — A Biography*, 12-13.

10 Alexander, 13-14.

11 D'Amore, 3.

12 Alexander, 15.

13 Ibid.

14 D'Amore, 5; Alexander, 16.

15 Alexander, 16-17.

16 Alexander, 18; D'Amore, 5

17 Lloyd Johnson and Miles Wolff, eds., *The Encyclopedia of Minor League Baseball*, 2nd ed., 197.

18 Lee Allen and Tom Meany, *Kings of the Diamond: The Immortals of Baseball's Hall of Fame*, 124; Rogers Hornsby with Bill Surface, *My War With Baseball*, 36-37.

19 Alexander, 19' D'Amore, 7; Hornsby and Surface, 37.

20   Alexander, 21-22.

21   Alexander, 25.

22   Alexander, 26; D'Amore, 11.

23   Hornsby and Surface, 38; D'Amore, 11-12; Alexander, 26-27; Frederick G. Lieb, "Hornsby Badges — Blazing Bat, Sharp Tongue," *The Sporting News*, January 19, 1963, 12.

24   D'Amore, 15.

25   In the offseason the Cardinals had tried to sell Hornsby to Little Rock in the Southern League for $500, or $100 less than they had paid for him, but even that price was too steep so Little Rock passed. St. Louis had also signed Roy Corhan out of the Pacific Coast League, intending him to be their shortstop for 1916. D'Amore, 11; Alexander, 27.

26   Alexander, 31-32.

27   D'Amore, 17.

28   Alexander, 33.

29   D'Amore, 22; Alexander, 46-47.

30   Alexander, 47-48.

31   Bartell, 348.

32   Alexander, 54-55.

33   Tom Meany, *Baseball's Greatest Hitters*, 81.

34   Alexander, 74-77; D'Amore, 43-44.

35   Alexander, 79-80; D'Amore, 45.

36   Alexander, 81-83; 46-47.

37   Hornsby had thrown up his hands in frustration while at bat after getting the take sign from the dugout. He continued complaining loudly in the clubhouse after the game, and when confronted by Rickey, called him every unprintable name imaginable. Lee Lowenfish, *Branch Rickey — Baseball's Ferocious Gentleman*, 145-146; Alexander, 80-81.

38   D'Amore, 47.

39   Alexander, 87; D'Amore, 48.

40   Alexander, 90; D'Amore, 49.

41   Alexander, 95.

42   J. Roy Stockton, tongue-in-cheek, once explained that, "Hornsby was unfamiliar with pop flies because he hit so few himself." Broeg, *Super Stars of Baseball*, 128.

43   Bartell, 256.

44   Alexander, 95.

45   Alexander, 96-97.

46   Breadon had twice earlier tried to get Hornsby to take over as manager, but this time offered to finance his purchase of a minority interest in the ballclub. Alexander, 92, 100-101; D'Amore, 51.

47   Skipper, *A Biographical Dictionary of Major League Baseball Managers*, 152.

48   He so dominated in the big three categories that he finished 36 percentage points above the next highest batting average, 15 home runs ahead of the next leading home run hitter, and 13 runs batted in above the closest contender.

49   Peter Golenbock, *The Spirit of St. Louis — A History of the St. Louis Cardinals and Browns*, 102-103; John C. Skipper, *Billy Southworth — a Biography of the Hall of Fame Manager and Ballplayer*, 51.

50   Hornsby and Surface, 44-45.

51   Bill Southworth's three-run home run in the seventh inning iced the 6-2 victory.

52   Alexander, 118-119; D'Amore, 69; Jack Kavanagh, *Ol' Pete — the Grover Cleveland Alexander Story*, 103; John C. Skipper, *Wicked Curve — The Life and Troubled Times of Grover Cleveland Alexander*, 119.

53   Alexander, 119.

54   Gorman, 211-216; Lowenfish, 167-169.

55   Hornsby and Surface, 193.

56   Grover Cleveland Alexander said, "There is a great fellow if there ever was one. Who couldn't pitch for Rog? … He makes this a great ballclub." Alexander, 120. Catcher Bob O'Farrell later called Hornsby "a great manager," saying "He never bothered any of us. He just let you play your own game." Lawrence Ritter, *The Glory of Their Times*, 254-55.

57   J. Roy Stockton called him "a dynamic leader" whose best characteristics were "courage, honesty, bluntness, and determination." Alexander, 115.

58   Alexander, 125; Lowenfish, 170-172.

59   Hornsby and Surface, 29.

60   Joseph Durso, *The Days of Mr. McGraw*, 190-191; Peter Williams, *When the Giants Were Giants — Bill Terry and the Golden Age of New York Baseball*, 83-84. Mrs. John McGraw downplayed any conflict between the two, asserting that her husband had only "profound respect" for the Rajah. Mrs. John J. McGraw, edited by Arthur Mann, *The Real McGraw*, 314. It is interesting, however, to note that McGraw in his autobiography, even while naming him to his all-time team, uniformly referred to Hornsby as "Roger" rather than "Rogers," a common error that Hornsby detested. John J. McGraw, *My Thirty Years in Baseball*, 201, 226, 228, 262.

61   Robert S. Fuchs and Wayne Soini, *Judge Fuchs and the Boston Braves*, 55-58; D'Amore, 90, 93-94; Frank Graham, *Baseball Extra — An Album of Profiles*, 199-202; Robert H. Shoemaker, *The Best in Baseball*, 90-91.

62   Golenbock, *Wrigleyville*, 207-208.

63   Rick Huhn, *The Sizzler — George Sisler, Baseball's Forgotten Great*, 229-230.

64   Fuchs and Soini, 58-62; D'Amore, 97; Alexander, 148-149.

65   Alexander, 155-156; D'Amore, 102-103.

66   Alexander, 158-159; D'Amore, 102-103.

67   Rogershornsby.com/quotes.htm

68   The next day Hornsby, with one foot in a plaster cast and the still sore from bone spurs, hobbled out to home plate to accept his MVP award for 1929. Alexander, 161; D'Amore, 103.

69   Alexander, 161-162; D'Amore, 103.

70 Alan H. Levy, *Joe McCarthy — Architect of the Yankee Dynasty*, 144-145; When McCarthy refused to manage the final four games in 1930, Hornsby stepped in immediately to take over the team. The Cubs won all four games. Roberts Ehrgott, *Mr. Wrigley's Ball Club: Chicago and the Cubs During the Jazz Age*, 255; Alexander, 163; D'Amore, 104.

71 Alexander, 165; D'Amore, 104-105.

72 Bill Veeck with Ed Linn, *Veeck — As in Wreck*, 25.

73 Veeck, 30.

74 Ehrgott, 262, 270-171; Robert S. Boone and Gerald Grunska, *Hack — The Meteoric Life of One of Baseball's Superstars: Hack Wilson*, 105, 109; William F. McNeil, *Gabby Hartnett — The Life and Times of the Cubs' Greatest Catcher*, 168; Clifton Blue Parker, *Fouled Away — The Baseball Tragedy of Hack Wilson*, 131-133, 140-141; Ronald T. Waldo, *Hazen "KiKi" Cuyler — A Baseball Biography*, 159-161, 168-169.

75 Peter Golenbock, *Wrigleyville — A Magical History Tour of the Chicago Cubs*, 226.

76 Alexander, 171-172, 177-178; D'Amore, 115; Ehrgott, 280; David Pietrusza, *Judge and Jury: The Life and Times of Judge Kenesaw Mountain Landis*, 318; Peter Golenbock, *Wrigleyville*, 229-230; William F. McNeil, *Gabby Hartnett — The Life and Times of the Cubs' Greatest Catcher*, 168.

77 Ehrgott, 303-306.

78 Hornsby appealed the decision to Commissioner Landis, to no avail. Alexander, 180; D'Amore, 115-116; Ehrgott, 363-64; 375; Pietrusza, 337.

79 D'Amore, 121.

80 Bill Werber and C. Paul Rogers, III, *Memories of a Ballplayer — Bill Werber and Baseball in the 1930s*, 52.

81 D'Amore, 119.

82 Alexander, 214-215.

83 He also worked briefly that spring as a batting instructor and imparted wisdom in Florida that rookie Ted Williams never forgot: "Get a good ball to hit." *Ted Williams, My Turn at Bat* (New York: Fireside Books, 1988), 63.

84 Alexander, 221.

85 Alexander, 223-225; Patrick K. Petree, *Old Times to the Goodtimes — Oklahoma City Baseball*, 20-21.

86 Alexander, 226-227; Hornsby was the only player who received the three-fourths majority vote required for election that year as luminaries like Frankie Frisch and Mickey Cochrane fell short. D'Amore, 125.

87 Jeff Guinn with Bobby Bragan, *When Panthers Roared — The Fort Worth Cats and Minor League Baseball*, 51-53.

88 Hornsby was quoted as saying, "There's no place left for me in the game here. United States baseball has forgotten me." Alexander, 231.

89 89. Alexander, 232.

90 Pietrusza, 316-322.

91 Richard Leutzinger, *Lefty O'Doul — The Legend That Baseball Nearly Forgot*, 115, 129.

92 Eddie Robinson with C. Paul Rogers, III, *Lucky Me — My Sixty-Five Years in Baseball*, 72-73.

93 Alexander, 233-234, 237.

94 Alexander, 239; D'Amore, 130.

95 Alexander, 240-248.

96 Dick Dobbins, *The Grand Minor League — An Oral History of the Old Pacific Coast League*, 100-101.

97 Dan Raley, *The Story of the Seattle Rainiers*, 144-160; Dobbins, 98-103, 133-35.

98 Dobbins, 101.

99 Alexander, 251, 253.

100 Dobbins, 103.

101 Paul Dickson, *Bill Veeck — Baseball's Greatest Maverick*, 197; Alexander, 254; D'Amore, 131.

102 Larry Tye, *Satchel — The Life and Times of an American Legend*, 230; Dickson, 202-203.

103 Peter Golenbock, *The Spirit of St. Louis — A History of the St. Louis Cardinals and Browns*, 339-343.

104 According to one story, Hornsby didn't go to the mound to change pitchers because once when he did, the pitcher talked Hornsby into letting him stay in the game, swearing that he could get the next batter out. About the time Hornsby returned to the dugout, that batter hit a home run. From then on, he didn't want to risk being talked out of removing a pitcher. Guinn, 52.

105 Ned Garver, with Bill Bozman and Ronnie Joyner, *Touching All the Bases*, 49; Golenbock, *The Spirit of St. Louis*, 341-343.

106 Only catcher Clint Courtney, a Hornsby favorite, came to the Rajah's defense, calling him a fine manager and saying he "was like a father to me." Alexander, 266; D'Amore, 133-134. To his credit, two weeks after he was fired, Hornsby was quoted as saying that the Browns "were a fine bunch of fellows who gave me one hundred percent of their ability." Alexander, 267; Rogers Hornsby, *My Kind of Baseball*. 171.

107 Hornsby, *My Kind of Baseball*, 175-177.

108 Veeck, 235-240; Dickson, 203.

109 Alexander, 269.

110 William A. Cook, *Big Klu — The Baseball Life of Ted Kluszewski*, 42.

111 Author's interview with Bubba Church, June 1994.

112 Earl Lawson, *Cincinnati Seasons — My 34 Years with the Reds*, 93-107; William A. Cook, 47-50; Alexander, 276-278.

113 Alexander, 287. Earlier, in 1953, a woman named Bernadette Harris, whom Hornsby had lived with and whom he described as his "good friend and secretary," committed suicide in Chicago, leaving him more than $25,000 in her will. Alexander, 279-280; D'Amore, 137; Cook, 49.

114 One 1957 participant at Hornsby's baseball camp remembered him coming to the camp for three days and being "real ornery." The camper also remembered how Hornsby, at 61 years of age, laced a line drive

over his head in right field. David Cataneo, *Hornsby Hit One Over My Head*, 183-184.

115　The veteran sportswriter Fred Lieb claimed that Hornsby told him that he was a Ku Klux Klan member. Fred Lieb, *Baseball As I Have Known It*, 57. If he was, biographer Charles Alexander believes, he was only semi-active and probably not a member for long. Alexander, 146-147.

116　Although the assessment seems rather harsh given the competition, Bill James has characterized Hornsby as perhaps the biggest "horse's ass" in baseball history, ahead of even Ty Cobb. Bill James, *Whatever Happened to the Hall of Fame?*

CLAUDE JONNARD

By William H. Johnson

CLAUDE JONNARD, THE LESSER-KNOWN half of the Jonnard brothers battery, was a prominent right-handed relief pitcher in the 1920s, leading the National League in saves with the New York Giants in 1922 and 1923, and in pitching appearances with 45 in 1923. By the end of the decade his skills had diminished, but he still appeared in 12 games for the 1929 Cubs during their National League pennant chase. Between April 28 and July 26 of that year, he pitched just over 27 innings for Chicago, but a series of poor performances in July led to his release well before the World Series against the Philadelphia Athletics. Jonnard was done with the major leagues at the age of 31, only six years after his solid showing in two games during the Giants' 1923 World Series against the Yankees.

Claude Alfred Jonnard was born on November 23, 1897, in Nashville, Tennessee, an hour before his twin brother (future catcher and scout Clarence Jonnard), to Joseph Thomas Jonnard, a railroad foreman, and his wife, Maud (May). Claude was soon nicknamed Big Bubber in contrast with Clarence's sobriquet of Little Bub. The term reportedly derived from "brother." "Bubber" stuck to Clarence once he reached the major leagues; it was his nickname throughout his subsequent playing and coaching career. Claude, though, generally was called by his name. The siblings, a rare pitcher-catcher battery comprising identical twins, each developed and displayed their baseball skills at Hume-Fogg High School in Nashville until 1916.[1]

That Claude completed a major-league career in which he tallied 14 wins against 12 losses, with a career earned-run average of 3.79, for three pennant-winning teams was even more impressive because he was blind in his right eye. There is no remaining documentation of when or how he lost the use of the eye, whether it was from birth or occurred later, but the disability makes his performance all the more remarkable.

As a 19-year-old, Claude signed with the hometown Nashville Volunteers of the Class A Southern Association in 1917. Nashville dispatched him to the Talladega Tigers of the Class D Georgia-Alabama League, but he was back with Nashville the next season, winning 16 games and losing 25 in 46 appearances over the 1918 and 1919 seasons. His ERA in 1919 was an impressive 2.33.

Based on his work with the Volunteers, the Detroit Tigers purchased the pitcher's contract in the middle of the 1920 season and moved him to the Little Rock Travelers in the same league. In 1920 and 1921 Jonnard played for the combative manager Kid Elberfeld alongside three other future major-league pitchers, Tom Knowlson, Chief Yellow Horse, and Hank Robinson, as well as future major-league regulars Bing Miller and Travis Jackson. The talent and the attitude on the team presented a stark contrast to his Nashville time, and his two seasons in Arkansas led the New York Giants to acquire him for a late-season cup of coffee in 1921.

Jonnard made his major-league debut on October 1 in Philadelphia. He pitched four innings in relief of Red Causey and struck out seven of the 15 batters he faced while earning the save in the Giants' 3-0 victory. (The save is retrospective; official statistics on saves were not kept until 1969.) He remained with the Giants for the next three seasons. During those years he posted a 13-9 record in 112 games and leading the National League in appearances (45) in 1923 and saves (five each season) in both 1922 and 1923. Those were Jonnard's best years, and included two World Series pitching appearances in 1923 and one in 1924.

Jonnard's first World Series appearance, in 1923, came in the top of the eighth inning of Game Four, in relief of Hugh McQuillan with the Giants trailing the Yankees, 8-0. He got Joe Dugan to ground out to third, then gave up a line-drive double to Babe Ruth. After Bob Meusel fouled out, Jonnard walked Wally Pipp but got second baseman Aaron Ward to ground into a fielder's choice. The Yankees won, 8-4. He pitched again the next day, in the bottom of the eighth inning, with the Yankees up 8-1. This time he survived Ruth's deep fly to center field,

111

induced Meusel into a weak grounder back to the pitcher and struck out Pipp.

Jonnard's only other postseason appearance was in Game Three of the 1924 World Series, against the Washington Senators. This time, with New York ahead 6-3, Jonnard entered the game in the ninth inning after Rosy Ryan had loaded the bases with one out. With Bucky Harris on third, Goose Goslin on second, and Joe Judge on first, Jonnard walked Ossie Bluege to make the score 6-4. Manager John McGraw replaced Jonnard with Mule Watson, who recorded the last two outs to preserve the win.

Jonnard had developed a sore arm during the 1924 season.[2] After the season he informed the Giants that his arm felt fine, but New York still opted to release him. That year he married a 26-year-old Canadian émigrée named Marie. They later divorced, without children, and there is little detail available about her life. Jonnard signed with Toledo of the American Association,[3] and his sore arm was presumably cured, because he went 22-19 in 333 innings for the Mud Hens. That performance stimulated rumors that the Giants might re-sign Jonnard, but he instead chose to sign a $5,000 contract with the St. Louis Browns. After two losses and one save in 12 games in 1926, the Browns released him. He landed back in the American Association, this time with the Milwaukee Brewers, and won 42 games for the club over the 1927 and 1928 seasons.

The net result was that Jonnard was given one more shot at the majors, this time with the 1929 Chicago Cubs. Making his first appearance for the team on April 28 at Cincinnati, he proved to be the most effective Cubs pitcher of the day, holding the Reds scoreless in 1⅓ innings in a 17-12 loss. He pitched in three games in May, including one notably rough outing against the Braves on the 13th. Jonnard started the game and gave up four runs before being replaced in the first inning by the ultimate winner, Charlie Root, who shut down Boston the rest of the way.

After a few more chances, in which Jonnard's ERA dropped back to 3.72, he endured a disastrous appearance in long relief on June 21 against the Pirates, yielding six runs and ten hits in 6⅓ innings of a 14-3 loss at home. Over the next month Jonnard appeared only four more times, and allowed 13 runs in 11⅔ 12 innings. Jonnard's

final major-league appearance came on July 26 in Chicago against the Philadelphia Phillies. In three innings he gave up seven hits and four runs, and soon thereafter the Cubs sent him to Indianapolis (American Association) and acquired pitcher Ken Penner in his place.[4]

Although he never returned to the majors, Jonnard was not quite finished playing baseball as the 1930s began. In the winter of 1930 he went to Cuba to play for the island's Marianao team. In 1931 he led Cuba's Campeonaro Unico league in complete games (four) and wins (five), but his performance wasn't enough to earn him another chance to work at the major-league level.[5]

Meanwhile, Jonnard continued his career in the minors. At Indianapolis he pitched in 34 games in 1930 and suffered a 5.70 ERA. He remained in the American Association through 1933, with Milwaukee and Louisville, but he had difficulty keeping his ERA below 5.00. In 1934 he dropped to the Class A Texas League, pitching for the Dallas Steers and Fort Worth Cats in that season and for Fort Worth in 1935.

A right-handed pitcher, Jonnard made his final 12 appearances in a six-year major-league career for the Cubs in 1929. In 21 seasons in the minors, he won 210 and lost 210 games. (Retro Images Archive. George Brace Collection)

By 1936 it was becoming clear that Jonnard would not get another shot at the major leagues, and he never made it out of the South, finishing his player-only days with the Galveston Buccaneers of the Texas League. In 1938, at 40, Jonnard managed and pitched for, the Shreveport Sports in the Texas League. He used himself sparingly on the mound, making only three appearances all season, and the team finished in the lower division despite a roster that included an assortment of future major leaguers. Jonnard moved on to manage the Joplin Miners in the Class C Western Association in 1939, and guided the team to the playoffs before bowing to Topeka.

Between 1940 and 1942 Jonnard managed the Amarillo Gold Sox of the Class D West Texas-New Mexico League, earning Manager of the Year honors in 1940, and left only when the league disbanded on July 5, 1942, during World War II. He did not manage again until 1947, this time with the Grand Forks (North Dakota) Chiefs of the Class C Northern League, and spent the following four years managing the Lenoir Red Sox, the New York Giants' affiliate in the Class D Western Carolinas League. After the team posted a record of 40-70 in 1951, Jonnard switched careers, and he began full-time scouting for the Giants. He also moved to the Melbourne, Florida, area.

A baseball man almost to the end, Jonnard suffered a heart attack in 1957 and returned to Nashville, where he took up residence with an aunt. Two years later, on August 27, 1959, and after suffering several cardiac complications, Jonnard died at 61 after surgery to remove a blood clot from his aorta at Nashville's Baptist Hospital.[6] He is buried at Nashville's Mount Olivet cemetery, beneath the Jonnard family memorial.

NOTES

1   Bill Traughber, *Looking Back: The Vols' Jonnard Twins*, May 31, 2010, milb.com/news/print.jsp?ymd=20100531&content_id=10639290&vkey=news_t556&fext=.jsp&sid=t556

2   "Giants Turn Jonnard over to Toledo Mud Hens," *The Sporting News*, February 12, 1925, 3.

3   Ibid.

4   "Chicago Cubs Head for Pair of Titles," *The Sporting News*, August 8, 1929, 1.

5   Peter Bjarkman, *A History of Cuban Baseball, 1864-2006* (Jefferson, North Carolina: McFarland, 2007), 118.

6   Claude Jonnard clippings file at the National Baseball Hall of Fame and Museum, Cooperstown, New York.

PAT MALONE

GREGORY H. WOLF

THE KNOCK AGAINST PAT MALONE, A big, hard-throwing right-hander who debuted for the Chicago Cubs in 1928 after seven years in the minors, was that he enjoyed the night life too much and didn't take baseball seriously enough. Discarded by New York Giants manager John McGraw for his wayward behavior, Malone found his mentor (and a longer leash) in Cubs skipper Joe McCarthy. Malone responded by winning 18 games as a rookie and then leading the National League in victories in his next two seasons. "Malone was a big, strong, rough-tough character," recalled longtime Cubs trainer Ed Froehlich. "On the mound he didn't hesitate to knock you down. When the visiting team came to town, they would dread it."[1] Forming one of baseball's best pitching trios with Guy Bush and Charlie Root, Malone helped lead the Cubs to the NL pennant in 1929 and 1932. Malone clashed with Marse Joe's successors, Rogers Hornsby and Charlie Grimm, and was ultimately traded to the St. Louis Cardinals, who sold him to the New York Yankees in 1935 without him ever playing a game for them. Malone, overweight and past his prime, was reunited with his mentor McCarthy, pitched his final three seasons as an effective reliever and occasional spot starter, and was a member of World Series championship teams in 1936 and 1937.

Perce Leigh Malone was born on September 25, 1902, in Altoona, Pennsylvania, the second of two children born to Christian and Anna (Murphy) Malone. Altoona, located in the Allegheny Mountains, about 100 miles east of Pittsburgh, was a bustling industrial city and booming railroad hub made famous by the Horseshoe Curve, an engineering marvel permitting trains to traverse the steep Appalachian terrain. Christian worked as an assistant yard master in the Altoona rail yards while mother Annie and sister Evelyn found piecemeal work. As a youngster Malone thought the name Perce sounded too "sissy" and demanded, sometimes with fisticuffs, that he be called Pat.[2] He was never called Perce again, at least not to his face.

Malone, a tough kid, enjoyed fighting and raising hell. He was a leader of a band of boys who stole food from neighbors and took it to a nearby shanty in a ravine where they concocted their next plan. By the age of 14, Malone had quit school and was working for a parcel carrier, Adam's Express. Around the same time he became interested in baseball. By the age of 15 he was playing left field on a local semipro team. "I caught the ball and let loose with a peg to first base with such speed," Malone recalled, "that George Quinn, the manager, immediately decided a fellow with an arm like that ought to be a pitcher."[3] Brash and fearless, he falsified his age to land a job as a fireman on the Pennsylvania Railroad at the age of 16. A year later he enlisted in the US Army and was assigned to F Troop of the First Cavalry at Fort Douglas, Arizona. An all-around athlete, Malone played football and baseball and boxed in the service, and was discharged after one year. He returned to Altoona and the railroad, boxed as an amateur under the alias Kid Williams and had a short stint as a football player at Juniata College in Huntingdon, Pennsylvania. Malone enjoyed his greatest success on the diamond for the semipro Altoona Independents in a local industrial league. His foray into professional baseball was the product of luck, good timing, and fate. A friend, Pat Blake, had signed as a catcher with the Knoxville (Tennessee) Pioneers of the Class D Appalachian League, re-inaugurated after a six-year absence. On Blake's advice Knoxville signed the 18-year-old Malone for the 1921 season. After he compiled a 13-12 record in 219 innings for Knoxville, John McGraw and the New York Giants bought Malone on the recommendation of scout Dick Kinsella for a reported $5,000.[4]

Malone discovered at the Giants' spring-training camp in 1922 that his drinking and rowdy behavior were unacceptable to the reigning world champions. "[Manager] McGraw was on me the first spring," he recalled.[5] He was dispatched to the Waterbury (Connecticut) Brasscos in the Class A Eastern League, where he pitched well (6-8 with a 2.31 ERA in 140 innings), but openly flouted manager Billy Gilbert's team rules. Consequently, Malone was summoned in midseason by McGraw, who had caught wind of his continued excessive living. "[McGraw] said he was going to suspend me on general principles," recounted Malone. "I told him that I would save him the time by quitting."[6] He returned to Altoona and resumed playing semipro ball. When he hurled a no-hitter, the Giants demanded that he honor his contract and return to Waterbury. "I refused to report," said Malone, "but told [McGraw] that I'd consider Toledo."[7] Malone's insubordination earned him a late-season promotion to the Mud Hens of the Double-A American Association.

Malone's second shot with the Giants in spring training in 1923 was followed by a horrendous year at Toledo. He won just nine games, lost 21, and posted a 5.64 ERA in 241 innings. But at 6-feet-2 and weighing over 200 pounds, the hard-throwing Malone had potential, and McGraw was reluctant to give up on him. At the Giants' new camp in Sarasota, Florida, in 1924, the players were assigned to two hotels. While McGraw stayed with the veterans at the brand new Mira Mar Hotel, Malone continually broke curfew and ran wild a half-block away in the less glamorous Watrous Hotel. Finally McGraw's patience ran out and he sold Malone outright to the Minneapolis Millers of the American Association. At just 21 years of age, Malone had established his reputation as an undisciplined swashbuckler who was wasting his talents.

Malone spent 1924 and 1925 playing Class A ball for the Beaumont Exporters and Shreveport Sports in the Texas League with late season call-ups to the Millers. Frustrated and angry, Malone pitched poorly (a combined 3-10 with a 7.96 ERA in 1924 and 12-15, 5.23 in 1925). "[McGraw] didn't give me a chance in the National League," Malone brooded years later, failing to accept blame for his predicament. "He kept me from going up for three years."[8]

With a career record of 44-66 through his first five seasons of professional baseball, Malone's season with the Des Moines Demons of the Class A Western League in 1926 was unanticipated. He harnessed his fastball (a league-leading 190 strikeouts) and improved his control (only about half as many walks per nine innings as his previous career average) to set career-highs in wins (28) and innings (349) while becoming one of the most unhittable pitchers

in the league. A first-team all-star, Malone helped lead the Demons to the league title.

Malone was quick to credit his recent marriage to Marion Seeley of Milan, Ohio, as the reason for his miraculous turnaround. He claimed that a quiet home life and early nights helped him rededicate his life to baseball. They had one child, Patricia. During the offseasons, the Malones lived in Milan, Altoona, and in Los Angeles when the pitcher was among the highest-paid members of the Cubs, earning a reported $22,500 annually. Malone was an avid hunter and fisherman and enjoyed golf.

Minnesota Millers owner and manager Mike Kelley recognized that his acquisition of Malone in 1924 might soon pay big financial dividends. Pitching exclusively for the Millers in 1927, Malone proved that he was a bona-fide major leaguer by leading the American Association in strikeouts (214) and ranking in the top five in almost every important pitching category, including wins (20), innings (319), and games (53). By the end of the season, teams were clamoring to purchase Malone's contract. The Chicago Cubs had an advantage. Cubs' skipper Joe McCarthy and Kelley were friends and had known each other since at least 1919, when McCarthy began managing the Louisville Colonels in the American Association. Kelley sold Malone to the Cubs for a reported $25,000, including an immediate $15,000 payment with an option of either the balance due or the return of Malone to Minneapolis by the June 15 trading deadline the following season.

Malone joined the 1928 Cubs pitching staff, which included three established starters, led the previous season by 26-game-winner Charlie Root, lefty Guy Bush, and dependable Sheriff Blake. Struggling with his control during most of spring training on Catalina Island, California, Malone lost out to 35-year-old former Giant Art Nehf and 28-year old Percy Jones as the team's fifth starter. His big-league career began as a nightmare, as he lost five of his first six appearances. On April 12 at Redland Field in Cincinnati, Malone debuted in the seventh inning in relief of Jones. He yielded three hits and issued two walks in 1⅔ innings, was undone by sloppy fielding that led to six runs (all unearned), and was charged with the

9-3 loss. Malone's luck turned around in early May. After an impressive five-inning relief performance against the Phillies in which he struck out eight to earn his first major-league victory, Malone pitched a complete-game six-hitter to defeat John McGraw's Giants, 4-2, on May 12. The Cubs moved into sole possession of first place five days later behind Malone's first of 15 big-league shutouts, a five-hitter against Boston. Though they spent only four more days in first, the Cubs battled the Cardinals and Giants for the pennant the entire season and finished in third place, just four games behind league champion St. Louis.

Malone proved to be the Cubs' most successful and consistent pitcher, especially during the pennant race in the last two months of the 1928 season. He won nine of ten decisions in August and September, hurled complete games in eight of his last nine starts, relieved in four other games, and notched a 2.41 ERA in 89⅔ innings. For the season, he paced the team with 18 wins, 250⅔ innings, and 42 appearances (25 starts). His 155 strikeouts and 5.56 strikeouts per nine innings were second only to Brooklyn Robins ace Dazzy Vance, with whom he was compared because of his size and fastball. Malone earned McCarthy's trust, and Marse Joe leaned on the big, broad shoulders of Pat Malone for the next two years.

In 1929 the Cubs won their first pennant since 1918 behind the heavy hitting of offseason acquisition and eventual MVP Rogers Hornsby (39 home runs, 149 RBIs, and a .380 average) and slugger Hack Wilson (39-159-.345), and the league's best pitching trio, Malone, Root, and Bush, who won a combined 59 games. Malone got off to a hot start, winning his first five starts, including two shutouts. On June 12 he struck out a career-high 12 Phillies in a complete-game victory, and then struck out ten Cardinals in his next start, another complete-game win. An Associated Press story suggested that Malone had "probably the fastest ball in the major leagues."[9] Cubs beat reporter Edward Burns praised Malone's "comet ball," which was even deadlier with a recently honed change-of-pace.[10] As the Cubs pulled away from Pittsburgh and New York, Malone concluded the season with a yeoman's performance, completing his last five starts and winning four of them. On September 19 at

Wrigley Field, he exacted revenge against the Giants by tossing his league-leading fifth shutout to notch his NL-best 22nd victory, 5-0. With four games of at least ten strikeouts (there were only ten such games in the entire major leagues in 1929), Malone broke Vance's seven-year hold on the strikeout title with a career-best 166.

Facing the overwhelming favorite Philadelphia Athletics in the World Series, Malone was clobbered in Game Two. In 3⅔ innings he yielded five hits, walked five, and gave up six runs (three earned) in crushing 9-3 loss. Following two-thirds of an inning in relief during the horrendous bottom of the seventh inning in Game Four, Malone cruised through the first eight innings in his start two days later in Game Five, surrendering just two hits. Mule Haas tied the game in the ninth with a two-run blast. Four batters later, Malone was tagged for a two-out walk-off Series-ending double by Bing Miller.

The Cubs were preseason favorites to return to the World Series in 1930, but their season was an unmitigated disaster defined by injuries and an increasingly acrimonious and tension-filled clubhouse. Hornsby, injured most of the year, undermined McCarthy's relationship with Cubs owner William Wrigley, who held Marse Joe responsible for the World Series loss to the Athletics. In the Year of the Hitter (the NL posted a record-high 4.97 ERA), Malone was the team's most consistent and effective pitcher, and came to McCarthy's rescue throughout the season. His complete-game victory over Brooklyn on August 14 kept the Cubs in first place. The Black Knight (as papers often called him in reference to his military background) pitched the final two innings in relief on August 29 to earn the victory over the Cardinals in a 13-inning contest and keep the Cubs in first place by a season-high 5½ games. But disaster struck in September. The Cubs won only 9 of 22 games to begin the month and squandered their lead as the Cardinals won 21 of their last 25 games to grab the pennant. The final insult of the season occurred when McCarthy was unceremoniously fired with four games left in the season and replaced by Hornsby. The NL's most dominant pitcher, Malone led the league in wins (20) and complete games (22); he also set personal bests with 45 appearances, 35 starts, and 271⅔ innings.

The relationship between Malone and Hornsby started off bad in 1931 and worsened throughout the season. Hornsby blamed the Cubs' collapse the previous September on Malone's (and other pitchers') poor conditioning and vowed to make changes in spring training. Without the even hand of McCarthy, Malone bristled under Hornsby's tyrannical approach to managing. Malone missed much of spring training because of shoulder problems and began the season slowly (just three wins through May), which further exacerbated his rapport with Hornsby. The hostilities came to a boiling point after a terrible outing by Malone on June 26 against the Braves, when he yielded four runs in just a third of an inning. Hornsby called the pitching "distasteful" and publicly intimated that Malone was a flop.[11]

With his thunderous laugh, Malone was described as an "overgrown boy" and prankster who played practical jokes on everyone around him.[12] Sportswriter Frank Graham called him "one of the most popular players ever to wear a Cubs uniform … [who] never let his fans down."[13] He was an acknowledged vocal clubhouse leader and supportive teammate. But Malone was also temperamental, upset easily by umpires or fans' razzing, and needed gentle coaxing from a supportive manager. McCarthy tolerated Malone's excesses, drinking, and occasional attention-grabbing headlines, such as his arrest for disorderly conduct at a South Side bar in 1930.[14] General manager William Veeck even paid the expenses for Malone's wife to accompany the team on road trips to chaperone Malone. But with McCarthy gone, Malone was seen as a "problem child" during the remainder of his Cubs tenure.[15]

By 1931 roommates Hack Wilson and Malone were inseparable drinking buddies with reputations as barroom brawlers. And their careers seemed to be veering out of control. In September *The Sporting News* reported that the Cubs "passed a vote of censure against Pat Malone who has rebelled against social conventions" (a euphemism for drinking).[16] The low point of Malone's career came on September 5 when he beat up two sportswriters in a Pullman wagon in Cincinnati while Wilson looked on. It wasn't the first time Malone assaulted writers. Hornsby was livid and vowed that "Wilson and Malone will not be with my ball club in 1932."[17] Embarrassed by their

players' actions, Wrigley and Veeck suspended Wilson and fined Malone $500. Never one to take himself or baseball too seriously, Malone shrugged off the incident and pitched complete-game victories in his next three starts. He finished with 16 wins. Cubs reporter Irving Vaughan's headline "Malone Draws Reprieve from Cubs" underscored the team's approach to Malone, who was either the hero or villain.[18]

The Cubs began the 1932 season as an aging team searching for a new identity after the offseason death of owner William Wrigley. Wilson was jettisoned in the winter, but "Phat Pat" was back on the North Side.[19] Like the rest of the team, Malone was mired in mediocrity (10-10, 3.34 ERA), when Hornsby was replaced by his polar opposite, Charlie Grimm, a laid-back player-manager. In Jolly Cholly's first game as skipper, Malone tossed a complete-game victory over the Phillies. The victory marked the beginning of a 23-5 stretch that catapulted the Cubs from a five-game deficit to a seven-game lead

Hard-throwing Malone led the NL in wins (22), shutouts (5), and strikeouts (166) for the Cubs in 1929. After seven seasons and 115 wins with the Cubs, he played his final three seasons with the New York Yankees where he was reunited with manager Joe McCarthy and won two World Series titles. (Retro Images Archive. George Brace Collection)

in the pennant race. For the red-hot Cubs, Malone concluded the season as a tough-luck loser, winning just four of 11 decisions (the Cubs scored one run total in three of the losses; two other losses were by one run). Malone won 15 games, and for the fifth consecutive and final time in his career logged at least 200 innings (237). He also lost a career-high 17 games.

For the surprising NL pennant winners, Malone was the odd man out as Grimm opted for a three-man rotation (19-game winner Bush, 22-game winner Lon Warneke, and a rejuvenated 33-year-old Root) against the prohibitive favorite New York Yankees in the World Series. The Bronx Bombers were piloted by ex-Cub manager Joe McCarthy. Malone's only appearance was in Game Three. He replaced Root after Charlie gave up another set of consecutive blasts to Ruth (his famous "called shot") and Gehrig, and pitched 2⅔ scoreless innings in a 7-5 loss. The Yankees clobbered the Cubs in Game Four (13-6) to sweep the Series.

For the second consecutive winter, trade rumors swirled around Malone, and they continued into the season. At various times he was reported on his way to the Braves, Reds, and Phillies. Malone was bothered by season-long nagging shoulder problems, and his campaign was a study in contrasts. He posted winning streaks of four (all complete games) and three games; but his three-, six-, and especially a five-game losing streak (during which he logged just 23½ innings and posted an 8.49 ERA) suggested his demise. He was relegated to the bullpen for the final four weeks of the season and made just three relief appearances.

Malone's holdout prior to the 1934 season rekindled reports that he was "hard to handle" and "frivolous in nature."[20] *The Sporting News* described him as a "champion [in night clubbing]."[21] After splitting his first four decisions, Malone lost his position in the starting rotation. He made his first start in almost a month in the second game of a doubleheader on May 30 (after seven consecutive relief appearances), but pitched inconsistently. Malone's victory over the Phillies on July 19, in which he yielded three hits over seven innings, inaugurated an unlikely six-game winning streak. The *Chicago Daily*

Tribune declared that Malone "is the only consistently good Cubs pitcher" on an underachieving team.[22] Malone concluded the streak with arguably the most dominant game in his career, a two-hit shutout over Philadelphia on August 18 at Wrigley Field. He also tied his career high with 12 strikeouts. It proved to be his last win as a member of the Cubs. After his next start (a loss to Brooklyn), on August 24, Malone was mysteriously pulled from the starting rotation and made just two relief appearances the rest of the season. While the Cubs hit bottom in September with a 12-14 record, the tension between Malone and Grimm was palpable as sportswriters attempted to sort out details of Malone's benching. The Cubs kept quiet on the subject, but Malone publicly berated the team, claiming that his unofficial suspension was a ploy to rob him of bonuses he would earn with each win beginning with his 15th.[23] "Anywhere will do just as long as it isn't with the Cubs," said Malone when asked where he anticipated playing in 1935.[24]

On October 26, 1934, the Cubs sent Malone and cash to the Cardinals for minor-league catcher Ken O'Dea (a capable backup to Gabby Hartnett for the next four years). The trade marked the end of the NL's most successful and durable pitching trio from 1928-34. In their seven years together, Bush (121-64, 1,587⅓ innings), Malone (115-79, 1,632), and Root (100-79, 1,556⅔) accounted for 336 wins and 4,776 innings. Some players were disappointed to see Malone leave. "[Wilson and Malone] were two of the most lovable hoodlums in baseball," said catcher Gabby Hartnett. "Never a dull moment in the clubhouse, dugout, or hotel lobby with either of those two Indians around."[25]

Malone refused to report to the Cardinals after hearing that general manager Branch Rickey expected him to take a reported 50 percent salary cut to $5,000.[26] Rickey thought he had an ace in the hole to make some money. On December 17, 1934, he placed Malone on waivers and no one claimed him. "If Rickey says that all the clubs have waived on me, I'll do a little gambling with him," Malone said mistrustfully about the waiver shenanigans. "I knew this was coming way back last fall and I asked if I could buy my release. Rickey will never see me for that kind of money."[27] Malone and Rickey eventually reconciled their differences, enabling the pitcher to report to spring training, but Malone was unexpectedly sold on March 26, 1935, to the Yankees. The waiver transaction caused a controversy. Brooklyn had originally claimed Malone the first time Rickey placed Malone on waivers, on October 29 (St. Louis withdrew him after Brooklyn's claim), and argued that Rickey did not go through the proper channels when placing him on waivers the second time.

Malone spent his final three years in the big leagues reunited with his trusted manager, Joe McCarthy, who had attempted to acquire him in the spring of 1934.[28] Malone's limited personal success (at least compared to his tenure with the Cubs) was offset by enormous team success and two world championships.

The big right-hander arrived at the Yankees' spring training in St. Petersburg overweight, out of shape, and with a sore shoulder, which raised questions about whether Rickey knew of the injury. Malone's season was a washout. He made just two ineffective starts among his 29 appearances and logged only 56⅓ innings. Malone's precipitous fall (3-5 with a 5.43 ERA) was shocking, especially considering McCarthy and Rickey anticipated that he was still a front-line starter capable of winning 15 games.

Despite Malone's terrible season, McCarthy gave him another chance in 1936. "I am going to pitch Malone into winning form," said Marse Joe, "or run him out of the league."[29] Malone sensed the seriousness of his predicament. He replaced his rotten teeth, a longtime source of chronic pain and a cause of headaches. Feeling strong and rested, Malone pitched four-hit, one-run ball over six innings of relief in his second appearance of the season. It was his best performance since August 1934 and earned him a spot start. Malone responded by hurling a complete-game eight-hitter against the Browns, striking out nine in an 8-2 victory. At the All-Star break, Malone was a surprising 8-2 with five saves, but owned a high ERA (5.54). In the second half of the season, the Yankees ran away with the pennant behind the league's most potent offense (scoring 1,065 runs) and stingiest pitching staff (surrendering 731 runs). And Malone played an important role as a fireman, posting an impressive 2.12 ERA in 68 relief innings. Relying on his three-quarters-to-overhand curveball as much as his fastball, he concluded the season with two consecutive complete-game victories to push his record to 12-4. His nine saves (an unofficial statistic at the time) led the league; his 3.81 ERA (in 134⅔ innings) was second-best on the team for pitchers with at least 100 innings.

In New York Malone endeared himself to his teammates, coaching staff, and especially to the sportswriters. On teams expected to win, he seemed to lighten the pressure with his pranks, practical jokes, and sometimes adolescent humor. Writers and players called him "Blubber" in reference to his whale-like physical stature; even Malone took to the moniker. At this point in his career, he regularly weighed 230 pounds. A team player, Malone responded to McCarthy's style of leadership, and though he was known to still enjoy a few beers in a tavern, he did not have the kinds of fights and incidents with reporters that marred his tenure in Chicago.

In the 1936 World Series against the New York Giants, the first all-Gotham Series since 1923, Malone relieved Bump Hadley to start the ninth inning of Game Three and earned a save in the Yankees' tension-filled 2-1 victory. With the Yankees up three games to one, he returned to the mound to start the seventh inning in Game Five with the game tied, 4-4. After pitching three no-hit, scoreless innings, Malone yielded a leadoff double to Jo-Jo Moore, who later scored the eventual winning run on player-manager Bill Terry's long sacrifice fly to center field in the tenth inning. Malone had two strikes on Terry and seemingly had a third, but the pitch was called outside by home plate umpire Cy Pfirman. The Yankees failed to score off starter Hal Schumacher, and lost the game, 5-4. Notwithstanding Malone's "underserved loss," the Yankees pummeled the Giants, 13-5, in Game Six to win the Series.[30]

Described as a "stout-hearted has-been of another era," Malone earned another championship in 1937, though he did not pitch in the World Series.[31] Unable to duplicate the magic from the previous season, he faltered to a 4-4 record with a career-worst 5.48 ERA in 92 innings. The Yankees released him in January 1938, but McCarthy vowed to help find him a job.

Malone's final season in Organized Baseball was a forgettable one. McCarthy, still loyal to his big right-hander, pulled in a favor from Mike Kelley and the Minnesota Millers, who bought Malone's contract.[32] Unfortunately, Malone lasted for only one relief appearance before he abruptly quit the team in April. He had been suspended after a drunken melee at the team's hotel in Indianapolis before Opening Day, and his relationship with the team soured quickly. After Baltimore of the Double-A International League purchased his contract, Malone split the season with the Orioles and the Chattanooga Lookouts of the Class A1 Southern Association, where he was reunited with new manager and former nemesis Rogers Hornsby. Malone posted a combined 6-16 record and 4.62 ERA for the three teams. Baltimore sold his contract to the Oakland Oaks of the Double-A Pacific Coast League in the offseason, but Malone chose to retire on February 20, 1939, instead of reporting.

Malone never shied away from challenging anyone. "[He] was a stuff pitcher," said Ed Froehlich. "He didn't have finesse, didn't nibble the corners. He threw straight down the middle of the plate and beat you with his stuff."[33] In his ten-year big-league career, Malone won 134 and lost 92, logged 1,915 innings, posted a 3.74 ERA (111 ERA-plus), and was on four pennant winners. In eight seasons in the minors, he recorded 98 wins and 113 losses.

The 36-year-old Malone returned to his home town in the Allegheny Mountains with his wife and daughter and opened a saloon in downtown Altoona. Less than six years after he played his last big-league game, big Pat Malone died on May 13, 1943, of acute pancreatitis, a disease that can be caused by alcohol abuse. He was just 40 years old. Even in retirement, he never lost his love for the game. "You go out on the mound one day, feeling great and thinking you have a lot of stuff," Malone once said of the thrills and frustrations of pitching. "Then the opposition pins your ears back in a couple of innings. You warm up, feel out of shape, know you haven't any speed, and realize your curve isn't breaking. But you go out and pitch a two-hit game. That's baseball."[34]

SOURCES

Chicago Daily Tribune

New York Times

The Sporting News

Ancestry.com

BaseballLibrary.com

Baseball-Reference.com

Retrosheet.com

Pat Malone player file at the National Baseball Hall of Fame, Cooperstown, New York

NOTES

1   Peter Golenbock, *Wrigleyville. Magical History Tour of the Chicago Cubs* (New York: St. Martin's Press, 1999), 197.

2   *The Sporting News*, November 9, 1933, 3.

3   "How I Got My Start in Baseball by Pat Malone as Told to Irving Vaughan," *Chicago Daily Tribune*, April 25, 1932, 21.

4   J.R. Hillman, "Pat Malone. Threw Hard and Played Harder," *Sports Collectors Digest*, February 7, 1997, 170.

5   Edward Burns, "Clubhouse Confessions of Our Cubs," *Chicago Daily Tribune*, May 12, 1929, A5.

6   *The Sporting News*, November 9, 1933, 3.

7   Ibid.

8   Edward Burns, "Clubhouse Confessions of Our Cubs," *Chicago Daily Tribune*, May 12, 1929, A5.

9   "Cubs Depend on Pat Malone," (Associated Press), *Meriden* (Connecticut) *Daily Journal*, September 24, 1929, 3.

10 Edward Burns, "Maybe Pat's Out for Fun, but He's Won a Lot of Games," *Chicago Daily Tribune*, September 28, 1929, 19.

11 *The Sporting News*, July 9, 1931, 1.

12 Edward Burns, "Maybe Pat's Out for Fun, but He's Won a Lot of Games," *Chicago Daily Tribune*, September 28, 1929, 19.

13 Frank Graham, "Setting the Pace." No source given. Undated article from Pat Malone player file, National Baseball Hall of Fame.

14 "Pat Malone Is Freed by Court, Pays Cafe Bill," *Chicago Daily Tribune*, May 10, 1930, 18.

15 Edward Burns, "Cubs to Trade Malone at League Meeting," *Chicago Daily Tribune*, February 4, 1934, B1.

16 *The Sporting News*, September 10, 1931, 4.

17 *The Sporting News*, September 17, 1931, 4.

18 *The Sporting News*, October 8, 1931, 1.

19 Edward Burns, "Cubs Gain in Pennant Race, Whip Phils, 7-0," *Chicago Daily Tribune*, July 8, 1932, 19.

20 Edward Burns, Cubs Dispose of Malone; Want Hallahan," *Chicago Daily Tribune*, October 11, 1934, 21.

21 *The Sporting News*, February 15, 1934, 5.

22 Edward Burns, "Malone Fans 12 Phillies; Cubs Win, 2-0," *Chicago Daily Tribune*, August 19, 1934, A1.

23 *The Sporting News*, October 25, 1934, 1, and July 27, 1939, 4. Bonuses paid to players achieving statistical milestones were frowned upon at the time and were often gentlemen's agreements not stipulated in contracts. Commissioner Kenesaw Landis considered bonuses detrimental to the interests of the game because they were "special incentives which rich owners could hold to his athletes while poorer clubs were placed at a disadvantage." See *The Sporting News*, September 18, 1946, 18. Malone's alleged bonuses were reported to range from $250 per game beginning with his 15th victory and $3,000 if he reached 15 victories.

24 *The Sporting News*, October 25, 1934, 1.

25 *The Sporting News*, February 27, 1936, 3.

26 *The Sporting News*, February 21, 1935, 7.

27 Ibid.

28 *The Sporting News*, April 4, 1935, 1.

29 *The Sporting News* April 2, 1936, 2.

30 *The Sporting News*, October 15, 1936, 8.

31 *The Sporting News*, March 4, 1937, 4.

32 *The Sporting News*, February 24, 1938, 5.

33 Peter Golenbock, 197.

34 *The Sporting News*, November 9, 1933, 3.

NORM MCMILLAN

By Bill Nowlin

THE SHORTEST HOME RUN IN MAJOR-league history? It was hit in 1929 by South Carolina's Norm McMillan, who played every position except left field, catcher, and pitcher, but was remembered in his obituary for hitting that homer.

He was born in the small town of Latta in northeastern Dillon County. His father, Sidney Alexis McMillan, ran the general store in town — a town for which he'd surveyed and laid out the first street. Sidney also had a tobacco and cotton farm. Sidney and his wife, Sue Rogers, appear to have had two sons, Norman and Ernest, and a daughter, Aileen, who became head of the music department at Columbia Women's College. Ernest became the superintendent of schools in Union, South Carolina.[1]

Norm was born on October 5, 1895, graduated from the Latta public schools, and attended Clemson A&M (now Clemson University) for three years, concentrating on veterinary science. With World War I in full swing, he was called to service during his junior year and wound up in the United States Navy, serving aboard the battleship Mississippi until he was discharged in December 1918.

McMillan was offered the opportunity to start a professional baseball career at age 23 with the Sally (South Atlantic) League's Greenville Spinners. He was a shortstop, playing in 58 games in 1919 (he was ill much of the year) and a full 126 games in 1920. He hit .288 in his first season, and then .294 in 1920 with 14 home runs. He was a little porous on defense, making 69 errors in 1920 for a .907 fielding percentage. He did complete his studies and graduated after playing varsity baseball all three years. (He was graduated after three years when he was called to service in 1917.) McMillan was named All-Southern third baseman in his last year.

He was still of interest to the New York Yankees, who purchased his contract on August 3, 1920. They thought McMillan a promising prospect but wanted him to get more playing time in the minor leagues, though they did promote him all the way from Class C to Double-A on

March 22, 1921, assigning him to play in the International League with the Rochester Colts. It didn't hurt McMillan's batting average, which climbed to .318 while his slugging percentage remained more or less stable. Although with just six home runs, he hit 23 triples. His defense had improved, playing the full season at third base. His success in 1921 boosted him to the big-league club.

Batting fourth and playing right field, McMillan made his major-league debut on April 12, 1922, at Washington, going 0-for-4. He was 2-for-4 with a triple and a run batted in the next day and 3-for-5 with four RBIs against Boston on the 18th. Playing under manager Miller Huggins, the 175-pound "Bub" McMillan stood an even 6 feet tall, but he was fast and several times was inserted as a pinch-runner for Babe Ruth, who was not.[2] Though an infielder in the minor leagues, he served as a regular in New York's right field and center field for the first several weeks of the season, while Ruth and Bob Meusel were serving five-week suspensions issued by Commissioner Kenesaw Mountain Landis for barnstorming after the 1921 season. Meusel's suspension was lifted on May 20, and he began to play that day in St. Louis. Even though McMillan was hitting .309 through April 30, he appeared in only two May games. Major-league veteran Whitey Witt was hitting over .400, and Witt got preference in the outfield, appearing in 140 games and batting .297. With Ruth and Meusel back and Witt hitting so well, McMillan became a reserve outfielder. He appeared in 33 games and hit .256 in 78 at-bats.

McMillan had two at-bats in Game Five of the 1922 World Series, but did not get a base hit. He did earn a share of the World Series money.

Red Sox owner Harry Frazee was hopeful of getting McMillan for his team, but the Yankees weren't all that ready to let him go. They wanted Shano Collins or Joe Harris or Herb Pennock in exchange. Frazee drove a reasonably tough bargain and sent Pennock to New York but received McMillan, George Murray, Camp Skinner, and $50,000. The trade was executed on January 30, 1923, and worked out well for the Yankees; Pennock was later elected to the Hall of Fame.[3] The *Boston Globe* thought it a deal done at the request of incoming Red Sox manager Frank Chance, who was in dire need of a third baseman. The *Boston Post* declared that the Red Sox team "was squeezed of the last drop of blood" when it let Pennock go; he was the only remaining member of the 1918 world-championship Red Sox team. The Yankees now had ten former Red Sox players on their 1923 roster, and the Red Sox had 14 former Yankees. In 1923 New York won its first World Series; Boston finished in last place.

McMillan played third base, second, and short in 1923 and appeared in 131 games, but batted only .253 and drove in 42 runs. At least a couple of times his errors in the field cost the team games and put him in the headlines. He committed 35 errors in 1923.

McMillan appeared set to become Boston's first-string third baseman for 1924 but was suddenly traded to the St. Louis Browns on April 14 for Homer Ezzell. New Red Sox manager Lee Fohl was hoping for an upgrade in batting. McMillan hit .279 for St. Louis, but played in only 76 games. Ezzell hit a comparable .271 in 90 games.

In January 1925 St. Louis was evidently very high on catcher Leo Dixon, and sent Pat Collins, Raymond Kolp, and McMillan to the St. Paul Saints of the American Association to get him. As if that weren't enough, the Browns also sent some cash and allowed the Saints the use of two other players. McMillan played three seasons for Double-A St. Paul — 1925, 1926, and 1927. He played second base all three years and played some of his best defense, as measured by fielding percentage. He hit .287 in 1925, and then improved to .289 in 1926 and .305 with 11 homers in 1927, at age 31.

By executing 213 double plays in 1927, the Saints set an American Association record. *The Sporting News* ran a photograph of McMillan, Oscar Roettger, and Leo Durocher, and wrote, "McMillan, in particular, [was] a star in instigating double plays."[4] McMillan also led the league in stolen bases, with 42. An assessment in print: "McMillan gave the impression here [in St. Paul] earlier that he was a good front runner, but this opinion was shattered last season when he stayed in there for practi-

cally every game and hustled from first to last. Only by hustling could he have been such an important cog in that infield, which hung up such an awe-inspiring mark."[5]

On October 4, 1927, McMillan was selected by the Chicago Cubs in the annual draft. He made the team out of spring training on Catalina Island and appeared in 39 games, splitting his time almost equally between second base and third base (though showing much better fielding at second). Manager Joe McCarthy used him as a utility infielder, not for his bat. McMillan hit only .220 in 1928, but third baseman Clyde Beck switched roles with McMillan in 1929, with Beck becoming the backup and Bub taking over as first-string third baseman. An unattributed typescript found in McMillan's player file at the National Baseball Hall of Fame says that Cubs manager Joe McCarthy's "gesture was one of either sublime faith or dark despair when he finally told McMillan one day last June to 'go out there and play that third base for the rest of the season.'" McMillan played in 124 games and hit .271, while Beck hit .211 in 54 games. Although he led the National League in errors at third base that year, it was McMillan who played for the Cubs in the 1929 World Series against the Philadelphia Athletics. The Cubs lost in five games, and McMillan managed two singles in 20 at-bats. He struck out six times and neither scored nor drove in a run.

On August 26, 1929, however, McMillan hit the ball thought to have been the shortest home run ever hit in big-league history. It went about 100 feet. The Cubs were home at Wrigley Field, hosting the Cincinnati Reds. Chicago had been on the short end of a 5-2 score heading into the bottom of the eighth. By the time McMillan came up to bat, the score was tied and the bases were loaded with two outs. "I hit a ball that bounded over third base," he told *The Sporting News* years later. It bounced foul and into the Cubs' bullpen and slipped up inside the discarded jacket of relief pitcher Ken Penner, which had been lying on the ground "about ten feet behind the base. As it turned out, the ball went up the sleeve of the jacket and while the Reds' left fielder, third baseman, and shortstop were all looking for the ball, we all raced home."[6] Penner appeared in only nine major-league games, four in 1916 and five in 1929, but his jacket helped win this

The starting third baseman for the Cubs in 1929, McMillan batted .271 in his final of five seasons in the majors. (Retro Images Archive. George Brace Collection)

game for the Cubs, 9-5, on McMillan's 100-foot grand slam. The Associated Press may not have seen it, either, dubbing it a "freak home run which took a bounce into the stands."[7] McMillan may have exaggerated the distance; the *Chicago Tribune*'s veteran sportswriter Irving Vaughn said that Penner's jacket was about 60 feet past third base — which would still make it a 150-foot home run. Vaughn explained that the Reds fielders never did find the ball, even though one of them picked up and shook Penner's jacket while in the hunt, thus excusing a perhaps-hastened AP dispatch. It was only after the game when Penner put on his jacket that he found the ball lodged inside his sleeve.[8]

On December 5 Cubs president Bill Veeck traded McMillan to Double-A Kansas City for a right-handed pitcher, Lynn Nelson (who was something of a phenom), a player to be named later, and a "bundle of cash."[9]

McMillan hit .326 playing second base for the Kansas City Blues in 1930. When shifted to third in 1931, he didn't fare well in the field (an .871 percentage) — though he

excelled at the plate, batting .354. After 30 games he was traded to Chattanooga and appeared in 27 games there, hitting .271. In January 1932 Reading obtained McMillan from Chattanooga and he played in his last 38 games of Organized Baseball, hitting .315 (often pinch-hitting) and back at his more comfortable position at second base for the 20 games he played on defense.

After baseball McMillan returned home to his beloved bird dogs in South Carolina and married Sara Lucretia Varn in April 1932. He prospered as a pharmacist during the Depression, noted in 1935 as owning a chain of drugstores in South Carolina.[10] He also became a cotton and tobacco farmer. He maintained an interest in baseball and coached American Legion ball for many years, one of his teams winning the South Carolina state championship. He said he'd always taught his teams to play for one run at a time, the way he had when he'd been a ballplayer.[11]

Norman McMillan died of emphysema in Marion, South Carolina, on September 28, 1969.

SOURCES

In addition to the sources noted in this biography, the author also accessed McMillan's player file from the National Baseball Hall of Fame, the *Encyclopedia of Minor League Baseball*, Retrosheet.org, and Baseball-Reference.com.

NOTES

1   *Chicago Tribune*, September 21, 1929.

2   This work earned him this headline for his obituary in the September 30, 1969, *Boston Record American*: "McMillan, Pinch Runner For Babe Ruth, Dies, 73."

3   *New York Times*, December 22, 1922, and *Boston Globe*, January 31, 1923.

4   *The Sporting News*, December 1, 1927.

5   *The Sporting News*, December 8, 1927.

6   *The Sporting News*, October 11, 1969.

7   See, for instance, the *New York Times* of August 27, 1929.

8   *Chicago Tribune*, July 3, 1931.

9   *Chicago Tribune*, December 6, 1929.

10 *Hartford Courant*, April 28, 1935.

11 *The Sporting News*, October 11, 1969.

JOHNNY MOORE

BY C. PAUL ROGERS, III

JOHNNY MOORE'S ONE GLIMPSE OF fame, if it can be called that, is that he was the Cubs center fielder over whose head sailed Babe Ruth's supposed called-shot home run in the 1932 World Series. Otherwise, it is hard to imagine a more completely forgotten yet outstanding player from any era than Moore. Even excellent recent histories of baseball in the 1930s, oral and otherwise, have completely omitted him.[1]

In ten big-league seasons spanning 1928 through 1937 and then again briefly in 1945, Moore batted an impressive .307 for the Chicago Cubs, Cincinnati Reds, and Philadelphia Phillies as a left-handed-hitting outfielder. At 5-feet-10 and 175 pounds, he had surprising pop in his bat. His lack of notoriety is certainly due in part to the fact that he spent most of his career with bottom-dwelling teams, as compared to his near namesake JoJo Moore, who patrolled the outfield for the high-profile New York Giants during the same time span.[2]

Moore apparently didn't gain much respect during his playing days either. Although he was among the league leaders in hitting for five consecutive seasons with the Phillies, topping out at .330 in 1934, he was never named to the National League All-Star Team. And, after hitting .319 in 96 games in 1937, he found himself without a major-league job. He showed he still had a lot left in the tank, winning a Pacific Coast League batting title and finishing second another year in eight productive seasons with the Los Angeles Angels.[3] Although Moore hit well above .300 in seven of those eight PCL years, he didn't appear in a major-league game again until the tail end of the war-depleted 1945 season when, as a 43-year-old he pinch hit in seven games.

John Francis Moore was born in the Waterville neighborhood of Waterbury, Connecticut, on March 23, 1902. He was drawn to baseball at an early age, but at about the age of 14 entered a trade school to learn tool and die making. When he graduated, he went to work for the major tool and die company in Waterbury, which afforded him the opportunity to play on the company's baseball

and basketball teams. Moore "thought Santa Claus had come."[4]

Moore was an outstanding basketball player and played against the Original Celtics (a barnstorming team of the 1920s not related to the Boston Celtics of the NBA) and other top teams. But his first love was baseball and at the age of 21 he caught the attention of Neal Ball, a scout for the New Haven Profs of the Class A Eastern League, which was owned by George Weiss.[5] Moore, who had married when he was 18, was unsure if he should give up a steady, good-paying job to try professional baseball.

Moore and his wife, Rita, decided to have him give pro baseball a try.[6] He showed immediate promise, batting .323 in 31 games and 124 at-bats during his initial year in the fast Class A Eastern League. That earned Moore a return invitation to New Haven for 1925. In his first full season he dipped to .267 in 116 games for the fourth-place Profs. Moore had a day to remember that year, however, going 6-for-6 in a midseason game.[7] He split 1926 between New Haven and his hometown Waterbury Brasscos, batting a robust .323 in 136 games and 523 at-bats.

In 1927 Moore was back with New Haven and played in all 154 games, batting .285 for the fifth-place Profs. That performance earned him, finally, a promotion to the Reading Keys in the Double-A International League, where he hit an impressive .328 in 1928 while driving in 117 runs in 146 games. The Chicago Cubs were impressed enough to purchase Moore's contract after the minor-league season concluded. In four late-season games with the Cubs, he batted four times without a hit.

The Cubs invited Moore to spring training in 1929 and he showed enough to make the team. Playing time was sparse, however, for Chicago had Kiki Cuyler, Riggs Stephenson, and Hack Wilson patrolling the outfield. Although with the team the entire season, he got into only 37 games, hitting .286 in 69 plate appearances. Sixteen of those were as a pinch-hitter, as were four of his 18 hits for the year. Manager Joe McCarthy did not, however, use Moore in the World Series, won by the Philadelphia Athletics in five games.

To gain Moore regular playing time, the Cubs sent him to the Los Angeles Angels of the Pacific Coast League for 1930. He proceeded to bat .342 for the year and made the All-Star team in a league many considered a third major league.[8] Still, the Cubs didn't call until midway through 1931. Moore was batting .366 in 80 games when Chicago finally summoned him back to the big leagues. For the balance of 1931 he managed only a .240 average for the fourth-place Cubs in 39 games, 16 as a pinch-hitter.

Hack Wilson wore out his welcome in Chicago in 1931 and was traded in December, finally opening a spot in the Cubs' outfield for Moore. Normally hitting fourth or fifth in the lineup, he responded with a fine 1932 season in center field for the pennant-winning Cubs, batting .305 in 119 games.

In the World Series the Cubs were swept by the New York Yankees. Moore struggled at the plate, going 0-for-7 while starting Games One and Three. It would be Moore's only World Series. In fact, 1932 was the only full season he played on a team contending for the pennant.

When Babe Ruth allegedly called his shot in Game Three, the ball reached the stands just over Moore's outstretched glove in center field. When asked, Johnny said he couldn't tell from his vantage point whether or not Ruth actually pointed to the stands. He just knew that he wasn't able to catch Ruth's blast.[9]

After the season the Cubs shipped Moore along with catcher Rollie Hemsley, outfielder Lance Richbourg, and pitcher Bob Smith to the Cincinnati Reds for outfielder-first baseman Babe Herman. The Reds had finished in the cellar in 1932 and repeated the feat in 1933, completing the season 33 games out of first place. Moore was installed in center field in 1933 but slumped to .263 in 562 plate appearances. It was his lowest full-season batting average by 42 points. His home-run total also tailed off from 13 with the Cubs to only one with the Reds.

Moore got off to an even slower start with the Reds in 1934 and after 16 games was hitting only .190. The Reds

Moore played in 15 games in the outfield for the Cubs in 1929. He batted .307 in parts of ten seasons in the majors. (Retro Images Archive. George Brace Collection)

were again going nowhere and on May 16 they traded Moore and pitcher Syl Johnson to the equally inept Philadelphia Phillies for pitcher Ted Kleinhans and outfielders Art Ruble and Wes Schulmerich. It would turn out to be one of the few good trades the Phillies of that era ever made as Moore averaged over .325 for the next four years in the City of Brotherly Love. He began by hitting a lusty .343 and driving in 93 runs in 116 games for the 1934 Phillies, who finished in seventh place, five games ahead of the last-place Reds. Both marks led the team while his 11 home runs were second to the 12 hit by first baseman Dolph Camilli. Moore followed that superb season by appearing in all 153 Phillies games in 1935 and batting .323 to lead the team in hitting for the second year in a row. His 93 runs batted in again led the team while his 19 home runs were second on the club to Camilli's 25. The team was still mired in seventh place but finished 26 games ahead of the woeful Boston Braves, who lost a then-record 115 games.

Moore played right field for the Phillies in 1935 in front of the infamous short but high right-field fence in the old Baker Bowl. Given the Phillies' weak pitching, he had plenty of practice and quickly became expert at playing the caroms off the poles and metal fence.[10]

In 1936 the Phillies reacquired Chuck Klein from the Cubs to play right field and it was thought that Moore would be relegated to the bench. But by the end of May he was hitting .360 while patrolling the more spacious left field. He ended up leading the team in hitting for the third straight season, batting .328 with 16 home runs, as the team slipped into the cellar, winning only 54 games. Moore had a career day on July 22, hitting three consecutive home runs and driving in six runs in a 16-4 win over the Pittsburgh Pirates at Baker Bowl. Moore later recalled that he almost had four in a row. The first three were high fly balls that he pulled over the short right-field wall, but the fourth was a line smash that was caught at the base of the fence.[11]

On August 27 of that year Moore made a triumphant return to Waterbury, as the Phillies played an exhibition game against a team of local amateur all-stars. He smashed three home runs as the major leaguers prevailed, 10-8, in a slugfest that was called after eight innings because the teams had run out of baseballs.[12]

The Phillies climbed to seventh place in 1937 and Moore was again one of their leading hitters with a .319 batting average. Injuries limited him to 72 games in the outfield and 329 plate appearances. In 20 pinch-hit appearances he came through with seven hits. He had another memorable day on August 17 against the Dodgers in Ebbets Field, slugging two home runs with five RBIs to lead the Phillies to an 11-1 victory. Although it seemed a meaningless game to most, it was not so for the participants because it propelled the victors out of the cellar, changing places with Brooklyn.

Phillies owner Gerry Nugent was notorious for selling his ballplayers to make ends meet, and that is just what he did with Moore after the 1937 season, peddling him to the Los Angeles Angels of the Pacific Coast League. Although the Dodgers were reputedly also interested in acquiring Moore, the Angels offered more money.[13] Thus, at the age of 35 Moore was suddenly out of the big leagues, although some would argue that the better Coast League

teams were superior to major-league tail-enders like the Phillies.

According to one source, Moore spent offseasons playing bridge and basketball, bowling, and fishing.[14] Beginning in 1933, the Moores lived in Sarasota, Florida, in the offseason. Moore passed the Florida real-estate examination after the 1937 season and began working in the real-estate business in preparation for life after baseball.

Moore became a fixture with the Angels, however, and stayed with the team for eight years. He was a regular for the first five seasons, hitting over .300 each year. In 1940, for example, Moore got off to a torrid start for the Angels, batting .448 after 25 games before finishing the year at .311.[15] In 1941, at the age of 39, he led the league in hitting with a .331 average, slugging 18 home runs and driving in 100 runs in 134 games. He struck out only 12 times in 518 plate appearances. At 40 the following year, he did even better, hitting .347 in 537 plate appearances. He was also an outstanding flychaser with the Angels, making more than three errors in a season only once and ranking in the top five in fielding average every year but one.[16]

By 1943 Moore was a part-time player and frequent pinch-hitter, hitting .290 in 81 games. He followed in 1944 with a .325 average in 134 appearances, mostly as a pinch-hitter. He exceeded that in 1945 at the age of 43. Used exclusively as a pinch-hitter for the Angels, he batted a robust .354 in 65 at-bats. He drove in 26 runs with his 23 hits, and slugged four pinch-hit homers. In the ninth inning of an August game against the Portland Beavers, Moore blasted a pinch-hit grand slam to turn an 8-5 Angels deficit into a 9-8 walk-off win.

Angels manager Bill Sweeney called Moore the best pinch-hitter he had ever seen and "conservatively" estimated that Moore had won at least ten games for the Angels that year.[17]

Moore's 1945 performance earned finally earned him a trip back to the big leagues when the Cubs, who were in the middle of a tight pennant race, purchased his contract in early September. Cubs manager Charlie Grimm used him sparingly down the stretch, however. In seven pinch-hit appearances, Moore singled in two runs and drew a walk as the Cubs won the pennant by three games over the St. Louis Cardinals. He missed being eligible for the World Series roster by only one day.[18]

Moore retired as an active player that winter, after a 22-year professional playing career. The Cubs offered him a minor-league managerial position, but he instead signed as a West Coast scout for the Boston Braves.[19] He served the Braves organization for 22 years. He quickly became one of the best judges of talent in the game, signing Eddie Mathews in 1949 and Del Crandall in 1950 as amateurs and finding Lew Burdette, who was languishing with the San Francisco Seals when they were the worst team in the Pacific Coast League.[20]

Moore first saw Mathews play when he was 14 years old and followed him through his high-school career. Eventually 15 of the 16 major-league clubs contacted Eddie. But Mathews was impressed by Moore's honesty and candor and signed with the Braves for considerably less money, because he knew he wouldn't be rushed to the big leagues before he was ready.[21]

Moore was so astute at finding prospects that at one point in the early 1960s he had signed five of the Braves' 25-man big-league roster, even though the Braves had 24 full-time scouts on the payroll.[22] The Montreal Expos lured Moore away as their West Coast scout when they came into existence in 1968 before he retired in the winter of 1971 at the age of 68. On that occasion both Montreal president John McHale and general manager Jim Fanning lauded Moore as one of the most respected and best scouts in the game.[23] Overall, he had signed more than 200 players to professional contracts.

After retirement, Moore and his wife, Rita, settled in Bradenton, Florida. He became a three-handicap golfer and a top player on the local seniors circuit, once beating his old rival Paul Derringer in a playoff for the Sarasota Seniors Championship.[24]

Johnny Moore died in Bradenton on April 4, 1991, at the age of 89. He left behind his wife, Rita, two children, six grandchildren, and a great-grandchild. In 2009 Moore was elected to the Original Pacific Coast League Hall of

Fame. Although he was largely under the radar, his was a fine baseball career as both a player and scout.

SOURCES

Beverage, Richard E., *The Angels — Los Angeles in the Pacific Coast League, 1919-1957* (Placentia, California: Deacon Press, 1981).

Ehrgott, Roberts, *Mr. Wrigley's Ball Club — Chicago & the Cubs During the Jazz Age* (Lincoln: University of Nebraska Press, 2013).

Johnson, Harold (Speed), *Who's Who in Major League Base Ball* (Chicago: Buxton Publishing Co., 1933).

Johnson, Lloyd, and Miles Wolff, eds., *The Encyclopedia Minor League Baseball* (Durham, North Carolina: Baseball America, Inc., 2nd ed., 1997).

Klima, John, *Bushville Wins! The Wild Saga of the 1957 Milwaukee Braves* (New York: Thomas Dunne Books, 2012).

Mathews, Eddie, and Bob Buege, *Eddie Mathews and the National Pastime* (Milwaukee: Douglas America Sports Publications, 1994).

Spalding, John E., *Pacific Coast League Stars — Ninety Who Made It to the Majors* (Manhattan, Kansas: Ag Press, 1997).

Wells, Donald R., *The Race for the Governor's Cup — The Pacific Coast League Playoffs, 1936-1954* (Jefferson, North Carolina: McFarland & Co., Inc., 2000).

Westcott, Rich, *Diamond Greats — Profiles and Interviews With 65 of Baseball's History Makers* (Westport, Connecticut: Meckler Books, 1988).

Westcott, Rich, and Frank Bilovsky, *The New Phillies Encyclopedia* (Philadelphia: Temple Univ. Press, 1993).

Bloodgood, Clifford, "The Interesting Career of Johnny Moore, *Baseball Magazine*, August 1937.

Johnny Moore clippings file of the Baseball Hall of Fame Library.

NOTES

1　For examples of excellent histories of the 1930s baseball without a trace of Johnny Moore, see Charles Alexander, *Breaking the Slump — Baseball in the Depression Era*; Donald Honig, *Baseball When the Grass Was Real - Baseball from the 20's to the 40's Told by the Men Who Played It*; Eugene Murdock, *Baseball Between the Wars — Memories of the Game by the Men Who Played It*; and Fay Vincent, *The Only Game in Town — Baseball Stars of the 1930s and 1940s Talk About the Game They Loved*.

2　Moores were rampant in the National League outfield during the 1930s. In addition to Johnny and JoJo, Gene Moore roamed the outfield for the Cardinals and Randy Moore for the Braves. Also, Austin "Cy" Moore pitched for the Dodgers and Phillies and Whitey Moore for the Reds.

3　Overall, Moore batted .326 in 10 Pacific Coast League seasons. John E. Spalding, *Pacific Coast League Stars — Ninety Who Made It to the Majors, 1903 to 1957*, 110.

4　Rich Westcott, *Diamond Greats - Profiles and Interviews With 65 of Baseball's History Makers*, 109.

5 Neal Ball's primary claim to fame was that he made an unassisted triple play during his playing days with the Cleveland Indians.

6 The couple had three children: Johnny Jr., who played minor-league baseball for a couple of seasons during the early 1940s, Rita, and Irving. Clippings dated May 7, 1942, and June 22, 1944, from the Johnny Moore clippings file of the Baseball Hall of Fame Library; Rich Westcott, 110.

7 Clifford Bloodgood, "The Interesting Career of Johnny Moore," *Baseball Magazine*, August, 1937, 398.

8 That season Moore played in one of the best PCL outfields of all-time. In addition to his .342 average, Jigger Statz hit .360 and Wes Schulmerich .380. Fourth outfielder G.W. Harper hit .308.

9 Westcott, 109.

10 Westcott, 108.

11 Westcott, 109-110.

12 Clipping dated August 27, 1936, from the Johnny Moore clippings file of the Baseball Hall of Fame Library.

13 Westcott, 108.

14 Harold (Speed) Johnson, *Who's Who in Major League Baseball*, 291.

15 Clipping dated May 23, 1940, from the Johnny Moore clippings file of the Baseball Hall of Fame Library.

16 Spalding, 110.

17 Unidentified article dated September 6, 1945, from the Johnny Moore clippings file of the Baseball Hall of Fame Library.

18 Unidentified articled dated July 7, 1963, from the Johnny Moore clippings file of the Baseball Hall of Fame Library.

19 Ibid.

20 Ibid; John Klima, *Bushville Wins — the Wild Saga of the 1957 Braves*, 32-33, 39, 41-42.

21 Eddie Mathews and Bob Buege, *Eddie Mathews and the National Pastime*, 5-6.

22 In addition to Eddie Mathews and Del Crandall, they were Denny Lemaster, Lee Maye, and Dan Schneider. Unidentified article dated July 7, 1963, from the Johnny Moore clippings file of the Baseball Hall of Fame Library.

23 Montreal Expos Press Release, January 5, 1971, in the Johnny Moore clippings file of the Baseball Hall of Fame Library.

24 Westcott, 110.

ART NEHF

By Gregory H. Wolf

WHEN MANAGER JOHN McGRAW needed a clutch win for his New York Giants during their four-year run as National League champions (1921-1924), he often relied on ace southpaw Art Nehf, winner of 184 games for four teams in his 15-year career (1915-1929). Described as a "money pitcher" by sportswriter Frederick G. Lieb, Nehf won the deciding game of the World Series in both 1921 and 1922 by tossing a shutout and a five-hitter respectively against the New York Yankees.[1] His World Series résumé also includes a six-hit shutout against the Yankees in 1923 and an epic 12-inning complete-game victory versus Walter Johnson and the Washington Senators in 1924. "Nehf is one of the finest, gamest pitchers the game has ever known," McGraw once said.[2] Plagued by arm and hand miseries, Nehf was waived by the Giants in 1926, but resurrected his career with the Chicago Cubs and helped them to the fall classic in 1929.

Arthur Neukom Nehf was born on July 31, 1892, in Terre Haute, Indiana, to Charles and Wilhelmine "Minnie" (Neukom) Nehf. The German-American Nehfs were a prosperous and well-respected family and owned a jewelry store in town. They raised their only child to appreciate education, music, and sports. A slightly built left-hander, Nehf gathered most of his initial baseball experience from school teams. Upon graduation from Wiley High School in 1910, he enrolled at Rose Polytechnic Institute (now known as Rose-Hulman Institute of Technology), where he played football, basketball, and baseball. He set a school record with a 99-yard touchdown as a quarterback in 1911, but was even more spectacular on the diamond. Described by Sporting Life as the "premiere pitcher in the Indiana College League" in 1911 and 1912, Nehf was a strikeout artist who supposedly fanned 98 batters in eight games, including 20 in a no-hitter.[3] In the summer of 1912, Nehf signed with Negaunee of the independent Iron and Copper League of northern Michigan. "The spectators were mostly miners," recalled Nehf. "The fights they used to have among themselves over close games were more thrilling than the games."[4]

Nehf's foray into Organized Baseball got off to a rocky start when he signed with the Kansas City Blues of the Double-A American Association in 1913. Homesick, dejected, and feeling out of place, Nehf pitched just twice in relief before being transferred to the Sioux City (Iowa) Packers in the Class A Western League. He won his first professional game and posted a 5.01 ERA in 32⅓ innings with the Packers but ended his season prematurely so that he could return to college.

In 1914 Nehf graduated with a degree in electrical engineering from Rose Polytechnic, but decided to give baseball another shot when he discovered the poor wages engineers earned at the time. After getting his unconditional release from Kansas City, he signed with the local Terre Haute Terre-iers of the Class B Central League, for whom he won 11 of 18 decisions and logged 174⅔ innings in less than two-thirds of the season.

Freed from the confines of his academic schedule, Nehf showed his potential in his first full year of professional baseball, in 1915. His Terre Haute minor-league team was now known as the Highlanders. By midseason, scouts from the Chicago White Sox, New York Giants, Philadelphia Athletics, and Washington Senators, as well as the Federal League flocked to see "Little Arthur," the stocky, 5-foot-9, 170-pound hurler whose accomplishments included a no-hitter and a league-record 17 strikeouts in another game.[5] The Boston Braves, acting on a tip from Terre Haute infielder Joe Evers (whose brother Johnny Evers played for Boston), dispatched scout Fred Mitchell to follow the 22-year old southpaw. Lauded as "brilliantly spectacular," Nehf posted a 19-10 record and led the league with 218 strikeouts and a minuscule 1.38 ERA.[6] On August 4 the Braves purchased Nehf's contract for a reported record $3,500 and secured his immediate transfer to the big-league club. In a widely circulated contemporary story, Johnny Evers had the opportunity to sign Nehf in 1913 when the Hall of Fame infielder was player-manager of the Chicago Cubs; however, Evers dismissed Nehf after a tryout as too small.

Nehf joined the reigning World Series champion Boston Braves, who were struggling to play .500-ball. With his star hurler, Bill James, suffering from arm miseries, manager George Stallings desperately needed an effective pitcher. After tossing batting practice for a week, Nehf made his big-league debut on August 13 against the first-place Philadelphia Phillies at the Baker Bowl. In relief of starter Dick Rudolph, he threw two scoreless innings with no hits allowed in a 5-3 loss. His first big-league start came on August 21 at Braves Field in the second game of a double header. The southpaw shut out the Pittsburgh Pirates on seven hits and singled in both sixth-inning runs of a 2-0 victory. Described as a "one of the best left-handed pitchers who have broken into the National League in years," Nehf tossed shutouts in two of his next three starts (including the first of three career one-hitters) to blank the Brooklyn Robins, 6-0, in Boston on September 4.[7] The reinvigorated Braves challenged the Phillies for the pennant, but eventually ended seven games behind to settle for second place. In a seamless transition to the big leagues, Nehf went 5-4, tying veteran Tom Hughes for the team lead in shutouts (4), and carved out a robust 2.53 ERA in 78⅓ innings.

In an era when critics considered baseball players uncouth and immoral, Nehf was a shining exception. Erudite, studious, and cultivated, Nehf had interests other than baseball. He was an excellent piano and organ player, earning the nickname "The Organist" from teammates when he played vaudeville during his years with the New York Giants. "The way [Nehf] ambles over the piano keys pounding out real harmony," opined a contemporary paper, "makes some folks wonder why he picked baseball as a profession."[8] Nehf enjoyed the company of sportswriters, and according to Frederick G. Lieb "was a skilled conversationalist who could talk well on most any subject.[9]

In 1916, Nehf's first full season began with great anticipation. "Stallings has a star in Nehf,"[10] wrote Grantland Rice, but the left-hander was derailed by a season-long battle with what physicians initially feared was typhoid fever (it wasn't). In early September, Nehf was hospitalized and missed three weeks of action.[11] Rested and seemingly cured, he returned for the final two weeks, but finished with a disappointing 7-5 record and only 13 starts.

Nehf completed 121 innings, along with an ERA of 2.01, as the Braves finished four games behind in third place.

Upon receiving his contract calling for a substantial pay cut for the 1917 season, Nehf threatened to quit baseball.[12] Unlike most players, Nehf had viable career options: he was a trained engineer and worked as a jeweler in his home town of Terre Haute. James E. Gaffney, owner of the cash-strapped Braves, ultimately acquiesced to Nehf's demands, and the lefty reported to spring training in Miami. However, Stallings wasn't pleased and relegated Nehf to the bullpen for the first six weeks of the season. On June 2 he finally started (a complete-game victory over the Cincinnati Reds) and proved to be the most consistent winner on a weak, sixth-place team. During a dominant stretch of five starts in September, Nehf hurled 41 consecutive scoreless innings, tying Jack Chesbro (Pirates in 1902) and Grover Cleveland "Pete" Alexander (Phillies in 1911) for the second-longest such streak in NL history behind Ed Reulbach's 44 innings in 1908 (with the Chicago Cubs). Nehf's scoreless streak accomplishment ties him for ninth-longest in NL history as of the end of the 2014 season. The streak included three overpowering outings (the latter two on three days' rest) on the road: a three-hitter against the Pittsburgh Pirates, followed by a 14-inning tie versus the St. Louis Cardinals and a four-hitter against the Reds. Nehf finished the season with a 17-8 record, completed 16 of 23 starts among his 38 appearances, and posted a stellar 2.16 ERA in 233⅓ innings.

Nehf was primarily a breaking-ball pitcher with a good fastball that belied his small stature. His success, the *New York Times* once suggested, came from the combination of "speed and immaculate control."[13] He also altered his pitching motion, much to the chagrin of batters. *Baseball Magazine* noted that he had a "puzzling underhand or sidearm delivery alternating occasionally with an overhand movement."[14] By 1920 he had also developed a slowball that was described as a "floater" or "fingernail ball" and fluttered much like a knuckleball.[15]

The 1918 season, played against the backdrop of a world war and General Enoch Crowder's "work or fight" decree, ended four weeks early, on Labor Day. While the seventh-place Braves fell precipitously from their "miracle" championship just four years earlier, Nehf rose to new heights. He completed a NL-leading and career-best 28 games (in 31 starts), including 18 in a row. The streak concluded in a marathon on August 1 at Braves Field. Nehf held the Pittsburgh Pirates scoreless on eight hits for 20 innings. In the 21st frame he was tagged for four hits and two runs, and collared with a heartbreaking 2-0 loss in which he faced 77 batters. He split his 30 decisions and posted a 2.69 ERA in a career-best 284⅓ innings.

Nehf experienced an uncertain offseason. While World War I cast doubts on the 1919 season, owners took advantage of the situation to release all players (in effect, granting them free-agent status) with a "gentleman's agreement" not to sign each other's players. Consequently, Nehf inked a contract to play semipro ball in the competitive Triangle Factory League in Dayton, Ohio, where he also worked to support the war effort.[16]

In fulfillment of sportswriters' predictions for a last-place finish, the Braves started the 1919 season with nine consecutive losses. The dubious streak was broken by Nehf's 11-inning, complete-game victory over the New York Giants which also reignited offseason rumors of New York's eventual acquisition of the hurler with an "elusive, tantalizing curve."[17] The trade was finally consummated on August 1 when the Giants sent pitchers Red Causey, Johnny Jones, and Joe Oeschger, catcher Mickey O'Neil, and an "immense sum" of money (reportedly $40,000 to $55,000) to the Braves.[18]

Nehf's arrival in New York was met with universal approval by fans and sportswriters who thought the left-hander would play the deciding role in the Giants' quest for a pennant. "[Nehf] is like a high-class horse hitched to a dray. He showed a lot of class but could get anywhere," read one report.[19] Following frustrating losses in his first two starts, Nehf commenced one of the most impressive stretches in his career. He won a career-best nine consecutive decisions, hurled eight complete games during his last ten starts, and posted a microscopic 1.45 ERA in 87 innings; nonetheless, the Giants still lost ground to the eventual pennant winning Cincinnati Reds. In a season

shorted by 14 games, Nehf finished with 17 wins and a 2.49 ERA in 270⅔ innings for the Braves and Giants.

Manager John McGraw counted on the "sweetest staff in the NL" to guide the Giants to the pennant in 1920, but the team got off to an unexpectedly slow start, fighting to play .500 ball through July.[20] After a brutal start to the season (34 hits and 18 runs in just 14 innings), the "priceless portside flinger" Nehf finally found his rhythm by winning nine of ten decisions from June 24 to August 2.[21] The

In his 15th and final season in the majors, Nehf notched eight of his 184 career wins for the Cubs in 1929. A two-time 20-game winner, the southpaw anchored the New York Giants' staffs that won four consecutive pennants and two World Series titles in the early 1920s. (National Baseball Hall of Fame)

Giants came roaring back in August and September (38-20) to challenge Brooklyn and Cincinnati, but ultimately finished in second place for the third straight season. Nehf showed his mettle by hurling a 17-inning complete game on three days' rest to defeat the Reds at Redland Field, 6-4, on August 27 during the first game of a doubleheader. Allowing just five earned runs in 41⅓ innings in September, Nehf closed out the season on a tear, finishing with a career-high 21 wins and joining Jesse Barnes (20-15) and Fred Toney (21-11) to form the NL's first trio of 20-game winners since the 1913 Giants. Nehf also helped his cause by recording a record-tying 11 double plays (Curt Davis broke the mark with 12 in 1934).

In 1921 the Giants waged a season-long battle against the Pittsburgh Pirates for supremacy in the NL. The league's highest-scoring offense was led by a quartet of future Hall of Famers, youngsters Frankie Frisch, Ross Youngs, and High Pockets Kelly, and veteran Dave Bancroft; however, "Little Napoleon" McGraw leaned on his pitchers Nehf, Barnes, Toney, and Phil Douglas, who combined for 68 of the team's 94 victories and logged almost 1,000 innings. Nehf came through when the Giants needed him most by defeating the Pirates seven consecutive times (all by complete game) and posting a 1.14 ERA. "The name of Nehf produces the same effect upon a Pirate as a conjurer's imprecation," wrote the *New York Times*.[22] The Giants overcame a 7½-game deficit on August 23 to take the lead on September 9 and held on to capture their first of four consecutive pennants. Nehf paced the staff with 20 wins and 260⅔ innings. "Once [Nehf] gains the upper-hand, he is poison," wrote syndicated columnist and AL umpire Billy Evans about the southpaw's emerging reputation as a big-game pitcher.[23]

The New York Giants and their tenants in the Polo Grounds, the New York Yankees, squared off in what H.G. Salsinger called "probably the best World Series ever played."[24] The third and final installment of the experimental best-of-nine format, the series was a clash of philosophies, pitting McGraw's Deadball Era tactics of "small ball" versus Miller Huggins's "long ball" embodied by Babe Ruth. During the regular season, the Yankees had hit 134 homers compared with the Giants' 75. In spite of the media's new-found fascination with the home run,

the World Series contained an epic battle between two pitchers, 21-year-old right-hander and future Hall of Famer Waite Hoyt (19-13) of the Yankees and Nehf.

Nehf held the vaunted Yankees lineup to just three hits and one earned run in Game Two, but lost, 3-0, as Hoyt subdued the Giants on two hits. In Game Five Nehf surrendered six hits and three runs, but his teammates could manage only one unearned run on ten hits against Hoyt. On two days' rest, Nehf and Hoyt squared off for the third time with the Yankees on the brink of elimination. In what was described as "one of the most brilliant games ever twirled in a World's Series," Nehf exacted revenge in Game Eight, holding the Yankees to four hits in his third straight complete game.[25] In the bottom of the ninth, nursing a precarious 1-0 lead, Nehf dispatched pinch-hitter Ruth, (who was suffering from an infected arm and bad back and did not play in Game Six or Seven), then walked Aaron Ward. The game ended when Home Run Baker grounded out and Ward was thrown out going for third. "If courage is the test of heroism," wrote *The Sporting News* of the Giants gaining their first championship since 1905, "then Art Nehf … is the pitching hero of the World Series."[26]

The NL's stingiest pitching corps (3.45 ERA) and a high-octane offense led the Giants to the pennant in 1922. Nehf, the unequivocal staff ace, led the team in innings (268⅓), starts (a career-high 35), complete games (20), and wins (19). His 3.29 ERA ranked fifth in the NL. "Nehf is a wonder," said McGraw, trying to explain his lefty's durability and success despite his size.[27] An excellent, nimble fielder, Nehf either led or tied for the lead with NL pitchers in putouts for the second time in three years, and ranked in the top four every year from 1918 to 1923.

The 1922 Series was back to a best-of-seven status. In the Opening Game of the World Series rematch, Nehf limited the Yankees to six hits and two runs (one earned) in seven innings of work. He was lifted for Earl Smith, who unsuccessfully pinch-hit with the bases loaded in the bottom of the seventh. A three-run rally in the eighth inning provided the Giants their only runs in a hard-fought victory. Game Two had ended in a ten-inning 3-3 tie. The

Giants took the next two games by scores of 3-0 and 4-3 to go up three games to none on the Yankees. On a rainy, overcast day, Nehf took the mound in Game Five on October 8 with the Giants on the verge of another championship. In a sense of déjà vu, Nehf, "the master of situations,"[28] hurled a complete-game five-hitter, surrendering just three runs. The Giants' three-run rally in the eighth inning made Nehf the winner, 5-3, and the Giants the kings of New York.

Nehf had an unexpectedly erratic season in 1923 during which he completed just seven of 27 starts and posted the league's fourth-highest ERA (4.50 in 196 innings). "Nehf is breaking down," wrote John B. Foster;[29] while Henry L. Farrell noted that the lefty was "awfully good or terribly bad."[30] For the first time in his life, Nehf was bothered by chronic arm pain all season long.[31] With an ERA well over 5.00 by the end of July, Nehf was relegated to a once-a-week starter and occasional reliever in August and September. The extra rest seemed to pay dividends, as the 30-year-old hurler sliced his ERA by nearly a run at season's end. Nehf's shutout against Brooklyn in his last start of the season rekindled fans' hope that the staff ace would be ready to face the New York Yankees for the third consecutive year in the World Series.

With the World Series tied one game apiece, Nehf (13-10) started Game Three at Yankee Stadium, inaugurated just that year and located across the Harlem River from the Polo Grounds. Described as the "diminutive star" by the Associated Press, Nehf blanked the Yankees on six hits to earn the victory, 1-0, courtesy of Casey Stengel's home run.[32] Nehf's wizardry over the Yankees ended in the deciding Game Six at the Polo Grounds. Through 7⅓ innings, he was dominant, surrendering just two hits and a run. Then the bottom fell out. He gave up two singles and walked the next two batters on eight pitches. With one run in and the bases loaded, Nehf was mercifully removed and sobbed on his way to the dugout.[33] The Yankees blasted reliever Rosy Ryan for four runs (three charged to Nehf) to win the game and the first championship in their history.

McGraw told the press even before the 1924 campaign started that he was not "banking on Nehf."[34] The "Terre

Haute Terror," as Nehf was sometimes called, pitched sparing through July, starting just nine times in an effort to save wear and tear on his arm. McGraw, bracing for an annual battle for the pennant, counted on his experienced pitcher during the final, tense two months during which the Giants lost a nine-game lead. "Surpassing McGraw's expectations," Nehf tossed nine complete-game victories in 12 starts between July 29 and September 25 and reclaimed his place as the staff ace.[35] Always adept with the bat (.210 career average), Nehf went on a slugging rampage during this stretch, belting five of his career eight home runs and knocking in 11 runs in just 30 at-bats. Nehf's 14th and final victory of the season completed a three-game sweep of the Pittsburgh Pirates on September 25 and effectively clinched the Giants' fourth consecutive pennant with two games remaining.

The World Series opened in Griffith Stadium in Washington, D.C., where Nehf took the mound against the Washington Senators' legendary ace, 36-year old Walter Johnson, winner of 377 games and pitching in his first fall classic. Through 11 innings the two veterans battled to a 2-2 tie before the Giants rallied for two runs off the Big Train in the 12th frame. Calling on his "cunning and endurance," Nehf extinguished the Nationals' rally to earn the victory, 4-3.[36] The exciting win was tempered by news that Nehf had injured his hand batting down a line drive. His next start was pushed back to Game Six with the championship on the line. Through seven innings, Nehf yielded just four hits and two runs before being lifted for pinch-hitter Frank Snyder in the eighth. The Giants managed just one run off southpaw Tom Zachary to make Nehf the hard-luck loser. Nehf hurled two-thirds of an inning of relief in Game Seven which ended on Ed McNeely's "bad-hop" walk-off double scoring Muddy Ruel in the 12th inning to give the Senators their first and only championship in D.C.

Eighteen months after his duel with Walter Johnson, Nehf's career seemed washed up. Since as early as 1924, he had suffered from what physicians ultimately diagnosed as neuritis, a debilitating disease that caused numbness in his fingers, making holding a ball, not to mention throwing one, a difficult task. After logging just 155 innings while winning 11 of 20 decisions in 1925, Nehf was sold on May 11, 1926, to the Cincinnati Reds in a waiver transaction. He pitched in only nine games combined for the Giants and Reds in 1926, followed by 21 for the Reds in 1927 before he was given his unconditional release on August 30.

Nehf signed with the Chicago Cubs as a free agent two days after his release and experienced an unexpected rebirth. Thrown into a pennant race, Nehf made eight appearances in just over three weeks, tossed his first shutout in more than two years, and notched an impressive 1.37 ERA in 26⅓ innings. More importantly, he pitched his way to a contract for 1928.

Nehf vindicated manager Joe McCarthy's decision to keep him by shutting out the Reds on six hits in the third game of the 1928 season. The veteran southpaw became one of a core group of six hurlers (Sheriff Blake, Guy Bush, Pat Malone, Charlie Root, and Percy Jones) who started between 19 and 30 games and cumulatively won 87 of the team's 91 victories. Nehf, the oldest of the sextet by almost six years, flourished in his role as a once-a-week starter. He showed his former skipper, John McGraw (against whom he carried a grudge and supposedly refused to speak to for having sold him to Cincinnati) that he could still pitch by holding the Giants to one unearned run over 13 innings in a an eventual 2-1 Cubs victory in 15 frames during the first game of a doubleheader then threw 12 innings of a 13-inning, 3-2 loss, during consecutive starts in July. The dagger in the heart of his former team came on September 27 in the first game of a double header at the Polo Grounds. With New York just one game out of first place, Nehf hurled a masterful six-hitter versus rookie Carl Hubbell to earn a 3-2 victory. In a tight three-team pennant race, the Cubs finished in third place, four games behind the St. Louis Cardinals. Nehf's comeback season included a 13-7 record and the NL's third-best ERA (2.65) in 176⅔ innings.

Described by reporter Edward Burns as the "fine and cultured patriarch of the Cubs," Nehf divided his time between starts and relief appearances in 1929.[37] He went 8-5, but was hit hard, posting a career-worst 5.59 ERA in 120⅔ innings for the pennant-winning Cubs. In Chicago's much anticipated World Series with the

Philadelphia Athletics, Nehf pitched a scoreless inning of relief in the Cubs' Game Two loss. In what proved to be his last appearance in the big leagues, Nehf relieved Charlie Root in Game Four with one out and two runners on in the seventh in one of the epic collapses in Series history. The first batter Nehf faced, Mule Haas, hit a towering, but routine fly ball that center fielder Hack Wilson lost in the sunlight. The ball dropped for an inside-the-park, three-run homer. After walking Mickey Cochrane, Nehf was replaced by Sheriff Blake, the third of four Cubs pitchers in that fateful inning during which they collectively yielded ten runs in a 10-8 loss to go down three games to one. The A's captured the title two days later with another comeback rally in Game Five.

Nehf announced his retirement in the offseason, bringing his 15-year career to an end. He won 184 and lost 120 while posting a 3.20 ERA in 2,707⅔ innings. In five World Series he split his eight decisions, carved out a 2.16 ERA in 79 innings (seventh-most as of the end of 2014), and held the opposition to a minuscule .174 batting average.

Nehf and his wife, Elizabeth (May) Neff, settled in Phoenix, where they had established their home in the mid-1920s. They raised three children — Arthur, Daniel, and Elizabeth. A respected and successful businessman, Nehf suffered a debilitating heart attack in 1932 that forced him into permanent retirement. He remained actively interested in local semipro leagues in Phoenix, and helped arrange tryouts for several players, most notably All-Star outfielder Hank Leiber, who had a ten-season career with the New York Giants and Chicago Cubs. Nehf was inducted into the Arizona Sports Hall of Fame in 1959, and posthumously into the Indiana Baseball Hall of Fame in 1989.

In poor health the last few years of his life, Nehf passed away at the age of 68 on December 18, 1960. The cause was cancer. Honorary pallbearers at the funeral service included Del E. Webb, co-owner of the New York Yankees, and Horace C. Stoneham, president of the San Francisco Giants. Nehf was cremated and his ashes were interred at the Greenwood Memorial Park in Phoenix. Rose-Hulman Institute of Technology renamed its baseball field Art Nehf Field in his honor, and later inducted him into its athletic hall of fame.[38]

SOURCES

Chicago Daily Tribune

New York Times

The Sporting News

Ancestry.com

BaseballLibrary.com

Baseball-Reference.com

Retrosheet.org

SABR.org

Art Nehf player file, National Baseball Hall of Fame, Cooperstown, New York.

NOTES

1   *The Sporting News*, December 28, 1960, 36.

2   Associated Press, "Drama of Series Enacted in Team Dressing Rooms," *Altoona (Pennsylvania) Tribune*, October 16, 1923, 8.

3   "Blues Sign Pitcher Nehf," *Indianapolis News*, July 11, 1913, 14.

4   "The Man Who Gave The Braves Their Final Spurt," *Baseball Magazine*, November 1915, 34.

5   Ibid.

6   Ibid.

7   "The Man Who Gave The Braves Their Final Spurt," 33.

8   "JOB, McGraw Puts End To Rumors About Ross Youngs," *San Antonio Evening News*, March 5, 1920, 17

9   *The Sporting News*, December 28, 1960, 36.

10 Grantland Rice, *Sporting Life*, March 25, 1916, 16.

11 *Sporting Life*, September 16, 1916, 4.

12 "Art Nehf balks," *Indianapolis News*, February 19, 1917, 13.

13 "Giants Down Cards as Corsairs Lose," *New York Times*, September 27, 1921, 16.

14 "The Man Who Gave The Braves Their Final Spurt," 33.

15 "McGraw Puts His Faith in His Three Aces," *Nevada State Journal* (Reno, Nevada), April 18, 1920, 5.

16 "More Diamond Stars join Factory League," *Fort Wayne Journal-Gazette*, August 4, 1918, 9.

17 "Braves Find Giants In Relenting Mood," *New York Times*, May 9, 1919, 18.

18 W.A. Phelon, "Who Will Win the Big League Pennants?," *Baseball Magazine*, October 1919, 329.

19 "Critics Size Up Arthur Nehf," *Terre Haute Saturday Spectator*, October 4, 1919, 33.

20 "Hurlers Fail to Make Grade in Major Loops," *Indianapolis News*, April 21, 1920, 18.

21 "Giants Win When Nehf Tames Cubs," *New York Times*, June 25, 1920, 13.

22 "Nehf Weaves Spell Over Pirates," *New York Times*, August 28, 1921, 93.

23 Billy Evans, "Billy Evans Sizes Up New York Giants an Good, Not Great, But Game Ball Club," *Fort Wayne Journal-Gazette*, October 1, 1921, 11.

24 *The Sporting News*, October 20, 1921, 1.

25 "Giants Win World Series; Nehf Beats Hoyt, 1-0 in Thrilling Finish," *New York Times*, October 14, 1921, 1.

26 *The Sporting News*, October 20, 1921, 1.

27 "McGraw Names an All-Star Baseball Team For The National League," *San Francisco Chronicle*, December 2, 1922, 3.

28 "Giants Take Series Without Defeat; Win Last Game, 5-3," *New York Times*, October 9, 1922, 1.

29 John B. Foster, "Hard Fight to Keep Giants at the Top," *Harrisburg Telegraph*, July 16, 1923, 13.

30 Henry L. Farrell, "Pirates Are Most To Be Feared By M'Graw's Giants," *News-Herald* (Franklin, Pennsylvania), May 17, 1923, 8.

31 "Not Banking on Nehf," *Evening News* (Harrisburg, Pennsylvania), January 10, 1924, 21.

32 Associated Press, "Nehf May Pitch for Giants and Pennock Yankees," *Morning Sun* (Yuma, Arizona), October 10, 1923, 1.

33 Associated Press, "Drama of Series Enacted in Team Dressing Rooms," *Altoona (Pennsylvania) Tribune*, October 16, 1923, 8.

34 Not Banking on Nehf," *Evening News* (Harrisburg, Pennsylvania), January 10, 1924, 21.

35 Norman E. Brown, "Jack Bentley and Art Nehf Are Hot To Beat in Older Organization," *San Bernardino County Sun* (San Bernardino, California), August 2, 1924, 16.

36 Associated Press, "Mogridge and Johnson Stand Between Giants and Winning Flag," *Post-Crescent* (Appleton, Wisconsin), October 7, 1924, 5.

37 Edward Burns, "Stephenson and Grimm Hit 'Em, Nehf Holds 'Em," *Chicago Daily Tribune*, May 8, 1929, 29.

38 "Art Nehf," Rose-Hulman Fightin' Engineers. .edu/athletics/athletic-hall-of-fame/current-hall-of-fame-inductees/nehf.aspx.

BOB OSBORN

By Nancy Snell Griffith

BOB OSBORN WAS A RIGHT-HANDED pitcher for the Chicago Cubs and the Pittsburgh Pirates in parts of six seasons from 1925 until 1931. A spot starter and reliever in 1926 and 1927 for the Cubs, Osborn spent all of 1928 and most of 1929 in the minor leagues before Chicago made him a late-season call-up during its exciting pennant run in the latter year. He pitched only three times for the North Siders in 1929 and was not on their World Series roster.

John Bode Osborn was born on April 17, 1903, in San Diego (Duval County), Texas, the son of Adolphus, a railroad conductor, and Lillian Bode Osborn. By 1923 he was playing for the Wichita Falls Spudders of the Class A Texas League, part of the Cubs organization. He didn't have a very stellar season that year. He won two games and lost five, gave up 56 hits and 22 walks in 52 total innings, and finished the season with an earned-run average of 4.67.

Despite this rather lackluster showing, the Cubs gave Osborn a look in 1924, but by April 7 he had been sent back to Wichita Falls with outfielder Marty Callaghan and infielder Pete Turgeon in exchange for shortstop Ralph Michaels.[1] He won 13 and lost 17 that year, with an ERA of 4.39. He was also with Wichita Falls for most of the 1925 season, winning 16 and losing 10, and posting an ERA of 3.94 before being called up by the Cubs in mid-September. Osborn's major-league debut came on September 16, 1925, when he appeared in relief during the second game of a doubleheader against the Boston Braves. He pitched the sixth and seventh innings, and gave up six hits and two runs.

In March 1926 Osborn spent spring training with the Cubs, and this time he made the team. He had trouble with his control during the season, giving up large numbers of hits in the majority of his appearances. He was also walking too many batters, sometimes averaging a walk an inning. On June 27 he gave up ten walks in 9⅔ innings. On September 5, he gave up 11 hits, one walk, and six runs in just 5⅔ innings and left the game with the Cubs trailing, but was awarded the win under the scoring decisions of that era. He pitched in 31 games that year, starting 15 of them, and had a won-lost record of 6-5. In the course of 136⅓ innings he gave up 58 walks, but ended the season with an ERA of 3.63, the lowest mark he posted in a full season during his major-league career.

Osborn was back with the Cubs in 1927. On May 17 in Boston, he took over the mound against the Braves in the ninth inning. The game went on for 22 innings, with the Cubs coming out on top, 4-3. According to the *Miami News,* "Bob Osborn was the hero of the 22-inning struggle. He took the box for Chicago in the ninth and held the Braves to six hits. For 14 innings — from the seventh to the 22nd, the rivals battled without a score. Not a hit went for more than two bases."[2] Osborn appeared in 24 games during the season, starting 12 of them, and completing two. He ended the season with a 5-5 record and an ERA of 4.18.

On March 30, 1928, the Cubs traded Osborn and an outfielder to be named later to the Los Angeles Angels of the Pacific Coast League for infielder Ray Jacobs.[3] He pitched in 26 games (120 innings) for the Angels, winning five and losing nine. His ERA was 5.70. The following February, the Cubs bought Osborn back from Los Angeles, but by April 1929 he had been sent on option to the Reading Keystones of the International League.[4] He didn't pitch well for the Keystones, and by June 5 he had lost five in a row.[5] By mid-August his record was 8-11.[6] After pitching in 34 games (182 innings) for Reading, he was called up by the Cubs for the final weeks of the season. His record at Reading was 11-14, with an ERA of 4.10.

When Osborn was called up from Reading, the Cubs were in the midst of a pennant race. During the remainder of the season, he pitched in three games (nine total innings) for the Cubs, starting only one. He appeared in relief in the last inning of a 9-6 loss to the Brooklyn Robins on September 17. He pitched one inning as a reliever during a 7-3 loss to the New York Giants on September 18, giving up two hits and one run. He started against Cincinnati on October 4, pitching seven innings and giving up six hits and two runs in a 6-3 Cubs extra-inning victory. During the offseason, Osborn returned to live with his mother, Lillian, in El Paso, Texas.

By March 1930 Osborn was back at Cubs training camp. One sportswriter noted that he had "had several tryouts and … is long over due."[7] By May, Cubs manager Joe McCarthy was reportedly worried about his pitching staff. He was carrying a roster of 12 pitchers, seven of them rookies, and had to make final cuts by June 15. By that time Osborn had started four games for Chicago and had appeared as a reliever in nine others. He remained on the roster and, according to sportswriter John B. Foster, he had "come up to snuff for the Cubs. The big fellow always had enough strength to eat six meals a day. He had been too wild to get much out of him. This year he has won five games for his club and lost only one to the Phillies. Those five games are worth a heap to the Cubs right now."[8] By July 19 Osborn's record was 8-1, which ranked among the best in the National League.[9] On August 28 Osborn came in during the ninth inning and pitched until the end of a marathon 20-inning loss to the Cardinals. On September 1 he gave up five hits, the fewest of his career in a complete game, in a losing effort against Cincinnati. By the end of the 1930 season Osborn had appeared in 35 games (126⅔ innings), 13 of which he started. His record was 10-6, and his ERA was 4.97.

Despite this promising season, on April 22, 1931, Osborn was sold to the Pittsburgh Pirates. This move caused some surprise in baseball circles because "[t]he young hurler did fine work last year for the Cubs and appeared destined to star in the senior loop, but he being unable to reach form this year, was allowed to go."[10] Pirates manager Jewel Ens had high hopes for Osborn, especially because pitchers Ervin Brame and Remy Kremer were "out with illness," and Steve Swetonic had an injured elbow.[11] The Pirates used Osborn mostly as a short reliever, and by June he had three wins and no losses, which one sportswriter declared "good enough for him for the time being."[12] He played his final major-league game with the Pirates on September 24, 1931. He appeared in 27 games

(64⅔ innings) during the season, starting only two. He ended the season with a record of 6-1 and an ERA of 5.01, and his six wins in relief led the NL.

On January 29, 1932, the Pirates traded Osborn and catcher Eddie Phillips to the Kansas City Blues of the Double-A American Association, part of the Cardinals organization, in exchange for pitcher Bill Swift. Commenting on the trade, sportswriter Fred Wertenbach went so far as to call Osborn "the colorless Bob Osborn."[13] Pirates manager George Gibson said that he hated to let Osborn go: "I wanted to keep Osborn. But I also wanted Swift, and the Blues wouldn't listen to a trade unless I gave them Osborn."[14] Osborn never made it back to the majors. He finished with 121 career games, starting 43 of them, and logged 446 innings. His record was 27-17, and his ERA was 4.32.

During 1932 Osborn played for both the Blues and the Columbus Red Birds of the American Association, another Cardinals affiliate. In 1933 he played for two other

A right-handed pitcher, Osborn made three appearances for the Cubs in 1929. He won 27 games in six years in the majors. (Retro Images Archive. George Brace Collection)

Cardinals affiliates, Springfield of the Class B Mississippi Valley League and Elmira of the Class A New York-Pennsylvania League. According to Osborn's friend (and El Paso sportswriter) Bob Ingram, Osborn did not appreciate the treatment he was given by the St. Louis organization: "He balked at taking a big salary cut and walked out on Organized Baseball. He was bitter at the then Cardinal farm system and advised young players against going into it."[15]

Osborn was back in El Paso by September 1933, when he was recruited by the semi-pro Hugo & Millers of the International League to pitch in the championships.[16] He remained in El Paso in 1934, where he was being wooed by Jodie McCormick of the semi-pro Mitchell Brewers.[17] By 1935 Osborn was pitching and managing for the semipro Crane Oilers of the Permian Basin Baseball League.[18] He was still with the Oilers in 1938.

Sometime between 1930 and 1938, Osborn married Hallie Nell McPherson. A son, John Bode Osborn, Jr., was born to them in Crane County on October 22, 1938, but he died in El Paso County only a month later. In 1940 Bob and Hallie were still living in Crane, Texas, where he was working as a tool dresser. He apparently then returned to El Paso, where, according to the *El Paso Herald Post*, he was living in 1948. By 1949 he was managing the semipro Tigua Cubs.[19] And he was always hanging around the sandlots in El Paso, "looking over youngsters, helping coach some of them, giving others a few pointers."[20]

Some years later, Osborn and his wife relocated to Paris, Arkansas, where he planned to raise cattle. He wasn't a farmer for long, however, and soon became the recreation director for the town of Paris. According to Bob Ingram, "Baseball was his big love and he couldn't get away from it." Osborn died of a heart attack in Paris, Arkansas, on April 19, 1960. He was 57 years old. His death came as a surprise; at the time he was lining up the teams for the area Little League.[21] He is buried in Oaklawn Cemetery in Paris. His wife died in 1991.

SOURCES

Baseball-Reference.com

Retrosheet.org

Ancestry.com

NOTES

1 "Alexander Shows Fans His Arm is Still Far from Being Dead," *Spokane Daily Chronicle*, April 7, 1924, 14.

2 "Boston-Chicago Play Twenty-Two Innings," *Miami News*, May 18, 1927, 12.

3 "Sport Jabs," *Beaver County* (Pennsylvania) *Daily Times*, March 30, 1938, Section 2, 10.

4 "Reading gets Osborn from Cubs," *New York Times*, April 17, 1929, 31.

5 "Trailing the Keys," *Reading Eagle*, June 5, 1929, 16.

6 "Trailing the Keys," *Reading Eagle*, August 15, 1929, 18.

7 Associated Press, "Cubs Confident of Repeating in 1930," *Palm Beach Post*, March 5, 1930, 19.

8 "John B. Foster, "Ex-Boston Pitcher Wins Six in Row for New York," *Oakland Tribune*, July 1, 1930, 30.

9 United Press, "McCarthy Confident Cubs Will Win National Pennant," Sheboygan (Wisconsin) Press, July 29, 1930, 12.

10 Arcadia (California) Tribune, May 1, 1931, 3.

11 "Pirates' Purchase of Osborn Bad Omen for Swetonic," *Pittsburgh Press*, April 26, 1931, sports section, 5.

12 John B. Foster, "National League Pitchers Having Very Good Seasons," *Appleton* (Wisconsin) *Post Crescent*, June 10, 1931, 12.

13 Fred Wertenbach, "Bucco Pilot Confident of Improvement," *Pittsburgh Press*, January 31, 1932, sports section, 5.

14 Bob Ingram, "As I Was Saying," *El Paso Herald-Post*, April 5, 1933, 8.

15 Bob Ingram, "As I Was Saying," *El Paso Herald Post*, April 21, 1960, 34.

16 "Clint, Hugos Add Pitchers for Title Set," *El Paso Herald-Post*, September 30, 1933, 6.

17 "Losing Teams Angling for New Players," *El Paso Herald Post*, April 16, 1934, 6.

18 Bob Ingram, "As I Was Saying," *El Paso Herald-Post*, August 31, 1935, 7.

19 "Tigua Cubs Beat White Sands Nine," *El Paso Herald-Post*, June 22, 1949, 17.

20 Bob Ingram, "As I Was Saying," *El Paso Herald Post*, April 21, 1960, 34.

21 Bob Ingram, "As I Was Saying," *El Paso Herald Post*, April 21, 1960, 34.

KEN PENNER

By Chip Greene

Kenneth William Penner was a baseball lifer. From the time he broke into organized ball as a 17-year-old pitcher in 1913, until his final pitch, thrown at the age of 47, Penner spent parts of 28 seasons in the minor leagues, pitching for 17 teams in 11 leagues and four classifications. In between, the right-hander realized two brief stints 13 years apart in the major leagues, and when he was through as an active player, spent another 15 years as a minor-league manager and major-league scout before succumbing at the relatively young age of 63.

Penner's formative years are largely a mystery. Born April 24, 1896, in Booneville, Indiana, he was the son of W.D. Penner and Florence (Cox) Penner.[1] While Florence was a presence in Penner's life well into the 1940s, beyond the initials W.D., we know nothing about his father. By all appearances, W.D. died early in Penner's life, as the 1900 census lists the future major leaguer living with his mother, then 27 years old and "widowed," in the home of Penner's maternal grandmother, Mary M. Cox, in Spencer, Indiana. Also residing in the home at that time were eight more of Mary's ten children, plus Mary's parents, John W. and Millie Lamar. With 13 people living under the same roof, it must have been rather cramped quarters for the 4-year-old Ken.

From that point until his start in professional ball, we lose sight of Penner as a young man. In 1913, though, his professional career began as he made five appearances with the Columbus (Mississippi) Joy Riders, of the Class D Cotton States League, pitching a total of 35 innings. How he joined that team is unknown, but by the following year Penner was a full-fledged ace, as he moved to the Cadillac Chiefs of the Class D Michigan State League and tossed a team-leading 277 innings in 38 games, winning 14 and losing 18. (Penner walked 94 batters in his 277 innings; it was the first of several seasons in which he posted impressive control totals.) In 1915 Penner moved on to the Keokuk (Iowa) Indians of the Class D Central Association, where he was even better, posting an 18-14 record in 269 innings over 37 games with a WHIP (walked

plus hits per inning pitched) of 1.056, a performance that earned him a brief promotion to the Class B Central League, where he pitched twice for the Grand Rapids (Michigan) Black Sox. There, he dazzled, walking just one batter in 11 innings and finishing with a WHIP of just 0.818. He was just a year away from appearing on the major-league stage.

Little evidence can be found that might provide a clue to Penner's pitching skills. Online resources are devoid of strikeout totals, and box scores of his games are equally scarce, so it's difficult to judge what kind of pitcher he might have been. Rather than possessing overpowering stuff, however, it's more likely, given his totals of hits allowed totals and minimal walks, that Penner was a nibbler, a control pitcher, more than a strikeout artist. If so, in 1916 he was at the top of his game. That season found him in Marshalltown, Iowa, pitching for the Marshalltown Ansons of the Class D Central Association. He and a left-hander named Phil Slattery, who had pitched three games for the Pittsburgh Pirates the previous season, each posted 22-11 records, with Slattery tossing a team-leading 303 innings, and Penner 287. Penner walked just 62 with a WHIP of 0.997 and a miserly 1.41 earned-run average; he allowed just 45 earned runs in his 51 appearances. So impressive must Penner have been that year that in July a newspaper reported that "Cleveland is now after pitcher Ken Penner of Marshalltown. There is little doubt but what the former Keokuk starter will go up at the end of the season."[2] In addition to Cleveland, the New York Yankees had also expressed interest in Penner, reports also said. In the end, the Indians obtained his services; in September, Penner was sold to Cleveland.

Penner made his major-league debut on September 11, 1916, pitching the seventh and eighth innings of a 9-1 home loss to Detroit. The next day he again faced the Tigers, allowing one hit in two-thirds of an inning. In neither of those appearances did he allow any runs. On the 15th, again at home, Indians manager Lee Fohl called on the 20-year-old rookie to start against the Philadelphia Athletics, and Penner got his only major-league win, tossing seven strong innings while allowing just six hits and two earned runs in a 3-2 Cleveland victory. Penner also started the team's final game of the season, the second game of a doubleheader on October 1 at Cleveland's Dunn Field, but this time he was not as effective: In three innings he allowed four hits and four earned runs, and was the losing pitcher as the Indians lost to the White Sox, 8-4. In his brief trial, Penner had split two decisions and posted an ERA of 4.26 in 12⅔ innings. They were the only games he ever pitched in the American League.

When spring training rolled around, Penner was back in the minor leagues, and with a new team. In January 1917 the Portland Beavers announced that they had obtained Penner from Cleveland, and he went on to have a solid year in the Pacific Coast League — 21 wins and a 3.33 ERA in 59 games and 375⅓ innings. It was the first of many stops over the next 13 years, as Penner's career took a nomadic turn. Between 1917 and 1928 he pitched for teams in Portland, Oregon; Salt Lake City; Portland

After a 13-year absence from the big-leagues, right-hander Penner made five appearances for the Cubs in 1929. In 27 seasons in the minors he won more than 300 games. (National Baseball Hall of Fame)

again; Sacramento; Vernon, California; Wichita, Kansas; Vernon again; and then three seasons with the Houston Buffaloes. Throughout, he proved a durable, effective starter, averaging over that span 39 games, 280 innings and 13 wins per season. Four times he was a 20-game winner.

Perhaps Penner's wins would have been greater but for a freak automobile accident in 1918. That year he joined the Salt Lake City Bees of the Pacific Coast League. The Bees trained in Porterville, California. Having started slowly in the spring because of a case of measles, Penner had recovered by the end of March and was positioning himself as the ace of the Bees' staff. On March 24, the Bees traveled from Porterville to Bakersfield for a game. Boosters had supplied the team with a fleet of automobiles in which to travel, and Penner was a passenger in one of the vehicles. En route, the driver of Penner's car lost control, a tire blew, and the car swerved and tipped over. All the occupants were pinned underneath the car. All escaped serious injury except Penner, who suffered a cracked collarbone broken ribs. His injuries kept him out for more than a month; Penner returned on May 2, but for the season he appeared in just 16 games, tossing 117⅔ innings. It appears to be the only serious injury he ever incurred.

By 1920 Penner, still just 24 years old, had already logged seven seasons in the minor leagues and totaled 98 wins. That season he joined the PCL's Sacramento Senators and began one of his longest sustained engagements, four consecutive seasons. Indeed, for the remainder of his life Penner's baseball career would be primarily identified with California's capital.

As with many of the pitcher's moves, tracking down the specifics of how he came to join the Sacramento club is difficult. Although he pitched for Portland in 1919, there's some indication that Sacramento wasn't his initial destination in 1920. Reporting in January about the proliferation of athletes, specifically baseball players and boxers, taking up golf as a way to stay in condition ("Many Ball Players Take to the Links to Keep in Shape for Coming Season" was the headline in the January 16 edition of the *Twins Falls Daily News*), the press noted the "number of athletes in both classes making use of the Los Angeles municipal golf links in Griffith Park." Penner was one of the players identified as a regular visitor to the links, but he was identified as "Penner of the *Vernon* club (author's italics)." He wouldn't take the mound for Vernon until 1924. In 1920 Penner led Sacramento in innings pitched and hurled five shutouts. In his four full seasons in Sacramento, he pitched in 181 games, an average of 45 per season, and averaged 282 innings per year. In all, usually toiling for bad teams, he won 59 games for Sacramento, with a 3.64 ERA, and walked just 269 batters in 1,126 innings. Eventually, Penner also made Sacramento his home.

If Penner found winning difficult in Sacramento (his overall winning percentage was just .453), his fortunes were dramatically different in Houston. Following a poor start at Vernon in 1925 (2-6, 5.47 ERA in 18 games), the right-hander had been sold outright to Wichita Falls, a Cardinals affiliate in the Class A Western League, where he'd again been a big winner, crafting a record of 19-6. In the offseason, though, as had become customary, Penner was sold to the Buffaloes, where he spent the next three seasons. There, he finally joined a winner, although with the conclusion of each season his return was always questionable. After a largely pedestrian 1926 campaign, in 1927 Penner won 19 games and the league ERA crown (2.54); his wins and innings pitched were second on the team. The following season was even better. Finishing with a record of 20-8, Penner combined with pitchers Bill Hallahan, Jim Lindsey, and Frank Barnes to win 88 games and the Texas League pennant. It was Penner's final 20-win season.

One game during the 1926 season gives a glimpse into Penner's other baseball skills. On July 12, in a game against the San Antonio Bears, the pitcher was called on to pinch-hit with two outs in the bottom of the ninth with the Buffaloes trailing 1-0 and the bases empty. "After he hit for two bases in a pinch," a sportswriter said, "Ken Penner spoiled an excellent chance to score when he tried to stretch the hit into a three-bagger and was thrown out on third, retiring the side to give the Bears the opening game of the series, 1-0."[3] It's not known if Penner frequently pinch-hit, but by all accounts he was a relatively good hitting pitcher: In 2,410 at-bats, he batted .242 and hit 15 home runs.

Despite Penner's impressive performances for the Buffaloes, each winter of his stay with the team found him moved to another affiliate. In February 1927 Houston president Fred Ankenman "announced that pitcher Sylvester Johnson had been traded to the Syracuse, International League, team for Kenneth Penner. Penner pitched for the Buffaloes last summer, and was sold in the fall to Syracuse." Johnson, however, "protested against coming to Houston," and thus Penner was sent back to the Buffaloes.[4] Then, in August of 1927, it was announced that "Ken Penner of Buffs Will Go to Syracuse: Penner and Tex Carleton have been sold to the Syracuse International league club in an outright cash deal," effective at the close of the season.[5] In November it was reported that "six or seven Syracuse batterymen are likely to go to the Cardinal Training Camp [sic] when it opens" including "four or five pitchers, one of whom is almost certain to be Ken Penner."[6] Yet again, though, Penner opened the season with Houston, as in February 1928 team president Ankenman announced, "The official release to the Houston Buffaloes of two pitchers, Ken Penner … and Frank Barnes." Curiously, the story related that Penner and Barnes "are procured from Rochester, International League … in a deal that takes pitcher Herman Bell and an unannounced sum to Rochester."[7] There was no explanation how Penner ended up with Rochester.

Nor is it clear how he wound up with his new team in 1929. As the season began, Penner had joined the Indianapolis Indians of the American Association. That stay turned out to be one of his best performances in several years, as Penner, who typically allowed over a hit per inning (entering the season he had given up 4,392 in 4,235 frames, an average of 1.03) allowed only 170 hits in 191 innings while walking just 51, a 1.157 WHIP; with a 3.25 ERA, he also won 13 of 20 decisions. More importantly, though, the right-hander drew the attention of major-league scouts, and on August 2, 13 years after his previous major-league stint, Indianapolis announced the "sale of Ken Penner, to the [first place] Chicago Cubs."[8] (The deal also included pitcher Claude Jonnard and cash.) Penner, who was in Kansas City with the Indians on August 1, the day the deal was made, was to leave that night and join the Cubs the next day in Chicago, in time for the beginning of their four-game series with Brooklyn.

If, in the end, the 33-year-old Penner failed to make much of a splash with the Cubs, neither did he prove a mistaken signing. After making his first appearance in the Brooklyn series, on August 6, when he held the Robins hitless over the final 1⅔ innings of a 5-4 Cubs loss, he appeared four more times before the season's end. In four of his five outings Penner did not allow an earned run, although sloppy fielding by the Cubs in his final game, on September 4 in St. Louis, charged Penner with six unearned runs and the loss, his only decision. Penner's final ERA of 2.84 in 12⅔ innings was the highlight of the month he spent on the mound as a Cub. When Chicago lost to the Philadelphia Athletics in the World Series, Penner was not on the Chicago roster.

In nine major-league games, Penner finished 1-2, with a 3.55 ERA in 25⅓ innings.

Whether or not he was ever again considered for a chance to pitch in the major leagues is unclear. In any event, if his time with the Cubs proved eventful, it was undoubtedly eclipsed by his marriage that year to Thelma Lamar. They remained married until Penner's premature death; by all accounts they were childless.

In 1930 Penner joined the Louisville Colonels of the American Association. He remained with the Colonels for six years, through the 1935 season, and managed the team his final two seasons. Over the next four years, now in his 40s, he pitched for and managed teams in Crookston, Minnesota; Montgomery, Alabama; and Bellingham, Washington; in 1940 he managed the Pocatello (Idaho) Cardinals, in the Class C Pioneer League.

During his time in the Cardinals organization it's likely that Penner met Pepper Martin. In 1941 and 1942, when the Gas House Gang alumnus was managing the Sacramento Solons of the Pacific Coast League, Penner was a coach for the team. In 1943 he succeeded Martin as the Solons' manager, and over those two seasons, Penner, now past 40, pitched the final ten games of his minor-league career. He finished with a 28-season record of 331-284.

Penner's final season in uniform was as manager of the Rochester Red Wings of the International League in 1944.

It was only fitting that Penner remained in the game virtually until the end of his life. In 1945 he joined the St. Louis Cardinals scouting staff, and by 1957 he was the team's West Coast scouting supervisor. In that year Penner was diagnosed with ALS (Lou Gehrig's disease), and the end came relatively quickly.

By October 1958 Penner was bedridden and required 24-hour attention. More than 30 major and minor leaguers who resided in the Sacramento area appeared in a benefit game at Sacramento's Edmonds Field that raised over $4,000 for the popular former major leaguer who had spent 43 years in the game he loved.

Penner died on May 28, 1959, at his home in Sacramento. He was cremated at Sacramento's East Lawn Crematory.

SOURCES

Sincerest appreciation is given to SABR member Bill Mortell for his diligent genealogical research.

Penner's player file from the National baseball Hall of Fame, Cooperstown, New York.

Corsicana (Texas) Daily Sun

Galveston (Texas) Daily News

Joplin (Missouri) New Herald

Ogden (Utah) Standard

Oakland (California) Tribune

San Antonio Express

San Antonio Light

Syracuse Daily Herald

Twin Falls (Idaho) Daily News

Waterloo (Iowa) Evening Courier

Sporting Life

Baseball-reference.com

Retrosheet.org

NOTES

1   Curiously, while both online sources and Penner's death certificate list Booneville as his birthplace, multiple sources in his National Baseball Hall of Fame file say that he was a native of Florence, Alabama.

2   *Waterloo (Iowa) Evening Courier*, July 14, 1916.

3   *San Antonio Express*, July 13, 1926.

4   *Galveston* (Texas) *Daily News*, February 27, 1927.

5   *Corsicana* (Texas) *Daily Sun*, August 24, 1927.

6   *Syracuse Herald*, November 29, 1927.

7   *San Antonio Light*, February 29, 1928.

8   *San Antonio Express*, August 2, 1929.

CHARLIE ROOT

By Gregory H. Wolf

PERHAPS UNFAIRLY, CHARLIE ROOT'S name and legacy are indelibly intertwined with one of baseball's most enduring and intriguing legends: Babe Ruth's "called shot" in Game Three of the 1932 World Series. Overlooked is Root's reputation as one of the most dependable, durable, and hardest-throwing pitchers of his generation. With the most victories in Chicago Cubs history (201), Root paced the National League with 26 wins in 1927 and helped lead the North Siders to four World Series appearances (1929, 1932, 1935, and 1938) during a ten-season span. After his active playing career, Root was a well respected minor-league manager and major-league pitching coach, most notably for the 1957 champion Milwaukee Braves.

A baseball career was far from foretold when Charles Henry Root was born on St. Patrick's Day, March 17, 1899, the eighth of nine children of Jacob and Mary Root in Middletown, Ohio, situated about halfway between Cincinnati and Dayton. Called the Kaiser for his authoritarian personality and preference for speaking German at home, Jacob worked in the local steel mill, Armco, and envisioned for his four sons a life of hard work in factories.[1] Young Charlie was a class clown in grade school and often found himself in trouble with his teachers. When a teacher reprimanded 13-year-old Charles for his disruptive behavior, "I quit school," he recalled. "And I never spent another day in the classroom."[2] Jacob, who placed little value in formal education and considered athletics folly, accepted his son's decision and demanded that Charlie find a job to help support the financially strapped family. Charlie began "driving a grocery wagon" and then toiled in a box factory, but admitted that he spent more time playing baseball on vacant lots, collecting baseball cards from tobacco packs, and hunting bumblebees. Approaching his 18th birthday, Root took a job at Armco as a patternmaker. Aided by a growth spurt, he pitched and played shortstop for the factory team. Showing promise as a pitcher, Root played semipro ball for the Middletown Eagles, earning $5 a game on Sundays in 1919. When the nearby Hamilton Engine Works offered him $35 per game to pitch for them and a job paying $50 a week, Root jumped at the opportunity, and led manager Carl Link's team to the championship in the Southern Ohio industrial league. Industrial leagues were fertile grounds for professional baseball at the time and were scouted heavily. St. Louis Browns pitcher and scout Carl Weilman, who lived in Hamilton, saw Root pitch several times, including in an exhibition against the Browns, and signed Root to a professional contract.

Almost 22 years old, Root reported to manager Lee Fohl at the Browns' spring-training camp in Bogalusa, Louisiana, in 1921. "A promising youngster" was the report on the tough right-hander, but the Browns, whom some considered to be serious contenders in the American League, had little use for such a green player.[3] Root was optioned to the Terre Haute Tots in the Class B Illinois-Indiana-Iowa (Three-I) League, but his promising maiden season (8-7 with a 3.57 ERA) was cut short when he broke his leg sliding into third base. Returning to Terre Haute the following season, Root helped lead the Tots to the pennant by winning 16 games, including a no-hitter, and impressed management with his versatility as a starter and reliever.

With a career in the major leagues beckoning, Root joined the Browns at their spring-training facility in San Antonio in 1923 and made the team. Coming off a surprise second-place finish in 1922, the Browns had a veteran staff, led by Urban Shocker, and topped the AL in ERA. Pitching out of the bullpen, Root made his major-league debut on Opening Day, April 18 and retired all three batters he faced in the ninth inning. Throwing almost exclusively fastballs, Root pitched typically in mop-up situations (the Browns lost 23 of the 27 games in which he appeared) and finished with a 0-4 record and 5.70 ERA which earned him a ticket out of the major leagues. "I was glad to go," Root said. "Those fellows just murdered my fast one and they were the best I had in the bag."[4]

In the offseason new Browns manager George Sisler traded Root, utilityman Cedric Durst, pitcher Rasty

Wright, and catcher Josh Billings to the Los Angeles Angels in the Pacific Coast League for pitcher George Lyons and catcher Tony Rego in a deal later called Sisler's Folly.[5] Veteran pitcher Doc Crandall took Root under his wing, taught him a hard curveball and helped him develop a changeup. The results were spectacular: Root won 21 games and logged 322 innings. The Chicago Cubs purchased his contract after the season for an estimated $30,000 and two players.[6] After participating in the Cubs' spring training at Catalina Island, Root was optioned back to the Angels for more seasoning. He excelled, winning 25 games, lowering his ERA almost one full run to 2.86, logging 324 innings, and leading the league in strikeouts.

Commencing in manager Joe McCarthy's first year at the helm of the Cubs and marking the advent of 14 consecutive winning seasons for the team (1926-39), including four NL pennants, Root's career has two distinct phases. As the staff workhorse from 1926 to 1933, he averaged 18 wins per season, 40 appearances, (31 starts), and 252 innings pitched; from the age of 35 in 1934 through 1941, Root was an invaluable spot or fourth starter and reliever, averaging 8 wins, 35 appearances (12 starts), and 140 innings per season.

Described as the "pitching find of the season" in 1926, Root (whose first name was spelled both Charley and Charlie in newspaper reports his entire career) began auspiciously, winning his debut by going the distance against the Reds on April 14.[7] Almost immediately, the 27-year old Root established himself as the staff ace, capable of starting every fourth day and occasionally relieving. More than anything, he earned McCarthy's trust; in turn, McCarthy depended on Root more than any other pitcher in their five years together. Completing 21 of 32 starts (two of them were ten-inning outings) and appearing ten times as a reliever, Root logged 271⅓ innings and won 18 times; however, had the Cubs provided him even average run support in his losses, he might have won 25, instead of leading the NL with 17 defeats. In 13 of his losses, the Cubs scored two runs or less (a total of 13 runs).

"Cool" and "graceful," Root was one of the great fastball pitches of his era.[8] Though he never led the league in

Root won 19 games and lost just six for the Cubs in 1929. An important contributor on four Cubs pennant-winners (1929, 1932, 1935, and 1938), Root held as of 2014 team records for victories (201), games pitched (605), and innings (3,197 1/3). (Retro Images Archive. George Brace Collection)

strikeouts, he ranked in the top five for six consecutive seasons (1926-1931) in both strikeouts and strikeouts per nine innings. *The Sporting News* said he had a "mysterious delivery" and could baffle hitters with his overhand, three-quarters, and side-arm delivery depending on the batter or pitch count.[9] With a commanding mound presence, the tobacco-juice spitting Root intimidated batters and freely threw inside, thus earning his nickname Chinski (a ball near the batter's chin). His curveball, a self-described "wrinkle ball" ("It slews a little like the wrinkle in a piece of suit," he said), was known to freeze hitters.[10]

In 1927 Root had one of the best seasons for a pitcher in Cubs history, leading the National League with 26 wins, 309 innings, and 48 games pitched. For the first time since their last pennant, in 1918, the Cubs remained in contention until a September collapse. Hailed as the "best pitcher in the league" and the "sensation of the major leagues," Root won his 22nd game on August 16 by tossing his second consecutive shutout and defeating the Dodgers in Brooklyn, 3-0, giving the Cubs a season-high six-game lead over the Pirates.[11] "Root, once a discarded disappointment, was brought back to life and ambition by McCarthy," lauded the *New York Times*.[12] With six weeks remaining in the season, fans and sportswriters wondered if Root could be the first NL hurler to win 30 since Pete Alexander in 1917. Lacking confidence in his other pitchers and in a tight race, McCarthy pitched Root on short rest and used him in relief between starts. Root won his 24th game on August 27 (after pitching in relief in both games of a doubleheader); overworked, exhausted, and weak (he lost 15 pounds), he won just twice the rest of the season as the Cubs faltered with a 12-17 record in the last month to finish in fourth place.

One constant in Root's rise from semipro ball in Ohio to success with the Cubs was the unwavering support of his wife, Dorothy, Throughout Root's 16 years with the Cubs, she was a permanent fixture at home games at Wrigley Field and often traveled with the team to road games. They were so inseparable that *The Sporting News* labeled them "baseball's ideal family" in a special report about Dorothy.[13] They met in Charlie's hometown, Middletown, eloped to Newport, Kentucky, to marry on May 9, 1918, and had two children, Della and Charley Jr., who were also regulars at the Cubs games.

Largely responsible for keeping the Cubs near the top of the NL in 1927, the 5-foot-10, 190-pound Root reported to camp about 15 pounds overweight in 1928 and battled his waistline all year. After he lost his first three decisions and with an ERA over 5.00, it appeared as though Root was burnt out and suffering the consequences of overwork the previous season. With Pat Malone, Sheriff Blake, Art Nehf, Guy Bush, and Root, McCarthy had five legitimate first-line starters and no longer needed to rely on one pitcher. Root never got untracked and finished with a disappointing 14 wins, a team-high 18 losses, and a 3.57 ERA, and finished only 13 of 30 starts.

Rumors of a trade involving Root for Boston Braves second baseman Rogers Hornsby proved incorrect when the Cubs acquired the cantankerous infielder for five other players and an estimated $120,000 to $200,000,

instantly making the Cubs the favorite to win the pennant in 1929.[14] Relying on his fastball and fast curve, Root enjoyed arguably his best season, winning 19 games and leading the league with a .760 winning percentage. Behind Malone, Root, and Bush (who ranked 1, 2, and 4 in the NL in wins), the Cubs demolished competition in July and August, going a combined 44-18, and cruised to the pennant. Consistent the entire season, Root was best when the Cubs needed him, especially in September, when he tossed five consecutive complete games, winning four.

Finishing with 98 wins, their most since 1910, the Cubs faced the juggernaut of the Philadelphia Athletics, winners of 104 games and an 8-1 favorite to win the World Series.[15] Instead of 22-game winner Malone, McCarthy unexpectedly chose 30-year-old Root, noting his "greater experience," to start Game One at home.[16] Unflappable on the mound, Root was temperamentally sound, level-headed, and not easily rattled. In the most effective start of his four World Series with the Cubs, Root surrendered just three hits in seven innings, including a home run by Jimmie Foxx, but was lifted for a pinch-hitter in the seventh inning. His mound opponent, submariner Howard Ehmke, pitched the game of his life, struck out a then-World Series record 13 batters, and won, 3-1. Given the start at Shibe Park in Game Four with Chicago down two games to one, Root cruised into the seventh inning with an 8-0 lead before surrendering a towering home run to Al Simmons. After a single by Foxx, Hack Wilson lost Bing Miller's fly ball in the sun and Root came undone, giving up singles to three of the next four hitters before being replaced by Art Nehf. Owing to another Wilson miscue, Root was charged with six runs in 6⅓ innings, but not the loss as Philadelphia scored ten runs during the inning in a crushing 10-8 Cubs' loss. The A's closed out the Series two days later with a ninth-inning comeback win.

With great expectations for another pennant, the Cubs got off to a sluggish start in 1930, further enraging team owner Bill Wrigley, who was still smarting from the World Series defeat. Root buttressed the team with nine wins in his first 13 starts, including eight complete games and three shutouts. With their offense firing on all cylinders, the Cubs enjoyed a 5½-game lead over the New York Giants when Root left in the first inning of a defeat to the Pirates on August 27 after surrendering four runs without retiring a batter. Diagnosed with shoulder problems, he was limited to 13⅔ innings over the remaining five weeks of the season. Chicago lost 13 of its next 19 games to fall out of contention. McCarthy resigned with four games remaining, Wrigley's trust in him irrevocably damaged.

McCarthy's easy-going demeanor was sharply contrasted with new manager Rogers Hornsby's authoritarian and tyrannical rule over players in his year and a half as skipper. Root rebounded in 1931 from a lackluster 1930 season to post 17 wins and led the staff in innings (251), starts (31), complete games (19), and appearances (39, tied with Guy Bush),while lowering his ERA almost one run to 3.48; however, the Cubs were undone by injuries, poor pitching, and age. Alienating players, Wrigley, and general manager William Veeck, the egotistical Hornsby led the team to a disappointing third-place finish.

The mood in the Cubs' clubhouse changed overnight when first baseman Charlie Grimm replaced Hornsby as manager after 99 games in the 1932 season. The tactful and approachable Jolly Cholly let his team play and they responded by winning 26 of 32 games and cruising to the pennant. Root, noticeably relaxed after his relegation to the bullpen for two weeks in July under Hornsby, pitched his best ball of the season after Grimm took over, winning seven of nine decisions in August and September on his way to a 15-10 record. At 33 Root was still a vital member of the staff, which led the NL in ERA and included 22-game winner Lon Warneke and 19-game winner Bush.

With losses in the first two games of the World Series to the overwhelming favorite Yankees in New York, the Cubs returned to Chicago for Game Three. After surrendering a towering three-run blast to Babe Ruth in the first inning and a solo shot to Lou Gehrig in the third, Root entered the fateful fifth inning in a 4-4 game. According to Root, Cubs players had been riding Ruth the entire game. After the first strike Ruth supposedly yelled at him "That's only one strike" and then gestured to him after the second strike.[17] On the next pitch Ruth

clouted a shot over the center-field bleachers. Gehrig followed with his second home run and Root was replaced after becoming the first pitcher in World Series history to surrender four home runs in a game. The Bronx Bombers won, 7-5. On the next day, the Yankees completed their resounding sweep of the Cubs.

Neither Root nor Ruth made references to a "called shot" after Game Three and contemporary sportswriters did not mention one either, except for Joe Williams of the *New York Telegram*, whose columns were syndicated nationally. Soon, the story of Ruth's "called shot" spread like wildfire, helped by the sheer stature of the game's greatest player. Eyewitness accounts differ about what actually happened, and an amateur 16mm film of Ruth's at-bat, discovered in the 1970s, has not quelled the enduring controversy. "Ruth most certainly did not call his home run in that game," said Root years later. "I ought to know. I was there."[18] Root claimed that he would never have allowed Ruth to show him up without retaliating: "I'd have put one in his ear and knocked him on his ass."[19] Longtime teammate and friend Grimm added, "Root never squawked as the legend grew that Ruth had called his shot for baseball's most celebrated home run."[20] Never seeking the spotlight, Root, adamantly opposed any dramatizations of the event that exaggerated Ruth's at-bat and refused to cooperate with a Hollywood film of the event.

In 1933, Grimm's first full season as manager, the Cubs plodded along and never challenged for the pennant. The 34-year-old Root pitched solidly, completing 20 of 30 starts, notching 15 wins, and posting a career-low 2.60 ERA. He pitched four extra-inning complete games, including a career-high 13 innings in a 3-2 loss to the Phillies on September 9. The Cubs scored three runs or fewer in all of his ten losses (a total of 15 runs), an oft-repeated refrain for the season.

After a poor spring, Root had an auspicious beginning in 1934 by hurling a complete-game victory on April 21 while hitting a solo home run against rival St. Louis, winning 2-1. A capable hitter with 11 career home runs, Root had a career .180 batting average (196-for-1,086) and 93 RBIs. Failing to get on track after his initial victory,

Root, battling his weight, was demoted to the bullpen after a dismal two-inning outing in which he surrendered four runs to the Giants on June 20. Root didn't start another game all season, and finished with a 4-7 record that ushered in suggestions of his demise as a pitcher.

The 1935 season put the suggestions to rest. No longer capable of starting every fourth or fifth day, the 36-year-old Root proved his worth as an effective spot starter, completing six of eight starts while appearing in 16 games as a reliever in the first four months of the season. "I had developed a roll of fat across my shoulders," he said of his problems the season before. "It bothered my delivery."[21] He said that during the offseason he had seriously contemplated quitting the game. But with the endless encouragement of Dorothy, Root began a regimen of rowing and arrived at spring training lighter than in previous seasons, ready to prove he wasn't washed up. His fastball no longer a threat, the 36-year-old Root developed an effective hard knuckleball to go with his breaking balls and transformed himself into a wily, cerebral pitcher whom newspapers called the "grandpappy" of the Cubs staff.[22]

Entering September in the middle of a pennant race, just 1½ games behind St. Louis, the Cubs began an unprecedented run by winning 23 of their last 26 games, including a club-record 21 in a row from September 4 through September 27, on their way to the NL pennant. Joining Warneke, Bill Lee, and Larry French as the primary starters during the September stretch, Root won four consecutive starts, including an 11-inning, complete-game masterpiece over the Phillies on September 5. Root got credit for the Cubs' presence in the pennant race.[23] "[Root] was a big help, not only as a pitcher," recalled first baseman Phil Cavaretta, "but as a coach to our younger pitchers."[24]

Sporting a 15-8 record and a 3.08 ERA in 201⅓ innings, the sturdily-built Root, whom teammates called Old Bear, started Game Two in the 1935 World Series with a chance to exorcise demons from his performances in 1929 and 1932.[25] Facing the vaunted batting order of the Detroit Tigers boasting four future Hall of Famers (Mickey Cochrane, Charlie Gehringer, Goose Goslin, and Hank Greenberg), Root was lifted after surrendering four runs

in the first inning without getting an out. He had one more chance to pitch in the Series (two scoreless innings in relief during Game Four), before the Cubs were defeated in six games.

After an ineffective season as primarily a reliever in 1936 (3-6 with a career-low 73⅔ innings), Root won 13 games in 1937, prompting *The Sporting News* to report that he "still stands out as the only reliable performer" on a maddening inconsistent staff.[26] When he relieved Roy Parmelee on August 13 and pitched 7⅓ innings to earn the victory in a 22-6 drubbing of the Reds, the Cubs owned a 6½-game lead over the Giants, but went cold, going 27-24 down the stretch to finish in second place for the second consecutive year.

Used mainly in relief during most of the 1938 season while the Cubs floundered in third or fourth place, Root experienced his final moments of glory in the tension-filled last month of the 1938 season as the Cubs staged a dramatic comeback under the direction of player-manager Gabby Hartnett (who had replaced Grimm in midseason) to win the pennant on the next-to-last day of the season. With the Cubs down by seven games on September 4, Root pitched a complete-game 11-inning 2-1 victory over the Reds at Crosley Field to initiate a 21-5 run the rest of the season. In the best month of his season, Root started five games, relieved in three, won four games, and posted a 2.49 ERA. His last two victories were among the most important of his career: With a scoreless inning of relief against the Pirates on September 28, Root earned a victory when catcher-manager Gabby Hartnett hit his celebrated game-winning "homer in the gloamin'" in the bottom of the ninth to go into first place. Two days later, Root pitched a complete game to defeat the Cardinals 10-3 in Sportsman's Park, securing the pennant for the Cubs. Despite Root's success at the end of the season, Hartnett opted for a three-man rotation of 22-game winner Bill Lee, oft-injured Dizzy Dean, and Clay Bryant for the World Series against the Yankees. The Cubs were swept, and in his only appearance, Root relieved Lee in Game Four and pitched three innings, allowing one run).

On the biggest stage in baseball, Root inexplicably had some of his worst games in his career. In the Cubs' four

World Series defeats, Root was winless, lost three, surrendered 26 hits in 22⅔ innings, and was charged with 18 runs (17 earned) for a 6.75 ERA. Root's woes in the World Series have contributed to his neglected legacy as one of the era's most dependable pitchers. Never one to make excuses, Root admitted that he never learned to pace himself and had a tendency to overpitch.[27]

Pitching three more seasons and winning an additional 18 games, "Old Mr. Troubleshooter" had the distinction of being the oldest player in 1940 and 1941 and the last player born in the 19th century to play in the major leagues.[28] Released at the end of the 1941 season, the 42-year-old Root finished his career with 201 wins and 160 losses and a 3.59 ERA,. At the end of 2012, Root's 605 appearances as a Cub led the franchise by a wide margin.

A baseball lifer, Root pitched for the Hollywood Stars from 1942 through 1944. In his second season with the club, he was the team's player-manager. In 1945-46 he was the player-manager of the Columbus (Ohio) Red Birds, the Cardinals' affiliate in the American Association. In 1948, at the age of 49, Root pitched his final game in Organized Baseball for the Billings Mustangs in the Class C Pioneer League. He finished with 111 victories in his minor-league career.

Root was the pitching coach of the Cubs for three seasons (1951-53) before former teammate Charlie Grimm hired him in 1956 as a coach for the Milwaukee Braves. Root was known for his "Nine Hill Commandments." With his pitchers he stressed conditioning, ball control, fielding, mastering pitches before experimenting with new ones, running every day, bunting, pacing, developing a changeup, and finally an unteachable quality: "heart."[29] After leading the National League in ERA in 1956, the Braves ranked second in their 1957 championship season. "We all respected Root," eight-time All-Star Del Crandall told the author.[30]

In a surprise move, Root and coaches Johnny Riddle and Connie Ryan were fired within weeks after the Braves won the World Series over the Yankees. "Chances are that no club in major league history went through a shake-up like that after the World Series," reported The

Sporting News.[31] "Puzzled" by the firing, Root felt insulted by how the Braves, and especially manager Fred Haney, who replaced Grimm in 1956 and wanted his own coaching staff, presented the news to the public. "The club," reported The Sporting News, "made it clear that [Root] had been 'replaced' and had not resigned."[32] When Grimm returned as manager of the Cubs in 1960, Root joined him for one final season of coaching before retiring from baseball.

Among the highest-paid players in baseball in the 1930s, Root invested wisely during the Great Depression and lived within his means. After living in Los Angeles during the offseason for many years, he and Dorothy later lived on their 1,000-acre Diamond-R Ranch in Paicines, 120 miles southeast of San Francisco, where Root became a successful cattle rancher and enjoyed hunting and fishing. After an extended illness, Root died on November 5, 1970, at the age of 71 near his home in Hollister, California. He was cremated at Garden of Memories Memorial Park in Salinas, California, and his ashes were scattered.

SOURCES

Newspapers

Chicago Tribune

Milwaukee Journal

Milwaukee Sentinel

The Sporting News

Websites

Ancestry.com

BaseballLibrary.com

Baseball-Reference.com

Retrosheet.org

SABR.org

NOTES

1   Roger Snell, *Root for the Cubs. Charlie Root and the 1929 Chicago Cubs* (Nicholasville, Kentucky: Wind, 2009), 8.

2   *The Sporting News*, March 2, 1933, 7.

3   "Browns to be in Flag Fight," *New Castle* (Pennsylvania) *News*, March 10, 1921, 20.

4   "Charley Root Has the Makings of a Truly Great Hurler," *Zanesville* (Ohio) *Times Signal*, December 19, 1926, 14.

5   *The Sporting News*, March 7, 1933, 7.

6 "Cubs Pay $50,000 for Charley Root," *Wisconsin State Journal* (Madison), August 10, 1924, 27.

7 *New York Times*, August 2, 1926, 13.

8 "Charley Root Has the Makings of a Truly Great Hurler."

9 *The Sporting News*, June 7, 1926, 1.

10 "Charley Root Has the Makings of a Truly Great Hurler."

11 *New York Times*, March 19, 1928, 27; *Milwaukee Journal*, August 13, 1927, 11.

12 *New York Times*, August 28, 1927, 53.

13 *The Sporting News*, November 9, 1939, 4.

14 Glen Stout, *The Cubs: The Complete Story of Chicago Cubs Baseball* (Boston: Houghton Mifflin Harcourt, 2007), 123.

15 "A's 8-1 Favorite to Win World Series, Associated Press, *Fredericksburg* (Virginia) *Freelance Star*, October 11, 1929, 1.

16 "Root to oppose Grove," Associated Press, *Pittsburgh Press*, October 7, 1929, 20.

17 Peter Golenbock, *Wrigleyville: A Magical History Tour of the Chicago Cubs* (New York: St. Martin's Griffin, 1999), 237.

18 *The Sporting News*, May 12, 1948, 10.

19 Geoffrey C. Ward and Ken Burns, *Baseball: An Illustrated History* (New York: Knopf, 2010), 210.

20 Peter Golenbock, 236.

21 "Charlie Root Tries Again" Associated Press, *Windsor* (Ontario) *Daily Star*, October 7, 1935.

22 "New Yorkers Tumble Far Behind Leaders," *Palm Beach* (Florida) *Post*, September 19, 1935, 6.

23 "Charley Root Main Factor in Chicago's Drive in the National League," *Saskatoon* (Saskatchewan) *Star-Phoenix*, July 23, 1935, 11.

24 Peter Golenbock, 255.

25 Ibid.

26 *The Sporting News*, July 22, 1937, 5.

27 *The Sporting News*, April 4, 1956, 11.

28 *The Sporting News*, March 7, 1940, 1.

29 *The Sporting News*, April 4, 1956, 11.

30 Author's interview with Del Crandall on July 30, 2012.

31 *The Sporting News*, November 6, 1957, 3.

32 *The Sporting News*, November 6, 1957, 3-4.

JOHNNY SCHULTE

By James Lincoln Ray

A BACKUP CATCHER IN ALL OF HIS FIVE years in the Major Leagues, Johnny Schulte found greater success as a coach under manager Joe McCarthy. Schulte was a Yankees coach during almost all of McCarthy's tenure with the team. After McCarthy left the Yankees in the middle of the 1946 season, Schulte stayed on with the Yankees until the end of the 1948 season, coaching under managers Bill Dickey, Johnny Neun, and Bucky Harris. In 1949 he rejoined McCarthy, who was then managing the Boston Red Sox. When McCarthy retired in 1950, Schulte also left the game. A year later he turned up in Cleveland, where he worked as a scout for more than a decade before retiring for good in 1963.

John Clement Schulte was born on September 8, 1896 in Fredericktown, Missouri, a town in the foothills of the Ozarks about seventy-five miles south of St. Louis. Schulte's parents were Michael Charles Schulte, a bank clerk, and the former Amelia Rosar. John was one of seven children, three girls and four boys. He was the third child and the second son.

Schulte began playing baseball in grade school and competed in the citywide *St. Louis Post-Dispatch* tournament in 1912, at the age of fifteen. He signed his first professional baseball contract in 1915, with the Oklahoma City Senators of the Class D Western Association. Schulte, an eighteen-year-old outfielder, batted .167 in twenty-eight games. In 1916 he played for three teams, Newport News of the Class C Virginia League, and Wheeling and Terre Haute of the Class B Central League. Overall he batted .202 in eighty-two games.

Schulte served in the Navy during World War I, playing baseball at the Great Lakes Naval Training Station. He missed the 1917 and 1918 seasons, but when he returned to baseball in 1919, he seemed to have found his batting eye. With the Terre Haute Browns of the Three-I League, Schulte hit .304 In 102 games, mostly as an outfielder.

With Terre Haute again the next season, Schulte played in 131 games and batted .278. In 1921, he moved up to the Mobile (Alabama) Bears of the Class A Southern Association, where he was switched from the outfield to catcher, his position for the rest of his baseball career. Schulte had the best season of his career in 1922, leading the Southern Association in batting (.357), home runs (12), and slugging (.597)for the pennant-winning Bears.

After the season the St. Louis Browns purchased Schulte's contract. He made his Major League debut on Opening Day 1923, as a late-inning substitute at first base. The next day he pinch-hit, drew a walk, and scored. After a month, in which he appeared in seven games, Schulte was sent to the San Antonio Bears of the Class A Texas League, where he stayed the rest of the season, hitting .269 in fifty-nine games and showing none of the power he had displayed the year before in Mobile.

The five-foot-eleven, 190-pound Schulte spent the next three seasons (1924 through 1926) at the Class Double-A level, at the time, the minor league's highest classification. Playing in the American Association in 1924–1925, and in the International League in 1926, he regained his batting ability and played strong defense. He began the 1927 season in the International League, but made it back to the majors, with the St. Louis Cardinals, on May 29. Schulte was 3-for-5 in his National League debut, with four runs batted in as the Cardinals defeated Cincinnati, 11–3. The next day he was 2-for-3 with a walk. Just over a week later, on June 8, Schulte smacked his first Major League home run, a two-run shot off Hal Goldsmith of the Boston Braves.

Schulte remained with the Cardinals for the rest of the 1927 season. He hit .288 in 208 plate appearances, with an impressive on-base percentage of .456. He hit nine home runs and had thirty-two RBIs. However, the Cardinals had a surplus of catchers and traded Schulte after the season to the Philadelphia Phillies. He appeared in sixty-five games for the Phillies in 1928, many of them as a pinch-hitter, and batted .248.

On January 17, 1928, Schulte married twenty-year-old Gladys Moran of St. Louis, a professional singer. The marriage lasted until Schulte's death more than fifty years later.

The Phillies sold Schulte to the Columbus (Ohio) Senators of the American Association in January 1929, but before he could play for Columbus, the Chicago Cubs purchased his contract. As a reserve catcher and pinch-hitter on the pennant-winning team managed by Joe McCarthy, Schulte hit .261 in thirty-one games. He had no appearances in the World Series, which the Cubs lost to the Philadelphia Athletics in five games.

Schulte didn't play in the 1930 season but returned to baseball in 1931 with the Los Angeles Angels of the Pacific Coast League, where he served as a catcher and pinch-hitter, appearing in 101 games and hitting .283. The Browns picked him up in the off-season, but he was released in

Schulte made 22 starts as catcher for the Cubs in 1929. He played for five teams in parts of five seasons in the big leagues. (Retro Images Archive. George Brace Collection)

early August after playing in just fifteen games. A few days later he signed with the Boston Braves, but played in just ten games for them. Schulte was one of a select group of players that hit a home run in his last Major League at bat; it came off Freddie Fitzsimmons of the New York Giants on September 20, 1932, in the Polo Grounds. He finished with a career Major League batting average of .262 in 374 at-bats.

Schulte caught on as a coach on Charlie Grimm's Cubs staff in 1933. In 1934 Joe McCarthy, in his fourth year as manager of the Yankees, recalled how well Schulte handled the pitchers on the 1929 Cubs and hired Schulte as the Yankees' bullpen coach and pitching instructor. Schulte spent the next fifteen seasons in the Bronx, coaching on seven pennant winners, six of which won the World Series.

In addition to his coaching duties, Schulte occasionally worked as a scout for the Yankees. In 1936 he persuaded Yankees chief scout Paul Krichell to sign a skinny young shortstop who had been passed over by the Brooklyn Dodgers and the New York Giants. The kid was Phil Rizzuto, and though Krichell originally wasn't impressed, he agreed to send him to the Yankees lowest minor league club if Schulte would pay Rizzuto's $20 train fare from New York City to Bassett, Virginia.

Six years later, in 1942, Schulte spotted an awkward-looking, wild-swinging seventeen-year old catcher playing in an American Legion game in St. Louis. The catcher, Yogi Berra, blasted two home runs and Schulte got the Yankees to sign him, for $500.

When Whitey Ford first tried out for the Yankees in 1946, he did so as a potential first baseman. As with Rizzuto, the head scout was not impressed and was ready to send the eighteen-year-old home. But when Ford told Schulte that he could pitch, Schulte grabbed his catcher's mitt and said, in classic Missouri fashion: "Show me." Ford showed him, and the Yankees signed the left-hander, who went on to win more games than any other Yankee pitcher.

Schulte died on June 28, 1978, in St. Louis at the age of eighty-one, and was survived by his wife and his son, John Jr. He is buried in St. Louis's Calvary Cemetery.

SOURCES

"Cubs Get Ed Baecht For 7 Players, Cash," *New York Times*, November 7, 1930.

Bob Broeg, "Schulte: 1 of Baseball's Top Scouts" (obituary) St. *Louis Post-Dispatch*, July 1, 1978.

"Phils Release Ring Outright, Sell J. Schulte to Columbus," *New York Times*, January 6, 1929.

Robert L. Burns, "Eagle Eye Johnny Schulte" (obituary), *St. Louis Globe-Democrat*, July 4, 1978.

Walter E. Orthwein, "Whatever Happened to Johnny Schulte," *St. Louis Post-Dispatch*, January 1978.

Neil Russo, "John Schulte Recalls Happy Years as Scout," *St. Louis Post-Dispatch*, January 15, 1961.

Newyorkyankees.com

wikipedia.com

RIGGS STEPHENSON

By Gregory H. Wolf

"IGGS STEPHENSON IS A BRILLIANT hitter, steady fielder, and a southern gentleman," wrote Chicago Cubs beat reporter Edward Burns in 1929, as the rugged Alabaman was en route to a .362 batting average and 110 runs batted in for the pennant-winning Cubs.[1] Blessed with eagle eyes, but cursed with a poor throwing arm, the career .336 hitter over 14 big-league seasons had a hard time breaking into the starting lineup. He joined the Cleveland Indians in 1921 straight from the campus of the University of Alabama, but his fielding woes at second base, third base, and the outfield exasperated manager Tris Speaker, who finally discarded the five-year veteran with a .337 average to the minor leagues in 1925. A year later Stephenson was granted a new lease on life when new Cubs skipper Joe McCarthy acquired him. Placed in left field to hide his weak arm, Stephenson was a model of consistency, albeit an oft-injured one, on successful Cubs teams of the late 1920s and early 1930s.

Jackson Riggs Stephenson was born on January 5, 1898, in a small hamlet "out in the country," about ten minutes away by horse from the small Alabama town of Akron (population about 350), located 80 miles from Birmingham in the east-central part of the state.[2] His parents, James and Addie (Wilson) Stephenson, were born when slavery was still legal, and like most families in Hale County, were farmers. According to various census reports, Riggs was the final of six children the family welcomed to the world. As a child, Riggs often accompanied his father, who also served as a rural mail carrier, on a horse and buggy as he made his rounds to the outcrops that dotted the bucolic landscape. He was introduced to baseball by his brother Samuel Gardner (six years older), who was a pitcher in 1913 and 1914 for the Anniston (Alabama) Moulders in the Class D Georgia-Alabama League. By the age of 15, Riggs was playing infield for his local town team, showcasing his talent against other area nines in small towns up and down the rail line leading to New Orleans. By all accounts, Riggs was a natural athlete, who

also played football and basketball, and ran track in high school.

Riggs followed Samuel's footsteps and enrolled at the University of Alabama in 1917, where he earned three letters each in football and baseball, and one in basketball. He received a scholarship from the state, but also worked in the school cafeteria to pay for his education. Riggs' arrival in Tuscaloosa corresponded with the university's ascent to national prominence on the gridiron. A two-way player throughout his career (fullback and defensive back), Stephenson scored five touchdowns against Ole Miss as a freshman in 1917. While the 1918 season was canceled because of World War I, Stephenson served in the student training corps in the Army. Under coach Xen Scott, the sturdily built, 5-foot-10, 185-pounder was hailed as the "Greatest Fullback in the South" and earned All Southern Conference honors (the precursor to the Southeastern Conference) in 1919 and 1920.[3] Riggs is a "better football player than Jim Thorpe," said Scott of his pugnacious player, who once rushed for 286 yards versus Sewanee and helped lead the Crimson Tide to successive records of 8-1 and 10-1, the school's first season with double-digit victories.[4]

As good as Alabama's football team was, its baseball team was equally flush with big-league talent. Stephenson's teammates included future Hall of Famer Joe Sewell, Luke Sewell, Lena Styles, brothers Dan and Ike Boone, and Frank Pratt, all of whom debuted in the major leagues between 1919 and 1922. With an infield anchored by Stephenson at shortstop and Joe Sewell at second base, the Crimson Tide posted records of 13-4, 16-2, and 15-2 from 1918 to 1920 and won three consecutive Southern Intercollegiate Athletic Association (SIAA) titles for coach Loonie Noojin.[5] Stephenson played in the independent Delta League of Dixie during the summers from 1918-1920.

Stephenson's big-league career got a boost from his football coach, Xen Scott, a former horse-race writer in Cleveland who had contacts with the Indians. "[Scott] said it looked like I had good, big wrists," Stephenson once said. "And the boys told him I was a pretty good ball player, so he recommended me."[6] Without having seen Stephenson play, Scott took him as well as Joe Sewell to the Indians spring-training camp in New Orleans in 1920. They both worked out with the team; while Sewell was signed by the New Orleans Pelicans of the Class A Southern Association, Stephenson was told to come back the following year.

Still a collegian, Stephenson made a positive impression on Indians manager Tris Speaker of the reigning World Series champions at spring training in 1921, in Dallas. "The very first day [Stephenson] stepped on the diamond, he looked like a polished big league workman," gushed sportswriter Wilbur Wood.[7] Stephenson's prospects to make the team were not good. His college teammate, Joe Sewell, had made a successful switch from second base to shortstop and had started all seven games of the World Series. Second base was occupied by veteran Bill Wambsganss; consequently, Stephenson was dispatched back to Tuscaloosa, where he still had one year of eligibility. But when Wambsganss and utility infielder Harry Lunte were sidelined with injuries as Opening Day approached, Stephenson reaped the benefits. "They called me two days before the season," he said, "and I joined the team in St. Louis. Speaker signed me for $300 a month."[8]

"I had never played second base," said Stephenson. But after two days of practice, Stevie, as the press began to call him, occupied the keystone position on Opening Day 1921. Always a streaky hitter, Stephenson could not have imagined his immediate success. He went 2-for-4 against spitballer Urban Shocker of the St. Louis Browns in his debut. In his next seven games, he banged out 14 hits in 25 at-bats, and scored nine times. Stephenson, now batting .552 and slugging .655, drew comparisons to the Browns' George Sisler, who had batted .407 the previous season. "He's been hitting the ball squarely on the nose and his speed has canned the critics," wrote Indians beat reporter Francis J. Powers.[9] Sewell, catcher Steve O'Neill, and Stephenson were dubbed "SOS" (Sewell-O'Neill-Stephenson) for their early-season hitting exploits at the bottom of the order.[10] The rookie second baseman was equally sharp in the field, committing only one error in

his first 18 games. ("He has a wonderful set of hands," said Powers.[11]) But he committed 14 in his next 30 games and was replaced by Wambsganss on June 8 despite batting .347. Limited to just 17 games and 30 at-bats for the rest of the season, Stephenson was a forgotten man on Speaker's club, which succumbed to the Yankees in the September pennant drive. The Sporting News called Stephenson the "greatest enigma in camp" in 1922.[12] "[He] has one of the best batting eyes that has come into the league in many seasons. … He [can] do everything but make snap throws."[13] Relegated to role player, Stephenson made 21 starts at second base and 29 at third base. He culled together 233 at-bats, posted a .339 batting average and .511 slugging percentage (both second to Speaker), and walloped 24 doubles for the fourth-place club.

Stephenson was widely seen as a budding star, but his defensive deficiencies tormented Speaker, and it seemed as if everyone had advice to offer. Critics suggested that

Among the most overlooked players in baseball history, leftfielder Stephenson batted .362 and drove in 110 runs for the Cubs in 1929. In 14 years in the majors, he batted .336 and collected 1,515 hits. (National Baseball Hall of Fame)

Stephenson could replace the aging Larry Gardner at third, or eventually move to the outfield once Speaker retired; even Connie Mack, owner-manager of the rival Philadelphia Athletics, chimed in, arguing that Stephenson should be converted to a first baseman because he hit too well to sit on the bench.[14] Nicknamed Old Hoss for his reliable hitting, Stephenson was candid about his fielding woes: "I wasn't such a good defensive player. I had trouble making the double play on the pivot."[15]

After the season, Stephenson joined other big-league stars including Waite Hoyt, Herb Pennock, Luke Sewell, Irish Meusel, and Casey Stengel on Herb Hunter's all-star team which toured Japan, Korea, China, and the Philippines. "[Stephenson is] one of the most gentlemanly athletes in the game and is certain to reflect credit to baseball in foreign lands," wrote *The Sporting News*.[16] Speaker thought the opportunity for Stephenson to play third base every day would "smooth out the rough spots" and enable him to challenge for a starting position.[17]

Stephenson was shunted to the far end of the bench in 1923 when rookie Rube Lutzke won the third-base job. With only 24 at-bats through July 1, the infielder was the object of constant trade rumors, yet suitors were anxious about his reputation for "mighty hitting but not so mighty fielding."[18] He got his chance to play regularly when a broken finger sidelined Wambsganss in early July. Beginning on July 3, Stephenson made 64 starts at second base, batted .329, and knocked in 63 runs in just 277 at-bats in the longest stretch of playing time in his career to that point. He was tabbed the second baseman of the future, and Wambsganss was traded in the offseason.

More relaxed at the plate and in the field during 1924 than in previous seasons, Stephenson was batting .365 and had committed only one error when he injured his leg on May 1.[19] "I ran down to first base playing the Chicago White Sox. The first baseman Earl Sheely jumped up for a ball and I tripped over his leg," said Stephenson.[20] In his absence Chick Fewster (who had come over in the trade for Wambsganss) took over. Stephenson was sidelined for a month and his movement was limited for the remainder of the season. But the Indians, who fell to sixth place, desperately needed his hitting. Over an

11-game stretch beginning on August 28, Stephenson pounded out 25 hits in 44 at-bats and knocked in 17 runs en route to a .371 average (in 240 at-bats).

Stephenson was a classic line-drive and spray hitter who enjoyed hitting in Cleveland's League Park (also called Dunn Field beginning in 1916). Its architectural trademark was a short right-field fence (290 feet compared with 375 in left field) and its 60-foot-high wall. "I used to hit a few off that right-field wall," he said, claiming that he approached right- and left-handed pitchers the same.[21]

Stephenson's big-league career came crashing down in 1925 when he was optioned to the Kansas City Blues of the Double-A American Association in June. He had been moved to right field to start the season, but "Old Hoss" struggled at the plate and in the field. "I was very disappointed," said Stephenson. "I went down with the intention of giving it all I had. But if it didn't do any good, I was going to quit … but I hit pretty good."[22] He was with Kansas City for only two months before the Indians sent him and two other players to the Indianapolis Indians of the same league in exchange for the rights to a hot infield prospect, 19-year-old Johnny Hodapp.[23]

Despite his .337 batting average in parts of five seasons with Cleveland, Stephenson's stock had dropped precipitously. The 28-year-old began the 1926 season with Indianapolis needing to prove he could play the outfield; managers across baseball already knew he could hit. In 51 games he torched the ball for a .385 average, and also had some luck. Prior to the season the Chicago Cubs had hired manager Joe McCarthy, whose experience as skipper of the American Association's Louisville Colonels had given him ample opportunity to assess Stephenson's strengths.

On June 7, 1926, Stephenson got a shot at redemption when the Cubs sent outfielder Joe Munson, infielder Red Shannon, and cash to Indianapolis for Stephenson and utilityman Hank Schreiber. Two days later Stephenson was installed in left field, one of the team's glaring weaknesses.

"My arm wasn't strong enough to play right field," said Stephenson bluntly. "You gotta have the best arm on the team in right field. I was lucky to get to Chicago. They needed a left fielder. Maybe my (throwing) arm wasn't even average. I was accurate but I couldn't throw long distances."[24]

After going 0-for-4 in his Cubs debut on June 9, the streaky Stephenson cranked out 14 hits in his next 31 at-bats, including the first of three games during his major-league career with two home runs. "[He's] upheld his hitting reputation," wrote Chicago sportswriter Irving Vaughan.[25] After the club had gone through three managers during a last-place finish in 1925, McCarthy had the team playing inspired ball and fighting for a pennant. Stephenson wrenched his back on August 31 with the Cubs in fourth place but only five games off the lead. The Cubs sorely missed Stephenson's bat in September, when they stumbled to a 13-14 record. In a seamless transition to the National League and Wrigley Field, the transplanted Southerner led the Cubs with a .338 average (in 281 at-bats).

With the NL's leading pitching staff (3.26 ERA in 1926), the Cubs were expected to compete for the pennant in 1927. McCarthy moved a "surprised" Stephenson to third base, the team's sore spot, to start the season.[26] The experiment lasted only six games as Stephenson struggled in the field and at the plate. He was reinserted in left field and never played another position in his big-league career. Third base remained a mess all season with five additional players splitting time at the hot corner. Batting fifth in the overwhelming majority of his games, Stephenson was an ideal protector for the NL's most feared home-run slugger, center fielder, Hack Wilson, who like Stephenson was a castoff from another team. "No sane pitcher is going to pass anybody to get him," wrote Irving Vaughan about Stephenson.[27] The stocky West Virginian Wilson belted 30 round-trippers to lead the NL for the second of three consecutive seasons. Stephenson, healthy all season long, played in 152 games (exceeding his previous career high by 61), batted .344 (fourth in the NL), rapped a career-high 199 hits, including an NL-best 46 doubles, and scored 101 times. In a tight race with the Pittsburgh Pirates all season, the Cubs moved into first place on August 1 and increased their lead to six games on August 16. While the North Siders struggled thereafter (16-28) and fell to

fourth place, the Pirates went 22-9 in September to take the flag by 1½ games over the St. Louis Cardinals.

In the offseason Cubs owner William Wrigley made a big splash when he acquired speedy outfielder Hazen "Kiki" Cuyler from the Pirates in exchange for infielder Sparky Adams and utiltyman Pete Scott. The 29-year-old Cuyler (at the time a .336 career hitter who clashed with Pirates manager Donie Bush) formed with Wilson and Stephenson Chicago's version of Murderers' Row. However, the Cubs slogged through the first three months of the season, playing uninspired ball, and languished in fourth place at the beginning of July. A model of consistency, Stephenson battled a severe case of influenza in late May and subsequent hospitalization while establishing his reputation as the club's clutch hitter. The Cubs went 47-26 over the last 73 games of the season to pull within two games of the St. Louis Cardinals in mid-September, but it was too little, too late. Old Hoss batted .450 (27-for-60) in his first 16 games of September to finish with a team-high .324 average and knocked in 90 runs for the third-place club.

Newspapers reports often characterized Stephenson as "unsung."[28] Henry L. Farrell wrote, "[Stephenson is] one of the immensely valuable players who doesn't command the spotlight. The Chicago fans know how valuable he is, but the customers in other cities know more about Gabby Hartnett, Hack Wilson, and others."[29] On teams loaded with stars, Stephenson was content to be in the background. "[He is] the Cubs' most vicious batsman and mildest citizen," wrote Cubs reporter Edward Burns."[30] Stephenson had an air of Southern gentlemanly aristocracy; sportswriters often made reference to his collegiate background and his slow, Southern drawl. In contrast to some teammates who were well acquainted in the speakeasies located all over Chicago's North Side, Stephenson did not drink or smoke, apparently was genuinely liked by his teammates, who gave him the sobriquet Blossom, and was a favorite of manager McCarthy.[31]

Sparing no cost in pursuit of a championship, Cubs owner William Wrigley acquired baseball's best all-around hitter, second baseman Rogers Hornsby, from the Boston Braves in the offseason, making the Cubs an odds-on favorite to win the NL pennant. "With sluggers Cuyler, Hornsby, Wilson, and Stephenson to depend on," opined sportswriter Ralph Davis, "it is apparent that the Cubs are going to exhibit a punch this season."[32] Even in a year of inflated offensive numbers, the aforementioned 3-4-5-6 hitters comprised one of the most feared lineups in league history, combining for 520 runs batted in, 493 runs scored, and a .362 batting average. Stephenson clicked on all cylinders early in the season, going 24-for-46, drawing 11 walks, and scoring 17 times over a 12-game span from April 23 to May 7. Batting primarily in the sixth position, Stephenson knocked in a career-high 110 runs, including a personal-best seven in the last of his three two-home-run games, an 11-11 tie with the St. Louis Cardinals on July 1.

Stephenson played in 136 mostly pain-filled games. He injured his left knee on June 4, missed ten days, and his already slow gait was hindered even more. On August 22 he ruptured an abdominal muscle and was feared lost for the season. However, he was back in left field a week later (after several pinch-hitting appearances), even though the Cubs enjoyed a double-digit lead in the pennant race. "[Stephenson's] hitting and work in left field have been important factors in the Cubs overpowering the competition in the NL," read an Associated Press report.[33] Stephenson concluded the season on another tear (36-for-86) to wrap up his best season with a .362 average on 179 hits, and also banged out a career-high 17 home runs.

In the much anticipated World Series, the underdog Cubs (98-54) faced the Philadelphia Athletics (104-46), whose offensive production almost matched that of the North Siders, and whose pitching staff was baseball's finest. The tone of the Series was set in Game One when Connie Mack surprised everyone by starting 35-year-old Howard Ehmke, who struck out a then Series record 13 to defeat the Cubs, 3-1, for his last win as a big-leaguer. On the verge of tying the Series at two games apiece, the Cubs squandered an 8-0 lead in Game Four when the A's exploded for a Series-record ten runs in the seventh inning. The Cubs never recovered emotionally after that defeat and lost the Series in five games. Stephenson batted a quiet .316 (6-for-19) with at least one hit in each game, but scored just three times and knocked in three runs as the vaunted A's pitchers subdued the Cubs sluggers, limiting them to just 17 runs and a team .249 batting average.

A shoulder injury suffered in spring training in 1930 plagued Stephenson all season long and limited him to just 79 starts in left field and 29 pinch-hit appearances. Despite the team's offensive prowess (an NL-best 171 home runs and the second-most runs, 998), the Cubs played inconsistently all season. "When [Stephenson] is in the lineup, the Cubs are a different team," opined writer Francis J. Powers.[34] With a 5½-game lead over the New York Giants on August 30, the North Siders seemed poised to capture their second consecutive pennant. But the team came unraveled by infighting and poor performances, and lost 14 of their next 21 games and ultimately finished in second place, two games behind the Cardinals, who won 21 of their last 25 contests. "We couldn't win anything," said a worn-out Stephenson, who batted just 7-for-35 in September. "Our pitching was bad and someone always came back to beat us."[35] In one of the most disappointing seasons in Cubs history, McCarthy was forced out with four games remaining and was replaced by Hornsby, who had undercut his authority all season long while limited to just 104 at-bats. Despite his injuries, Stephenson batted a team-high .367 (125-for-341).

Even before the start of spring training in 1931, newspapers reported that slugger Johnny Moore (who batted .342 with the Los Angeles Angels of the Pacific Coast League in 1930) would replace Stephenson in left field. But a healthy Old Hoss withstood the challenge until the snake-bit player suffered a season-ending injury on July 27. In the first inning of that day's game, he collided with a former teammate, Philadelphia Phillies pitcher Sheriff Blake, at first base, and stepped awkwardly on the bag, breaking his ankle and tearing muscle.[36] In 80 games Stephenson batted .319 for the third-place Cubs.

Stephenson's injury cast doubts on his future with the club. Paul Michaelson of the Associated Press wrote, "[Stephenson] cannot be counted on to play regularly so a replacement in necessary."[37] But the Old Hoss was not yet ready to be sent out to the pasture. "[He] has been uncorking hits … [and] galloping around the outfield with more abandon than he displayed last season," wrote

Irving Vaughan of Stephenson's seemingly miraculous recovery from a devastating injury.[38] The Cubs chafed under manager Hornsby's autocratic and increasingly authoritarian rule, leading to his replacement by first baseman Charlie Grimm, whose laid-back, jovial personality was in stark contrast to the Rajah's. Jolly Cholly reinvigorated his teammates, who went 37-18 to take the pennant by four games over the Pirates. Like his skipper, Stephenson was a source of calm professionalism in a tumultuous season, indeed a year which began with the death of the club's innovative owner, William Wrigley, in January. "I just swoop 'em in a pinch," replied Stephenson when asked to explain his approach to hitting.[39] He "just goes along day after day giving the best that's in him," wrote Vaughan. "The things that Stevie can't do well are run and throw. If things break badly, he seldom offers a complaint."[40] The oldest starting position player on the team at 34, Stephenson led the squad in batting (.324) runs batted in (85), and doubles (49).

A balanced offensive team with the NL's leading staff, the Cubs still were no match for the New York Yankees (107-47 and piloted by former Cubs manager Joe McCarthy), who swept them in four games in the World Series which is perhaps best remembered for Babe Ruth's "called shot" in Game Three. Stephenson led the team with 8 hits in 18 at-bats and 4 RBIs, but only one extra-base hit as the Cubs were outscored 37-19. "We just didn't have the power to beat the Yankees with Babe, (Lou) Gehrig, (Tony) Lazzeri, and (Bill) Dickey," Stephenson said.[41]

Plagued by myriad maladies (broken finger, sore shoulder, and malaria) in 1933, Riggs batted a team-high .329, but managed just 346 at bats. The elder statesman was reduced to a little-used pinch-hitter and occasional left fielder in 1934 as running became increasingly difficult for the 36-year-old. As a testament to his value to the organization, Stephenson was honored in a "sentimental ceremony" and given an engraved watch when he was released on October 30. "Stephenson's release," wrote Edward Burns, "was no ordinary bounce of the sort usually accorded to players who have outlived their usefulness."[42] The 14-year big-league veteran concluded his career with a .336 batting

average (22nd-highest in major-league history as of 2014) and recorded 1,515 hits in 1,310 games.

Stephenson remained in Organized Baseball for five more years. In 1935 he played in 147 games and batted .343 for the Indianapolis Indians of the Double-A American Association. The following season, he accepted the Cubs' offer to serve as player-manager for team's new affiliate in the Class A1 Southern Association, the Birmingham Barons. He led the team in hitting (.355 in 120 games), and more importantly to the league title over the New Orleans Pelicans before succumbing to the Texas League champion Tulsa Oilers in the Dixie Series. Released the following season after the Barons finished sixth in an eight-team league, Stephenson led the Helena (Arkansas) Seaporters of the Class C Cotton States League to a second-place finish as player-manager in 1938. He managed the Montgomery (Alabama) Rebels in the Class B Southeastern League for a half-season in 1939.

Stephenson retired to his home town of Akron, Alabama, where he had spent his offseasons throughout his playing career. In 1934 he had married Alma Chadwick, with whom he had two children, Jack and Marla. Far away from the bright lights of major-league baseball, Stephenson farmed and had a number of successful business pursuits, including a car dealership, sawmill, and lumber yard. In 1971 Stephenson was inducted into the Alabama Sports Hall of Fame.

On November 15, 1985, Riggs Stephenson died at the age of 87 at his home in Tuscaloosa. He was buried at the Tuscaloosa Memorial Park.

SOURCES

Chicago Daily Tribune
New York Times
The Sporting News
Ancestry.com
BaseballLibrary.com
Baseball-Reference.com
Retrosheet.com
SABR.org

Riggs Stephenson player file at the National Baseball Hall of Fame, Cooperstown, New York.

NOTES

1   Edward Burns, "Stephenson to Swoop 'Em in the Pinches," *Chicago Daily Tribune*, September 23, 1929, 25.

2   Charles Land, "Riggs Stephenson: From Akron to the American League," *Tuscaloosa* (Alabama) *News*, January 26, 1964, 10.

3   Ibid.

4   Paul W. Bryant Museum, bryantmuseum.com/index.asp.

5   2013-2014 University of Alabama Baseball Media Guide. rolltide.com/sports/m-basebl/media-guide.html

6   Land.

7   *The Sporting News*, March 17, 1921, 1.

8   Eugene Converse Murdock, "Interview with baseball player Riggs Stephenson" (MP3), Cleveland Public Library Digital Collection, 1977.

9   *The Sporting News*, April 21, 1921, 1.

10   *The Sporting News*, April 28, 1921, 1.

11   *The Sporting News*, April 21, 1921, 1.

12   *The Sporting News*, March 16, 1922, 2.

13   Ibid.

14   *The Sporting News*, November 16, 1922, 1.

15   Murdock.

16   *The Sporting News*, October 5, 1922, 1.

17   *The Sporting News*, February 1, 1923, 2.

18   *The Sporting News*, November 16, 1922, 1.

19   *The Sporting News*, March 13, 1924, 5.

20   Murdock.

21   Murdock.

22   Murdock.

23   *The Sporting News*, August 20, 1925, 2.

24   Murdock.

25   *The Sporting News*, June 17, 1926, 2.

26   Irving Vaughan, "McCarthy to Bench Freigau for Stephenson," *Chicago Daily Tribune*, March 31, 1927, 19.

27   *The Sporting News*, April 21, 1927, 1.

28   Irvin Vaughan, "Record Crowd of 48 Thousand See Cubs Win," *Chicago Daily Tribune*, April 23, 1928, 21.

29   Henry L. Farrell, "National League's Most Valuable," *Freeport* (Illinois) *Journal- Standard*, August 27, 1928, 11.

30   Edward Burns, "When Greek Meets Greek, It's All Greek to Hank," *Chicago Daily Tribune*, May 13, 1928, 5.

31   "McCarthy Thinks Well of Stephenson," *Kingston* (New York) *Daily Freeman*, January 28, 1928, 8.

32   *The Sporting News*, April 25, 1929, 5.

33   Associated Press, "Threat to Cubs Grows," *Kansas City Star*, August 29, 1929, 14.

34   Francis J. Powers, "Hack Wilson Adds Real Punch to Winning Stride for Cubs," *San Bernardino* (California) *Sun*, June 3, 1930, 14.

35   Murdock.

36   "Second X-ray Shows Stevie's Ankle Broken," *Chicago Daily Tribune*, July 29, 1931, 17.

37   Paul Michaelson, "Hornsby Sees More Power for Cubs But No Title," Associated Press, *Evening Huronite* (Huron, South Dakota), December 22, 1931, 9.

38   *The Sporting News*, March 31, 1932, 5.

39   Irving Vaughan, "A Guy Named Stephenson's Still a Cub," *Chicago Daily Tribune*, January 24, 1932, A2.

40   Irving Vaughan, "Old Faithful Stephenson Big Help to Cubs," *Chicago Daily Tribune*, September 16, 1932, 25.

41   Murdock.

42   Edward Burns, "Cubs Give Riggs Stephenson Release and Engraved Watch," *Chicago Daily Tribune*, October 31, 1934, 19.

DANNY TAYLOR

By Nancy Snell Griffith

ANNY TAYLOR, AN OUTFIELDER known for his hitting and his speed, was a product of the sandlots of Western Pennsylvania. He put together a 16-year career in Organized Baseball, starting with his first appearance with the Buffalo Bisons in 1926 and ending as player-manager of the Harrisburg Senators in 1942. During the baseball seasons of 1926 and 1929 through 1936, Taylor played in the major leagues, first with the Washington Senators, and then with the Chicago Cubs and the Brooklyn Dodgers. He was with the Cubs during their championship year in 1929, but only briefly at the beginning of the season.

Daniel Turney Taylor was born in Cowansburg in Sewickley Township of Westmoreland County, Pennsylvania, on December 23, 1900.[1] He was the son of coal miner Henry Judson Taylor and his wife, Emma. At the time of the 1900 census, the Taylors were living in Sewickley Township with five children: Mordecai, Anna, Lela, Abram, and Charley. By 1910 Henry Taylor had died, and Emma was living in Sewickley Township with Abraham (19), Charley (14), and Daniel (9). Danny Taylor didn't attend high school, but started working as a weighmaster in the coal mines as a teenager. According to his daughter, Madge Taylor Hula, Danny actually missed his eighth-grade graduation because he was playing in a pickup baseball game.[2] He also began playing for a semipro baseball team in nearby West Newton, earning $3.50 per game.[3] According to Madge Hula, such baseball teams were very popular at the time, touring the area and even playing local African-American teams like the Homestead Grays.[4] In 1924 Taylor was playing for the Uniontown (Pennsylvania) Elks, and "his bat played a pretty song on the short fences at the local park."[5] In 1925 he started out playing for West Newton, but then became a star outfielder for the Barnesville Hilltops of the Eastern Ohio League.[6] At some time during this period, Taylor married Hallie M. Seneff; their daughter, Madge, was born in 1926.

In February 1926 Taylor was signed by the Buffalo Bisons of the Double-A International League. The *Uniontown Morning Herald* said he was the "fence buster of the in-dependent circuit.… Taylor has long been an outstanding figure in sandlot baseball here about and is rated as the best hitter on the independent circuit, for the past five years, being particularly a home run clouter. Last season with the champion West Newton team he cracked out 19 home runs and established a new record for long distance hitting by slamming out a pair of circuit clouts in one inning…Buffalo is a big jump for a sandlotter. If Danny can keep up his hitting stride there is little reason to doubt that he can make good."[7]

Taylor played in 34 games for Buffalo that season, batting .306 with a slugging percentage of .556. By late June the Washington Senators had exchanged pitcher Alex Ferguson for Taylor.[8] He made his major-league debut against the Red Sox in Boston on June 30, 1926, at the age of 26. He had three hits, including a home run, in four at-bats. He played 21 games for Washington, batting .300, before being traded to the Memphis Chickasaws of the Class A Southern Association in August for pitcher Horace Lisenbee.[9]

Taylor remained with Memphis in 1927. Newspapers called him a "speedy, hard hitting outfielder," but said that "Danny does not like the idea of playing in that climate but feels that a season with a team like Memphis will do him much good."[10] By early July he led the Southern Association with 11 home runs and was the best base stealer in the league.[11] By the end of the season, he led the league with 27 triples, tying the record held by Elliott Bigelow and Ike Boone.[12] He played in 151 games for the Chicks that year, batting .286 with a .518 slugging percentage.

By 1928 the Brooklyn Robins had recruited Taylor, but they sent him back to Memphis in late March.[13] On July 25 the Chicago Cubs purchased him, but he was not to report until 1929. According to the *Uniontown Morning Herald*, "Although the purchase price has not been made known it is understood that President W.L. Veeck of the Cubs laid out a fancy figure for the outfielder."[14] During his stint with Memphis in 1928, Taylor played in 155 games, the most of any outfielder in the league, and led the league in bases on balls (115) and putouts by an outfielder (322).[15] He batted .374 with a slugging percentage of .655.

Taylor was with the Cubs for just over four weeks of the 1929 season. He struck out as a pinch-hitter in the ninth inning in a game against St. Louis on April 23. On May 14 he was brought into right field as part of a defensive switch in the sixth inning in a game against Boston. He had three plate appearances, walking once. He was then sent to the Reading Keystones of the Double-A International League, where he batted .371 and had a slugging percentage of .620. He was clearly having more success against minor-league pitching.

Taylor was back for another trial with the Cubs in 1930. By late August Hugh Fullerton of the United Press was singing his praises: "By his brilliant work as substitute for 'Old Hoss' Riggs Stephenson, young Danny Taylor

Taylor played in just two games for the Cubs in 1929. He batted .297 in nine seasons in the majors. (National Baseball Hall of Fame)

has just about won himself a regular place in the Chicago Cubs' outfield. Taylor, who finished the Cubs' triumph over Brooklyn a week ago by driving in the winning run in the final game, did the same thing to the New York Giants yesterday in a more sensational fashion and put Chicago five full games ahead in the National League pennant struggle with a 3-2 triumph. Taylor stole home in the ninth inning when the score was tied, the bases full, two men out and two strikes on the batter."[16] Writing several years later, sportswriter John Drebinger described Taylor as "the fleet outfielder who once, while wearing the livery of the Chicago Cubs, dismayed the Giants by stealing home in the ninth inning of a crucial battle, while Joe Heving stood on the pitching mound reflecting upon the stitching on the ball."[17] Taylor appeared in 74 games for the Cubs that year, batting .283 with a slugging percentage of .402.

Taylor remained with the Cubs in 1931. On July 31 he hit two triples in three at-bats during a 10-3 rout of St. Louis. He played in 88 games that season, with a batting average of .300 and a slugging percentage of .448. He started the 1932 season with the Cubs, playing in six games and batting only .227. Manager Rogers Hornsby was apparently not satisfied, and on May 7 the Cubs sold Taylor to the Brooklyn Dodgers. Taylor immediately caught fire, and had the best season of his major-league career. On July 17, in a Brooklyn victory over St. Louis, he had four hits in four at-bats, including two doubles during the second game of a doubleheader. On August 9, in an extra-inning loss to Cincinnati, he had two home runs and a double in four at-bats. He played in 105 games for the Dodgers, batting .324 with a slugging percentage of .499, 11 home runs, 48 RBIs, and 13 stolen bases.

Taylor was back with Brooklyn in 1933. While his hitting was important to the team, some felt his fielding left something to be desired.[18] He did, however, pull off an unassisted double play on June 20, something that was not duplicated in the National League by a center fielder until Curt Flood of St. Louis did it on June 19, 1967.[19] On August 2 Taylor had four hits, including two doubles, in four at-bats in an 8-5 loss to Boston. Two weeks later he hit two solo home runs in a 2-1 Dodgers extra-inning victory over Pittsburgh. In 103 games with the Dodgers that year, he batted .285 with a slugging percentage of .469 He remained with the Dodgers in 1934. On May 20 he walked twice and stole two bases during Brooklyn's 5-1 defeat of the Cubs. He played 120 games that year, batting .299 with a slugging percentage of .440. He was fourth in the National League with 12 stolen bases.

Taylor, at 5-feet-10, was apparently having trouble with his weight. He appeared for spring training in 1934 weighing 200 pounds, but with new recruit Stanley "Frenchy" Bordagaray threatening his spot in left field in 1935, he came to camp at a trim, fit 185 pounds.[20] On June 1 he got four hits, including two doubles, in an 8-4 Brooklyn victory over Philadelphia. During the season he played in 112 games for the Dodgers, batting .290 with a slugging percentage of .432.

Taylor was back with the Dodgers for the first half of the 1936 season. On May 24 he had three hits, including a double and a home run, in four at-bats. He drove in a career-high five runs in this 11-2 rout of the Boston Bees. He was retired as a pinch-hitter in the seventh inning of his final major-league game, on July 10, 1936. Over his 43 games with Brooklyn that year he batted .293 and had a slugging percentage of .397. He played in 674 major-league games, batting .297 with a slugging percentage of .447. His fielding percentage was somewhat less stellar at .979. He had 650 hits with 44 home runs, and drove in 305 runs. He got four hits in ten of his games, and three hits in another 46.

On July 11, 1936, the Dodgers sold the 35-year-old Taylor to the Indianapolis Indians of the Double-A American Association. He played in 16 games for them, batting .302. He remained with Indianapolis in 1937, playing in 146 games and batting .327. In 1938 Taylor played for three teams in the American Association. He started the season with Indianapolis, but by June he was with the Minneapolis Millers. One of his teammates in Minneapolis was Ted Williams. He was soon traded to the Columbus Red Birds for catcher Earl Grace.[21] He was leading the American Association with a .364 batting average.[22] Over the course of the season, he played in 125 games and batted .333.

In February 1939 the Syracuse Chiefs of the Double-A International League bought Taylor from Indianapolis. According to the *Syracuse Herald*, "Taylor is listed as liking the idea of being back in the International League. He thrived in his only two years in the circuit which finds [him] not distant from his home in West Newton, Pa., where he resides with his wife and 13-year-old daughter, Madge."[23] He played in 126 games that year, batting .306. During 1940 he was a player-coach with Syracuse, batting .316 in 15 games.

In 1941 Taylor was hired by the Lansing Senators of the Class C Michigan State League as a player-manager. He appeared in 20 games during his time in Lansing, batting .351. By June 10 he had resigned at Lansing and was soon the player-manager of the Harrisburg Senators in the Class B Interstate League.[24] The 40-year-old Taylor was a big help to the Senators that season. During the last half of June he batted safely in 12 straight games.[25] He played in 83 games, batting .335 with a slugging percentage of .500. He remained with Harrisburg in 1942, but his numbers were way down. His batting average was only .243, his slugging percentage .286, and his fielding percentage .971. This was Taylor's final year in Organized Baseball. During his 11 whole or partial seasons in the minor leagues he played with seven Double-A teams (then the highest minor-league classification), two Class A teams, two B teams, and one C. He played in 1,069 games and batted .327 with a slugging percentage of .507 and a fielding percentage of .972.

By 1943 Taylor was back in Westmoreland County, and was a Republican candidate for county sheriff.[26] He lost that race, and worked for a time as a salesman for Stoney's Brewery in Smithton. Mostly, though, after he retired from baseball he became pretty much of a homebody. His wife, Hallie, was trained as a teacher. She returned to teaching when there was a shortage of teachers during World War II, and continued teaching after the war ended.[27]

Danny Taylor died at 71 on October 11, 1972, in Latrobe, Pennsylvania. He is buried in the West Newton cemetery. His wife, Hallie, died in 1978. He is a member of the Westmoreland County Hall of Fame, and was inducted

into the Mid-Mon Valley All Sports Hall of Fame on
June 26, 1998.[28]

SOURCES

Ancestry.com

Baseball-reference.com

Retrosheet.org

Telephone interview with Danny Taylor's daughter, Madge Taylor Hula,
August 21, 2013

NOTES

1   Most sources say that Taylor was born in Lash, Pennsylvania. He was
actually born in Cowansburg, which used the nearby Lash post office.

2   Telephone interview with Madge Taylor Hula, August 21, 2013.

3   "Taylor One of West Newton's Baseball Best," *Valley Independent*
(Monessen, Pennsylvania), June 13, 1998, S1; Harold Seymour, *Baseball:
The People's Game* (New York: Oxford University Press, 1990), 263.
Accessed online at *books.google.com/books?id=oJuwTnbkmUMC&pg=PA
263&dq=%22danny+taylor%22+outfielder&hl=en&sa=X&ei=Prr_Uf3Q
CYf48gTcjoG4Cg&ved=oCEcQ6AEwBQ#v=onepage&q=%22danny%20
taylor%22%20outfielder&f=false,* August 5, 2013.

4   Madge Taylor Hula interview.

5   "Former Elks' Player Bought by the Cubs," *Uniontown* (Pennsylvania)
Morning Herald, July 25, 1928, 11.

6   *Uniontown Morning Herald,* August 11, 1925, 10; "Hilltops Trim Noakers
and Tie for First," *Zanesville* (Ohio) *Times Recorder,* July 18, 1925, 10.

7   "Danny Taylor to Play Ball With Buffalo." *Uniontown Morning Herald,*
February 20, 1926, 10.

8   "Washington Swaps Pitcher Ferguson for Danny Taylor." *San Antonio
Light,* June 24, 1926, 10.

9   "Washington Swaps Pitcher Ferguson."

10   "Taylor Joins Memphis," *Coshocton* (Ohio) *Tribune,* February 21, 1927, 6.

11   "Taylor Champion Home Run Hitter for Memphis Team," *Charleroi*
(Pennsylvania) *Mail,* July 8, 1927, 16.

12   "Taylor One of West Newton's Baseball Best."

13   "Taylor Goes to Minors," *Uniontown Morning Herald,* March 24, 1928, 10.

14   "Former Elks' Player Bought by the Cubs," *Uniontown Morning Herald,*
July 25, 1928, 11.

15   "Taylor One of West Newton's Baseball Best."

16   Hugh S. Fullerton, United Press, "Cubs Triumph over Giants; Cards
take 2," *Southeast Missourian* (Cape Girardeau, Missouri), August
25, 1930, S2.

17   John Drebinger, "Grantham in Fold; 23d Giant to Sign," *New York Times,*
February 3, 1934, 16.

18   Cleon Walfoort, "The Sport Dial," *Sheboygan* (Wisconsin) *Press,* June
10, 1933, 12.

19   baseballlibrary.com/ballplayers/player.php?name=Curt_
Flood_1938&page=chronology Accessed August 5, 2013.

20   "Training Camp Sidelights," *Ironwood* (Michigan) *Daily Globe,* March
6, 1935, 8.

21   "Baseball," *Ironwood Daily Globe,* June 17, 1938, 2.

22   "Columbus Player Tops Association Batters with .364," *Appleton*
(Wisconsin) *Post-Crescent,* June 18, 1938, 14.

23   "Chiefs Buy Outfielder Taylor," *Syracuse Herald,* February 15, 1939, 18.

24   "Such is the Plight of a Manager," *Benton Harbor* (Michigan) *News-
Palladium,* June 10, 1941, 7.

25   "Danny Taylor Big Help to Harrisburg," *Charleroi* (Pennsylvania) *Mail,*
July 5, 1941, 7.

26   Paul Horn, "The Sporting Way," *Charleroi Mail,* June 11, 1943, 5.

27   Madge Taylor Hula interview.

28   "Taylor one of West Newton's Baseball Best."

ZACK TAYLOR

By Norm King

THE LONG AND THE SHORT OF IT IS that Zack Taylor was the manager who sent 3-foot-7 Eddie Gaedel to the plate to pinch-hit for the St. Louis Browns against the Detroit Tigers in 1951. But Taylor was not simply a straight man in an owner's stunt, for he spent 58 years in professional baseball as a respected player, coach, manager, and scout. He had legendary teammates like Rogers Hornsby and Babe Ruth, was involved in some of the game's greatest and goofiest moments, and learned from great managers like John McGraw and Joe McCarthy.

James Wren Taylor was born on July 27, 1898, in Yulee, Florida, the son of William Taylor, described in *The Sporting News* as a turpentine distiller, and Mattie Taylor.[1] James was a baseball prodigy with skill beyond his years; he was so good that the baseball coach at Rollins College in Winter Park, Florida, brought him up at age 14 to catch for the college team.[2]

Taylor combined playing baseball with his studies at Rollins for three years. When he was 17, he caught the eye of Birmingham Barons manager Carlton Molesworth and shortstop Roy Ellam when the Barons played Rollins in an exhibition series. Molesworth and Ellam recommended the youngster to Dutch Jordan, manager of the Valdosta Millionaires of the Class D Florida-Alabama-Georgia League. Taylor signed with Valdosta in 1915, thus beginning his long career in Organized Baseball.

It's quite impressive that Taylor had such a long career in the game because one wouldn't guess that based on his minor-league progression. Before reaching the majors in 1920, his path through the minors looked like a bad report card. From 1915 through 1919, he played in succession at Classes D, D, D, A, and C. And like a bad report card, his statistics at Valdosta weren't anything you'd be proud to show Mom and Dad; in 64 games that first year, he hit only .150 and showed very little extra-base power, with only five doubles, but no triples or home runs.

In 1916 Taylor joined the Dothan (Alabama) club, which, with Valdosta, had moved from the now defunct Florida-Alabama-Georgia League to the new Class D Dixie League. His numbers were slightly better with his new team; in 61 games, his batting average rose to .224, but he still suffered from a power shortage, with only five extra-base hits, all two-baggers.

Taylor played for Dothan again in 1917, then moved up to the Chattanooga Lookouts of the Class A Southern Association the following year. Statistics aren't available for either season, but Taylor's 1918 campaign is noteworthy because that's the year he received his presidential nickname. According to a biographical article on Taylor in *The Sporting News* in 1948:

"The new (St. Louis) Brownie manager picked up the nickname Zack in 1918 while with Chattanooga. The moniker is a contraction of the first name of the twelfth president of the United States — Zachary Taylor — although the new Brownie manager is not even a distant relative. … According to Zack, a stepdaughter of Zeke Lohman, a pitcher for Chattanooga at the time, was responsible for the nickname. A great kidder, she ribbed the catcher about being related to old Rough and Ready Taylor, and the players and baseball writers proceeded to hang the name on him."[3]

Zack and Zeke were teammates for only that one season, as Taylor dropped down to Class C with the Charlotte Hornets of the South Atlantic League in 1919. By this time he was 20 years old and more physically mature. He hit .282 and began to show more extra-base power, with 12 doubles, 4 triples and even a home run. He played in 94 games, his highest total up to then, according to the available statistics.

Taylor's play was good enough to catch the attention of Brooklyn Robins scout Nap Rucker, who signed Taylor to a contract. The signing was conditional upon Taylor's recovering from a knee injury, but it healed in time for the 1920 season.

It would be fair to say that Taylor spent virtually all of his first three seasons with the Robins riding the pines. In his first year, the Robins won the National League pennant, but he played in only nine regular-season games and didn't appear at all in the World Series. In fact, from 1920 through 1922, Taylor got into just 46 games with the Robins, and managed only a cumulative .217 batting average with zero home runs and a total of 15 RBIs. The team finally sent him down to the Memphis Chickasaws of the Southern Association during that 1922 season to get him some playing time. With the Chickasaws, Taylor got into 54 games and hit .247. The time spent actually playing served Taylor well in establishing him as a legitimate major-league catcher beginning with the 1923 season.

In the early 1920s, the Robins did not have what would today be considered a "Number One" catcher. In 1920 Otto Miller appeared in 90 games behind the plate, while Ernie Krueger saw action in 52 games, and Rowdy Elliot was in the lineup for 41. Miller again caught the majority of games in 1921, 91, while Krueger appeared in 65 and Taylor 30. In 1922 Hank DeBerry saw action in 85 games, while the aging Miller appeared in 59 games, Bernie Hungling 39, and Taylor 7. Perhaps manager Wilbert "Uncle Robbie" Robinson, for whom the Robins were named, was quite particular about what he expected from his catchers, having carved himself a Hall of Fame career at the position.

Nonetheless, in 1923, when Taylor was finally ready to assume a larger share of the catching responsibilities, Robinson still did not name an everyday catcher; Taylor started the most games, 83, while DeBerry started 58 contests and rookie Charlie Hargreaves 11. Any illusions that Taylor had of being a power hitter must have been gone by this time, because he had no home runs, but he hit a solid .288 with a respectable 46 RBIs in 337 at-bats. It is difficult to assess Taylor's defensive statistics for the season, for while he tied for the league lead in assists (118) and runners caught stealing (66), he also had the most errors by a catcher (16) and the most passed balls (13). He deserves credit for being at the top in assists and runners caught stealing because he caught fewer than 90 games. Taylor actually tied Chicago Cubs catcher Bob O'Farrell for the league lead in assists, but O'Farrell

caught in 40 more games. As for Taylor, leading in errors and passed balls indicates that he was inconsistent defensively that year.

Robinson divided the catching duties again in 1924, with Taylor starting the most games (92), followed by DeBerry (59) and Hargreaves (3). Taylor had a good year offensively, hitting .290. He also hit his first major-league home run, a solo shot off the Philadelphia Phillies' Jimmy Ring on June 1 at Ebbets Field. Defensively, he led the league in fielding percentage at his position (.988), and wasn't among the league leaders in errors or passed balls.

Taylor started 89 games at catcher in 1925, and had an excellent season offensively. He hit .310 with three home runs, both career highs. He had another up-and-down year behind the plate—second in the league in errors (17) and assists (102). He again led the league in passed balls (9) and both stolen bases allowed (64) and runners caught stealing (60).

Although Taylor and DeBerry competed for playing time, they were good friends off the field. In fact, they both married girls from the same small town, Atoka, Tennessee. Taylor and his wife, Marguerite, stayed married until Taylor's death in 1974 and had one son, Ed.

The teammates also weren't above ribbing each other. On September 8, 1925, DeBerry, who was Dazzy Vance's regular catcher, wasn't available to catch for Vance during the first game of a doubleheader against the Philadelphia Phillies, so Taylor donned the "tools of ignorance." Vance pitched a one-hitter for a 1-0 Robins win, prompting Taylor to tell DeBerry that he didn't know how to catch for Vance. Five days later, also in the first game of a doubleheader and with DeBerry behind the plate, Vance pitched a no-hitter in a 10-1 trouncing of the Phillies.

"Hank was fully entitled to give me the works with: 'Well, I guess I showed you how to catch (Vance) today,'" said Taylor.[4]

Camaraderie and a good season aside, the Robins traded Taylor to the Boston Braves on October 6, 1925, as part of a six-player deal. The change of scenery allowed Taylor to claim the catching spot as his own, at least for the 1926 season. He appeared in a career-high 125 games for the Braves, and batted .255 with no home runs and 42 RBIs. Defensively, he again led the league in several categories, some good, some bad, including assists (123), double plays turned as a catcher (17), passed balls (13), stolen bases allowed (59), and runners caught stealing (59).

Taylor got off to a slow start with the Braves in 1927, hitting only .240 with one home run, when on June 12 he found himself part of another multiplayer trade, this time to John McGraw's New York Giants as part of a deal that landed the Braves infielder Doc Farrell. Taylor got into 83 games with the Giants, and finished the season with a .234 average. The unimpressed Giants put him on waivers, and the Braves picked him up again just before the 1928 season.

Taylor tied his career high in games played in 1928 with 125. He hit only .251 with two home runs and 30 RBIs. His glove work again left people scratching their heads, as he led the league in both passed balls (11) and stolen bases allowed (62), while finishing third in fielding percentage, at .985.

Until this point in his career, Taylor hadn't known any postseason success. That all changed in 1929, a year in which he experienced the lows and highs of being a professional athlete. The low was when the Braves put him on waivers in early July. The high came on July 6, when the pennant-bound Chicago Cubs claimed him to replace future Hall of Famer Gabby Hartnett, who missed virtually all of the 1929 season with a sore arm. For the season, Taylor played in 98 games and batted .266 with one home run and 41 RBIs. He even got a vote for MVP. As an article in the *Pittsburgh Press* stated:

"The beginning of the present season for Zack was a dreary enough prospect — catching whatever balls batters opposing the Braves whimsically chose to let drift pass — but now it looks like the world series for Mr. Taylor."[5]

Taylor also got to play in a World Series for the first time, although maybe he wished he hadn't. That year the Cubs lost to the powerhouse Philadelphia Athletics in a five-game affair and Taylor was behind the plate in all of them.

That Series included two of the most famous games in World Series history. Amazingly, Taylor was not one of Howard Ehmke's 13 strikeout victims when the A's veteran set a World Series strikeout record in Game One, although Taylor had only two at-bats and didn't play the whole game. He was also behind the plate in Game Four, when the A's scored ten runs in the seventh inning to erase an 8-0 deficit. Taylor at least had a sacrifice fly to drive in a run, which probably didn't make up for having to watch the A's turn the field into a life-size pinball machine in that one frame. For the Series, he batted .176 with three RBIs.

Taylor's playing career dwindled after 1929. He remained a backup with the Cubs until 1933, played four games for the Yankees in 1934, and returned to Brooklyn for 26 games in 1935. Overall in those six seasons, he appeared in 107 games and batted .184, with one home run and 19 RBIs.

When Taylor was acquired from the Boston Braves in July 1929, he took over as catcher and stabilized the team's most glaring weakness. A baseball lifer, Taylor played in the majors for 16 years, coached and managed in the in the majors and minors, and scouted for two decades. (National Baseball Hall of Fame)

During his final stint in Brooklyn, Taylor was sent to the Reading/Allentown Brooks of the Class A New York-Pennsylvania League as a player-manager. This was the first stop in his long post-playing career in baseball. Taylor went on to cut his Baltimore chops with managerial posts in San Antonio of the Class A1 Texas League and in Toledo of the Double-A American Association. After a coaching stint with the St. Louis Browns in the early 1940s, he got his first taste of managing a major-league team when he replaced Luke Sewell as Browns pilot late in the 1946 season and compiled a 13-17 record with a team that went 66-88 for the season.

Taylor expected to get the manager's reins for 1947, but didn't, and so caught on with the Pittsburgh Pirates. He lasted one season in Pittsburgh before returning as the Browns skipper for 1948.

The Browns were poor cousins to the other occupant of Sportsman's Park, the Cardinals. (The Browns owned the ballpark and the Cardinals were their tenants.) One of the lesser-known ways in which World War II turned everything upside down was that the Browns won the pennant in 1944, the only time in the franchise's time in St. Louis that they made the World Series. Playing both "home" and "away" games in the same ballpark, they lost to the Cardinals in six games.

When players returned from the war to the major leagues, the Browns crashed to reality, and it was this ragtag outfit that Taylor managed from 1948 to 1951. In his four years as manager, the team's records were 59-94, 53-101, 58-96, and 52-102. These terrible won-lost totals reflected less on Taylor's managerial skills and more on how the Browns operated. Good players were few and far between, and those who showed any talent were sold off to pay the team's debts.

In Taylor's last season as skipper, Bill Veeck bought the club and pulled some stunts in order to bring fans to the ballpark, stunts that brought the team notoriety but little else.

Oddly enough, the idea of using a little person in a game was not new to Taylor. When Veeck approached him about doing it, Taylor told him that John McGraw once had the idea of having one on the team in case the Giants needed a base on balls in the ninth inning of a game. Veeck made sure no rules barred the idea, and on August 19, 1951, Gaedel led off the second game of a doubleheader against the Detroit Tigers. "We got Detroit out in their half of the first inning," said Taylor. Frank Saucier was our leadoff man but I sent up the midget to hit for him."[6]

Naturally, Tigers manager Red Rolfe and home-plate umpire Ed Hurley questioned Gaedel's appearance. Taylor produced a legitimate player's contract, so Gaedel was able to take his rightful place in the batter's box. He walked on four pitches, was replaced by a pinch-runner, and was never heard from again.

Five days after that, a section of fans made Taylor's evening easier by getting to vote "yes" or "no" on certain strategy options in the Browns' August 24 game against the Philadelphia Athletics. Whether the fact that the Browns won the game 5-3 influenced Veeck's decision to fire Taylor at the end of the season is not known.

Taylor continued on in baseball for another 22 years. He finally retired in 1973 at the age of 75 while serving as a scout for the Montreal Expos and that was only because the state of Florida wouldn't renew his driver's license due to his eyesight.

"If you can't drive, you can't get out to see the players….," he said.[7]

He also ran a catching school for youngsters from 1968 almost until his death.

Taylor died at age 76 on September 19, 1974, of an apparent heart attack at his home in Orlando, Florida.

SOURCES

AP, "Fans Will Direct St. Louis Browns in Game Tonight," *Florence (Alabama) Times*, August 25, 1951.

Richman, Milton, "Above Everything Else, Zack Taylor Was For Real," *Warsaw (Indiana) Times-Union*, September 20, 1974.

Baseball-Reference.com

SABR.org

NOTES

1   "Zack's Tracks," *The Sporting News*, November 12, 1947.

2   Rollins College baseball records go back only to 1947.

3   "Zack's Tracks."

4   "Zak [sic] Taylor Was an Actor in Many Baseball Thrills," *Pittsburgh Press*, December 24, 1944.

5   "Sun Shining Now for Zack Taylor," *Pittsburgh Press*, August 27, 1929.

6   "Taylor Still Likes to Talk About Midget," *Florence* (Alabama) *Times*, March 13, 1960.

7   Milton Richman, "Above Everything Else, Zack Taylor Was For Real," *Warsaw,* (Indiana) *Times-Union*, September 20, 1974.

CHICK TOLSON

By Chip Greene

TWO AND A HALF MILES SOUTHEAST of the United States Capitol, situated along the Anacostia River, lies the historic Congressional Cemetery. Founded in 1807 by Congress as the first national burial ground, the 35-acre historic site is the final resting place or memorial for more than 65,000 people, including senators, Cabinet members, a Supreme Court justice, scores of representatives, and even a vice president, not to mention perhaps the most celebrated personality interred there, former FBI Director J. Edgar Hoover.

But not all who rest at the historic site were politicians; also included are many 19th-century Washington families who had nothing to do with the federal government, but were nonetheless important to the growth and development of the nation's capital. Of those, 83 bore the last name Tolson.[1]

Four miles west of the cemetery, situated prominently on the Anacostia's southwest waterfront, stands Nationals Park, the home field of the Washington Nationals. Looking south across the river from the stadium, one can view Anacostia, a neighborhood in the Southeast quadrant of the city. As with many of the Tolsons buried at the Congressional Cemetery, Anacostia was the birthplace of the former major leaguer Charles Julius Tolson, known during his playing days as Chick. It was a place that throughout his lifetime, Tolson never really left.

Nearly all the members of Tolson's family tree are buried in the Congressional Cemetery, including his parents and grandparents. One of the most prominent was his paternal grandfather, Julius, from whom Tolson took his middle name. At the turn of the 20th century in Anacostia, Julius was a lumber merchant. His was a family business, with three sons employed as salesmen and a daughter as the company's bookkeeper. One of the sons was Charles Watkins Tolson, who, together with his wife, Annie, gave birth to Charles Julius, the future major leaguer.

Exactly when that birth took place is open for conjecture. In most contemporary baseball references, Chick Tolson's birth date is given as May 3, 1895. However, census information contradicts that date. In the 1900 census young Charles was recorded as one year old; in 1910, as 11; and in 1920, as 21. That would place his birth some time in 1898 or '99, not in 1895, as commonly accepted. Conversely, by 1930 the young man had apparently lost four years, as his age was then recorded as around 27, which would have made his birth year sometime around 1903. Somewhere along the way Tolson seems to have altered his age. Yet given the earliest documents and also the fact that when he died in 1965 his obituary listed his age as 66, it's most likely that Tolson was born no more than a year or two prior to 1900. The best guess that can be gathered from genealogical research is November 6, 1898. That's the date Tolson listed on his draft registration, as well as the one that appeared in the Social Security Death Index. Therefore, it's the one we've accepted as true.

Much as with his true age, Tolson's childhood is also largely a mystery. During his career the ballplayer seems to have gotten little attention from the press, as searches for interviews or biographical sketches proved mostly fruitless. In the 1940 census, though, it was noted that Charles's highest completed school grade was the eighth, most likely around 1915.

During the ballplayer's youth, the Tolsons seem to have been a rather close-knit family. In 1900 Julius and his wife, Alice, lived with eight of their children, including a married daughter, at 322 Lincoln Street in Anacostia, while Chick lived close by with his parents and older sister, Myrtle, at 533 Jefferson Street. Charles Watkins Tolson most likely worked for his father during Chick's childhood, but in 1907 things probably changed. For that year, Julius claimed bankruptcy. It was the first of multiple tragic events experienced by the young Tolson.

The next two events were significantly more devastating. In February 1912 Chick's mother, Annie Vermillion Tolson, died. Chick was 12 or 13 years old. Then, three years later the *Washington Post* reported that "Charles W. Tolson [Chick's father], 41, 2108 Nichols Ave., Anacostia, was found dead in his bed yesterday morning by his brother, W.W. Tolson." Charles, the paper continued, "was a sufferer from heart trouble, from which he died."[2] Thus, when Chick was around 16 years old, he and his siblings were orphaned.

His grandfather took them in. In 1920 Chick, his younger brother, Chester, and his sister Mary (older sister Myrtle had married and was living elsewhere with her husband), resided with their grandparents at 1739 W Street, in Northwest Washington. By all appearances it was Chick's last stop; he was still there in 1940, and from then until his death, it appears to be the only address he ever reported. Born and raised along the banks of the Anacostia River, despite his far-flung baseball career, Tolson never wandered far from his roots.

If Tolson's formative years are difficult to piece together, tracing the roots of his baseball career is equally as murky. Nothing has been found regarding his earliest development in the game. In 1922, however, according to author Peter Stewart in his book *Early Professional Baseball in Hampton Roads: A History, 1884-1928*, "Charles Tolson tried out for first base" with the Norfolk Tars of the Class D Virginia League. How that tryout came to pass is unclear, but there is no record that Tolson either made the team that season or, if he did, that he played; a fragment in his Hall of Fame file seems to suggest that he was released by Norfolk in the spring of 1922. By the next season, Tolson had signed with the Salisbury (Maryland) Indians of the Class D Eastern Shore League, and there he produced a performance that started him on a path to the major leagues: In just 57 games with the Indians, Tolson batted .355 with 27 home runs and a .789 slugging average. That impressive power display apparently brought him to the attention of the Danville (Virginia) Tobacconists, in the Class C Piedmont League, for Tolson's HOF file also suggests that he was sent there in the summer of 1923. Again, there's no record of Tolson seeing action with Danville, but in 1924 the big slugger finally spent his first full season in the minor leagues, this time with the Charlotte Hornets, in the Class B South Atlantic League. There, he delivered a performance that elevated him to the doorstep of the major leagues.

Tolson started 29 games at first base in place of the injured Charlie Grimm in 1929. He played in 144 games in parts of five seasons in the majors. (National Baseball Hall of Fame)

It's not difficult to envision Tolson as a player. At a reported 6 feet tall and 185 to 190 pounds, the right-handed hitter was a large man for his era. With baseball's evolution to a more lively offense beginning in 1920, he also came along at just the right time to utilize his size in developing as a power hitter. Indeed, this vision of the big man crushing the ball is reinforced by one of his more fanciful nicknames: In addition to the moniker Chick, which was then commonly adopted by players named Charles (Chick Hafey, Chick Stahl, Chick Galloway), Tolson was also tagged with the nickname Slug.

If Tolson had developed any skeptics during his eye-popping half-season totals at Salisbury in 1923, his next two seasons proved that he was in fact a heavy hitter. Playing each year at successively higher classifications, he not only bolstered his potential as a home-run hitter, but also proved his skills as an all-around batsman. Beginning with Charlotte, where he supplemented 22 home runs and a .594 slugging average by batting .341, in 1925 Tolson advanced to the Nashville Volunteers of the Class A Southern Association. (Tolson's HOF file states he was drafted by Birmingham in November 1924, but there's no evidence he ever played for that club.) Playing at the now-legendary Sulphur Dell ballpark, he produced another 19 home runs and raised his batting and slugging marks to .361 and .605, respectively, while also totaling 15 triples, giving him 31 in two seasons. Meanwhile, Tolson proved an equally adept first baseman, as over those two seasons he amassed fielding averages of .985 and .989. Somewhere along the line, he drew the attention of major-league scouts.

While the course of events is unclear, at the beginning of July 1925, Tolson was sold to the Cleveland Indians. It would prove to be a very brief tenure. At the time, manager Tris Speaker's club was mired in the lower half of the American League with a record of 30-41. Regular first baseman George Burns was enjoying a solid season to that point, a .325 average on July 2, but whether he was hurt or just needed a day off, on July 3, with the White Sox in town at Cleveland's Dunn Field, Speaker inserted his newly arrived first baseman into the starting lineup. Batting fifth behind Speaker and Joe Sewell, that afternoon Tolson made his major-league debut, playing a flawless first base while collecting a single and a walk in five plate appearances against future Hall of Fame right-hander Ted Lyons. The next day, with the same lineup again versus Chicago, Tolson started both ends of an Independence Day doubleheader and recorded a combined 2-for-8, including a single in the second game against another future Hall of Famer, Red Faber. In all, over the three games Tolson produced three singles in 12 at-bats and also handled 34 defensive chances without a miscue. It appeared a solid if unspectacular debut.

Then, inexplicably, Tolson went home.

It was his decision. (In Tolson's Hall of Fame file, the transaction states "released back to Nashville at request after three days trial.") Interviewed four years later, Tolson recalled that day. Curiously, he credited the reason for his leaving to the wrong opponent. A newspaper story in October 1929 after Tolson's lone World Series appearance (the article is riddled with mistakes) related that "Tolson … made a previous stand in the big leagues, but

it was of one day's duration. He was a little bit homesick [but] could have weathered that had it not been for Tyrus Raymond Cobb. Tolson reported to the Indians during the season of 1926 [actually 1925] and broke into the lineup. … [W]hile the Tribe was playing Detroit. The big fellow, fresh from a starring role with New Orleans of the Southern League, got off to a fine start when he singled his first trip to the plate.

"Later in the game, Cobb, in beating out one of his infield hits, spiked the giant Tolson on the foot. Tolson stuck in there, despite … Cobb and his mates … [who] tried hard to make him step away from the bag when taking throws.

"In the eighth inning, with the Indians two runs behind and two men on, Tolson came up and walloped a long fly to center field, so long that at first it looked as though it would go for a home run. But Cobb, speeding toward and under the ball, caught it just as it was about to bang into the fence.

"After the game, Tolson announced that he did not want to play big league ball and that he was going back to New Orleans. 'If you have to hit 'em farther than that one Cobb caught of mine in this league,' Tolson said, 'It ain't the league for me.'

"And he went home, too."[3]

Thus was ended Tolson's first major-league foray.

His second one came the next season. Returning to Nashville, he completed the 1925 season. At some point in the offseason Tolson signed for 1926 with the Chicago Cubs. It was understood that his playing time would be limited. With incumbent Charlie Grimm firmly ensconced at first base, manager Joe McCarthy planned to find at-bats for Tolson primarily as a pinch-hitter and as Grimm's backup. That's exactly how Tolson's season unfolded. Seeing action in just 57 games, just 13 of them in the field, the big slugger got 89 plate appearances and batted .313. He was 14-for-40 in 44 games as a pinch-hitter. After pinch-hitting in 14 of his first 15 appearances, on June 20 Tolson made his first start, in the second game of a doubleheader during a five-game series at Cincinnati. That series proved the highlight of his limited season.

Future Hall of Famer Eppa Rixey was the primary victim of Tolson's offensive outburst. On June 21 Tolson started at first base against the southpaw Rixey. In a game Cincinnati won, 6-5, in 16 innings, Tolson produced three hits in seven at-bats, including a double and two RBIs, off Rixey and three relievers. Two days later he delivered an even bigger blow. With the game tied at 3-3, one on and two outs in the top of the tenth inning, Rixey relieved Cincinnati starter Dolf Luque. Joe McCarthy sent Tolson to the plate as a pinch-hitter, and Tolson drilled a two-run homer that gave the Cubs a 5-3 victory. It was the first of Tolson's four major-league home runs.

Tolson's second came the next season and was even more dramatic … to a degree. He had returned to the Cubs for another stint on the bench. With Grimm once again manning first, Chick's playing opportunities were limited, and he saw even less action than he had the previous year, appearing in just 39 games, only eight in the field, for a total of 54 at-bats. On May 1 against the Pittsburgh Pirates at Wrigley Field, he pinch-hit against Pittsburgh reliever Percy Jones with the bases loaded in the seventh inning and the Cubs trailing, 5-2, Press accounts the next day described the end result dramatically:

"Astonishingly bad pitching in the ninth by [reliever] Charlie Root … handed the ball game to the Pirates, 7-6 … [and] kept Charles Julius Tolson of Washington, D.C. … from being a hero." With the Cubs leading, 6-5, Root had entered the game in the top of the eighth inning. As the Cubs pitcher began to work the ninth, however, "Tolson must have been swearing softly at Root from the Cubs dug-out as he witnessed the ball game he apparently won flit away. Tolson had hit a tremendous homer into the center field bleachers with the bases full in the seventh to put the Cubs that run in front." In the ninth after the first two batters made outs, "Root walked three consecutive batters to load the bases, then gave up a single to Paul Waner" which scored what turned out to be the eventual tying and winning runs.[4] For the deflated Tolson, it had been his second career home run and only grand slam. With it, he became the first Cub in history whose first two major-league home runs came as a pinch-hitter. If only Root could have performed as well that day.

The 1928 season brought Tolson a change of scenery. It also finally gave him the opportunity to once again play every day. He spent the entire season with the Los Angeles Angels of the Pacific Coast League. As if to make up for lost time, he was brilliant at the plate, batting .351 with 28 home runs and a .609 slugging mark. That performance prompted a return to the Cubs; after the season the Cubs reacquired him from the Angels for $7,500."[5] However, when the 1929 season opened, Tolson was once again in Los Angeles, for in February he had been returned to Los Angeles in a deal for pitcher Bob Osborn.[6] That season Tolson's production virtually mirrored 1928: a .359 batting average, .602 slugging average, and 28 home runs. Despite two years of relative activity on the Cubs bench, the slugger had proved he could still produce.

As it was, Tolson wasn't quite finished with the Cubs. Sparked by Rogers Hornsby, newly acquired from the Boston Braves, the Cubs raced to a first-place lead over the Pirates that by August 20 reached 9½ games. That day, though, first baseman Grimm fractured his arm during a game against the Giants, and doctors predicted that he might be lost for the season. McCarthy recalled Tolson, and over the remainder of the season Chick batted .257/.325/.330 in a career-high 109 at-bats. Grimm recovered in time for the Cubs' World Series appearance against the Philadelphia Athletics, but Tolson made the postseason roster as a bench player. His lone appearance in the Series came in Game One when, pinch-hitting for pitcher Guy Bush in the bottom of the ninth with Chicago runners on first and third, Tolson struck out to end the Cubs' 3-1 loss. That whiff was the 13th strikeout recorded by Philadelphia's Howard Ehmke, who set a Series single-game record (since broken) for strikeouts.[7]

The 1930 season was Tolson's last in the major league. After making the club in the spring, he managed just 20 at-bats in 13 games before he was sent at the end of August to the Minneapolis Millers of the American Association in a deal that brought future Hall of Fame first baseman George "High Pockets" Kelly to the Cubs. Tolson saw action in 28 games in 1930, then played one final game with the Millers in 1931. In April 1932 newspaper stories reported "the unconditional release of Charles Tolson"[8] from Minneapolis and his subsequent signing by the

Atlanta Crackers, of the Class A Southern Association, but there's no record that Tolson ever played for that club. With that, his career in Organized Baseball came to an end. He was 33 years old.

In 144 major-league games Tolson batted .284 with a .350 on-base percentage and a .393 slugging average. He hit 4 home runs and had 45 RBIs. In 2,360 minor-league at-bats over parts of seven seasons, the slugger averaged an impressive .351 and slugged .621, with 132 round-trippers.

Finding a trace of Tolson's life after baseball is as difficult as tracing the rest of his life. At the time of the 1940 census he was living with his grandmother, now 85 (Julius had died in the 1930s) in her house at 1739 W Street, N,W., in Washington. Sometime between 1935 and 1940 he married Elizabeth, a buyer for a department store, who had been born in Germany. At the time, Tolson listed no occupation. There's no record that the two had children. In 1944 *Washington Post* columnist Shirley Povich reported that Tolson was "employed as a guard by the British Purchasing Commission," a World War II agency that acquired airplanes and other war materials from the US.[9] The commission occupied the entire ninth floor of the Willard Hotel.

Charles Julius Tolson died at the D.C. Village, a retirement home, on April 16, 1965, from a stroke. Going by Census information, he was 66 years old. Unlike his kin, Tolson rests at the Harmony Cemetery in Landover, Maryland, a ten-mile ride from his Anacostia home.

SOURCES

Washington Post

Joplin (Missouri) *Globe*

Decatur (Georgia) *Review*

Blytheville (Arkansas) *Courier News*

Salt Lake Tribune

Oakland Tribune

Charleston (West Virginia) *Gazette*

San Antonio Light

congressionalcemetery.org/welcome-historic-congressional-cemetery

baseball-reference.com

retrosheet.org

Chick Tolson Hall of Fame player file, Cooperstown, New York

The author extends his sincerest appreciation to SABR member Bill Mortell for his diligent genealogical research.

NOTES

1   One of the more famous Tolsons interred at the Congressional Cemetery is Clyde Tolson, longtime right-hand man to FBI director J. Edgar Hoover. There is nothing to indicate that Clyde and Chick Tolson were related.

2   *Washington Post*, October 18, 1915.

3   Unidentified clipping in Tolson's Hall of Fame player file.

4   *Decatur* (Georgia) *Review*, May 2, 1927.

5   Associated Press via *Blytheville* (Arkansas) *Courier News*, November 16, 1928.

6   Associated Press via *Oakland Tribune*, February 21, 1929.

7   sportsillustrated.cnn.com/baseball/mlb/2001/worldseries/news/2001/10/28/worldseries_strikeouts_ap/

8   Associated Press via *San Antonio Light*, April 27, 1932.

9   Ibid.

HACK WILSON

By Thomas E. Schott

A FEW GUYS POPULATE BASEBALL'S Hall of Fame who deserve the title of "hard luck hero." Addie Joss comes to mind, a superb right-handed pitcher from the first decade of the 20th century who died of tuberculosis at the age of 31 after nine seasons, 160 wins, a perfect game, a no-hitter, seven one-hitters, and the second lowest career ERA (1.89) ever. Or Ross Youngs, an equally superb outfielder for the New York Giants in the '20s, ten seasons, .322 lifetime hitter, and dead at age 30 of Bright's disease. An on-field foot injury shattered Dizzy Dean's career, chronic arm problems truncated Sandy Koufax's, while catcher Roy Campanella was crippled in an auto accident after playing only ten major-league seasons.

We might be tempted to add Lewis Robert "Hack" Wilson to this list. (The most convincing tale of how he earned his nickname has him named after a professional wrestler George Hackenschmidt, whom he resembled.) Wilson's 12 seasons in the big leagues added up to only about ten full seasons. His claim to a place among baseball immortals rests on five seasons —four excellent ones from 1926 through 1929, and a fifth for the ages in 1930 when his star rose to the outer edge of the firmament. Yet he too had a disease-shortened career: For through all of those seasons and till the end of his short life, Wilson was an incorrigible alcoholic. You cannot read anything longer than 500 words about the man that doesn't mention the problem. And yet even today, the disease that killed Wilson's baseball career and eventually the man himself still carries about it the whiff of moral opprobrium and illegitimacy, despite its ravages and untold number of victims.

Lewis Robert Wilson was born in Ellwood City, Pennsylvania, a steel town some 30 miles northwest of Pittsburgh, on April 26, 1900, of undistinguished parents, both alcoholics, who never married. Mom Jennie Kaughn was only 17 years old, a street kid from Philadelphia, who died of appendicitis when her son was only 7 years old. Hack's father was a 24-year old steelworker named Robert Wilson, who after paying for Jennie's funeral, pretty much

abandoned his son to be raised by the woman known as Grandma Wardman who owned his boarding house. Her son Connie, in turn, became a mentor of sorts to Hack and introduced him to the game of baseball.

Without warning one day, Robert Wilson took his son and moved to Chester, another gritty industrial town on the other side of the state, just southwest of Philadelphia. Then they took off to nearby Eddystone. At the age of 16, having progressed through the sixth grade, young Lewis quit school to go to work, not an uncommon course for a poor kid living a rough childhood. For two years, 12 hours a day, and for $4 a week, Wilson labored as a printer's devil at an Eddystone print works. It was hot, dangerous work: While there, Hack said, "I had carried a million pounds of lead and was getting to be a big husky lad."[1]

Which, to say the least, was an understatement. Hack's appearance elicits as much comment as his drinking. He was built like an oil barrel. He stood 5-feet-6-inches tall, had a huge torso with short, stubby legs and weighed between 190 and 230 pounds depending on the year. He had a large head, flattened in the face, 16-inch biceps, and an 18-inch neck, but small hands — his bat handles had to be skinnied down for him to get a good grip — and even tinier feet. Sources put his shoe size no larger than 5½. Although people considered him odd-looking at the time, today we recognize in Wilson all the telltale signs of fetal alcohol syndrome, which in addition to physical peculiarities can also result in various mental disorders, such as delayed development, learning disorders, and behavioral issues like short attention span and poor impulse control. In other words, Hack Wilson entered life, and baseball, with the proverbial two strikes already against him. That his life was tragic is beyond question; that he succeeded to such an extent against the odds is remarkable.[2]

In 1921 Wilson moved to Martinsburg, West Virginia, the town of record for him and his family, to begin his rise to stardom. By this time he had played a lot of baseball, mainly as a catcher, on sandlots, amateur, and semipro teams. In his first game with the local club, the Martinsburg Blue Sox of the Class D Blue Ridge League, Hack broke his leg sliding into home, an event that had a pronounced effect on his life. For it led to his meeting a local woman, 34-year-old Virginia Riddleburger, whom he married in the following year, and the injury messed up his leg for a couple of years so he had to switch from catching to the outfield.

A talent like Wilson's — in 114 games, he averaged .364 with a 1.050 OPS (a statistic not calculated at the time) and 35 homers — could not remain in Class D long. Shortly after the start of the 1923 season, the Portsmouth Truckers of the Class B Virginia League bought him for the princely sum of $500, and by the end of the year, John McGraw of the New York Giants, urged by the Truckers' owner, had bought him as the tag-along player in a deal

The 5-foot-6, 190-pound Wilson walloped 39 home runs, led the NL with 159 RBIs, and batted .345 for the Cubs in 1929. The following season he increased those totals to 56, a big-league record 191, and .356. (National Baseball Hall of Fame)

for a pitcher he really wanted from Portsmouth. Thus did Hack Wilson, "a loud vulgarian draped in a $17.95 checkered suit," make it to the bigs. He appeared in three games, debuting on September 29, 1923.[3]

McGraw wasn't much impressed the following year, and Hack, despite some flashes of power and speed in the outfield, which amazed observers, began the 1924 season on the bench. Stubby and pudgy, he just didn't look like a big leaguer, and even when he produced as a substitute player, he didn't earn a starting job until mid-June. A month later he had to be carried off the field after spraining an ankle in center field and was out for a week. (Ever after, Wilson taped his ankles for every game.) He reinjured the ankle in early September, but finished out the season and played in all seven games of the World Series against the victorious Washington Senators.

In 1925, despite hitting the longest home run in the history of Ebbets Field on April 19, and two homers in one inning on July 1, Hack's troubles hitting the curve, which had begun the year before, continued. With Wilson struggling in a 5-for-26 slump and batting just .239, McGraw finally lost patience with his chunky center fielder and sent him down to the Giants' Double-A farm club at Toledo in early August. And although the ambitious young outfielder was thoroughly humiliated, the demotion opened the doors of the Hall of Fame for him by allowing the Chicago Cubs to draft him in the offseason, "one of the most infamous blunders on the part of McGraw and the Giants."[4] The Giants failed to exercise their option on Wilson, thus opening him up for the draft. The last-place Cubs jumped on him for the bargain price of $5,000. It seems clear now that McGraw simply didn't want him — he had been mistaken, he told reporters, in "rushing him along" — though other explanations have been advanced.[5]

Wilson found the brawling City of the Big Shoulders (and the domain of Al Capone's mob) congenial to his rollicking spirit.[6] But the sentiment would not have been possible without the enabling influence of the new Cubs manager, Joe McCarthy. The two men had what we would call chemistry. McCarthy, who liked Wilson anyway, knew just how to apply discipline. He would exact punishment in sweat equity, rarely dollars, and he refused to use curfews or after-hours spies on his players.[7] For his part, Wilson displayed an almost childlike compliance when it came to team strictures on alcohol. "I never played a game drunk," he told Gabby Hartnett. "Hung over, yes. But drunk, no."[8] And because he always came to the park ready to play, McCarthy would bail him out of jail, something he would never do for other famous carousers like Grover Cleveland Alexander.[9] "What could a manager say to such a loyal player," he once mused, "who had a weakness he could not handle?"[10]

Wilson would have strained his resources anyway. During his first year with the club, Hack got stuck in a window trying to escape a police raid on a Capone speakeasy — for which he was fined one dollar, only one of many incidents involving Wilson, cops, and Demon Rum. Hack and his drinking buddy pitcher Pat Malone proved to be a source of endless trouble. The center fielder had never, from his earliest days, ducked a fight, and his time in Chicago was punctuated by several celebrated ones. He charged into the stands once and pummeled a foul-mouthed heckler, and later survived a retaliatory lawsuit. During the second game of a July 4 doubleheader at Wrigley Field in 1929, he raged into the Cincinnati Reds dugout after pitcher Ray Kolp called him a "bastard" several times (a particularly sensitive slur for Hack). Later that evening and connected to the same incident, he decked another Reds pitcher, Pete Donohue, on a railroad platform, knocking him out, splitting his lip, and earning a three-day suspension and $100 fine from the league. McCarthy managed around this and a lot more for five years. According to sportswriter Frank Graham, McCarthy shielded Hack from the teetotaling Cub owner William Wrigley, and he "understood [Wilson], made allowances for him when he failed and rewarded him with praise when he did well." And although he could be "strict and stern" with players, "he never was with Hack, and Hack repaid him by playing as he never had before, nor would again."[11]

Wilson's remarkable five years with the Chicago Cubs during the Prohibition Era have earned enough ink over the years that the outline of them is known to most baseball fans. From 1926 through 1930, he led the league in home runs four times and RBIs twice. During those

five years, he *averaged* per season: 183 hits, 117 runs scored, 35 home runs, 142 RBIs, and .331/.419/.612 with a 1.031 OPS. He was off the charts in 1930, setting the modern NL record for home runs (56) that stood until steroids, and the practically impervious mark for RBIs in a season, 191. (Originally counted as 190, the latter figure was upped to 191 in 1999 as a result of research and documentation by SABR members. The missing RBI, originally credited to Charlie Grimm, came from the second game of a doubleheader against the Reds on July 28.)[12] Moreover, in a situation that could not happen today, Wilson lost credit for an additional homer and RBI when he crushed a ball in Cincinnati into the right-field bleachers that hit the seats so hard it ricocheted back onto the field. Reds backup catcher Clyde Sukeforth saw it happen from the bullpen. "The umpire had a bad angle on it and ruled it hit the screen and bounced back." Naturally, Sukeforth said nothing, "[b]ut Hack really hit 57 that year."[13]

Aside from the extracurricular activities, brawls, and brushes with umpires, one other on-field blemish mars Wilson's five golden seasons; indeed, it may be as famous as the RBI mark. This would be his notorious flubs in center field during the 1929 World Series. In Game Four, with the Cubs looking to tie the Series at two games apiece and leading the Philadelphia Athletics 8-0 in the bottom of the seventh, Wilson lost two fly balls hit to center in the sun, both instrumental in opening the floodgates for a ten-run rally by the A's. The Cubs lost that game and the Series two days later, four games to one. According to his teammate Kiki Cuyler, Hack was "inconsolable" about the mistakes, uncharacteristically brushing through the crowd after the game, eyes glistening with tears. Wilson never forgot it. The nightmare inning played endlessly in his memory.[14]

Had Wilson realized what the Fates had decreed for him after his magical 1930 season, he might have had to stifle another sob or two. Both his career and his life headed south in a swift, seemingly pre-ordained decline. Wilson's guardian angel Joe McCarthy left to pilot the Yankees in 1931, and Hack was thrust into the none-too-tender mercies of new Cubs manager Rogers Hornsby, an abstemious, stern disciplinarian who instituted curfews, weight controls, and tighter discipline at the plate on free-swinging sluggers like Wilson. He was everything the gregarious, hard-drinking and partying Wilson was not. Hack had a reciprocal arrangement with the fans and the kids: He loved them and gave freely of his time to sign autographs and banter; they in turn made him "the most loved player anywhere … the toast of the town," according to his son Robert. Hornsby had "the coldest eyes I ever saw," said rookie Billy Herman. The two men couldn't stand each other.[15]

And it wasn't long before Hornsby brought the hammer down. After a lousy spring, Hack started the 1931 season in his customary slow fashion and didn't improve. Hornsby benched him for a few games at the end of May and continued to throughout the summer. Finally at the end of August, he relegated Wilson to a few pinch-hitting appearances, after an ugly August 24 incident at the Polo Grounds when after being thrown out of the game by plate umpire Beans Reardon, Wilson refused to leave and had to be dragged off the field by his teammates. A couple of weeks later, he was fined and suspended without pay for the rest of the season for not intervening while his teammate Pat Malone beat up two baseball writers in a train station.

Altogether it had been a miserable year. In addition to $6,500 in fines, the mighty Hack Wilson had put up dismal season numbers. In 112 games only 13 homers, a .261 average, and 61 RBIs. It was as if the Superman of 1930 had been exposed to kryptonite the following year. To some observers, Hack's season-long slump was inexplicable, but in fact, Wilson's own reckless behavior as much as Hornsby's management style, or perhaps more accurately, McCarthy's absence, had spawned this disastrous season.[16]

Obviously, Wilson's days with the Cubs were numbered. On December 11 the club traded him to the St. Louis Cardinals. Stunned by the tone of Wrigley's announcement of the trade, Hack received an even bigger shock when his new team's general manager, Branch Rickey, proffered a contract of $7,500 — a 77 percent cut. Wilson indignantly refused to sign; he would not work for that under "any conditions," he said. After more than a month of public bickering and endless speculation about Wilson's

worth in the papers, Rickey traded him to the Brooklyn Dodgers for a minor-league pitcher and cash. Hack still took a huge pay cut — he signed for $16,500 — but he had salvaged his pride somewhat, and he repaid the Dodgers by having a solid year in 1932 — .295/.366/.538 with 23 homers and 123 RBIs in 135 games — but hardly the kind of year to reestablish his credentials as a premier slugger, not with the kind of numbers others were putting up that decade.[17]

On record as saying he was "not going to sign any pledge or make any drastic changes in my mode of living," Hack lived up to his word in 1933.[18] The drinking got worse, his weight ballooned to around 230 pounds: he looked about five years older than his 33 years. And his performance on the field fell off badly. He could no longer hit for power or even consistently. He slipped more frequently into the role of pinch hitter and part-time player. He ended up with numbers slightly worse than those of the fateful 1931 season. And yet he had the audacity to hold out the following winter when the Dodgers offered him a contract for $11,000. According to one writer, Dodger management considered Hack "just a fat and fussy little fellow who hit for a meager .266 last year and covered the outfield like a man with a trunk on his back." In fact, the club had "challenged Wilson to arrange a trade for himself. … Which ever [sic] way Hack turns, he bumps into the fact that nobody wants him."[19]

It wasn't quite literally true, because Brooklyn took Wilson on again for 1934, but he didn't make it through the season; the club released him on August 9. He claimed no animosity between him and new manager Casey Stengel — "as grand a fellow as I ever worked for" — but confessed to being "disappointed."[20] He thought the club would let him finish out the season. Hack managed to hook on with the Philadelphia Phillies for seven more games. On August 25, 1934, he appeared in his last major-league game, singling in two runs as a pinch-hitter. The following year he played 59 games for Albany in the International League. And then it was over.[21]

All that remained were what Wilson's biographer calls "the wandering years." Hack went back home to Martinsburg, played some ball with the town's semipro team, opened a rec and pool hall in town with a partner, and spent a lot of time with his old drinking buddies, all the while drifting further from his wife and son, Bobby. A terrible businessman, Hack gave away too many things for free at the pool hall, and eventually his partner bought him out. In 1937 his troubled marriage gave way, and Virginia filed for divorce, claiming that she had been deserted by her husband who was immorally cohabiting with one Hazel Miller, a girl who worked at the pool hall. Both charges were true. Wilson later married Hazel, and she spent the rest of her life waiting for her husband to get home.

Hack Wilson spent the balance of the 1930s an aimless drifter, working odd jobs up and down the East Coast. He and Hazel moved to Baltimore in 1941 and he went to work in an aircraft assembly plant. In August of 1942, he quit the defense industry and began bartending near his apartment. Amazingly, this job lasted until June 1948, when he quit it. The city of Baltimore took pity on Hack and gave him work in the parks and recreation department. His last job was as an attendant at a public swimming pool.

As the fates sometimes so weirdly have it, Wilson got a final chance to speak publicly from his heart just days before his death. Already a sick man, he accepted an invitation to travel to New York and appear on *We, the People*, a CBS radio talk show (famed for its unusual testimonies of real people). During the course of the interview, Wilson frankly admitted to drinking his life away. He had had a lot of time to think during a recent hospital stay, he said. "There are kids, in and out of baseball, who think because they have talent, they have the world by the tail. It isn't so. In life you need things like good advice and common sense. Kids, don't be too big to take advice. Be considerate of others. That's the only way to live."[22] A week after the interview, Wilson took a fall in his apartment, and he was taken to Baltimore City Hospital. A few days later, on November 23, 1948, his alcohol-ravaged body gave up the ghost. He was 48 years old.[23]

In an almost perfect metaphor of his fall from the heights of fame to obscurity, Wilson's body lay in the mortuary unclaimed for three days; his son refused to accept re-

sponsibility for it. His drinking buddies up and down the North Street taverns in Baltimore tossed into a hat to help pay for a funeral service, with enough left over for a gravestone; the National League sent a check for $350. Originally scheduled to be interred in Baltimore, Wilson was buried — in a donated plot –in Martinsburg on November 28 at the request of his widow. One of the numerous floral arrangements came from Joe McCarthy. The funeral procession, according to reports, was "one of the longest seen here in many years."[24]

Election to the Hall of Fame eluded Wilson for 40 years. He finally achieved that honor in 1979 when the veterans committee voted him in. Even today some experts would argue that he doesn't deserve inclusion.[25] But if Hack Wilson doesn't deserve the title "hard luck hero" and a place alongside Joss, Koufax, and Campanella, who does?

NOTES

1   Biographical references from Clifton Blue Parker, *Fouled Away: The Baseball Tragedy of Hack Wilson* (Jefferson, NC: McFarland, 2000), 7-10.

2   Mark Kram, "Why Ain't I in the Hall?" April 11, 1977, sportsillus-trated.cnn.com/vault/article/magazine/MAG1092281/index.htm; Wickersham's Conscience, "Book Review: Fouled Away, the Story of Hack Wilson," wickershamsconscience.wordpress.com/2010/05/11/book-review-fouled-away-the-story-of-hack-wilson/; "Fetal Alcohol Syndrome," mayoclinic.com/health/fetal-alcohol-syndrome/DS00184 (all accessed, November 12, 2013).

3   Kram, "Why Ain't I in the Hall?"

4   Parker, *Fouled Away*, 42-43.

5   Parker, *Fouled Away*, 39.

6   Wilson and Capone knew each other. Hack would frequent Capone's club, and the gangster would come to ballgames. On one occasion after Hack greeted Capone in his seat behind the Cubs dugout, Commissioner Kenesaw M. Landis called him on the carpet and complained. What was he doing talking to thugs, Landis demanded angrily. "Well, Judge," Wilson replied, I go over to his place, so why shouldn't he come to mine?" Kram, "Why Ain't I in the Hall?"

7   Arthur Daley, "A Tragic Figure," *New York Times*, November 25, 1948.

8   William F. McNeil, *Gabby Hartnett: The Life and Times of the Cubs' Greatest Catcher* (Jefferson, North Carolina: McFarland, 2004), 98.

9   Art Ahrens, *Chicago Cubs, 1926-1940*, (Charleston, South Carolina: Arcadia, 2005), 117.

10 Alan Howard Levy, *Joe McCarthy: Architect of the Yankee Dynasty* (Jefferson, North Carolina: McFarland, 2005), 105.

11 Parker, *Fouled Away*, 54; *Brooklyn Eagle*, February 12, 1930.

12   "Remaking history: Hack Wilson's RBI record turned up—69 years later," cnnsi.com/baseball/mlb/news/1999/06/22/wilson_rbi/index.html (Accessed November 13, 2013).

13   Donald Honig, *A Donald Honig Reader* (New York: Simon & Schuster, 1975), 141-42. See also Walt Wilson, "Hack Wilson in 1930: How to drive in 191 runs," *Baseball Research Journal* 29 (2000): 27-29.

14   David F. Neft and Richard M. Cohen, *The World Series: Complete Play-by-Play of Every Game, 1903-1989* (New York: St. Martin's, 1990), 130; Ronald T. Waldo, *Hazen Kiki Cuyler: A Baseball Biography* (Jefferson, North Carolina: McFarland 2012), 138.

15   Parker, *Fouled Away*, 131, 133.

16   Parker, *Fouled Away*, 127-41; "Cubs' Play Boys Feel Iron Hand of Hornsby for Breaking Rules," unidentified newspaper clipping, July 2, 1931; Thomas Holmes, "If Hack Stands Up Through May, Club Should Regain Money," *Brooklyn Eagle*, January 25, 1932, both in National Baseball Hall of Fame Library, Cooperstown, New York.

17   "Hack Wilson Balks at $25,000 Pay Cut," *New York Times*, January 9, 1932; Parker, *Fouled Away*, 149, 155.

18   "'I'll Be in Condition,' Says Hack as He Trains in Home Gym He Built," *Brooklyn Eagle*, January 24, 1932.

19   Harold Parrott, "Club Challenges Hack to Make His Own Deal; Wright to Be Released," [c. January, 1934], unidentified clipping in HOF Library.

20   Tommy Holmes, "Hack's Heart Strong as Body Was When He Made Diamond History," *Brooklyn Eagle*, August 10, unidentified clipping in HOF Library.

21   "Hack Wilson" baseball-reference.com/players/w/wilsoha01.shtml and baseball-reference.com/minors/player.cgi?id=wilson001lew (both accessed November 12, 2013).

22   "60 Years Ago—'We, the People' Ushered in the Radio-Television Simulcast" emmytvlegends.org/blog/?p=1101 (Accessed March 17, 2014); Wilson quoted in Parker, Fouled Away, 191.

23   Parker, *Fouled Away*, 165-92.

24   Edwin A. Lahey, "Hat Passed in Saloon for Wilson Burial Fund," and G. C. McKown, "Wilson Laid to Rest in Blue Ridge Town Where He Started Climb to O.B. Fame," both in *The Sporting News*, December 8, 1948, clipping in HOF Library.

25   Bill James, *Whatever Happened to the Hall of Fame? Baseball, Cooperstown, and the Politics of Glory* (New York: Free Press, 1994), 72.

JOE MCCARTHY

By John McMurray

ELF-EFFACING AND RELENTLESSLY confident, Joe McCarthy was a relatively silent yet authoritative force behind the success of the New York Yankees during 1930s and most of the 1940s. McCarthy's Yankee teams regularly dominated the American League, and in many seasons New York faced little competition for the pennant. Although he was once famously scorned by Jimmy Dykes as a "push-button manager" who won largely because of his teams' superior talent, McCarthy's former players regarded him as indispensable to the success of seven World Series-winning teams in New York.[1] "I hated his guts," said former Yankee pitcher Joe Page, "but there never was a better manager."[2]

The first manager to win pennants in both leagues, McCarthy managed the Chicago Cubs to the World Series in 1929. Overall, his teams won seven World Series in nine appearances, and his career winning percentages of .615 in the regular season and .698 in the postseason remain major-league records. At the end of his career, McCarthy managed the Boston Red Sox. Although his Red Sox teams won 96 games in both 1948 and 1949, he was never able to manage Boston to the World Series, leading many Red Sox fans to view him as aloof and gruff rather than the taciturn managerial genius that so many Yankee fans embraced.

McCarthy was born in Philadelphia on April 21, 1887. When he was only 3 years old, his father was killed in a cave-in while working as a contractor. McCarthy's impoverished upbringing forced him to do everything from carrying ice to shoveling dirt. Still, his prowess playing baseball in the Germantown section of Philadelphia soon earned him attention. He was a member of his grammar-school team as well as a local team in Germantown.

He broke his kneecap as a youth while playing in Germantown, which likely limited his chance to one day be a major-league player. "It left me with a loose cartilage which cut down on my speed," said McCarthy. "But I didn't do so good against a curved ball, either."[3] Even so, McCarthy was productive enough to be offered a scholar-ship to Niagara University to play baseball starting in the fall of 1905, in spite of never attending high school. McCarthy lasted at college for two years, but the strain of not making any money was too great and he left school to play minor-league baseball.

The 5-foot-8½-inch, 190-pound, right-handed-batting McCarthy signed with Wilmington of the Tri-State League to start the 1907 season. His first game was on April 24, against Trenton, and he got one of his team's four hits and stole a base while playing shortstop in a 9-3 road loss. In 12 games with Wilmington, McCarthy had seven hits in 40 at-bats without getting an extra-base hit or more than one hit in a game. McCarthy was never much of a hitter, and during his entire minor-league career, he batted better than .300 in a full season only once, when he hit .325 for Wilkes-Barre in 1913.

When manager Pete Cassidy was fired and McCarthy's job was given to another player, McCarthy jumped to Franklin of the Inter-State League, where he batted a more impressive .314 with two home runs for the rest of the season while making $80 a month. Three and a half years of minor-league ball with Toledo under Bill Armour followed before McCarthy went to Indianapolis of the American Association for the final half of the 1911 season in a trade for Fred Carisch. It wasn't always smooth in Indianapolis: In a game on April 26, 1911, McCarthy made four errors in seven chances at third base.

In 1912 and 1913, McCarthy played for Wilkes-Barre of the New York State League, where Bill Clymer was the team's president and manager. Eventually his salary rose to $350 a month. In 1914 and 1915, McCarthy played for Buffalo of the International League, along with future major leaguers Joe Judge and Charley Jamieson.

McCarthy jumped his contract to sign with Brooklyn of the Federal League in 1916, but the league collapsed and McCarthy never got to play for Brooklyn. That period was particularly confusing for McCarthy, as he received a call from the New York Yankees for a tryout around the same time, but he instead received what author Harry Grayson called "the runaround" when the team refused to commit to McCarthy, saying it might be sold.[4] Instead, McCarthy spent the final six years of his minor-league career (1916-1921) with Louisville of the American Association after being awarded to the team in the dispersal of players from the Federal League.

In spite of his long minor-league playing career, McCarthy was never able to get to the major leagues as a player. As Joe Williams wrote in *The Sporting News* in 1939 when McCarthy was in his 14th season as a major-league manager, "More than half of McCarthy's baseball life was spent in the brambles of mediocrity. He was the confirmed and perpetual busher [in the minor leagues]. He played the tank towns, rode the day coaches, had a gustatory acquaintance with all the greasy-spoon restaurants. He played second base and was an adroit fielder. He hit well enough, especially in the clutches, with men on base. But he was slow. The broken kneecap had left an enduring mark. 'If it wasn't for that knee, we'd recommend you,' the scouts always said."[5]

McCarthy was a versatile player during his minor-league career. He began as a shortstop, moved to third base, later became an outfielder, and ultimately found his greatest success at second base. When Bill Clymer left his job as Wilkes-Barre's manager after the 1912 season, McCarthy received his first managerial job, at the age of 25. He did quite well as the youngest manager in professional baseball, leading his team to a second-place finish only 1½ games behind Binghamton.

McCarthy got the chance to manage again in Louisville. "In those early years in Louisville, I became convinced that I never would set the woods on fire as a player," he later recalled. "My mind began to work along managerial lines. I studied the systems of successful managers of the period. My chance came midway through the 1919 season when Patsy Flaherty resigned."[6] McCarthy took over as manager of Louisville on July 22, 1919, and won his first game, 6-2. His pitcher that day was Bill Stewart, later a National League umpire.

An insult from a teammate precipitated McCarthy's retirement as a player. During a game against St. Paul in September 1920, McCarthy was playing second base when St. Paul's Bert Ellison was caught in a rundown. When Louisville first baseman Jay Kirke made a throw that was too late, the ball hit McCarthy in the chest and went into center field.

"What made you do a thing like that?' said McCarthy. "Why didn't you give me the ball sooner?"[7]

Kirke, according to writer Joe Williams, "looked the manager of the Colonels in the eye and imperiously said, 'What right have you got trying to tell a .380 hitter how to play ball?'"[8]

That incident affected McCarthy. According to Williams, "McCarthy was hitting only .220 at the time, so instead of becoming outraged, he bowed to the logic of Mr. Kirke's criticism, and that night he announced his retirement from baseball as an active player. From that point on, he would sit on the bench and tell the players what to do."[9]

After retiring as a player, McCarthy went on to manage Louisville to its first American Association pennant in 1921 (he did play in 11 games that year). The Colonels defeated the Baltimore Orioles in the Little World Series, five games to three. In every year but one after that, McCarthy's teams finished in the top four in the league. He managed the Colonels for four more seasons, leading the team to a second pennant in 1925. This time the Colonels lost the Little World Series to the Orioles, by an identical five games to three, then played a series with San Francisco of the Pacific Coast League, losing five games to four.

After that season William Wrigley, Jr., the Cubs' owner, offered the Cubs managerial position to McCarthy. The Cubs in 1925 had, in the words of James Enright, "flopped into the coal hole," employing three managers and finishing in eighth place in the National League with a 68-86 record.[10] McCarthy had hoped to keep word of his new contract with the Cubs out of the press until after the Colonels' postseason series with the San Francisco Seals, but word that he had signed a two-year contract with Chicago soon leaked out.

Before McCarthy began with the Cubs, writer Irving Vaughn noted: "For several years in the American Association, they have regarded [McCarthy] as sort of a miracle worker, but the new graduate into the big leagues can't explain his success. He has no pet theories about managing a team. He says he merely studies each individual player under him and then studies the opposition."[11]

As Joseph Durso recounted, McCarthy was quickly introduced to the star system when he joined the Cubs. Discussing a strategic scenario in the clubhouse, McCarthy reportedly said, "Now, suppose we get a man on second base? …" Star pitcher Grover Cleveland Alexander lit a cigarette and retorted: "You don't have to worry about that, Mr. McCarthy. This club will never get a man that far." A month later, McCarthy sold Alexander to the St. Louis Cardinals. Shortly thereafter, Wrigley told McCarthy: "Congratulations. I've been looking for a manager who had the nerve to do that."[12]

In McCarthy's first season with the Cubs, the team showed marked improvement. A sportswriter wrote, "There has been more interest in the Cubs in Chicago this year than ever before. Their unexpected showing also stimulated business on the road and it is a fair bet when the team holds its annual meeting President William Veeck will be able to tell the few stockholders that a juicy melon is in the safe ready for cutting."[13]

McCarthy's success, the writer said, was even more remarkable considering that Alexander and Wilbur Cooper were both gone from the pitching staff. "Naturally much credit is being cast in the direction of McCarthy and he seems entitled to every nice thing that is said."[14]

The Cubs finished in fourth place in both 1926 and 1927 behind the strong hitting of Gabby Hartnett, Riggs Stephenson, and Hack Wilson. While the pitching was solid if not spectacular, the Cubs struggled to win on the road. Even in 1928, when they finished with 91 wins, it was the team's struggles to win away from Chicago that kept it from being more competitive.

McCarthy's managerial decisions paid more dividends in 1929. According to one newspaper account, "It is gener-ally agreed now that McCarthy made a move for improvement when he broke away from the batting layout he had established for himself early in the Spring. This involved only the heavy caliber members of the attack. [Kiki] Cuyler had been third, [Rogers] Hornsby fourth, Wilson fifth, and Stephenson sixth. Now Cuyler has been shunted in fifth place and Hornsby and Wilson have been elevated to third and fourth, respectively."[15]

Although McCarthy was never a particular favorite of the media, his managerial style was appreciated early in his career. Said one account in 1929: "[McCarthy] has one quality which endears him to those who know what a manager has to face in the way of heckling. He stands by his players. … Tell him his team is weak here, or weak there, and he will not fly off the handle. On the contrary, he will tell you where it is strong and going along to suit him."[16]

After leading the Cubs to a pennant in 1929, McCarthy was forced out as manager with four games remaining the following season. He later led the New York Yankees to seven World Series titles. (Retro Images Archive. George Brace Collection)

While with the Cubs, McCarthy became known by the nickname Marse Joe, a name that followed him throughout his life. Writer Will Wedge contended: "It is suspected that Marse Joe was hung on Joseph Vincent by a Windy City scribe after he had risen from a rather Little Joe, not so very seriously considered at first, to a veritable Master Joe by his forcing the Cubs up from the ruck into a championship in the space of five years. … When you come to think of it that Marse Joe label has a quiet sound, a safe sound. It isn't the name you'd hang on a person who goes off half cocked. It's the title of an overseer who's sane and balanced. And McCarthy is just that."[17]

McCarthy's finest moment with the Cubs ultimately resulted in his undoing there. He led the Cubs to a 95-win season in 1929 and to the World Series. The Cubs, however, lost the Series in five games to the Philadelphia Athletics. Not only did McCarthy's team lose the first game when Connie Mack surprisingly started aging Howard Ehmke, who won, 3-1, and struck out a then-record 13 batters, but the team also allowed the Athletics to overcome an eight-run deficit in Game Four by allowing 10 runs in the seventh inning, keyed by Hack Wilson's losing Mule Haas's fly ball in the sun.

Even with a second-place finish in 1930 supported by Hack Wilson's National League record 56 home runs, McCarthy was not offered a contract by the Cubs at the end of that season and was replaced by Rogers Hornsby. The 1930 Cubs endured an injury to pitcher Charlie Root in September as well as a particularly weak showing on a late-season East Coast trip.

Still, the loss in the 1929 World Series was never truly forgotten. As Joseph Durso later wrote, "neither the Chicago fans nor Mr. Wrigley ever quite forgave Mr. McCarthy for that." Wrigley, in fact, was quoted as saying, "I have always wanted a world's championship, and I am not sure that Joe McCarthy is the man to give me that kind of team."[18] Hornsby also reportedly had "openly censured" McCarthy for using pitcher Art Nehf during that miserable seventh inning in Game Four of the 1929 World Series.[19]

For whatever lack of enthusiasm followed McCarthy out of Chicago, he was eagerly pursued by the New York Yankees to replace Bob Shawkey. Still, McCarthy's arrival in New York was held up since he had promised first to talk to the Red Sox about their managerial vacancy. An unattributed newspaper clipping in McCarthy's Hall of Fame file reports, "The offer [the Red Sox] made was not attractive to him, however, and he felt free to talk to Col. Jacob Ruppert and Edward G. Barrow, which he did last Friday night."[20] In the end, McCarthy turned the Red Sox down for a two-year contract with the Yankees.

Even before McCarthy's hiring was officially announced by New York, one reviewer thought well of it. Another Hall of Fame clipping reads: "The coming of McCarthy to the Yankees is regarded in New York as a ten-strike for the Yankees and the American League, as well it should be. After all, here is a man who built up a winning team in Chicago and managed it intelligently — so well did he manage the torn and battered Cubs this year that he came within an ace of winning the pennant again. What he will do with the Yankees is, of course, problematical, but the chances that he will be as successful in New York as he was in Chicago are tremendously in his favor. Managerial ability isn't a matter of geography and a manager who does well in one town should do well in another, provided he isn't hampered by his new surroundings."[21] Yet there were initial jitters: after McCarthy flubbed Colonel Ruppert's name during an early meeting with the press, Ruppert replied: "Maybe McCarthy will stay around long enough to learn my name."[22]

Babe Ruth, who was said to have been disappointed not to get the New York managerial job himself, reportedly praised McCarthy when the latter was hired and said that the two would get along well. One paper in October 1930 even went so far as to say that "the coming of McCarthy to New York is one of the biggest achievements of the American League since Colonel Ruppert engaged the late lamented Miller Huggins 12 years ago. McCarthy is a figure of national importance. He is enjoying the friendship and sympathy of millions of fans who want to see him vindicated."[23]

"I have no illusions about the task ahead of me with the Yankees," McCarthy wrote in a piece published in the *Philadelphia Record* in February 1931 (the Yankees had finished third in 1930). "The pitching staff showed signs of crumbling under Miller Huggins (who last managed in 1929)." He cited the arrival of Joe Sewell, which he felt could help form "an efficient infield combination." McCarthy also placed a lot of stock in rookie players, saying, "This ought to be a pretty good year for the rookie, as I am an American League rookie myself and stand willing to be convinced."[24]

So began one of the most impressive managerial tenures in major-league history. In McCarthy's first 13 seasons with the Yankees, his teams finished in first or second place in every season but one. From 1932 to 1943, his teams won eight American League pennants and seven World Series. His teams won more than 100 games in a 154-game season six times, and the Yankees won 90 games or more 11 times during that span.

Speaking in 1956, McCarthy listed his team's 1932 World Series victory over the Cubs as his greatest thrill. "Perhaps you understand why," he said. "First it was my first World Series winner. Secondly, it was against the Cubs."[25]

McCarthy's skill was often praised even while he never was particularly warm or introspective with the media. A representative review appeared in the *New York Times* of September 24, 1937, after the Yankees had again won the pennant: "McCarthy deserves much credit for this year's Yankee success, having turned in the best of all his managerial jobs. He won despite a series of injuries to prominent hitters and an epidemic of lame arms which threw the pitching staff out of kilter. As he went along, Marse Joe proved himself to be an excellent handler of pitchers. He manipulated the staff adroitly, especially through the many weeks in which it was not up to full strength."[26]

Still, McCarthy's troubles with the press limited his appeal. Writing in 1950, Arthur Daley remarked, "Marse Joe was never easy to know. He was a suspicious man with the press and it was only on the rarest occasions that he'd let down his guard and talk expansively. Yet even then he'd suddenly whip up his guard and start sparring cautiously."[27]

Managing perhaps the broadest collection of stars in major-league history with New York — including Bill Dickey, Lou Gehrig, Joe DiMaggio, Babe Ruth, Tony Lazzeri, and Lefty Gomez, among others — McCarthy was an understated presence, a teacher who insisted on consistent effort and outstanding performance. As Arthur Daley said in the *New York Times*: "Few men in baseball were ever as single-minded as he. That was to be both his strength and his weakness. Baseball was his entire life and it never was lightened by laughter because he was a grim, humorless man with a brooding introspection which ate his heart out."[28]

At the time of his death, Durso remarked: that McCarthy "was a stocky 5-foot-8-inch Philadelphian with a strong Irish face, an inexpressive manner, a conservative outlook — the master of the noncommittal reply and the devotee of the 'set' lineup. He had neither the quiet desperation of Miller Huggins who preceded him as the Yankee empire builder, nor the loud flamboyance of Casey Stengel." As Durso recalled, Joe DiMaggio said, "Never a day went by that you didn't learn something from McCarthy."[29]

With the Yankees, McCarthy maintained strict standards. Shortly after Jake Powell joined the team, for instance, Powell tried to give a teammate a hotfoot while the Yankees were waiting for a train. According to sportswriter Jim Ogle, McCarthy quickly said to Powell: "You're a Yankee now, we don't do that."[30]

As Joe McKenney recounted, McCarthy insisted that "his ball players play the part of champions at all times. Their dress and deportment in hotels and on trains was always McCarthy's concern and so successful were his methods that it was always easy to pick out a Yankee in a crowded lobby, even in Boston."[31]

McCarthy, as John Drebinger recounted, had "an extraordinary ability in judging young players." Oscar Grimes, a utility infielder, committed three ninth-inning errors that lost a game for New York. After the game Grimes was sure that he would be sent to the minor leagues. According to Grimes, "Instead, McCarthy slapped me on the back and said, 'Oscar, you'll never believe this, but I once had a worse inning than that at Louisville. Now get out there and win this second game for me.' You know, you've got to play your guts out for a man like that."[32]

McCarthy also succeeded in managing Babe Ruth. According to one writer, "No matter what his thoughts might have been, Joe ran the rest of his club and left Babe to his own devices. Ruth never bothered Joe much either. He did just about as he pleased, just showed up for the games and gave McCarthy four pretty good seasons. It was hard to tell what he thought of the manager."[33] There were, however, reports that Ruth's jealousy of McCarthy led to Ruth's release by the Yankees and signing by the Boston Braves in 1935.

Still, in spite of his successes, McCarthy's teams were not up to the same standards during the latter part of World War II. From 1943 to 1945 the Yankees never finished above third place, as many of his star players had retired, left for other teams, or gone into the armed forces. On May 26, 1946, in a telegram from his farm at Tonawanda, New York, to team president Larry MacPhail, McCarthy resigned. "It is with extreme regret," McCarthy wrote, "that I must request that you accept my resignation as manager of the Yankee Baseball Club, effective immediately. My doctor advises that my health would be seriously jeopardized if I continued. This is the sole reason for my decision, which as you know, is entirely voluntary on my part."[34]

The *New York Times* reported that McCarthy had suffered a recurrence of a gall-bladder condition that necessitated his retirement and that he would remain with the team in an advisory capacity. "McCarthy was the most cooperative manager with whom I have ever been associated in baseball," said MacPhail at the time.[35] Longtime Yankee catcher Bill Dickey was named as McCarthy's replacement. There were also persistent rumors that McCarthy resigned because of a personality conflict with Larry MacPhail, with whom he did not have as close a relationship as he had with Ed Barrow.

Said one contemporary article: "There is no question that McCarthy is a sick man, but the prime reason that he is not returning to the Yankees is not his ailments but Larry MacPhail, new president of the club. … Now apparently the more he cogitates on MacPhail's blast about the

Yankees not hustling, the more determined he becomes to stay in Buffalo and terminate his connection to the club."[36] MacPhail had also publicly scorned McCarthy for a confrontation with Joe Page during a flight from Cleveland to Detroit five days earlier.

After two years out of baseball, McCarthy was hired by the Boston Red Sox. Boston had finished 14 games behind the Yankees in 1947, and McCarthy's hiring was part of a larger shakeup that included shifting manager Joe Cronin to the general manager's position. Cronin sounded impressed also: "Joe's going to have more power than probably any manager since McGraw. He will have complete charge of the team and will have the power to make any deal he wants."[37]

Even though McCarthy's Boston teams finished in second place in each of his two full seasons with the Red Sox, it was not enough to satisfy Boston fans who were eager for him to duplicate the World Series-winning success he had in New York. Boston lost a one-game playoff for the American League pennant to Cleveland in 1948 and finished second to the Yankees in 1949, losing the pennant on the last weekend of the season.

In 1969 McCarthy got together with Ted Williams and recalled that Williams had been the last player to leave the locker room after Boston's loss in the 1948 one-game playoff. As recounted by Buffalo sportswriter Cy Kritzer:

" 'Do you remember what I said to you that day?' Joe inquired.

" 'How could I ever forget those kind words?' Williams replied. 'They were the kindest words ever spoken to me in baseball.'

"Marse Joe had told his star slugger, 'We did get along, didn't we? And we surprised a lot of people who said we couldn't.'"[38]

According to Kritzer, Williams also appreciated how McCarthy never criticized his players in the press.

Still, said Ed Fitzgerald in *Sport* magazine: "The sportswriters of the town, who greeted [McCarthy] with open arms when he took over the job, have been beating him over the head ever since. Not all of them, but most of them. … They criticize his handling of his players, his relations with the press, his every positive or negative act."[39]

And when McCarthy resigned from Boston's managerial position on July 22, 1950, again citing ill health, his critics were ready to pounce. But an admirer, Arthur Daley, wrote in the *New York Times*, "Marse Joe failed at Boston. It's unfortunate that his departure had to come on such a sour note because the small-minded men who don't know any better will definitely remark that he could never manage a ball club anyway and add that it's good riddance. They'll even add that the records are false in proclaiming that the square-jawed Irishman from Buffalo won more pennants than John McGraw and Connie Mack."[40]

Retiring to his farm home in Tonawanda, New York, McCarthy was done with professional baseball for good. He liked, as one report said, "to putter around the garden." In retirement, he was busy: "I don't have time to do any fishing now, either," he said in 1970 when he was 83. "This place is big enough to take care of, so I never get out. I do a few things around the house. A little gardening. Not much. I plant tomatoes and beans and stuff like that."[41] He called his home "Yankee Farm."[42] Joe's wife, Elizabeth McCarthy, died in October 1971 at the couple's 61-acre farm.[43]

McCarthy was elected to the Hall of Fame by the Veterans Committee in 1957 along with former Detroit Tigers star outfielder Sam Crawford.

McCarthy died of pneumonia at the age of 90 on October 13, 1979, at Millard Fillmore Hospital, near his home in Tonawanda. He had been hospitalized twice in 1977, once for a fall and later for pneumonia. He was buried in Mount Olivet Cemetery in Tonawanda.

An earlier version of this biography originally appeared in the book *Spahn, Sain, and Teddy Ballgame: Boston's (Almost) Perfect Baseball Summer of 1948*, edited by Bill Nowlin and published by Rounder Books in 2008.

SOURCES

McCarthy's biography and World Series statistics on baseball-reference.com.

Clippings from McCarthy's file at the Baseball Hall of Fame.

NOTES

1   Joseph Durso, "Joe McCarthy, Yanks' Ex-Manager, Dies at 90," *New York Times*, January 14, 1978.

2   Joseph Durso, "Whether They Liked It or Not, McCarthy Did Things His Way," *New York Times*, November 15, 1978.

3   Harry Grayson, "McCarthy Recalls Pine St. Baseball Parade That Turned Him from Cricket to Diamond." Unattributed article from player's Hall of Fame file.

4   Ibid.

5   Joe Williams, "Busher Joe McCarthy," *Saturday Evening* Post, April 15, 1939.

6   Harry Grayson, "McCarthy Recalls Pine St. Baseball Parade That Turned Him from Cricket to Diamond." Unattributed article from player's Hall of Fame file.

7   Joe Williams, "Busher Joe McCarthy."

8   Ibid.

9   Ibid.

10 James Enright, "Will Luck of the Irish Revive Faded Cubs?" *The Sporting News*, March 23, 1963.

11 Irving Vaughan, "McCarthy Signs to Pilot Cubs for Two Years: Louisville Manager Closes With Veeck," *Chicago Tribune*.

12 Joseph Durso, "Joe McCarthy, Yanks' Ex-Manager, Dies at 90."

13 "No Kick on Cubs in Chicago This Time: Joe McCarthy's Debut Year All That Could Be Asked," September 30, 1926. Unattributed article from player's Hall of Fame file.

14 Ibid.

15 "Good for Joe," July 25, 1929. Unattributed article from player's Hall of Fame file.

16 Ibid.

17 Will Wedge, "That Marse Joe Nickname," 1931. Unattributed article from player's Hall of Fame file.

18 Joseph Durso, "Joe McCarthy, Yanks' Ex- Manager, Dies at 90."

19 "Yankees to Sign Joe M'Carthy When Series Moves Off Stage," October 9, 1930. Unattributed article from player's Hall of Fame file.

20 Ibid.

21 "Yankees to Sign Joe M'Carthy When Series Moves Off Stage."

22 Joseph Durso, "Joe McCarthy, Yanks' Ex-Manager, Dies at 90."

23 "Yankees to Sign Joe M'Carthy When Series Moves Off Stage."

24 "McCarthy Admits Yankees' Hurling Must Stiffen Much," *Philadelphia Record*, February 23, 1931.

25 Cy Kritzer, "Marse Joe's Biggest World Series Thrill? Sweep Over Cubs Who Fired Him," *Sporting News*, May 2, 1956.

26 "Yankees Owe Flag Largely to Marse Joe: McCarthy Shows His Ability in Solving Fielding Problems," *New York Times*, September 24, 1937.

27 Arthur Daley, "Exit for Marse Joe," *New York Times*, June 25, 1950.

28 Arthur Daley, "Delayed Tribute," *New York Times*, September 2, 1951.

29 Joseph Durso, "Joe McCarthy, Yanks' Ex-Manager, Dies at 90."

30 Jim Ogle, "Joe McCarthy: A Tribute," *My Yankee Scrapbook*, 1978.

31 Joe McKenney, "Hub Prospects Rejuvenate McCarthy," *The Sporting News*, October 29, 1947.

32 John Drebinger, "Marse Joe Coming Home." *New York Times*. Undated. Player's Hall of Fame file.

33 Leo Fischer, "Joe Welcomed the Honor but Not at Players' Expense," February 6, 1957. Unattributed article from player's Hall of Fame file.

34 James P. Dawson, "McCarthy Resigns: Dickey Yank Pilot," *New York Times*, May 1946.

35 Ibid.

36 Charles Segar, "M'Carthy to Quit Yank Post," July 31, 1945. Unattributed article from player's Hall of Fame file.

37 Ed Fitzgerald, "Nobody's Neutral About McCarthy," *Sport*, August 1950, 82.

38 Cy Kritzer, "Glory Days Come Alive: Ted Visits McCarthy," September 8, 1969. Unattributed article from player's Hall of Fame file.

39 Ed Fitzgerald, "Nobody's Neutral About McCarthy."

40 Arthur Daley, "Exit for Marse Joe."

41 "Marse Joe McCarthy, at 83, Has Scant Time for Baseball," United Press International, January 14, 1970.

42 "Marse Joe Has 88th," United Press International, April 22, 1975.

43 "Mrs. Joe McCarthy," Obituaries, *New York Times*, October 20, 1971.

JIMMY BURKE

By Gary Livacari

JIMMY BURKE, A COACH FOR THE 1929 Cubs, was the quintessential baseball lifer. A marginal ballplayer at best, he somehow managed to hang around in the game for 38 years. His long career as player, manager, coach, and scout began in 1896 with the Peoria Distillers of the Western Association, where he felt privileged to play the game he loved for a modest $125-a-month salary. In later years he jokingly remarked that he would have gladly played for even $25. For nearly four decades Burke was never without a job in baseball. He crisscrossed the country on countless train rides over tens of thousands of miles, ready to play for any team that wanted him and offered a baseball paycheck. When deteriorating health brought his career to an abrupt end in 1933 he retired in comfort to the city of his birth, St. Louis, Missouri.

James Timothy "Sunset Jimmy" Burke was born on October 12, 1874, in St. Louis, the son of John Burke and Catherine McGary, immigrants from Ireland's County Cork. Other known siblings included a brother John and an unidentified sister. Little is known of Jimmy's early years. The schools he attended are unknown and he did not attend college. His introduction to organized baseball came in the early 1890s with the Shamrocks, a sandlot club of kids who wore flamboyant white flannel suits trimmed with green caps, green belts, and green stockings. The Shamrocks were considered the best independent team in the St. Louis vicinity, and many major leaguers emerged from their ranks. His wife was named Lottie, but details of her life, their courtship, and the date of their marriage are also unknown. Lottie died at an early age, leaving Jimmy a young widower with one child, his beloved daughter Marion, who died while Jimmy was a coach for the Boston Red Sox in the 1920s. Jimmy remained an unmarried widower for the rest of his life.

Burke is often remembered as the manager who in 1911 "canned" Joe McCarthy from the minor-league Indianapolis Indians. As he said at the time, "McCarthy couldn't hit his weight."[1] McCarthy never held a grudge against Burke over this dismissal, claiming in later years

that it was the best thing that ever happened to him. He admitted that he was over his head at Double-A Indianapolis, and his focus shifted from playing to where his talents lay: leadership. This became the first step on McCarthy's path to his Hall of Fame managerial career. In a wonderful slice of baseball irony, Burke and McCarthy later became fast friends. Burke became McCarthy's trusted right-hand man during a successful pennant run in Chicago and a world championship in New York. Burke may have been directly responsible for McCarthy's landing his first big-league managerial job. While managing the Double-A Toledo Mud Hens in 1924, Jimmy recommended McCarthy to Cubs owner William Wrigley, who shortly after inked McCarthy as the new Cubs skipper. Burke is also remembered, along with Rogers Hornsby, Branch Rickey, Gabby Street, and Marty Marion as the only managers who took the helm of both St. Louis teams, the Cardinals and the Browns. Of this group, he is the only one who was also a St. Louis native.

Burke did not look like a ballplayer. He was small in size at 5-feet-7 and 160 pounds. With his red hair, florid complexion, steel-blue eyes, ready smile, and sunny disposition, he was the personification of a strapping Son of Ireland. He was blessed with the Irish gift of gab and always had a baseball anecdote on the tip of his tongue ready to share with his many friends on and off the field. He hailed from St. Louis's famous Kerry Patch district, located north of downtown. It was described by sportswriter Fred Lieb as a "breeding ground for big leaguers."[2] It may be a bit of a reach to characterize the Patch as the San Pedro de Macoris of its day — that small Dominican town that turns out so many of today's finest Latin ballplayers. Like San Pedro, Kerry Patch produced an inordinate amount of major-league talent, but in this case the players were Irish.

Burke was typical of many second-generation Irish ballplayers from the early decades of the 20th century: Often diminutive in stature, they made up for their lack of size and limited skills with a combative nature, a competitive spirit, and a willingness to use their fists wherever and whenever the occasion arose. Like their role model John McGraw and his feisty Baltimore Orioles, they hated to lose and loved to fight. They battled umpires and opposition teams with equal intensity. In 1931, when Jimmy was a Yankees coach near the end of his career, he reflected on his combative approach to the game:

"I had to be a fighting ballplayer. That's how I got by. I wasn't a great ballplayer, so I made the best of such assets as I possessed. I put all of the fight and enthusiasm I could into my work. So even if I had shortcomings, owners knew I always worked and hustled for them. Besides, in the old days a player had to have a reputation as a fighter in self-defense. It didn't do to be too meek. Everyone would step on you."[3]

Burke made his major-league debut at the age of 23 on October 6, 1898, as a scrappy, slick-fielding third baseman for the National League Cleveland Spiders. In 13 games

A baseball lifer, Burke was manager Joe McCarthy's trusted coach in Chicago (1926-1930) and in New York (1931-1932). (Retro Images Archive. George Brace Collection)

he hit a less-than-robust .105 (4-for-38). That year also saw a return to the Peoria (Illinois) Distillers of the Class B Western Association and stops with the Milwaukee Brewers and Minneapolis Millers of the Class A Western League.

Burke had a two-game cup-of-coffee with the National League St. Louis Perfectos in 1899, but spent most of the year with the Rochester (New York) Bronchos of the Class A Eastern League. In 1900 he was a member of the Milwaukee Brewers of the newly named American League. The AL was a Class A minor league that year, having evolved from the Western League under Ban Johnson, and elevated itself to major-league status in 1901. That season Burke played with three different American League teams, the Milwaukee Brewers, Chicago White Sox, and Pittsburgh Pirates. He spent all of 1902 with the pennant-winning Pirates. It was his best season offensively, as he hit .296 in 60 games. In 1903 he was traded for infielder Otto Krueger, this time to his hometown St. Louis Cardinals. He became the team's player-manager in early May 1905, succeeding Kid Nichols. Burke finished his major-league playing career that year, appearing in his last major-league game on October 8, 1905. In his seven-year major-league career he played in 550 games and compiled a modest batting average of .244. With his major-league playing days over, he commenced on his second career, which included jobs as manager, coach, and scout in the major and minor leagues. This second career continued unbroken for 27 years.

Burke had minor-league managerial stints from 1906 to 1912 with three American Association teams, the Kansas City Blues, Louisville Colonels, and Indianapolis Indians; and with the Fort Wayne Billikens of the Class B Central League. He returned to the majors with Detroit from 1914 to 1917 as a coach and scout for manager Hughie Jennings, a future Hall of Famer. Next came three years (1918-1920) as manager of the St. Louis Browns succeeding the unpopular Fielder Jones. Jimmy's outgoing, optimistic personality made a striking contrast with the dour Jones and he was received warmly. He had limited success with the Browns, finishing no higher than fourth. In his four years as a major-league manager his teams had an unimpressive 206-236 record.

The St. Louis years were followed by three as a Red Sox coach under another future Hall of Famer, Hugh Duffy, and then back to the minors for two years as manager of the Toledo Mud Hens in the American Association. In 1926 he returned to the National League for five years as McCarthy's lieutenant in Chicago, which included the first of McCarthy's nine pennants, in 1929. When Marse Joe fell out of favor with owner William Wrigley in 1930 and was dropped as manager, his first item of business after being hired by the Yankees was to secure the services of his loyal friend and adviser Burke to succeed retiring coach Charlie O'Leary.

In 1932 Burke played an important role in the Yankees' sweep of the Cubs in the World Series, one remembered for Babe Ruth's purported called home-run shot off Charlie Root at Wrigley Field. As a former Cubs coach, Burke knew their weaknesses especially the throwing ability of their outfielders. This proved to be valuable information, which he readily shared with the players. His contribution to the Yankees' championship was summarized by a sportswriter:

"As a result of this knowledge on the part of their coach, such lumbering players as Gehrig, Ruth, and Bill Dickey scored from second on short hits to the outfield on which ordinarily they would have had to pull up at third or be thrown out at the plate."[4]

Over his long career, Burke played with many of the game's stars. Toward the end of his career, he was asked whom he regarded as the greatest player he ever saw. He replied without hesitation: Honus Wagner, ranking him ahead of Speaker, Cobb, and even Ruth:

"I think he was the greatest because he was such a marvelous defensive ballplayer in addition to his brilliant batting and baserunning ability. Wagner was without doubt the greatest shortstop, but he was just as great in center field or at first base. When I first went to Pittsburgh ... Wagner played center field and I never saw anyone, not even Speaker, play the position any better. If a ball was hit to center, left, or right, Hans always yelled: 'I got it.' And the Dutchman was a smart ballplayer, as smart as they came. He didn't look it but the man who played alongside of him or with him knew it."[5]

After the World Series victory in 1932, Burke was unceremoniously released by the Yankees at the age of 58 as part of league-wide cost-cutting measures. The Yankees decided two coaches were enough and felt coaches Art Fletcher and Cy Perkins were more valuable. Given his unconditional release by Yankees business manager Ed Barrow, Burke, like McCarthy before him in 1911, took his dismissal like a man, held no grudges, and laughed as he quoted from, as he called it, his "walking papers": "We regret to inform you that your services will no longer be required, etc., etc."[6] Speaking of his dismissal, Burke remarked:

"I'm glad of it. You know a fellow'll never quit in this game. He'll carry on and on and on. The years seem to whistle by — one after another — and he sticks to his job. But this release means that Jimmy's going to enjoy a vacation. I haven't spent a full summer in St. Louis since 1895. The town's grown considerable since then and I want to see what's been going on since I put on my first uniform."[7]

The move proved to be unpopular with the players and fans and the Yankees soon reconsidered. They offered Burke the opportunity to return to the team for the 1933 season. However Jimmy suffered a debilitating stroke that spring and was unable to continue with his coaching duties. His career was over and he had no choice but to retire. The stroke left Burke an invalid and he spent his remaining days chair-bound in his home at 5477 Queens Avenue in St. Louis. After a ten-year battle with Parkinson's disease he was admitted to St. John's Hospital on March 20, 1942, and died on the 26th of complications from pneumonia. Burke was 67. He was buried in Calvary Cemetery in St. Louis and was survived by a brother, John, and a sister.

Although his *Baseball Encyclopedia* entry reveals unimpressive career statistics as a player and manager, baseball lifer Burke could boast of membership on five pennant-winning teams. Not many ballplayers can say the same. Although he was never a candidate for the Hall of Fame, he played an important advisory role as a loyal coach to Joe McCarthy, the most successful manager in baseball history. He survived in the game he loved for 38 consecutive years — much longer than almost anyone else from his generation. He did it with the successful combination of his endearing personality, his unquestioned loyalty and love for the game, and his acknowledged baseball "smarts." When Jimmy Burke died in 1942, the game lost one of its most colorful and beloved figures.

SOURCES

Farrington, Dick, "It's Better Game Today — Jimmy Burke," *The Sporting News*, date unknown, clipping from Jimmy Burke's Hall of Fame player file.

Keener, Sid, "Sid Keener's Column," *St. Louis Star*, 1933, clipping from Jimmy Burke's Hall of Fame player file.

Lee, Bill, *The Baseball Necrology* (Jefferson, North Carolina: McFarland and Company, 2003).

Lieb, Fred, "Cutting the Plate With Fred Lieb," *The Sporting News*, February 24, 1931, clipping from Jimmy Burke's Hall of Fame player file.

New York Times, obituary for Jimmy Burke, March 27, 1942.

Reichler, Joseph, *The Baseball Encyclopedia*, Ninth Edition (New York: Macmillan, 1993).

Spatz, Lyle, *The SABR Baseball List & Record Book* (New York: Scribner, 2007).

Baseball-Reference.com

BaseballQuest.com

Retrosheet.org

Baseball Hall of Fame Library, player file for Jimmy Burke.

NOTES

1 *The Sporting News*, date unknown, clipping from Jimmy Burke's Hall of Fame player file.

2 *The Sporting News*, February 24, 1931.

3 Ibid.

4 Unknown author and publication (probably *The Sporting News*), November 24, 1932, clipping from Jimmy Burke's Hall of Fame player file.

5 *The Sporting News*, February 24, 1931.

6 Sid Keener, *St. Louis Star*, 1933, clipping from Jimmy Burke's Hall of Fame player file, exact date unknown.

7 Ibid.

MICKEY DOOLAN

By Paul Mittermeyer

THE PROTOTYPE GOOD-FIELD, NO-HIT shortstop, Mickey Doolan was blessed with a remarkable ability to snap the ball accurately to first base from the most difficult of positions. Sportswriter Fred Lieb once remarked that Doolan "could throw standing on his head" and favorably compared his defense to that of his elite contemporaries Honus Wagner and Joe Tinker. Lieb's comparison holds up under scrutiny. Between 1906 and 1913, Doolan led the National League in putouts four times, assists five times, double plays five times, and fielding percentage once. According to Bill James's Win Shares system, the Philadelphia captain was the National League's pre-eminent fielding shortstop four times.

Doolan, who was a coach for the Chicago Cubs from 1926 to 1929, was born Michael Joseph Doolittle in Ashland, Pennsylvania, on May 7, 1880, to James and Anna (Kennedy) Doolittle. (Ashland is in the eastern Pennsylvania coal-mining region, about 85 miles northwest of Philadelphia.) His adopted surname was variously spelled "Doolan" and "Doolin" throughout his 71 years. Mickey suffered a childhood injury to his throwing arm and had to overcome residual stiffness. Unable to make the long overhand throw from shortstop to first base, he compensated by developing a "snap" throw, wristing the ball from a side-arm to three-quarters orientation. It worked. As a teen Mickey played amateur ball throughout southeastern Pennsylvania, and in 1900 and 1901 he played shortstop for Villanova College, where he also acquired an education in dentistry (which, of course, earned him the ubiquitous nickname of Doc).

Because baseball was Doolan's passion, his offseason occupation had to take a back seat for the time being. From 1902 through 1904 he played for Jersey City of the Class A Eastern League, which was managed by future Philadelphia Phillies manager Billy Murray. In 1903 Mickey was the regular second baseman, contributing solid defense and a respectable .287 batting average as Jersey City captured the pennant, registering 92 wins against only 33 defeats for a lofty .736 percentage. Brooklyn

moved to draft him, but the Superbas erroneously drafted Pop Dillon instead. Mickey returned to Jersey City, which subsequently traded him to the Phillies for infielder/outfielder Bill Keister and $2,500.

Becoming Philadelphia's everyday shortstop in 1905, Doolan responded by hitting .254, 24 points above his eventual major-league career average. Despite his weak bat, the three men who managed the Phillies over the next nine seasons penciled his name into the lineup nearly every day, and in 1909 he was even named team captain, a position he held through 1913. Doolan's best year at the plate in the majors was 1910, when he logged personal highs for at-bats (536), hits (141), doubles (31), batting average (.263), and on-base percentage (.315). Yet those modest marks represented rarefied air for Doolan, who was one of the truly bad hitters of an offense-starved era, incapable of hitting for average or power. Doolan's 1911 campaign, in which he batted .238 with a .313 slugging percentage, was more typical of his output. By 1913 his batting average had plummeted to .218 with a woeful .270 slugging percentage.

After the 1913 season Doolan agreed to join a world tour organized to promote the great American game overseas. Modeled on a similar excursion in the late 19th century, the trip included such luminaries as Connie Mack, Charles Comiskey, and John McGraw. In an odd premonitory run-in prior to the tour's departure, the Phillies attempted to prevent Doolan from leaving unless a life-insurance policy for $10,000 was taken out by the ballplayer to indemnify the club. A leader of the Players Fraternity, Doolan balked at the stipulation and maintained that he was legally a free agent. At the last minute McGraw, who had been interested in acquiring Doolan to play third base for the Giants, agreed to pay the premium on the player's behalf.

When the grand world tour docked in New York harbor at the completion of the trip, Doolan was one of two players to sign on the spot with the neophyte Federal League. The Baltimore Terrapins offered Doolan a salary of $6,000, a better than 70 percent increase over his 1913 pay and a sum no National League club was prepared to match. It is unknown whether Phillies owner William Baker offered any salary increase whatsoever. Baker's reputation spurs doubt. Mickey had received only one raise since 1908, when the Phillies hiked his salary to $3,500 prior to the 1911 season.

Doolan played one full season with Baltimore, then moved over to the pennant-bound Chicago Whales when the last-place Terrapins traded him for infielder Jimmy Smith and cash late in the 1915 season. After the collapse of the Federal League, Doolan was awarded to the Chicago Cubs, for whom he saw limited action in 1916 before his inclusion in the midseason trade sending infielder Heinie Zimmerman to the Giants for second baseman Larry Doyle. In McGraw's employ at last, he played infrequently in New York as well, and was back in the minors by 1917. Signing as player-manager of the International League's Rochester (New York) Hustlers, Doolan guided the team to fifth place, an improvement of eight games and two

places in the standings over the previous season, but he was nonetheless let go after the season. He returned to the National League as a second baseman for the Brooklyn Robins in 1918, appearing in 92 games and batting a mere .179 with just 10 extra-base hits in 308 at-bats.

After stints in the International League with Reading and Jack Dunn's powerhouse Baltimore Orioles, Mickey re-emerged in the majors in 1926 as a coach for the Cubs, a role he held into the 1929 season. Starting in 1930, Doolan served three years as a coach for the Cincinnati Reds, leaving the majors for good after the 1932 season. With his baseball career behind him, Doolan practiced dentistry until 1947. Upon retiring, he and his wife, Emma, relocated to Orlando, Florida, where Mickey suffered a stroke in late 1949. A subsequent leg injury left him a partial invalid. Acute appendicitis beset Doolan in late October 1951; the appendix ruptured and he succumbed to the resultant peritonitis early in the morning of November 1. Emma survived Mickey by just over three months, dying in February 1952. They had no children.

Note: A slightly different version of this biography appeared in Tom Simon, ed., *Deadball Stars of the National League* (Washington: Brassey's, Inc., 2004).

SOURCES

The Baseball Encyclopedia, Eighth Edition, (New York: Macmillan Publishing Company, 1990).

Bready, James H., *Baseball in Baltimore*, (Baltimore: Johns Hopkins University Press, 1998).

Light, Jonathan Fraser, *The Cultural Encyclopedia of Baseball* (Jefferson, North Carolina: McFarland & Company, 1997).

Johnson, Lloyd, and Miles Wolff, *The Encyclopedia of Minor League Baseball* (Durham, North Carolina: Baseball America, Inc., 1997).

O'Neal, Bill, *The International League: A Baseball History 1884-1991* (Austin, Texas: Eakin Press, 1992).

Okkonen, Marc, *The Federal League of 1914-1915: Baseball's Third Major League* (Pittsburgh: Society for American Baseball Research, 1989).

Pietrusza, David, Matthew Silverman, and Michael Gershman, eds., *Baseball: The Biographical Encyclopedia* (New York: Total Sports Publishing, 2000).

A coach for the Cubs from 1926 to 1929, Doolan was a slick fielding shortstop during his 13-year career in the majors (1905-1918). (National Baseball Hall of Fame)

GROVER LAND

By Gary Livacari

IKE MANY MARGINAL BALLPLAYERS from the Deadball Era, Grover Land has been largely forgotten with the passage of time. His career as a player and coach spanned 27 seasons (1904-1930). He logged seven years as a major leaguer, the first five as backup catcher for the Cleveland Naps in the American League and the last two as the primary catcher for the Brooklyn Tip-Tops of the "outlaw" Federal League. His well-traveled minor-league career consisted of parts of 13 seasons. He spent seven years as a coach with the Pittsburgh Pirates, Cincinnati Reds, and Chicago Cubs. The highlight of his career was serving as a coach for the 1929 pennant-winning Cubs, his only World Series experience. Grover Land is best remembered for his occasional flashes of defensive brilliance on the diamond, and for more than a few flashes of his volatile temper off the field. He is also remembered for involvement in two bizarre on-field incidents.

Grover Cleveland Land's entries in the *Baseball Encyclopedia* and on Basebal-Reference.com gives September 22, 1884, as his date of birth and Frankfort, Kentucky, as his place of birth. However, responding in 1922 to a *Baseball Magazine* request for personal information, he submitted a hand-written entry indicating his birthday as September 22, 1886, and his place of birth as Shady Grove, Kentucky.[1] The 1886 birth date is also found on Land's Heilbroner Baseball Bureau player card. Land was named after Grover Cleveland, the president at the time of his birth (assuming the 1886 date is accurate). His parents were W.G. Land, a native of Kentucky, and Mary C. (Ward) Land, originally from Virginia. Only one other sibling is known, a sister of unknown name who died in 1910. Little is known of Land's early years. His grade school and high school are unknown, and he did not attend college. His wife was named Sara Lee and they were married on the morning of May 11, 1914, before the Tip Tops' game that afternoon. There is no information on Sara's place or date of birth. The couple had at least one child, Grover Land, Jr., who served in the US Army in World War II.

Land made his major-league debut on September 2, 1908, with the Cleveland Naps in a 5-3 loss to the Detroit Tigers at Bennett Park in Detroit. During his years in the big leagues, all in the Deadball Era, the burly 6-foot, 190-pound catcher compiled a career batting average of .243 in 293 games with no home runs and an anemic slugging average of .279. His career fielding average was a mediocre .964. Land was a catcher for his entire career, except for one game at first base in 1911. He played his last major-league game on September 25, 1915, with Brooklyn. His minor-league record was not better, with a career batting average of .234 in 780 games. His name appears on one dubious major-league list: He is tied for 13th place with six other players on the list of "Most hits in a season with no extra-base hits." This occurred in 1910, when Land had 23 hits in 34 games for Cleveland, all singles.

Land began his well-traveled baseball career in 1904 with the Paducah Indians of the Class D Kitty League for a salary of $75 a month. He played on various American Association teams until 1908 when he was traded to the Naps by the Toledo Mud Hens for pitcher Tex Pruiett and infielder-outfielder Charlie Hickman. Land bounced between Cleveland and Toledo five times until 1914. He made so many stops between Toledo and Cleveland that he once joked: "Why, I used up something like $300 worth of transportation between Cleveland and Toledo. In fact, I believe these two burgs declared large dividends for the Lake Shore Railroad annually. It was a common occurrence for conductors to say: 'Hello Grover, are you with us again?' "[2]

In five years with Cleveland Land hit a dismal .189 in 95 games. In 1914 the allure of big money enticed him to jump to the Brooklyn Tip-Tops of the new Federal League. Brooklyn dangled a three-year contract worth $10,000, which Land found hard to resist. But there was a problem: He had already signed a contract with Sioux City of the Class A Western League, and had drawn a $500 advance on his salary. Western League President E.J. Hanlon threatened legal action to prevent Land from violating his contract. No suit ever materialized, and he landed with Brooklyn. Land had his best year in the majors with the 1914 Tip-Tops, hitting .275 in 102 games for manager Bill Bradley. He slumped to .259 in 96 games in 1915. After the demise of the Federal League, Land spent 1916 with the Minneapolis Millers of the American Association as part of the "peace agreement" that disbanded the upstart league. In 1917 he played for the St. Paul Saints, also of the American Association.

In World War I Land enlisted in the Army in February 1918 and served for ten months, assigned to a field-artillery unit in Jefferson City, Missouri. It is not known whether he saw action overseas. After the war, a final six games with the Seattle Rainiers of the Pacific Coast League in 1919 ended his minor-league career. From 1919 to 1922 he played for semipro teams in cities including Oakland; Victoria, Texas; Little Rock, Winston-Salem: Danville, Virginia; and Charleston. He then worked as a coach and scout for the Pittsburgh Pirates under manager Bill McKechnie for the 1923 and 1924 seasons and for the Cincinnati Reds under manager Jack Hendricks in 1925 and 1928. He was released by the Reds in December 1928 when they decided to keep only one coach and chose Ivey Wingo. His final two years of major-league service found him on the coaching staff of Joe McCarthy with the Cubs in 1929 and 1930 (including Marse Joe's first of nine pennant winners in 1929. At one point during his coaching days, Land was described as "one of the most popular coaches in the game … and one of the most valuable advisors in baseball."[3] *Land's tenure with the Cubs ended after the 1930 season, when McCarthy was not offered a Cubs contract for 1931, left for the Yankees, and took coach Jimmy Burke from the Cubs with him.*

While never much of an offensive threat, Land had a reputation as a bulldog behind the plate who was not easily intimidated. Various newspaper accounts at the time described him as a defensive standout, noting particularly his ability to block the plate. In 1910 one reporter commented: "Grover has few superiors as a backstop when he tends to business"[4] Another said:

"All the players claim Grover Land is the hardest catcher in the business to slide into the plate on. It is absolutely necessary to go around him, he blocks the plate so effectively. He has caught the best ball of his career this year."[5]

But Land carried this aggression off the field. At one point his volatile temper came to the attention of the president of the American League: "The war-like disposition of Mr. Land was so protuberant that Ban Johnson used to write him notes and tell him about it. … He was quite a fighter."[6] An article in 1911 reported his arrest for assault and battery after he struck the gatekeeper of the Cleveland Park who had refused to admit two of Land's friends and "grossly insulted them when they applied for admission."[7] Land was fined $100. The same year he was arrested in Frankfort, Kentucky, for allegedly shooting the "keeper" of a Greek restaurant over an undisclosed dispute. In a 1926 domestic quarrel, his wife, Sara, testified that Land "became intoxicated and fired a revolver at me in a fit of temper."[8] She was granted an "absolute divorce, with the decree carrying an allowance of $1,500 alimony annually."[9] Despite the finality implied in this ruling, there apparently was a reconciliation. Sara was named as Land's wife on his death certificate and in his obituaries in 1958.

Land was involved in a bizarre event on Opening Day of 1915 at Brooklyn's Washington Park. It happened in the seventh inning of a game between the Tip-Tops and the Buffalo Blues. Land was sent in to pinch-hit for pitcher Bill Upham with one on and the score tied. Land singled, and a pinch-runner was then sent in for him. In the next inning, Land unexpectedly re-entered as the Tip-Top catcher and finished the contest — even though he was officially out of the game! No explanation was given for why the umpires allowed this violation of a fundamental rule to stand. Newspaper accounts suggested that such incidents gave the impression that the Federal League did not deserve major-league status and that they may have contributed to its demise.

During the summer of 1914, Land was the principal player in an unusual home run. Umpire Bill Brennan was the lone arbiter in a Federal league game between the Tip-Tops and the Chicago Whales. Brennan grew tired of running to the dugout for new balls every time a foul ball was hit into the stands, so he piled up the extra balls into a pyramid just behind the pitcher's mound. In one account of the incident, Land came to the plate and smashed a low line drive that smacked right into the pile, sending the extra balls flying in every direction.

"Land realized he had caused some confusion," the account said. "He kept running around the bases while every Chicago infielder and the pitcher and catcher grabbed a loose ball and tried to tag him. After he crossed home plate, there was nothing left for the umpire Brennan to do but award an 'inside the diamond home run' — because no one could identify the legally batted ball that started the play. It was the shortest home-run hit on record. The ball was known to have traveled 70 feet."[10] The story may be apocryphal, despite numerous accounts found in Land's Hall of Fame player file, or perhaps the home run was later disallowed. Land has no home runs recorded in the *Baseball Encyclopedia* for 1914.

After his discharge from the Army in 1918, Land tried to get his share of "easy money" by cashing in on his war-service notoriety. Stars like Joe Tinker, Christy Mathewson, and Rube Waddell were drawing huge salaries on the vaudeville circuit and Land thought he could do the same. However his one chance in front of the klieg lights ended in miserable failure. A contemporary account described the incident, noting that Land was "bold as a lion on the field, but he was as bashful as a June bride upon the stage … and he was unable to deliver his two-word line."[11] He froze with stage fright. People in the audience threw bouquets of flowers at his feet. He picked one up to hide his face — and an enormous cabbage fell out. Overwhelmed with embarrassment, the hot-tempered Land launched into an emotional, profanity-laced tirade as the audience howled with laughter. So ended Grover Land's disastrous, short-lived experience in show business.

While a coach with the Reds in 1928, Land was involved in an unusual incident that resulted in injury to Reds manager Jack Hendricks and may have contributed to Land's eventual dismissal. During a spring-training game, Land was filling in as the home-plate umpire with pitcher Ray Kolp on the mound and Jack White at the plate:

"Hendricks was just behind Land, watching the delivery of the various pitchers and coaching the youngsters in batting and suddenly Hendricks called: 'Let the next one

A former catcher, Land spent seven seasons as a coach in the major leagues. Chicago was his last stop in 1929. (National Baseball Hall of Fame)

go by.' Land believed the remark addressed to him, and so it happened that when the husky Kolp let go, Land stepped aside and the ball hissed past White and Land and socked the Red Leg rajah on the left knee, knocking him flatter than linoleum."[12]

Details of Land's life after baseball are unknown. In later years he was employed as a host by the Luke Greenway Post No. 1 of the American Legion in Phoenix, Arizona. He died at the Veterans Hospital in Phoenix on July 22, 1958, of an aortic aneurysm one day after admittance. Land was 73. He was survived by his wife, Sara (from whom he was previously divorced), and his son, Grover

Land, Jr. He was buried in Greenwood Memorial Park in Phoenix. He had been a resident of Phoenix from 1921 until the time of his death.

SOURCES

Heilbroner, Louis, *The Baseball Blue Book* (Fort Wayne, Indiana: Heilbroner Baseball Bureau), information card for Grover Land.

Lee, Bill, *The Baseball Necrology* (Jefferson, North Carolina: McFarland and Company, 2003).

Reichler, Joseph, *The Baseball Encyclopedia*, Ninth Edition (New York: Macmillan, 1993).

Spatz, Lyle, ed., *The SABR Baseball List & Record Book* (New York: Scribner, 2007).

Phalon, W.A., "Shall Baseball Cease," *Baseball Magazine*, December, 1918, 102 (clipping from Land's Hall of Fame file).

Sawyer, C. Ford, *Baseball Magazine* (personal information card submitted by Land to Sawyer, 1922).

Associated Press, unnamed article, March 30, 1926.

Baseball Magazine

Kansas City Star, August 10, 1917.

Leslie's Weekly, April 29, 1915.

New York Times

Sporting Life

The Sporting News, February 27, 1972.

Obituary for Grover Land, publication unknown, July 30, 1958.

Baseball-Almanac.com

TheBaseballCube.com

Baseball-Reference.com

BaseballGauge.com

Retrosheet.org

(Some of the sources listed above are from Land's player file at the Baseball Hall of Fame Library, Cooperstown, New York.)

NOTES

1   SABR's Biographical Research Committee gives 1884 as the year of Land's birth.

2   *New York Times*, August 19, 1914.

3   Associated Press, March 30, 1926, unnamed publication, clipping from Land's Hall of Fame player file.

4   *Sporting Life*, April 30, 1910, 11.

5   *Sporting Life*, September 26, 1914, 15.

6   *Baseball Magazine*, December, 1918, 102.

7   *New York Times*, August 19, 1914.

8   Associated Press, March 30, 1926, unnamed publication, clipping from Land's Hall of Fame player file.

9   Ibid.

10 *The Sporting News*, February 27, 1972.

11 *Baseball Magazine*, December, 1918, 102.

12 Unnamed publication, March 7, 1928, clipping from Land's Hall of Fame player file.

BILL VEECK, SR.

By David Fletcher and George Castle

I T WOULD NOT BE INACCURATE TO CALL the 1929 Cubs team president William L. Veeck's crowning achievement.

Arguably baseball's strongest franchise — even the Ruth/Gehrig New York Yankees could not have been rated higher at this juncture — the Cubs had been built player by player over a decade by Veeck, with assistance from keen scout Jack Doyle. The last building block came aboard, thanks to owner William Wrigley, Jr.'s impetus and healthy checkbook, via second baseman Rogers Hornsby. Few could even dream to match up with the Cubs' lineup, anchored by Hornsby and Hack Wilson, and backed by a Big Four pitching rotation led by Charlie Root.

Catcher Gabby Hartnett, who would miss much of the 1929 season with a right-arm injury, was the first piece of the puzzle, acquired from Worcester of the Eastern League before the 1922 season. Veeck crafted savvy trades with the Pittsburgh Pirates to garner first baseman Charlie Grimm in 1924 and right fielder Kiki Cuyler late in 1927.

Hack Wilson, who did not stick with the New York Giants during a subpar 1925 season, was traded to Toledo, from where Veeck performed a salvage job by drafting the short, stocky player who John McGraw felt would never be productive. The Cleveland Indians' decision makers inexplicably did not see the long-term merits of infielder Riggs Stephenson even after he batted .371 in 1924. Veeck did, and installed him in left field to great effect in Cubs Park. Root failed as a reliever during a cameo appearance with the St. Louis Browns in 1923, but Veeck snared him for the Cubs and he was a rotation mainstay by 1926.

Veeck found 1929 Cubs manager Joseph McCarthy (and the future manager of the Yankees dynasty) toiling as a minor-league manager in Louisville and hired him in 1926.

It was Veeck who engineered the building of the 1929 Cubs, believed by many baseball historians as their best team ever, even surpassing the Cubs "mini-dynasty" teams of 1906-1910.

But like the namesake son he raised and who adored his memory till the end of his own colorful life in 1986, the elder Veeck was no one-trick pony with his construction of the 1929 Cubs. He was as multidimensional and dynamic a sports executive as existed in his era. As his son wrote in his seminal book *Veeck — As In Wreck*, "He was a man of imagination … the greatest innovator of his time."[1] In fact, when the record is laid out, one can argue that William L. Veeck was the best executive in Cubs history; the franchise was never the same after his sudden and early death at 56 in 1933. As a team-builder and talent procurer, Veeck had no match in Chicago National League annals. The juggernaut that was tripped up in the 1929 World Series by the Philadelphia Athletics did not just die out, even though owner Wrigley was heartbroken to fall short of his coveted championship.

Many of the same players went on to win NL pennants in 1932 and 1935. Hartnett was a dual threat, slugging the historic, season-turning "Homer in the Gloamin'" while sparking the Cubs as player-manager to the 1938 flag. Other young Cubs coming through the pipeline under Veeck after 1929, like second baseman Billy Herman, shortstop Billy Jurges, third baseman Stan Hack, and outfielder Frank Demaree, proved mainstays on the pennant winners through 1938. Hack still was starting at the hot corner on the wartime 1945 NL champion Cubs.

But there was a lot more in Veeck's actions and personality, as the game's most respected executive in his era and an unsung hero who had long-lasting positive effects throughout the major leagues.

The list is long:

*Veeck took the first firm action against the gambling that had infested the game like a wooden house sagging under termites' hunger. Thwarting a possible fixed game in Wrigley Field in 1920, Veeck's quick work contributed to the probe that exposed the Black Sox Scandal.

*Related to the threat of gambling and fixes, Veeck was a key early supporter of Kenesaw Mountain Landis for the job as baseball's first commissioner. Landis was far from the perfect baseball czar, with his apparent obstacle to integration his biggest demerit, but he brought a semblance of order to a situation threatening to descend into chaos.

*Contrary to many sports owners' beliefs at the time, Veeck was a strong proponent of broadcast exposure to popularize the Cubs; radio listeners soon became ticket buyers — an attendance record of nearly 1.5 million in 1929. His advocacy was proved right against fearful, misguided team moguls as far as 80 years into the future. That's when the Chicago Blackhawks' Rocky Wirtz ended his father Bill's home-game TV blackout to enjoy wire-to-wire sellouts for a two-time Stanley Cup champion. Fittingly, the 1980s Cubs became a "national" team via heavy exposure on satellite-borne superstation WGN-TV.

Among the most influential and most innovative executives in baseball history, Veeck engineered the building of the 1929 Cubs. (National Baseball Hall of Fame)

*Under Veeck the Cubs built the fan base far beyond the typical macho, cigar-chomping, cussing, straw-skimmer-topped male crowd. Even before Chicago began to contend in 1926, he instituted Ladies Day on the North Side. The weekly games in which admission was free for women were an instant hit. Thousands of women streamed into the ballpark, with the largest-ever Wrigley Field baseball crowd, more than 51,000 (19,000 paid) in 1930, a Ladies Day product.

*Veeck was one of the early supporters of the All-Star Game, conceived as a one-shot exhibition to tie in to Chicago's Century of Progress world's fair in 1933. His influence prompted the other NL teams to support the game. Thanks to a massive crowd at old Comiskey Park and Babe Ruth's well-timed showmanship, the game immediately became an annual affair. Now, its winner determines World Series home-field advantage for the team's league. The All-Star Game evolved far beyond Veeck's original idea.

*Interleague play was proposed by Veeck more than 60 years before its implementation. Regular-season interleague clashes were introduced in 1997 by Commissioner Bud Selig as part of sweeping schedule changes that included wild-card playoff teams and the Divisional Series implemented during the 1995 postseason. Baseball does evolve, but often more slowly than its visionaries desire.

*Veeck was the first major-league executive to promote a woman into an executive level when he appointed Margaret "Midge" Donahue the Cubs club secretary in 1926; she was the Cubs vice president by the time her career ended in 1958.

*Veeck was the philosophical grounding of his far better known son. Although possessed of different personalities, the dignified William L. Veeck and Barnum-like promoter Bill Veeck shared a customer-service philosophy and an ability to think beyond hidebound tradition. It's not hard to conceive that had the elder Veeck lived longer, he would have taken his son under his wing in the Cubs front office as his possible successor. History would have dramatically changed individually and teamwise. Since P.K. Wrigley, William Wrigley, Jr.'s son, admired almost everything his father did and tried to copy many of his decisions, passing on the power generationally in the Veeck family could have provided the Cubs management stability the franchise never possessed.

Indeed, in the real timeline, the death of William L. Veeck from leukemia that is now treatable robbed the Cubs of the team's guiding light and the face of the franchise that was adorned on all of the Cubs scorecards. The first preference of P.K. Wrigley was for Veeck to run the team, with near-ownership power, as he did for William Wrigley, Jr. But after Veeck's death in October 1933, P.K. Wrigley, dissatisfied with the short presidency of William L. Walker, appointed himself president even though he admitted to Chicago sportswriters that he knew little about baseball. Wrigley's reasoning for taking the day-to-day helm was that he could not find "another Bill Veeck." (But he passed up Veeck's right-hand "man" Margaret Donahue though many sportswriters felt that she should be have been tabbed to succeed William L. Veeck.)

Without that buffer of a knowledgeable, popular leader respected throughout the game who was placed between himself and team operations, Wrigley began to impose schemes rooted either in business or his own personal, baseball-ignorant beliefs. The Cubs completed a steady decline, culminating in the manager-less "College of Coaches" and an athletic director hired from the Air Force in the early 1960s, a decline begun as the last of the Veeck-developed players left the organization.

Due to the traditional lack of strong Cubs scouting and player development, it can be argued that Veeck's death had an impact stretching into the present day, and that it — not the 1964 trade of Lou Brock or the 1992 free-agent loss of Greg Maddux — was the most grievous setback in Cubs history.

Son Bill Veeck, Lou Brock, and Greg Maddux are far better known than William L. Veeck. A crash course in history should be in order for all Cubs executives and fans to understand his impact.

William L. Veeck succeeded in an old-fashioned, All-American manner very rarely duplicated today. He followed his dream from his small-town birthplace — Boonville, Indiana, 20 miles east of Evansville, in 1877 — to relative success as a sportswriter in the big city, Chicago. A combination of talent and the open-mindedness of William Wrigley, Jr. led to Veeck's ascendancy to the top of the baseball world. In transforming themselves from sportswriters to baseball honchos, only the likes of Fred Claire and Ned Colletti with the Los Angeles Dodgers have come close to the Veeck story in recent decades.

After breaking into the newspaper business in Boonville, Veeck joined the *Courier-Journal* in Louisville, the nearest medium-sized city. That job led to sportswriter positions on Chicago newspapers, including the *Evening American*. Switching to the pen name "Bill Bailey" in 1908, Veeck enjoyed a prosperous decade covering both the Cubs and White Sox. Then came a 1918 dinner at William Wrigley, Jr.'s Pasadena, California, home that changed his life — and the eventual direction of the Cubs.

Enjoying the lively art of conversation with a group of sports scribes, Wrigley was particularly interested in Veeck's analysis of the Cubs. He asked if Veeck "could do any better" than present management. "I certainly couldn't do any worse," Veeck replied.

"Contrary to published reports, Veeck's articles were not scathing diatribes against the Chicago Cubs (or any sports team). Instead, they were thoughtfully crafted analyses, with some providing vivid, striking details and portrayals," wrote Jack Bales regarding the myths about Veeck's hiring by Wrigley, who would soon have the power to reshape the Cubs when financially strapped team president Charles Weeghman turned over most of his stock to Wrigley.[2] Now the most influential of the Cubs owners, Wrigley and the board of directors named Cubs manager Fred Mitchell team president and Veeck vice president and treasurer after the 1918 season. When Mitchell felt too burdened by his dual role as field manager/president in July 1919 and desired to just manage, Veeck took over as president.

His first distinguishing act was to take two courageous stands in 1920 against the rampant gambling in the game. First he dealt with Cubs infielder-outfielder Lee Magee, who admitted to Veeck in February 1920 that he tried to "toss" a game with the Boston Braves when he was with Cincinnati in 1918. Magee claimed that notorious game fixer Hal Chase had double-crossed him and so he stopped payment on a check to Chase. On February 20, 1920, Veeck released Magee, who sued the Cubs for his 1920 salary of $4,500, charging that his livelihood as a ballplayer had been destroyed because he was released after he admitted to game-fixing. The case went to trial in Federal Court in Cincinnati with Veeck testifying. Magee lost his suit and was banned by baseball.

The Magee incident set the stage for Veeck's most heroic act, one that arguably ended up saving baseball. Before an August 31, 1920, game against the Phillies at Cubs Park, Veeck received six unsolicited, anonymous telegrams and two phone calls within a 45-minute span warning him that the day's game would be fixed. Veeck quickly went to manager Mitchell, who immediately removed scheduled starter Claude Hendrix. Grover Cleveland Alexander, who had already won 22 games on his way to 27 wins for that season, was inserted as the starter, and was offered a $500 bonus to win the game. But the Cubs still lost, 3-0.

A September 4 letter to the *Chicago Herald and Examiner* detailed betting on the August 31 game. Veeck hired the Burns Detective Agency to investigate while asking the Chicago baseball beat writers — his former colleagues — for help in uncovering the sordid mess. Eventually, Hendrix, first baseman Fred Merkle, second baseman Buck Herzog, and pitcher Nick Carter were left off the traveling roster by Veeck for a road trip to Pittsburgh. The events prompted the impaneling of a Cook County grand jury to investigate gambling in baseball. The grand jury instead turned its attention to the 1919 World Series between the White Sox and Reds, which had long been rumored to have been fixed. The genie was out of the bottle, thanks to Veeck's bold action.

Veeck testified that he had uncovered no actual plot to fix the August 31 game or found any evidence that his players were bribed. Nevertheless, the game's cleanup needed a trigger, something that brought the sordid underworld of baseball out in the open. Veeck took de-

cisive action while other top baseball executives largely looked the other way.

The domino effect led to the appointment of Landis as baseball's first commissioner, the indictment and acquittal of the eight Black Sox, and Landis's subsequent lifetime ban of the players. Episodes of gambling, even involving Hall of Famers Ty Cobb and Tris Speaker, kept churning throughout the 1920s. But the tide had turned. No additional Black Sox-level scandals would muddy baseball's reputation.

"Veeck not only was actuated by the highest principles in the case, but he also acted with great wisdom and for the best interests of the Chicago National League club and baseball," wrote John P. Sheridan in 1920.

"When the cleanup is made, when baseball is purged of its polluters, the name of William Veeck will stand high in the history of the game with that of A.G. Spalding, who as president of the same Chicago Club made the first great fight on the gamblers who threated to destroy the game some 43 years ago, as a man who helped protect professional baseball from utter and total disintegration and destruction."[3]

Surviving these gambling scares, Veeck settled down to a productive life, steadily building back the Cubs. Off-duty, he settled into a suburban lifestyle with his wife, Grace, who was somewhat embarrassed that she was older than her husband. (Grace Veeck ordered that this secret would not be revealed even after her death; her gravestone in the Hinsdale, Illinois, cemetery where she is buried next to her husband omits her birth year.)

Young Bill Veeck did not have to go to the North Side to get his baseball fix — it came to him. Among dinner guests at the Veeck home in Hinsdale, a western suburb of Chicago, was John McGraw, the greatest manager of the time. One day McGraw took note of the talent disparity between his New York Giants and the Cubs in the elder Veeck's early days as Cubs' boss, as recalled by Bill Veeck: "We could have beaten you even with our batboy in the lineup."

Away from his baseball cares, William L. Veeck was an involved, doting father. He read to his children each night he was home. Young Bill went on to average three books read each week, gaining him a widespread knowledge of nonbaseball subjects.

Bill Veeck certainly took note of his father's supervision of the building of the modern symbols of the Cubs. With attendance on the rise, a second deck was installed at the newly-renamed Wrigley Field over the course of 1926-1928. The Ladies Days promotions made the Cubs a favorite of female fans, a status that continued. "Crowd Overflows Cubs Stands, Jams Field" … "Lock Gates After 50,000 Enter," blazed the headlines of August 7, 1929, trumpeting the fact that 25,733 ladies (and future paying customers) had come to the game.[4]

On one crowded Ladies Day, Veeck encountered a distraught woman in an aisle just inside the entrance. He offered to find a seat for her. But the woman replied that she was merely walking by Wrigley Field when the surge of females into the ballpark swept her through the gates.

Perhaps the longest-lasting and most impactful Veeck policy was broadcasting. From the beginnings in 1925, when *Chicago Daily News* station WMAQ ("We Must Ask Questions") began airing all Cubs home games, Veeck went against baseball's grain in believing broadcast exposure would develop more fans. The Cubs allowed any station desiring to broadcast games access to the ballpark without charging a rights fee. By 1929, five radio stations carried the Cubs, a number that increased to seven by 1931. Network stations in surrounding states signed up. The Cubs developed a regional following with out-of-town license plates common on cars parked around Wrigley Field.

The strategy worked like a charm before the Great Depression. In 1926 the Cubs lead the NL in attendance for the first of seven consecutive years (1926-1933).

Other owners tried to ban baseball broadcasts, but the Cubs held firm. In the late 1930s all three New York teams colluded to keep their games off the radio until Dodgers owner Larry MacPhail broke the embargo by hiring Cincinnati announcer Red Barber. Yet the Yankees per-

sisted in the radio tuneout. In 1941 none of the at-bats of Joe DiMaggio's record 56-game hitting streak was broadcast on a New York station.

Similarly, in postwar America, most baseball owners developed a Superman-to-kryptonite relationship with heavy TV coverage. Eventually, though, they yielded with the rise of cable TV, the accompanying mega-millions (now billions) in broadcast rights and consistently rising attendance. Veeck's philosophy indeed leaps out of the past to impact the game today.

Veeck also convinced a reluctant P.K. Wrigley that the All-Star Game was a good idea, reminding him the *Chicago Tribune*, the employer of All-Star Game founder Arch Ward, was a valuable publicity conduit for the Cubs. Wrigley Field missed hosting the inaugural 1933 game via the losing side of a coin flip.

One Veeck idea that did not fly was interleague play. He proposed a limited series of NL-AL games to boost flagging attendance during the pit of the Depression in 1933. The All-Star Game turned out to be an exception to team moguls' traditional abhorrence of new ideas. The idea was tabled, not to see reality until 1997.

While Veeck looked into the future, he generally presided over player contentment in the present. Infielder Woody English recalled how management paid the highest salaries in the game. English's own $15,000 payout in 1930 enabled him to buy a home for his parents. Slugger Hack Wilson landed a $33,000 contract off his 56-homer, 191-RBI season in 1930.

But the Cubs president also had his tough side. He traded Wilson after an indifferent 1931 season, tired of cleaning up after Hack's nightly alcohol benders. Meanwhile, Veeck had to take another broom to Rogers Hornsby's mess.

Hornsby was a favorite of William Wrigley, Jr. He was appointed Cubs manager with four games remaining in 1930 when Joe McCarthy could not win a World Series fast enough. Hornsby created constant tension in the clubhouse. Between his .400-hitter's persnickety, unbending attitude toward his players and a weakness for the racetrack, Hornsby presided over an underachieving team that threatened to become fractious. Hornsby had borrowed money from multiple players to cover his horse-racing debts. Landis began sniffing around the situation, his ears always perked for reports of gambling in the game.

Veeck reportedly was never a fan of Hornsby the manager. With Wrigley Jr.'s death in January 1932 from heart disease, Veeck gained even more authority and looked critically at Hornsby's stewardship. Finally pulling the trigger, Veeck fired Hornsby on August 2, 1932, in Philadelphia, agreeing to pay off the Rajah's contract as agreed until season's end. The move was a breath of fresh air for the Cubs. They took off with first baseman Charlie Grimm now doubling as manager and zoomed to the pennant and their date with Babe Ruth and his "Called Shot" in the World Series as the Cubs were swept by the McCarthy-led Yankees.

Sadly, the era of Veeck having full authority over the Cubs and keeping Phil Wrigley away from disastrous decision-making lasted only two seasons. Veeck apparently fell ill with the flu after watching the Cubs play the Giants in inclement conditions in Chicago on September 14, 1933. He continued to run the team from his sickbed in Hinsdale even as his condition worsened. At one point, he could keep down only wine or champagne, still technically illegal in the last days of Prohibition. An emotionally stricken son Bill Veeck contacted the Capone family, who delivered two cases of French champagne to his father with a note, "Compliments of Al Capone" (then jailed in federal prison after his income-tax conviction).

Deathly ill, William Veeck was admitted to St. Luke's Hospital, where he was diagnosed with leukemia. There was no treatment for the blood disease in 1933. He died on October 5.

Tributes poured in from throughout baseball. Hundreds, including the Cubs players, attended his funeral. Baseball mourned his loss and lowered the flag to half-staff during the World Series in his honor. Veeck's casket passed through two rows of ushers standing in tribute. Landis reportedly cried in discussing the loss of his old friend.

Veeck left a legacy to his son, summed up in comments to writer Harry Neily a few weeks before his death:

"I go to baseball meetings, but nobody suggests how we can get more patrons into our parks. I am not certain what can be done, but we are conducting our business on the basis of two decades ago.

"Every other line of endeavor has changed its tactics, but we go along in the same old rut.

"I do not know what can be done, but baseball cannot stand still and survive."[5]

Those are words that ring as true in the 21st century as in 1933.

In 2012 the Chicago Baseball Museum began a campaign to get William L. Veeck on the Hall of Fame ballot to join his son in Cooperstown and become the second father-son combination in the Hall of Fame behind Larry and Lee MacPhail.

NOTES

1   Bill Veeck with Ed Linn, *Veeck — As In Wreck* (New York: Putnam, 1962), 25.

2   Jack Bale, "It Was His Fairness That Caught Wrigley's Eye: William L. Veeck's Journalism Career and His Hiring by the Chicago Cubs," *Nine* (Vol. 20.2, 2013), 1-14.

3   John Sheridan, *The Sporting News*, September 30, 1920, 4.

4   *Chicago Tribune*, August 7, 1929.

5   Harry Neily, "Hard-Fisted Policies Only Masked Human Side of Veeck," *The Sporting News*, October 26, 1933, 7.

MARGARET DONAHUE
PIONEERING FEMALE CUBS EXECUTIVE LEFT HER MARK ON THE '29 CUBS AND MLB

By David Fletcher and George Castle

BASEBALL FANS AND HISTORIANS have doubtless wondered about the mystery woman in Cubs team photos of the late 1920s that often show her sandwiched between Cubs owner William Wrigley, Jr. and Cubs president William L. Veeck.

There was good reason why the woman was front-and-center in the team family. If Rogers Hornsby, Hack Wilson, Wrigley, and Veeck were the popular faces of the 1929 Cubs, then Margaret Donahue was its behind-the-scenes beating heart and was the first female front-office executive in Major League Baseball who was not also an owner.

At ease with the Murderer's Row of that great team and with lost children she consoled in her ballpark office, "Midge" Donahue was baseball's pioneering female executive. Veeck hired her as a stenographer in 1919, and promoted her to corporate secretary in 1926. By the 1950s she was a vice president in the organization and was considered the leading expert on baseball waiver transactions before she retired in 1958.

A woman as a major-domo executive of a big-league baseball team, the ultimate boys club? Consider how groundbreaking it was in 1926 for a woman to be an executive with a big-league team, let alone any corporation. Just six years previously, women had first received the right to vote nationwide.

History often overlooks the some of the greatest achievers. Donahue was just such a person for the Cubs for nearly four decades before finally retiring with high honors from both owner Phil Wrigley and her many friends in baseball. She was every bit William Veeck's right-hand man, only this time of the other gender.

The 1929 Chicago Cubs had become big business in their first pennant season of the Wrigley family ownership, and Donahue was crucial to maintaining the bottom line for Wrigley and Veeck. The big bosses did not try to hide her crucial role, as evidenced by her prominent placing in team photos.

Donahue, hired soon after Veeck became team president in 1919, had only two years' education, including secretarial school.

Yet after seven years working for Veeck, he announced a startling promotion at a New York meeting. "I haven't signed any players recently," Veeck said, "but I'll tell you what I have done that means much to our club. I have, or rather our board of directors has elected a new club secretary, a woman, the only woman secretary in organized ball. Her name is Miss Margaret Donahue. … We feel that in Miss Donahue we have added a real asset to our club organization."[1]

Her promotion shattering baseball's glass ceiling made national news. *The Sporting News* ran a story about her, and her new job was featured on the front page of the *Chicago Tribune's* sports section, where she was pictured sitting at a desk.[2]

Bill Veeck biographer Paul Dickson wrote: "As though he thought the title might be underappreciated, he pointed out that the secretary was one of five jobs at the club that required annual reelection by the board of directors. Donahue — who had been the team's bookkeeper and had handled season tickets, press passes, cash receipts, and transfers for the Cubs and all other Wrigley Field events — was the first female baseball executive who rose from the ranks."[3]

Along the way of this amazing career that has largely gone under the radar in baseball history, she came up with the idea of season tickets in 1929, later adopted by the rest of baseball and other sports. She came up with other novel promotional ideas that are now commonplace, from selling tickets off-site at Western Union locations to offering a discounted ticket price for youngsters under 12 years old.

Donahue inaugurated the practice of selling season tickets prior to the 1929 season, which was an immediate success. On February 25 Veeck announced that demand for tickets had broken all Cubs records, with thousands of "pasteboards" sold more than a month before the season began. "It's the greatest preseason rush in Cub history," he said.[4]

"She said that they would often save seats for people on game day, and sometimes they didn't come," said her niece Margaret Manning. "And they were saving some of their best seats, and people weren't coming. So she thought they would probably be forced to come if they bought the tickets in advance."[5]

Donahue had arranged for tickets to be available at any Western Union telegraph office, rather than only at the box office, and after a three-year battle she succeeded in instituting a reduced price for children under 12. "She thought it would be convenient to give people the option of buying tickets at other locations than the park," Manning said.

"(Donahue is) as astute a baseball operator as ever came down the pike," wrote Wrigley Field colleague Bill Veeck, son of William L. Veeck, in 1954. "She has forgotten more

Donahue began a 40-year career with the Cubs as a stenographer in 1919. In 1926 she became the first female executive in big league history when she was promoted to corporate secretary. She retired in 1958. (Retro Images Archive. George Brace Collection)

baseball in her 40 years with the Cubs than most of the so-called magnates will ever know."[6]

Donahue ended up being a major influence on Bill Veeck, future owner of the Chicago White Sox, St. Louis Browns, and Cleveland Indians, and the Triple-A Milwaukee Brewers. The younger Veeck worked with Donahue after his father died in 1933.

"They worked side by side in the Cubs front office (in the 1930s)," Dickson said at the Chicago Baseball Museum's September 2012 "One Family One City Two Teams Symposium" on William L. Veeck and Bill Veeck. "She fed him this idea that baseball wasn't just about the men in the ballpark, that a ballpark should also have a family atmosphere."[7]

In fact, she was such a groundbreaking baseball executive that Cubs history could have forever have been changed if she had been named the Cubs president in October 1933 after the sudden death of the elder Veeck during the '33 World Series.

"They (the Cubs) should have made (Donahue) the club president in the 1930s," a *Chicago Tribune* article in July 2013 quoted this author as saying. "If they did that, they probably would have avoided their downfall."[8]

P.K. Wrigley commented later that he had hoped to find another Bill Veeck (Senior) to be the next Cubs president to fill the huge void that occurred after Veeck's death. Wrigley failed to tap the one person who had the talent and experience to fill William Veeck's shoes until his son Bill Veeck was experienced enough to guide the Cubs future. Instead, Wrigley's poor choices in hiring lackluster general managers Jim Gallagher, Wid Matthews, and John Holland are among the main reasons for the Cubs' decline and subsequent decades of mediocrity.

P.K. Wrigley, who inherited the Cubs from his father in January 1932, got the opportunity to see how a baseball team should be run in the two seasons, including the pennant winning year of 1932, with William L. Veeck at the helm and Midge as his "right-hand man."

Wrigley failed to tap the knowledge that Donahue learned from the elder Veeck. Her comments when she retired in 1958 about the Cubs' poor strategy in player develop-ment still ring true in the 21st century. "I believe we fell behind the parade because we didn't go into the farm business soon enough," Donahue said. "Late in the '30s, when others were developing their players, we were still trying to buy them. And we also refused to pay bonuses until recently."[9]

While recognizing the Cubs' biggest Achilles heel, Donahue also realized the missed opportunities she witnessed at the franchise's peak in 1929. Passed down to her family were memories of a gloomy train ride back to Chicago from Philadelphia after the disastrous end to the 1929 World Series.

Until her dying day Midge was haunted, as modern-day fans are by the "Steve Bartman game" in the 2003 NLCS, with the recurring memory of Hack Wilson stumbling in the sun-soaked Shibe Park center field in Game Four in 1929. Wilson dropped a fly ball that would have stopped the floodgates of the Athletics' ten-run seventh inning after the Cubs had led 8-0 and were about to tie the Series two games apiece, guaranteeing a return trip to Chicago for Game Six at Wrigley Field.

But her positives will be remembered far longer than that depressing moment. Donahue finally got some latter-day recognition. In 2014 she was honored as part of Wrigley Field's centennial celebration. Cubs co-owner Laura Ricketts considered her an inspiring figure. By the time Donahue retired in 1958, she was vice president and execu-tive secretary of the Cubs. Her reputation at Wrigley Field had long been well-established and respected.

"I was trained by Mr. Veeck to do my best to make cus-tomers leave the ballpark happy, no matter what happens," Donahue, who got her job via a help-wanted ad, said in a 1955 interview.[10]

"I wanted a job somewhere in the Loop," Donahue said. "... I declined the job (but William Veeck) offered me far more than what I was making (at a laundry supply company) and persuaded me to take it. At the end of the season, I tried to quit again but he countered by making my hours 10 A.M. to 4 P.M., and I stayed."[11]

The existing record of Donahue, who never married or had children, has been faithfully kept by her nieces in their native Huntley, 50 miles northwest of Chicago. Their most prized possession was Donovan's "golden pass" signed by Major League Baseball's ruling leaders in 1958, which offered her free lifetime access to any game in any major-league stadium. She received this honor for her "long and meritorious service" with the Chicago Cubs.

After her retirement, in 1958, Philip K. Wrigley issued a proclamation on behalf of the Cubs' board of directors stating Donahue was "a nationally acknowledged authority on the intricacies of baseball rules and regulations."

Donahue was born on a farm on December 13, 1892, when Huntley, Illinois, was just a tiny agriculture-based com-munity. She was the second of eight children of Daniel and Hannah Connor Donahue. In recent years the farm became the site of Huntley's Wal-Mart. After retiring from the Cubs and living with three unmarried siblings in Chicago, Donahue returned to her family home in Huntley, where she lived until her death on January 30, 1978.

The night of her funeral she was eulogized on WGN by Jack Brickhouse, whom she had welcomed to Chicago at the start of his longtime broadcasting career. *Sports Illustrated* announced her death in its February 13, 1978, issue.

Donahue, who is buried in St. Mary Cemetery in Huntley, became more than just a point of pride for her relatives, who knew her as Aunt Midge. She was like an associate mother to three nieces in Huntley.

In July 2013 Mary Beth Manning and Barbara Ernesti sat down with sister Margaret Manning at the latter's dining-room table in Huntley. Surrounded by memora-bilia of Aunt Midge, they recalled a woman — way ahead of her time — who combined an impressive business mind with a delicate human touch for both her family and Wrigley Field fans.

"She was a very gentle person, very friendly with all of us," Margaret Manning said. "But still a very strong person, quite an organizer. She had things pretty much under control at home and at work. She could get right in at the crux of the matter."[12]

Said Mary Beth Manning: "I think she grew into the job. She was hired in 1919 and was named secretary by 1926. So she must've shown her ability in that short of a period that pushed her into that big job that had never been filled by a woman before."

"They all came about gradually, her responsibilities, and she handled them well," said Ernesti. "She was not pushy at all. People — the men — didn't feel intimidated by her. She handled details apparently very well. She had the ability to accept more and more responsibility. She was the authority on waivers and trades, and did all the paperwork."

Pointing to a vintage photo, Mary Beth Manning sketched her aunt's personality: "She's very young, but you can see the intensity at her desk, in her eyes."

From their 21st-century vantage point, the sisters could see how Aunt Midge broke barriers, certainly helped by the forward-thinking William L. Veeck.

"She had this great organizational ability to see what was wrong," said Margaret Manning.

Donahue came up with the season-ticket idea for simple economic reasons. "She was upset because they'd save tickets, people didn't show up and that was a waste," said Margaret Manning. Later, she created the forerunner of TicketMaster, TicketTron and all the electronic ticket-selling services. Donahue arranged for Cubs tickets to be sold at the downtown Western Union office.

Aunt Midge was a gracious host to the Huntley girls — whether at Wrigley Field, her home in Evanston (after previously living in Chicago's Rogers Park neighbor-hood), at other events in Chicago, or even at the World Series in Milwaukee.

"As time went on, and we grew older, we used to go into there to visit, and they'd take us downtown on Saturday," Margaret Manning said. "She got us tickets to plays, the Ice Follies because being involved with the Cubs, she'd have access to tickets. At the Ice Follies, we had front-row

seats. She was sitting right there. One of these clowns jumped right into her lap."

"Frick and Frack," said Mary Beth Manning.

"She had a horrified look on her face," said Margaret Manning. "She had on a new fur coat. The clown was all sweaty. She laughed about it and said that's what you get for getting a free ticket. They know you're right there in front."

A trip to Philip K. Wrigley's office in the Wrigley Building also was a side benefit of hanging with Aunt Midge.

"I remember she used to have an office down in the Wrigley Building," Ernesti said. "We went down on a Saturday, and (Wrigley) wasn't there. She said let's go in (to Wrigley's office) and look out over the lake. Wrigley's secretary was there."

Even more fringe benefits were available to young Donahue kinfolk.

"When I'd go and stay with them in Evanston, I'd go down (to Wrigley Field) later," Margaret Manning said. "She'd leave a ticket for me. One day there was a great big guy sitting in the box with me, and he said you're going to be on television because this is a busman's holiday for me. He was Tom Gorman, the umpire. He taught me the official way to keep score."

Donahue probably had more varied duties than any other Cubs employee. In addition to signing checks — Ernie Banks' payout bore one of her later signatures — and contracts while confirming waivers, she distributed the baseballs to the umpires before each game. The balls were stored in a cabinet in her office. Running the ballpark office staff, she also supervised first aid and gave comfort to lost children.

"It's a rare day when I get to watch a complete game even though the team is playing but a few steps from my door," Donahue said in 1955.[13] She worked in a wood-paneled office under the grandstand.

"When I stayed with her on weekends and went to games, there was someone who was hit with a broken bat," Margaret Manning said. "She spent a lot of time dealing with those incidents at the park, making sure they got to first aid. We'd hear some of those things at night from her."

Donahue kept candy, gum, and baseball stickers to soothe the nerves of children who temporarily got separated from their family at games. She also had cleaning fluid on hand for the kids after they spilled concessionaires' products on their clothes.

Donahue literally rode shotgun for the Bears' gate receipts in the decades the NFL team played at Wrigley Field. After George Halas paid the players, the officials, and other team workers, Donahue and two Chicago police officers took the remaining cash in a cab to store overnight in a safe in the Palmer House until the bank opened Monday morning.

Standing out among the nieces' memorabilia was a letter dated May 13, 1980, two years after her death, by Bill Veeck. The then-White Sox owner gave thanks to Donahue's sister, Mabel Hemmer. The Cubs front office of Bill Veeck's youth was obviously a fond time.

"My sincere appreciation for sending along the photograph of my daddy, which you found among Margaret's effects," Veeck wrote to Hemmer. "It truly was a delight to receive the picture, which I might add arrived in excellent condition. It will be kept among my treasured possessions. Many thanks for your thoughtfulness in remembering me."

The piles of letters and newspaper clippings, along with photos and other tidbits, were kept in boxes originally by Donahue's parents and sister. Eventually they found their way to Hemmer and in turn to her three daughters.

But what Donahue left behind paled in comparison to the oral history her nieces could recall.

Margaret and Mary Beth Manning and Barbara Ernesti got to spend time with Donahue in her senior years when she and her three siblings — two sisters and a brother — returned to be close with family in Huntley.

The farm-oriented town, about 12 miles northwest of Elgin, once had Al Capone's associates bring his car to a local repair shop to throw off potential saboteurs or as-

sassins. Huntley was still rural when Donahue returned. Used to long workdays at Wrigley Field, she did not exactly become inactive.

Mary Beth Manning recalled how Aunt Midge volunteered for various activities. An appreciative family, remembering how good a hostess she was back in Chicago, would cook for her.

As her health declined, some who worked with her tried to re-establish contact. One was ex-GM Jim Gallagher.

Donahue experienced stress working with Gallagher, according to her nieces. But her former boss was profound in a January 13, 1978, letter — also part of the Huntley memorabilia collection — to her family, two weeks before she died at 85. Gallagher wrote that he had "neglected to express my affection until it was too late" and added "how much she meant to me. … Please tell Margaret that I love her."

The letters flowed out from the family, too. Midge's nieces debriefed the Cubs' Ricketts ownership family in an April 22, 2013, letter, a copy of which was provided by the three sisters:

"We appreciate your efforts, as the present owners, to initiate plans both to preserve Wrigley Field as an iconic destination and the Cubs' 'home base,' and to guide the team into the future — one that we all hope has a World Series appearance in it! In fact, we were relieved to learn only last weekend that you've secured an agreement with Mayor Emanuel and the City of Chicago.

"We ask now that you consider Margaret Donahue's career with the Cubs, and we hope you will agree that she merits a commemorative tribute at the park where she worked for almost four decades — perhaps a 'Midge Day' as part of a special 'Women in Baseball' type of event.

"It is securely a part of club history that the Cubs were ahead of the times in promoting a woman to such a high-profile position. Notably, however, a book appeared last year that underscores the importance of her career all over again: Paul Dickson's *Bill Veeck: Baseball's Greatest Maverick*. He writes engagingly, to be sure, about Bill Veeck, Jr.'s, storied tenure in professional baseball.

However, Mr. Dickson also covers the early history of the Chicago Cubs organization involving Bill's father, William, Sr., and — most exciting to our family he even provided us with new information about Aunt Midge!

"Our aunt's accomplishments as part of the Chicago Cubs organization have been a source of pride to us and our extended families for all of these years. Her role with the team is the largest contributing factor to the fact that we all bleed 'Cubby blue' to this day.

"As you embark on a new era at Wrigley Field, we would welcome the opportunity to discuss potential ways to commemorate and honor Margaret Donahue's meritorious service to the Cubs organization. It has been our dream all these years to see the development of a meaningful recognition of Aunt Midge's career. We can assure that we would love nothing better — except seeing the Cubs in a World Series, of course!"

NOTES

1   Paul Dickson, *Bill Veeck: Baseball's Greatest Maverick* (New York: Walker and Company, 2012).

2   "She's a Baseball Boss," *Chicago Tribune*, December 14, 1926.

3   Paul Dickson, *Bill Veeck: Baseball's Greatest Maverick*.

4   Paul Dickson, *Bill Veeck: Baseball's Greatest Maverick*.

5   Author interview with Margaret Donahue's nieces, Huntley, Illinois, in the summer of 2013. All interviewees' quotes appeared in a two-part story at ChicagoBaseballMuseum.org.

6   John Owens, "1929 female Cubs executive left her mark on the big leagues," *Chicago Tribune* July 22, 2013.

7   Excerpt of speech by Paul Dickson at September 2012 event honoring Veeck family at Chicago History Museum.

8   John Owens, "1929 Female Cubs executive."

9   Edgar Munzel, *Chicago Sun-Times*, 1958.

10 International News Service, *St. Petersburg Times*, 1955.

11 Edgar Munzel, *Chicago Sun-Times*, 1958.

12 Author interview with Margaret Donahue's nieces.

13 International News Service, *St. Petersburg Times*, June 5, 1955. 8

THE FRIENDLY CONFINES OF WRIGLEY FIELD

BY SCOTT FERKOVICH

IT WAS BUILT ON THE SITE OF A FORMER theological seminary (of all places). It is one of the most renowned addresses in baseball history, nestled in a vibrant urban neighborhood that takes on the atmosphere of a block party on game days. It has seen the Babe's called shot, Gabby's Homer in the Gloamin', and the curse of the billygoat. It was the stamping grounds of High Pockets and Kiki, of Jolly Cholly and Hack, of the Mad Russian and Mad Dog, of Mr. Cub, Ryno, and the Hawk. It is as well-known for its famous foliage and its Bleacher Bums as it is for some of the heartbreak and incompetency that it has seen on the field. For decades, it stubbornly refused to evolve, becoming a symbol of "baseball as it was meant to be played." To many, it is a kind of pastoral palace, a living fossil where folks can cling to their own rose-colored versions of the past. It has been a lovable dinosaur where progress died faster than the fleeting hopes of April and May. It is the unexpected answer to one of the more intriguing trivia questions you are likely to hear: What sporting venue has hosted the most NFL games ever? It has been immortalized in songs, in movies, in television commercials, and in its own cottage industry of coffee-table books and tributary tomes. It remains a must-see tourist attraction in a city full of them. It is the Friendly Confines of Wrigley Field.

Rewind way, way back, to a time when the Woodrow Wilson family resided at 1600 Pennsylvania Avenue, when Charlie Chaplin starred in his first film, and when the Ford Motor Company announced an eight-hour workday and a minimum wage of $5 a day. Back to 1914. The ballpark that sprouted up at 1060 West Addison Street in Chicago's Lake View neighborhood was initially the home of the Chicago entry in the Federal League. The team was known as the Federals (Chi-Feds for short) and was owned by Charles Weeghman, who named the park after himself. The Federal League, then in its first year of existence, was an upstart circuit in direct competition with the established National and American Leagues. The Chi-Feds were able to lure such established stars as the Cincinnati Reds' shortstop Joe Tinker (of Tinker-to-Evers-to-Chance fame), and pitcher Mordecai "Three Finger" Brown of the Chicago Cubs. The Chi-Feds finished second in 1914, then changed their name to the Whales for 1915, a season in which they finished tied with the St. Louis Terriers for first place. The Federal League was gone by 1916. Weeghman, however, bought the National League's crosstown Chicago Cubs, who played at old West Side Park, and immediately moved them into Weeghman Park. The Cubs played their first game in their new home on April 20, 1916. The home team beat the Cincinnati Reds in 11 innings.

At this time, the park at Clark and Addison was a single-decked structure of steel and concrete. Weeghman had hired Zachary Taylor Davis (the architect of Comiskey Park, on the South Side of Chicago) to design the ballpark. The grandstand on the Clark Street (third base) side extended halfway to left field. The grandstand on the Addison Street (first base) side extended all the way to the right-field corner. One of the old seminary buildings loomed beyond the left-field fence, until it was demolished after the 1914 season, to be replaced by a bleacher section. The houses on Waveland Avenue (beyond the left-field wall) and Sheffield Avenue (beyond the right-field wall) have for the most part remained strikingly unchanged. In 1915 the scoreboard, which had originally been in left field, next to the seminary building, was moved to center. During these early years, only a brick wall extended from the right-field corner to center field. In 1916, while the Cubs cavorted on the field inside the park, a genuine cub bear frolicked in a cage stationed directly outside the park on Addison Street.

Weeghman earned the favor of the fans during this period, as he made it a policy to allow spectators to keep any ball hit into the stands. This was an especially novel idea for a time when fans were required to return any balls hit their way.

One of the more remarkable games in baseball history took place at the park on May 2, 1917. Hippo Vaughn of the Cubs and Fred Toney of the Cincinnati Reds both threw no-hit ball for nine innings. Vaughn retired the first Red in the top of the tenth, then gave up two consecutive hits, resulting in a run. Toney set the Cubs down in order in their half of the inning, getting the win and the no-hitter. At the time the game was considered a "double no-hitter," but under current rules only Toney is credited with a no-no. It remains the only game in which neither team got a hit in regulation.

A new era was ushered in at the corner of Addison and Clark in 1918. That was when Weeghman sold his interest in the Cubs to minority shareholder William Wrigley, Jr., the magnate who had made his money in the production of chewing gum. By 1921, Wrigley had bought out the other shareholders and taken complete control of the club. The ballpark, which had been known at various times (in addition to Weeghman Park) as the North Side Ball Park, the Federal League Ball Park, and Whales Park, was by now going by the name of Cubs Park.

Baseball wasn't the only game in town on the North Side. In 1921, George Halas's Chicago Staleys, a team in the fledgling American Professional Football Association (which became the National Football League in 1922), played their first game at 1060 West Addison. By the next

season, they would change their nickname to the Bears. The blue and orange, "the pride and joy of Illinois," would be a gridiron fixture in Lake View for the next half-century. The first NFL Championship game ever was held on December 17, 1933, at Wrigley Field. The Bears defeated the New York Giants, 23-21. That team, coached by Halas, featured NFL greats halfback Red Grange and fullback Bronko Nagurski.

To William Wrigley's credit, he was never hesitant to spend money on expansion and upkeep of his ballpark. The grandstand was double-decked in time for the 1928 season, and new bleachers were added from the right-field corner to center field, increasing the capacity from 18,000 to 32,000. However, a perennial problem during Wrigley's early tenure as owner was the disorganized appearance and surly attitude of ushers at the ballpark. Incredibly (to modern practice), ushers were simply recruited the day of the game from random men (or kids) off the street. They often were derelict in their duties, keeping the best seats for themselves and their friends, and taking bribes from folks looking for better seats. Then one afternoon, Andy Frain approached Wrigley's box seat and told him that he could do a better job of organizing men to work the aisles. Frain had had some success doing the same

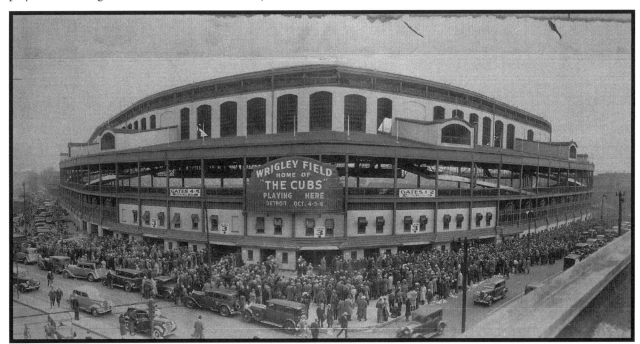

Wrigley Field at the corner of Clark St. and Addison St. The iconic marquee was installed in 1934. (National Baseball Hall of Fame)

thing at Chicago Stadium, for Blackhawks hockey games. Wrigley agreed to Frain's proposal, and he was immediately put in charge of hiring and organizing the Wrigley Field ushers. Through Wrigley's capital investment, Frain outfitted his employees with their traditional blue and gold uniforms, and instructed them in how to act politely and professionally. Andy Frain later expanded his business to ballparks and stadiums around the country. The company that bears his name still flourishes.

The Cubs had gone to the World Series in 1918 (losing to the Red Sox in six games), but the team finished in the second division for half of their seasons during the 1920s. Despite lackluster play on the field, the Cubs were developing a growing legion of fans, thanks to William Wrigley's marketing savvy. The Cubs became one of the first teams in baseball history to fully take advantage of the new phenomenon called radio. Most team owners feared that game broadcasts would reduce attendance, as fans would stay at home and listen for free. But Wrigley had the foresight to see that games on radio were the ideal marketing tool. Also, since all games were played in the daytime, many of the fans listening to Cubs broadcasts were housewives. Wrigley took advantage of this emerging demographic through the promotion of Ladies Day games, which frequently drew packed houses to the ballpark and became a staple for years. By the summer of 1927, Cubs Park had been renamed Wrigley Field. That year, the Cubs drew over one million paying customers, becoming the first National League team to top the million mark. They continued to do so through 1931. The crowds that came out to Wrigley Field during these years got a firsthand look at some of the best Cubs teams ever assembled.

The team that Wrigley and team president William Veeck put together was a colorful, talented group of players who were a perfect fit for the Roaring Twenties. In 1929 manager Joe McCarthy's club won 98 games to take the National League pennant. The team's outfield that year was exceptional, with Kiki Cuyler, Riggs Stephenson, and Lewis "Hack" Wilson hitting a combined .355 and each driving in over 100 runs. Thirty-three-year-old Rogers Hornsby, in his last great year as a player, hit 39 home runs with 149 RBIs, while hitting .380. First

baseman Charlie Grimm knocked in 91 runs to complement a .298 average. The pitching staff featured 19-game-winner Charlie Root, 18-game-winner Guy Bush, and Pat Malone, who topped the National League with 22 wins.

The 1929 World Series was the first one played at Wrigley Field. (Their home games for the 1918 Series had been moved to Comiskey Park, which had a higher seating capacity.) Their 1929 opponents were Connie Mack's Philadelphia Athletics, a team featuring future Hall of Famers Mickey Cochrane, Jimmie Foxx, Al Simmons, and Lefty Grove. The Mack Men trounced the Cubs, winning in five games.

The team finished a close second in 1930. In a year when offense exploded around professional baseball, Hack Wilson put on one of the most stunning displays of hitting ever seen. He slugged 56 homers, setting what was the National League record at the time, while batting .356. He batted in 191 runs, a record that stands as of 2014. But his career sank like a stone after that. In 1931 he managed only 13 homers, 61 RBIs, and a .261 average. Before the next season, Wilson was sent packing, initially to the St. Louis Cardinals and then to the Brooklyn Dodgers. He was out of baseball by 1934.

During an exhibition game at Wrigley Field in 1931, Cubs catcher (and future Hall of Famer) Gabby Hartnett got his picture taken in a rather compromising position. The famous photo shows a smiling Hartnett casually leaning over a low wall in front of the first-row box seats. Occupying the seats are none other than gangster Al Capone and his young son Sonny, for whom Hartnett appears to be autographing a baseball. Capone is looking gleefully back at Hartnett. The photo, which was printed in newspapers throughout the country, eventually reached the desk of baseball Commissioner Kenesaw Mountain Landis. Landis immediately wired Hartnett, telling him, in so many words, to refrain from such fraternization in the future. As the story goes, Hartnett wired him back, "OK, but if you don't want me to have my picture taken with Al Capone, you tell him."[1]

With the passing of William Wrigley, Jr. in January of 1932, his son, Philip K. Wrigley, took over the ownership reins of the team. "P.K.," as he was affectionately called, would always consider the Cubs, and Wrigley Field especially, among his most cherished possessions. One of the reasons Wrigley Field has lasted so long is that both Wrigleys, father and son (as well as Charles Weeghman before them), always took such good care of the park. Whatever Philip Wrigley's shortcomings as a baseball owner, it cannot be denied that he was a clever marketer. He clearly understood that by beautifying Wrigley Field, and keeping it clean and well-manicured, he could draw paying crowds to an afternoon of baseball in the sunshine, even if the team on the field was only ordinary. Every year, the ballpark got a fresh coat of paint. During the season, the place was kept in immaculate condition.

The Cubs made it back to the fall classic in 1932, taking on the New York Yankees. This was the Series that featured the most debated and dissected event in Wrigley Field history. It was Babe Ruth's "Called Shot." The seemingly endless dispute about whether Ruth did or did not point to the center-field bleachers before slamming his second home run off Charlie Root in Game Three is one of those questions that keep baseball historians up at night. According to the story, the Cubs bench jockeys had been riding The Babe during the first two games of the Series. When he stepped up to the plate, he supposedly made a gesture in the general direction of center field. Some witnesses claim he was merely pointing toward the Cubs dugout. Whatever the case, Ruth hit a shot that carried to the right of the center-field scoreboard, sailing past the temporary bleachers that had been built just beyond the park's outer wall. Estimates had the ball traveling 490 feet. It was Ruth's last World Series home run. New York, led by former Cubs manager Joe McCarthy, swept the Cubs in four games.

Today, the prevailing sentiment among most Wrigley Field patrons is that baseball (and the Cubs in particular) goes better with a cold beer or two. Or three. It wasn't until the 1933 season, however, that beer was first sold at Wrigley Field. Even then, it was only on tap, and it was only 3.2 percent alcohol. When Prohibition was finally repealed in December of that year, a bevy of bars and restaurants opened up around the ballpark.

The main entrance at the corner of Addison and Clark is noted for its neon Art Deco marquee with the words "Wrigley Field Home of Chicago Cubs." It was designed by the Federated Sign Company. For decades, it was blue with white lettering, but in 1965 it was repainted the red and white color scheme that still existed in 2014.

In 1937 a significant remodeling of Wrigley's outfield bleachers took place. A new brick wall now ringed the entire outfield. The bleachers were expanded, and, most importantly, raised. They had been at field level, but would now be elevated to their present height of just above the brick fence. While Wrigley claimed this was done in order to give fans in that section a better view, in truth the change was as much a product of necessity as anything else: the grounds crew needed the space created beneath the new bleachers to store their mowers, rollers, and chalkers. Hence the metal doors in the brick wall (which for years were maroon-colored, unlike the green of later years).

As part of the refurbishment, the hand-operated scoreboard was built above the center-field bleachers. Fluttering atop the scoreboard are colorful flags, one for each National League team, showing the order of that day's standings from top to bottom. Another enduring scoreboard tradition at Wrigley was the raising of a white flag sporting a blue "W" for a Cubs win or a blue flag with a white "L" for a loss. The flags were made easily visible to neighborhood residents strolling along Sheffield or Waveland Avenue, or commuters passing by on the nearby elevated train. A crossbar was attached to the top of the scoreboard, with a green light on one end, for a victory, and a red light on the other end, for a loss. This was for the benefit of train riders passing by late at night. The rear of the scoreboard, as seen from outside above the bleacher entrance, also became iconic, with the words "Chicago Cubs" in white block lettering on the image of a waving blue flag. At night, the letters light up in bright neon red.

Not only do the scoreboard team flags indicate the order of the NL standings, they also reveal which way the wind is blowing. This is of vital importance at Wrigley Field, which can be either a hitter's haven or a pitcher's paradise on any given day, depending on whether the Lake Michigan breezes are blowing out or in.

By the end of 1937, the world's best-known example of parthenocissus tricuspidata, or Boston Ivy, had been planted around the entire base of the brick wall. Bill Veeck (son of William Veeck, who died in 1933), claimed in his autobiography that he, along with a couple of grounds-keepers, planted the mix of bittersweet and Boston Ivy one night by the light of incandescent bulbs strung along the outfield wall for that very purpose. The veracity of Veeck's version of events is open to question. Whoever planted it and when, the Boston Ivy soon overtook the bittersweet, and the rest is horticultural history. Outfielders patrolling Wrigley Field are duly instructed to throw both arms up as a signal to the umpires when a struck baseball is hidden within the ivy, rather than search for the sphere; thus keeping the play alive.

Everybody loves a good walk-off home run, and Gabby Hartnett's Homer in the Gloamin' at Wrigley Field remains one of the most legendary. To set the scene: The Cubs and Pirates went into their game of September 28, 1938, with Chicago trailing Pittsburgh by a half-game in the standings. The contest entered the ninth inning tied at five runs apiece. As the late-afternoon gloom descended at the corner of Addison and Clark, the umpires made the announcement that if the game remained tied after regulation, it would be called on account of darkness. According to the rule in place at the time, the game would have to be replayed in its entirety the next day, necessitating a doubleheader. The Cubs came to bat in the bottom of the ninth. On the hill for the Pirates was hard-throwing reliever Mace Brown. After Brown got the first two batters out, Gabby Hartnett stepped up to the dish. He quickly found himself in an 0-and-2 hole. Then, in a classic example of fact trumping fiction, Hartnett stroked a home run that landed in the left-center-field bleachers. The darkening ballpark exploded in bedlam, with players

No ivy yet. Wrigley Field with a standing-room-only crowd on the edge of the outfield. Bill Veeck, Jr., the son of the former Cubs GM, planted ivy on the walls in 1937. (Retro Images Archive. George Brace Collection)

and fans running onto the field. The Cubs won the game, 6-5, and took over first place by a half-game. They beat the Pirates the next day as well, to sweep the three-game series. They eventually took the National League pennant by two lengths over Pittsburgh.

Baseball history is full of what-ifs. What if Ted Williams had played in Yankee Stadium with its short right-field porch? What if Joe DiMaggio had played in Fenway Park with its Green Monster? What if the Mets had drafted Reggie Jackson instead of Steve Chilcott? Then there is the question, "What would have happened if the Japanese hadn't bombed Pearl Harbor?" The answer to that one is easy. Wrigley Field would have had lights installed for the 1942 season. Philip Wrigley was never a fan of baseball under the stars, but in order to boost attendance he reluctantly decided to give it a try. The club had even obtained light towers, which were sitting under the stands at Wrigley Field, waiting to be erected. With the tragic events of December 7, 1941, however, America was thrust into World War II. Wrigley chose to donate the lights and the metal towers to the war effort. Soon after, Wrigley proclaimed that as long as he was alive, night baseball would never happen at the park that bore his name. He turned out to be a prophet.

Wrigley Field's other tenant, the Chicago Bears, had one of their most successful decades in the 1940s. Known as the Monsters of the Midway and led by quarterback Sid Luckman, they appeared in five NFL Championship games from 1940 to 1946, winning four of them.

One of the more legendary subtexts in Wrigley Field history is the Curse of the Billygoat. In 1945 the Cubs faced off against the Detroit Tigers in the World Series. A Chicago tavern owner, Billy Sianis, tried to enter the park with his pet goat. After all, he had a ticket for the goat, so why not? Sianis and the billygoat were let in, and made their way down to their box seats. As the story goes, some of their immediate neighbors were put off by the odor emanating from the goat. The goat and his escort were swiftly shown the exit doors. Later, Sianis supposedly put a curse on the Cubs for insulting his goat. They lost that Series to the Tigers in seven games. Of course, curses don't mean a thing. And of course, the Cubs haven't made

it back to the fall classic since. (Sianis's nephew, Sam Sianis, ventured down down to Wrigley Field in 1973, again with a goat, and was again asked to make tracks. Sam was invited onto the field in 1994, along with a goat, in order to remove the curse.)

Looking back on the years 1929 to 1945, one can easily make the argument that they were a kind of Golden Age for the Cubs at Wrigley Field. During that 17-year period, the team went to the World Series five times (1929, '32, '35, '38, and '45), although they didn't win any of them. From 1926 to 1938 they led the National League in attendance eight times, while five times they drew the second-most at the gate. The 1938 season was the last in which the Cubs led the league in attendance. After their final World Series appearance, in 1945, the club finished third in 1946 with a record of 82-71, 14½ games off the pace. They would not have a season over .500 for the next 16 years.

If 1929 to 1945 was indeed a Golden Age, then the decades of the 1950s and 1960s were a nadir at Wrigley Field. Attendance was annually near the bottom of the league, and an aging Philip Wrigley was no longer as vigilant about keeping his ballpark in pristine condition. The surrounding neighborhood, while not exactly deteriorating, was getting a bit rough around the edges. Most importantly, the Cubs were becoming irrelevant in Chicago, as team owner Bill Veeck and his White Sox were growing in popularity, buoyed by their 1959 "Go-Go Sox" team that went to the World Series. From 1951 to 1965, Comiskey Park drew over one million fans every year but one, while the Cubs topped the million mark only once (1952). In 1962 the Cubs lost 103 games to finish ninth behind the expansion Houston Colt .45s, and were led by Philip Wrigley's "College of Coaches," an eight-man committee in lieu of a full-time manager.

Perhaps the low point of the organization was the 1966 season, when the team again lost 103 and finished tenth, which allowed the New York Mets to escape last place for the first time as a franchise. Only 635,891 fans passed through the turnstiles that year. (On September 21 a small get-together of only 530 fans bothered to show up.) But in the midst of these quiet days at Wrigley, a small group of young fans, who regularly sat in the sparsely populated bleachers, decided to form a loose club. They were extremely vocal in their encouragement of their favorite Cubs (and equally strident in their discouragement of the opposition). They showed up to games wearing yellow hard hats, ready to yell, sing, and drink beer (they were even known to drink with the players at local watering holes after the games.). As their numbers grew, so did their legend, and the Bleacher Bums were born. By the early 1970s, many of the original members had drifted away, to be replaced by new blood. The nickname endured, however, and over time the Wrigley Field bleachers took on more and more of a party atmosphere, which carries on.

After nearly two decades of mediocre baseball, 1969 saw the first pennant race on the North Side since 1945. Suddenly the fans began to pack Wrigley Field, to the tune of 1,674,993, at the time a club attendance record. What they witnessed was a talented team managed by Leo Durocher, with four future Hall of Famers (Billy Williams, Ron Santo, Ferguson Jenkins, and Ernie Banks). Banks was the feel-good story of the year. Having forged a brilliant career at the Friendly Confines since joining the Cubs in 1953, and seemingly doomed to endure one dismal season after another, it looked as though Mr. Cub, at age 38, would have his best chance to reach the postseason.

The 1969 Cubs never spent a day in second place the first five months of the season. On August 16 they had a nine-game lead over the surprising second-place New York Mets. From that point, it was a disaster of epic proportions. The Mets seemingly refused to lose, carving out two big winning streaks of nine and ten games while the Cubs won just eight of 25 games in September. When the dust settled, a season that had begun with so much promise for Chicago ended up in bitter defeat. And it wasn't even close. The Mets took the NL East division by eight games over the Cubs.

For Banks, it proved to be his last productive season. His final moment of glory at Wrigley came on May 12, 1970, when he hit his 500th career home run. He retired as a player in 1971. His infectious love for the game, and for Wrigley Field, made him a favorite of Cub fans, and his familiar "Let's play two!" has become one of the game's enduring catch-phrases.

After an infamous 1970 Opening Day in which several rowdy bleacher fans leaped over the ivy-covered brick wall, the Cubs decided to make a change. They installed a wire screen along the top of the wall, which angled 42 inches out over the playing surface. To modern bleacher patrons, it is a well-known feature, also serving to help prevent littering onto the field.

Ever since the late 1950s, professional football was becoming increasingly popular. But it was also becoming increasingly clear that Wrigley Field was inadequate as a football facility. The beginning of the end came with the merger of the National Football League and American Football

A view of Wrigley Field from the outfield in 1929. (Library of Congress)

League in 1966. In order to accommodate more paying customers, the new NFL dictated that all stadiums were to have a minimum capacity of 50,000. Cozy Wrigley Field obviously did not. The Bears played their final game at Addison and Clark on December 13, 1970, a victory over their archrival Green Bay Packers.

To generations of Wrigley Field patrons, the voice of public address announcer Pat Pieper was a familiar part of the game-day experience. Pieper, a former popcorn and peanut vendor at old West Side Park, served as the announcer at Clark and Addison from 1916 until his death in 1974. His signature call at the beginning of every contest was "Attention! ... Attention please! ... Have your pencil ... and scorecards ready ... and I'll give you ... the correct lineup ... for today's ballgame!"

The decades of the 1960s and 1970s saw baseball undergo seismic shifts, and the ballpark landscape was not immune to this change. Teams were abandoning their classic old ballparks and moving into modern stadiums. The vast majority were multipurpose facilities surrounded by parking lots rather than neighborhoods. Many of them featured that bane of '70s baseball, artificial turf. They were better suited to football than baseball, and were totally lacking in charm or distinctiveness. They were derisively called "cookie cutters," or "concrete doughnuts" because of their circular sameness. Richie Hebner once said of them, "I stand at the plate in the Vet (Veterans Stadium in Philadelphia) and I don't honestly know

whether I'm in Pittsburgh, Cincinnati, St. Louis, or Philly. They all look alike."[2]

In the midst of this progress, Wrigley Field remained as familiar as always. (Incredibly, however, Philip Wrigley had seriously considered installing artificial turf at the park in the late '60s.) On the field, the Cubs endured some lean years in the '70s. Nevertheless, the fans continued to come out to the old ballpark, as the club annually topped the million mark in attendance. That the Cubs were able to draw this well despite the mediocre team on the field, is amazing when one considers the team's philosophy regarding ticket sales. According to Stuart Shea in his book, *Wrigley Field: The Unauthorized Biography*, "The Cubs had a long-standing practice of selling all 3,250 bleacher seats, as well as all lower- and upper-deck grandstand tickets, only on the day of the game."[3] Shea added, "P.K. Wrigley believed that fans should have the walk-up option, and all grandstand and bleacher seats were day-of-game sales only while he continued to own the club."[4] Philip Wrigley died in 1977, and four years later the Wrigley family sold the team to the Chicago Tribune Co. By the late '80s, no more "day-of-game" tickets were sold at Wrigley.

WGN was the local Chicago television station (Channel 9) which aired every Cubs game. In 1978 it began broadcasting nationally via the emerging medium of cable TV. Not many American TV sets were cable-ready at this time, but within a few years the number of subscribers had grown astronomically. WGN, along with Atlanta's

WTBS, which (at the time) broadcast all Atlanta Braves games, became what were known as "superstations." Fans from all over the country could tune in to WGN in the summertime and catch a Cubs game. The Cubs, and Wrigley Field, were getting more national television exposure than they ever had before.

Harry Christopher Carabina, born in 1914, and better known as Harry Caray, was the longtime radio and TV broadcaster, at various times, for the St. Louis Cardinals, St. Louis Browns, Oakland Athletics, and crosstown White Sox. He joined WGN in 1981, eventually pairing with former Cub and White Sox pitcher Steve Stone in 1983. The dry-witted, tell-it-like-it-is Stone was the perfect foil for Caray in the broadcast booth. As an announcer, Caray was an unrepentant homer. From his over-the-top glee at every Chicago victory ("Cubs win!! Cubs win!! Cubs win!!), to his frustration at their frequent failures ("Heee popppped it upp!"), he made it sound as if you were listening to your lovable old uncle broadcast the game. Still, Caray was an astute observer of the game who knew when the Cubs deserved criticism. He was notorious for butchering player names; Bret Barberie, Heathcliff Slocumb, and Mark Grudzielanek were always an adventure. But Caray was most famous for his ritual of belting out "Take Me Out to the Ballgame" on the Wrigley Field public address system during the seventh-inning stretch, and getting the crowd to sing along with him. It was a tradition he had actually started back in his Comiskey Park days after a suggestion from Bill Veeck during his second tenure as the White Sox owner. (After Caray's death in 1998, the team began a new Wrigley Field tradition of having a different celebrity sing the song at every game.)

In 1984 the Cubs, led by MVP second baseman Ryne Sandberg, came out of nowhere and won the NL East Division with a record of 96-65. That season also marked the first year of the Cubs drawing over two million fans to Wrigley Field. In the best-of-five National League Championship Series, against the San Diego Padres, Chicago won the first two games at Wrigley Field. The television networks salivated at the prospect of a Cubs-Tigers World Series, but it wasn't to be. The Cubs lost the next three in San Diego, and it was the Padres who

would advance to the World Series against Detroit (and lose). A glorious season for Chicago had ended in heartbreak.

To many baseball purists during these years, Wrigley Field had become the perfect antidote to the modern cookie-cutter stadium. In a baseball world that had grown weary of artificial turf, sterile domes, and concrete dough-nuts surrounded by parking lots, Wrigley (along with Boston's Fenway Park) came to symbolize baseball played on grass, in an intimate setting, where you were closer to the players. A game at Wrigley had a neighborhood feel, where people on rooftops across the street could set up a few lawn chairs and a grill, and make an afternoon of it. And the most wonderful thing of all, for Cubs fans, was that Wrigley Field remained the last major-league ballpark without lights. Games were played in glorious sunshine. You could take the afternoon off from work, hop on the El train, buy a cheap bleacher ticket, take your shirt off, and enjoy the festive atmosphere. As Bill Veeck once said, "An afternoon in the bleachers is the greatest buy in the country. Drinking a few beers and telling a few lies, you can't beat the entertainment."[5]

After the 1984 season, mounting pressure had been put on the Cubs, from both the National League and the major television networks, to install light towers. A heated debate grew among Wrigleyville residents. Many felt that the introduction of night games would result in an increase in noise and rowdiness, while others, particularly bar and restaurant owners, welcomed the change, feeling it would bring in more business. A compromise was reached. Lights would be installed, but there would be a limit of 18 night games per season, an average of less than one per week. The first night game was scheduled for August 8, 1988, versus the Philadelphia Phillies. However, by the fourth inning, rain began to fall hard, and after a two-hour delay, the contest was finally called. The first official night game, therefore, was August 9. The Cubs beat the Mets, 6-4, in front of 36,399 fans. Wrigley Field had been the last major-league ballpark without lights, a distinction it held for 40 years, ever since Briggs Stadium (later renamed Tiger Stadium) installed lights in 1948.

Another economically necessary upgrade, but one that received less sentimental fanfare, was the construction in 1989 of 67 luxury suites directly below the upper-deck stands, from foul line to foul line. A new press box was also built.

In 1990 Wrigley Field hosted its first All-Star Game in nearly 30 years, a 2-0 American League victory. It was only the third All-Star Game ever played in the Friendly Confines. The first was in in 1947, when the American League bested the National League, 2-1. In 1962 the AL trounced the NL, 9-4, during the second All-Star contest played that season.

As the final decade of the 20th century approached, the cookie-cutter stadiums, which had been universally panned almost from the beginning, were now increasingly obsolete. Fans in Pittsburgh, Cincinnati, St. Louis, Philadelphia, and other baseball towns waxed nostalgic about their long-lost fields of dreams. After the 1990 season, Comiskey Park on Chicago's South Side would succumb to the wrecking ball. Of the classic ballparks, only three remained: Wrigley, along with Fenway Park in Boston and Tiger Stadium in Detroit. (Four, if one were to include a rebuilt Yankee Stadium in the list.) But a new era of ballpark design was about to emerge. In 1992 Oriole Park at Camden Yards in downtown Baltimore opened its doors. Groundbreaking in design, it harkened back architecturally and esthetically to the grand old ballparks, while giving fans all the modern amenities. The Retro Park movement had begun in earnest. Planners and designers of these new ballparks would look to the Friendly Confines and the other classic yards for inspiration.

The Cubs, meanwhile, continued to come up short in their quest for a world championship. In their last six playoff appearances (1984, 1989, 1998, 2003, 2007, and 2008), they have been swept three times. With the exception of the 2003 NLDS against the Atlanta Braves, as of 2014 the Cubs have not won any other postseason series, let alone a championship, since 1908.

And so Wrigley Field endures. In the 2004 season, the Cubs drew over three million fans to Wrigley Field for the first time. Its place in the American sporting con-

sciousness is secure, yet the ballpark is on the cusp of major changes. Current Cubs owner Tom Ricketts understandably wanted to tap new revenue sources from the aging park, and one of those ways was with more and more advertising signage. Newer luxury suites were also proposed. There were plans for renovated concourses, able to accommodate fancier concession stands and souvenir shops. Also proposed was a controversial high-definition Jumbotron above the left-center-field bleachers. Purists may howl, but the metamorphosis of Wrigley Field was well under way. Once a haven for daytime baseball, the 2014 Cubs schedule included more than 40 home night games. Ricketts insisted that in order for the Cubs to win a World Series, Wrigley Field would have to be transformed into a thoroughly modern venue. Regardless of what the future held for this classic park as it celebrated its 100th birthday in 2014, it would still remain the Friendly Confines to legions of baseball fans.

SOURCES

Benson, Michael, *Ballparks of North America: A Comprehensive Historical Reference to Baseball Grounds, Yards and Stadiums, 1845 to Present* (Jefferson, North Carolina: McFarland & Company, 2009).

Dickson, Paul, *Bill Veeck: Baseball's Greatest Maverick* (London: Bloomsbury Publishing, 2012).

Ehrgott, Roberts, *Mr. Wrigley's Ball Club: Chicago and the Cubs During the Jazz Age* (Jefferson, North Carolina: McFarland & Company, 2013).

Gillette, Gary, and Eric Enders, *Big League Ballparks: The Complete Illustrated History* (New York: Metro Books, 2009).

Jacob, Mark, and Stephen Green, *Wrigley Field: A Celebration of the Friendly Confines* (New York: McGraw Hill, 2003).

McNeil, William, *Gabby Hartnett: The Life and Times of the Cubs' Greatest Catcher* (Jefferson, North Carolina: McFarland & Company, 2004).

Shea, Stuart, *Wrigley Field: The Unauthorized Biography* (Dulles, Virginia: Potomac Books, 2004).

Smith, Ron, *The Ballpark Book: A Journey Through the Fields of Baseball Magic* (St. Louis: The Sporting News, 2000).

Stout, Glenn, *The Cubs: The Complete Story of Chicago Cubs Baseball* (New York: Houghton Mifflin, 2007).

Baseball-Reference.com

NOTES

1   William McNeil, *Gabby Hartnett: The Life and Times of the Cubs' Greatest Catcher* (Jefferson, North Carolina: McFarland Publishing, 2004), 147.

2 Charles A. Santo, *Sport and Public Policy: Social, Political, and Economic Perspectives* (Champaign, Illinois: Human Kinetics), 73.

3 Stuart Shea, *Wrigley Field: The Unauthorized Biography* (Dulles, Virginia: Potomac Books, Inc., 2004), 266.

4 Ibid.

5 Paul Dickson, *Bill Veeck: Baseball's Greatest Maverick* (London: Bloomsbury Publishing, 2012), 329.

PENNANT BEES WERE BUZZING:
CATALINA ISLAND, WILLIAM WRIGLEY JR., AND THE FAMED SPRING TRAINING GROUNDS OF THE CHICAGO CUBS

By Zachary Michael Jack

I N February 1919 the recently pro-claimed principal owner of the Chicago Cubs, William Wrigley, Jr.; his wife, Ada; and a real-estate broker, Captain David Blankenhorn, boarded the good ship Hermosa and set off across the San Pedro Channel for an hours-long reconnaissance in search of a California island Wrigley had purchased sight unseen for several million dollars.

"My goodness. It is a mountain, I thought it was flat," the chewing gum magnate opined, as the fog lifted and he beheld for the first time the rocky shores of Santa Catalina in all their Mediterranean-esque splendor.[1] After a night of deep and dreamy sleep induced by the lullaby of the deep blue Pacific outside their suite at the St. Catherine Hotel, the Wrigleys awoke even more sold on their impulse buy. Unable to contain his enthusiasm, the Cubs owner gathered reporters around him that first morning to report that wife Ada had gone to the window and declared that she would like one day to make this remote place her home. "I had never seen a more beautiful spot," Wrigley gushed. "Right then and there I determined that the island should never pass out of my hands."[2]

A mere two years later, in a bold, synergistic move that would become his hallmark, Wrigley married the twin passions of his late middle age, the Chicago Cubs and Santa Catalina Island, in a union that would last some 30 years, decreeing that his Cubs should use his temperate island as their perennial spring-training grounds. And yet the quiet announcement of the marriage in a February 1921 issue of the *Catalina Islander* hardly belied the future importance of Wrigley's bold move in team branding. Cubs manager Johnny Evers, the hometown newspaper reported, had agreed to let his team take on a team of islanders calling themselves the Catalina Cubs in Avalon. "That the game will be an interesting one for the island

fans is the general opinion," the nondescript newspaper article read.[3] Wrigley, though, had far bigger plans for the Cubs/Catalina merger, plans that would bear fruit in a World Series appearance in 1929.

In the spring of 1921, when the Cubs played their first spring-training game in Catalina's principal city of Avalon, America's great philanthropist, Andrew Carnegie, had been dead for nearly two years. William Wrigley, Jr. was mere months from turning 60 and had begun, predictably, to reflect on his legacy. He had achieved worldwide renown in turning a reported $32 in pocket change into a confectionery and chewing-gum empire worth tens of millions; he had broken ground on an architectural land-mark, the Wrigley Building, on Chicago's North Michigan Avenue; and he had purchased, expanded, and refurbished what would come to be called the Wrigley Mansion in Pasadena — one of six residences the Wrigleys maintained around the country. He had made many of his sharehold-ers wealthy many times over, and had more than secured the financial future of Ada and their two children, Dorothy and Philip, but he had not necessarily made the world a better place in the humanitarian sense, unless one considered his Juicy Fruit and Doublemint gums a balm to life's slings and arrows.

A black cloud hung over baseball in 1921, and it was Wrigley who was said to have recommended to his fellow owners the appointment of tough-as-nails Judge Kenesaw Mountain Landis as a commissioner with enough power to put baseball's house in order after the Black Sox scandal. Baseball, Wrigley felt, ought to be America's great demo-cratic game, and running a club ought to be as much a public service as a money-making proposition. A good, clean game well-played, he firmly believed, would help America regain its confidence in itself and its institutions and heroes; it would help American women, in particular, find a pastime they could share with their families and feel good about supporting with their hard-won dollars. Baseball, he fervently hoped, would give hundreds of thousands of workaday residents in places like Chicago something to get behind and feel patriotic about. It was a "whale of a business," Wrigley enthused, claiming to draw from the diamond "larger dividends in fun and personal satisfaction than … in money."[4] Likewise, Catalina Island was intended to be a feel-good rather than strictly profit-generating enterprise. Predicting that the development of Catalina would be "one of the greatest pleasures of my life," Wrigley hastened to add, "While my motive in purchasing the island is largely a romantic one, I am going to leave no stone unturned to make it a refuge from worry and work for rich and poor."[5]

In his statement, Wrigley might have swapped out "rich" and "poor" for life's "winners" and "losers," as he intended the island to be accessible to both. However, in 1920 his Cubs were neither winners nor losers, but were instead Mr. In-Betweens, middling in the National League in 1919 with a winning percentage barely over .500 despite a World Series appearance in 1918. Players had begun to grumble about the mediocre facilities in Pasadena, where the Cubs had trained since 1917, prompting Wrigley to take a detachment of his boys on a brief reconnaissance mission "26 miles across the sea," as the Four Preps would later croon it, to check out spring-training prospects on

William Wrigley purchased controlling interest in Catalina Island in 1919. Two years later he constructed a baseball facility for the Cubs who conducted spring training there until 1951. (Retro Images Archive. George Brace Collection)

Santa Catalina Island. There, on March 16, 1920, the team climbed aboard an open-air bus locals fondly referred to as the Catalina Goat, no doubt for its resemblance to a cattle truck, and rode along the bay waving at the adoring fans who had plastered a "Chicago Cubs Welcome to Our Island" sign on the Goat's rear end.

Locals liked what they saw in the spring of 1920, and so did Wrigley, and as the president of the Wrigley Company began to make a winner of the Cubs, his aspirations for both his team and his far-flung island predictably increased. Still, the remoteness of the island inevitably tempered the innate ambition of Wrigley's building program. As late as 1922, the Cubs were still doing much of their training on the isle's sandy beaches, while Wrigley and his team of engineers scouted for a level location suitable for a ballfield on the rugged, steeply sloped terrain. At 34, Cubs manager Reindeer Bill Killefer was just one year removed from his playing days in 1922, and still young enough to throw the hardball on the beach with the pitchers and the catchers who arrived early every year in hopes of rinsing off the rust.

Eventually Wrigley's scouts found their field in Avalon Canyon, adjacent to the oldest continuously operating golf course west of the Mississippi River, a nine-holer built by the island's original developers, the Bannon Brothers. By the middle of the 1920s the field itself and the boys of spring who played there had become the island's principal winter tourist attraction, and the third-known Wrigley Field, behind the Cubs home base back in Chicago and Wrigley Field in Pasadena, the headquarters of the Wrigley-owned Los Angeles Angels of the Pacific Coast League.

Early blueprints of the field demonstrated that the Chicago businessman intended to spare no expense in his twin desire to turn Catalina, and the Cubs, into bona-fide winners. The "Plan for Training Grounds for the Chicago Cubs at Avalon" showed an irrigated, sodded field romantically set at the base of Avalon Canyon and laid out to reproduce exactly the dimensions of Wrigley Field in Chicago.[6] Bulkhead lattice would be used for the fence and a clubhouse would be located along the first-base line with first-class amenities such as a massage and rubbing room, and a dedicated area behind home plate for the increasing number of newsmen accompanying the team on their annual island frolic. Along the third-base line, next to a row of eucalyptus trees planted for shade and protection from errant golf balls from the adjacent course, architects included a dedicated spectators' entrance to grandstands projected to seat 1,000.

Beyond the right-field fence, prescient planners drafted into their blueprints a series of bungalows or "casitas" designed for players and staff with families in tow. About 1,500 feet beyond the bungalows, directly down an extrapolated first-base line, Wrigley built a spring training bungalow for himself and his family on top of a 350-foot hill he dubbed Mount Ada in honor of his wife. While Wrigley claimed that he sited his mansion thusly because it would receive the best of both the morning and the afternoon sun, observers noted that the owner's perch afforded him direct sightlines to the field where, with a telescope, the paternalistic leader could oversee the action from his hilltop office. Players he deemed underperforming would receive a summons to run up the precipitous zigzag of terraced trails leading to Wrigley Road and upward to the mansion, where, breathless and itchy in their woolen uniforms, they would be asked to bid Mr. Wrigley a penitential good night.

Star second baseman Rogers Hornsby didn't have to make many punitive jogging trips up Mount Ada, if any, as he shared his boss's insistence on excellence. Hornsby later recalled of his hard-driven but fair-minded boss, "Like most successful men Mr. Wrigley was a man of strong likes and dislikes. If you showed him you were on the level he was for you right down the line. But if you ever did anything to show that your heart was not in your work, or that you would not help to make his the best rowboat, or the best steamship, or the best island, or the best ball club, he had no time for you, and did not want to see you in the picture any longer."[7]

In typical Wrigley fashion, the clubhouse originally designed for the first-base line was soon scrapped in favor of a more spacious and picturesque locale on the hillside across Avalon Canyon Road, beyond center field. Finished in time for the 1928 camp, it was lavish, designed in the mission style with red tiled roof and inset Catalina clay tiles. True to Wrigley's philanthropic ideal, while the Cubs were away the whole complex was to be used by the semipro Catalina Cubs, whose manager, Harry D. Diffin, exercised his islanders on what was likely the finest and most picturesque stadium enjoyed by a semipro team anywhere in the land. Diffin's family ran the local grocery store, which sponsored scorecards advertising Wrigley Field as the home of the Catalina Cubs, while promising "food products with personality." Indeed, Catalina and the Chicago Cubs were both strong on the personality front, owing in part to the larger-than-life persona of their shared owner. "If this is part of the Cub ball club treatment to players then a pennant should be forthcoming ere long," Cubs coach Bobby Wallace told the *Chicago Tribune* in 1923.[8] Wallace had been in the big leagues for 24 seasons, he went on to say, and "had never seen the equal of the spring training Bill Wrigley had resolved to provide his players."

Perhaps not coincidentally, as the Cubs began a period of dramatic improvement subsequent to a last-place finish in 1925, Wrigley saw to it that the island kept pace, further joining the fates of his two most beloved civic enterprises. In his development of the island as a spring retreat, Wrigley, a believer in good, clean fun, walked a fine line. On the one hand, economic development of his paradise depended on the offering of all the allures Roaring Twenties socialites expected of their vacation haunts. On the other hand, Wrigley wanted neither his island nor his team tarnished by crass commercialism and corruption in an era when ballplayers increasingly mingled with, and lived like, fast-living celebrities.

"There is to be nothing of the Coney Island flavor about Santa Catalina," Wrigley warned. "It would be unthinkable to mar the beauty of such a spot with roller coasters and the like."[9] Wrigley, however, allowed that the Cubs and their boosters must have high-quality music and dancing, even though he himself did not care to dance, and they must likewise have access to what he termed "adequate theaters." Even these he regarded as potential distractions, preferring instead to market the island's simpler pleasures, including glass-bottomed boats from which tourists could view "marine gardens" unequaled anywhere else in the world. "There are hills to climb and flowers to pluck," Catalina's patron insisted, implying that racier diversions were best left to the mainland.[10]

Wrigley and his marketing team aimed to create a world of health, fitness, naturalness, and curative restfulness — all fixtures of spring training dating back to before Wrigley's tenure, when the Cubs would travel to Hot Springs, Arkansas, to "boil out" — literally killing off what Chicago Colts (forerunner to the Cubs, 1890-1897) manager Cap Anson and his trainers dubbed the "alcoholic microbes" built up in boozy offseasons. While Catalina didn't offer out-of-shape Cubs the balm of geothermal waters, it did offer isolation from distraction, plenty of sunshine, a paucity of femmes fatales, the absence of racetracks and gambling halls, and, coupled with an 11 P.M. curfew, relatively little chance to get into trouble steeper than barroom fisticuffs.

A growing number of fans back in wintry Chicago were encouraged to partake in the rest and relaxation that, by 1926, had helped turn the Cubs back into winners. Ads from the era showed animated suns smiling down atop cavorting bear cubs happily playing ball against the backdrop of Catalina's sun-kissed climes. "The Cubs Are Here!" one ad read. "Why don't you come, too?"[11] Other ads in the local *Catalina Islander* urged residents and ballplayers alike to "Keep trim with the ballplayers at Santa Catalina Island."[12] Newsreels that came along several years later documented the perennial rejuvenation that happened on what Wrigley's admen branded a "magical isle."

Newspaper dispatches of the time likewise portrayed the frolicsome Cubs involved in wholesome, manly pursuits that didn't involve late-night skulduggery or shadowy bookies. The *Chicago American* delighted in reporting, for example, how coach Oscar Dugey and trainer Andy Lotshaw had hooked a giant eel and devilfish from the pier outside the Cubs' beach-side locker room. With much ado, Wrigley's boys went on an annual mountain-goat hunting expedition, and the subsequent struggles of the players' wives to prepare goat meat would be enthusiastically documented. The *Chicago Daily News* detailed harrowing backcountry horseback rides undertaken by pitcher Tony Kaufmann and infielder Howard

Freigau that made them "so stiff … they can't climb into the saddle."[13] Photographers captured pitchers Pat Malone and Lon Warneke with rifles over their shoulders and dead goats pinned beneath their cleats. At night Charlie Grimm provided entertainment on the banjo and piano, leading sing-alongs of feel-good country songs, while the *Chicago Herald and Examiner* reported that, in the absence of the usual glut of music halls and tin pan alleys, a handful of Cubs had stepped up to form their own band.

The success of the Catalina spring training, coupled with judicious trades, a growing fan base, and an owner determined to pay the asking rate for the league's best talent, created winners of both the island and the club. By 1929, when Wrigley opened a 12-story dance hall and movie theater on the island that boasted the world's largest uninterrupted dance floor and space aplenty for 1,800 simultaneously whirling couples, Catalina had been put firmly on the map as a place of pilgrimage for the recreation-hungry and winter-weary.

That same year all signs pointed to an especially auspicious spring training for the Cubs and the regular season to follow. Manager Joe McCarthy had led his team to fourth- and third-place finishes respectively in 1927 and 1928, and his front office had made a blockbuster offseason trade, by obtaining and signing the previous year's league-leading hitter from the Boston Braves, Rogers Hornsby, for $40,000. Hornsby would join heavy hitters Hack Wilson, Kiki Cuyler, and Riggs Stephenson in a home-run-hitting foursome the Associated Press dubbed "The Four Bludgeoneers."[14] More promising still, as the Cubs prepared to leave Chicago for Catalina in the second week of February, Cubs president William Veeck, Sr. gleefully reported that there would be no spring-training holdouts.

At exactly 1:35 P.M. the train carrying McCarthy and Cubs pitchers and catchers pulled out of Chicago Union Station to crowds the Associated Press reported were larger and more enthusiastic than ever before. "With Rogers Hornsby batting and fielding for us, it looks like we are going to win the flag at last," the Cubs' usually reticent manager crowed.[15] No less than Babe Ruth agreed, predicting that the Cubs and the Yankees would take their respective pennants.

In their predeparture meetings with local newsmen, the crowing North Siders were in such "superb voice," noted the *Tribune's* somewhat sanguine Edward Burns, that it seemed as if they had would win their first 20 games by the time they reached Catalina. Overconfidence aside, Burns wrote, Wrigley's boys began the training season "under auspices remarkably favorable to Cub success."[16] This year, sensed Burns and the other correspondents traveling with the team, Catalina could prove definitive. "Spring training trips do not always produce news for the fans," he observed, "… but Catalina should be different, perhaps to a greater degree than any training camp of recent years." Burns went on to claim that "many pertinent hints" as to the ball club's pennant chances would be uncovered "right off that big Pacific rock which is entitled Catalina Island."[17]

All along the Cubs' route, high expectations were apparent, as swarms of fans greeted the hopefuls at each successive depot heading west. At the sight of so many fanatics, the typically reserved Burns declared, "The extent of these demonstrations set a precedent in the matter of off-season baseball interest."[18] The 1929 Cubs enjoyed an unprecedented experience upon their arrival in California, too, prompting Burns to observe, "Cub getaways, like the patronage during the regular seasons, grow bigger and better. There were only ten [Cubs] to make up the second squad that set sail yesterday for the Catalina camp, but those ten were enough to draw into the Santa Fe train shed about five hundred frostbitten bugs who literally climbed over one another to get autographs, handshakes, or close-ups of the diamond notables."[19]

Adoring fans weren't the only welcome sight greeting the team as they disembarked from the Sante Fe terminus to the worst cold snap in Southern California in 40 years. As was the fashion on the long trip out West, the Cubs caravan would be joined by players and coaches who had scattered across the country during the offseason. At Los Angeles the Cubs were joined by left-hander Art Nehf, the pilot-pitcher who had flown himself in from Phoenix; fellow hurler Pat Malone, who had been working in a Southern California stone quarry in the offseason; and Cubs ace Charlie Root, who had likewise wintered on the Coast and showed up at the railyard with what

Edward Burns described as a comeback glint in his eye and in "high spirits and the best of health."[20] Veteran catcher Gabby Hartnett and his new bride were serenaded dockside by the faithful before boarding the early-morning steamship to Catalina, where camp kicked off with a rigorous afternoon hike.

Dispatches on February 22 came as a relief to winter-weary fans back in the Midwest: "The Chicago Cubs Have Played Their First Game of the Season." A day earlier McCarthy had surprised his boys by announcing that the day's workout would conclude with a scrimmage, the stated goal being to "harden the Cub pitchers and catchers."[21] Per the custom for such intrasquad games, the Cubs would be split into two teams, each with distinctive calling cards. As training camp that spring of 1929 wore on, the rival sides would typically suit up as the Avalons versus the Catalinas, but for this first game, McCarthy and Co. took the field as the Regulars, led by Hartnett, versus the Hooligans, headlined by pitcher Pat Malone.

As the Hooligans upset the Regulars beneath the shade of Wrigley's eucalyptus trees in Avalon Canyon, half a continent away the Associated Press reported that the second detachment of Cubs, this one made up of infielders and outfielders, had left Chicago to join their mates. This particular platoon was be led by Danny Cahill, arguably the Cubs' first true superfan. A pint-sized retired firefighter, Cahill demonstrated a devotion to the North Siders so great that Wrigley and the rest of the Cubs

The Chicago Cubs' "Wrigley Field" on Catalina Island. (Retro Images Archive. George Brace Collection)

invited him to sit front and center in many of the official spring-training photos taken on the island.

All indications early in 1929 pointed to a pitching and catching staff in unusually good shape. Hartnett and Malone, it was noted, both came in slightly above their ideal fighting weight, but physically the Cubs were starting well ahead of where they had been at the start of camp the previous year. Watching the early practices on the island from the press box, Burns noted that the pitchers were "in excellent condition" and that the fans who were accustomed to "viewing training camps as congresses of sore-armed gents" would be shocked to learn that the services of trainer Andy Lotshaw were hardly in demand.[22]

That very morning at the Hotel St. Catherine, reported the *Tribune*, William Wrigley, Jr. had come galloping up on horseback with good news: advance sales for the Cubs' season opener against the Pittsburgh Pirates on April 16 were already greater than they had been the eve of the Cubs' first game the previous year — and his squad was still nearly two months away from their first official at-bats of the season. "The King of Catalina" also reported that the exhibition games the Cubs had scheduled with the minor-league Los Angeles Angels and the Detroit Tigers on the mainland appeared set to break all spring exhibition-game records for attendance. "I'm getting a whale-kick out of the situation," Wrigley enthused, "because I know the fans can't be disappointed with the gang McCarthy is going to put in the field this year."[23]

The one lingering doubt coming out of the Catalina camp in the February of 1929 was the state of the Cubs' pitching. Starting pitcher Root had been up and down in previous seasons, including posting a league-leading 17 losses in 1926, only to win a major-league-leading 26 games in 1927, before returning to his losing ways in 1928 with 18 losses to 14 wins. In a dispatch dated February 19, the AP's Thomas L. Gard wrote, "As the first detachment of the Chicago Cubs speed their way to Mr. Wrigley's personal island of Catalina for the start of the spring-training grind (the Cubs will be) endeavoring to find some magical fluid that will restore Charlie Root's pitching arm to its 1927 cunning."[24] Indeed Gard went so far as to claim that

the Cubs' pennant chances hinged on whether or not Root regained his earlier form.

For his part, "Boss Joe" McCarthy resolved to crack the whip once his unusually promising squad of swatters arrived in Avalon, and at his urging, his stable of pitchers "bore down heavier than ever … in contemplation of the arrival of the Cub powerhouse squad."[25] Several days in advance of the arrival of his hitters, McCarthy curtailed visits to the Catalina's major attractions — the golf course, the world-class aviary Wrigley had recently built, and the mountain-goat hunting grounds themselves — in favor of two-a-day practices to replace the two-hour, morning-only practice sessions he had broken in his team with.

On February 26 the city of Avalon awoke to anticipation of the landing of Rogers Hornsby and rest of the Cub contingent. William Wrigley's steamship Catalina, Burns reported, was scheduled to dock at noon "amidst the tooting of a band, the notes of the Avalon carillon, the roar of hydroplanes, and the insolent slapping of trainer Andy Lotshaw's flock of trained sea gulls."[26] Big Ben, Catalina's giant seal," Burns added, tongue firmly in cheek, "…is the only prominent resident who will not be at the dock, according to current plans." Joining the squad on special request of manager McCarthy were two first-string pitchers from the Los Angeles Angels to join the 15 pitchers McCarthy had already retained for his Catalina camp in hope of testing and sharpening his brigade of bludgeoneers, perhaps most especially Hack Wilson, the cantankerous, heavy-set, and occasionally brilliant hitter the *Tribune's* Irving Vaughn had described that preseason as "round enough to roll up without effort" and with "at least fifteen pounds of excess beef clinging to his frame."[27]

The real headliner in February 1929, though, and the man projected to replace Wilson as the Cubs' cleanup hitter, was Rogers Hornsby, the sweet-swinging if not somewhat taciturn second basemen known for his ability to knock the leather off the ball. "California never has seen the great Rajah in a baseball uniform, except during the winter league season, the young man having always done his spring training in Florida," noted the *Tribune's* man in Avalon.[28] By March 1 even the AP writers stuck in still-wintry Chicago were abuzz with secondhand news of the Rajah's exploits, noting, "Reports drifting back from Catalina Island so far are unanimous that Rogers Hornsby and his big stick have already made a hit with manager Joe McCarthy and his ambitious Cubs."[29]

By the end of a first week in which his pitching staff had comported themselves well against the gifted battery of Cubs long-ballers, McCarthy declared his team fit to begin play against Mr. Wrigley's other team, the Angels of the Pacific Coast League. On March 7 Burns filed the following dispatch post-departure: "The Cubs this afternoon gave Catalina Island back to Mr. Wrigley and this evening are lolling about in the plush divans at their mainland headquarters in the city."[30] Though the Cubs would return to the island for a four-day stint after their weekend tilt with the Angels, 1929's auspicious sojourn on the magical isle began to seem a distant memory, as Cub thoughts turned to the coming season. While Wrigley had built his island to wholesomely entertain, the mountain goats and paucity of girls and glam didn't sit well with some of the city boys on the squad and a few of the more urbane reporters, all of whom relished the return to the mainland. Those in the know tacitly agreed with Burns's prediction that the remaining few days of camp on the island wouldn't be the same after the Cubs had re-experienced "the thrill of the electric signs, the big movie palaces, the orange huts, and one thing and another racing through their veins."[31]

Once back in the City of Angels, the Cubs would spend an evening at the Mayfair Hotel receiving detachments of loyal fans who couldn't stomach, literally or figuratively, the 30-mile steamship trip to Catalina. Manager McCarthy declared to reporters that he intended to win every one of the 32 exhibition games Wrigley's front office had scheduled for his club on its five-week journey back to Chicago. The hard-driven manager warned that "mid-season procedures"[32] would be followed even in these warmup tilts, and pitchers would be unceremoniously yanked if they found themselves in trouble early on.

"I want the players to get into the habit of winning ball games," the skipper told reporters. "The 'it-doesn't-mean-anything' attitude toward exhibition games is bunk with me. I'm a tough loser and I don't care who knows it."[33]

"Boss Joe" could talk the talk and back it up both in the spring of 1929 as the pennant bees were buzzing more loudly than ever when the Cubs pummeled the Angels, 11-6, in their first exhibition game of the season, delighting the reported 8,000 fans on hand for the novelty of a match between two teams owned by William Wrigley. Hornsby, the man the *Tribune* estimated 7,500 of the 8,000 fans had turned out to see, didn't disappoint, socking his first home run in a Cubs uniform against a professional team, while clouting two doubles for good measure. At first base Charlie Grimm kept the basepaths hopping, going 4-for-4 while playing errorless ball in the field.

Like his manager, William Wrigley, Jr. didn't much like a loser, either in business or in baseball, and both his fantasy island, Catalina, and his Cubs paid impressive dividends. In the ten years from 1919 to 1929, the exploits of Wrigley and his team had increased the number of visitors to the island from 90,000 to 750,000. And even in down years like 1925, when the Cubs finished at the bottom of the pack, the organization finished second in the league in attendance. By the end of a fairy-tale 1929 season that culminated in an appearance in the World Series, the Cubs had drawn an estimated 1.5 million fans to Wrigley Field — 500,000 more than had visited the chewing-gum magnate's increasingly popular island.

The Cubs and Catalina — the arranged marriage between them would be both affectionate and prolific in a 30-year run lasting until 1951. During that time Avalon served as a training ground for several hundred players, including 16 future Hall of Famers with names like Grover Cleveland Alexander, Dizzy Dean, and Rogers Hornsby, whose collective glamour and glory would help turn Catalina into an enclave for Hollywood stars and starlets in the 1930s and beyond.

"I am putting more than $1,000,000 a year into Catalina," Wrigley reminded still-dubious reporters as he neared his death in the early 1930s. "I may be foolish in doing this. I do not think so. I love the island, and before I pass on I hope to have a larger portion of my fortune invested there. I feel that I am doing something definite and useful for humanity in developing it."[34] Indeed, the King of Catalina loved his island home sufficiently to be interred there after his death in January 1932, taking up what all assumed would be his perpetual residence in a custom-built sarcophagus at the base of a reinforced concrete and Catalina tile mausoleum said to be 80 feet tall and 180 feet deep, though in World War II the family moved body to Pasadena, citing increased security concerns.

Naysayers and boo-birds called Wrigley a fool for pouring his assets into a desert island and an apparently accursed team that would go more than a century without a World Series title, but the numbers suggest that Wrigley's may have been the last laugh. Each year Catalina draws an estimated 1 million visitors to its far-off shores, while the Cubs themselves, despite a record of middling seasons and dubious trades, top the *Forbes* list of most profitable teams in baseball.

SOURCES

Associated Press, "Cub Battery Men on Their Way to Camp," *Sterling* (Illinois) *Daily Gazette*, February 14, 1929, 9.

—————-"Cubs Back to Catalina For More Training," *Alton* (Illinois) *Evening Telegraph*, March 11, 1929, 10.

—————-"Cubs Leave Catalina to Tackle Angels." *Alton* (Illinois) *Evening Telegraph*, March 14, 1929, 10.

"Boys in Blue: Chicago Cubs and Spring Training on Catalina Island," exhibit curated by John Boraggina, Catalina Island Museum, Avalon, California.

Burns, Edward, "McCarthy's Men Limber up Wings in Catalina Camp," *Chicago Tribune*, February 20, 1929, 19.

—————-"Mr. Burns Gives The Rajah 100 in Deportment," *Chicago Tribune*, March 6, 1929, 23.

—————-"Cubs Moundsmen Spike Cub Siege Guns; Cubs Win," *Chicago Tribune*, March 7, 1929, 19.

—————-"Hornsby Hits Homer as Cubs Beat Angels," *Chicago Tribune*, March 9, 1929, 21.

—————-"Angels Beat Cubs, 11-8, in Riotous Battle," *Chicago Tribune*, March 10, 1929, A1.

—————-"Bounding Main Fails to Agree with Our Cubs," *Chicago Tribune*, March 12, 1929, 27.

—————-"Bush, Malone Fail in Cubs' Training Test," *Chicago Tribune*, March 13, 1929, 2.

—————-"Cubs Cut Loose in Final Island Game; Avalons Win," *Chicago Tribune*, March 14, 1929, 21.

—————-"Cubs Bid Avalon Adieu, Aim to Clip Wings of Angels, *Chicago Tribune*, March 15, 1929, 25.

Catalina Islander Newspaper Collection, Collection of the Catalina Island Museum, Avalon, California.

Chicago Tribune Press Service, "Best Clubs of N.L. Training on Coast, It Seems," *Chicago Tribune*, March 24, 1929, A8.

"Cubs See Action at Catalina," *Chicago Tribune*, February 22, 1929.

Gard, Thomas L. (Associated Press), "McCarthy, Cubs Manager, Is Real Diplomat," *Carbondale* (Illinois) *Daily Free Press*, March 26, 1929, 3.

"Greetings from Catalina Island: Spring Training Home of the Clubs from 1921-1951," *Spring Training*. (1977). springtrainingmagazine.com/history2.html

Howser, Huell, "California's Gold #6004: Catalina Cubs," DVD, Huell Howser Productions, Los Angeles.

Snell, Roger, *Root for the Cubs: Charlie Root and the 1929 Cubs*. (Nicholasville, Kentucky: Wind Publications, 2009).

Vaughn, Irving, "Cubs' Big Parade Ready for March to Training Grounds," *Chicago Tribune*, February 12, 1929.

Vitti, Jim, *The Cubs on Catalina Island: A Scrapbook of Memories about a 30-year Love Affair between One of Baseball's Classic Teams and California's Most Fanciful Island* (Darien, Connecticut: Settefrati Press, 2003).

—————*Chicago Cubs Baseball on Catalina Island* (Charleston, South Carolina: Arcadia Publishing, 2010).

Windle, Ernest, *Windle's History of Santa Catalina Island* (Avalon, California: Catalina Islander Newspaper Press, 1931).

Zimmerman, William, *William Wrigley Jr.: the Man and his Business* (Chicago: R.R. Donnelley and Sons Co., 1935).

NOTES

1   Ernest Windle, *Windle's History of Santa Catalina Island* (Avalon, California: Catalina Islander Newspaper, 1931), 19.

2   William Zimmerman, *William Wrigley Jr.: the Man and His Business* (Chicago: R.R. Donnelley and Sons Co., 1935), 238.

3   "Catalina Cubs vs. Chicago Cubs," *Catalina Islander*, February 1921.

4   Zimmerman, 221.

5   Ibid.

6   "Plan for Training Grounds for the Chicago Cubs at Avalon," collection of the Catalina Island Museum, Avalon, California.

7   Zimmerman, 235.

8   Jim Vitti. *The Cubs on Catalina Island: A Scrapbook of Memories About a 30-year Love Affair Between One of Baseball's Classic Teams and California's Most Fanciful Island* (Darien, Connecticut: Settefrati Press, 2003), 14.

9   Zimmerman, 241.

10 Zimmerman, 242.

11 Jim Vitti, *Chicago Cubs Baseball on Catalina Island* (Charleston, South Carolina: Arcadia Publishing, 2010), 17.

12 Collection of the Catalina Island Museum, Avalon.

13 Vitti, *The Cubs on Catalina Island*, 94.

14 Associated Press, "Cub Bludgeoneers Gird for Flag Fight," *Carbondale* (Pennsylvania) *Daily Free Press*, March 8, 1929, 8.

15 Associated Press, "Cubs' Advance Guard Leaves for Catalina," *Alton* (Illinois) *Evening Telegraph*, February 14, 1929, 8.

16 Edward Burns, "Cub Pitchers Start for Catalina Today," *Chicago Tribune*, February 14 1929,

17 Ibid.

18 Edward Burns, "Cubs Spin West; Reach Catalina," *Chicago Tribune*, February 15, 1929, 25.

19 Edward Burns, "Cub Batteries Anticipate Arrival of Swat Squad," *Chicago Tribune*, February 24, 1929, A2.

20 Edward Burns, "Cubs Pitch Camp at Avalon," *Chicago Tribune*, February 18, 1929, 21.

21 Associated Press, "The Chicago Cubs Have Played Their First Game of the Season," *Alton* (Illinois) *Evening Telegraph*, February 22, 1929, 6.

22 Edward Burns, "Wrigley Tells Cubs How Fans Await April 16," *Chicago Tribune*, February 25, 1929, 25.

23 Ibid.

24 Thomas Gard, Associated Press, "First Chicago Cub Detachment to Catalina," *Carbondale* (Illinois) *Daily Free Press*, February 19, 1929, 2.

25 Edward Burns, "Cub Batteries Anticipate Arrival of Swat Squad, *Chicago Tribune*, February 24, 1929, A2.

26 Edward Burns, "Second Group of Cubs Reaches Avalon Today," *Chicago Tribune*, February 26, 1929, 23.

27 Irving Vaughn, "Second Cubs Squad Off for Avalon Today," *Chicago Tribune*, February 23, 1929, 17.

28 Edward Burns, "Second Group of Cubs Reaches Avalon Today," *Chicago Tribune*, February 26, 1929, 23.

29 Associated Press, "Hornsby Makes Big Hit With Cubs," *Sterling* (Illinois) *Daily Gazette*, March 1, 1929, 13.

30 Edward Burns, "Mr. Wrigley's Boys Quit Island For the Big Town," *Chicago Tribune*, March 8, 1929, 23.

31 Ibid.

32 Ibid.

33 Ibid.

34 Zimmerman, 238.

ED BURNS

By Chip Greene

AMONG A LIFETIME OF LIVELY anecdotes, perhaps none better evokes the colorful and adventurous life of Ed Burns than that told by another renowned sportswriter from the profession's glory days, Red Smith. Writing four days after Burns's untimely death, on January 27, 1955, at the age of 64, Smith suggested that his colleague "probably was the only sports reporter in America who was prodded into the craft by the muzzle of a sawed-off shotgun."[1]

The episode took place in Chicago during the Al Capone-era Prohibition days of gangland warfare. At the time, Burns was in his second incarnation with the *Chicago Tribune*. Having joined the paper as an artist early in 1918, his employment was interrupted in July of that year when Burns was drafted into the Navy, where, Smith reported, he was "valorous in defense of the Brooklyn Navy Yard."[2] After discharge, Burns rejoined the *Trib*, but this time as a news reporter, assigned variously to the Federal building and criminal courts. On the latter beat, Burns "became personally acquainted with commanders, lieutenants and foot soldiers of the underworld's several clashing forces."[3]

One day while Burns was walking down Michigan Avenue, he was joined by one of these nefarious characters, who engaged him in conversation. When it came time for the two to part, the associate seemed reluctant to leave Burns's side; he kept Burns talking for a considerable time. The next day, Burns encountered a member of a rival gang, who asked, "You bumped into Big Tony yesterday, didn't you? Did you happen to notice a car following you along the curb?" When Burns answered no, the man explained, "Some of us boys were in it. We were gonna take care of Big Tony, but we didn't leave him have it because you were in line."[4]

Moments later, Burns stood before his managing director and told him, "I have come to the conclusion that sportswriting is my true métier."[5]

For almost 30 years, sports fans were thrilled that he had made the switch.

As a boy, Burns had the perfect role model for a journalism career. Born in Frankfort, Indiana, on January 17, 1891, Edward Harold Burns, Jr. was the second son (the first son, Robert, died at 5 in 1892; and sister Blanche was born in 1894) of Edward and Flora Burns. After a stint as editor of the *Frankfort Banner*, in 1887 Edward Sr. became a partner and joint editor of the *Frankfort Evening News*, which he later owned. For four years beginning in 1906, Edward Sr. also served as Frankfort's postmaster.

Edward Jr. began his career in the newspaper business at 14 by gathering personal items for his father's newspaper. (In his obituary, it was also noted that Burns later worked on several newspapers, in Crawfordsville, Indiana, where he attended school, as well as in Illinois, at the *Joliet Herald-News* and the *Chicago Examiner*, but the timeline is unclear.) Around 1909, Burns then enrolled at Wabash College, in Crawfordsville, where he was a member of the Delta Chi fraternity. Whether Burns majored in journalism at Wabash is unknown, but after graduation he expanded his creative nature by studying at the Chicago Art Institute and the Academy of Fine Arts, before he joined the staff of the *Chicago Herald* in 1914. Four years later, he moved to the *Tribune* and took a job in the art department.

With his artistic talents, Burns's career might have turned out differently, although he eventually merged both journalism and art. In reporting upon Burns' being drafted in 1918, the *Tribune* wrote, "If he can draw a bead on a Teutonic dome with half the cleverness with which he portrays their features on paper there will be fewer Fritzes to return to the fatherland."[6] After his service in the Navy, Burns returned to Chicago and took a job in the art department of an advertising agency, which he held for two years. In 1923, however, he returned to the *Tribune* as their crime reporter. His switch to sports took place in 1927.

It was the last position Burns ever held (the exception being supplementary work he did for years with *The Sporting News*); for the rest of his life, almost literally until the day he died, Burns reported on sports for the *Tribune*. A big, jovial man, who was a master of satire and an expert in the art of ribbing and needling,[7] in addition to baseball, Burns also covered football and hockey, and "won (a) reputation for his whimsical writing style."[8] (Burns was a charter member of the National Hockey League selection committee that yearly named the All-Star players and winners of hockey's Lady Byng, Hart, and Calder trophies. When he died, Burns's impact on hockey, it was claimed, would best be remembered by a suggestion he made to widen the blue lines on the rink from a thin, obscure marker to one 12 inches wide. Burns also originated the term "feathering the puck," then standard in describing the practice of ragging the puck to kill penalty time.[9])

Burns couldn't have been more physically different from the athletes he covered. Indeed, he was a rather large man. Writing about their young artist in 1918, when Burns left the paper for the Navy, the *Tribune* first reported that he "weigh[ed] something more than 200 [pounds.]"[10] In 1973 sportswriter Edgar Munzel, a contemporary of Burns for many years at *The Sporting News*, with whom Burns spent many springs during the 1930s at Chicago Cubs training camps on Catalina Island, offered an even more inflated account when he recalled Burns as "the 300-pound *Tribune* chronicler."[11] And perhaps Red Smith said it best when he wrote, in his own inimitable style, of Burns as both possessing a "large spherical silhouette" and a man who was also "corpulent and sedentary."[12] Together with his jovial personality, "delicious wit" and "wide friendliness," the bespectacled Burns endeared himself to his contemporaries in the press box.[13]

That wasn't always the case with the athletes, though. In days when writers often glossed over the foibles of the men whom they covered, Burns, recalled Red Smith, "could see deeper than a sweatshirt and, having measured an athlete's talents accurately, could sum up his judgment succinctly." "No hero worshipper" was Burns, wrote Smith, "enshrining demigods on pedestals of prose."[14] (When the Cubs blew a six-game lead in 1930, Burns wrote:

"Don't shoot your rifles at that thar balloon, boys — the Cubs are in it." Later, he blamed the team's collapse on a pair of peacocks Rogers Hornsby had bought from the late William Wrigley, Jr.'s Catalina Island bird farm during spring training. Peacocks, he insisted, were bad luck. "Back home in Indiana," he wrote, "we tolerated 'em only on millinery. And then only on certain folks."[15])

More than once, Burns's bluntness and criticism provoked outrage and anger from an aggrieved athlete; and yet, "if occasionally there were threats of violence from some ballplayer he had written about with what the athlete deemed an excess of candor," Burns nonetheless remained undisturbed. "He had no patience with professionals who came complaining when he'd written the truth about them, whining, 'You're taking away my bread and butter.'"

"How do they think I earn my bread and butter?" Burns would retort. Of course, it helped that "he outweighed most ordinary infielders by 100 pounds or so."[16]

Sometimes Burns's critical commentary could be relentless. Witness the feud he had one season with Cubs shortstop Dick Bartell. One day during 1939 spring training with the Cubs on Catalina Island, recalled Munzel, Burns was walking across the ball field with Cubs traveling secretary Robert Lewis, another man of large girth, after

Burns covered the Cubs for the *Chicago Tribune* from 1927 until his death in 1955. (Meet the Sportswriters; Baseball-Fever.com)

a team workout. Spotting the two men, Bartell yelled, "When does the balloon go up?"

"And did Rowdy Richard [Bartell] pay for the remark!" exclaimed Munzel. "Burns was on Bartell for the rest of the year. It was never a vicious frontal attack, but big Ed jabbed the needle in day after day by tabulating Bartell's errors … Another boot by Dick Bartell, his 22nd of the season, cost the Cubs the game … Bartell's 31st error of the season set up another run for the Cardinals. And on and on it went, with Bartell unwittingly playing right into Burns's hands. He had a terrible season."[17]

In his 1988 autobiography, Bartell himself remembered that year. "Dizzy Dean, Woody English and I were walking up the path to the ballpark. Up ahead was a rotund, heavyset guy. He had to turn sideways to get through the gate.

"I called out, 'Hey what time does the balloon go up?' It was a common barb we used to throw at overweight players.

"Dean said, 'Do you know who that is?'

"I said no.

"Dean said, 'That's Ed Burns, the writer for the Chicago Tribune.'

"Burns turned and pointed a finger at me. 'You'll hear from me all summer,' he said.

"Well, the season started and I was being charged with errors on plays where there was no error, like a double play we didn't finish. But Burns was the official scorer. He would give me one, anyhow. And anything that might have been called a hit for me, he'd charge the other team with an error. …

"The other writers in the press box heard "Error, Bartell" so often, every time I booted one or threw it into the stands, everyone sang out, "Error, Bartell."'

Burns's enmity would rarely last, though. Years later, according to Bartell, Burns apologized "for coming down so hard on me that year."[18]

By the time Burns joined the *Tribune* sports department in 1927, another *Tribune* sportswriting legend, Irving Vaughan, was beginning his second decade of Chicago sports coverage. From that point on, Burns and Vaughan alternated their reporting between the city's two baseball teams. A typical article that appeared in a July 1937 edition of *The Sporting News* accurately conveyed their teamwork.

"Switching time is at hand for the Chicago scribes," the article explained. Unlike "some of the New York boys" who covered three teams yet usually switched their coverage "willy nilly," Burns and Vaughan always traded places at midseason. "The Trib pair have arranged an intricate switch. Burns, who will leave the Cubs to cover the White Sox in Detroit, July 5, en route to the All-Star game, will rejoin the Cubs in Pittsburgh for three days en route home, then will return to Chicago to join the Sox for the remainder of the season. Vaughan will pick up the Cubs at a night game in Cincy, July 12."[19] Their changes almost always went off seamlessly.

The two also yearly alternated spring trainings. (In 2002 veteran journalist Godfrey Sperling, who enjoyed a 59-year career with the *Christian Science Monitor*, recalled that Vaughan and Burns were "my favorite sports writers in those days. … How I envied them their assignments, covering the White Sox and the Cubs. They would start out with one team at spring training and then trade teams at midseason."[20]) Burns's first spring with the Cubs at Catalina Island occurred in 1929, the year the Cubs won the National League pennant. That spring was also the first time Burns met Cubs owner Philip Wrigley. Writing in 1947, during his first visit back to Catalina after a five-year hiatus, Burns declared, "I felt pretty proud being greeted by Mr. and Mrs. Wrigley when I got off the boat the other day. First time I ever met P.K. was right on that same wharf. He was helping unload a snow white Arabian stallion. Don't imagine the hoss is still about his business hereabouts."[21]

Filing dispatches from whichever locale happened to be his assignment was, of course, paramount for Burns, but once his working day was through, he always found the nightlife appealing. (Of Burns's writing method, Sperling wrote, "In later years, I happened to meet Burns, who told me he always wrote his stories in longhand and that there was one Tribune (Linotype) operator who always handled his stories because he was the only one who could decipher Burns's handwriting."[22]) During his early years at Catalina, Burns stayed at the St. Catherine Hotel, where he would often entertain friends. "Bob Lewis [the traveling secretary] used to fix it with the management so I had the same room each year," Burns wrote. "It was on the third floor north front, overlooking the ocean. … Once a gent … came to my room [for drinks]. … As we sat for several hours discussing world problems, my guest forgot where he was. Furthermore, it was high tide and the waves were roaring up to the walk under my window. My landlubber friend heard the roar, looked out, blinked as he beheld nothing but water, then cried: "My gawd, we're at sea. I've been shanghaied. Then he fainted. Quite a mess getting him to his own bed."[23]

By 1947 Burns had relocated. "I'm a little sad about the dormant state of the St. Catherine hotel, but delighted with my quarters in the Atwater. Never in all the years I've been coming here had I set foot in the place, although I spent many hours on my feet and otherwise in a neighborhood establishment when it was known as the White Cap. That was when we used to get up and come down for the 4 a.m. show. There was a banjo player who had a three piece orchestra and he billed his unit as "Professor Burns and his Thirty Dirty Fingers."[24]

If Burns gained national renown and respect for his *Tribune* work (in 1942 he became chairman of the Chicago chapter of the Baseball Writers Association of America; in 1947, president of the national BBWAA; and in 1952, a member of the BBWAA board of directors), he possibly exceeded that work elsewhere. As baseball writer-turned-baseball executive Garry Schumacher opined in a 1961 *TSN* article when he named Burns and *New York Herald-Tribune* writer Bill Hanna as the best writers of his time, "Actually, Burns did his best work for *The Sporting News*."[25] There, Burns often combined his writing with his art.

In 1937 Burns interviewed Cubs coach John "Red" Corriden, who had been in the game for 30 years, concerning "inside baseball" and the variety of signs used by managers and coaches. In the piece, Burns accompanied

the narrative with a panel of his own humorous drawings, such as a coach touching the brim of his hat with his left hand, while with his right simultaneously touching his ear lobe. This action, Burns wrote, "is an absent-minded coach touching skin and clothing simultaneously. If you understand baseball signs you know this kind of careless business is likely to make an obedient ball player try to run in opposite directions at the same time thus precipitating havoc. Or he might hit a triple when he was supposed to bunt." Another cartoon shows a coach holding an open pouch of tobacco in his left hand while in his right he pinches a bit between thumb and forefinger. In this case, wrote Burns, "A coach taking a chew in this fashion would mean one thing. Pouring the scrap into his face direct from the pouch might mean an entirely opposite message with disastrous results."[26] Several months later he also produced "Burns-Eye Views of Big Time Parks," a 15-part serial that featured, in intricate and exacting detail, Burns's handwritten drawings of every stadium in the major leagues accompanied by "a paragraph here and there about the fan inmates thereof, together with miscellaneous historical matter and maybe an anecdote or two."[27] At the time of his death almost 20 years later, he was hoping to resume his *Sporting News* column, "Bouncing Around With Ed Burns." Truly, these works represented Burns at the peak of his creativity.

The end came over a span of six months. On June 1, 1954, Burns was in Boston while traveling with the White Sox when he was stricken with an illness that turned out to be cancer. After several operations, he returned to his Oak Park, Illinois, home to recuperate. (A lifelong bachelor, for many years he lived with his sister Blanche and her family on South Maple Drive in Oak Park.) That November, Burns returned to the *Trib* when he covered his 28th Purdue-Indiana football game. His final assignment was Christmas night, 1954, at the opening of the Hollywood Ice Revue in Chicago Stadium. After his story was completed, Burns collapsed. For three weeks he lay in a coma at Chicago's Wesley Memorial Hospital, before a clot on a brain artery took his life.

Two days after his death, Ed Burns was laid to rest beside his parents in Chicago's Rose Hill Cemetery. Among his pallbearers was his good friend, Irving Vaughan.

SOURCES

Sincerest appreciation is expressed to SABR member Bill Mortell for his invaluable contribution to this biography. Bill utilized Geneaology.com and Ancestry.com, as well as several online sources referenced below.

Newspapers/Magazines (online):

Seattle Times

Chicago Tribune

Catalina Islander

The Sporting News

Christian Science Monitor

Baseball Digest

NOTES

1   "Red Smith: Views of Sport," *Seattle Times*, January 31, 1955.

2   Ibid.

3   Ibid.

4   Ibid.

5   Ibid.

6   *Chicago Daily Tribune*, July 27, 1918.

7   "Ed Burns, Columnist for the Sporting News, Dies," *The Sporting News*, February 2, 1955.

8   Ibid.

9   Ibid.

10   *Chicago Daily Tribune*, July 27, 1918.

11   "Munzel - 44 Years of Spring Fun and Frolic," *The Sporting News*, March 10, 1973.

12   "Red Smith: Views of Sport," *Seattle Times*, January 31, 1955.

13   "Ed Burns, Columnist for the Sporting News, Dies," *The Sporting News*, February 2, 1955.

14   "Red Smith: Views of Sport," *Seattle Times*, January 31, 1955.

15   "Ed Burns, Columnist for the Sporting News, Dies," *The Sporting News*, February 2, 1955.

16   Ibid.

17   "Munzel - 44 Years of Spring Fun and Frolic," *The Sporting News*, March 10, 1973.

18   "Dingers & Zingers," Phily.com, August 9, 1995.

19   "Switching Time for Chi Scribes," *The Sporting News*, July 1, 1937.

20   *Christian Science Monitor*, July 23, 2002.

21   *Catalina Islander*, February 20, 1947.

22   *Christian Science Monitor*, July 23, 2002.

23   *Catalina Islander*, February 20, 1947.

24   Ibid.

25   *The Sporting News*, March 29, 1961.

26   *The Sporting News*, April 29, 1937.

27   *The Sporting News*, June 24, 1937.

IRVING VAUGHAN

BY CHIP GREENE

IN THE SUMMER OF 1919, THE YEAR THE Black Sox threw the World Series, 30-year-old sportswriter Irving Vaughan joined the staff of the *Chicago Tribune*. It wasn't his first newspaper job, but it would be his last. When he retired 38 years later, having covered more than 7,000 baseball games during a career that spanned almost 50 years, Vaughan was considered the "dean of the nation's baseball writers"[1] and was one of the most knowledgeable, best-informed and respected men in the press box.

It was the simplicity of his writing that elevated Vaughan to the top of his profession. Indeed, eulogizing its former star reporter upon his death in 1963, the *Tribune* recounted that "Irv, as he was known to his colleagues, wrote baseball in a straight-away style unaffected by the flamboyancy that characterized sports articles during the earlier stages of his development. Pretentious figures of speech, metaphors and flowery phrases typical of those times had no part in his terse, accurate accounts. He saw action on the field and put it thru his typewriter."[2] Such ability to starkly convey the happenings on the diamond won for Vaughan a legion of dedicated readers.

If Vaughan undoubtedly came by his literary talent naturally, still, it's likely his brother deserved some degree of credit for his success. Born Mark Irving Vaughan on December 14, 1888, in Racine, Wisconsin, Irving was the second child of John Vaughan, a laundryman, and his wife, Lelia. Manning was two years older. (The Vaughans also had a daughter, Dorothy, who later wed Herb Graffis, a well-known golf writer for the *Tribune*, whom Irving likely introduced to his sister.) In 1906 Manning Vaughan began his own career as a sportswriter when he joined the *Milwaukee Sentinel*. Three years later, the 20-year-old Irving also started his sportswriting career with the *Sentinel*. We can only speculate whether Manning brokered his brother's employment.

(During research for this biography, tracking down a record of Vaughan's education proved mostly futile. The only references found were a single line on Baseball-fever.

com that said he had been "educated in schools at Milwaukee,"[3] and an entry in the 1940 census that noted he had completed four years of high school.)

It didn't take long for Vaughan's talent to propel him toward a bigger stage; within less than a year of joining the *Sentinel*, he moved to Chicago. On January 2, 1910, at the behest of a sports editor named Gus Axelson, who was familiar with Vaughan's work, Vaughan joined Axelson's sports department at the *Chicago Record-Herald*. The following year Vaughan covered his first World Series, as the Philadelphia A's won their second consecutive world championship, over the New York Giants in six games. Thereafter, Vaughan covered virtually every one of the next 46 fall classics. In October 1914 he moved to the *Chicago Examiner*, where he remained until June 1919, when he joined the *Tribune*.

Over the years Vaughan understandably became a student of the game, and his writing on a broad range of baseball topics in addition to the play on the field reflected his extensive familiarity with the nuances and facets of the sport. His subject matter was wide-ranging:

In December 1921, concerning the status of players who had jumped to other leagues, Vaughan wrote: "Organized baseball is said to have undergone a change of heart in regard to its rules against players who either failed to report or jumped to the so-called 'outlaw' ranks. Certain minor league players who were put outside the fold for neglecting to observe the reserve clause already have received overtures to return, and it was learned yesterday that the big leagues shortly will take similar steps to bring the wayward sons back home."[4]

Several years later, discussing an increase in offense resulting from a livelier ball, he wrote, "Mechanical devices had resulted in stitching that leaves the seam practically at a level with the rest of the cover. … With most hurlers the seam has always been utilized as a means of getting a better grip on the ball. With the ends of the fingers directly over a part of the seam it is far easier to get a spin on the pellet as it leaves the hand and it is the spin — forwards, backwards or sideways — that causes the object to curve, hop or dip. If the seams have been depressed, as the makers claim it is possible, then the pitchers aren't getting the stuff on the ball as they did before, and with less deception the batters are swinging freer and connecting oftener."[5]

And in 1943, with most of the game's stars away in the service, Vaughan defended the talents of their "inferior replacements," stating that although the "homer, to a certain extent, has been eliminated," the "game isn't on its last legs." Rather, "these supposedly inferior replacements … have brought back into the game something that had been lost since the magnates went home run crazy"; namely, "this or that fellow in the minors who could field but not hit."

"Fielding as a whole," suggested Vaughan, "is something worthy of fans' interest." A lot of the replacement players "consistently produce plays that in the live ball days were rarities. And even when such plays were made in those

Bill Veeck, Sr. and Irving Vaughan (r). For almost 38 years Vaughan covered both the Chicago Cubs and White Sox for the *Chicago Tribune*. (National Baseball Hall of Fame)

times they attracted little attention. Only the homer meant anything.

"Fans like the new fielding touch … taking the long hitters have [sic] evened up the game."[6] Clearly, Vaughan loved baseball in its purest form.

While Vaughan often expounded on all manner of themes peripheral to the players and the games, his primary subjects were always, of course, the hometown teams. From the time he arrived in the Windy City, Vaughan covered in equal measure both the Cubs and White Sox. In 1927 he was joined on the *Tribune* sports staff by a rotund former artist named Ed Burns. Together, each year until Burns's premature death in 1955, the two men shared reportage of the Chicago baseball landscape. They also became close friends. (Vaughan was a pallbearer at Burns's funeral.) Each season they would alternate both spring training and the regular season, covering one team from the outset and then swapping assignments at the All-Star break, at which point they'd finish the season with the other team. It was an arrangement that brought great balance to the reading public's perception of both teams.

What was most important about Vaughan's work, particularly given his proximity to his subjects ("he associated closely with men whose names have become legendary in sports," offered the *Trib*, "Ty Cobb, Babe Ruth, Lou Gehrig, Walter Johnson, Judge K.M. Landis, Charles A. Comiskey I and many others"[7]) was the impartiality of his reporting. Whether Chicago's teams were good or bad, Vaughan simply told things as they were, with no attempt to influence popular opinion. After the Cubs' last-place finish in 1925 ushered in Joe McCarthy and a rebuilding project, Vaughan wrote in December of that year, "When it comes to making over a ball team in short order, the Cubs have to be awarded the palm. It is no simple matter to change almost the entire personnel of a squad in one season but the officials of the local team have done that very thing and when Joe McCarthy, the new manager, hits the Catalina Island training camp next February, he is going to have a real job on his hands trying to figure out what is worth keeping and what isn't so good."[8]

Likewise, after the Cubs won the 1929 NL pennant, energizing their fans, Vaughan presciently predicted, "There may be a few shootings and some exhibitions of pineapple tossing over tickets for the impending World's Series strife. That's how bad the situation looks at the present time, and the tickets haven't even been issued. When they finally appear and a lot of folks who now feel they're fixed, find they are not, there will be such a stampede that the club officials may have to take to the tall timbers. … Plenty of folks think the (S)eries … should be staged at Soldier's Field where there are seats for more than 100,000, but the stadium was not built for baseball."[9]

Later it was written of Vaughan, in regard to a 1933 piece he wrote for *The Sporting News*, "In a recent issue Irving Vaughan comes out and says that he has a growing suspicion that the Cubs are not the ball club they were cracked up to be; that their successful drive last year was no glory to the Cubs, but … was the result of Pittsburgh's almost unbelievable breakdown when it appeared the Pirates were 'in.'"[10]

And of the White Sox: "Becoming [the] Joke of [the] Major Leagues," Vaughan wrote in 1934, "the White Sox have less than half a dozen players of major league caliber. One major leaguer recently said that if he had his pick of the Sox he would choose only two, Simmons and Bonura. There are no more than three or four others worthy of a place on a big league team. The Sox have a futile scouting system. They have no young players coming up. The situation looks as bad, or worse, than it did after the Black Sox scandal."[11]

Such was the candor of Vaughan's work.

During the 1930s Vaughan entered into his third decade as a sports reporter. Around that time his writing, which was already nationally syndicated, became even more widely read when he became a correspondent for *The Sporting News*. There, he drew on his longevity in the business to pen a series entitled "Freak Happenings in Ball Games," which featured such bizarre occurrences as St. Louis Browns third baseman Art Griggs, who once, with a runner on third, had a bad-hop grounder carom off his head into the stands at Boston's Huntington Avenue Grounds, allowing the runner to score; Cubs

third baseman Norm McMillan, who hit a 75-foot home run during the 1929 pennant chase; Indians catcher Steve O'Neill, who in a 1917 game versus the White Sox, struck out on a wild pitch that should have been an out, took first and moments later scored the winning run; and the afternoon when Frank Chance, then managing the New York Yankees, batted twice in the same inning during a rally, yet in two different spots in the order, once as a pinch-hitter in the ninth spot and in his next trip in the eighth spot.

Also, in the beginning of the 1930s, Vaughan, who was well compensated for his work (according to the 1940 census, his salary was $5,000 annually), became a world traveler. On July 9, 1918, he had wed Loretto Lalor, who was called Peggy. They remained together until Vaughan's death 45 years later. Childless, the two became enthusiastic tourists. In 1931 the couple spent time wandering around Europe, and during four successive winters made trips around the world. On one of those excursions their traveling partners were reportedly Mr. and Mrs. George Herman Ruth.

Whether the latter trip occurred before or after the 1932 World Series is unclear, but in that Series Vaughan was a witness to Ruth's "called shot" home run. It occurred in the fifth inning of Game Three. That day, neither Ed Burns, whose story of the game appeared on page 1 of the *Tribune*, nor Vaughan, whose account led off the sports page, made mention of Ruth's pointing to center field or calling his home run. As Vaughan wrote, "There was something more surprising about the wallop than the distance it traveled or the fact that it was made off a slow pitch. That was the conditions under which Ruth turned it loose." After pitcher Charlie Root "blazed in two strikes, Ruth turned to the Cubs dugout and bellowed, 'That is only two strikes, boys, I still have one coming.'"[12] Then Ruth knocked the next pitch into the center-field bleachers. It's intriguing to envision Ruth and Vaughan discussing the hit on their around-the-world adventure, but if that talk ever happened, it seems Vaughan never confessed.

Undoubtedly Vaughan lived those times with a heavy heart. On April 7, 1932, while he was in Kansas City with the Cubs he received word that his brother Manning had died. A week before, while in Memphis, Tennessee, covering the American Association's Milwaukee Brewers, Manning, who had left the *Milwaukee Sentinel* and was now sports editor of the *Milwaukee Journal*, was found unconscious in his room at Memphis's Frisco Hotel. Manning was taken to Hot Springs, Arkansas, for treatment by a physician, and was later transferred to Barnes Hospital in St. Louis, where he was pronounced dead. Irving told the press that Manning had collapsed in the lobby of the Memphis hotel; the coroner later returned a verdict of a fractured skull suffered when Manning fell out of bed. In either case, Irving had lost his brother. That day, Irving flew to St. Louis to handle Manning's funeral arrangements. Manning Vaughan was 45 years old. (The Milwaukee Braves later created the Manning Vaughan Award, in recognition of the team's MVP. Among the recipients were Joe Torre and Hank Aaron.)

For the remainder of his career, as Vaughan continued to report on Chicago's sports fortunes (when the baseball season was over, he followed his second love, college football), he simultaneously ascended the hierarchy of his profession's local and national assemblage, the Baseball Writers Association of America. In April 1933 Vaughan was elected secretary of the BBWAA's Chicago chapter, and two years later assumed the role of chairman, during which he played an important role in negotiations for the first All-Star Game, sponsored by the *Trib*. Three years later, in their annual meeting, held in New York, Vaughan was elected vice president of the BBWAA. And finally, on October 9, 1937, he was unanimously elected president of the BBWAA. There was no opposition. (Under Vaughan's presidency, the BBWAA voted to change the method in which MVPs in two major leagues were selected. While previously two committees composed of one writer from each of eight cities selected each league's MVP, under Vaughan a committee of 24 writers, three from each city, made the selections. The point-scoring system for voting was also changed. In 1947, when Ed Burns was elected president of the BBWAA, Vaughan was named to the board of directors.)

In 1952 Vaughan was one of six veteran writers from the BBWAA's Chicago chapter selected to name the first

official all-time, all-star Cubs team. (The choices were pitcher Mordecai Brown, catcher Gabby Hartnett, and outfielder Hack Wilson, all named unanimously, as well as pitchers Jim Vaughn, Lon Warneke, and Charlie Root; infielders Charlie Grimm, Billy Herman, Billy Jurges, and Stan Hack; and outfielders Kiki Cuyler and Riggs Stephenson.[13])

A year later, Vaughan produced for syndication "Baseball Worth Remembering," a series of "True Life Stories of Baseball Greats" that "recall[ed] many of the history-making games and amusing incidents that have made baseball America's favorite sport and baseball players the idols of American youth."[14] ("Ever hear of a double-no-hit baseball game in which the final score was 1 to 0? If not, turn to the *Times Signal* sports section tomorrow";[15] "If you are not old enough to speak with authority on the memorable feat of Charley Robertson who pitched a perfect game for the Chicago White Sox in 1922";[16] "Like to know how the Chicago Cubs broke Rube Marquard's 19-game victory string? Fine. Just turn to the *Times Signal* sports section."[17])

On November 1, 1957, Vaughan, aged 68, announced his retirement from the *Tribune* sports staff. At the time he was the only baseball writer to have covered two perfect games, Charley Robertson's 2-0 triumph for the White Sox over the Detroit Tigers on April 30, 1922, and Don Larsen's World Series win for the Yankees over the Brooklyn Dodgers in 1956. Additionally, he had reported on numerous other no-hit performances, including those of Ed Walsh, Joe Benz, Jimmy Lavender, Vern Kennedy, Bill Dietrich, and Bob Feller. In 1941 the Vaughans had moved to Lake Villa, Illinois. In July 1963 they moved to Waukegan, Illinois, where Vaughan, after a long illness, died at his home in the early morning of November 22, 1963, at 74. He was cremated, and his ashes were placed in a crypt beside those of his brother Manning, in Valhalla Cemetery, Milwaukee.

SOURCES

Chicago Tribune

Chicago Star Publications

Decatur (Illinois) *Review*

Janesville (Wisconsin) *Gazette*

Kansas City (Missouri) *Star*

Lacrosse (Wisconsin) *Tribune*

Madison (Wisconsin) *State Journal*

Madison (Wisconsin) *Capital Times*

Manitowoc (Wisconsin) *Herald News*

Mason City (Iowa) *Globe Gazette*

Moorhead (Minnesota) *Daily News*

Salt Lake (Utah) *Tribune*

San Antonio (Texas) *Express*

The Sporting News

Valparaiso (Indiana) *Vidette Messenger*

Waterloo (Iowa) *Evening Journal*

Waterloo (Iowa) *Daily Courier*

Zanesville (Ohio) *Signal*

Baseball-reference.com

Baseball-fever.com

Sincerest thanks to SABR member Bill Mortell for his diligent genealogical research.

NOTES

1 *Janesville* (Wisconsin) *Gazette*, November 1, 1957.

2 *Chicago Tribune*, November 23, 1963, via baseball-fever.com.

3 Baseball-fever.com/showthread.
php?57538-Meet-The-Sports-Writers/page2.

4 *Decatur* (Illinois) *Review*, December 9, 1921.

5 *Waterloo* (Iowa) *Evening Courier*, July 2, 1925.

6 *Salt Lake Tribune*, July 4, 1943.

7 *Chicago Tribune*, November 23, 1963, via baseball-fever.com.

8 *The Sporting News*, December 24, 1925.

9 *The Sporting News*, September 12, 1929.

10 *Waterloo* (Iowa) *Daily Courier*, May 11, 1933.

11 United Press, *Moorhead* (Minnesota) *Daily News*, August 9, 1934.

12 Robert Markus, "Three Chi Writers Saw Ruth's Homer Differently," *The Sporting News*, December 12, 1970.

13 *Madison* (Wisconsin) *Capital Times*, February 5, 1952.

14 *Chicago Star Publications*, January 20, 1953.

15 *Zanesville* (Ohio) *Signal*, February 14, 1953.

16 *Zanesville* (Ohio) *Signal*, March 21, 1953.

17 *Zanesville* (Ohio) *Signal*, March 28, 1953.

BOB ELSON

By Fred Taylor

OB ELSON BROADCAST CHICAGO Cubs games over the radio from 1929 through 1941. A radio pioneer, Elson got his start at a time when only home games were broadcast live. (Some road games were "re-created" after the fact from ticker-tape transmissions.[1]) This gave Elson the opportunity to also do Chicago White Sox home games when the Cubs were on the road. Elson was named "Announcer of the Year" by *The Sporting News* in 1940 and 1941. He signed on with the Navy from 1942 through 1945, rising to the rank of commander, and forevermore became known as "The Commander" (or "the Old Commander") while broadcasting for the White Sox from 1946 through 1970.

Robert Adolph Elson was born in Chicago on March 22, 1904, to Charles Otto Elson and Anne Elizabeth (Chambers) Elson. He was of German and Swedish ancestry and the oldest of four children. His father alternatively listed his occupation as bookkeeper and salesman for a glass company. Several years before his death in 1941, Charles was a clerk at the Cook County Treasurer's Office. At the age of 9, Bob displayed his singing talents with the Paulist Chorister Choir of Chicago and toured Europe. He attended Loyola University in Chicago before transferring to Northwestern University in suburban Evanston to study medicine. "I was going to be a doctor," Elson said in 1979. "I would have killed thousands of people by now if I had."[2]

While on vacation in St. Louis in 1928, Elson stayed at the Chase Park Plaza Hotel. Its top floor was home to radio station KWK, and Elson decided to take a tour. "I'd never been in a studio in my life," he later recalled. He wound up in a line with about 40 other men, and the receptionist mistakenly thought he was there for an audition contest the station was running. "They told me not to be nervous. Nervous? I didn't even know what I was doing," a surprised Elson recalled after he was selected to become the station's new announcer.[3] The story made its way to the newspapers in Chicago and Elson was quickly hired by the station manager at WGN Radio in Chicago.

The first owner to see radio's promise was William Wrigley of the Cubs. Unlike the owners in New York and Brooklyn, who by 1932 had banned all radio transmission of their games, Wrigley and his son, Phil, invited Chicago stations to carry Cubs games free of charge. "Forget sponsors, nobody paid for the privilege of carrying games," according to Hal Totten, another early Cubs broadcaster.[4] By 1929, seven Chicago stations aired the Cubs and White Sox, Elson joining with Quin Ryan on WGN. Elson broadcast baseball games by day and announced big-band music at night.

Elson continued his dual role of broadcasting Cubs and White Sox games for 13 years through 1941. Beginning in 1929, he was selected by Baseball Commissioner Kenesaw Mountain Landis to serve as one of the broadcasters for the World Series, the first of his 13 years as a World Series commentator ending with the 1941 Series. "I'll have to admit my friendship with Landis helped," Elson said in 1970.[5] He was a frequent luncheon companion of the commissioner. "Today everyone you know is on some kind of a diet. I never ate lunch with the judge when he didn't order three big ears of corn and a piece of cherry pie. And the guy never had a sick moment," Elson related in in a 1966 interview.[6]

Landis had several rules for anyone announcing World Series games. He dismissed one announcer for his criticism of the umpires and he had a standing requirement for movie actors in the stands: Don't mention any movie stars attending the World Series "even if they slide into second base. They haven't been around all year, but they're here now. Gentlemen, I don't want any of those Hollywood characters named on the radio. The World Series is for baseball people."[7]

Elson witnessed Babe Ruth's purported "called-shot" home run during Game Three of the 1932 World Series at Wrigley Field. He was probably in the minority who thought the moment was real. "I definitely know he pointed to center field, There was no doubt about it, he did call his shot," Elson said. "It was only right" was a typical Elson laconic response to another famous Ruth homer — at the first-ever All-Star Game, played in 1933 at Comiskey Park.[8] Elson broadcast nine All-Star Games in the 1930s and 1940s.

In 1931 Elson conducted the first on-field radio interview, running a wire from the broadcast booth to the field in order to talk to Connie Mack. "Judge Landis said it was okay to run a wire from the booth. At first players were antsy. Before long they got the swing," was Elson's description many years later.[9] He once said he enjoyed interviews as much as or more than doing play-by-play.

When asked in 1966 to name his most memorable baseball moments, Elson said they were Gabby Hartnett's "homer in the gloamin'" on September 28, 1938, at Wrigley Field and Ted Williams winning the 1941 All-Star Game with a three-run homer in the bottom of the ninth inning at Tiger Stadium. He listed his favorite players as Joe DiMaggio ("the greatest player I saw in 40 years,") Lou Gehrig, Babe Ruth, and Willie Mays.[10] But interviewing the Yankee Clipper was a different matter: "DiMaggio was my toughest interview. He was the world's greatest introvert."[11]

Elson was instrumental in bringing Jack Brickhouse to Chicago as his assistant broadcaster in 1940. "I'd gotten to know Bob when he came (to Peoria, Illinois, where Brickhouse was a broadcaster) for personal appearances, and we got to be friendly," Brickhouse related years later, "so without me even knowing it, he arranged an audition." On the wall of Brickhouse's home he kept the original telegram for years: "Expect call from WGN as a staff announcer and sports assistant. Remember, if asked, you know all about baseball. Best of luck, Bob Elson."[12] When Elson went into the Navy in 1942, Brickhouse was his replacement.

Elson was a many-faceted person who excelled in so many areas besides baseball that he might be called a Renaissance Man. He was an expert at gin rummy; Elson said he was so good that "just about no players in the cities we visit will play with me anymore."[13] When sportswriter Jerome Holtzman asked for lessons, Elson told him "That is like asking Jascha Heifetz to teach you to play the violin. I give lessons, but they will cost you."[14] White Sox manager

Paul Richards banned his players from playing with Elson in the early 1950s because they were losing so much money. Later, another manager, Al Lopez, said Elson could memorize the cards that had been discarded better than anyone he ever saw.

Elson claimed that John Kuenster, the longtime editor of *Baseball Digest*, lost enough money to him playing gin to finance the wedding of one of Elson's daughters. During one "slaughter," Kuenster didn't notice until after the game that Elson was reading Kuenster's cards from a mirror conveniently placed on the wall behind Kuenster's back.

Elson's proclivity for betting on anything was well-known. Stationed at the Great Lakes Naval Training Center in World War II, he frequently wagered on his ability at basketball by taking on his fellow seamen in free-throw contests. He usually won, until he challenged future tennis pro Bobby Riggs. Elson bet $1,000 on Notre Dame against Army in a 1946 football contest with Army, then had headphones attached to the broadcast of that game while he did play-by-play for a Big 10 football contest. The

A radio pioneer, Elson broadcast Cubs games and served as one of the broadcasters for the World Series from 1929 to 1941. (National Baseball Hall of Fame)

Army-Notre Dame game ended in a 0-0 tie. At the other extreme, Elson was known to pitch pennies with parking-lot attendants.

In describing himself and fellow announcer Red Barber, Elson said, "We were first and foremost newsmen, not some jock announcer, and we both followed the news of the front page and outside world more continually, more avidly, than anything some sports page might headline."[15] For years, starting in the 1930s, Elson hosted a radio program from Chicago's Pump Room restaurant in the Ambassador East Hotel. He spoke with everyone from politicians (Jack and Robert Kennedy) to entertainers (Frank Sinatra and Elizabeth Taylor) to leaders of industry to auto mechanics. He did the same at Chicago's LaSalle Street Station, interviewing VIPs as they boarded or exited the Twentieth Century Limited train. If a guest gave too short an answer, Elson's distance from the microphone and his demeanor would indicate to the interviewee that more was expected. He would therefore often get comments that surprised even the person who said them.

Elson's style both in and out of the broadcast booth was low on feeling but high on enunciation. His vocal inflections were always within a polite range. Both his words and the long pauses between them were crisply created. He was never a rambling radio voice. In baseball and other sports, Elson kept a distance between himself and the game, unlike Harry Caray, who was literally part of the event. Elson reported it more than announced it. You got the feeling that Elson did not really need the game in front of him to do a broadcast, possibly a result of the many re-created games he did in the 1930s, when broadcasters frequently had to embellish and improvise. The re-creations were some of his least favorite duties. "I'll tell you after doing a ticker doubleheader, six or seven hours in that hot little studio, you were talking to yourself," he told a journalist.[16]

Elson was never very emotional, something that increased criticism of him in his later years. Unlike the "back … back … back … Hey! Hey!" of Brickhouse or Caray's "It might be, it could be, it IS!!!!, a home run, Holy Cow!!"

Elson would say, "It's a home run" or invoke the name of the sponsor for a "Coca-Cola wallop."[17]

Elson blistered people he considered phonies, not only in sports but in politics and show business as well. He vented his opinions to close friends over dinner, but never on the air, where he was always a booster.

One of Elson's broadcast partners was Milo Hamilton, who considered him to be a "notorious freeloader" in a good-natured way.[18] Whenever they dined out, Elson always arranged for the younger, less-experienced Hamilton to pay the bill as well as the tip. Hamilton said that Elson "always had a caddy — a guy who would carry his briefcase, come to the station, take him to the ballpark, or pick him up at the airport after a road game. He never paid the guy in cash. He gave him tickets to games."[19]

On one occasion, Elson agreed to give his caddy half his speaking fee since it involved driving him 80 miles round-trip from Chicago to Joliet, Illinois. While Elson was in the men's room, the chairman handed the caddy an envelope with six $50 bills enclosed to pay Elson for his speech. The caddy, Vincent Garrity, opened the envelope and pocketed two of the bills. On the way home, Garrity handed the envelope to Elson, who opened it and didn't say a word. When Elson got out of the car, he threw a $50 bill at Garrity and said, "Would you believe those cheap sons-of-bitches only gave me $100?"[20]

Like a number of broadcasters, Milo Hamilton could do an excellent imitation of Elson's voice. Said Hamilton, "when people tell me I sound like him, they couldn't give me a greater compliment."[21]

By 1970, many fans believed Elson was too "old hat" and boring and was driving people away from the ballpark. White Sox owner John Allyn fired him as part of a desperate attempt to restore sagging attendance on the South Side of Chicago. The "generation gap," a term coined in the 1960s, had caught up with Elson. The younger generation wanted more color, more "tell-it-like-it-is" analysis. Elson belonged to a more laid-back, relaxed era. Like Jack Brickhouse, he was not going to criticize the players or the club paying his salary.

Fired by Charles Finley after one year of broadcasting Oakland A's games in 1971, Elson returned to Chicago. He broadcast Chicago Blackhawks hockey, something he had done for about 20 seasons starting in 1935. (Elson was also a Chicago Cardinals announcer for years until the NFL team moved to St. Louis in 1960.) He also resumed doing interviews for a Chicago radio station.

Elson once said that his only regret as a broadcaster was the time he had to spend away from his wife, three children, and other family members. In 1975 Elson's wife of many years, Jeanne Helen Kuhl, a former model, died. In 1979 Elson became the third recipient of the Ford C. Frick Award from the Baseball Hall of Fame, following Red Barber and Mel Allen.

Sportswriter Dave Condon said of Elson, "He was of the John Wayne mold. Though he could have retired in luxury, he remained behind the microphone and on the banquet circuit until a failing heart forced him to lighten the load.[22] On January 22, 1981, Elson was admitted to Augustana Hospital in Chicago because of continuing problems with heart trouble. He was never released and died there on March 10 at the age of 76. Almost until the end, he believed he would recover to continue the vocation he had pursued all of his working life. Regarding his never-completed autobiography, Elson said "The world has been good to me. The hard part is that if I wrote 1,000 pages, I still wouldn't be able to credit all the people who helped me."[23]

Despite Elson's accolades, there was no shortage of negative reaction to his broadcasting style. The broadcasting historian Curt Smith, hearing him for the first time, thought Elson "ungodly dull" and added, "He should have folded before the dealer closed."[24] White Sox historian Rich Lindberg was more direct "(W)e were put to sleep by the droning of Bob 'The Commander' Elson. if Marconi had heard Elson do a broadcast, he would have thrown the radio out the window."[25]

Another writer compared Harry Caray's arrival in the Comiskey Park booth in 1971: "Harry was much different, after so many seasons of the droll and dry broadcasts of Bob Elson, who was anything but part of the event. He would spend time talking about his recent gin rummy

conquest in the Bard's Room, or (Chicago restaurateur) Ernie Carroll's chili on a cold night, or the pitching exploits of Lon Warneke from ages past. Harry Caray, on the other hand, found countless ways to add excitement to his calling of action on the field."[26]

Elson felt sorry for players of limited skills who worked so hard to reach the majors, then tripped over their inadequacies and fell back into the minors. "They never had a chance to make it, so why should I add to their troubles?" he said. "I never knocked the umpires either. I thought they were at least 95 percent right. I made it a point to never criticize a player on the air, never second-guess a manager, never rap an owner. … People can question my abilities, but I hope they say as long as Bob Elson was on the air, he never hurt anybody."[27]

SOURCES

The author thanks Bill Mortell for his email assistance in this endeavor. Bill also furnished genealogical research on Bob Elson's family. Matthew Bohn generously shared his files of newspaper clippings on Elson and Bill Francis of the National Baseball Hall of Fame and Museum provided the Hall of Fame clip file on Bob Elson. All of their help was invaluable.

Hamilton, Milo, and Dan Schlossberg with Bob Ibach, *Making Airwaves* (Champaign, Illinois: Sports Publishing LLC, 2006).

Lindberg, Rich, *Stuck on the Sox* (Evanston, Illinois: Sassafras Press, 1978).

Pietrusza, David, *Judge and Jury* (South Bend, Indiana: Diamond Communications, 1998).

Smith, Curt, *Voices of the Game* (New York: Simon & Schuster, 1992).

Smith, Curt, *Voices of Summer* (New York: Carroll and Graf, 2005).

Thorn, John, and Pete Palmer, eds., *Total Baseball* (New York: Warner Books, 1989).

Condon, David, "Elson a celebrity who kept common touch," *Chicago Tribune*, March 12, 1981.

Craig, Jack, "sporTView," *The Sporting News*, June 13, 1970.

Lundquist, Carl, "35 Years on Airplanes, and Elson Flashes Zest of a Chisox Rookie," *The Sporting News*, August 6, 1966.

Monahan, Anthony, "The game is never over until Bob Elson says it is," *Chicago Sunday Sun-Times, Midwest Magazine*, February 28, 1971.

Olmstead, Bob, "Elson Mass on Friday, ex-'voice' of Cubs, Sox, *Chicago Sun-Times*, March 12,1981.

Powers, John, "Bob Elson, Dean of the Ballpark," *Chicago Magazine*, August 1979.

Shnay, Jerry, "The Years Have Been Good to Bob Elson and Vice Versa," publication unknown, from Hall of Fame clipping file on Elson.

Sons, Ray, "Elson voiced the style of a generation," *Chicago Sun-Times*, March 12, 1981.

"Ex-'voice' of Chisox, Cubs ex-med student," *Augusta* (Georgia) *Chronicle*, August 8, 1979.

"Holy Cow! When Harry came to town — fun at the old ballpark," allthingswhitesox.com, accessed February 2014.

NOTES

1   Early in Ronald Reagan's career as an entertainer, he broadcast re-creations of Cubs games over radio station WHO in Des Moines.

2   "Ex-'voice' of Chisox, Cubs ex-med student," *Augusta* (Georgia) *Chronicle*, August 8, 1979.

3   Ibid.

4   Curt Smith, *Voices of Summer* (New York: Carroll and Graf, 2005), 11.

5   Jack Craig, "sporTView," *The Sporting News*, June 13, 1970, 34.

6   Carl Lundquist, "35 Years on Airplanes, and Elson Flashes Zest of a Chisox Rookie," *The Sporting News*, August 6, 1966, 8.

7   David Pietrusza, *Judge and Jury* (South Bend, Indiana: Diamond Communications, 1998), 344.

8   Jerry Shnay, "The Years Have Been Good to Bob Elson and Vice Versa," publication unknown, from Hall of Fame clipping file on Elson.

9   Smith, *Voices of Summer*, 18.

10   "Ex-'voice' of Chisox, Cubs ex-med student."

11   Ray Sons, "Elson voiced the style of a generation," *Chicago Sun-Times*, March 12, 1981.

12   Ibid.

13   Craig.

14   Sons.

15   Curt Smith, *Voices of the Game*, 48.

16   Anthony Monahan, "The game is never over until Bob Elson says it is," *Chicago Sunday Sun-Times, Midwest Magazine*, February 28, 1971, 14.

17   John Powers, "Bob Elson, Dean of the Ballpark," *Chicago Magazine*, August 1979.

18   Milo Hamilton, *Making Airwaves* (Champaign, Illinois: Sports Publishing LLC, 2006), 63.

19   Hamilton.

20   Hamilton.

21   Hamilton.

22   David Condon, "Elson a celebrity who kept common touch," *Chicago Tribune*, March 12, 1981.

23   Smith, *Voices of Summer*, 20.

24   Smith, *Voices of Summer*, 17.

25   Rich Lindberg, *Stuck on the Sox* (Evanston, Illinois: Sassafras Press, 1978), 21.

26   Bob Olmstead, "Elson Mass on Friday, ex-'voice' of Cubs, Sox," *Chicago Sun-Times*, March 12, 1981. "Holy Cow! When Harry came to town — fun at the old ballpark," allthingswhitesox.com

27   Olmstead.

CHICAGO CUBS
1929 SEASON SUMMARY

By Gregory H. Wolf

ALL HEADLINES ARE FROM THE NEXT day's edition of the *Chicago Daily Tribune*, unless otherwise noted.

April 16. **50,000 SEE PITTSBURGH BEAT CUBS, 4-3. PIRATES GATHER 3 RUNS AGAINST ROOT IN FIRST.**

On a cold, 47-degree day, an estimated 48,000 spectators and another 3,000 in the park flooded Wrigley Field. With fans pouring out onto the field, ground rules were enacted more than an hour before the game. The Pirates loaded the bases in each of the first three innings off Charlie Root but managed only three runs until they plated another tally in the seventh. Thirty-five-year-old Burleigh Grimes, coming off a career-high 25 wins the previous season, held the Cubs scoreless until the eighth, when Riggs Stephenson singled home Kiki Cuyler for the first Cubs run to make it 4-1. With the bases filled, pinch-hitter Gabby Hartnett struck out. The Cubs rallied for two more runs in the ninth, but came up short as they stranded 12 runners on base.

The Cubs' Opening Day lineup was:

Woody English	SS
Clyde Beck	3B
Kiki Cuyler	RF
Rogers Hornsby	2B
Hack Wilson	CF
Riggs Stephenson	LF
Charlie Grimm	1B
Mike Gonzalez	C
Charlie Root	P

April 17. **CUBS HOME RUN BARRAGE BEAT PIRATES, 13-2. STEVIE, GRIMM, AND HORNSBY HIT FOR CIRCUIT.** The Cubs Murderer's Row assaulted four Pirates pitchers for 15 hits and drew six walks. The attack commenced in the first inning when Hack Wilson smacked a two-run double and Riggs Stephenson belted a three-run homer to give the Cubs a five-run lead. Big

Pat Malone corralled the Pirates on six hits. Wilson had a season-high four hits and Rogers Hornsby drove in four runs.

April 18. **BLAKE GIVES ONLY 4 HITS; CUBS WIN, 11-1. CHARLEY GRIMM EARNS PLACE IN SLUGGERS UNION.** First Baseman Charlie Grimm, the only left-handed hitter in the Cubs lineup, launched a grand slam in the third inning and Hack Wilson hit his first homer of the season as the Cubs scorched the Pirates for 13 hits in an assault that beat reporter Edward Burns called "ruthless." Fred "Sheriff" Blake handcuffed the Pirates on four singles.

April 19. Pittsburgh Pirates at Chicago: rained out.

April 20. St. Louis Cardinals at Chicago: rained out.

April 21. **51,000 WATCH CUBS DEAFEAT CARDINALS, 4-0. RAJAH PROVES TROUBLE-MAKER. YES, SIR! 'N' HOW!** In front of the largest crowd ever assembled at Wrigley Field, Rogers Hornsby went 4-for-4 with two doubles and drove in the first two runs of the game against his former team. Guy "Mississippi Mudcat" Bush tossed a three-hitter to silence the Cardinals bats.

April 22. **MALONE'S ARM, HORNSBY'S BAT CHECK CARDS.** With hits in his first two at-bats, including a home run, Hornsby registered seven consecutive hits over three games. The Rajah and Kiki Cuyler (3) recorded half of the team's ten safeties off ex-Cub Grover Cleveland "Pete" Alexander. Big right-hander Pat Malone tossed a five-hitter to lead the Cubs to a 3-0 victory in front of 32,000.

April 23. **TWO CUBS CATCHERS HURT AS CARDINALS WIN, 9 TO 6.** The Cubs catching corps was the team's weak link all reason, with inspirational leader Gabby Hartnett suffering from a mysterious dead arm that limited him to just one game behind the plate all season. The situation worsened when 38-year-old

Miguel "Mike" Gonzalez, from Cuba, injured his hand in the fifth inning, leading to the big-league debut of two catchers in the same frame. Twenty-two-year-old Earl Grace's debut was cut short, literally, when the first ball he caught sheared off a fingernail. He was replaced by Tom Angley, who played in his first of five big-league games. The Cubs pounded out 15 hits off slowball whiz, Bill "Wee Willie" Sherdel," including a 4-for-4 performance by left fielder Riggs Stephenson. But Frankie Frisch's three hits and three runs batted in led the Cardinals 16-hit attack en route to a 9-6 victory.

April 24. CUBS LOSE TO PIRATES, 5-4, IN 13 INNINGS. Chicago inaugurated a season-high 19-game Eastern swing with a three-game set at spacious Forbes Field in Pittsburgh. The Pirates' Burleigh Grimes held the Cubs to seven hits over 11 innings and Steve Swetonic hurled the final two scoreless frames to earn the win on Earl Sheely's walk-off double scoring Pie Traynor. Tom Angley went 3-for-5 with two runs batted in, and 155-pound right-hander, Trader Horne was a tough-luck loser in his major-league debut after tossing three-hit ball over 6⅓ innings of relief.

April 25. Chicago at Pittsburgh: rained out.

April 26. HORNSBY'S TRIPLE HELPS CUBS WIN, 9-6. Down 3-0 after two innings, the Cubs exploded for five runs in the third inning off Ray Kremer, led by Rogers Hornsby's bases-loaded triple. Catcher Johnny Schulte, purchased two days earlier from the Columbus (Ohio) Senators in the American Association, chipped in with two hits in his Cubs debut. Guy Bush pitched erratically (six hits, six walks, and six runs over eight innings) but he still picked up the win.

April 27. SCHULTE HELPS ON ATTACK, THEN HALTS CORSAIRS' RALLY. En route to their sixth win in eight games, the Cubs experienced a scare in the ninth inning, when Hornsby muffed Pie Traynor's routine double-play grounder. Pittsburgh scored three runs to make it a game, 8-7, and had a man on second base with no outs. Sheriff Blake whiffed Dick Bartell and then Johnny Schulte did the rest by catching Erv Brame's foul pop and fielding Bob Linton's tapper in front of home plate and rifling a throw to first sacker Charlie Grimm

to secure the win. Schulte also chipped in with a career-high four runs batted in.

April 28. REDS OUTRACE CUBS, 17-12. NO FOOLIN', FOUR BRUIN PITCHERS GOT A TANNING. The Cincinnati Reds exploded for 12 runs in the first three innings off Cubs starter Hal Carlson and reliever Trader Horne. The Cubs came roaring back in the fifth inning when they batted around (highlighted by Hack Wilson's two-run home run and two-run single), scoring eight times to pull within one run, 12-11. But left-hander Art Nehf, making his first appearance of the year, gave up four runs in the bottom of the fifth. The Cubs hurlers surrendered a season-high 21 hits and their catchers also committed two errors. Catcher Schulte was spiked in the third inning, reducing the team to just one catcher (Tom Angley). Schulte would not don the tools of ignorance again until May 30.

April 29. CHARLEY FANS 8, TURNS IN 4-3 TRIUMPH. Right-hander Charlie Root picked up his first victory of the season by holding the Reds to three runs and nine hits in a complete game. The Cubs scored all four of their runs in the sixth inning. Charlie Grimm belted a two-run double, Angley singled home Riggs Stephenson, and Root connected for a single to drive in Grimm for the game-deciding run.

April 30. MURDERERS' ROW SLUGS, BUT REDS BEAT CUBS, 5-4. Quiet for the first seven innings, the Cubs took leads in the eighth (home run by Rogers Hornsby and RBI single by Riggs Stephenson) and again in the ninth inning (RBIs by Hack Wilson and Charlie Grimm), but the Reds answered back each inning off starter Sheriff Blake. Hughie Critz ended the game on a walk-off sacrifice fly that scored pinch-runner Pinky Pittenger.

NL Standings, after games played on April 30, 1929

Team	Won	Lost	Tie	Pct	GB
Boston Braves	7	2	0	.778	·
Chicago Cubs	7	5	0	.583	1.5
St Louis Cardinals	7	5	0	.583	1.5
New York Giants	4	4	0	.500	2.5
Cincinnati Reds	5	7	0	.417	3.5
Philadelphia Phillies	4	6	0	.400	3.5
Pittsburgh Pirates	4	6	0	.400	3.5
Brooklyn Robins	4	7	0	.364	4

May 1. REDS AND CUBS PLAY TO 13-INNING TIE, 4-4. The final contest of a four-game series at Redland Field was called after 13 innings because the Cubs had to rush to Union Terminal in Cincinnati to catch their train for Philadelphia. The Cubs were leading, 4-2, with two outs in the bottom of the ninth inning when Guy Bush surrendered a two-run double to Hughie Critz to force the game into extra innings. After Bush's season-high 11-inning effort, Charlie Root pitched two crafty innings of relief. With a man on third and one out in each inning, he intentionally loaded the bases, but didn't yield a run.

May 2. Chicago at Philadelphia rained out.

May 3. Chicago at Philadelphia rained out.

May 4. CUBS TROUNCE PHILLIES TWICE, 16-0 AND 9-7. GRACE, CUYLER AND HORNSBY CLOUT HOMERS. Two successive rainouts forced a doubleheader at the Baker Bowl on Saturday afternoon. The North Siders exploded for 16 runs in the first game, led by Hornsby scoring four and Hack Wilson three. Six Cubs hitters notched at least two hits, including three by Wilson, Charlie Grimm, and pitcher Pat Malone, who also knocked in three runs. Malone tossed a 10-hit shutout, surrendering at least one hit in each inning, for his fourth consecutive victory.

Down 2-0 after one inning in the second game, the Cubs exploded for nine runs combined in the second and third innings. Catcher Earl Grace launched a three-run homer for his first big-league hit, and right fielder Kiki Cuyler connected for his first round-tripper of the season. Left fielder Riggs Stephenson continued his torrid pace, going 2-for-4. The notoriously streaky hitter has gone 21-for-38 (.553) in his last ten games with 12 runs scored and 10 walks for a .646 on-base percentage. McCarthy let his favorite pitcher, Charlie Root, go the distance despite allowing 12 hits, seven earned runs, and five walks.

May 5. No Game in Philadelphia scheduled. Strict blue laws in the City of Brotherly Love prohibited professional baseball games on Sunday. The first legal Sunday game took place on April 8, 1934.

May 6. BLAKE ALLOWS 4 HITS, TWO ERRORS HELP QUAKER CAUSE. Sheriff Blake pitched masterfully through eight innings, holding the Phillies to just two singles and one unearned run. But the Cubs offense stalled and managed only five hits and a run off Claude Willoughby. With one out in the ninth, Blake committed a costly error, dropping Charlie Grimm's throw while covering first base. Blake gave up two more singles, the latter a game-winning walk-off single by Pinky Whitney which, according to Edward Burns, was a "humiliating licking," 2-1.[1]

May 7. STEPHENSON AND GRIMM HIT 'EM, NEHF HOLDS 'EM. In the first start of his final season, 15-year veteran, southpaw Art Nehf tossed a nine-hit complete-game to defeat the Brooklyn Robins, 9-4. Riggs Stephenson went 2-for-4, with four runs batted in and a season-high four runs scored. Charlie Grimm belted two home runs in a game for the second and last time in his career.

May 8. CUBS TAKE LEAD; HARTNETT TOLD ARM IS O.K. The Cubs moved into sole possession of first place for the first time all season behind the strong pitching of Guy Bush, who limited the Robins to seven hits to win his third straight decision, 4-2. The Cubs did their damage in the sixth, scoring three times courtesy of Hack Wilson's single and shoddy Brooklyn defense. The big news of the day concerning catcher Gabby Hartnett gave the Cubs hope. Physicians at the Johns Hopkins Hospital in Baltimore after examining his right shoulder deter-

Preparing for a night out. Pitcher Guy Bush, catcher Gabby Hartnett and pitcher Charlie Root. (Retro Images Archive. George Brace Collection)

mined that "nothing was wrong" and that he could begin throwing.[2]

May 9. CUBS SWEEP BROOKLYN SERIES; WIN 11 TO 2. The vaunted Cubs offense victimized three Robins pitchers for six runs in the first inning. In a balanced 11-hit attack, Hack Wilson connected for a home run while shortstop and leadoff hitter Woody English scored three times, and right fielder Kiki Cuyler reached base five times. Big Pat Malone won his fifth consecutive decision in convincing fashion, holding Brooklyn to six hits and whiffing seven.

May 10. ROOT, GRACE LEAD CUBS ATTACK; GIANTS FALL 11-4. Catcher Earl Grace (2-for-4 and three RBIs) and hurler Charlie Root (2-for-3 with a career-high four runs batted in and a home run) led a 13-hit Cubs attack in the Polo Grounds. Riggs Stephenson continued his hot hitting (.434 for the season so far) by collecting three hits. The Cubs improved to 13-6.

May 11. CUBS HELD TO TWO HITS AS GIANTS WIN, 6-0. New York right-hander Larry Benton, who had tied for the NL lead with 25 victories the previous season, picked up his first win of the season in dominant fashion, allowing only six balls out of the infield, including the Cubs two hits. The Cubs suffered their first of five shutouts of the season. Tough-luck hurler Sheriff Blake lost his third straight start despite yielding just five earned runs in 23⅔ innings during the stretch.

May 12. CUBS TIE GIANTS, 6-6; HARTNETT GETS HOMER. An estimated 55,000 spectators showed up on a Sunday afternoon to watch the Cubs and Giants battle at the Polo Grounds to a 6-6 tie before the game was called in the 11th inning because of rain. The Cubs pounded Carl Hubbell, who had no-hit the Pittsburgh Pirates in his previous outing, for nine hits and five runs in seven innings, including pinch-hitter Gabby Hartnett's only home run of the season, a three-run blast. The Giants chased starter Art Nehf in the sixth inning and later tagged Guy Bush, in his first relief outing of the season, for five hits and two runs (one earned) in three innings.

May 13. CUBS REGAIN FIRST PLACE; BEAT BRAVES, 6-4. Playing without regular outfielders Kiki Cuyler and Hack Wilson, who were both injured the previous day in New York, the Cubs got on the winning track. Slumping leadoff hitter Woody English was dropped to the two-hole and responded by rapping four hits and scoring twice. Center fielder Johnny Moore had a day of firsts: in his first big-league start, he picked up his first two hits and three RBIs of his career. Charlie Root replaced Cubs starter Claude Jonnard after just two-thirds of an inning, and hurled 8⅓ innings of six-hit shutout ball to earn the win.

May 14. CUBS DROP 12 INNING DUEL TO BRAVES, 6-5. Against surprising third-place Boston, the Cubs managed just nine hits off Braves starter Ben Cantwell and reliever Johnny Cooney. The Cubs' Pat Malone went the distance, issuing seven walks and allowing 14 hits, including the walk-off double by catcher Al Spohrer with one out in the 12th as the Cubs fell back into a tie for first place with the St. Louis Cardinals.

May 15. CUBS TURN BACK BRAVES IN FINAL; HOME TOMORROW. The Cubs' 7-4 victory finished a grueling 19-game Eastern swing with an impressive 11-6 record, plus two ties. In a deliberate effort, every Cubs position player, except catcher Mike Gonzalez, hit safely, led by Riggs Stephenson's three hits. Kiki Cuyler returned from a two-day absence and connected for his fourth homer. Diminutive left-hander, Mike Cvengros (5-feet-8 and less than 160 pounds) relieved the normally sure Guy Bush and tossed 5⅓ innings of one-hit, shutout ball to pick up his first victory of the season.

May 16. No Game Scheduled.

May 17. CUBS BEAT REDS, 9 TO 3, IN HOMECOMING GAME. M'CARTHY MEN NOW ALONE ON TOP OF LADDER. In their first game in the friendly confines of Wrigley Field since April 23, the Cubs benefited from 19 baserunners (11 hits and eight walks) to win in a laugher. Hack Wilson returned after a three-game absence to bash a grand slam, his seventh homer of the season, and drove in four runs a total matched by Charlie Grimm, who belted his fifth round-tripper of the season. Sheriff Blake tossed a six-hit complete game and yielded just one earned run to pick up the victory.

May 18. ROOT WINS NO. 5 AS CUBS ROUT REDS, 7-0. The Cubs' 1-2-3 hitters (Norm McMillan, Woody English, and Kiki Cuyler) went a combined 9-for-13 and drove in all seven runs to propel the Cubs to victory. Charlie Root tossed a six-hit shutout to push his record to 5-1 and move the Cubs to a season-high 1½-game lead in the pennant race.

May 19. 45,000 SEE PIRATES TROUNCE CUBS, 4-1. The Pirates' Burleigh "Ol Stubblebeard" Grimes, who had tied for the NL lead with 25 victories the previous season, improved his record to 6-0 with a convincing seven-hitter. Pat Malone lost his second consecutive start, yielding nine hits and six walks in eight innings to disappoint a large crowd at Wrigley Field on a Sunday afternoon.

May 20. STEVE SWOOPS ONE FOR BUSH WITH THREE ON. The Cubs were leading the Pirates 2-1 in the eighth inning when Riggs Stephenson connected for a triple off rookie Steve Swetonic, clearing the bases. Hack Wilson reached base four times (two hits and two walks) and scored twice, as did Kiki Cuyler, who also recorded two hits. Guy Bush returned to form, tossing a five-hitter in a game that lasted only one hour and 41 minutes.

May 21. CUBS COME FROM FAR BACK TO BEAT PIRATES, 8-6. RAJAH'S HOMER LOFTS BRUINS OUT OF DEPTHS. On Boys Day at Wrigley Field, the Cubs found themselves in a 6-2 hole in the bottom of the fifth inning. They scored three runs in the fifth, highlighted by Rogers Hornsby's two-run home run, then took the lead the next inning on pinch-hitter Clyde Beck's RBI single and Woody English's groundout to drive in slow-footed catcher Mike Gonzalez. Trader Horne pitched 1⅓ innings of relief to earn his first and only big-league victory (though he won 229 in 21 years in the minors). The Cubs moved a season-high ten 10 games above .500.

May 22. No Game Scheduled.

May 23. CARDS WREST FIRST PLACE FROM CUBS. M'CARTHY MEN TOTTER BEFORE HIGH'S BIG BAT. The Cubs traveled to St. Louis for the first time this season for a battle of pennant frontrunners at Sportsman's Park. The Cubs tagged 37-year-old Clarence Mitchell for 11 hits, led by Woody English's four, but scored just three times. The NL's leading hitter at .420, Andy High collected three hits, including a home run, and knocked in four. Sheriff Blake absorbed the loss.

May 24. CUBS DEFEAT CARDINALS, 5-4. Wee Willie Sherdel, a 21-game winner in 1928, kept the Cubs scoreless until with one out in the sixth Rogers Hornsby's two-run single got Chicago to within a run, 3-2. Chicago took the lead in the eighth on RBI doubles by Hornsby, Hack Wilson, and Charlie Grimm. Pat Malone went the distance to pick up the victory after losses in his previous two outings; however, the Altoona, Pennsylvania, native was shaky, surrendering ten hits and issuing a then career-high eight walks (he would yield nine in a game against St. Louis in 1933).

May 25. CARDINALS DEFEAT CUBS IN 12TH INNING, 7 TO 6. VICTORY PUT ST. LOUIS BACK IN FIRST PLACE. The Cubs scored three runs in the eighth inning to take the lead, 6-5. But according to *Chicago Daily Tribune* writer Edward Burns, the Cubs "were guilty of one of their ninth inning blowup specials."[3] The Cardinals loaded the bases with no one out, but managed to score only one run to tie the game. Cardinals' relief pitcher Syl Johnson lined a walk-off single with one out in the 12th inning to win the game for himself. The loss kept the Cubs winless (three losses and two ties) in five extra-inning games for the season.

May 26. CUBS REGAIN LEAD BY DEFEATING REDS. Back home for just one game before departing on a road trip, the Cubs regained first place by handing the Reds their ninth consecutive loss. The Cubs' 4-5-6-7 hitters (Hornsby, Wilson, Stephenson, and Grimm) each collected two hits while the Rajah connected for his sixth round-tripper. Guy Bush scattered eight hits in a complete-game victory, 5-1.

May 27. REDS END LOSING STREAK; RALLY BEATS CUBS, 8-5. The Cubs were in command, 4-2, at Redland Field for a two-game set until the flood gates opened in the eighth inning. The Reds connected for six straight hits off starter and loser Sheriff Blake and reliever Charlie

Root en route a six-run outburst. Norm McMillan, Woody English, and Hornsby combined for eight of the team's ten hits, but the five through nine batters went a collective 2-for-19.

May 28. Chicago at Cincinnati rained out.

May 29. PIRATES BEAT CUBS IN BATTLE FOR FIRST PLACE, 7-2. In Pittsburgh to begin a three-game series at Forbes Field with the streaking second-place Pirates, Cubs starter Pat Malone was chased in the fifth inning after yielding six runs. The Cubs managed only one extra-base hit among their 11 safeties and left nine men on base in a lackluster performance to drop into second place.

May 30. CUBS DROP TO 3D PLACE; SPLIT WITH PIRATES. BRUINS VICTORS IN OPENER, 5-1, THEN LOSE, 4-0. In the first game of a doubleheader, Cubs starter Art Nehf scattered six hits over eight innings and yielded just one unearned run to notch his second victory of the season. Hack Wilson led the 13-hit assault by going 3-for-4 with three runs batted in to end the Pirates' eight-game winning streak. Rogers Hornsby continued his hot hitting, going 2-for-4, giving him 13 hits in his last 23 at-bats.

In the second game, Pirates starter Burleigh Grimes continued his dominance over the North Siders by tossing a seven-hit shutout and profiting from three double plays. Charlie Root had blanked Pittsburgh through seven innings before the Pirates exploded for four runs (three earned) as the Cubs experienced yet another late-game blow up. The team's fifth loss in the last eight games dropped them into third place.

May 31. No Game Scheduled.

NL Standings, after games played on May 31, 1929

Team	Won	Lost	Tie	Pct	GB
St. Louis Cardinals	26	15	1	.634	·
Pittsburgh Pirates	23	14	1	.622	1
Chicago Cubs	22	14	2	.611	1.5
Philadelphia Phillies	19	17	0	.528	4.5
New York Giants	17	17	1	.500	5.5
Boston Braves	15	23	0	.395	9.5
Brooklyn Robins	14	22	0	.389	9.5
Cincinnati Reds	12	26	1	.316	12.5

June 1. GIANTS CRUSH CUBS, 7-4, BEFORE 30,000. The Cubs returned to Wrigley Field to play just their 13th home game out of 39 so far this season. With the Cubs leading the New York Giants 4-3 through five innings, shortstop Clyde Beck (in his third game subbing for the injured Woody English) and third baseman Norm McMillan committed errors leading to four unearned runs off starter Guy Bush. Bush went the distance in the sloppy contest, but could not overcome 11 hits, five walks, and his teammates' four errors, and thus was the losing pitcher for the first time this season. The Cubs managed only eight hits off Carl Mays and Jack Scott and were defeated for the fourth time in five games.

June 2. GIANTS AGAIN BEAT CUBS, 4-1, BEFORE 40,000. BENTON THROWS 'EM PAST OUR "MURDER" ROW. The Cubs lost for the third consecutive game and fifth in six games as Giants right-hander Larry Benton corralled the North Siders on five hits. Norm McMillan's first home run of the season, in the bottom of the ninth, was the Cubs' only bright spot on a Sunday afternoon as Cubs starter Sheriff Blake fell to 2-7.

June 3. GIANTS WHIP CUBS, 8 TO 1; MAKE IT THREE STRAIGHT. HUBBELL SHOWS BRUINS THEY'RE ONLY LAMBSKINS. Chicago lost a season-high fourth straight game as the team's hitters continued to hibernate, managing just eight singles off Carl Hubbell, whose screwball the Cubs pounded in the dirt the entire game. The Giants became the first NL team since 1899 to play an entire game without making an outfield putout. After his 5-0 start to the season, Pat Malone was shelled for six runs and nine hits in five innings to lose for the fourth time in his last five starts, during which he has surrendered 25 earned runs in 38 innings. Part-time catcher Tom Angley, who appeared in five games during the last week of April, was given his unconditional release. The Cubs remained in third place as they fell to a season-high 3½ games off the NL lead.

June 4. CUBS HOME RUN STORM DROWN GIANTS, 10-9. The Cubs broke out of their offensive slump by smashing five home runs. With the game tied, 4-4, in the bottom of the fifth, Rogers Hornsby, Hack Wilson, and Charlie Grimm homered to propel the Cubs into a 9-4 lead. Wilson launched his second round-tripper in the seventh for much-needed insurance and a 10-7 lead. Cubs pitchers continued to struggle at home as starter (and winner) Art Nehf and reliever Charlie Root were victimized for 14 hits and nine runs.

June 5. CUBS WIN, 4-3, AS ROBINS TAKE FLIGHT IN NINTH. With the Brooklyn Robins leading, 3-0, in the ninth inning, future Hall of Fame shortstop Dave Bancroft booted two sure chances for double plays. Norm McMillan drove in the first run in the fateful frame by drawing a bases-loaded walk with one out. Still down by a run, pinch-hitter Gabby Hartnett lined starter Doug McWeeny's 3-2 pitch into center field to drive in Charlie Grimm and McMillan for the walk-off single. In the only start of his big-league career, the Cubs' Trader Horne yielded six hits and seven walks in five innings. Hal Carlson pitched a scoreless ninth to pick up his first win of the season.

June 6. BROOKLN GETS THE JUMP, BUT CUBS WIN, 8-6. "The Cubs are good clean livers," wrote Edward Burns, "and the gods again rewarded them for their righteous behavior."[4] The Robins clobbered starter Guy Bush for six runs before Pat Malone entered in relief with no outs in the third inning and hurled seven innings of shutout ball. Chicago managed only six hits (including solo home runs by Rogers Hornsby and Malone), but drew seven walks in a come-from-behind victory thanks to some shoddy defense as both teams committed three errors.

June 7. CUBS WIN, 11-2; SWEEP 3 GAME BROOKLYN SERIES. The Cubs won their fourth consecutive game and swept a three-game series for the first time since May 7-9 (also versus the Robins) by demolishing Brooklyn. Johnny Moore, starting in left field during the second of seven straight games for the injured Riggs Stephenson, had four hits, including his first home run of the season, drove in three runs, and scored twice. Charlie Grimm also knocked in three runs and Hack Wilson two in a strong team effort. Charlie Root tossed a four-hitter for his sixth victory.

June 8. CUBS DISSIPATE FOUR RUN LEAD, SO BRAVES TAKE OPENER, 5-4. Chicago was cruising along with a 4-0 lead when the wheels came off with two on in the seventh inning against starter Sheriff Blake. Shortstop Woody English made two consecutive errant throws on potential double-play balls; then Blake surrendered a three-run homer to George Harper. Boston right-hander Bob Smith scattered ten hits, but was also the victim of his team's porous defense as four Braves errors led to three unearned runs.

June 9. WILSON'S 11TH HOMER WINS FOR CUBS, 2-1. 35,000 WATCH NEHF, CANTWELL IN MOUND DUEL. In what Edward Burns described as "the classiest show of the year," 36-year-old Art Nehf, a 184-game winner in his 15th and final big-league season, and third-year veteran Ben Cantwell (who compiled a 76-108 record in 11 seasons) each tossed complete-game four-hit masterpieces.[5] With Rogers Hornsby on first base courtesy of a walk, Hack Wilson belted a two-run home run in the seventh inning to give the Cubs all the runs they needed to secure their fourth win in five games and remain in third place, 1½ games behind the league-leading Pittsburgh Pirates.

June 10. CUBS OUTSLUG BRAVES, 10 TO 8; GAIN ON PIRATES. Starter Hal Carlson and reliever Mike Cvengros were tagged for ten hits and eight runs in just 4⅔ innings before rubber-armed Guy Bush, who led all major-league pitchers with 50 appearances in 1929, held the Braves scoreless on three hits over the final 4⅓ innings to earn the win. Like their foes, the Cubs' mighty batters were swinging on all cylinders, pounding four Boston hurlers for 15 hits, led by Woody English's four. Johnny Moore, Norm McMillan, and Earl Grace each scored twice, as eight Cubs hitters knocked in a run.

June 11. Boston at Chicago: rained out.

June 12. CUBS DEFEAT PHILS, 7-3, AS MALONE FANS 12. Pat "The Black Knight" Malone struck out a career-best 12 batters (achieved twice) in a complete-game eight-hitter and led the offensive attack with two doubles as the Cubs rolled to their seventh win in eight games. In the seventh inning shortstop Woody English was knocked cold when Phillies first baseman Don Hurst collided with him on a stolen-base attempt. English was removed by stretcher and missed four games.

June 13. **RAIN RUINS FIVE INNINGS' OF LABOR FOR CUBS, PHILS.** On Ladies Day at Wrigley Field, rain forced the game to be called after five innings with the Cubs and Phillies tied, 0-0. Chicago's Charlie Root allowed only four hits while his counterpart, Philadelphia's Claude Willoughby, permitted just three. It was the Cubs' third of four ties on the season.

June 14. No Game Scheduled.

June 15. **HORNSBY'S HOMER SCORES 4; CUBS BEAT PHILS 8-7.** In their sixth extra-inning game of the season, the Cubs finally won one. In a scoreless game, the Phillies exploded for five runs off starter Guy Bush in the sixth inning. The Cubs roared back in the seventh, scoring six runs, highlighted by Rogers Hornsby's grand slam to take a 7-6 lead. Phillies' first baseman Don Hurst tied the game, 7-7, with a run-scoring single in the ninth inning. With one out and the bases filled in the tenth, pinch-hitter Riggs Stephenson (batting for the first time since June 4) popped a high foul ball which both Hurst and catcher Spud Davis went after. Reacting quickly, manager Joe McCarthy, coaching third base, sent Norm McMillan racing home for the winning run after the catch was made as the plate was left uncovered. The heads-up move was a thrilling end to a victory that elevated the Cubs into second place (by percentage points) over St. Louis.

June 16. **13 CUBS STRIKE OUT; PHILLIES WIN, 7 TO 2.** Phillies right-hander Ray Benge struck out a career-high 13 batters in an overpowering five-hit complete game.

Woody English, Charlie Root and Sheriff Blake pose before a game. (Retro Images Archive. George Brace Collection)

Cubs starter and loser Art Nehf was victimized for ten hits and three runs in five innings while reliever Hal Carlson continued his season-long struggles, surrendering three runs in one-third of an inning to raise his ERA to 14.21. The Cubs' loss dropped them into third place, just a game behind league-leading St. Louis.

June 17. **CARDINALS ROUT TWO CUBS PITCHERS; WIN 13-3.** The Cubs suffered their worst defeat of the season thus far as the Cardinals banged out 15 hits, including seven for extra bases, in a laugher. St. Louis scored eight runs in the sixth inning off starter and loser Charlie Root and struggling Trader Horne to make it 12-1, before Claude Jonnard was summoned from the far reaches of the bullpen for 3⅓ innings of mop-up work.

June 18. **CUBS BEAT CARDINALS, 13-6; WILSON HITS 2 HOMERS.** The Cubs scored as many runs on this Tuesday afternoon as they had in the previous four games combined. Hack Wilson smashed a two-run homer in the first, followed by a grand slam in the Cubs' seven-run fifth inning. Third baseman Clyde Beck went 3-for-6 with three runs batted in and Charlie Grimm scored three times in the 14-hit attack. Sheriff Blake pitched 6⅓ shaky innings (nine hits, five walks, and five runs) to end a four-game losing streak, and also took part in the slugfest by going 2-for-3 and scoring twice.

June 19. **CUBS TAKE LEAD; BEAT CARDS, 7-3 AND 11-3. 45,000 WATCH PANORAMA OF BRUIN BASE HITS.** With a doubleheader sweep of their archrivals, the Cubs moved into a tie for first place with the Pittsburgh Pirates. However just 3½ games separated them from the fourth-place New York Giants. In the first game, Rogers Hornsby went 4-for-4 with two doubles, drew a walk, and scored three times, while Hack Wilson connected for his third homer in two games and knocked in three runs. Pat Malone struck out ten in a complete game for his tenth victory.

In the second game, the Cubs scored three runs in the first and third innings and five in the sixth to trounce the Cardinals 11-3. All Cubs reached base, courtesy of nine hits and seven walks. Kiki Cuyler, Riggs Stephenson, Charlie Grimm, and Mike Gonzalez had two runs batted in each, while Cuyler scored three times, and Rogers

Hornsby and Hack Wilson twice. Guy Bush tossed a complete-game ten-hitter to improve to 7-1.

June 20. CUBS BEAT CARDS, 7-6. TIGHTEN GRIP ON LEAD. Hack Wilson continued his torrid hitting, slugging two more home runs (numbers 15 and 16) and driving in three runs, and Rogers Hornsby belted his 10th round-tripper as the Cubs beat the Cardinals for the fourth consecutive time. En route to his career-high and league-leading 43 stolen bases for the season, Kiki Cuyler swiped three bases for the third and last time in his career. Starter Art Nehf yielded five runs in five innings but still got the win. Charlie Root tossed four innings of relief. During the five-game series, the Cubs and Cardinals combined for 72 runs and 106 hits. The offensive show between the teams kept both managers busy as 21 pitchers were sent to the mound during the four days.

June 21. PIRATES TAKE FIRST PLACE; WHIP CUBS 14-3. 19,000 WOMEN WATCH GRIMES SUBDUE BRUINS. The Pirates' veteran spitball pitcher Burleigh Grimes disappointed what the *Chicago Tribune* described as the "largest ladies crowd in the history of baseball" by handing the North Siders their most lopsided defeat of the season this far.[6] The Cubs managed nine hits, including Hack Wilson's sixth home run in five games. Three Cubs pitchers, starter and loser Mike Cvengros (who lasted just two-thirds of an inning), Claude Jonnard, and Trader Horne, were pummeled for 18 hits.

June 22. PIRATES DEFEAT CUBS, 7-4; INCREASE LEAD. CORSAIRS PLANT 2D VICTORY IN TREASURE CHEST. For the third consecutive game, the Cubs starting pitcher struggled; this time it was Sheriff Blake, who permitted 15 baserunners (10 hits and five walks) and five runs in just 5⅔ innings. Charlie Grimm belted a two-run homer in the sixth to pull the Cubs to within one, 5-4. However, the Pirates tagged Charlie Root, in his second long relief outing in three days, for two runs, while Pittsburgh starter Ray Kremer tossed a seven-hit complete game.

June 23. PIRATES WHIP CUBS, 8 TO 7, BEFORE 50,000. The Cubs chased 33-year-old rookie hurler Heinie Meine in the third inning, but the Pirates' offensive juggernaut, led by the Waner brothers (Lloyd and Paul)

knocked out Pat Malone in the fifth inning in yet another poor outing by a Chicago starter (seven runs in 4⅓ innings). McCarthy used 19 players (and every position player) in search of a much-needed win. Pinch-hitter Gabby Hartnett stroked a double in the seventh inning to tie the game, 7-7. But Lloyd Waner's third hit of the game, a single in the eighth off loser Art Nehf, drove in what proved to be the deciding run. The Cubs' three-game losing streak dropped them 2½ games behind the Pirates.

June 24. CUBS' HOMERS TAKE FINAL GAME FROM PIRATES, 4-3. The Cubs banged out three homers, including Kiki Cuyler's solo shot, Hack Wilson's two-run clout, and finally Rogers Hornsby's solo blast in the eighth inning with the score tied, 3-3. The hero of the game might have been left fielder Riggs Stephenson. The often maligned fielder made a running, over-the-shoulder catch of Charlie Hargreaves' blast in the ninth inning to keep the runner (Earl Sheely) on second from scoring, and then ended the game when he threw a perfect strike to home plate to cut down Sparky Adams (pinch-running for Sheely) on Dick Bartell's long single. Charlie Root tossed a ten-hit complete game for his seventh victory. The Cubs ended their 23-game homestand (including one rainout) with a record of 12 wins, nine losses, and one tie.

June 25. No game scheduled.

June 26. No game scheduled.

June 27. HORNSBY HITS HOMER AS CUBS BEAT CARDS, 5 TO 4. In the first game of a five-game series at Sportsman's Park in St. Louis, Rogers Hornsby's 12th home run of the season broke a 4-4 tie in the eighth inning to give the Cubs the deciding run in a 5-4 victory. Hornsby and Woody English collected three hits each in the Cubs' 14-hit attack. Guy Bush tossed an eight-hit complete game.

June 28. CUBS ROUT CARDS, 9 TO 5; TAKE FIRST PLACE. The Cubs exploded for seven runs in a second-inning "batting orgy" that included home runs by Rogers Hornsby, Hack Wilson, and pitcher Pat Malone off St. Louis starter Jesse Haines, just as the NL-leading Pirates' loss to the Cincinnati Reds was posted on the scoreboard.[7]

Malone hurled a complete game, though he gave up 11 hits and six walks, as the Cardinals left 11 men on base. The Cubs victory moved them into first place, just percentage points in front of the Pirates.

June 29. CUBS' ATTACK IN EARLY INNINGS DEFEATS CARDINALS, 10 TO 7. The Cubs put the Cardinals in a 5-0 hole after a half-inning on Rogers Hornsby's home run (his fourth consecutive game with a round-tripper) and Charlie Grimm's grand slam. Kiki Cuyler went 3-for-5 with two runs scored and two runs batted in as the Cubs collected nine of their ten hits and all ten runs off Cardinals starter Bill Sherderl in 3⅔ innings. Sheriff Blake picked up the win, though his performance – seven hits, five walked and seven runs (five earned) – was anything but inspiring.

June 30. CUBS SPOT CARDINALS SIX RUNS; THEN WIN 14 TO 8. St. Louis put Chicago in a deep hole when they scored six runs (only two earned) off starter Charlie Root in the second inning. Trailing 8-1 after three innings, the Cubs scored 13 unanswered runs for their fifth successive victory, and eighth consecutive win over the Cardinals. The Rajah led the Cubs' 19-hit attack by going 4-for-5 (giving him 11 hits in 20 at-bats in the series against his former team); Hack Wilson and Charlie Grimm each went 3-for-5 with three runs batted in, while Grimm and Woody English scored three times. Hal Carlson held the Cardinals hitless over the last four innings to earn the victory. The Cubs won 17 and lost 9 (and tied one) in the month.

NL Standings, after games played on June 30, 1929

Team	Won	Lost	Tie	Pct	GB
Chicago Cubs	39	23	3	.629	·
Pittsburgh Pirates	40	25	1	.615	.5
New York Giants	38	29	1	.567	3.5
St Louis Cardinals	36	30	1	.545	5
Brooklyn Robins	31	36	0	.463	10.5
Philadelphia Phillies	28	39	1	.418	13.5
Boston Braves	27	41	0	.397	15
Cincinnati Reds	24	40	1	.375	16

July 1. CUBS AND CARDS TIE, 11-11; IN SIX INNINGS. In a game shortened by three innings so that they could catch their train to Chicago, the Cubs escaped St. Louis with their fourth and final tie of the year, but concluded the five-game series at Sportsman's Park undefeated. The unequivocal star of the game was Riggs Stephenson, who belted two home runs for the third and last time of his career, scored three times, and knocked in a career-best seven runs. Footsie Blair, the 28-year-old rookie third baseman and leadoff hitter, collected three hits including his first major-league home run.

July 2. CINCINNATI BOWS TO CUBS IN 11 INNINGS, 5-4. The Cubs returned to Wrigley Field for a four-game series against the Cincinnati Reds. Trailing 4-2 in the bottom of the ninth, pinch-hitter Gabby Hartnett lined a triple off the Reds' starter, southpaw Eppa Rixey, to drive in Cliff Heathcote, pinch-running for catcher Mike Gonzalez. Fleet-footed pitcher Sheriff Blake took over as pinch-runner for Hartnett, and scored on Clyde Sukeforth's passed ball to send the game into extra innings. Hack Wilson ended the game in the 11th inning on a long sacrifice fly off Dolf Luque scoring Woody English from third. Guy Bush relieved Charlie Root after nine innings and held the Reds hitless in the extra frames to pick up the win.

July 3. CUBS WIN SEVENTH IN A ROW; BEAT REDS, 7-5. Trailing, 3-2, Cincinnati starting pitcher Red Lucas intentionally walked Riggs Stephenson to load the bases in the fifth inning to escape a jam. But the plan backfired as Cubs captain Charlie Grimm rapped a bases-clearing triple to give the North Siders a 6-2 lead. Hot-hitting Rogers Hornsby went 3-for-5 and scored three times (29-for-57 with 23 runs in his last 14 games). Guy Bush overcame a shaky seventh when the Reds scored three unearned runs to go the distance for his tenth win in 11 decisions. The Cubs won their seventh straight (excluding the July 1 tie) and maintained their half-game lead over the Pirates.

July 4. CUBS WIN, 10-5; LOSE 9-8; DROP TO 2D PLACE. In just their fourth doubleheader of the season, but the first of six they will play in July, the Cubs lost, 9-8, to the Cincinnati Reds in the first game, which was called after eight innings. In a poorly pitched game by both squads, the Cubs pounded out 15 hits, led by Charlie Grimm's three. Starter Pat Malone was pummeled for 11 hits and seven runs in six innings while reliever Hal Carlson was tagged with the loss.

Trailing 4-0 in the second game, the Cubs erupted for six runs in the third inning, highlighted by Rogers Hornsby's RBI triple and Kiki Cuyler's two-run homer. All eight starting position players collected a hit in the North Siders' 13-hit attack, led by Norm McMillan's three hits and three runs batted in and two hits and two RBIs by Woody English and Hornsby. Sheriff Blake tossed a complete game (allowing 11 hits and six walks) to earn the win. The Pirates' doubleheader sweep of the Cardinals in Forbes Field dropped the Cubs to second place, a half-game off the pace.

Tempers between the two clubs were flaring since the first game of the series, when Riggs Stephenson slid hard into second base, severely injuring Reds' captain and second baseman Hughie Critz's left knee (Critz missed the next six weeks). The doubleheader on July 4 was marred when Hack Wilson slugged Reds pitcher Ray Kolp (who was not pitching) in the second game. For his pugilistic behavior, Wilson was given a three-game suspension by league President John A. Heydler. Later that evening, as the two teams departed from Union Station, Wilson pummeled Reds pitcher Pete Donohue, starter of the second game.

July 5. No Game Scheduled.

July 6. **CUBS HELD TO FIVE HITS; LOSE TO BRAVES, 3-1.** The Cubs' four-city, 17-game swing to the Northeast began with a thud as the Boston Braves' Socks Seibold held the Hack-less North Siders to five hits and one run. Cubs starter (and loser) Art Nehf tied the score, 1-1, with a double in the seventh. When he loaded the bases in the bottom of the frame, he was relieved by Guy Bush, who surrendered a two-run single to Seibold for the game-winning runs.

July 7. **CUBS' 19 HITS ROUT BRAVES BY 15 TO 4.** Woody English and Mike Gonzalez each knocked in three runs in the Cubs' offensive explosion. Charlie Grimm scored four times, Rogers Hornsby rapped a homer, triple, and double, while a trio of other hitters (Riggs Stephenson, Norm McMillan, and Gonzalez) also

collected three hits. Charlie Root went the distance for his eighth victory, striking out a season-high nine. The victory kept the Cubs in second place, a half-game behind the Pirates.

July 8. **CARLSON STOPS BRAVES; CUBS HAMMER OUT 11 TO 3 VICTORY.** Hal Carlson, the 37-year-old elder statesman of the Cubs' pitching staff, tossed his first complete game since August 26, 1928, shutting down the Braves on five hits. Third baseman Norm McMillan (3-for-5) and Cliff Heathcote, starting in his third successive game for Hack Wilson (3-for-5), paced the Cubs' 15-hit attack, which saw eight different batters collect at least one RBI.

July 9. **BRAVES STOP CUBS WITH 5 HITS, 6 TO 2.** For the second time in four games, the Cubs were held to just five hits. This time, right-hander Ben Cantwell (who won only four of 17 decisions the entire season) did the honors. Cubs starter Claude Jonnard was rocked for six hits and five runs in 2⅔ innings of what proved to be his last big-league start. Hack Wilson returned to the lineup and rapped a double, the North Siders' only extra-base hit.

July 10. **BUSH HURLS CUBS TO VICTORY OVER THE GIANTS.** Rubber-armed Guy Bush tossed his fourth consecutive complete-game victory (with two relief appearances in between) to improve his record to 11-1 during the 6-2 victory. In their methodical approach, the Cubs chased New York Giants starter (and loser) Carl Hubbell after the fifth inning, leading 3-1. The North Siders scored one run in six different innings, capped off by Hack Wilson's 20th home run, his first since June 28. The Cubs remained in second-place, 1½ games behind the streaking Pirates, winners of nine of their last ten games.

The big news of the game focused on catcher Zack Taylor, acquired in a waiver transaction from the Boston Braves on July 6. In his first game behind the plate for the Cubs, the 30-year-old backstop went 2-for-3 and scored twice. Taylor stabilized the weakest link in the Cubs armor, and started 60 of the Cubs' next 81 games.

July 11. **PIRATES GAIN AS CUBS AND GIANTS DIVIDE.** An estimated 32,000 spectators showed up at the Polo Grounds for a doubleheader between the second- and third-place clubs. The Cubs scored the first eight runs of the game (all off Giants starter Fat Freddie Fitzsimmons) for an 8-3 victory. Norm McMillan hit a three-run home run for his third round-tripper of the season, and pitcher Pat Malone lined a double, knocking in two runs. Malone went the distance, giving up seven hits to improve his record to 12-4.

The two teams combined for 37 hits and 28 runs in the second game with the Cubs on the losing end, 16-12. Hack Wilson led the Cubs' 19-hit barrage with three hits, including his fifth two-home-run game of the season, and knocked in five runs. The Giants took a 5-0 lead in the first inning off starter Sheriff Blake who lasted just two-thirds of an inning. Giants batters gave Trader Horne, Art Nehf, and Claude Jonnard a similar greeting in their highest-scoring game of the season. The Cubs fell to two games behind the Pirates.

July 12. **GIANTS WHIP CUBS, 4-3, ON JACKSON'S HOME RUN.** The Cubs were scoreless through the first six innings, then scored one run in the seventh and eighth, and took the lead, 3-2, in the ninth on Woody English's sacrifice fly scoring Norm McMillan. Pat Malone came on in relief to save the game but surrendered a two-out, game-tying triple to Mel Ott. With the game tied, 3-3, shortstop and future Hall of Famer Travis Jackson sent Malone's first pitch in the tenth inning into the left-field seats for a dramatic walk-off home run. The Cubs lost two consecutive games for the first time since June 22-23, and fell three games behind the Pirates.

July 13. **HAL CARLSON HOLDS GIANTS TO FOUR HITS; CUBS WIN, 4-0.** Hal Carlson tossed his best game in almost four years by blanking the Giants on four hits in the final game of a five-game series. Rogers Hornsby connected for three hits, including a home run and a double, driving in two runs. Riggs Stephenson launched his sixth homer as all Cubs position players collected at least one hit.

July 14. No Game Scheduled.

July 15. **CUBS WIN TWO FROM PHILLIES; GAIN ON PIRATES.** In the first game of a doubleheader sweep of Philadelphia at the Baker Bowl, the Cubs won, 9-6, thanks to timely hitting and three Phillies errors leading to two unearned runs. Hack Wilson walloped his 23rd home run. Guy Bush yielded 15 hits and six runs but went the distance to improve his record to 12-1.

The Cubs collected four hits and five runs off Phillies starter Luther Roy, who lasted just a third of an inning in the second game; however, they managed only four additional hits and two runs off a quartet of Phillies relievers in a 7-6 win. In a shaky start, Sheriff Blake gave up ten hits, and six walks in 7⅔ innings. Chuck Klein's 26th home run, a grand slam with two outs in the eighth inning, pulled the Phillies to within one, 7-6, and forced Blake's removal. Art Nehf and Charlie Root retired four of the last five Philadelphia batters to secure the Cubs' third straight victory, which moved them to 2½ games behind the Pirates.

July 16. **WILLOUGHBY'S CURVES ARE PUZZLE TO BRUINS. PHILS HOME RUNS DEFEAT CUBS, 6 TO 5.** Chuck Klein, Philadelphia's 24-year-old outfielder in his first full season, continued his home-run barrage. He connected off Cubs starter (and loser) Pat Malone twice (his 27th and 28th) for his sixth home run in four games and his fifth in the last three to tie a major-league record. The Cubs collected 13 hits off Phillies starter Claude Willoughby, but only two went for extra bases, and they stranded 11 runners.

July 17. **CUBS GAIN ON PIRATES; DEFEAT PHILS, 16-3.** The Cubs matched their season high in runs scored during an 18-hit barrage against the sixth-place Phillies in the final game of the series. All nine Cubs collected at least one hit; seven delivered two or more each. Rogers Hornsby was the star among stars with three hits, including his 18th home run and four runs batted in. Woody English scored four times and Zack Taylor matched his career high with three runs scored. Charlie Root tossed a complete game for his ninth win and chipped in with a double, triple, and three runs batted in.

July 18. **CUBS OUTSLUG ROBINS, 11 TO 7; TRIM PIRATES LEAD.** In what was described by Irving

Vaughan as a "bone-crushing attack," the Cubs scored seven runs in the first inning, which included eight hits (two by Cliff Heathcote) and a walk off two Brooklyn pitchers.[8] Every Cubs position player notched at least a hit and eight different players drove in at least one run. A Brooklyn rally in the sixth drove an ineffective Hal Carlson from the mound (nine hits and six runs in five innings). In the ninth inning, Riggs Stephenson fell for the hidden-ball trick. After stealing second on Norm McMillan's strikeout, "Old Hoss" did not notice that second baseman Billy Rhiel (upon snagging the throw from the catcher) had handed the ball to shortstop Dave Bancroft. Stephenson gradually moved off the bag and was tagged out by Bancroft. The Cubs moved to within a game of the Pirates.

July 19. Game canceled because of bad weather. Doubleheader scheduled for the following day.

July 20. **CUBS WIN TWO; TAKE LEAD AS PIRATES SPLIT.** Brooklyn jumped on Cubs starter Guy Bush for four runs in the first inning of the first game of the double-header. But the Mississippi Mudcat settled down and allowed just one more run in a ten-inning complete game for his 13th win against just one loss. With two outs in the fifth inning, the Cubs collected five consecutive hits and scored three times to take the lead, 5-4. In the tenth inning, Charlie Grimm connected for a two-out single to drive in Kiki Cuyler for the eventual game-winning run in a 6-5 victory.

In a well-pitched contest by both teams, the Cubs scored all four of their runs in a third-inning rally off Brooklyn starter Johnny Morrison. Sheriff Blake tossed a six-hitter to notch his fourth victory in his last five starts. Hack Wilson had a single to extend his hitting streak to a career-best 27 games, during which he batted .393 (42-for-107, 9 HRs, 27 runs and 30 RBIs). The 4-1 Cubs' victory, their fourth in a row, put them back into first place, but only by percentage points (.646 to .643) over the Pirates due to the teams' uneven schedules

July 21. **CUBS LOSE TO ROBINS, 3-1; PIRATES LEAD. VANCE DAZZLES BRUINS; FANS 10, YIELDS FIVE HITS.** In a rare pitching duel during a season of unprecedented scoring (the NL set a new big-league record with 6,609 runs), two of baseball's hardest-throwing pitchers squared off at Ebbets Field. Pat Malone limited the Robins to just one hit in the first six innings, but yielded three hits in the following frame, including Del Bissonette's two-run triple. Thirty-eight-year-old Dazzy Vance, whose seven-year reign as strikeout king of the NL came to a close in 1929, held the Cubs to five hits and struck out a season-high ten in a commanding complete-game victory. The Cubs went 11-6 on their 17-game road trip.

July 22. No Game Scheduled.

July 23. **GIANTS FALL BEFORE CUBS, 2-0; PIRATES LOSE.** Back in the friendly confines of Wrigley Field for the first time since a doubleheader on July 4, the Cubs inaugurated a season-changing 16-game homestand during which they will begin to pull away from the other pennant contenders. An estimated 30,000 spectators packed the park on a Tuesday afternoon to watch Charlie Root blank the New York Giants on four hits. The Cubs also managed only four hits, all of them off starter and loser Carl Hubbell. Hack Wilson and Charlie Grimm drove in the runs for Chicago.

July 24. **CUBS LEAD LEAGUE; NOSE OUT GIANTS, 8-7.** Cubs starter Guy Bush cruised through the first five innings, yielding just two hits. But in the sixth inning, when a driving rainstorm temporarily halted action, the Giants' bats woke up, scoring seven runs (only two earned) off Bush and reliever Art Nehf, to take the lead, 7-4. The Cubs came roaring back in the seventh inning off Freddie Fitzsimmons in his third inning of relief of starter Jack Scott. Hack Wilson launched his second home run, a game-tying three-run blast; three batters later, Norm McMillan drove in Riggs Stephenson (scoring his third run of the game) for the eventual game-winning tally. Pat Malone, Mike Cvengros (who got the win), and Charlie Root combined for four innings of scoreless relief. The victory moved the Cubs a half-game ahead of the Pirates into sole position of first place where they remained for the rest of the season.

July 25. **CUBS BEAT GIANTS, 8 TO 5; SWEEP 3 GAME SERIES.** Held scoreless through the first five innings, the Cubs erased two deficits for their third straight win over New York. With the Cubs trailing, 2-0,

Charlie Grimm rocketed a two-run single back through the mound to tie the score in the sixth. Down 5-4 in the eighth inning, pinch-hitter Gabby Hartnett drove in Norm McMillan with a sacrifice fly to tie the score. Footsie Blair put the Cubs ahead when he scored on second baseman Andy Cohen's error. Hack Wilson rounded out the scoring in the inning by doubling in two insurance runs. Reliever Mike Cvengros hurled a scoreless inning in the eighth to win for the second consecutive day.

July 26. PHILS GET 7 RUN LEAD; LOSE TO CUBS 13-10.
Philadelphia erupted for seven runs during the first two innings. But the Cubs' offensive juggernaut came back with 11 combined runs in the third and fourth innings. Cliff Heathcote tied his career high with five hits; Rogers Hornsby, Hack Wilson, and Riggs Stephenson each drove in three runs, as the North Siders collected 18 hits. The Phillies mounted a rally in the eighth, scoring twice to make it 13-10. With the bases filled and two outs, manager Joe McCarthy brought in Guy Bush, who retired Denny Sothern and followed that with a hitless ninth to preserve the victory.

July 27. CUBS TRIM PHILLIES TWICE, 48,000 CHEER.
A big crowd turned out on a Saturday afternoon to watch the Cubs sweep their third doubleheader in 12 days. Phillies starter Lou Koupal held the Cubs to two hits for 5⅔ innings before Rogers Hornsby smacked a two-run homer to get the North Siders on the board in a four-run sixth. Hornsby's 2-for-4 performance with three runs batted in concluded an awe-inspiring 38-game stretch during which he batted .428 (68-for-159) with 44 runs, 12 homers, and 47 RBIs. Cliff Heathcote collected a career-best three doubles in the Cubs' 6-1 victory. Pat Malone went the distance, scattering nine hits.

Cubs starter Charlie Root started off shaky, surrendering five runs in the first three innings. Trailing 5-2 in the fourth, the Cubs scored five runs to take the lead, which they didn't relinquish. Root tied the game with a two-run double, then scored the go-ahead run on Cliff Heathcote's grounder to first base which Don Hurst misplayed. Root connected for another two-run double in the fifth to match his career high with four RBIs, to make it 9-5. Hack Wilson's solo home run in the sixth concluded the Cubs' scoring in their 10-7 victory. Root went the distance for his 11th win.

July 28. CUBS WIN SEVENTH IN A ROW; BEAT PHILS, 7-2. BRUIN MACHINE RUNS SMOOTHLY; BUSH AT WHEEL.
Guy Bush dispatched the Philadelphia Phillies on six hits for his ninth consecutive victory and pushed the Cubs' record to 60-30. Chicago pounded Phillies starter Lester Sweetland for six runs in the third inning, highlighted by Riggs Stephenson's three-run clout.

July 29. CUBS OUTSLUG PHILLIES, 12-10, INCREASE LEAD.
In a game featuring 29 hits, five home runs, and 22 runs, Chicago was the last team standing to record a rare five-game series sweep. Rogers Hornsby's two-run blast tied the game, 2-2, as part of a four-run first inning. Chicago increased its lead to 9-4 after five innings, but in the sixth Art Nehf, in relief of starter Mike Cvengros, surrendered five runs, topped off by Don Hurst's second home run, a grand slam, and the score was tied, 9-9. Hack Wilson put the Cubs back in front with a two-run home run in the eighth inning. Pat Malone allowed one run over the final 3⅓ innings to record his 14th victory, increasing the Cubs' lead over the Pirates to 3½ games.

July 30. CUBS BEAT BOSTON, 4-0, FOR NINTH IN ROW.
Sheriff Blake needed only one hour and 28 minutes to toss the last of his 11 career shutouts, a five-hitter, to defeat the Boston Braves and extend the Cubs' season-best winning streak to nine games. Led by Riggs Stephenson's two-run homer, the Cubs scored three runs in the fourth inning off Braves starter Bruce Cunningham. Hack Wilson recorded two runs batted in, giving him 103 in just 90 games.

July 31. CUBS STRING ENDED AT NINE; SPLIT TWIN BILL.
In the first game of the doubleheader, Socks Seibold (48-85 career record) put a definitive end to the Cubs winning streak by tossing an impressive seven-hit complete game during Boston's 7-1 victory. Braves leadoff hitter Lance Richbourg belted three triples and scored four times to pace the invaders' 13-hit attack. Cubs starter Charlie Root allowed nine hits and five runs in seven innings to lose for the first time since June 17.

Hack Wilson's two home runs and four runs batted in powered the Cubs to a 6-3 win in the second game, increasing their lead to five games over Pittsburgh. Perhaps more important than the victory was the return of Kiki Cuyler, who patrolled right field for just the second time since July 10, when he suffered a leg injury that limited him to pinch-hit duties for eight games. Pat Malone went the distance, scattering 11 hits, to earn his 15th victory. In one of the best and most productive months in Chicago Cubs' history, the team posted a 24-8 record (with one tie) and scored 239 runs.

NL Standings, after games played on July 31, 1929

Team	Won	Lost	Tie	Pct	GB
Chicago Cubs	63	31	4	.670	·
Pittsburgh Pirates	58	36	1	.617	5
New York Giants	55	45	1	.550	11
St Louis Cardinals	49	49	2	.500	16
Brooklyn Robins	43	54	0	.443	21.5
Boston Braves	42	58	0	.420	24
Cincinnati Reds	40	57	1	.412	24.5
Philadelphia Phillies	38	58	1	.396	26

August 1. **CUBS BEAT BRAVES, 1-0, AS BUSH WINS NO. 15.** Guy Bush needed only one hour and 33 minutes to toss a five-hit shutout and join teammate Pat Malone as a 15-game winner. The Cubs' only run came in the first inning when Woody English doubled and later scored after Braves starter Ben Cantwell issued three walks. The Cubs tallied just three hits for the game. The *Chicago Daily Tribune* announced the acquisition of 33-year-old right-hander Ken Penner from the Indianapolis Indians of the American Association in exchange for the struggling Claude Jonnard (31 hits and 19 runs in his last 18 innings) and cash.

August 2. The final game with the Braves was rained out.

August 3. **BRUINS LEAD BY SIX GAMES. CARLSON PRESIDES ON MOUND. KEEPS FOES IN CHECK.** The Cubs assaulted three different Brooklyn Robins pitchers for 15 hits in an overwhelming victory, 12-2. Kiki Cuyler led the barrage with four runs batted in, Zack Taylor had a season-high three RBIs, and the Cubs' two through six hitters (English, Hornsby, Wilson, Cuyler, and Stephenson) each scored two runs. Hal Carlson tossed a complete-game eight-hitter to help the Cubs extend their lead over the Pirates to six games. It matched

the Cubs' lead from August 16, 1927, the day before they began a 10-22 skid to fall out of contention.

August 4. **45,000 SEE CUBS DEFEAT ROBINS, 6 TO 4.** On a Sunday afternoon, the Cubs came back twice from two-run deficits to tie the game, 2-2 and 4-4, the latter on Riggs Stephenson's solo home run. In the seventh inning, team captain Charlie Grimm belted a single with the bases loaded driving in two, giving the Cubs enough margin for their fourth straight win. Sheriff Blake went the distance for his ninth win.

August 5. **CUBS GO 16 INNINGS TO BEAT VANCE, ROBINS.** Hack Wilson hit a game-winning walk-off single off Dazzy Vance (who had pitched 8⅓ innings of relief), driving in Woody English in the 16th inning to give the Cubs their fifth consecutive win, 9-8, the 14th victory in their last 15 games. What started out as a pitching duel between Chicago's Charlie Root and Brooklyn's Johnny Morrison turned onto a slugfest that produced 30 hits. After squandering a 5-1 sixth-inning lead, the Cubs scored two runs in the eighth inning to tie the game, 7-7. In the bottom of the 10th, down 8-7, Riggs Stephenson collected his fourth RBI of the game by lining a single driving in Kiki Cuyler to avert the loss. Rogers Hornsby set a career high by drawing five walks. Guy Bush hurled eight innings of relief, but the victory went to Art Nehf, who held the Robins scoreless in the final frame.

August 6. **CUBS LOSE; LOCK GATES AFTER 50,000 ENTER.** On a Tuesday afternoon an overflow crowd was bitterly disappointed to see the Cubs lose for just the second time during their 16-game homestand. Trailing 2-1, the Cubs took a precarious 3-2 lead in the seventh inning on Norm McMillan's long fly ball that rolled into the crowds lined up along the outfield wall for a ground-rule two-run double. But Chicagoans' hope for a happy ending before the Cubs boarded a train for Philadelphia was dashed the following inning when Brooklyn engineered a game-winning three-run rally off starter and loser Pat Malone. Despite the 5-4 loss, the Cubs captured their seventh consecutive series.

August 7. No Game Scheduled.

August 8. No Game Scheduled.

August 9. **CUBS HOLD LEAD; DEFEAT PHILLIES, 12-6.** The Cubs began an 18-game Eastern swing by trouncing Philadelphia in a one-game series before departing later that evening for Boston. Chicago scored all of its runs in three big innings. Riggs Stephenson's bases-loaded, two-run single highlighted a three-run first. After the Phillies scored five times in the second to take the lead, the Cubs retook the lead in the third inning on two-run home runs by Rogers Hornsby and Stephenson. The Cubs tacked on five more in the ninth. In the Cubs' 13-hit attack, all eight position players notched at least one hit and scored a run. Guy Bush tossed a complete game for his tenth consecutive victory.

August 10. **CUBS GAIN ON PIRATES; DEFEAT BOSTON, 4-1.** Braves right-hander Socks Seibold, who had permitted the Cubs just two runs during a pair of complete-game victories in July, blanked the Cubs for the first seven innings before issuing a bases-loaded free pass to Woody English in the eighth inning. Right fielder Cliff Heathcote followed with a two-run infield single for a 3-1 lead. Sheriff Blake tossed seven effective innings to earn his fifth consecutive victory and even his record at 10-10 (he was 2-8 on June 8).

August 11. **CUBS WIN, 3-1; LEAD PIRATES BY 8 GAMES.** Five of Chicago's six hits came from former Boston Braves players, Rogers Hornsby and catcher Zack Taylor. Hornsby knocked in all of the Cubs runs on three hits, including his 25th home run. Charlie Root needed just one hour and 35 minutes to toss a complete game and notch his 12th win

August 12. **CUBS LOSE IN TENTH, 4-3, ON BLAIR'S ERROR.** Trailing 2-0, the Cubs scored three runs in the sixth inning, led by Hack Wilson's RBI single and Riggs Stephenson's two-run blast to take the lead, 3-2. Cubs starter Pat Malone was relieved with one out in the seventh after he issued a bases-loaded walk to Les Bell forcing in pitcher Ben Cantwell with the tying run. With two outs in the eighth inning, the Cubs faced another bases-loaded jam, but Guy Bush entered in relief of Art Nehf to put out the fire. After Braves starter Cantwell tossed a scoreless tenth, he led off the bottom of the

inning with a single off Bush. Third baseman Footsie Blair misplayed Lance Richbourg's bunt, tossing it so far away from first baseman Charlie Grimm that Cantwell raced home with the winning run and ending Bush's personal ten-game winning streak.

August 13. **CUBS TAKE 8-GAME LEAD; BEAT BRAVES, 4-2.** Cubs' starter Hal Carlson tossed a six-hitter to win his sixth consecutive decision and lead the Cubs to their third victory in a surprisingly competitive four-game series against seventh-place Boston. Trailing 2-0, Chicago finally tallied a run when pinch-hitter Cliff Heathcote hit a long fly ball to drive in Kiki Cuyler in the sixth. In the seventh Riggs Stephenson whacked a two-run single with the bases loaded to give the Cubs a 3-2 lead, which they increased by a run the following inning on Rogers Hornsby's third hit of a game, a double driving in Woody English. While the Pittsburgh Pirates won just 7 of 19 games since July 22, the Cubs went 18-3 to open a seemingly insurmountable 8½–game lead in the pennant race.

August 14. No Game Scheduled.

August 15. **CUBS DIVIDE DOUBLE HEADER; INCREASE LEAD.** In the first game of a doubleheader against the Brooklyn Robins at Ebbets Field, each of the Cubs position players notched at least one safety during a 14-hit attack against a quartet of pitchers. Rogers Hornsby belted his 26th home run and Kiki Cuyler went 3-for-4 with two RBIs and two runs scored. Starter Guy Bush shook off a relief loss three days earlier by going the distance to pick up the win, 9-5. The victory was marred by an ugly scene in the bottom of the ninth. As Robins pinch-hitter Rube Bressler ran from first to second on a ball hit by teammate Wally Gilbert, he was nicked on the heel and called out by third-base umpire Edward McLaughlin. While Bressler and McLaughlin engaged in a heated argument, fans tossed bottles on the diamond. After order was restored, the next batter, Johnny Frederick, launched a two-run home run, making it 9-5. Fans once again pelted the field with bottles.

The Cubs' Sheriff Blake and the Robins' Dazzy Vance tossed complete games in the second game of the doubleheader, which Brooklyn won, 5-4. Charlie Grimm and

Riggs Stephenson accounted for six of the Cubs' ten hits; Kiki Cuyler connected for his first home run since July 4, but the North Siders could not muster enough offense against the hard-throwing Vance to overcome a 4-0 deficit after two innings.

August 16. BROOKLYN CUTS CUBS' LEAD; WINS, 5-2. BRUINS FEAR OF POP FLY PAVES WAY FOR ROBINS WIN. In the bottom of the seventh inning in a scoreless game, Robins right fielder Babe Herman hit a high fly ball just inside the left-field foul line. Cubs fielders Riggs Stephenson, Woody English, and Footsie Blair all converged on the ball, but let it drop, opening the floodgates for three Brooklyn runs. Robins starter Ray Moss blanked the Cubs until one out in the ninth when Gabby Hartnett, pinch-hitting for starter Charlie Root, smashed a two-run double. The Cubs lost consecutive games for the first time since July 11-12.

August 17. CUBS BEAT ROBINS, 10-4. BRUINS BATS ROUT 4 PITCHERS. Norm McMillan, Rogers Hornsby, and Hack Wilson connected for home runs as the Cubs erupted for ten runs on 11 hits (and drew eight walks) to salvage a series split with Brooklyn. Swingman Art Nehf went the distance for the first time since June 9 to pick up his seventh win.

August 18. MALONE LEADS CUBS IN 1-0 WIN OVER GIANTS. 35,000 spectators showed up on a Sunday afternoon at the Polo Grounds to see a classic pitching duel between the Cubs' Pat Malone and the Giants' Larry Benton. Kiki Cuyler led off the seventh with a long double and moved to third on Riggs Stephenson's bunt. After Charlie Grimm walked, manager Joe McCarthy pinch-hit for the slow-running catcher Zack Taylor to avoid a potential inning-ending double play. The strategy worked as pinch-hitter Cliff Heathcote hit a long fly ball that drove in Cuyler for the game's only run. Malone went the distance, yielding just five hits while whiffing seven to record his 16th victory.

August 19. No Game Scheduled

August 20. CUBS LOSE, 4-1; THEN WIN, 1-0; GAIN GAME. Despite managing just 12 combined hits and two runs, the Cubs split a doubleheader with the New York

Giants and increased their lead over the fading Pittsburgh Pirates to a season-high 9½ games. In the first game, the Giants' Freddie Fitzsimmons silenced the Cubs on six hits. He would have secured a shutout had first baseman Bill Terry held on to his throw after he fielded Riggs Stephenson's bouncer back to the mound. Rogers Hornsby scored on the error. Cubs' starter Guy Bush picked up the hard-luck loss. In seven innings he yielded six hits, no walks, and two runs (one unearned).

The Cubs and Giants pitchers continued their pitching duel in the second game of the doubleheader. In the fourth inning of a scoreless game, Rogers Hornsby smashed a long triple off Giants starter Carl Hubbell. With the infield drawn in and hoping for a play at the plate, Hack Wilson lined a single to drive in Hornsby for the game's sole run. Hal Carlson hurled a six-hitter to win his seventh consecutive decision. The shutout proved to be the right-hander's 17th and final in his big-league career. Less than a year later, he died tragically at the age of 38 on May 28, 1930, from a stomach hemorrhage. The Cubs' victory was costly as first baseman Charlie Grimm injured his left hand.

August 21. CUBS BEAT GIANTS, 9-2, IN FINAL; LEAD BY 10 1/2 GAMES. The Cubs began the day with the news that first baseman and team captain Charlie Grimm would be out at least a month. X-rays after yesterday's doubleheader determined that he had splintered a bone in his left hand when he crashed into the grandstand while chasing a foul ball hit by Edd Roush in the eighth inning. Utilityman Footsie Blair took over first-base duties for the next six games until Charlie "Chick" Tolson reported from the Los Angeles Angels of the Pacific Coast League. The North Siders responded to the loss of their inspirational leader by bashing a trio of Giants hurlers for 14 hits and nine runs. Riggs Stephenson and Kiki Cuyler each homered and drove in two runs. Charlie Root went the distance, scattering ten hits and striking out eight. The victory moved the Cubs to 40 games above .500 (76-36) and a 10½-game lead over Pittsburgh.

August 22. CUBS BATTER DOWN PHILS, 16-7, WITH 21 HITS. The Cubs matched their highest-scoring game of the season with an offensive barrage in the Baker Bowl. Catcher Zack Taylor equaled his career bests with four hits and three runs scored, Woody English enjoyed one of his five games with four hits during the season, and Hack Wilson and Kiki Cuyler each knocked in three runs. The Cubs' slugfest offset a poor outing by Sheriff Blake, who was lifted after 3⅔ innings having yielded 12 hits and six runs, and made a winner out of reliever Mike Cvengros.

August 23. **CUBS HOMERS DEFEAT PHILS, 6-1, FOR 11 GAME LEAD.** Late-inning round-trippers by Rogers Hornsby, Hack Wilson, and Zack Taylor provided the Cubs all six of their runs. Wilson's three-run blast was his 33rd of the season, tying the Phillies' Chuck Klein and the New York Yankees' Babe Ruth for the major-league lead. Cubs starter Pat Malone needed just one hour and 40 minutes to toss his second consecutive five-hitter for his 17th win.

August 24. **CUBS OVERCOME PHILS, 9-6.** The Cubs made a dramatic late-inning comeback to improve their record to 12-4 on this road trip. Trailing 5-1, Chicago rallied for three runs in the seventh inning, beginning with a run-scoring single by Riggs Stephenson (pinch-hitting for starter Art Nehf). The Phillies increased their lead to two in the bottom half of the inning, courtesy of a bobble by second baseman Rogers Hornsby and three singles by the Phillies. The Cubs scored once in the eighth, setting up a dramatic finish. With the bases loaded and two outs in the ninth, Kiki Cuyler lined a two-run single to put the Cubs in front for the first time in the game. Mike Cvengros hurled his second scoreless inning of relief in the ninth to earn his fifth victory of the season (which also proved to be his 25th and last one in his big-league career).

August 25. **CUBS DIVIDE WITH REDS; COME HOME TODAY.** In the teams' first meeting since the fisticuffs during and after their doubleheader on July 4, the Cubs and Reds split a peaceful twin bill in front of more than 35,000 spectators at Redland Field on a Sunday afternoon. In the opening game, Reds right-hander Red Lucas scattered eight hits, three of them by Norm McMillan, for a convincing complete-game, 6-3 victory.

Lucas led the NL with 28 complete games (in 32 starts) in 1929. The Reds scored all of their runs off Cubs starter Hal Carlson, who lasted just 3⅓ innings and took the loss.

The second game was scoreless until the Cubs exploded for eight runs in the seventh inning off Reds starter Pete Donohue and reliever Dolf Luque. The scoring started when Riggs Stephenson, pinch-hitting for catcher Mike Gonzalez, belted a bases-loaded single driving in two runs. Doubles by Woody English and Cliff Heathcote produced three more. Luque replaced Donohue and was greeted by Hornsby (an RBI single) and Kiki Cuyler (a two-run double) as the Cubs extended their lead to 8-0. Guy Bush went the distance for his 18th win (against just 3 losses), 10-1. It proved to be Bush's last victory of the regular season. The Cubs concluded their 18-game road trip with an impressive 13-5 record.

August 26. **CUBS' 8TH INNING RALLY ROUTS REDS, 9-5.** The Cubs were back in the friendly confines of Wrigley Field for the first time since August 6, but an estimated 30,000 spectators had little to cheer about through the first 7½ innings. The North Siders had managed just two runs off Cincinnati Red southpaw Eppa Rixey, while Charlie Root had been banged around for 10 hits and five runs. Much to the delight of the cheering faithful, the Cubs exploded for seven runs in the eighth inning. After the Cubs scored three runs with four consecutive hits, Norm McMillan crushed a pitch from Reds reliever Rube Ehrhardt with the bases loaded. It appeared to be a double, but rookie left fielder Evar Swanson had trouble finding the ball, which had rolled into the gutter near the Cubs bullpen. McMillan raced home for his first and only inside-the-park home run. (It also proved to be his sixth and final big-league home run.) The offensive outburst made a winner out of Root; Pat Malone tossed a scoreless ninth.

August 27. **HORNSBY GETS 4 HITS; CUBS BEAT REDS, 4-1.** The Rajah tallied four of the Cubs' seven hits, scored twice and knocked in a run to help the Cubs beat the Cincinnati Reds, 4-1. It marked the Cubs' third con-secutive victory and eighth of previous nine, and moved them to a season-high 14½ games ahead of the Pirates. A Tuesday afternoon crowd estimated by the *Chicago*

Daily Tribune at 25,000 also witnessed Sheriff Blake hurl a six-hitter to even his record at 11-11.

August 28. **CUBS LOSE DOUBLE HEADER TO PITTSBURGH.** After a two-game respite at home, the Cubs were back on the road, where they were swept by the Pittsburgh Pirates in a doubleheader at Forbes Field. "[The Cubs] hurling was ineffective, their fielding provoked laughs and their attack scattered," wrote Irving Vaughan of the *Chicago Daily Tribune*.[9] Trailing 3-1, the Pirates scored a combined nine runs in the sixth and seventh inning off Cubs' starter Pat Malone en route to a victory in the first game, 10-3. The Cubs committed three errors and managed only nine hits off Pirates starter Burleigh Grimes, who improved to 17-3.

In the second game, the Cubs had a seemingly comfortable lead, 6-2, after 6½ innings. Chicago had battered Pirates starter Ray Kremer for ten hits, including Rogers Hornsby's 30th home run, and two clutch singles by Mike Gonzalez driving in three runs. The Pirates scored three runs off reliever Ken Penner in the seventh, and then added two more in the eighth to win the game, 7-6. Reliever Mike Cvengros was collared with the loss.

August 29. **PIRATES WIN; CUT CUBS LEAD TO 11 GAMES.** Trailing 2-0 after just one inning, the Cubs battered 34-year-old southpaw, Jessy Petty, for nine hits and all four of their runs in the first five innings. First baseman Chick Tolson knocked in two runs on a single in the second inning; Rogers Hornsby and Hack Wilson each drove in a run in the fifth to give the Cubs a 4-2 lead. But the "Silver Fox" Petty yielded just one hit over the last four frames. Cubs starter Hal Carlson was nicked for a run in the fifth and two more in the sixth to pick up the 5-4 loss. The Cubs lost three consecutive games for the first time since June 21-23.

August 30. **PIRATES WIN FOURTH IN A ROW FROM CUBS.** The Cubs suffered their worst defeat of the year, 15-0. They managed just three hits off 33-year-old Heinie Meine, who tossed his first career shutout. Cubs' starter Guy Bush was clobbered for ten hits and charged with eight runs in just 3⅓ innings to absorb the loss; reliever Art Nehf fared almost as poorly, yielding 11 hits and seven runs in 4⅔ innings. Pirates third baseman Pie Traynor

equaled his career high with five hits. The Cubs' four-game losing streak matched their longest of the season.

August 31. **CUBS WHIP PIRATES, 7-6; HOME TODAY.** In their fifth game against Pittsburgh in four days, The Cubs found themselves in familiar territory. Trailing 3-1 to begin the seventh inning, the Cubs rallied to tie the score, courtesy of Woody English's two-run single off Burleigh Grimes, in relief of starter Steve Swetonic. The Pirates reclaimed the lead in the bottom of the frame by scoring a run off Pat Malone, in relief of Cubs starter Charlie Root. Chicago staged an exciting comeback with one out in the ninth inning by loading the bases on three walks by Grimes. Hack Wilson hit what appeared to be a sure double-play grounder to shortstop Stu Clarke, but the 5-foot-6, 190-pound slugger beat the relay throw to first base, enabling pinch-hitter Johnny Moore to score the tying run. The next batter, Kiki Cuyler, put the Cubs in the lead with a two-run double. Riggs Stephenson connected for his third single to drive in the speedy Cuyler and make it 7-4. The Pirates rallied for two runs off Guy Bush, who had been battered the day before, but Pittsburgh came up short, 7-6.

NL Standings, after games played on August 30, 1929

Team	Won	Lost	Tie	Pct	GB
Chicago Cubs	83	41	4	.669	·
Pittsburgh Pirates	71	52	1	.577	11.5
New York Giants	67	57	1	.540	16
St Louis Cardinals	61	60	2	.504	20.5
Brooklyn Robins	56	66	0	.459	26
Philadelphia Phillies	54	69	1	.439	28.5
Cincinnati Reds	52	72	1	.419	31
Boston Braves	48	75	0	.390	34.5

September 1. **CUBS BEAT CARDINALS, 10-3; PLAY TWO TOMORROW.** After losing four out of five in Pittsburgh, the Cubs were back in Chicago for a three-game series with St. Louis for part of the Labor Day holiday weekend. Trailing 1-0, the Cubs scored four runs in the fourth inning on bases-loaded hits by Kiki Cuyler and Chick Tolson to take a 4-1 lead. After the Cardinals cut the lead to one on catcher Jimmie Wilson's two-run single in the sixth, the Cubs tacked on three more when Hack Wilson launched his 34th home run and Tolson and pitcher Sheriff Blake followed with run-scoring hits.

The Cubs banged out 12 hits, led by Cuyler's three (and three runs batted in), and Woody English scored three times. Blake tossed a complete-game ten-hitter, for his 12th victory.

September 2. **CUBS BEAT CARDS TWICE; GAIN ON PIRATES.** In a separate admission doubleheader on Labor Day, the Cubs supplied the fireworks (36 hits and 23 runs) to defeat the St. Louis Cardinals, 11-7 and 12-10 and extend their winning streak to 11 (excluding the tie on July 1) over the reigning NL pennant winners. Edward Burns of the *Chicago Daily Tribune* reported that the crowd of 38,000 spectators for the pre-lunch game "broke all records" in Chicago, and the combined attendance of 81,000 had been surpassed only in Yankee Stadium.[10]

In the first contest, Hack Wilson knocked in five runs, three of which came on his 35th home run in the Cubs' six-run third inning to break the game open. Rogers Hornsby collected three hits, including his 31st home run, while Woody English scored four times. Pat Malone went the distance to win his league-leading 19th game and struck out ten, but was also touched for 14 hits.

Cubs starter Hal Carlson spotted the Cardinals four runs in the first inning, but the North Siders scored five in the second inning and three times each in the fourth and fifth en route to the series sweep. Hornsby once again led the attack with another home run and three runs batted in. Carlson enjoyed a career day at the plate (2-for-3 with a career-best three runs scored and three runs batted in) and picked up his 10th win despite being pounded for 14 hits and nine runs (eight earned) in six innings.

September 3. No Game Scheduled.

September 4. **CUBS DIVIDE WITH CARDS; LOSE 14-8, WIN 8 TO 3.** In the first game of the doubleheader at Sportsman's Park in St. Louis, the Cubs committed four errors that led to 12 unearned runs in a 14-8 loss. Trailing 7-2, Chicago scored five runs in the sixth inning, highlighted by Rogers Hornsby's 33rd home run, to tie the game. In the eighth inning, the Cardinals exploded for six unearned runs for the second time in the game. The inning started with first baseman Chick Tolson dropping Norm McMillan's throw, followed by the

Cardinals loading the bases with two outs before the scoring spree started. On the mound was Ken Penner, the Cubs' third hurler of the day. He yielded four hits and four walks in 1⅔ innings to absorb the loss in his last big-league appearance.

Cubs starter Charlie Root was tagged for three runs in the first inning of the second contest, but the hard-throwing right-hander shut down the Cardinals the rest of the way en route to a complete-game victory that improved his record to 15-5. The Cubs were scoreless until they erupted for six runs, including Riggs Stephenson's two-run round-tripper, off St. Louis starter Syl Johnson in the sixth inning, Hack Wilson had a productive twin bill, scoring four times and driving in five runs in the 8-3 win.

The two games scheduled for September 5 and 6 were canceled because of bad weather. The Cubs concluded their season series against the Cardinals with an impressive 15-5 record, averaging 8.3 runs per game, but also surrendering 6.45.

September 5. Cubs at St. Louis: rained out.

September 6. Cubs at St. Louis: rained out.

September 7. **CUBS SLUGGING BEATS BRAVES, 13 TO 6 AND 9 TO 2.** In front of an estimated 30,000 spectators in Wrigley Field, the Cubs exploded for a record-tying ten consecutive hits in the fourth inning in the first game of a doubleheader. The seven-run offensive outburst, highlighted by Kiki Cuyler's three-run home run, came an inning after the Cubs took the lead, 4-3, on Riggs Stephenson's bases-clearing double. Rogers Hornsby continued his hot hitting, belting a round-tripper in the seventh inning, giving him four homers and 12 runs batted in during the last five games on 12-for-20 hitting, and scoring ten times. Sheriff Blake went the distance, yielding ten hits and seven walks, for his 13th win.

In the second game of the doubleheader, Cubs' starter Pat Malone overcame a rough first inning (including walking three consecutive batters and yielding the Braves' two runs) to shut down Boston in overpowering fashion.

He surrendered just four hits while striking out 11 (his fourth game of the season with 10 or more punchouts) to earn his 20th victory of the season. The Cubs' 12-hit barrage off Braves' starter Ben Cantwell was led by Hack Wilson (3-for-3) who scored three times and knocked in two more runs with a triple in the seventh inning.

September 8. **CUBS ATTACK WASTED; BRAVES WIN, 13-11**. Trailing 7-0 after two innings and 9-3 after 5½ frames, the Cubs scored seven runs in the bottom of the sixth to take the lead, 10-9, to the delight of 35,000 spectators in Wrigley Field. But the Braves resumed their onslaught the next inning by scoring three times off reliever Hal Carlson en route to the victory. The Cubs tallied 16 hits, including a 4-for-5 performance with two doubles and a home run by red-hot Rogers Hornsby (19-for-31 in his last eight games). Cubs starter Guy Bush was clobbered for six hits and seven runs in just 1⅓ inning.

September 9. **CUBS SCORE TWICE IN THE 9TH; BEAT BRAVES, 4-3.** Notwithstanding the drizzling rain, which caused several delays and limited attendance to an estimated 10,000 at Wrigley Field, the Cubs won their 90th game of the season in exciting fashion. With the Cubs trailing 2-0 in the seventh inning, Hack Wilson tied the game with a two-run home run. Cubs starter Charlie Root issued a bases-loaded walk to Rabbit Maranville in the ninth inning to set the stage for an exciting finish. With one out Riggs Stephenson tied the game on his 16th round-tripper of the season. Chick Tolson followed with a single and then was waved home by Joe McCarthy on Zack Taylor's game-winning, walk-off double. The Cubs concluded their season series with the Braves with a 15-7 record.

September 10. No Game Scheduled.

September 11. **CUBS HOME RUNS DEFEAT PHILADELPHIA, 5-2.** The Cubs took advantage of solo home runs by Riggs Stephenson, Hack Wilson, and Chick Tolson to eke out a hard-fought 5-2 victory over the Phillies. Cubs starter Art Nehf tossed a complete-game five-hitter, yielding round-trippers to Chuck Klein and Don Hurst, to win his eighth game of the season. (It was the 184th and last victory of his career.) The Cubs improved to a season-best 48 games over .500 (91-43).

September 12. **CUBS LOSE TO PHILLIES, 7-1; NEED 3 VICTORIES.** Chicago's rubber-armed starting pitcher and fireman Guy Bush continued his late-season collapse. Since his victory on August 25 to improve his record to 18-3 and lower his ERA to 2.93, Bush up to today had allowed 40 hits, 31 runs (25 earned), and 18 walks in 20⅓ innings. He yielded 18 combined hits and walks, as well as six runs in 6⅔ innings during an ugly 7-1 loss to the Phillies. Philadelphia starter Claude Willoughby corralled the Cubs on seven hits, one of which was Hack Wilson's 39th home run.

September 13. **CUBS PENNANT RUSH HALTED BY PHILS, 7 TO 6.** The Cubs scored four runs in the fourth inning, keyed by Kiki Cuyler's two-run single, to give the Cubs a 5-3 lead. But Cubs starter Sheriff Blake, who had tossed complete-game victories in his last three outings, could not handle the Phillies, who scored twice in the sixth and twice in the eighth. The Cubs rallied in the ninth when Rogers Hornsby launched a solo shot with one out. Singles by Hack Wilson and Cuyler and a walk to Chick Tolson loaded the bases, but Claude Willoughby, the pitching hero from the previous game, in a relief role induced a double-play grounder from Zack Taylor to end the game. The Cubs won 17 of 22 against the Phillies during the season, averaging an impressive 8.3 runs per game.

September 14. **PAT MALONE HURLS 21ST VICTORY OF SEASON.** The Cubs managed only five hits off Robins starter Watty Clark, but three of them were in the fourth inning when Rogers Hornsby and Hack Wilson belted run-scoring doubles. The Cubs' final run came from Kiki Cuyler's "funny homer." Irving Vaughan of the *Chicago Daily Tribune* described how the ball went on a line to the right-field corner where Brooklyn outfielder Babe Herman was there to field it but "the ball took one hop and vanished from his sight. It had jumped into the extreme end of the grandstand, and being more than the prescribed 250 feet from the plate, it had to be rated a homer."[11] Pat Malone blanked the Robins on eight hits to notch his 21st win, 3-0, on the day the Philadelphia Athletics clinched the AL pennant.

September 15. **CUBS ROUT FOUR ROBINS PITCHERS; WIN, 13-4. BRUINS JUST ONE VICTORY FROM LEAGUE TITLE.** After spotting the Robins two runs, the Cubs torched rookie Bobo Newsom for six runs in the first inning, propelled by Chick Tolson's two-run single and Charlie Root's two-run triple, en route to a blowout. All nine players hit safely in the Cubs' 18-hit attack, led by Tolson's career-best four hits. Rogers Hornsby went 2-for-4, belted his 37th home run, scored twice, and knocked in three runs. Hack Wilson and Tolson also had three RBIs. Root tossed his third consecutive complete-game victory as the Cubs moved to a season-high 14½ games in front of the second-place Pittsburgh Pirates and 48 games over .500 (93-45) to match a season high. The Cubs scored ten or more runs for the 34th time in 142 games; over the remaining 14 games of the season, they would not score more than eight in a game (averaging just 4.0 per game) and won just five times.

September 16. Brooklyn at Chicago: rained out.

September 17. **PIRATES WIN, CUBS LOSE; STILL NEED 1 GAME.** In the first game of a doubleheader forced by the rainout the day before, the Cubs overcame a 6-0 deficit by scoring three runs in the fourth and four in the fifth off Robins starter Dazzy Vance to take a 7-6 lead. The latter four runs came courtesy of Kiki Cuyler's grand slam. Brooklyn rallied for two runs in the ninth inning against relievers Mike Cvengros and Sheriff Blake for the eventual victory, 8-7.

The second game of the doubleheader read almost like a carbon copy of the first. The Cubs fell behind early and were trailing 5-0 before they bounced back with five runs in the sixth and seventh innings combined. In the eighth inning Robins right-fielder Babe Herman launched a grand slam off reliever Pat Malone, the fourth of five pitchers used by the Cubs during this contest. The 9-6 loss was charged to Art Nehf, who surrendered hits to the only two batters he faced. With the two losses, the Cubs finished the season with a 16-6 record against the Robins.

September 18. **CUBS WIN PENNANT RACE AS PIRATES LOSE.** Despite losing, 7-3, to the New York Giants in the first game of a four-game series at Wrigley Field, the Cubs won their first pennant since 1918 when the Boston Braves defeated the Pittsburgh Pirates, 5-4, in the first game of a doubleheader at Forbes Field. While the Giants whacked Cubs starter (and loser) Sheriff Blake for ten hits and six runs in four innings, Chicago was unable to muster a comeback against New York starter Carl Hubbell, who went the distance, yielding ten hits. Rogers Hornsby had three of those hits and scored all three Cubs runs.

September 19. **CUBS' EARLY ATTACK BEATS GIANTS, 5-0.** The Cubs got some much-needed good pitching by Pat Malone who blanked the New York Giants on six hits to record his league-leading 22nd win and fifth shutout (he also paced the NL with 166 strikeouts). Rogers Hornsby started the Cubs scoring with a single in the first inning, driving in Cliff Heathcote, and later scored on Chick Tolson's single. Hack Wilson's two-run single was the North Siders' deciding blow in a three-run second inning.

September 20. No Game Scheduled.

September 21. **CUBS BAFFLED BY SOUTHPAW; GIANTS WIN, 4-1.** Chicago's heavily tilted right-handed hitting lineup had no answer for New York Giants left-hander (and eventual regular-season NL ERA champion) Bill Walker, who scattered eight singles to defeat the Cubs, 4-1. Hack Wilson's single to drive in Cliff Heathcote (the only left-handed hitter in the Cubs lineup) in the first inning provided Chicago with its sole run. Charlie Root held the Giants scoreless through seven innings before yielding two runs in the eighth (including Mel Ott's league-leading 40th home run) and two more in the ninth to pick up his sixth loss of the season.

September 22. **HARTNETT COMES BACK BUT CUBS LOSE, 5-4.** Cubs catcher Gabby Hartnett was in the starting lineup for his first and only game behind the plate this season and Guy Bush completed his first start since August 25, yielding ten hits and five runs (three earned), but it was not enough to keep Chicago from losing for the seventh time in ten games. The Cubs took the lead, 3-1, in the fourth inning on run-producing singles by Bush and Woody English. But in the seventh inning the Giants' Freddie Lindstrom lined a two-run single to center field, and then scored when center fielder Hack Wilson misplayed the ball, allowing it to roll past him for an error. The loss gave the Cubs a 12-10 record in the season series against the Giants.

September 23. No game scheduled. Cubs played an exhibition game in Aurora, Illinois.

September 24. No Game Scheduled.

September 25. No Game Scheduled.

September 26. No Game Scheduled.

September 27. No Game Scheduled.

September 28. **REDS BUNCH HITS ON MALONE; BEAT CUBS, 5-3.** In their first game in six days, the Cubs took the lead, 2-1, in the fourth inning on Kiki Cuyler's two-run home run, which bounced into the right-field grandstand at Wrigley Field. The Cincinnati Reds nicked Cubs starter Pat Malone for three runs in the fifth to retake the lead and added another run in the sixth. Cuyler's run-scoring single in the eighth inning helped ignite a potential rally, but Chick Tolson grounded into an inning-ending double play with the bases filled.

September 29. **HORNSBY'S 39TH HOME RUN BEATS REDS, 1-0. BRING ON THE MACKS! CHARLEY ROOT IS READY.** In one of his strongest performances of the year, Cubs starter Charlie Root tossed a six-hit shutout, whiffing four and walking one, to defeat the Cincinnati Reds, 1-0. Rogers Hornsby collected four of the Cubs' seven hits, including his 39th home run in the fourth inning off tough-luck loser Benny Frey to account for the lone run of the game. Cubs left fielder Riggs Stephenson's accurate throw to catcher Mike Gonzalez on Clyde Sukeforth's single cut down Ethan Allen at the plate for the second out to save the game in the ninth.

September 30. No Game Scheduled.

NL Standings, after games played on September 30, 1929

Team	Won	Lost	Tie	Pct	GB
x-Chicago Cubs	95	51	4	.651	·
Pittsburgh Pirates	86	64	1	.573	11
New York Giants	82	66	1	.554	14
St Louis Cardinals	76	73	2	.510	20.5
Brooklyn Robins	70	81	0	.464	27.5
Philadelphia Phillies	70	81	1	.464	27.5
Cincinnati Reds	64	84	1	.432	32
Boston Braves	54	97	0	.358	43.5

x-clinched pennant

October 1. **REDS BUNCH HITS OFF BUSH; BEAT CUBS, 3-2.** The Cubs traveled to Cincinnati for a five-game set with the Reds at Redland Field. Run-scoring singles by Riggs Stephenson and Norm McMillan in the second inning off Reds starter Red Lucas provided the Cubs their only runs. Chicago maintained the 2-0 lead until the bottom of the eighth, when the Reds scored all three of their runs off Cubs tough-luck loser, starter Guy Bush, who tossed a complete-game six-hitter. Reds third baseman Hughie Critz smashed a two-run triple to tie the score. The next batter, Curt Walker, hit an easy grounder to first baseman Charlie Grimm, playing in his first game since suffering a broken hand on August 20. Grimm made a "ludicrous throw" to home plate enabling Walker to score even though he should have been out by "15 feet."[12]

October 2. **CUBS HIT BEHIND BLAKE TO BEAT PESKY REDS, 7-4.** The Cubs broke out of their offensive slump by collecting 14 hits (all singles) and seven runs, their most since September 17. Riggs Stephenson led the attack with four hits and two runs batted in; Kiki Cuyler added three hits and also knocked in two runs. Ineffective in his previous two starts, Sheriff Blake tossed a complete-game eight-hitter for his 14th and final victory of the season. The Cubs' victory was just their third in the last ten games.

October 3. **CUBS WIN, 8-1; HACK GETS 4 HITS; KIKI STEALS 2 BASES.** In an all-around team effort, the Cubs enjoyed good hitting (16 hits), effective, error-free defense, and strong pitching. All eight position players collected at least one hit, led by Hack Wilson's four. Riggs Stephenson and catcher Johnny Schulte knocked in two runs, as did pinch-hitter Cliff Heathcote. In order to prepare his staff for the World Series, manager Joe McCarthy announced before the game that he would use a three-pitcher rotation, as he did during spring training.

Starter Hal Carlson tossed three scoreless innings and was awarded the victory.

October 4. **CUBS NIP REDS IN TENTH, 6-3. VICTORY NUMBER 19 FOR ROOT.** The Cubs took the lead after just two batters when Norm McMillan led off the game with a triple and scored on Clyde Beck's single. In the third inning Riggs Stephenson singled to drive in Rogers Hornsby, who scored his league-leading 156th run (the most by a right-handed batter in the 20th century). Kiki Cuyler stole his 43rd base to lead the NL for the second consecutive year and later scored on a rundown between third base and home plate during a double-steal attempt. In his only start of the season, the Cubs' Bob Osborn held the Reds to six hits and two runs in seven innings. Cincinnati tied the game, 3-3, in the eighth off reliever Charlie Root. In the tenth inning, Cubs catcher Zack Taylor belted a bases-loaded, two-run single for the eventual winning runs.

October 5. **REDS SHUT OUT CUBS, 9-0; SPOIL 100 WINS HOPES.** Cubs starter Mike Cvengros took one for the team, pitching all nine innings and yielding 14 hits while losing a 9-0 pounding during the team's last road game of the regular season. After the Reds took a 2-0 lead in the third inning, Joe McCarthy all but conceded the game by replacing second baseman Rogers Hornsby and center fielder Hack Wilson with Footsie Blair and Johnny Moore respectively. Reds hurler Rube Ehrhardt needed just 75 minutes to blank the Cubs on five hits for the last of his 22 big-league wins. The Cubs won 14 and lost eight against the seventh-place Reds during the season, and finished with a 46-29 record on the road.

October 6. **PIRATES BATTER GRAMPP; DEFEAT CUBS IN FINAL, 8-3.** There was no fairy tale ending for Hank Grampp in front of an estimated 27,000 spectators in the regular-season finale at Wrigley Field. After serving as the Cubs' batting practice pitcher for three years (and making two brief relief appearances in 1927), Grampp started his first and only game in his big-league career. As if taking batting practice, the Pittsburgh Pirates clobbered Grampp for six runs on four hits and three walks in two innings. The Cubs managed just six hits off Pirates rookie southpaw Larry French. The loss dropped

Chicago to 9-13 against the Pirates, the only team that had a winning record against the Cubs. The Cubs' home record was 52-25. They scored two fewer runs at home than on the road (490 to 492) and permitted ten fewer (374 to 384).

1929 NL Final Standings

Team	Won	Lost	Tie	Pct	GB
Chicago Cubs	98	54	4	.645	·
Pittsburgh Pirates	88	65	1	.575	10.5
New York Giants	84	67	1	.556	13.5
St Louis Cardinals	78	74	2	.513	20
Philadelphia Phillies	71	82	1	.464	27.5
Brooklyn Robins	70	83	0	.458	28.5
Cincinnati Reds	66	88	1	.429	33
Boston Braves	56	98	0	.364	43

1929 AL Final Standings

Team	Won	Lost	Tie	Pct	GB
Philadelphia Athletics	104	46	1	.693	·
New York Yankees	88	66	0	.571	18
Cleveland Indians	81	71	0	.533	24
St Louis Browns	79	73	2	.520	26
Washington Senators	71	81	1	.467	34
Detroit Tigers	70	84	1	.455	36
Chicago White Sox	59	93	0	.388	46
Boston Red Sox	58	96	1	.377	48

NOTES

1   *Chicago Daily Tribune*, May 7, 1929.

2   *Chicago Daily Tribune*, May 9, 1929.

3   *Chicago Daily Tribune*, May 26, 1929.

4   *Chicago Daily Tribune*, June 7, 1929.

5   *Chicago Daily Tribune*, June 9, 1929.

6   *Chicago Daily Tribune*, June 22, 1929.

7   *Chicago Daily Tribune*, June 29, 1929.

8   *Chicago Daily Tribune*, July 18, 1929.

9   *Chicago Daily Tribune*, August 29, 1929.

10   *Chicago Daily Tribune*, September 3, 1929.

11   *Chicago Daily Tribune*, September 15, 1929.

12   *Chicago Daily Tribune*, October 2, 1929.

JUNE 9, 1929 AT WRIGLEY FIELD
CHICAGO CUBS 2, BOSTON BRAVES 1
ART NEHF AND BEN CANTWELL HURL FOUR-HITTERS

By Gregory H. Wolf

NATIONAL LEAGUE TEAMS SET NEW records by averaging 5.36 runs and 10.28 hits per game in 1929, but on June 9 of that season the Boston Braves and the Chicago Cubs played what *Chicago Daily Tribune* reporter Edward Burns called "one of those old fashioned pitching duels, so rare in these days of the rubber baseball."[1]

With the offseason acquisition of second baseman Rogers Hornsby, the game's best hitter and arguably its most divisive player, the Cubs were considered preseason favorites to capture their first pennant since 1918. But the season had thus far not gone according to the script manager Joe McCarthy had written. With a record of 26-18, the Cubs were in third place, 2½ games behind the league-leading Pittsburgh Pirates and a game behind the reigning NL pennant-winning St. Louis Cardinals. However, the club was playing inconsistent, all-or-nothing team ball. Prior to their disappointing 5-4 loss to the Braves in the opening game of a three-game series the day before, the North Siders had scored just six runs combined in four consecutive losses followed by 33 runs in four straight victories. Unlike the Cubs, the Braves had no pennant aspirations. After three consecutive seventh-place finishes, the Braves owner, Judge Emil Fuchs, installed himself as manager in 1929, but the results were familiar. In sixth place with a record of 17-27, Boston was in a free-fall, having won just three of its last 19 games.

On the mound for the Cubs was 36-year-old southpaw Art Nehf, who had anchored the New York Giants staffs during their four-year hold on the NL crown (1921-1924). The college-educated, slightly built hurler (5-feet-9, 175 pounds) was in the last season of his 15-year career, during which he went 184-120. Often overlooked as one of the best pitchers of his era, Nehf revived his career with the Cubs in 1928, overcoming what appeared to be a career-ending arm injury in 1926, and served as a swingman in

1929. Boston's Ben Cantwell, who as of 2014 held the dubious extinction of being the last big-league hurler to lose at least 25 games in a season (which he did for the Braves in 1935), was a 27-year-old right-hander in the third season of an 11-year career during which he went 76-108.

An estimated 35,000 spectators packed Wrigley Field on a Sunday afternoon as the Cubs prepared for the ninth game in a 23-game, season-longest homestand. Through the first six innings, Nehf permitted only two hits (singles by the leadoff hitter, right fielder Lance Richbourg, in the first and by catcher Zack Taylor in the third) while an error by shortstop Woody English put center fielder Earl Clark on base. All three baserunners were erased by double plays, two of which were started by Nehf, considered one of the most agile and best-fielding pitchers of the period.

Cantwell matched Nehf's shutout, also allowing just three baserunners (only one hit) through six innings. Cantwell faced his first trouble when he issued leadoff walks to Rogers Hornsby and center fielder Hack Wilson in the fourth inning, but alert defense quickly quashed the rally. After catcher Taylor fielded first baseman Charlie Grimm's bouncer in front of the plate to force Hornsby at third base, Cubs third baseman Norm McMillan grounded back to Cantwell, who started an inning-ending double play.

In the tension-packed game, the seventh inning provided all of the scoring, though far from all of the excitement. The Braves struck first when second baseman Freddie Maguire launched a double to left center and then scored on left fielder George Harper's two-out single. Clark flied out to end the inning. With one out and Cubs right fielder Kiki Cuyler on first, courtesy of Cantwell's third and final walk, Hornsby smashed a "hot grounder to deep short" which shortstop Rabbit Maranville, Hall of Famer, fielded.

Described as "his second of two great stops," Maranville, on his knees, threw to second base to force Cuyler.[2] With Hornsby on first, reigning three-time NL home-run champion Wilson clouted his 11th round-tripper to give the Cubs a 2-1 lead.

Nehf and Cantwell shrugged off the seventh inning and resumed their dominance of the opposition in the last two frames. In the eighth inning, Cubs catcher Earl Grace collected his second single (and Chicago's fourth hit). The conclusion of the game brought the Cubs faithful to their feet in a mixture of anticipation and confusion. With two outs, Maguire hit a slow roller near the first-base foul line. Nehf and Grimm went after the ball and collided viciously. While Nehf fell to the ground, knocked out cold, Grimm retrieved the ball and apparently tagged the runner. According to Edward Burns, players, under the impression that the game was over, gathered around Nehf. When the pitcher was revived, umpire Cy Rigler ruled the ball foul.[3] Determined to finish what he had started, Nehf limped back to the mound and induced Maguire to foul out to Grace.

The victory moved the Cubs to 1½ games behind the Pirates. Described as "the classiest show of the year," both pitchers tossed four-hitters.[4] Nehf won his third consecutive decision, improving his record to 4-1, en route to an 8-5 record that year. Cantwell dropped his fourth straight and won only four of 17 decisions in 1929.

SOURCES

Baseball-Reference.com

Chicago Daily Tribune

Retrosheet.org

SABR.org

The Sporting News

NOTES

1   Edward Burns, *Chicago Daily Tribune*, June 10, 1929, 25.

2   Ibid.

3   According to the *Chicago Daily Tribune*, Rigler made the call; however, he is listed as the third-base umpire in box scores available on Baseball-Reference.com and Retrosheet.org. The home-plate umpire, who would have most likely made the call in the situation, was Edward McLaughlin

4   Ibid.

JUNE 15, 1929 AT WRIGLEY FIELD
CHICAGO CUBS 8, PHILADELPHIA PHILLIES 7
RIGGS STEPHENSON'S WALK-OFF POP-FOUL
WINS IT IN THE 10TH

By Gregory H. Wolf

AFTER LOSING THEIR FIRST FIVE extra-inning games of the 1929 season, the Chicago Cubs finally broke the dubious streak with a combination of timely hitting, good defense, and heads-up baserunning to defeat the Philadelphia Phillies, 8-7, on Saturday, June 15. "The Cubs and Phillies put on a drama," wrote Edward Burns of the *Chicago Daily Tribune*, "that hasn't been surpassed in these parts for many seasons."[1] Both teams arrived at Wrigley Field well rested to play the third game of the four-game series. Not only did they enjoy a rare Friday afternoon off, rain ended their Thursday Ladies Day game after five scoreless innings. Despite the tie, the Cubs had been playing their best baseball of the season, and had won seven of eight games to improve their record to 29-18, good for third place, just one game behind the Pittsburgh Pirates. After a surprisingly good start to the season (20-17 at one point), the Phillies had lost nine of their last 10 games (excluding the tie) and had fallen to fifth place.

The *Chicago Daily Tribune* reported that an estimated 20,000 spectators "spurned the American Derby"[2] — the biggest horse race of the year in the Windy City, which took place 30 miles south in suburban Homewood — to pack the friendly confines on the north side of town. The teams engaged in an unexpected scoreless pitchers' duel through five innings. Chicago's starter, Guy Bush (an impressive 6-1), had been victimized for six hits and six runs (five earned) during a no-decision in just two innings in his last start, on June 6, but had since pitched 6⅓ innings of scoreless relief in two separate appearances. Luther Roy, Philadelphia's 26-year-old journeyman right-hander, was 3-2 with a horrendous 7.47 ERA.

The offensive fireworks began in the top of the sixth. After Bush struck out right-fielder Chuck Klein, second baseman Rogers Hornsby booted cleanup hitter Don

Hurst's "easy roller" for his second error of the game, opening the floodgates.[3] Third baseman Pinky Whitney singled, and center fielder Denny Sothern followed with a double to drive in Hurst for the game's first run. With runners on second and third, Bush issued an intentional pass to shortstop Bernie Friberg to play for a twin killing with slow-footed catcher Spud Davis at the plate. The plan backfired as the 24-year-old backstop belted his first career grand slam to make it 5-0. Courtesy of a walk, Roy was the sixth consecutive Philadelphia player to reach base, before Bush registered the final two outs.

In the bottom of the inning, Hazen "Kiki" Cuyler finally put the Cubs on the board with a leadoff home run. Despite his lofty .346 batting average, the right fielder had been mired in a power slump, with just four extra-base hits and no home runs in his last 25 games.

En route to a career-best and an NL-leading 43 home runs in 1929, Phillies slugger Chuck Klein led off the seventh with his 16th round-tripper, which sent Bush to the showers. The "Mississippi Mudcat's" line was unimpressive: eight hits and six runs (five earned) in six innings. Trailing 6-1, the Cubs called on Trader Horne, in his first and only season in the big leagues, for mopup duty. The 30-year-old, 155-pound righty tossed an inning of scoreless relief.

The Cubs exploded for six runs in the bottom of the seventh. First baseman Charlie Grimm commenced the relentless attack by drawing a walk. After third baseman Norm McMillan beat out an infield single, rookie catcher Earl Grace drew one of his three walks to fill the bases. Pinch-hitting for Horne, Cliff Heathcote knocked in Grimm and reached base on a fielder's choice when Grace was forced at second. Leadoff hitter Clyde Beck drew one of his three free passes to load the bases again. Roy, who had issued six walks and yielded five hits in 6⅓ innings, was replaced by Les Sweetland. He faced the Cubs' emotional leader, catcher Gabby Hartnett, whose mysterious arm miseries had prohibited him from donning the tools of ignorance thus far in the season. Batting for left fielder Johnny Moore in just his sixth pinch-hitting appearance of the season, "Old Tomato Face" drew the Cubs' fourth walk of the inning, driving in McMillan.[4] With pinch-runner Footsie Blair on first and the bases still filled, reliever Phil Collins struck out Cuyler. Hornsby, batting an uncharacteristic .256 (11-for-43) in his previous 13 games, "squelched the howling wolves" and boo birds by blasting a grand slam off Collins to give the Cubs their first lead, 7-6.[5]

After a scoreless eighth, the Phillies rallied in the ninth. Mike Cvengros, the Cubs' fourth pitcher, walked left fielder Lefty O'Doul, who scampered to third on Klein's single. Hurst singled, driving in O'Doul to tie the game. With runners on the corners and the game on the line, manager Joe McCarthy brought in hard-throwing Pat Malone, who led the NL with 22 wins in 1929 but also made 10 relief appearances. Malone put out the fire when Whitney lined to shortstop Clyde Beck, whose throw to Grimm doubled Hurst off first base and completed the Cubs' fourth twin killing of the game. Malone fanned two in a 1-2-3 10th inning to give the Cubs another chance for a dramatic victory.

Grimm led off the Cubs' 10th with a double, the Cubs' seventh and last hit of the game. In a poorly executed sacrifice, McMillan bunted the ball back to Phillies' reliever Bob McGraw, who quickly threw to second baseman Fresco Thompson. The NL leader on both putouts and errors for second baseman in 1929, Thompson caught Grimm in a rundown but not before McMillan made it to second. McGraw walked Earl Grace intentionally to either create a force at third or play for an inning-ending double play. But McMillan unexpectedly stole third to put men on the corners with just one out.[6] McGraw intentionally walked Cliff Heathcote (the Cubs' 12th free pass of the game) to fill the bases for Riggs Stephenson, pinch-hitting for Beck. Stephenson, batting .370, but making his first appearance since June 4, popped a high foul ball that both first baseman Hurst and catcher Davis went after. Hurst caught the ball "half way between the dugout and the screen"; however, home plate was unguarded because neither pitcher McGraw nor third baseman Whitney had dashed to cover it. Reacting quickly, McCarthy, coaching third base, sent McMillan racing home to score the winning run standing up.

The heads-up move brought Malone his ninth win and was a thrilling end to a victory that elevated the Cubs into second place (by percentage points) over Pittsburgh.

SOURCES

Baseball-Reference.com

Retrosheet.org

NOTES

1　Edward Burns, "Hornsby's Homer Scores 4; Cubs Beats Phils, 8-7," *Chicago Daily Tribune*, June 16, 1929, A1.

2　Ibid.

3　Ibid.

4　Game reports from the *Chicago Daily Tribune* and the *Philadelphia Inquirer* ("Failure To Cover Home Plate Costs Phillies Victory," June 16, 1929, 1) provide the same sequence of events. Those papers as well as widely circulated Associated Press box scores credited Gabby Hartnett with an RBI (see "Win in Tenth," *Ogden* [Utah] *Standard-Examiner*, June 16, 1929, 13). These game summaries differ from the box scores available on Baseball-Reference.com and Retrosheet.org.

5　Burns.

6　Box scores from Baseball-Reference.com and Retrosheet.org do not credit McMillan with a stolen base; however, game reports, including those from the *Chicago Daily Tribune* and *Philadelphia Inquirer*, as well as the Associated Press, do.

AUGUST 1, 1929 AT WRIGLEY FIELD
CHICAGO CUBS 1—BOSTON BRAVES 0
GUY BUSH HURLS SHUTOUT TO WIN 10TH CONSECUTIVE DECISION

By Gregory H. Wolf

"THOSE AMONG BASEBALL FANS WHO insist that pitching is a lost art and that the lively ball has destroyed the defensive features of the game might do well to consider the battle between the Cubs and Boston Braves," wrote Herbert W. Barker of the Associated Press after the two teams played on August 1, 1929.[1] In a season of record-breaking offense, the game featured great pitching, only eight hits, and just one run.

Members of the Chicago Cubs felt confident on that Thursday afternoon as they made their way to Wrigley Field. Winners of 17 of their last 20 games, the Cubs had transformed a three-game deficit on July 12 into a five-game lead over the Pittsburgh Pirates in a two-team pennant race. Prior to the doubleheader split with the Braves the day before, the Cubs had strung together nine consecutive victories to kick off a 16-game home stand. The Braves, in sixth place with a 42-58 record, had recently been playing better and had won 10 of their last 18 games. The Braves' recent success was a product of good pitching, a seemingly annual bugaboo of the long-suffering team that had enjoyed only one winning season since 1916.

Cubs manager Joe McCarthy called on rubber-armed right-hander Guy Bush to continue Chicago's unrelenting march to their first pennant since 1918. The 27-year-old Bush, enjoying his breakout season, was the hottest pitcher in the National League, having won 14 of 15 decisions; he finished the season with an 18-7 record and led the majors with 50 appearances, including 30 starts. Forgotten by all but the most ardent baseball historians, Bush was one of the most consistent hurlers in the NL, winning 15 or more games seven years in a row (1928-1934), and compiled a 176-136 record during a 17-year career. Boston's starter, Ben Cantwell, was suffering through a dismal year (4-13), though his 4.47 ERA was almost a run lower than the league average (5.36). But recently, he had pitched some of his best ball against the Cubs, including a five-hit victory and a four-hit loss in his last two starts against them. With a career record of 76-108, Cantwell endured some of the worst Braves teams of the era, including the 1935 squad (38-115) for which he lost 25 games.

An eventful first inning saw six baserunners but only one run. Hoping to extend his career-best winning streak to ten decisions, Bush surrendered consecutive two-out singles to first baseman George Sisler and third baseman Les Bell before striking out left fielder George Harper to end Boston's early scoring chance. With one out in the bottom of the frame, Cubs shortstop Woody English sent a fly ball over the head of right fielder Lance Richbourg for a double — the Cubs' only extra-base hit of the contest. Cantwell, who normally possessed good control, issued walks to second baseman Rogers Hornsby and right fielder Kiki Cuyler to load the bases. Left fielder Riggs Stephenson drew a bases-loaded walk to drive in what turned out to be the game's sole run. First sacker Charlie Grimm, batting seventh, "slapped a low rakish liner to right center" that Richbourg managed to catch, preventing a possible bases-clearing clout.

After putting down the Braves in order in the second and third innings, Bush encountered trouble in the fourth. Thirty-six-year-old "Gorgeous George" Sisler, a lifetime .340 hitter, singled. Cleanup batter Bell hit a grounder to third baseman Norm McMillan, who bobbled the ball for an error. After the runners advanced on Harper's hopper to first baseman Grimm, Bush walked second baseman Freddie Maguire intentionally to load the bases and set up a double play with the slow-footed catcher Al Spohrer at the plate. The plan worked to perfection as the backstop bounced to Hornsby, who flipped to the shortstop English to start an inning-ending double play.

Averaging seven runs per game thus far on their home-stand, the Cubs had no answer for Cantwell, who, according to Irving Vaughan of the *Chicago Daily Tribune*, "curved and speed balled" all afternoon.[2] Hornsby, who had been on fire in his last ten games, collecting 18 hits in 44 at-bats (.409), scoring 13 times, and driving in 13 runs, managed a single in the third, but was doubled up by center fielder Hack Wilson. Hitless in the fourth through sixth innings, the Cubs mounted a threat to add to their slim lead in the seventh inning when Grimm led off with a single. After catcher Zack Taylor (acquired from the Braves in a waiver transaction on July 6) popped out, Cantwell erred as he misplayed a ball hit back to the mound by Bush. With Chicago runners on first and second, McMillan flied to center fielder Jimmy Welsh and English fanned to end the inning. In the eighth, Cantwell was replaced by 35-year-old swingman Dixie Leverett, back in the big leagues after a two-year absence. He retired the side in order.

An aggressive, fast worker on the mound (the game took just one hour and 33 minutes to play), Bush set down Braves in order in the fifth, yielded yet another single to Sisler, in the sixth, and got out of a jam in the seventh after Maguire tripled. With the tying run 90 feet from home plate, Bush was in no mood to play the odds and walk Spohrer intentionally to face the weak-hitting Cantwell. Bush induced Spohrer to pop up to end the inning, and then retired all six batters he faced in the eighth and ninth innings.

Bush won his tenth consecutive decision to improve his record to 15-1 and maintain the Cubs' five-game lead in the standings. The Cubs continued to play exceptionally well, winning 18 of their next 24 games to run away with the pennant, but the Braves slid to the basement, losing 40 of their last 54 games.

SOURCES

Baseball-Reference.com

Chicago Daily Tribune

SABR.org

The Sporting News

NOTES

1   Herbert W. Barker, "Guy Bush Has Fifteenth Win To His Credit" (Associated Press), *The Journal News* (Hamilton, Ohio), August 2, 1929, 36.

2   Irving Vaughan, "Cubs Beat Braves, 1-0, As Bush Wins No. 15," *Chicago Daily Tribune*, August 2, 1929, 15.

SEPTEMBER 14, 1929 AT WRIGLEY FIELD
CHICAGO CUBS 3, BROOKLYN ROBINS 0
PAT MALONE TOSSES SHUTOUT FOR 21ST WIN

By Gregory H. Wolf

WHEN THE BROOKLYN ROBINS and the Chicago Cubs squared off for the first contest of a four-game series at Wrigley Field on Saturday, September 14, 1929, there was little suspense about the NL pennant race. With a record of 91-45, the Cubs enjoyed a 13½-game lead over the Pittsburgh Pirates. Manager Joe McCarthy's squad had won nine of their last 13 games; however, they looked vulnerable losing their last two games to the sub-.500 Philadelphia Phillies. The Robins, guided since 1914 by their namesake, skipper Wilbert Robinson, were in fifth place (63-74), 28½ games off the Cubs' pace.

On the mound for Brooklyn was 27-year-old left-hander Watty Clark, en route to a breakout season, leading the majors in starts (39), and the league in innings pitched (279), but also in losses (19). Winner of 16 games in 1929, Clark emerged as the staff's ace, a designation long held by Dazzy Vance. "I'll pitch a curve roughly half the time," said Clark. "Even when my arm is sore I'd rather pitch a curve than a fastball.[1] Over a four-year stretch (1929-1932), Clark averaged 16 wins and 246 innings per year, making him one of the top southpaws in the NL. Hard-throwing right-handed fastballer Pat Malone got the call for the North Siders. In his second season, the 26-year-old Pennsylvanian had already established himself as one of the most feared and best hurlers in the game. He had struck out 10 and 11 batters respectively in his last two outings, both complete-game victories, to reach the 20-win benchmark for the first of two consecutive seasons. The workhorse on the Cubs staff from 1928 to 1932, Malone averaged 18 wins and 251 innings during that span.

An estimated 20,000 spectators turned out on a sunny afternoon for the Cubs' eighth game on a 17-game home-stand.[2] A "genuine autumnal bite to the breeze" blowing off Lake Michigan portended a low-scoring game.[3]

Lacking his overpowering fastball, Malone relied on guile and some good defense to keep the Robins scoreless in the first three frames. Brooklyn second baseman Eddie Moore led off the game with a single to left field in front of a diving Riggs Stephenson, and moved to second on center fielder Johnny Frederick's walk. But Chicago turned the first of three double plays to thwart a possible Brooklyn score. Malone began the second by issuing his second and final walk, to first baseman Del Bissonette. Third baseman Wally Gilbert hit a screeching liner back to Malone, who knocked the ball down. Second sacker Rogers Hornsby picked it up and started another twin killing. Brooklyn had another scoring chance in the third inning when Frederick tripled with two outs. Malone reared back and whiffed hot-hitting outfielder Babe Herman, who had entered the game batting .388.

Unlike Malone, Clark breezed through the first three innings, allowing only a second-inning single to Hack Wilson, who was erased on Brooklyn's first of three twin killings. Things changed in the fateful bottom of the fourth inning when Cubs third baseman Norm McMillan led off with a low line drive that "almost carried Clark's right ear with it."[4] McMillan moved to second on short-stop Woody English's sacrifice bunt. Hornsby, batting .511 in his previous 12 games (23-for-45) with 16 runs scored and 20 runs batted in, took advantage of Clark's mistake — an inside fastball. According to Thomas Holmes of the *Brooklyn Eagle*, the "Rajah" "pulled it through the left side of the infield a mile a minute" to drive in McMillan.[5] The next batter, Hack Wilson, slashed Clark's first pitch down the right-field foul line, scoring Hornsby to make it 2-0. The Cubs possessed a "real Jack Dempsey knack for finishing off a slightly groggy pitcher," wrote Holmes.[6]

Center fielder Wilson, often derided for his defensive deficiencies, saved a potential run in the sixth inning. With Herman on first, cleanup hitter Harvey Hendrick smashed a deep fly ball. According to Roscoe McGowen of the *New York Times*, Wilson "stood with his back

Kindred spirits on and off the field: pitcher Pat Malone and slugger Hack Wilson. (Retro Images Archive. George Brace Collection)

against the left centre-field screen" to rob Hendrick of a possible extra-base hit.[7] Herman, thinking the ball would not be caught, had rounded second. He quickly sprinted back to first base, but had neglected to touch second base. Hornsby took Wilson's throw and touched second base for the out.

Clark yielded only one "fluke" hit in the final five frames.[8] Right fielder Kiki Cuyler (batting .412 in his last 13 games, 21-for-51) hit a "funny homer." Irving Vaughan of the *Chicago Daily Tribune* described how the ball went on a line to the right-field corner, where outfielder Babe Herman was there to field it but "the ball took one hop and vanished from his sight. It had jumped into the extreme end of the grandstand, and being more than the prescribed 250 feet from the plate, it had to be rated a homer."[9] [The ground-rule double took effect in the

National League for the 1931 season and a year earlier in the American League.]

Brooklyn's Hendrick and Bissonette recorded the team's seventh and eighth hits with one out in the ninth. But Malone, despite permitting 11 baserunners (including one batter he hit), was effective in the pinches. After Gilbert flied to center, the game ended when Hornsby jumped to snare a "lazy liner" off shortstop Jack Warner's bat to preserve the Cubs' 3-0 victory.[10]

On the day the Philadelphia Athletics clinched the AL pennant, Malone registered his 21st victory and fourth shutout en route to leading the NL in both categories (22 and five respectively). Tough-luck loser Clark fell to 14-17. "It seems as though the Robins lacked the killer instinct to as great a degree as the Cubs possessed it," wrote Holmes.[11] Four days later, on September 18, the Cubs clinched their first pennant since 1918.

SOURCES

Baseball-Reference.com

Brooklyn Eagle

Chicago Daily Tribune

New York Times

SABR.org

The Sporting News

NOTES

1   Bill James and Rob Neyer, *Neyer/James Guide to Pitchers* (New York: Fireside, 2004), 165. Clark's quotation from *Baseball Magazine*, August 1930.

2   Crowd estimate from Roscoe McGowen, "Cubs Blank Robins; Move Nearer Flag," *New York Times*, September 15, 1929, S7.

3   Thomas Holmes, "Robins Outhit Cubs, But Heirs Apparent Win Game, 3 to 0," *Brooklyn Eagle*, September 15, 1929, C1.

4   Irving Vaughan, "Pat Malone Hurls 21st Victory of Season," *Chicago Daily Tribune*, September 15, 1929, A1.

5   Holmes.

6   Holmes.

7   McGowen.

8   Holmes.

9   Vaughan.

10 Vaughan.

11 Holmes.

THE 1929 PHILADELPHIA ATHLETICS

By Bob Buege

ONNIE MACK WON 3,582 GAMES AS manager of the Philadelphia Athletics. That's 999 games more than John McGraw, who ranks second all-time, won as skipper of the New York Giants. Mack's total will never be rivaled. He owned the team, so no matter how badly his club performed, he could not be fired. As a result, he held the reins for 50 years.

During his career Mack enjoyed two mini-dynasties. The first came shortly before World War I. The A's won four American League pennants in five years (1910-1914), each year except 1912, when they finished third. The Mackmen, as the newspapers customarily called them, were loaded with hitters, at least by the standards of the Deadball Era. What's more, they had a dominating pitching staff that included Jack Coombs plus a pair of future Hall of Famers, Eddie Plank and Chief Bender. The A's also won three World Series in those years, all except 1914, in which they were swept by the "Miracle Braves" of Boston.

After the 1914 season, with the newly formed Federal League throwing cash around and competing for players, Mack began breaking up his championship club rather than go head-to-head in a bidding war with the Federals. He was well off by ordinary measures, but he did not possess the level of wealth that most of his rival owners did. Mack claimed that his ballclub was placed at a serious financial disadvantage by Philadelphia's restrictive Blue Laws, enacted in 1794, when George Washington was president. These ordinances forbade the performance of any worldly business, including professional baseball games, on the Lord's Day. Most other big-league cities allowed baseball on the Sabbath; in fact, it was generally considered to be the most attended day of the week. Beginning in 1911, Mack campaigned to repeal the Blue Laws, without success.

In 1926 Philadelphia played host to a Sesquicentennial Exposition commemorating 150 years of American independence from England. The businessmen who sponsored the event determined that they needed to be open on Sundays in order to make a profit, and the city fathers

raised no objection. Mack decided that if the Exposition could conduct its business on the Sabbath, so could his Athletics. Despite threats of police action to keep Shibe Park closed, the A's played the White Sox on August 22, 1926, in flagrant violation of the law. The contest proceeded without incident, and the A's won, 3-2. Nevertheless, the allied forces against evil prevailed, and no more major-league games were played on Sunday in Philadelphia until after the law was repealed in November 1933.

The 1915 season found Mack's two ace hurlers, Bender and Plank, pitching in the Federal League and the A's firmly planted in last place in the American League, 58½ games behind Babe Ruth and the Boston Red Sox. In fact the A's remained in last place for seven consecutive seasons. After that, Mack gradually rebuilt his club into a respectable contender. The turning points occurred in 1924, after he acquired Al Simmons, and 1925, when he added Jimmie Foxx, Mickey Cochrane, and Lefty Grove. The signing of those four future Hall of Fame enshrinees made the Athletics a worthy opponent that steadily climbed in the standings. In 1927 the A's finished a distant second behind the fabled Murderers' Row New York Yankees. The next year Mack's team finished a close second to Gehrig and Ruth and their Bronx Bombers.

As spring training opened in 1929, the American League looked like more of the same. The Athletics appeared formidable; the Yanks seemed unbeatable. The A's were worried about the well-being of Al Simmons, slowly recovering from a bout with rheumatism. Actually the health watch went right to the top. Mack had been plagued all winter with an undiagnosed illness. In late January his friend Henry Killilea, like Mack one of the founders of the American League, died in Milwaukee. Mack was convalescing in Florida and felt too sick to attend the funeral. He worried about being able to make it through the full season and feared he might have to retire from the rigors of managing a baseball team. He recovered, though, and so did the A's.

Like any team, the Mackmen comprised a variety of attitudes and personalities and skills. They had a few individuals who were prone to fits of anger and boorishness, but overall they had remarkably little disharmony. They shared a competitive fire, an unquenchable will to win. The term was not in common use back then, but the A's had good team chemistry. In addition to Mack, they had one other carryover from their last pennant-winning team. Eddie Collins had been the second baseman of the 1914 Athletics. In fact, Collins that season had received the Chalmers Award as the league's most valuable player. Mack called him "the best all-around player in the game."[1] Collins had subsequently been away for a dozen years toiling with the Chicago White Sox through the 1926 season, but in 1929 he did a little pinch-hitting for the A's and coached at third base. He was skilled at stealing signs and passing them along to those Philadelphia hitters who wanted to know what pitch was coming. Some did and some didn't.

On a team loaded with highly combative men, no one was more fiercely motivated than catcher Mickey Cochrane, the 1928 American League MVP. Mack described him as "Ty Cobb wearing a mask."[2] Cochrane took every loss personally. He was indisputably the team leader. It was said that "as a master of the mechanics of catching, he had no peer."[3] During his undergraduate days at Boston University, Cochrane had distinguished himself in numerous athletic endeavors, including boxing and track. Baseball may have been his third best sport behind football and basketball. His exceptional running speed set him apart from most catchers. So did his ability to handle pitchers. Besides being remarkable behind the plate, Cochrane excelled with the bat. His lifetime batting average was .320. In 1929 he batted .331, and in 606 plate appearances, he struck out only eight times.

Like Cochrane, the A's left fielder, Al Simmons, absolutely hated losing, and he looked at the opposing pitcher as a mortal enemy, a demon trying to take food from his table. Simmons played the game in a rage, whether trying to line the ball back through the box to intimidate the man on the mound, or, like Ty Cobb, sliding viciously into a base with his spikes high. Simmons believed he was a warrior and that his bat and his spikes were his weapons.

He possessed the strangest batting stance of any of the great hitters. Although he batted right-handed, in the batter's box his left foot pointed toward the third-base dugout and he stepped down the baseline, earning the nickname "Bucketfoot Al." Somehow his swing compensated for his unusual setup, allowing him to spray the ball to all fields. He was one of the greatest right-handed batters ever, slamming more than 300 home runs and batting above .380 four times. In 1929 Simmons batted .365, belted 34 home runs, and drove in a league-leading 157 runs, three ahead of Babe Ruth.

Philadelphia first baseman Jimmie Foxx was temperamentally the antithesis of Simmons. Both men had muscular physiques and enormous upper-body strength, but Foxx was good-natured and easy-going. He played with intensity, but he usually did so with a smile on his face. He nevertheless blasted some prodigious home runs and would become the second man, behind Ruth, to record more than 500 four-baggers, including 58 of them in 1932. Foxx would also win the league's Most Valuable Player Award three times. Foxx's breakout season was 1929. He clubbed 33 home runs and, despite a September slump, batted .354. As a testament to his newfound stardom, he appeared on the cover of the July 29 issue of *Time* magazine. In doing so he joined his manager, Mack, who had appeared on the front of *Time* on April 11, 1927. (Mickey Cochrane would do likewise on October 7, 1935.)

Cochrane, Simmons, and Foxx were all great hitters destined for Cooperstown. They were not the team's only offensive threats, though. Outfielders Bing Miller and Mule Haas both hit over .300 and drove in 93 and 82 runs, respectively, in 1929. Jimmy Dykes, the number eight hitter in the lineup, could play anywhere except behind the plate, and batted .327. The lowest average among the starters, not counting the pitchers, belonged to second sacker Max Bishop. Max, however, was adept at getting on base by walks, a league-topping 128 times in 1929. On April 29, 1929, against the Yankees, Bishop drew five bases on balls. A year later he became the only ballplayer to accomplish the feat twice, also against the Yankees.

With all their firepower, it was no surprise that the Athletics didn't just defeat their opponents — they often crushed them. The Mackmen in 1929 became the first team ever to have five men score more than 100 runs. On May 22 they scored a dozen times in the fifth inning. Twenty times during the regular season the A's scored at least ten runs in a game. Twice they exceeded the 20 mark. On May 1 in Fenway Park in Boston, the Macks belted 29 hits and chased 24 runners across the plate.

Despite their batting prowess, and despite having the American League's best defense, the main reason the 1929 A's breezed to the pennant was their superior pitching. They allowed by far the fewest runs of any team in the American League, and 160 fewer than the Yankees did. Ten-year veteran right-hander Eddie Rommel provided strong relief and achieved a 12-2 record. Bill Shores and Jack Quinn (one of the last two legal spitballers still in the American League) worked as spot starters or out of the bullpen as needed. It was the A's Big Three, however — Rube Walberg, George Earnshaw, and Lefty Grove — who carried the club to the World Series.

Walberg was a hard-working southpaw who ate up innings every year and won more games than he lost. In 1929 he won 18 games against 11 defeats. George Earnshaw didn't make it to the big leagues until June 1928, when he was 28 years old. A towering figure with a high leg kick and an unpredictable fastball, Earnshaw won 24 games, highest in the majors in 1929, while losing eight. His 3.29 earned-run average was fourth best in the AL. The lowest ERA in the major leagues that season, 2.81, belonged to Earnshaw's mound mate, the great Lefty Grove.

Connie Mack never got Lefty's last name right. He always referred to him as "Groves" (his given surname). When talking to him, Mack called him Robert. Whatever the name, though, he knew the flame-throwing left-hander was his ace in the hole. Before Mack acquired Grove from minor-league Baltimore of the International League after the 1924 season, he said he thought he just needed one good pitcher to make the A's a contender. "That man is Groves of the Orioles," Mack stated. "He is the best pitcher I ever saw in the minors."[4]

Lefty certainly did not disappoint his manager. He brought with him a fastball some thought could rival that of Walter Johnson. In 1929 Lefty became a 20-game winner for the third straight year, a streak that would reach seven. He had a volcanic temper that caused his teammates to avoid talking to him on days when he pitched, but catcher Mickey Cochrane mostly kept him in line. Lefty put together a personal nine-game winning streak in 1929. On August 14 he beat the Cleveland Indians to run his record to 18-2. There simply was no better pitcher at that time. Some people would say ever.

The Athletics made a mockery of the 1929 pennant race. Their only setback occurred when rain postponed the opener in Washington. The next afternoon President Herbert Hoover threw the ceremonial first pitch, the A's exploded for 13 runs in the first five innings, and the Mackmen were off and running. After May 11 they were never out of first place. Beginning on May 17, they won 11 in a row and 17 of 18. As of June 17, they had lost back-to-back games only one time. On the Fourth of July the Athletics' record stood at 53-17, a winning percentage of .757, which as of 2014 still stands as the best ever in the American League on Independence Day. On Labor Day, September 2, the A's swept a doubleheader from the Yankees, and the pennant race was all but over as Philadelphia now had a 13½-game lead over New York. Mack's team officially clinched it on September 14. They ended the season with a record of 104-46, a full 18 games ahead of the second-place Yankees.

All around Philadelphia the cry was, Bring on the Cubs!

SOURCES

Baseball-Reference.com

Retrosheet.org

"Connie Mack Signs Eddie Collins for Long Term," *Evening Independent*, July 28, 1914.

Obituary, Associated Press Wire, June 27, 1962.

Kaplan, Jim, *Lefty Grove* (Cleveland: Society for American Baseball Research, 2000).

Kashatus, Bill. *Connie Mack's '29 Triumph* (Jefferson, North Carolina: McFarland and Company, Inc., 1999).

NOTES

1 "Connie Mack Signs Eddie Collins for Long Term," *Evening Independent*
   (St. Petersburg, Florida), July 28, 1914.

2 Bill Kashatus, *Connie Mack's '29 Triumph*. (Jefferson, North Carolina:
   McFarland and Company, Inc., 1999), 100.

3 Obituary, Associated Press Wire, June 27, 1962.

4 Jim Kaplan, *Lefty Grove* (Cleveland: Society for American Baseball
   Research, 2000), 70.

THE 1929 WORLD SERIES
GAME-BY-GAME SUMMARY

By Norm King

PERHAPS MORE THAN ANY OTHER World Series in history, the 1929 version between the Philadelphia Athletics and the Chicago Cubs served as a metaphorical bridge for changing eras in America. It was the last fall classic of the Golden Age of Sports, and just as the roar of the 1920s was waning, the dominant team of the decade, the New York Yankees, was supplanted, albeit temporarily, by a new dynasty, the Philadelphia Athletics. Even President Herbert Hoover, judging by the reaction he received when he arrived for Game Five of the Series, could not have known that the Series finished a scant ten days before the stock market crash abruptly ended the boom times and sent the country and the world spiraling into the Great Depression.

"The President received a rousing welcome when he entered Shibe Park from the thousands of fans who crowded every corner of the stands," wrote the *New York Times* in describing Hoover's arrival for Game Five.[1]

It is doubtful he would have received the same reaction one year later.

As for the Series itself, it was only the second time that decade that neither participant represented New York or Brooklyn. The A's were playing in the Series for the first time since 1914 and the Chicago Cubs for the first time since 1918. The two teams had met previously in 1910, with the A's prevailing in five games.

PHILADELPHIA ATHLETICS

Many people believe that the New York Yankees of 1927 were the greatest team of all time, but the men who played against them feel that the 1929 A's were just about as good.

"According to most old-timers who played in that era, the 1927 and '28 Yankees and the 1929 and '30 Athletics matched up so closely that they were nearly equal, with the A's given the nod in fielding and pitching and the Yankees in hitting," wrote William Nack in *Sports Illustrated*.[2]

In 1928 the A's won 98 games but finished 2½ games behind the Yankees. A's manager Connie Mack decided that only some minor adjustments were necessary, and so he chanced to tinker with the team by releasing 30-year-old first baseman Joe Hauser and inserting 21-year-old Jimmie Foxx in his place. Foxx, who batted .328 with 13 home runs and 79 RBIs in 118 games in 1928, responded to playing full-time with a .354 average, 33 home runs, and 118 RBIs in 1929.

Adding Foxx to the lineup enabled the A's to steamroll over the American League with a 104-46 record and an 18-game margin over the second-place Yankees. Of course it also helped that the team led the league in on-base percentage (.365), and was second in runs scored (901, behind the Tigers' 927) and home runs (122 to the Yankees' 142).

The pitching staff did its part, too, allowing the fewest runs in the league (616) and having the best ERA (3.44). Defensively the A's committed the fewest errors (148) and tied the St. Louis Browns for the highest fielding percentage (.975).

CHICAGO CUBS

True, the A's were a dynasty in the making, but the Cubs weren't slouches, either. They won 91 games in 1928 and finished four games out of first place, so they didn't need to make substantial changes to compete in 1929. That is, of course, if you call trading for Rogers Hornsby a minor adjustment. Chicago acquired Hornsby from the Boston Braves on November 7, 1928, for five players and $200,000, a huge sum for the period. Only two of the players Chicago gave up, second baseman Freddie Maguire and pitcher Percy Jones, were with the Cubs in 1928.

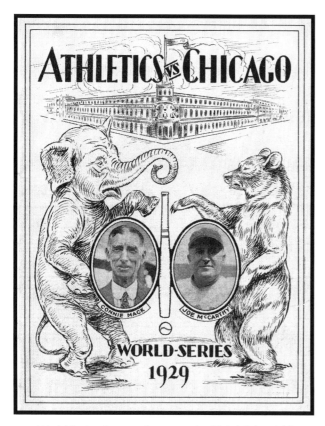

1929 World Series Program featuring the Philadelphia Athletics and Chicago Cubs. (National Baseball Hall of Fame)

The Rajah had a typical Hornsbyesque season in 1929, batting .380 with 39 home runs, 149 RBIs, and an amazing .459 on-base percentage. He wasn't the only one who could "tickle the ribbies," as three other players drove in more than 100 runs (Hack Wilson, 159; Riggs Stephenson, 110; Kiki Cuyler, 102). A fourth, Charlie Grimm, drove in 91 runs despite missing 34 games. With all this power, it's no surprise that the Cubs led the league in runs scored, with 982.

The Cubs also had a strong pitching staff. The team ERA of 4.16, although quite a bit higher than that of the A's, was actually second in the National League. They were also second in fewest runs allowed (759) and strikeouts (548) as a staff.

The pitching staff was helped by an excellent defense that committed the fewest errors in the league (154).

GAME ONE – TUESDAY, OCTOBER 8

With starters like George Earnshaw (24-8) and Lefty Grove (20-6) to choose from to start Game One at Wrigley Field for the A's, it only made sense for Mack to choose … Howard Ehmke?

Ehmke, a 35-year-old veteran of the American League wars, responded by pitching one of the most famous games in World Series history, a 3-1 complete-game win in which he established a record for strikeouts in a World Series game with 13. (Bob Gibson broke the record in 1968 when he fanned 17 Detroit Tigers in a World Series game.) Coincidentally, the Cubs were also the victims when Ed Walsh set the previous record of 12 in 1906 for the Chicago White Sox.

Although he was a surprise starter for the Athletics, the choice wasn't as strange as it seemed, judging by Ehmke's own reminiscence of events. That June, Mack wanted to send Ehmke to Portland of the Pacific Coast League for the remainder of the season and become manager there the next year. Ehmke persuaded Mack to let him stay on with the A's by telling him the Yankees were the team to beat and that he pitched well against them. He went 2-1 against the Yankees that season, and 7-2 overall with a 3.29 ERA as a spot starter. Friday, September 13, proved lucky for Ehmke, as he went eight innings in a 5-2 win over the White Sox in Philadelphia..

"It was following the White Sox game that Connie asked me if I could pitch in cold weather," said Ehmke. "I said, 'You mean October 8, the opening game of the World Series?' He said, 'That's exactly what I mean.'"[3]

The Cubs countered with a more conventional choice, Charlie Root (19-6), who seemed to have a penchant for being on the wrong end of famous World Series moments. He pitched in the other famous game of this Series, and was the pitcher for Babe Ruth's "called shot" in 1932.

The fame of Ehmke's performance hides the fact that the game was very close. The two pitchers traded goose-eggs on the scoreboard for six innings, until Jimmie Foxx broke the scoreless tie with a home run to left-center. Two errors by Cubs shortstop Woody English led to two more unearned runs to make it 3-0 going into the bottom of the ninth.

With one out, Cubs right fielder Kiki Cuyler made it to second base on a throwing error to first by A's third baseman Jimmy Dykes, and scored on a single by left fielder Riggs Stephenson to end Ehmke's shutout bid. First baseman Charlie Grimm followed with another single before pinch-hitter Footsie Blair bounced into a fielder's choice for the second out. With Chicago runners on first and third, Ehmke struck out pinch-hitter Chick Tolson to end the game.

For Connie Mack, whose career had more than its share of exciting moments, this game was special. "My greatest thrill was starting Howard Ehmke as [the] surprise pitcher against the Cubs in the first game of the 1929 World Series," he said in a 1941 interview.[4]

GAME TWO—WEDNESDAY, OCTOBER 9

In Game Two, Connie Mack continued using his pitchers in a manner inconceivable by today's standards, when he sent not one, but two 20-game winners to the mound in the same game. But hey, whatever works, right?

What promised to be a pitchers' duel between Earnshaw and Pat Malone (22-10) didn't work out that way, as the A's powered their way to a 9-3 win and a 2-0 lead in games as the Series headed to Philadelphia's Shibe Park.

Unlike Game One, it was obvious early that the Athletics meant business. Jimmie Foxx set the tone in the third with a three-run homer to left. Two hits, two walks, and an error in the fourth led to three more unearned runs and the rout was on.

The Cubs were nothing if not plucky, as they plated three runs, all earned, in the bottom of the fifth to make the game close, at least temporarily, as Stephenson, Grimm, and Zack Taylor each singled to reap an RBI in the inning. It was after the third run scored and with two out that Mack relieved Earnshaw with Lefty Grove, who held the Cubs scoreless on three hits the rest of the way.

Any thoughts of a Cubs comeback were dashed when the A's scored once in the seventh on Dykes' run-scoring single and twice in the eighth on Al Simmons' two-run shot.

GAME THREE—FRIDAY, OCTOBER 11

The Cubs had proved that Ehmke's 13-strikeout performance in Game One was no fluke by striking out the same number of times in Game Two. The top three batters in the lineup, including Hornsby, struck out twice each, while Cuyler swatted at air five times in the first two games. The only extra-base hits came off the bat of shortstop Woody English, who doubled in each game. If they wanted any hope of winning, the Cubbies were going to have to get some hits.

At least that's what conventional wisdom says. Instead, they won 3-1, despite getting only six hits, including three for extra bases that had no bearing on the scoring. In one inning, the sixth, Cubs hitters took advantage of their breaks with some timely hits, all singles, plus an error.

In another example of how differently pitchers were used before the days of pitch counts and multiple relievers, Mack went right back with Earnshaw. Guy Bush, who had an 18-7 regular-season record, and who had pitched the last two innings of Game One, started for the Cubs.

The game was scoreless until the bottom of the fifth inning, primarily because the A's didn't take advantage of their numerous opportunities. They left two on in the second and fourth innings, and the bases loaded in the third. Finally they got one across the small-ball way when Mickey Cochrane singled to short, moved to second on a groundout to Bush, and scored on a two-out single to center by right fielder Bing Miller.

Earnshaw committed a cardinal sin by walking the leadoff hitter in the top of the sixth. The mistake was compounded by the fact that it was the opposing pitcher, Bush. After third baseman Norm McMillan popped out to Cochrane trying to bunt, shortstop Woody English reached first on an error by third baseman Jimmy Dykes. Hornsby then singled to score Bush and, after a groundout by Wilson moved the runners up, Cuyler singled to center to drive in two. The A's last real chance for a comeback was in the seventh when they left runners on second and third. Bush put Philadelphia down in order the last two innings to get the complete-game victory.

"The gameness and smartness of Guy Bush won that ball game for the Cubs and brought them back into the series with a new fighting spirit," wrote Giants manager John McGraw.[5]

GAME FOUR — SATURDAY, OCTOBER 12

Some World Series games are spirit-breakers for the teams that lose them. Just ask the 1988 Oakland A's how they felt watching Kirk Gibson limping around the bases after his game-winning pinch-hit home run in Game One of that year's Series. The Los Angeles Dodgers' Series victory in five games over a team that had won 104 regular-season contests was almost a foregone conclusion after that.

Game Four of the 1929 World Series was like that for the Cubs. They snatched defeat from the jaws of victory in an unprecedented, bizarre manner and without a Steve Bartman in sight. Not only did they blow an 8-0 lead, they did it in ONE inning, as the A's scored ten runs in the seventh to make the ultimate outcome a mere formality.

The Cubs had a plenty of reason for optimism going into Game Four. Timely hitting and gritty pitching from Guy Bush had allowed them to win Game Three and seize the momentum from Philadelphia. Their confidence probably got another boost when Mack started 46-year-old journeyman Jack Quinn, who had an 11-9 record with a 3.97 ERA, instead of Lefty Grove. The Cubs started Charlie Root.

The Cubs went ahead 2-0 on a two-run homer by Grimm in the fourth, and then seemingly pulled away in the sixth. Four straight singles drove in two runs and sent Quinn to the showers to be replaced by Rube Walberg. With runners on first and second, Grimm got a bunt single, but Walberg's wild throw to first on the play scored two more runs and allowed Grimm to reach third. He scored on a sacrifice fly by catcher Zack Taylor. Another run in

the seventh gave the Cubs their seemingly insurmountable 8-0 lead.

Al Simmons led off the bottom of the seventh with a solo shot to left. Then the roof caved in for Root as five of the next six hitters singled, with the second of those hits a short fly ball that center fielder Hack Wilson lost in the sun. With the score 8-4 and runners on first and third, Art Nehf replaced Root and promptly gave up a fly ball to Mule Haas that Wilson also lost in the sun and ended up as a three-run inside-the-park homer. Now it was 8-7. A walk, followed by a two more singles, a hit batsman, and a two-run double (despite two additional pitching changes by Joe McCarthy), and the A's comeback was complete.

Philadelphia scored the 10 runs on 10 hits with Simmons, Foxx, and Dykes getting two hits each during the inning. Lefty Grove entered the game in relief for the last two innings and struck out four of the six Chicago batters he faced for his second save of the Series. The Cubs, who had been looking with anticipation of a Series tied at two games apiece, were now down three games to one.

"A one, or two, or three-run defeat in an ordinary ball game isn't bad," wrote Damon Runyon. "But a defeat that takes on the aspect of the ludicrous is a tough thing to overcome."[6]

GAME FIVE — MONDAY, OCTOBER 14

Pat Malone faced only four batters in the Game Four debacle, so with a day to rest because Philadelphia's Blue Laws forbade baseball on Sundays, McCarthy decided to start him in Game Five. Hoping to catch lightning in a bottle a second time, Mack went with Ehmke despite having Grove available (Grove pitched 6⅓ innings in the entire Series, all in relief).

The 13-strikeout game was a memory as Ehmke was down 2-0 when he left with two gone in the fourth. Cuyler started the two-out rally in that inning with a double. After Stephenson walked, singles by Grimm and Taylor scored Cuyler and Stephenson. Walberg, 18-11 during the regular season, came on for the A's, got the third out of the inning, and then went the rest of the way, allowing no runs while striking out six.

Malone was brilliant. Going into the ninth, he had given up only two hits. But as Game Four proved, the A's could be excused for thinking that they had the Cubs where they wanted them, even going into the bottom of the ninth down by two. With one out, Bishop singled to left and Haas followed with his second home run of the Series, a no-doubter over the right-field fence to tie the score. After Cochrane grounded out, Simmons doubled off the wall in center. Foxx came up with first base open and was walked intentionally, bringing Miller to the plate. Bing was able to start thinking about a white Christmas by doubling to center, driving in Simmons with the game and Series winner.

POSTSCRIPT

The two clubs continued to be successful as the "Dirty Thirties" began. The A's repeated as World Series champions in 1930, defeating the St. Louis Cardinals in six games after winning 102 during the regular season. The Cardinals returned the favor in 1931, winning the World Series in seven games over an Athletics club that had won 107 during the regular season. After that, age and trades caused the A's to decline steadily in subsequent years, to the point where they finished last in the American League nine times between 1935 and 1946.

The Depression-era Cubs, on the other hand, contended throughout the decade, reaching the World Series in 1932, 1935, and 1938 but losing every time. After a few lean years during World War II, they reached the Series again in 1945, losing in seven games to the Detroit Tigers. As of 2014, they had not returned to the World Series, and still awaited their first title since 1908.

SOURCES

news.google.com/newspapers

baseball-reference.com/teams/CHC/1929.shtml

books.google.ca/books

Huhn, Rick, *Eddie Collins: A Baseball Biography* (Jefferson, North Carolina: McFarland & Company Inc., Publishers, 2008)

NOTES

1   "Hoover is Cheered at Baseball Game," *New York Times*, October 15, 1929.

2   William Nack, "Lost in History," *Sports Illustrated*, August 19, 1996.

3   Ralph Bernstein, "Cinderella Pitcher of 1929 Series Tells Inside Story of Opening Game Victory" *The Daily Times* (Beaver and Rochester, Pennsylvania), February 19, 1945.

4   Associated Press, "Connie Mack Looks for Great Pitching Staff Next Season as He Observes 79th Birthday," *Pittsburgh Post-Gazette*, December 23, 1941.

5   John J. McGraw, "Cubs Chances Better — M'Graw," *Pittsburgh Press*, October 12, 1929.

6   Damon Runyon, "As Runyon Sees the Series," *Pittsburgh Post-Gazette*, October 14, 1929.

BY THE NUMBERS

By Dan Fields

CHICAGO CUBS IN 1929

1st

Pennant won by manager Joe McCarthy. He went on to win eight AL pennants and seven World Series titles with the New York Yankees.

2nd

Most Valuable Player award won by Rogers Hornsby. He was the 1925 NL MVP while playing for the St. Louis Cardinals.

3

Doubles by Cliff Heathcote in the first game of a July 27 doubleheader against the Philadelphia Phillies. The Cubs won 6-1.

3.47

ERA of Charlie Root, third lowest in the NL. Pat Malone was fourth with an ERA of 3.57, and Guy Bush was seventh with a 3.66 ERA.

4

Future Hall of Famers playing for the 1929 Cubs: Kiki Cuyler, Gabby Hartnett, Rogers Hornsby, and Hack Wilson. Manager Joe McCarthy was also a future Hall of Famer.

4

Players on the 1929 Cubs with at least 100 RBIs: Hack Wilson (159, most in the majors), Rogers Hornsby (149), Riggs Stephenson (110), and Kiki Cuyler (102). Hornsby, with 1,153 RBIs during the 1920s, was the only NL player with 1,000 during the decade.

5

Shutouts by Pat Malone, most in the majors. Charlie Root tossed four shutouts.

5

Singles (in five at-bats) by Cliff Heathcote in a nine-inning game on July 26. The Cubs beat the Phillies, 13-10.

5

Walks drawn by Rogers Hornsby in a 16-inning game on August 5. The Cubs beat the Brooklyn Robins, 9-8.

7

RBIs by Riggs Stephenson in a July 1 game against the Cardinals. He hit a grand slam in the first inning and a three-run homer in the sixth inning; he also hit a double. The teams tied, 11-11.

7

Multi-homer games by Hack Wilson, including six games from June 4 through July 31.

8

Saves by Guy Bush, tied for most in the NL.

9

Grand slams hit by the 1929 Cubs, still a team record.

22

Wins by Pat Malone, the only 20-game winner in the NL. Charlie Root tied for second in the league with 19 wins, and Guy Bush tied for fourth with 18.

27

Consecutive games with a hit by Hack Wilson, from June 20 through July 20. During the streak, he had 42 hits in 107 at-bats (.393), with 9 home runs, 28 runs scored, and 30 RBIs. Wilson's hot bat went cold on July 21, when he struck out four times in four at-bats against Brooklyn's Dazzy Vance. Wilson also had a 20-game hitting streak, from August 31 to September 21. During that streak, he had a .438 average, with 6 home runs, 20 runs scored, and 31 RBIs.

28

Consecutive scoreless innings by Chicago pitchers, from April 18 to April 23.

36

Hits by the Cubs during a doubleheader sweep (11-7 and 12-10) of the Cardinals on September 2, with 16 hits in the first game and 20 hits in the second game. Woody English, Rogers Hornsby, and Riggs Stephenson each had six hits that day, as did Jim Bottomley and Andy High of the Cardinals.

39

Home runs each by Rogers Hornsby and Hack Wilson, tied for third in the NL.

43

Stolen bases by Kiki Cuyler, most in the majors.

50

Games pitched by Guy Bush, most in the majors.

83

Strikeouts by Hack Wilson, most in the majors.

94

Extra-base hits by Rogers Hornsby, tied for most in the majors.

98

Wins by the 1929 Cubs, the most by the team since 1910, against only 54 losses. The Cubs finished 10½ games ahead of the second-place Pittsburgh Pirates.

156

Games played by Rogers Hornsby, most in the majors.

156

Runs scored by Rogers Hornsby, most in the majors in 1929 and most in the NL in one season since 1896; Hornsby's feat is still a Cubs single-season record. Hack Wilson was fourth in the major leagues with 135 runs, and Woody English was tied for sixth with 131.

166

Strikeouts thrown by Pat Malone, most in the NL. He led the majors with 5.596 strikeouts per nine innings.

169

Double plays turned by the 1929 Cubs, most in the majors.

229

Hits by Rogers Hornsby, the third most in the NL and still a Cubs single-season record.

.303

Batting average of the 1929 Cubs, tied for the second highest in the majors.

.380

Batting average of Rogers Hornsby, third best in the majors and still the highest by a Cub since 1895. Riggs Stephenson (.362) was fifth in the NL, and Kiki Cuyler (.360) was sixth.

409

Total bases by Rogers Hornsby, most in the majors. Hack Wilson was fourth in the NL with 355 bases.

The Cubs won 98 games in 1929 and captured their first pennant since 1918. They also won pennants in 1932, 1935, 1938 and 1945. (Library of Congress)

.459

On-base percentage of Rogers Hornsby, second highest in the NL.

.679

Slugging average of Rogers Hornsby, highest in the NL. This was the last of nine times that Hornsby led the league in slugging percentage.

.760

Won-lost percentage of Charlie Root, best in the NL. He had 19 wins against only 6 losses. Guy Bush was second in the league with a .720 percentage, and Hal Carlson and Pat Malone were tied for fourth with a .688 percentage.

982

Runs scored by the 1929 Cubs, most in the majors.

1.139

On-base percentage plus slugging average of Rogers Hornsby, tops in the majors. This was the tenth time that Hornsby led the NL in OPS.

1,485,166

Attendance at Wrigley Field during the 1929 season — a major-league record until 1946, and a Cubs record until 1969.

1929 WORLD SERIES

1st

World Series played at Wrigley Field. In 1918, Cubs played their home games during the Series in the larger confines of Comiskey Park.

1

Game won by the Cubs (Game Three). The Philadelphia Athletics won the Series in five games.

2

Home runs each by Jimmie Foxx, Mule Haas, and Al Simmons of the Athletics during the Series. The Cubs had only one home run, by Charlie Grimm in Game Four.

4th

World Series title won by Philadelphia manager Connie Mack, also won in 1910, 1911, and 1913. He went on to win one more title, in 1930.

10

Runs allowed by the Cubs in the bottom of the seventh inning of Game Four. Hack Wilson lost two balls in the sun, one for an inside-the-park homer that scored three runs. The Athletics overcame an 8-0 deficit to win 10-8. The next team to allow 10 runs in an inning in the World Series was the 1968 Cardinals, in the third inning of Game Six against the Detroit Tigers.

13

Strikeouts thrown by 35-year-old Howard Ehmke of the Athletics in Game One, a World Series single-game record until 1953. Among the attendees at that game was 9-year-old John Paul Stevens, who became a Supreme Court justice in 1975.

46

Age of Philadelphia pitcher Jack Quinn, who worked the first five innings of Game Four.

.471

Batting average of Hack Wilson, with 8 hits in 17 at-bats. Jimmy Dykes led Philadelphia batters with a .421 average (8-for-19).

AROUND THE MAJORS IN 1929

0

Hits allowed by Carl Hubbell of the New York Giants on May 8, in an 11-0 complete-game victory over the Pirates. It was the 13th of 253 wins and the only no-hitter in his career.

1st

Major-league pitch faced in which pitcher Clise Dudley of the Robins hit a home run, on April 27. He hit only two more home runs in his career. Earl Averill of the Cleveland Indians hit a home run in his first major-league at-bat, on April 16.

1st

Sunday baseball game in Boston, on April 28. Playing at Braves Field rather than Fenway Park, the Red Sox lost to the Athletics 7-3.

1st

Game in which opposing teams wore uniform numbers, as the Indians hosted the Yankees on May 13.

1st

Year of 12 consecutive years in which Jimmie Foxx hit at least 30 home runs and had 100 RBIs. It was also the first of nine consecutive years in which Lou Gehrig of the Yankees had a .300 batting average, 30 home runs, and 100 RBIs; he had previously accomplished the feat in 1927.

2

Grand slams by opposing pinch-hitters (Pat Crawford of the Giants and Les Bell of the Braves) in a May 26 game. The Giants won 15-8.

2

Consecutive games in which Babe Ruth of the Yankees hit grand slams, on August 6 and August 7 (first game of a doubleheader).

2.81

ERA of Lefty Grove of the Athletics. He was the only player eligible for the ERA title with an average under 3.00. Bill Walker of the Giants was best in the NL with an ERA of 3.09, which remains the highest average to lead the league since 1893.

3

Consecutive home runs by Babe Ruth, Lou Gehrig, and Bob Meusel of the Yankees in the seventh inning of a May 4 game against the White Sox. The Yankees won 11-9.

3

Triples by Lance Richbourg of the Braves during the first game of a July 31 doubleheader versus the Cubs at Wrigley Field, and by Charlie Gehringer of the Tigers in an August 5 game.

4

Players on the Phillies with at least 200 hits: Lefty O'Doul (254, an NL record that has never been topped), Chuck Klein (219), Fresco Thompson (202), and Pinky Whitney (200). The only team ever to match this feat was the 1937 Detroit Tigers.

4

Players on the Phillies with at least 115 RBIs: Chuck Klein (145), Don Hurst (125), Lefty O'Doul (122), and Pinky Whitney (115). No other team has ever matched this accomplishment.

5

Walks issued to Mel Ott of the Giants in the second game of an October 5 doubleheader against the Phillies. The walks helped deny Ott the NL home-run title. He and Chuck Klein began the day tied at 42 homers, and Klein hit his 43rd in the first game of the doubleheader.

5

Rookies who scored at least 100 runs in 1929: Roy Johnson of the Tigers (128), Johnny Frederick of the Robins (127), Dale Alexander of the Tigers (110), Earl Averill of the Indians (110), and Evar Swanson of the Reds (100).

6

Hits (in eight at-bats) by Lloyd Waner of the Pirates in a 14-inning game on June 15. Hank DeBerry of the Robins had six hits in seven at-bats in a 14-inning game on June 23.

9

Hits by Bill Terry of the Giants in a doubleheader against the Robins on June 18. He went 5-for-5 (including a three-run homer) in the first game and 4-for-5 in the second game. But the Giants could not capitalize on this feat; they were swept, 8-7 and 7-6.

10

Hits in 10 consecutive at-bats by Chick Hafey of the Cardinals, from July 6 to 9. He tied an NL record that still stands.

10

Wins by Burleigh Grimes of the Pirates in his first 10 decisions of the season. After compiling a record of 17-3 by late August, Grimes lost his last four decisions of the season.

12

Wins, with no losses, by Tom Zachary of the Yankees. He picked up nine wins as the starting pitcher. Zachary still holds the major-league record for most wins in a season without a loss.

14

Earned runs given up by Johnny Miljus of the Indians in the first three innings of a July 25 game against the Athletics. The Indians lost, 21-3.

19 and 9

Wins and saves, respectively, by Firpo Marberry of the Washington Senators. He was fourth in the AL in wins and tied for the major-league lead in saves. (The save figure is retrospective; there was no such statistic at the time.)

20

Triples by Lloyd Waner, most in the majors. Charlie Gehringer led the AL with 19.

20

Age of Mel Ott when he hit his 40th home run of the year, on September 21 against Charlie Root. Ott remains the youngest player to hit 40 home runs in a season.

21

Innings pitched by Ted Lyons of the Chicago White Sox in a 6-5 loss to the Tigers on May 24. George Uhle, who got the win, pitched 20 innings.

22

Losses by Red Ruffing of the Red Sox, most in the majors. Watty Clark of the Robins led the NL with 19 losses.

24

Wins by George Earnshaw of the Athletics, most in the majors. The other 20-game winners in the AL were Wes Ferrell of the Indians (21 wins) and Lefty Grove of the Athletics (20 wins).

27

Stolen bases by Charlie Gehringer, most in the AL.

28

Consecutive games with a base hit by Bing Miller of the Athletics, from May 30 through June 27.

28-6

Score by which the Cardinals beat the Phillies in the second game of a doubleheader on July 6. Jim Bottomley and Chick Hafey of St. Louis hit grand slams, and the team scored 10 runs in each of the first and fifth innings. The Phillies won the first game, 10-6. For the day, the two teams combined for 50 runs and 73 hits (43 hits by the Cardinals).

32

Consecutive innings in which the Yankees did not score a run, between August 21 and August 25.

46

Home runs by Babe Ruth, most in the majors. Chuck Klein led the NL with 43, a league record until the following year, when Hack Wilson hit 56.

52

Doubles by Johnny Frederick, the most in the majors and still a record for rookies. Three players tied for most in the AL with 45: Charlie Gehringer and Roy Johnson of the Tigers, and Heinie Manush of the St. Louis Browns.

53

Age of Nick Altrock of the Senators when he hit a single against the Red Sox on October 6.

104

Wins by the Athletics, against only 46 losses. The team won the AL pennant by 18 games over the second-place Yankees. It was the first of three consecutive years in which the Athletics won at least 100 games.

115

Consecutive games without striking out by Joe Sewell of the Indians, from May 19 through September 19. He led the majors, by far, with 144.5 at-bats per strikeout in 1929 (4 strikeouts in all).

128

Walks received by Max Bishop of the Athletics, most in the majors. He had 18 more walks than hits (110). Mel Ott led the NL with 113 walks.

131

Runs scored by Charlie Gehringer, most in the AL.

137

RBIs by Dale Alexander of the Tigers, a rookie record at the time. He also set rookie records for extra-base hits (83), total bases (363), and slugging average (.580).

157

RBIs by Al Simmons of the Athletics, most in the AL.

170

Strikeouts thrown by Lefty Grove, most in the majors. Teammate George Earnshaw was second in the AL with 149.

215

Hits each by teammates Dale Alexander and Charlie Gehringer, who tied for most in the AL. Another teammate, Roy Johnson, had 201 hits.

217-21-21

Hits, home runs, and stolen bases, respectively, by Babe Herman of the Robins. He became the first player with 200 hits, 20 home runs, and 20 stolen bases in the same season. Herman had a .381 batting average, second highest in the majors.

.294

Batting average of the entire NL. The AL had a batting average of .284.

.309

Batting average of the Phillies, highest in the majors.

334

Times on base by Lefty O'Doul, most in the majors and most in the NL since 1894. Lu Blue of the Browns led the AL with 296 times on base.

373

Total bases by Al Simmons, most in the AL.

.398

Batting average of Lefty O'Doul, tops in the majors and still the highest by a Phillie since 1899. Lew Fonseca of the Indians led the AL with a .369 average.

.465

On-base percentage of Lefty O'Doul, tops in the majors. Jimmie Foxx of the Athletics led the AL with a .463 OBP.

500

Career home runs by Babe Ruth as of August 11. He was the first to accomplish this feat. At the time, Ruth had more than twice as many as his nearest rival, Cy Williams of the Phillies (249 homers).

678

Hits by Lloyd Waner of the Pirates in his first three seasons (223 in 1927, 221 in 1928, and 234 in 1929), still a major-league record.

.697

Slugging average of Babe Ruth, tops in the majors.

.769

Won-lost percentage of Lefty Grove, highest in the majors. Teammate George Earnshaw was second in the AL with a .750 percentage.

1,036

Runs allowed by the Phillies — a whopping 6.73 per game.

1.128

OPS of Babe Ruth, highest in the AL.

1,338 and 1,002

RBIs by Babe Ruth and Bob Meusel, respectively, with the Yankees during the 1920s. Meusel was the third player with 1,000 or RBIs during his first ten seasons. Harry Heilmann had 1,131 RBIs during the 1920s, all with the Tigers.

1,413

Career wins by manager Miller Huggins when he died from blood poisoning on September 25 at the age of 51. He won 346 games with the Cardinals from 1913 through 1917 and 1,067 games (as well as six AL pennants and three World Series titles) with the Yankees between 1918 and 1929. At the time of his death, only four other managers (Connie Mack, John McGraw, Fred Clarke, and Clark Griffith) had won more games.

SOURCES

Nemec, David, ed., *The Baseball Chronicle: Year-by-Year History of Major League Baseball* (Lincolnwood, Illinois: Publications International, 2003).

Society for American Baseball Research, *The SABR Baseball List and Record Book.* (New York: Scribner, 2007).

Solomon, Burt, *The Baseball Timeline.* (New York: DK Publishing, 2001).

Sugar, Burt Randolph, ed., *The Baseball Maniac's Almanac* (third edition). (New York: Skyhorse Publishing, 2012.

baseball-almanac.com

baseballlibrary.com/chronology

baseball-reference.com

chicago.cubs.mlb.com

retrosheet.org

thisgreatgame.com/1929-baseball-history.html

THE CUBS AFTER 1929 — AN EPILOGUE

By Greg Erion

VEN THOUGH THE CHICAGO CUBS lost the World Series to the Philadelphia A's in 1929, they had the makings of a dynasty. William Wrigley had assembled a solid management team led by vice president and treasurer William Veeck, Sr. and manager Joe McCarthy. Wrigley supplied the capital, Veeck the organizational skills, and McCarthy the field leadership, having transformed the last-place baseball club he inherited in 1925 into the pennant winner of 1929. Poised to become a perennially dominant force in the National League, the Cubs faltered. An ill-advised management decision, a series of deaths, and the momentum to sustain excellence was lost. Decline was not apparent at first. Chicago won three pennants during the 1930s, seemingly a sign of continued success, but at the same time the firm sense of direction so necessary in achieving it gradually gave way to inconsistency and uncertainty. Into the 21st century the franchise had yet to regain any dependable sense of what they had attained during this era. Chicago's fall from grace had its origins in their fateful encounter with Philadelphia in the 1929 World Series.

The A's had decidedly manhandled Chicago. Howard Ehmke's quirky success in the opening game, their come-from-behind victory in Game Four after being down 8-0, and a last-inning rally to clinch the championship stunned the Cubs. Woody English recalled, "After we lost the final game it was pretty quiet in the clubhouse. Everyone was down, real bad."[1] Manager Joe McCarthy defended his players, insisting that the loss of the Series should not be pinned on Hack Wilson, whose fielding misplays highlighted the Cubs' collapse in the fourth game. Perhaps the loss was not Wilson's fault.

However, it was someone's. Despite McCarthy's success in leading the Cubs to their first pennant since 1918, he had not fulfilled William Wrigley's quest for baseball's ultimate prize. Upset after the A's ten-run outburst put the Cubs down three games to one, Wrigley found himself with *Chicago Tribune* sportswriter Irving Vaughn in a hotel elevator after the Series ended. Noting that McCarthy had another year on his contract, Wrigley

shared, "…and that was all he was going to get."[2] Wrigley spent the entire winter replaying the seventh inning of Game Four, visualizing McCarthy's seeming inaction in the face of catastrophe.[3] His mindset was not helped by the onset of the Great Depression, which had eaten into the Wrigley Company's finances. Any idea that McCarthy was imagining his boss's ire ended when former Chicago White Sox manager Ray Schalk, at the direction of Wrigley, was hired to replace one of McCarthy's coaches, Grover Land. Fatalism set in. During spring training McCarthy told his friend Warren Brown, a sportswriter for the *Chicago Herald and Examiner*, that "he would not be with the Cubs after the current season, win, lose or draw."[4]

Despite Wrigley's impatience and McCarthy's pessimism, Chicago was favored to win the pennant in 1930.[5] The team improved with the return of catcher Gabby Hartnett to the lineup, fully recovered from an arm injury that shelved him most of 1929. Veteran third baseman Les Bell, acquired from the Boston Braves, bolstered the infield.[6] Guy Bush, Pat Malone, and Charlie Root were in their prime, supported by Sheriff Blake and Hal Carlson on the mound, their combined record for 1929 a healthy 84-41.

Any illusions that Chicago might coast to another championship were quickly dashed as injuries assailed the team. Spring training saw Bush hurt his elbow and left fielder Riggs Stephenson damage his throwing arm. Bell developed a sore arm, missing most of spring training, others experienced nagging injuries.[7] The most serious injury however, was to Rogers Hornsby. During the latter part of the 1929 season, it became evident that Hornsby was not at full capacity, his lackluster .238 batting average during the World Series contributing to the Cubs' loss. During the offseason he had an operation to remove a bone spur from his right heel. Recovery was complicated; Hornsby was still limping as the campaign began. During the first few weeks, he played sporadically, mostly as a pinch-hitter. Toward the end of May, Chicago was sputtering along in fourth place behind St. Louis, five games out. Within a week, twin disasters hit the club.

Hal Carlson was scheduled to pitch on May 27; however, the game was rained out. Early the next morning, he died suddenly, the victim of a stomach hemorrhage. Carlson was only 38. On a pitching staff dominated by Bush, Malone, and Root, he filled a valued role, that of spot starter. In 1929 he was 11-5, in 1930 he had posted a 4-2 record, leading the team in victories when he died. The team was stunned.[8]

The day after Carlson's funeral, Chicago played a double-header against St. Louis. Hornsby, back in the lineup had just started to hit. In the first game, after hitting a double, he tried to move to third on a fly to right. Sliding to beat the throw, Hornsby broke his ankle. The man who had hit .380 with 39 home runs and 149 RBIs in 1929 was lost until late August, and then appeared mostly as a pinch-hitter.

Normally these incidents demoralized teams. However, 1930 was not a normal year. With the loss of Carlson, the Cubs pitching staff was suspect. But then, the pitching staff of the entire National League was suspect. The entire league hit .303, reflected in the senior circuit's 4.97 combined ERA, hitting enhanced by use of a lively ball wound with Australian wool.[9] Despite the loss of Hornsby, Chicago's offensive production improved over 1929 with a team batting average of .309, a league-record 171 home runs, and 6.4 runs scored per game. Hartnett hit 37 home runs, Kiki Cuyler batted .355, English .335, and Stephenson .367. It was not their hitting however, that captured the baseball world's attention, but teammate Hack Wilson's. He set a league record with 56 home runs and a major-league record 191 RBIs, a record still unsurpassed in 2014.[10]

With Wilson leading the way, Chicago fought its way back into the pennant race. And all along, Wilson and his compatriot Pat Malone spent the evenings carousing, stories of their escapades legion among followers of the game. Although McCarthy eventually gained a reputation as a stern taskmaster when managing the Yankees, this situation was beyond him. What am I supposed to do? Tell [Wilson] to live a clean life and he'll hit better?"[11]

By August 27 the Cubs had a 5½-game lead. McCarthy began breathing easier: "They can't stop us from winning a second consecutive pennant."[12] Ah, but they could. On August 28 Chicago lost a 20-inning game to St. Louis. The next day they beat the Cardinals in 13. The Cubs used nine pitchers during those two contests with three of them appearing on the mound in both games. The effort wore the staff out as Root developed a sore arm and Sheriff Blake's back went out.[13] St. Louis got hot, going 21-4 in September as the Cubs played .500 ball. As the Cubs' pitching gave way, McCarthy must have wistfully thought of what Carlson might have meant to the team.

When it became obvious that Chicago was not going to repeat, Wrigley's confidence in McCarthy ended. Hornsby, in the company of Wrigley much of the summer, had freely second-guessed his skipper. McCarthy, who had never played a day in the majors, was dwarfed in comparison with the greatest right-handed hitter in baseball, one who had piloted the Cardinals to a world championship just four years earlier.

Wrigley decided to replace McCarthy with Hornsby in 1931. As word of the impending change spread, McCarthy met with Wrigley and after being assured that his salary was to be honored through 1930, McCarthy left the team with four games to play. Hornsby took over, and Chicago won all four. It was too late; St. Louis finished two games ahead of the Cubs. Within weeks McCarthy became manager of the New York Yankees. He had not given Wrigley a world championship. He accomplished it seven times with the Yankees. Wrigley had the makings of a dynasty; several historians of the Cubs franchise cite the decision to fire McCarthy as the point from which it began to decline.[14]

With Hornsby at the helm and ready to play, many favored the Cubs winning the pennant in 1931 if they could avoid injuries. It was not to be. Chicago had benefited from the offensive explosion in 1930. After the season it was determined that the offensive onslaught must cease. The National League approved use of a ball with a thicker cover and raised stitching.[15] Woody English described the difference as it applied to Hack Wilson: "Hack that year (1931) was hitting fly-ball outs. The balls that used to carry into the stands were just long fly balls." The ball did not carry as far, moreover, with raised stitches; pitchers could get a better grip and achieve a higher level of control. Wilson plummeted to .261, 13 homers, and 61 RBIs. His decline brought out the worst qualities of his nature, and late in the season, after repeated incidents of breaking curfew, drunkenness, and altercations, he was suspended by the Cubs. During the winter, a series of trades put him on the Brooklyn Dodgers.

Wilson's offensive decline was somewhat made up for as Hornsby got back into the lineup, hitting .331 and driving in 90 runs. The aging Hornsby (he was 35) never fully recovered from his ankle injury and played in only 100 games; from then on, he was reduced to part-time play and pinch-hitting. Moreover, as in 1930, injuries did befall the club, the most serious when Stephenson broke his ankle in late July; the .319 hitter missed the rest of the season. Chicago was never a factor in the pennant race, finishing third behind St. Louis and New York, a distant 17 games out.

As disappointing as the season was, several developments gave promise of better days. In late August Hornsby took himself out of the lineup, inserting 22-year-old rookie Billy Herman at second. Billy Jurges, another rookie infielder, showed superb fielding skills. Still another rookie, right-handed pitcher Lon Warneke, joined the staff. Residual benefits of an organization built by the combined efforts of McCarthy and Veeck benefited the club throughout the 1930s.

But all the while most of the players seethed under Hornsby's leadership. Blunt, abrasive, he ruled based on authority, not respect. His insistence on batters taking 2-and-0 and 3-and-1 pitches took the bat out of players' hands.[16] Heeding only his own counsel, Hornsby increasingly made lineup and personnel changes that proved questionable. Eventually he interfered with Hartnett, who when he found out pitchers were shaking off his signals and was told Hornsby had decided to call pitches, stalked over to his manager and growled, "You catch."[17] Despite what was slowly developing into an incipient player rebellion, Hornsby still had the ear of Wrigley who, despite the team's lackluster performance in 1931,

A baseball lifer, "Jolly Cholly" Grimm played for the Cubs for 12 years and managed the club for parts of 13 seasons, leading the North Siders to pennants in 1932, 1935 and 1945. (Retro Images Archive. George Brace Collection)

affirmed to the *Tribune's* Vaughn that Hornsby was his manager "for life." Unfortunately for Hornsby, Wrigley had not specified whose life.

Within months of that pronouncement, Wrigley died on January 26, 1932. Ownership of the team passed to his son, Philip, who by most accounts did not share his father's passion for the game. Shortly after taking control, he said, "The club and park stand as memorials to my father. ..." Bill Veeck, Jr. later recalled, "Phil Wrigley assumed the burden out of his sense of loyalty and duty. If he has any particular feeling for baseball, any real liking for it, he has disguised it magnificently."[18] Initially young Wrigley was content to leave running the franchise in the capable hands of Veeck Sr. As years passed, he increasingly inserted himself into managing the franchise, making decisions characterized by lack of understanding of the game, often hiring lackluster personnel with ever-limited authority to make key decisions.[19] At one point he even hired a psychologist to study his players. This generated a great deal of derision without any results beneficial to the organization.[20]

As the 1932 season began, few sportswriters picked the Cubs to be a force in the pennant race. However, unsuspected forces came into play. First was the sudden and unexpected emergence of Warneke as the National League's premier pitcher. A mere 2-4 as a rookie in 1931, he went 22-6 in 1932, leading the league in wins and anchoring what was arguably the best staff in baseball. The pitchers received tremendous defensive support with Herman at second and Jurges at shortstop forming a double-play combination peerless in all of baseball. Chicago's combined pitching and fielding capabilities with Hartnett's catching, Charlie Grimm at first, and English playing third, allowed Chicago to jump off to a league-leading 17-6 start. By the morning of July 6, they had cooled off somewhat, a close third behind Boston and Pittsburgh, when calamity in the form of a chorus girl struck.

Jurges had joined the Cubs in 1931 and as a young bachelor quickly found himself attracted to Chicago's enticing nightlife, in particular, a chorus girl named Violet Valli. She wanted to take the relationship to a more serious level; Jurges did not. Valli determined to end things in her own way. On the morning of July 6, she confronted Jurges in his hotel room and shot him several times before he wrested her small-caliber gun away and preventing Valli from killing herself — her original plan. The incident provided great press for several days but despite its potential for tragedy soon blew over. Jurges chose not to press charges and quickly recovered, returning to the lineup in less than three weeks.

As if this were not enough to distract the team, Hornsby's personality and style of management had thoroughly alienated most of the team. By the end of the month, his assessment that the Cubs did not have what it took to win the pennant had pushed Veeck to the edge. At virtually the same time, Veeck learned that Hornsby was borrowing money from Cubs players to support his gambling habit, an untenable situation.

On August 2 Veeck fired Hornsby and made the affable Grimm manager. The Cubs were in second, five games out. Players rejoiced, and the change inspired the team to go 22-5 the rest of the month. The first-place Pirates were in the midst of a ten-game losing streak and a 1-14 run. By August 11, the team Hornsby had written off moved into first place. Chicago held its lead, and a 14-game winning streak that began late in August put the race away. The Cubs finished the season four games ahead of the Pirates, going 37-18 for Grimm.

They were to face the Yankees, under Joe McCarthy. New York had won 107 games, 17 more than Chicago. The team, headed by Ruth and Gehrig, went into the series decidedly alienated by the way Chicago had treated a former teammate, Mark Koenig. Koenig, picked up to replace Hornsby on the roster, hit .353 during the stretch drive. For some reason, the Cubs players voted him only a half-share of their World Series pot, infuriating the Yankees at what they perceived to be shabby treatment.[21]

Thoroughly aroused, New York beat Chicago in four straight games, outscoring the Cubs 37-19. Chicago had performed even worse than in 1929. The most memorable if not key moments of the Series came in the fifth inning of Game Three, when Ruth came to bat. The Cubs were razzing him unmercifully. Ruth, after taking two strikes, pointed into their dugout and said, "That's only two strikes." The next pitch went over the center-field fence. Whether Ruth was gesturing toward the Cubs or "called his shot," as legend has it, remains open to conjecture, a point of endless controversy. The homer broke a 4-4 tie; the next day, Chicago went down 13-6 to end the Series. The Cubs had been annihilated, as English recalled later, "All I remember about that Series was that they murdered us. We couldn't retaliate because they got too many runs."[22]

Chicago experienced a slight letdown in 1933 winning four games fewer. Grimm and Billy Herman fell off from their 1932 performance; outfielder Babe Herman, obtained in a trade with Cincinnati, failed to live up to expectations. The Giants, in Bill Terry's first full year as manager, improved enough to win the pennant, six games ahead of third-place Chicago.

In a way, the most significant development of 1932 occurred off the field. Less than a week after the season ended, Veeck died on October 5. Since the death of William Wrigley, Veeck had run the club with little interference. He oversaw a minor-league system that continually supplied Chicago with quality ballplayers. The success of young players like Herman and Jurges was followed in 1933 when Frank Demaree became a regular in the outfield, and in 1934 when Stan Hack took over at third. No successor ever had the autonomy Veeck enjoyed in running the franchise. William Walker, a stockholder in the Cubs who had made his fortune in the fishmongering business, was selected to succeed Veeck. Aside from being an investor in the Cubs, Walker had no previous experience in baseball.[23]

Before he died, Veeck, in an effort to improve the Cubs' offense, had been working on a deal to obtain slugger Chuck Klein from the Philadelphia Phillies to bolster the offense. Less than two months after Veeck's passing, Klein came to Chicago in exchange for three players (including Koenig) and $65,000. In Klein, Chicago had obtained an outfielder whose three previous seasons had averaged .351, 32 home runs, and 126 RBIs. The deal failed to take into account the extreme advantage Klein had in playing at Philadelphia's bandbox Baker Bowl. Wrigley Field, configured differently, transformed Klein's home runs into long outs.[24]

For the Cubs, 1934 was a repeat of 1933 in the standings as they won the same number of games and finished third again, this time eight games behind St. Louis. Klein disappointed, hitting only .301 with 20 home runs and 80 RBIs. Seeking to improve the Cubs' offense, Walker traded first baseman Dolf Camilli to Philadelphia for 1932's league RBI leader, Don Hurst. It was a mistake. Camilli saw better days with Philadelphia, then Brooklyn winning the MVP in 1941. Hurst hit only .199 in his last season in the majors, and failed to succeed first baseman Grimm, who was nearing the end of his playing career.

As the 1935 season began, *The Sporting News*, in its annual poll of writers, asking whom they favored to win the pennant. Chicago, having finished third two years running, was picked for third again, behind St. Louis and New York.[25] Although it was not appreciated at the time, the roster had undergone significant changes with the addition of solid young players. Third baseman Stan Hack had proved himself in 1934, as had right-hander Bill Lee. Outfielder Augie Galan showed promise. Toward the end of the season, Phil Cavarretta, just turned 18, played a handful of games at first base, and impressed. An off-season trade brought pitcher Larry French and veteran infielder Freddie Lindstrom from Pittsburgh in exchange for pitcher Guy Bush.

At the beginning of September, the baseball writers' spring predictions were holding true. On the morning of September 4, St. Louis was in first place, two games over New York and 2½ over Chicago. St. Louis went 19-12 in September, a solid performance. But Chicago went 23-3; beginning on September 4 they reeled off 18 consecutive victories, bringing them to St. Louis on September 25 three games ahead of the Cardinals with five games to play.

The first game of the series pitted 19-game-winners Lon Warneke and Paul Dean against each other. Cavarretta homered off Dean in the second inning to win the game, 1-0, assuring a tie. After a day off, they played a doubleheader. In the first game, Bill Lee bested Dizzy Dean, 6-2, clinching the pennant and joining Warneke as a 20-game winner. Chicago won the second game, 5-3, capping a 21-game winning streak.

The pennant was a team effort. Lee (20-6) and Warneke (20-13) were joined by French (17-10) and 36-year-old Root (15-8) to give the team the best pitching in the league. Augie Galan hit .314 and led the league with 133 runs scored. Both Hartnett and Billy Herman hit over .340, Frank Demaree hit .325, Stan Hack chipped in with a .311 average and Chuck Klein homered 21 times, their combined efforts generating the best offense in the National League. Cavarretta summed it up. "We won the pennant because of our complete team, the regulars who played every day and our pitching staff. They all did their job, and they did it right because the determination was there."[26]

Chicago faced Detroit in the World Series. Having lost to St. Louis in a hard-fought seven-game Series in 1934, Detroit was thirsting for redemption. Unlike their two previous appearances in the Series, the Cubs gave a good account of themselves. Warneke pitched well, shutting out a powerful (Mickey Cochrane, Charlie Gehringer, Goose Goslin, Hank Greenberg) lineup 3-0 on just four hits in Game One, and won Game Five as well, 3-1. He was Chicago's only winner. With the Cubs down three games to two, they entered the ninth inning of Game Six at Detroit's Navin Field tied 3-3. Hack led off the inning with a triple but was stranded there as the next three batters could not bring him home. With two outs in the bottom of the ninth, Goslin singled Cochrane home, giving Detroit its first world championship. Chicago had played well but Detroit, eking out three one-run victories, had done better.

It had been an ugly series as the Cubs reviled Greenberg mercilessly for his Jewish heritage. In the second game, after he homered in the first inning, he was hit by a pitch in the seventh, breaking his wrist and taking him out for the rest of the Series. Insults had reached a level that caused Commissioner Kenesaw Mountain Landis to warn that "uncivil and unprintable language" must cease immediately.

Chicago, as it had after winning a pennant in 1932, fell off the next two seasons, finishing second in 1936 and 1937, both times falling toward the end of the season to New York in close races. Failure to repeat was attributed in part to Warneke's developing a sore arm. After averaging more than 20 wins the previous four seasons, he finished 1936 at 16-13, seemingly a slight decline but enough to give New York, especially with Giants ace Carl Hubbell in his heyday, just enough of an edge to win the pennant. After the season Warneke was traded to St. Louis for Ripper Collins.

While the roster was changing, so was Wrigley Field. The club installed outfield bleachers, a scoreboard in center field, and, most prominently, ivy on the outfield walls. But no lights. Wrigley believed the sport should be played in the daytime, never mind that it shut out many who worked during the day.[27] (Lights were finally installed in 1988.)

While the changes improved the ballpark's attractiveness, they did not translate into wins. Wrigley, realizing the

Cubs needed a front-line pitcher, sent three players and $185,000 to St. Louis in April 1938 for Dizzy Dean, considered one of the best pitcher in baseball, if not the best. But Dean was not the best anymore. Having injured his arm in 1937, the fireballing Dean became a junk pitcher. The Cubs were unaware of his injury when the trade was made. Acquisition of Dean was seen a coup. Based in part on acquiring Dean, the Cubs were picked to win the pennant.

Despite the positive forecast, Chicago's play was mediocre. Grimm "seemed to be losing his drive," Cavarretta later recalled. Grimm's indifference and Chicago's play — they were in fourth place as the season passed the halfway point — cost him his job.[28] Hartnett took over. For several weeks there was no difference in how the club played under him or Grimm. On August 31, having gone 22-20 under Hartnett, they were seven games out, in fourth place behind Pittsburgh, New York, and Cincinnati.

Then, shades of 1935 … The team got hot with six- and ten-game winning streaks, and went 21-5 in September. By the 26th they had closed to within 1½ games of a slumping Pirate team. Pittsburgh came to Wrigley Field for a three-game series. Dean started the opener. His arm injury had severely limited Dean's appearances; he pitched in only 13 games (74⅔ innings) all season. However, when he pitched he was effective, coming into the game with a 6-1 record and a 1.91 ERA. He bested Pittsburgh's Jim Tobin, 2-1. The Pirates' lead was now just a half-game.

The next day's game proved one of the most memorable in Cubs history. Clay Bryant, who had picked up the slack caused by Dean's infrequent appearances, winning 19 games, proved ineffective; Pittsburgh knocked him out of the box in the sixth. Chicago fought back, entering the bottom of the ninth with the score tied 5-5. Imminent darkness made all realize this would be the last inning. Pittsburgh's premier reliever, Mace Brown, quickly got two outs, aided by an increasing gloom. Hartnett came to the plate and on Brown's third pitch, he hit a line drive into the left-field bleachers, beating a stunned Pirates team, 6-5. "The Homer in the Gloamin' " had given Chicago a half-game lead. The next day Lee posted his 22nd victory, 10-1 over a demoralized Pirates team.

Although they were just 1½ games out, the race was over; they lost three of their last four games to finish two games behind Chicago.

Chicago's offense was adequate, third in the league in runs scored, with Hack at .320 and veteran outfielder Carl Reynolds, salvaged out of the American Association, at .302, the team's only .300 hitters. Excelling on defense, they made a league-low 135 errors. The pitching staff recorded a league best 3.37 ERA. Lee's 22 victories led the majors, Bryant won 19, 39-year-old Root had an 8-7 record, Dean went 7-1. Now they had to face the New York Yankees, who had just won their third straight pennant and were looking for their third consecutive World Series win under Joe McCarthy.

New York, with players like Bill Dickey, Joe DiMaggio, Lou Gehrig, and Joe Gordon, crushed Chicago in four straight games, outscoring them 22 to 9. The closest Chicago came to a victory was in Game Two, when Dean teased the Yankees for seven innings, protecting a 3-2 lead. Frank Crosetti hit a two-run homer in the eighth, DiMaggio the same in the ninth. Chicago went quietly the next two games, 5-2 and 8-3, swept away just as they were in 1932 by McCarthy's club.

After winning the pennant in 1929, Chicago repeated every three years, winning in 1932, 1935, and 1938. They finished in second and third three times each, to go with their four pennants. After 1939, the club went into decline. Wrigley failed to appreciate the ability of a thriving farm system, placing little emphasis on developing players. Increasingly detached from success on the field, he viewed attending a game as the prime goal, "The fun, the game, the sunshine, the relaxation. Our idea is to get the public to go to see a ballgame, win or lose," summed up his philosophy.[29]

In 1939 the Cubs finished fourth, their lowest since 1927. Hartnett was dropped as manager in 1940, let go after a sub-.500, fifth-place finish. Wrigley hired Jim Gallagher, a sports reporter for the *Chicago Herald-American*, as the Cubs' general manager. Aside from writing about baseball, Gallagher had no experience in the game; but he was compatible with Wrigley. Former major-league catcher Jimmie Wilson, who had finished no higher than seventh

in five seasons managing the woeful Phillies, replaced Hartnett. Wilson had filled in as Cincinnati's catcher when Ernie Lombardi was hurt in 1940, and his play in the World Series helped the Reds take the championship. Previous managing performance aside, his heroics induced the Cubs to hire him.

Both appointments proved a disaster. Gallagher's lack of talent in judging players became immediately apparent in early 1941 when he traded Billy Herman to Brooklyn for two nonentities and cash. The trade gave the Dodgers what they needed to win the pennant. Numerous poor trades over the next several years along with Wilson's uninspired leadership brought the club no higher than fifth the next three years. Wrigley's indifference to the club's performance and his lack of concentration on strengthening the organization, especially in the minor leagues, established a general level of mediocrity that has continued into the 21st century.

However, not without one final burst of glory. Early in 1944 after a 1-9 start, Wilson was fired and Grimm was brought up from the American Association Milwaukee Brewers to manage. His return had the same effect as when he succeeded Hornsby in 1932. Chicago loosened up and after the disastrous start played well enough to finish fourth. This occurred against the backdrop of World War II, which deeply affected the level of play in the majors. The military called draft-age athletes to serve in the military, and teams had to scramble to fill their rosters with players rejected for medical reasons or those who were too old (or too young) for the draft. A team's performance could change radically based on the whims of the draft board. In this unusual environment, the baseball gods smiled on Chicago in 1945.

St. Louis had won the pennant three straight years, 1942-1944, the last two by convincing margins. In 1945 the Cardinals lost their best player, Stan Musial, and All-Star catcher Walker Cooper to the Navy. Chicago, meanwhile, more than any other team was able to retain most of its key personnel. The Cubs finished first three games ahead of St. Louis. Cavarretta hit .355 to win the batting title and was the league's Most Valuable Player. Stan Hack, who had retired in 1944 after deciding he could no longer play for Wilson, unretired and hit .323 in 1945. Second baseman Don Johnson chipped in with a .302 average. Andy Pafko, who had joined the club in late 1943, drove in 110 runs.

Chicago's pitching staff was led by Hank Wyse (22-10), Claude Passeau (17-9), Paul Derringer (16-11), and Ray Prim (13-8). Prim led the league with a 2.40 ERA. The paucity of talent was mirrored in the fact that Derringer and Prim were both 38. The pitcher who really put the Cubs over the top was midseason acquisition Hank Borowy. Borowy was 10-5 with the Yankees when on July 27 he was waived to the Cubs. Stories of why the best pitcher on the Yankees was put on waivers, let alone allowed to pass out of the American League, varied depending on whose view one accepted. Larry MacPhail, owner of the Yankees, claimed Borowy had a sore arm and could no longer complete his starts. He had not pitched well in few his last starts; moreover, he was subject to the draft.[30] That Chicago paid $97,000 to MacPhail for Borowy was not to be discounted. [31] In any case, Borowy went 11-2 for Chicago. With New York and Chicago, Borowy was 21-7, and was a valued addition to the Cubs staff.

Chicago had started slowly. By the end of May, the Cubs were in fifth. But by early July, they had gained first. During the season they swept 20 doubleheaders and feasted on second-division opponents, going 21-1 over seventh-place Cincinnati, 17-5 against the last-place Phillies and 15-7 against the sixth-place Braves. Their 53-13 record against the three teams allowed them to withstand St. Louis's 16-6 dominance.

Chicago faced the Detroit Tigers, their 1935 nemesis, in the World Series. Neither team came anywhere near having the quality players they had a decade earlier. Attempting to predict the likely World Series winner, Warren Brown of the *Chicago-Herald American*, after looking at both teams' collections of 4-F players, castoffs, and old veterans still in the game solely because of the war, observed, "I don't think either one of them can win it."[32]

Brown was not far off the mark. The classic went seven games highlighted by passed balls, misplays in the field and baserunning miscues. At the end of six games the teams were tied, and the seventh game was played at Wrigley Field before 41,590 fans.

Borowy, having relieved for four innings in Game Six, started Game Seven two days later. It was his fourth appearance in the series. He did not have it; by the end of the second, Chicago was down 6-1, the Cubs never recovered, and lost 9-3. They had been in five World Series beginning in 1929 and lost them all. Little did anyone realize when Don Johnson grounded to shortstop Skeeter Webb for a Series-ending force play that it was the last appearance of the Chicago Cubs in the World Series through 2014. In 1930 William Wrigley fired Joe McCarthy for not winning the World Series. Eighty-plus years later, the 43 managers who succeeded McCarthy have not fared any better.

NOTES

1   Peter Golenbock, *Wrigleyville, A Magical History of the Chicago Cubs* (New York: St. Martin's Press, 1996), 218.

2   Roberts Ehrgott, *Mr. Wrigley's Ball Club: Chicago & The Cubs During the Jazz Age* (Lincoln: University of Nebraska Press, 2013), 207.

3   Alan H. Levy, *Joe McCarthy, Architect of the Yankee Dynasty* (Jefferson, North Carolina: McFarland & Company, Inc., 2005), 144.

4   Golenbock, 234.

5   William Curran, *Big Sticks, The Phenomenal Decade of Ruth, Gehrig, Cobb and Hornsby* (New York: Harper Perennial, 1991), 258.

6   Acquisition of Bell came at a steep price. Wally Berger, who had starred with the Los Angeles Angels in the Pacific Coast League, was dealt to the Boston Braves. Berger who would probably not have cracked the Cubs outfield of Cuyler, Stephenson, and Wilson, joined the Braves and promptly set a record for home runs by a rookie with 38, a record that stood until 1987 when Mark McGwire of Oakland broke it with 47.

7   Ehrgott, 224-225; Stout, 127.

8   Ehrgott, 232-233; Stout, 128.

9   wikipedia.org/wiki/Hack_Wilson.

10   The record stood at 190 RBIs until 1999, when SABR researchers discovered that Wilson should have been credited with an RBI in the second game of a doubleheader on July 28, but that the RBI was mistakenly given to Charlie Grimm. Source: wikipedia.org/wiki/Hack_Wilson.

11   Ehrgott, 235.

12   Ehrgott, 243.

13   Levy, 143.

14   Golenbock, 224; Stout, 136.

15   Curran, 280-281.

16   Golenbock, 227.

17   Ehrgott, 278.

18   Golenbock, 240.

19   Stout, 158-159, and Golenbock, 271 each offer comments on Philip Wrigley's baseball management capabilities.

20   Christopher D. Green, "The Chicago Cubs and 'The Headshrinker,'" SABR's *Baseball Research Journal*, Spring 2011, 42-45.

21   Several myths came out of Chicago's bizarre experiences that season. It has been offered that Jurges' shooting inspired a similar scene in Bernard Malamud's *The Natural*, but the consensus is that a later shooting, that of the Phillies' Eddie Waitkus in 1949, most probably was the one that inspired Malamud. That Koenig replaced an injured Jurges is another popular misconception. Jurges was back in the lineup soon after being shot. Koenig replaced Hornsby on the roster after his release. Two weeks later Koenig replaced Jurges. whose playing was not up to par.

22   Golenbock, 235.

23   Golenbock, 243.

24   For 1931-33, Klein hit .429 with 71 HRs and 256 RBIs at Baker Bowl. On the road, the figures were .272, 26 HRs, 122 RBIs.

25   "Consensus of 194 Experts Favors Cards, Tigers to Repeat," *The Sporting News*, March 21, 1935, 3.

26   Golenbock 253.

27   Stout, 165.

28   Golenbock, 259

29   Golenbock, 268.

30   Lyle Spatz, in "Hank Borowy," SABR BioProject, sabr.org/bioproj/person/ea042adc, contains a plausible explanation of the transaction.

31   Golenbock, 307.

32   Stout, 188.

CONTRIBUTORS

Bob Buege was born on Luis Aparicio's 12th birthday. On the day Bob graduated from high school, Aparicio walked three times and scored the winning run as his Baltimore Orioles defeated the New York Yankees. Bob joined SABR in 1988 and has attended every SABR Convention beginning in 1990. He is the author of *The Milwaukee Braves: A Baseball Eulogy* and *Eddie Mathews and the National Pastime*.

George Castle is historian for the Chicago Baseball Museum and editor of its website, *www.chicagobaseball-museum.org*. Also author of 12 baseball books, Castle has covered baseball in Chicago for a variety of media outlets, including the *Times of Northwest Indiana* newspaper, for 35 years. He also hosted his own syndicated baseball radio show, "Diamond Gems," for 17 years.

Greg Erion and his wife Barbara, live in South San Francisco, California. Retired from the railroad industry, he currently teaches U.S. history part time at Skyline College. Greg has contributed several articles to the ongoing SABR Biography Project and is currently working on a book about the 1959 season.

Scott Ferkovich is the leader of the SABR Baseball Ballpark Project. His articles have appeared in numerous SABR publications. He is a contributing editor to the annual *Emerald Guide to Baseball*, and blogs about Detroit Tiger history for *Detroit Athletic Co*. He also writes for *seamheads.com*, *thenationalpastimemuseum.com*, and *Spitball* magazine. Scott is a graduate of Columbia College in Chicago. He lives in Michigan with his wife Cindy, daughter Zoey, and their Golden Retriever Spenser.

Dan Fields is a manuscript editor at the *New England Journal of Medicine*. He loves baseball trivia, and he regularly attends Boston Red Sox and Pawtucket (Rhode Island) Red Sox games with his teenage son. Dan lives in Framingham, Massachusetts, and can be reached at dfields820@gmail.com.

Dr. David Fletcher is founder and president of the Chicago Baseball Museum. A longtime SABR member and lifelong baseball fan, he is in the process of building the museum's first brick-and-mortar home in Whiting, Ind. Fletcher maintains the Jerome Holtzman Library, a collection assembled by the late baseball writer and MLB official historian. Fletcher is an occupational medicine specialist based in Champaign, Ill.

Ernie Fuhr is a high school teacher in Rockford, Illinois. Ernie was, admittedly, not a very good ballplayer while growing up, but he still loves the game. He is a loyal Milwaukee Brewers fan. The Hal Carlson story is his first biography for the SABR Baseball Project, but he has published other articles in local literary anthologies, *Secret Rockford* and *The Rockford Review*. Ernie and his wife Stephanie are the proud parents of two tuxedo cats.

Joseph Gerard has been a lifelong Pittsburgh Pirates fan. He grew up hating the Yankees despite being born and raised in Newark, NJ - his biggest regret in life is that he was only two years old in 1960. Because of Roberto Clemente, he developed an interest in Latin-American baseball history and has contributed biographies of five Latin players to the SABR BioProject. He lives in New York City with his wife Ann Marie and their two children, Henry and Sophie.

Chip Greene, a management consultant, has been a SABR member since 2006. He is a regular contributor to the Biography Project book series and is currently editing a BioProject book on the three time champion Oakland Athletics. Chip, the grandson of former Brooklyn Dodger pitcher, Nelson Greene, lives in Waynesboro, Pennsylvania, with his wife, Elaine, and daughters, Anna, and Haley.

Nancy Snell Griffith is the retired Archives and Special Collections Librarian at Presbyterian College in Clinton, South Carolina. She is a lifelong baseball fan, having grown up in Pittsburgh listening to Jim Woods and Bob Prince broadcast the Pirates' games.

Zachary Michael Jack is the author of many books on sports, earning nominations for the William Hill Sports Book of the Year Award and the Herbert Warren Wind Award. A devote of the Small Ball Theory, Zachary has been trusted by agents and executors to edit and anthologize the work of sportswriting legends such as Paul Gallico and George Plimpton in addition to working with a handful of the best contemporary practitioners on staff at *Sports Illustrated* and *Outside* magazine. He teaches occasional seminars in the Masters of Leadership Studies, Sports Leadership track at North Central College in Naperville, Illinois.

William H. Johnson is a retired Naval Flight Officer living in Cedar Rapids, Iowa. Since joining SABR in 1994, he has focused on Iowa's baseball heritage, including contribution of several essays to books for the BioProject. He is also co-author of the book *Norway Baseball: Gone But Not Forgotten*, with Shona Frese.

Norm King is a retired Canadian civil servant who delights in having the time to devote to SABR research. He still misses his beloved Montreal Expos and awaits the day when he will hear an umpire yell "Au jeu" again at the beginning of a ball game.

Russ Lake lives in Champaign, IL, and is a retired college professor emeritus. The 1964 St. Louis Cardinals remain his favorite team, and he was distressed to see Sportsman's Park (aka Busch Stadium I) being demolished not long after he had attended the last game there on May 8, 1966. His wife, Carol, deserves an MVP award for watching all of a 14 inning ballgame in Cincinnati with Russ in 1971 — during their honeymoon. In 1994, he was an editor for David Halberstam's baseball book, *October 1964*.

Len Levin, a resident of Providence, Rhode Island, has been a copyeditor for most of SABR's recent books and a Red Sox fan long before that. He is a retired newspaper editor, and currently works part-time editing the decisions of the Rhode Island Supreme Court.

Gary Livacari is a practicing dentist and a long-suffering Cub fan of over 55 years. A ten year SABR member, his hobby is identifying ball players in old photos and his numerous photo identifications appear on the *Baseball Fever* website. He was an Assistant Editor for the recent SABR project, *The Boston Public Library Leslie Jones Baseball Collection*, in which he participated in the identification of nearly 3000 baseball photos from the 1930's

and 40's. He has also contributed numerous articles to the SABR BioProject and SABR books projects, including *Go-Go to Glory* and *Pitching to the Pennant*. He and his wife Nancy reside in Park Ridge, Illinois.

John McMurray is Chair of the Society for American Baseball Research's Deadball Era Committee. He contributed to SABR's 2006 book *Deadball Stars of the American League* and is a past chair of SABR's Ritter Award subcommittee, which annually presents an award to the best book on Deadball Era baseball published during the year prior. He has contributed many interview-based player profiles to *Baseball Digest* in recent years.

Sixty one and at the cusp of formal retirement, **Paul Mittermeyer** anticipates a bi-coastal existence with his amazing wife. He plans to enjoy reading, writing, philosophy, history, politics, art horticulture, fermentation distillation, travel, dining, volunteering, swimming, walking, entertaining, golfing, bridge, scrabble, and all the individual and joint interests for which there never seems to be enough time enough days.

Jack Morris is a corporate librarian for a pharmaceutical company. He lives in East Coventry, Pennsylvania with his wife and two daughters. His baseball biographies have appeared in six books including *The Team That Forever Changed Baseball and America* (1947 Brooklyn Dodgers) and *Bridging Two Dynasties* (1947 New York Yankees). He is not the Jack Morris of World Series fame but, every once in a while, wishes he was.

Peter Morris of Haslett, Michigan, is a passionate fan of the Michigan State University volleyball team who has written six books about the early history of baseball, including "A Game of Inches: The Stories Behind the Innovations That Shaped Baseball."

Bill Nowlin is a lifelong Red Sox fan and bought a "Now I can die in peace" t-shirt after the Red Sox won the World Series in 2004. Earlier that same year, he was elected as vice president of SABR, a position he's held since then. Most Red Sox fans have probably always considered the Cubs a kindred team in the other league. White Sox fans were happy for 2005, but Cubs fans have waited longer than anyone. It's time.

James L. Ray is a lawyer in Center City Philadelphia. He grew up a Yankees fan, but gradually switched over to the Phillies during his 25 years living in the City of Brotherly Love. It is a decision that will cause him much pain, regret and heartache.

Paul Rogers is a law professor at Southern Methodist University, where he served as dean for nine years. When not writing about antitrust law or legal history, he has co-authored four baseball books, including two with his boyhood hero Robin Roberts, *The Whiz Kids and the 1950 Pennant* and *Throwing Hard Easy — Reflections on a Life in Baseball*. His most recent collaboration is *Lucky Me - My 65 Years in Baseball with Eddie Robinson*. He is also president of the Ernie Banks — Bobby Bragan DFW SABR Chapter, has authored a score of biographies for the SABR BioProject, and in 2013 served as a judge for the Casey Award.

Tom Schott is from New Orleans, but lives in Norman, Oklahoma, and still laments the sixth game of the 2011 World Series and the fate of his beloved Texas Rangers.

He's a professional historian, now retired, who spends his time reading, editing Civil War books, listening to music, and fooling around with various baseball projects, including writing bios and game stories for SABR and working on a compilation of every game in modern baseball history to end in a score of 1-0.

Fred Taylor is a retired tree planter living in southwest Iowa. A long time White Sox fan who now likes the Cubs ballpark better than where the White Sox play and still upset over what happened to the Phillies in 1964, roots for the Cubs whenever they play St Louis.

A lifelong Pirates fan, **Gregory H. Wolf** was born in Pittsburgh, but now resides in the Chicagoland area with his wife, Margaret, and daughter, Gabriela. A Professor of German Studies and holder of the Dennis and Jean Endowed Chair in the Humanities at North Central College in Naperville, Illinois, he edited the SABR book *"Thar's Joy in Braveland." The 1957 Milwaukee Braves*, and is working on a project about the 1965 Minnesota Twins.

Join SABR today!

If you're interested in baseball — writing about it, reading about it, talking about it — there's a place for you in the Society for American Baseball Research.

SABR was formed in 1971 in Cooperstown, New York, with the mission of fostering the research and dissemination of the history and record of the game. Our members include everyone from academics to professional sportswriters to amateur historians and statisticians to students and casual fans who merely enjoy reading about baseball history and occasionally gathering with other members to talk baseball.

SABR members have a variety of interests, and this is reflected in the diversity of its research committees. There are more than two dozen groups devoted to the study of a specific area related to the game — from Baseball and the Arts to Statistical Analysis to the Deadball Era to Women in Baseball. In addition, many SABR members meet formally and informally in regional chapters throughout the year and hundreds come together for the annual national convention, the organization's premier event. These meetings often include panel discussions with former major league players and research presentations by members. Most of all, SABR members love talking baseball with like-minded friends. What unites them all is an interest in the game and joy in learning more about it.

Why join SABR? Here are some benefits of membership:

♦ Two issues (spring and fall) of the *Baseball Research Journal*, which includes articles on history, biography, statistics, personalities, book reviews, and other aspects of the game.
♦ One expanded e-book edition of *The National Pastime*, which focuses on baseball in the region where that year's SABR national convention is held (in 2015, it's Chicago)
♦ 8-10 new and classic e-books published each year by the SABR Digital Library, which are all free for members to download
♦ *This Week in SABR* newsletter in your e-mail every Friday, which highlights SABR members' research and latest news
♦ Regional chapter meetings, which can include guest speakers, presentations and trips to ballgames
♦ Online access to back issues of *The Sporting News* and other periodicals through Paper of Record
♦ Access to SABR's lending library and other research resources
♦ Online member directory to connect you with an international network of SABR baseball experts and fans
♦ Discounts on registration for our annual events, including SABR Analytics Conference & Jerry Malloy Negro League Conference
♦ Access to SABR-L, an e-mail discussion list of baseball questions & answers that many feel is worth the cost of membership itself
♦ The opportunity to be part of a passionate international community of baseball fans

SABR membership is on a "rolling" calendar system; that means your membership lasts 365 days no matter when you sign up! Enjoy all the benefits of SABR membership by signing up today at SABR.org/join or by clipping out the form below and mailing it to SABR, 4455 E. Camelback Rd., Ste. D-140, Phoenix, AZ 85018.

SABR MEMBERSHIP RENEWAL FORM

	Annual	3-year	Senior	3-yr Sr.	Under 30
U.S.:	❏ $65	❏ $175	❏ $45	❏ $129	❏ $45
Canada/Mexico:	❏ $75	❏ $205	❏ $55	❏ $159	❏ $55
Overseas:	❏ $84	❏ $232	❏ $64	❏ $186	❏ $55

Add a Family Member: $15 for each family member at same address (list on back)
Senior: 65 or older before 12/31/2015

All dues amounts in U.S. dollars or equivalent

Participate in Our Donor Program!
I'd like to desginate my gift to be used toward:
❏General Fund   ❏Endowment Fund   ❏Research Resources   ❏_____
❏ I want to maximize the impact of my gift; do not send any donor premiums
❏ I would like this gift to remain anonymous.

Note: Any donation not designated will be placed in the General Fund.
SABR is a 501 (c) (3) not-for-profit organization & donations are tax-deductible to the extent allowed by law.

Name _____

Address _____

City _____ ST_____ ZIP_____

Phone _____ Birthday _____

E-mail: _____
(Your e-mail address on file ensures you will receive the most recent SABR news.)

Dues $_____

Donation $_____

Amount Enclosed $_____

Do you work for a matching grant corporation? Call (602) 343-6455 for details.

If you wish to pay by credit card, please contact the SABR office at (602) 343-6455 or visit the SABR Store online at SABR.org/join. We accept Visa, Mastercard & Discover.

Do you wish to receive the *Baseball Research Journal* electronically?: ❏ Yes   ❏ No
Our e-books are available in PDF, Kindle, or EPUB (iBooks, iPad, Nook) formats.

Mail to: SABR, 4455 E. Camelback Rd., Ste. D-140, Phoenix, AZ 85018

SABR BioProject Books

In 2002, the Society for American Baseball Research launched an effort to write and publish biographies of every player, manager, and individual who has made a contribution to baseball. Over the past decade, the BioProject Committee has produced over 2,200 biographical articles. Many have been part of efforts to create theme- or team-oriented books, spearheaded by chapters or other committees of SABR.

THE YEAR OF THE BLUE SNOW:
The 1964 Philadelphia Phillies
Catcher Gus Triandos dubbed the Philadelphia Phillies' 1964 season "the year of the blue snow," a rare thing that happens once in a great while. This book sheds light on lingering questions about the 1964 season—but any book about a team is really about the players. This work offers life stories of all the players and others (managers, coaches, owners, and broadcasters) associated with this star-crossed team, as well as essays of analysis and history.
Edited by Mel Marmer and Bill Nowlin
$19.95 paperback (ISBN 978-1-933599-51-9)
$9.99 ebook (ISBN 978-1-933599-52-6)
8.5"x11", 356 pages, over 70 photos

DETROIT TIGERS 1984:
What a Start! What a Finish!
The 1984 Detroit tigers roared out of the gate, winning their first nine games of the season and compiling an eye-popping 35-5 record after the campaign's first 40 games—still the best start ever for any team in major league history. This book brings together biographical profiles of every Tiger from that magical season, plus those of field management, top executives, the broadcasters—even venerable Tiger Stadium and the city itself.
Edited by Mark Pattison and David Raglin
$19.95 paperback (ISBN 978-1-933599-44-1)
$9.99 ebook (ISBN 978-1-933599-45-8)
8.5"x11", 250 pages (Over 230,000 words!)

SWEET '60: The 1960 Pittsburgh Pirates
A portrait of the 1960 team which pulled off one of the biggest upsets of the last 60 years. When Bill Mazeroski's home run left the park to win in Game Seven of the World Series, beating the New York Yankees, David had toppled Goliath. It was a blow that awakened a generation, one that millions of people saw on television, one of TV's first iconic World Series moments.
Edited by Clifton Blue Parker and Bill Nowlin
$19.95 paperback (ISBN 978-1-933599-48-9)
$9.99 ebook (ISBN 978-1-933599-49-6)
8.5"x11", 340 pages, 75 photos

RED SOX BASEBALL IN THE DAYS OF IKE AND ELVIS: The Red Sox of the 1950s
Although the Red Sox spent most of the 1950s far out of contention, the team was filled with fascinating players who captured the heart of their fans. In Red Sox Baseball, members of SABR present 46 biographies on players such as Ted Williams and Pumpsie Green as well as season-by-season recaps.
Edited by Mark Armour and Bill Nowlin
$19.95 paperback (ISBN 978-1-933599-24-3)
$9.99 ebook (ISBN 978-1-933599-34-2)
8.5"x11", 372 pages, over 100 photos

THE MIRACLE BRAVES OF 1914
Boston's Original Worst-to-First Champions
Long before the Red Sox "Impossible Dream" season, Boston's now nearly forgotten "other" team, the 1914 Boston Braves, performed a baseball "miracle" that resounds to this very day. The "Miracle Braves" were Boston's first "worst-to-first" winners of the World Series. Refusing to throw in the towel at the midseason mark, George Stallings engineered a remarkable second-half climb in the standings all the way to first place.
Edited by Bill Nowlin
$19.95 paperback (ISBN 978-1-933599-69-4)
$9.99 ebook (ISBN 978-1-933599-70-0)
8.5"x11", 392 pages, over 100 photos

THAR'S JOY IN BRAVELAND!
The 1957 Milwaukee Braves
Few teams in baseball history have captured the hearts of their fans like the Milwaukee Braves of the 1950s. During the Braves' 13-year tenure in Milwaukee (1953-1965), they had a winning record every season, won two consecutive NL pennants (1957 and 1958), lost two more in the final week of the season (1956 and 1959), and set big-league attendance records along the way.
Edited by Gregory H. Wolf
$19.95 paperback (ISBN 978-1-933599-71-7)
$9.99 ebook (ISBN 978-1-933599-72-4)
8.5"x11", 330 pages, over 60 photos

NEW CENTURY, NEW TEAM:
The 1901 Boston Americans
The team now known as the Boston Red Sox played its first season in 1901. Boston had a well-established National League team, but the American League went head-to-head with the N.L. in Chicago, Philadelphia, and Boston. Chicago won the American League pennant and Boston finished second, only four games behind.
Edited by Bill Nowlin
$19.95 paperback (ISBN 978-1-933599-58-8)
$9.99 ebook (ISBN 978-1-933599-59-5)
8.5"x11", 268 pages, over 125 photos

CAN HE PLAY?
A Look At Baseball Scouts and their Profession
They dig through tons of coal to find a single diamond. Here in the world of scouts, we meet the "King of Weeds," a Ph.D. we call "Baseball's Renaissance Man," a husband-and-wife team, pioneering Latin scouts, and a Japanese-American interned during World War II who became a successful scout—and many, many more.
Edited by Jim Sandoval and Bill Nowlin
$19.95 paperback (ISBN 978-1-933599-23-6)
$9.99 ebook (ISBN 978-1-933599-25-0)
8.5"x11", 200 pages, over 100 photos

SABR Members can purchase each book at a significant discount (often 50% off) and receive the ebook editions free as a member benefit. Each book is available in a trade paperback edition as well as ebooks suitable for reading on a home computer or Nook, Kindle, or iPad/tablet.

To learn more about becoming a member of SABR, visit the website: sabr.org/join

The SABR Digital Library

The Society for American Baseball Research, the top baseball research organization in the world, disseminates some of the best in baseball history, analysis, and biography through our publishing programs. The SABR Digital Library contains a mix of books old and new, and focuses on a tandem program of paperback and ebook publication, making these materials widely available for both on digital devices and as traditional printed books.

CLASSIC REPRINTS

BASE-BALL: How to Become a Player
by John Montgomery Ward
John Montgomery Ward (1860-1925) tossed the second perfect game in major league history and later became the game's best shortstop and a great, inventive manager. His classic handbook on baseball skills and strategy was published in 1888. Illustrated with woodcuts, the book is divided into chapters for each position on the field as well as chapters on the origin of the game, theory and strategy, training, base-running, and batting.
$4.99 ebook (ISBN 978-1-933599-47-2)
$9.95 paperback (ISBN 978-0910137539)
156 pages, 4.5"x7" replica edition

BATTING
by F. C. Lane
First published in 1925, Batting collects the wisdom and insights of over 250 hitters and baseball figures. Lane interviewed extensively and compiled tips and advice on everything from batting stances to beanballs. Legendary baseball figures such as Ty Cobb, Casey Stengel, Cy Young, Walter Johnson, Rogers Hornsby, and Babe Ruth reveal the secrets of such integral and interesting parts of the game as how to choose a bat, the ways to beat a slump, and how to outguess the pitcher.
$14.95 paperback (ISBN 978-0-910137-86-7)
$7.99 ebook (ISBN 978-1-933599-46-5)
240 pages, 5"x7"

RUN, RABBIT, RUN
by Walter "Rabbit" Maranville
"Rabbit" Maranville was the Joe Garagiola of Grandpa's day, the baseball comedian of the times. In a twenty-four-year career that began in 1912, Rabbit found a lot of funny situations to laugh at, and no wonder: he caused most of them! The book also includes an introduction by the late Harold Seymour and a historical account of Maranville's life and Hall-of-Fame career by Bob Carroll.
$9.95 paperback (ISBN 978-1-933599-26-7)
$5.99 ebook (ISBN 978-1-933599-27-4)
100 pages, 5.5"x8.5", 15 rare photos

MEMORIES OF A BALLPLAYER
by Bill Werber and C. Paul Rogers III
Bill Werber's claim to fame is unique: he was the last living person to have a direct connection to the 1927 Yankees, "Murderers' Row," a team hailed by many as the best of all time. Rich in anecdotes and humor, Memories of a Ballplayer is a clear-eyed memoir of the world of big-league baseball in the 1930s. Werber played with or against some of the most productive hitters of all time, including Babe Ruth, Ted Williams, Lou Gehrig, and Joe DiMaggio.
$14.95 paperback (ISNB 978-0-910137-84-3)
$6.99 ebook (ISBN 978-1-933599-47-2)
250 pages, 6"x9"

ORIGINAL SABR RESEARCH

INVENTING BASEBALL: The 100 Greatest Games of the Nineteenth Century
SABR's Nineteenth Century Committee brings to life the greatest games from the game's early years. From the "prisoner of war" game that took place among captive Union soldiers during the Civil War (immortalized in a famous lithograph), to the first intercollegiate game (Amherst versus Williams), to the first professional no-hitter, the games in this volume span 1833–1900 and detail the athletic exploits of such players as Cap Anson, Moses "Fleetwood" Walker, Charlie Comiskey, and Mike "King" Kelly.
Edited by Bill Felber
$19.95 paperback (ISBN 978-1-933599-42-7)
$9.99 ebook (ISBN 978-1-933599-43-4)
302 pages, 8"x10", 200 photos

NINETEENTH CENTURY STARS: 2012 EDITION
First published in 1989, Nineteenth Century Stars was SABR's initial attempt to capture the stories of baseball players from before 1900. With a collection of 136 fascinating biographies, SABR has re-released Nineteenth Century Stars for 2012 with revised statistics and new form. The 2012 version also includes a preface by John Thorn.
Edited by Robert L. Tiemann and Mark Rucker
$19.95 paperback (ISBN 978-1-933599-28-1)
$9.99 ebook (ISBN 978-1-933599-29-8)
300 pages, 6"x9"

GREAT HITTING PITCHERS
Published in 1979, Great Hitting Pitchers was one of SABR's early publications. Edited by SABR founder Bob Davids, the book compiles stories and records about pitchers excelling in the batter's box. Newly updated in 2012 by Mike Cook, Great Hitting Pitchers contain tables including data from 1979-2011, corrections to reflect recent records, and a new chapter on recent new members in the club of "great hitting pitchers" like Tom Glavine and Mike Hampton.
Edited by L. Robert Davids
$9.95 paperback (ISBN 978-1-933599-30-4)
$5.99 ebook (ISBN 978-1-933599-31-1)
102 pages, 5.5"x8.5"

THE FENWAY PROJECT
Sixty-four SABR members—avid fans, historians, statisticians, and game enthusiasts—recorded their experiences of a single game. Some wrote from inside the Green Monster's manual scoreboard, the Braves clubhouse, or the broadcast booth, while others took in the essence of Fenway from the grandstand or bleachers. The result is a fascinating look at the charms and challenges of Fenway Park, and the allure of being a baseball fan.
Edited by Bill Nowlin and Cecilia Tan
$9.99 ebook (ISBN 978-1-933599-50-2)
175 pages, 100 photos

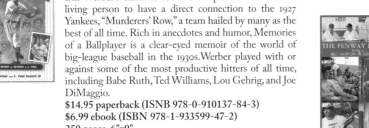

SABR Members can purchase each book at a significant discount (often 50% off) and receive the ebook editions free as a member benefit. Each book is available in a trade paperback edition as well as ebooks suitable for reading on a home computer or Nook, Kindle, or iPad/tablet.

To learn more about becoming a member of SABR, visit the website: sabr.org/join

Made in the USA
San Bernardino, CA
06 February 2015